Global Political Economy and New World Disorder

Drawing upon a range of resources of critique (including critical realist social theory, realist international relations theory, the sociology of globalization, the Marxist critique of imperialism, and dependency theory), this book is an essential contribution to the critical understanding of nationalism and imperialism in the global age. It conducts a sustained and in-depth analysis of the relations governing the asymmetry in the distribution of economic resources and powers of command, and the recent play of political events involving imperialist wars, including the Russo-Ukrainian and Israeli-Hamas wars. Crucially, Creaven argues that establishing these connections requires theorizing political economy in the so-called global age as comprised of neoimperial and neoliberal orders. As such, the author offers a new interpretation of the relations between neoliberalism and neoimperialism, and between modes of organizing social relations and resulting global disorders and instabilities. This book will therefore be of interest to researchers, scholars, and students working at the intersection of global political economy, international relations, and the sociology of globalization.

Sean Creaven is Senior Lecturer in Sociology and Criminology at the University of the West of England, UK. His research interests have included the sociology of modernity and postmodernity, sociological theory, critical theory, Marxism and post-Marxism, critical realism, and criminological theory. Most recently, these include also eco-sociology and the sociology of pandemics.

Global Political Economy and New World Disorder

Neoliberalism, Neoimperialism, and the Internationalization of Injustice

Sean Creaven

Routledge
Taylor & Francis Group
LONDON AND NEW YORK

First published 2025
by Routledge
4 Park Square, Milton Park, Abingdon, Oxon OX14 4RN

and by Routledge
605 Third Avenue, New York, NY 10158

Routledge is an imprint of the Taylor & Francis Group, an informa business

British Library Cataloguing-in-Publication Data
A catalogue record for this book is available from the British Library

ISBN: 978-1-032-98162-8 (hbk)
ISBN: 978-1-032-98164-2 (pbk)
ISBN: 978-1-003-59734-6 (ebk)

DOI: 10.4324/9781003597346

Typeset in Times New Roman
by Apex CoVantage, LLC

This is for Myrah, with love

Contents

Abbreviations and acronyms

- ACA—Arms Control Association
- AFTA—ASEAN Free Trade Area (and member states)
- APEC—Asia-Pacific Economic Cooperation
- ASEAN—Association of Southeast Asian Nations
- BAME—Black, Asian, and Mixed Ethnicity
- BRIC—Brazil, Russia, India, and China
- CEO—Chief Executive Officer
- CIA—Central Intelligence Agency
- CIS—Confederation of Independent States
- CPJ—Committee to Protect Journalists
- CRT—Critical Realist Theory
- DESA—Department of Economic and Social Affairs (UN)
- DfCI—Defence for Children International
- DU—Depleted Uranium
- DWP—Department of Wages and Pensions (UK)
- EEC—European Economic Community
- EPZ—Export Processing Zone
- ESRC—Economic and Social Research Council (UK)
- EU—European Union
- FAS—Federation of American Scientists
- FDI—Foreign Direct Investment
- FEZ—Free Enterprise Zone
- FPL—Federal Poverty Level (USA)
- G20—Group of Twenty Nations
- G7—Group of Seven Nations
- GATT—General Agreement on Tariffs and Trade
- GDP—Gross Domestic Product
- GFI—Global Financial Integrity Survey
- GNI—Gross National Income
- GUAM—Georgia, Ukraine, Azerbaijan, and Moldova (Organization for Democracy and Economic Development

- GUUAM—Georgia, Ukraine, Uzbekistan, Azerbaijan, and Moldova (Organization for Democracy and Economic Development
- HIC—High Income Country
- HMIC—Higher-Middle Income Country
- HRW—Human Rights Watch
- IAEA—International Atomic Energy Agency
- IAEA—International Atomic Energy Association
- ICC—International Criminal Court
- IDF—Israeli Defence Force
- IGO—International Government Organization
- IHRA—International Holocaust Remembrance Alliance
- IICHROT—Israeli Information Center for Human Rights in the Occupied Territories
- IISS—International Institute for Strategic Studies
- ILO—International Labour Organization
- IMF—International Monetary Fund
- IP—Internet Protocol
- ISIS—Islamic State of Iraq and Syria
- LDC—Least Developed Country
- LGBT—Lesbian, Gay, Bisexual, and Transgender
- LIC—Low Income Country
- LMIC—Lower-Middle Income Country
- LTV—Labour Theory of Value (in Marxian economics)
- MIC—Middle Income Country
- MITI—Ministry of International Trade and Industry (Japan)
- MNC—Multinational Corporation
- MNE—Multinational Enterprise
- NAFTA—North American Free Trade Agreement/Area
- NATO—North Atlantic Treaty Organization
- NEM—Newly Emerging Market
- NGO—Non-government Organization
- NHS—National Health Service (UK)
- NIC—Newly Industrializing Country
- NPI—Non-pharmaceutical intervention
- OECD—Organization of Economic Cooperation and Development
- ONS—Office for National Statistics (UK)
- OPEC—Organization of Petroleum Exporting Countries
- OPM—Official Poverty Measure (USA)
- PA—Palestinian Authority
- PCBS—Palestinian Central Bureau of Statistics
- PCHR—Palestinian Centre for Human Rights
- PCPSR—Palestinian Center for Policy and Survey Research
- PFP—Partnership for Peace (NATO programme)

- PLO—Palestinian Liberation Organization
- PMI—Purchasing Managers Index
- PRS—Poverty Reduction Strategy
- PSA—Production Sharing Agreement
- PSHRA—Prisoner Support and Human Rights Association
- RAT—Racism Awareness Training
- RIRT—Realist International Relations Theory
- SAP—Structural Adjustment Programme
- START—Strategic Arms Reduction Treaty
- TINA—"There Is No Alternative"
- TNC—Transnational Corporation
- TRPF—Tendency for Rate of Profit to Fall (in Marxian economics)
- TUC—Trade Union Conference (UK)
- UAE—United Arab Emirates
- UKCES—UK Commission for Employment and Skills
- UK—United Kingdom
- UNCESCR—UN Committee on Economic, Social and Cultural Rights
- UNCTAD—UN Conference on Trade and Development
- UNCTAD—United Nations Conference on Trade and Development
- UNDESA—UN Department of Economic and Social Affairs
- UNDP—UN Development Programme
- UNHCR—UN High Commission for Refugees
- UNHRC—UN Human Rights Committee
- UNHROHC—UN Human Rights Office of the High Commissioner
- UNICEF—UN International Children's Emergency Fund
- UNMOVIC—United Nations Monitoring, Verification and Inspection Commission
- UNOCHA—UN Office for the Coordination of Humanitarian Affairs
- UNRISD—UN Research Institute for Social Development
- UNRWA—UN Relief and Works Agency
- UNSCOM—UN Special Commission
- UNSC—UN Security Council
- UNSDG—UN Sustainable Development Goals
- UN—United Nations
- USA—United States of America
- USMCA—US–Mexico–Canada Agreement (trade zone)
- USNSC—US National Security Council
- USSR—Union of Soviet Socialist Republics
- WGP—World Gross Product
- WHO—World Health Organization
- WMD—Weapons of Mass Destruction
- WTO—World Trade Organization

Acknowledgements

Many people have assisted me over the course of producing this book. Too many to acknowledge by name. These include my colleagues and students at UWE Bristol for helping me clarify ideas in discussion and debate. This also includes all those at Routledge for supporting another project of mine that greatly exceeds the word length they would prefer. Alas, I'm incapable of writing shortish books! For this reason, my copy editor at Routledge warrants a special mention, because there was a lot of text to get through! I owe a particular debt as well to the reviewer who recommended this book for publication. His or her recommendations for improvement were insightful, and these inspired a 13,000-word rewrite. I thank you all.

There is one other I would like to acknowledge though—and by way of exception by name. Only it is paying homage that I have in mind rather than simply acknowledgement. This is John Pilger—investigative journalist, author, and documentary film-maker, who died in December last year. John Pilger was the absolute embodiment of everything critical, ethical, independent journalism should be, but rarely is. Never "embedded", John was a tireless campaigner for justice and a fearless opponent of power on behalf of the downtrodden and oppressed. His writings have inspired my own, though my academic work cannot match the power, passion, sensitivity, clarity, and warmth that his own exuded. He will be sorely missed. He is sorely missed.

Introduction

Our world is one of stunning asymmetries in the distribution of economic resources and powers of command. These are structural aspects of global systems. These asymmetries have, at the level of economic life, widened, not diminished, in recent decades, under the rule of a mode of politics that may be defined as neoliberal. We are also reminded in the most recent play of political events that our world is one in which imperialism and imperialist wars remain a potent force in world affairs.

As I write this introduction, Russia's brutal invasion of Ukraine—unleashed to prevent the country from being drawn into the NATO alliance and undermining Russia's security buffer against the West—has entered its twentieth month, with little prospect of this being ended for the foreseeable future, since this has become bogged down in the attritional stalemate of trench warfare. Simultaneously, Israel's murderous military assault on Gaza—in response to Hamas's cross-border attacks on Israeli civilian settlements and military targets—is now almost two-and-a-half months old, with more of the same promised for an unspecified period ahead. These events are, I contend, interconnected. This is because they have their conditions of existence in the aforesaid asymmetrical structuration of allocative (economic) and authoritative (political) resources in world systems.

Now, establishing these connections requires theorizing political economy in the so-called global age as comprised of neoimperial and neoliberal orders—or such is my argument. This is the purpose of this book. By way of introduction, I will summarize the main arguments set out in the analysis that follows and establish their ontological warranty in realist social theory. I will then set out the chief divisions (i.e. chapter by chapter) by which the analysis is set out.

Concepts and perspectives

Neoliberalism and neoimperialism are concepts that refer to forms of political governance that structure, organize, and administer global political economy today. To be clear from the outset, these orders are neither product of

DOI: 10.4324/9781003597346-1

globalization nor modes of globalization, because globalization is myth, for reasons that will be set out in these pages. However, international relations (i.e. the interstate system) and capitalist world economy (i.e. the corporate-market system) are of course real, whereas neoliberal and neoimperial modes of politics and governance are those which steer these systems. This is what establishes the international state system and capitalist world economy as neoliberal and neoimperial. Neoliberalism is a form of politics that is intended to maximize capitalist, business, or market freedoms—at the expense of public goods, non-market social services, and the bulk of waged employees—and especially those of the corporate-enterprise sector. Neoimperialism is a form of politics that seeks to preserve the predominance in global systems of the leading state-power actors (those essentially of the USA and the Western Alliance) in the postcolonial age where territorial empires are (mostly) no more.

These politics of international governance administer the two great engines of modernization—capitalist world economy and international state system. These systems are radically asymmetrical in terms of the resources they divide and distribute worldwide, generating huge inequalities in the power of command or authorization and in the control or ownership of property and wealth. This renders them systems of domination and subordination: of non-owning classes by owning classes; of lesser states by greater states. This also ensures that both are systems of competition, since domination can be secured for those elites who administer them only by competitive success in each of the systems. The world capitalist economy and the international state system are those in which the dominant actors (capitalist bosses and propertied elites in the economic sphere; state managers in the political sphere) seek to secure and extend their systemic advantages over their rivals (i.e. other capitals and other states). Neoliberalism and neoimperialism are modes of politics that are intended to secure these outcomes.

In theory, at the level of concepts, the international nation-state system and the capitalist world economy could operate as rival systems that obstruct or counteract each other in the service of opposed vested interests. The possibility is afforded by the fact that these are governed by and sourced in different modes of social power—the power of authorization versus the power of allocation, or the power of command over people versus the power of control over property.[1] But, in practice, the modernization process has more-or-less brought about a strategic alignment of polity and economy, of state and capital, of the power of ownership and the power of command—for reasons well theorized by Marx.[2] This is because economic powerholders need political powerholders to guarantee their control of allocative resources, just as political powerholders require economic powerholders to fund the institutions by which they deploy their authoritative resources.

So, capitalist world economy and international state system are parallel if intersecting systems of domination and subordination. But these are also closely *aligned* systems of domination (in the political sphere) and of exploitation (in the economic sphere). This is owing to the structural interdependence of state and capital at the level of each country and worldwide. On the one hand, the international state system is the life-support system of the capitalist world economy since this, contrary to the myths of globalization theory, cannot function in a borderless or deterritorialized world. Such is the bearer and defender of the world capitalist economy owing to its command of powers of authorization (political, military, and juridical) by which law and order is more-or-less maintained worldwide. And there can be no commercial order (based on legally sanctioned property rights and contractual obligations) without normative order. But, on the other hand, the interstate system can reproduce itself only because state authorities in each and every country draw on the economic resources generated by local capitalist enterprise within its borders and from its overseas operations to sustain themselves. The world capitalist economy thus bankrolls the interstate system and the protections of capitalist property and commerce (normative and otherwise) that this provides.

This relationship of structural interdependence of economy and polity in world systems ensures that the interests of powerholders in each are more-or-less congruent. This has rarely before been more transparent than it has become since the neoliberal era. This is because the neoliberal era has seen the dismantling of the postwar compromise between capital and labour (i.e. the social-democratic state) that was once seen as necessary to preserve capitalism itself. Nonetheless, the international order of states and capitals is hardly an integrated or harmonious systemic totality. This is exactly because both of its constituents are indeed systems of competition. Moreover, the logics of interest and competition in the two systems, though aligned, are not identical, so that tensions can arise between them.

On the one hand, capitals compete with other capitals for markets and profits in the economic sphere. This competition consolidates and often widens wealth and income differences by social class internationally and within national borders—as has been the pattern of recent decades. This is because capitalist success depends on reducing labour costs, driving up labour productivity, and increasing the surplus value extracted from the workers in production. On the other hand, states compete with other states in the political sphere to further the interests of their own home-grown capitals against others in the world market and to attract the inward investments of foreign capitals. This dynamic is what establishes the structural interdependence of state and capital locally and internationally.[3] Capitals and states everywhere share common interests in the subordination and exploitation of wage-labour at home and abroad. They are united on one side of the class divide.

Yet structural interdependence is not *functional* integration of state and capital, because despite the mutual dependence of state and capital their interests are not identical. Nationalism requires state managers to prioritize the interests of their own home-based and home-grown capitals against those of rival states and to assist these in their competition with foreign capitals overseas. This is because states must rely on their own national economies to resource their own operations of governance. Every national state authority must draw on within-border economic resources (taxation of wealth and income of its own citizens and residents) to sustain its own offices and functions. A nation-state must defend as a matter of first resort a *national capitalism*—even though the national capitals in question may also be internationally facing and competing with others on the world stage. This ensures as well that any state must relate to other states as rivals. This is to ensure economic success at home and to deny business opportunities to other states that would disadvantage it economically. But this ensures as well that any state must also relate to the capitals that grew up in other states as rivals of its own capitals.[4] This is because the security and stability of any state depends on the competitive success of those capitalist enterprises from which it derives the bulk of its income.

Ontological presuppositions

The capitalist world economy and interstate system, like all social systems, are not composed simply of human agency embedded in social practices. This is, as the critical-realist ontology (CRT) establishes, not merely an "interactional order" stretching out over space and time. Rather, the social practices that reproduce these systems day-to-day are embedded in the emergent structures generated by previously materialized social interaction.[5] These emergent structures are always the antecedent or anterior conditions of social practices that people find "ready-made" and which they are compelled to reckon with. These are basically "action-environments" in which people must act and relate to each other in response to the situational logics these confront them with. Structural emergence is what makes social life systemic. Social systems exist and are reproduced because they have structural properties. If this was not so, definite and particular regularities of social interaction over time, by consequence of which one can speak of its institutional or organizational forms or delineate specific types of society or social order, would not exist. Without structural properties, social life would be unsystemic, since social interaction would be endlessly, relentlessly, and randomly transformative, so that societies were radically ephemeral, unstable, and shapeless.

Structural emergence renders social life systemic because structures not only contextualize social practices, but they also situate these practices within a framework of constraints and facilitators that impart to the human agency that animates them directional guidance. This is what makes possible societal evolutionism rather than random chaotic historicity in the free play of events. However, the directional guidance that structures impart to social practices is not structural determinism. This is because constraints and enablers operate on the basis of involuntary placement of people within social relations *vis-à-vis* resource distributions generated by structures and in accordance with their vested interests in specific kinds of social agency that are fixed by these involuntary placements. The structural conditioning of human agency within social practices is not such that people are programmed to respond to it in specific ways. Behavioural and attitudinal flexibility is allowed by structural emergence since this manifests as a framework of fetters and enablers within which lives must be lived rather than as cultural hydraulics that permit of only one response to them.[6]

Structural conditioning cannot be structural hydraulics as well because of the nature of the objects of conditioning—people. The situational logics of human agency and social interaction (of involuntary placement and attendant vested interests) that are given by structures may be disregarded or misdiagnosed or resisted or subverted by those under their sway. This is possible because people make and remake structures, whereas structures do not make or remake people. Rather, structures merely influence or condition the people who do the making and remaking of social systems. Structures are not agents, only people are. And people are agents of societal reproduction and/or transformation because they, unlike structures, have needs (biological and social) that animate the pursuit of interests, just as they have causal powers of intentionality and subjectivity by which they recognize these needs as their own and are incentivized to act on them socially.

Realist theory and world systems

This is the basic critical-realist ontological theory (CRT) of social systems, which, I contend, provides the most elementary abstract model of the constitution of the international state system and world capitalist economy. The world order of polity and economy that exists at any time, from the CRT perspective, reflects the distribution of powers in the two systems. This distribution of powers at every point in the history of the systems is the outcome of structural emergence arising from hitherto processes of social interaction in the two systems. These result from success or otherwise in the processes of competition between the actors (states and capitals) up to that point to consolidate and extend their powers of authorization and their control of marketable assets. This renders world order a hierarchically or asymmetrically structured one, because competition begets winners and losers, and success or failure in the competition of states and capitals is itself shaped (in the sense of constrained and enabled) by the structural emergence of previously materialized processes of competition.

Patterns of domination and subordination or of advantage and disadvantage are thus not only established by structural emergence but are also reproduced by it. Hierarchized structural properties in the two systems sustain relations of asymmetrical interaction among the human agents that make or remake them, just as relations of asymmetrical interaction reproduce the hierarchized structural properties of the two systems. This developmental ratchet transports forward in time the structurally given patterns of domination/subordination and advantage/disadvantage from one phase of social interaction to the next. Processes of asymmetrical competition between capitals and states in the systems of world capitalist economy and international relations have, in other words, the directional tendency to reproduce and reinforce the hierarchical structures. This is owing to the prior uneven distribution of resources of and capacities for authorization and allocation among the agents of competition.

Moreover, since capitalism is a system that through business competition piles up ever more colossal resources for reinvestment rather than consumption, there is also a general tendency for money-power to become ever more concentrated and centralized in the hands of those already advantaged by or from previous cycles of business competition.[7] Centralization and concentration of capital (owing to the dynamics of accumulation and of merger and acquisition) consolidates and extends the powers of authorization of those states that administer and serve the interests of the most advanced and developed capitals (the MNCs) in their rivalries with other states. This is because these states can draw disproportionately on the prodigious surpluses that are generated by corporate-monopoly capitalism as a whole. The winners of structurally conditioned asymmetric inter-capitalist and interstate competition tend to accrue greater concentrations of authoritative and allocative resources. Structural emergence in the systems is thus a story of chronically reproduced inequality of outcomes. The most powerful capital-state actors that dominate are those which have inherited their structural advantages, and which are therefore best placed in competition to pass them on.

This "inheritance of inequality" as structural emergence is manifest in global political economy. For historical reasons, which are connected to uneven but combined development—colonial exploitation, postwar underdevelopment, asymmetrical dependency, and unequal exchange—the dominant players in both systems (whether capitals or states) are mostly though not entirely those of the Global North—or rather of the West in the North.[8] At the centre of this nexus of capital-state power actors are the USA, the other Western powers, and Japan. These are *metropole* states in the sense conveyed by dependency theory in sociology. This is inasmuch these states maintain their positions of advantage in global systems by virtue of the continued disadvantages of others. These are those which are chronically reproduced by relations of unequal exchange and asymmetrical competition, albeit supported by sustaining ideologies such as neoliberalism's free trade mantra, military power, diplomatic coercion (including by means of the levers of aid and debt), and the dominance of these states of key international political organizations.

These structural relations of economic and politico-military domination and subordination between the state-capital actors of the Global North and those of the Global South are also those which establish the world system as *imperial*.

These relations of basically unequal exchange fix the three domains—the developed, developing (or semi-developed), and underdeveloped worlds—of global political economy. These domains of world order relate to but do not exactly coincide with the chief geo-spatial division of the system into rival regional blocs of state-capital combines. These are the North American, European, and Southeast Asian hubs, which are the economic power-centres of world capitalism. As I will show,[9] these centres are where the bulk of the commodity trade, sales, and capital investments of the MNCs are situated. This amounts to a triadic centralization and concentration of money-power and means of production in specific places. By contrast, vast swathes of Africa, Central Asia, and the Americas remained locked in conditions of chronic economic underdevelopment since they are relatively cut off from the circuits of trade and investment that circulate within and across the Triad.[10]

The imperial system of states is multiple but subordinated to the primary imperialism of the USA. This is owing to the special role that the US state has taken on since World War Two—and which in the postwar era only it has been capable of delivering—of stabilizing the existing political and economic orders. The US state enjoys political leadership over the Western Alliance and Japan and political hegemony over the "free" world of liberal democracy and market economy more generally. This is because its state managers can draw on vastly superior economic (and hence military and ideological) capacities than can its coalition partners, or indeed those of any other state presently that would wish to disrupt or overturn its hegemony.

The USA's hegemonic role, as scholars of Realist International Relations Theory (RIRT) rightly argue,[11] entails acting as guarantor of worldwide order and security. This is not, of course, "order" or "security" of a neutral or objective or universal character, as it represents itself. Rather, this is the order and security of a world market fully open for corporate exploitation by American MNCs and by those of the other metropoles. All enjoy a share of the spoils derived from open and free markets that US power securitizes. Dominance in the interstate system of the HICs under US hegemony is also normalized and legitimized by virtue of supranational and reputedly multilateral political institutions of worldwide governance in which the rules and values of liberal markets are inscribed. These organizations—the UN, G7, WTO, IMF, World Bank, OECD, NATO, and so on—mobilize resources of command (whether political, ideological, or military) to reproduce the hierarchical structural properties of interstate polity and world capitalist economy.[12] This, of course, is their primary function.

Yet US political hegemony in and over the interstate system is under growing pressure, for a number of reasons. These include (1) the relative decline of American capitalism that would bankroll the "international security apparatus" that would sustain this hegemony; (2) the emergence of rival competitor-states that would either seek to subvert US leadership locally or regionally (e.g. Russia, Iran) or would even aspire to challenge it internationally (i.e. China); (3) the continued energy-dependence of Western-dominated world capitalism (which US powers seek to police) on the US state's alliances with authoritarian Arab regimes in the Middle East that lack democratic legitimacy and popular support and with the colonial-apartheid state of Israel that has illegally annexed Arab Palestine and brutally repressed its people; and (4) the fact that even partner states of the USA are also competitor-states, so that under certain circumstances, these have the potential to question US hegemony and assert themselves independently (e.g. if US power is perceived as weakening or posing greater dangers than benefits for national interests or the international security order that it is supposed to protect).

Consequences and prospects

Now, the present alignment of polity and economy under US hegemony that constitutes international order presents humanity with a fundamental, intractable problem. This is because the capitalist mode of production of our "global" age that the US-led interstate system administers has become a force of economic ossification and zombification. The system has been characterized for 50 years by weak growth, stagnation, and recession, so that its capacity to absorb major economic shocks (most recently, as generated by the COVID-19 pandemic) is radically compromised.[13] Yet those modes of political and economic governance that prevail in international relations (neoliberal and neoimperial) are those which can only seek to reproduce and consolidate the corporate-market mode and the existent asymmetrical distribution of allocative resources this prescribes.

Weberian sociologist David Lockwood's famous distinction between structural malintegration and social malintegration is relevant in this context.[14] The capitalist world economy today is *structurally* malintegrated owing to its inner institutional strains and antinomies—including the astronomical and widening gap between the incomes of rich and poor, its progressive tendency to subordinate human needs to capital growth, and the ecological havoc that it wreaks. The system is also *socially* malintegrated because from structural dissonance is flowing social disorder fanned by human discontent. This is why the "global" age has witnessed major convulsive upsurges of social conflict and the emergence of mass protest movements right across the world in response to the injustices and privations that the system imposes on billions of people worldwide.

Yet, in spite of this alignment of structural and social dissonance, corporate mega "zombie" capitalism perpetuates. It does so, not owing to its own robustness, but because the international nation-state system has been converted into its life-support system. This is due to the structural alignment of polity and economy that has been consolidated under neoliberal governance under the neoimperial hegemony of the USA and supported by the other "developed" countries. To put it simply, wherever social conflicts and political protests and other forms of resistance happen to arise (and these are typically responses to economic pressures and assaults on entitlements—often originating outside national borders), and in response to whatever trigger-events, these are more-or-less reigned-in by agents of state power. The universalization of social malintegration is countervailed by its splitting-up or compartmentalization into "localisms" that are ring-fenced by national borders and policed by individual sovereign states.

The two great systems of global political economy—the economic order of zombified mega-capitalism and the political order of rival nation-states—are thus *mutually reinforcing* structures of domination. So long as their strategic alignment remains intact, these constitute radical obstacles to further progress in human development and in the global civilization process. A sustainable future for humanity—economically, ecologically, and socially—depends on transcending both systems, or at least undermining the alliance of state power and capitalist power that is prolonging the demi-life of the latter.

Structure

The book is set out in four chapters. The first three chapters examine the emergent structures of contemporary global political economy. The first two chapters do this by focusing on the capitalist world economy under neoliberal governance. Chapter 1 addresses the dynamics of inequality and injustice, especially by social class and by nation but also by racial-class and feminized-class, in contemporary times under neoliberal corporate capitalism. Chapter 2 addresses primarily the question of how these injustices and other asymmetries and imbalances of capitalist world economy in the neoliberal age can be explained. The chapter also seeks to demonstrate how the inequities, asymmetries, and imbalances (i.e. the structural malintegrations) of world capitalism undermine globalization theory and establish our contemporary civilization of capital as zombified.

Chapter 3 focuses on the interstate system under neoimperial governance, albeit in relation to neoliberalism and world capitalism. Neoimperialism is interpreted as a form of politics that preserves the dominance of the Global North, the high-income countries, and the Western Alliance, over the Global South, and the middle-income and lower-income countries. This is primarily owing to defence of comparative advantage, by means of enforcing unequal exchange and neoliberalism's "free" markets, as these are underscored by US and Western dominance of the institutions of supranational governance and by US military power.

However, an important aspect of the neoimperial project is US patronage of surveillance states in areas of the world of geostrategic and/or economic importance to the goal of preserving the existing structures of advantage and disadvantage in the distribution of authoritative and allocative resources. Therefore, Chapter 4 explores one such case: the role of the state of Israel in the politics of the Middle East on behalf of US and Western powers. This case-study is pertinent because of the fundamental importance of this "watchdog" to reproduction of the neoimperial order of states under US hegemony. This is also pertinent because it foregrounds the willingness of neoimperialism's power-state actors to tolerate the expropriation of an entire people and their brutal repression by colonial authority for 75 years in defence of chronically reproduced injustices in world systems.

Sean Creaven
18 December 2023

Notes and references

1 Mann, M. (1986). The Sources of Social Power: A History of Power from the Beginning to AD 1760. Vol. 1. Cambridge: Cambridge University Press.
2 As elaborated in his theory of socio-historical materialism. See: Marx, K. and Engels, F. (1970). The German Ideology. [1845]. London: Lawrence and Wishart; Marx, K. and Engels, F. (1967). The Communist Manifesto. [1848]. Harmondsworth: Penguin; Marx, K. (1970). A Contribution to the Critique of Political Economy. [1859]. London: Lawrence and Wishart; Marx, K. (1978). The Poverty of Philosophy. [1847]. Peking: Foreign Languages Press; Marx, K. (1934). The Eighteenth Brumaire of Louis Bonaparte. [1852]. Moscow: Progress Publishers. For excellent introductions see: Callinicos, A. (1995). The Revolutionary Ideas of Karl Marx. 2nd edition. London: Bookmarks; Collier, A. (2004). Marx. Oxford: One World. For useful reconstructive defences, see: Callinicos, A. (1987). Making History: Agency, Structure and Change in Social Theory. Cambridge: Polity Press; Cohen, G.A. (1978). Karl Marx's Theory of History: A Defence. Oxford: Oxford University Press; Creaven, S. (2000). Marxism and Realism: A Materialistic Application of Realism in the Social Sciences. London and New York NY: Routledge; Creaven, S. (2007). Emergentist Marxism: Dialectical Philosophy and Social Theory. London and New York NY: Routledge; Levine, A. (1984). Arguing for Socialism: Theoretical Considerations. London: Routledge and Kegan Paul.
3 See especially: Harman, C. (1991). 'The State and Capitalism Today'. International Socialism, 2 (51), pp. 3–54.
4 See especially: Stopford, J. and Strang, S. (1995). Rival States, Rival Firms: Competition for World Market Shares. Cambridge: Cambridge University Press.
5 Archer, M. (1995). Realist Social Theory: The Morphogenetic Approach. Cambridge: Cambridge University Press; Bhaskar, R. (1998). The Possibility of Naturalism: A Philosophical Critique of the Contemporary Human Sciences. [1979]. 3rd edition. London: Routledge; Creaven (2000).
6 Archer (1995); Creaven (2000, 2007).
7 Marx, K. (1976). Capital. Vol. 1. Harmondsworth: Penguin, p. 929; Marx, K. (1971). Capital. Vol. 3. Moscow: Progress Publishers, p. 241.
8 See Ch. 1 and Ch. 2.
9 Ch. 2.
10 Callinicos, A. (2009). Imperialism and Global Political Economy. Cambridge: Polity Press.
11 See for example: Gilpin, R. (1981). War and Change in World Politics. Cambridge: Cambridge University Press; Gilpin, R. (1987). The Political Economy of International Relations. Princeton NJ: Princeton University Press; Gilpin, R. (2001). Global and Political Economy: Understanding the International Economic Order. Princeton NJ: Princeton University Press; Keohane, R. (1984). After Hegemony: Cooperation and Discord in the World Political Economy. Princeton NJ: Princeton University

Press; Kohout, F. (2003). 'Hegemonic Stability Theory'. International Political Science Review, 24 (1), pp. 55–6; Mearsheimer, J.J. (2001). The Tragedy of Great Power Politics. New York NY: W.W. Norton; Posen, B.R. (2003). 'Command of the Commons: The Military Foundation of U.S. Hegemony'. International Security, 28 (1), pp. 5–46.

12 Callinicos (2009).

13 See Ch. 2. See also: Brenner, R. (2006). The Economics of Global Turbulence: The Advanced Capitalist Economies from Long Boom to Long Downturn, 1945–2005. London: Verso.

14 Lockwood, D. (1964). 'Social Integration and System Integration'. G.K. Zolschan and H.W. Hirsch (eds) Explorations in Social Change. Boston MA: Houghton Mifflin.

1 Neoliberalism, inequality, and injustice

Neoliberalism

What is neoliberalism? In recent times, it has become an article of academic fashion to claim that the term is chaotic and over-generalized, often being applied inappropriately to all forms of right-wing authoritarianism.[1] Neoliberalism, it is said, refers "to too many heterogeneous and contradictory policy dynamics",[2] or "has become . . . an empty signifier that means everything and nothing simultaneously",[3] so that it may be considered as neither useful nor intelligible in political analysis. Certainly, in popular left-wing discourse, references to neoliberalism have often resembled a blanket condemnation of capitalism-friendly politicians, governments, states, and transnational political organizations. Moreover, in the left-wing academy, the concept of neoliberalism has typically been deployed as a catch-all for all of the injustices and privations associated with mega-capitalism and its political governance in the "global" age. As Adam Tooze puts it: "We tend to paint the term with a rather wide brush, decrying the state of late-stage capitalism and its deleterious effects as being the fault of the neoliberals and their hyper-capitalist economic stranglehold on the global market".[4]

There is indeed a case to answer. The use of neoliberalism as an explanatory concept has undoubtedly been over-extended in political commentary, supporting analytical reductionism—of social outcomes to a specific political programme.[5] This loses sight of the fact that the injurious impacts on worldwide social and economic life commonly laid at the door of specifically neoliberal policies and governments are as much if not more attributable to the internal machinations of international corporate capitalism and its world markets that neoliberalism seeks to serve. Capitalism itself in the corporate age generates much of those deleterious effects (deepening international inequalities by nation and class, financial crises, ecological devastation, de-unionization, undermining of community life and social solidarity, etc.) commonly attributed to a neoliberal politics that are fashioned in its own image. This also fails to get to grips with the role of what I have termed neoimperialism in sustaining and entrenching worldwide inequalities and injustices, especially those to the detriment of the

DOI: 10.4324/9781003597346-2

Global South and to the benefit of the Global North. Neoimperialism, as I will show, interfaces with corporate capitalism and neoliberalism in generating these perverse asymmetries in world systems.

Neoliberalism is undoubtedly real, however. The concept of neoliberalism, properly understood, is also far from chaotic, despite claims to the contrary. This is not an "empty signifier", which escapes definition. The meanings attributed commonly to the term are actually fairly consistent and common in critical political discourse. Indeed, "the most important literature on the topic" has been shown to overlap on "95 percent of . . . definitions".[6] In recent times, even senior economists in the service of the IMF have conceded that neoliberalism exists. Moreover, the definitions of neoliberalism they offer are also remarkably continuous with those of critics. Neoliberalism, these IMF economists have written, has pursued a political agenda aimed at deregulating labour markets worldwide, promoting the free circulation of money and commodity trade across national borders, downsizing the social and welfare aspects of government, and privatization or commercialization of social services and state enterprises. Not only that, for them, but the benefits of neoliberalism are also called into question in much the same way as they have been by left-wing commentators. "The authors cited statistical evidence for the spread of neoliberal policies since 1980, and their correlation with anaemic growth, boom-and-bust cycles, and inequality".[7]

Neoliberalism as political ideology is thoroughly permeated by neo-classical political economy and classical liberalism. To be clear, this does not make neoliberalism synonymous with these earlier traditions, though obviously this is where its roots lie. Unlike classical and neo-classical economics, neoliberalism is not a wholly economic programme, a reformulated laissez-faire, though a particular view of economics lies at the heart of it. This view is not that the role of government or the state is to restore "free" or self-regulating markets but to embed them in supposedly apolitical constitutional rules and technocratic procedures that would insulate them from political challenges and construct the institutional and normative frameworks that will allow them to prosper.[8] As Quinn Slobodian puts it, "the foundational neoliberal insight is comparable to that of John Maynard Keynes and Karl Polanyi: the market does not and cannot take care of itself". This makes neoliberalism, as Slobodian rightly says, "a form or variety of regulation rather than its radical Other".[9]

In all its forms, then, neoliberalism represents something of a break with classical laissez-faire economics, in the sense that it rejects the utopian idea of a "spontaneous" market order, a self-reproducing market economy, as integrated by the laws of supply and demand. Markets, for neoliberals, as for classical liberalism, are indeed virtuous, but unlike for classical economics, they do not make or protect themselves. For neoliberals, either it is the role of state or government to enforce market and property relations, or this is a role of the state in partnership with various other non-state actors and agencies (e.g. business leaders, regulators, auditors, benchmark-setters, consultants, commissioners, opinion-formers, logisticians, contractors), who are typically recruited from the corporate sector. Neoliberals differ in their view of the degree to which states and governments act as market enforcers *vis-à-vis* other institutions.[10] However, the neoliberal age has witnessed an increase in the number of international political organizations that function to oversee or support world capitalism or organize regional markets (e.g. EU, WTO, NAFTA/USMCA) and the strengthening of the authority of more longstanding ones (e.g. UN, World Bank, IMF).[11]

Nor does the neo-classical (*homo economicus*) core of neoliberalism render this as a uniform doctrine or intellectual monolith. Research into the genesis of neoliberalism (as well as explorations of the ideas of key founder intellectuals as these are developed in specific cultural milieus) has identified a number of different strands that have fed it. These include those that arose from schools, intellectual circles, think tanks, and other networks in places such as Vienna, Chicago, Virginia, Freiburg, and Geneva, from the 1920s until the 1970s. Each of these has a different position on the nature and role of the state and government, the scope and meaning of democracy, the exact relationship between market and government and society, and so on.[12] There is, in short, more to neoliberal origins than the so-called Washington Consensus, which was largely based on the ideas of Hayek and Friedman, even though this Anglo-American version of the doctrine certainly has been especially influential in the world of politics and set in motion the wheels of neoliberalism's global ascendancy.

Neoliberalism has also been characterized by various politico-ideological variants since its late 1970s origins in the pioneer nations of the UK and USA. Even though right-wing and conservative applications have been dominant since the start (as exemplified by Thatcherism and Reaganism in the founder countries), there have also been centrist, even mildly left-leaning incarnations, such as in the USA and the UK (under "Third Way" governments). Progressive neoliberalism in government, however, may be described as a politics committed as much as its right-wing predecessors and successors have been to the hard programme of free-market fundamentalism (and associated retrenching of welfare rights in favour of workfare "opportunities"), but conjoined with the trappings of an anaemic social liberalism, which was not permitted to encroach on the sacrosanct domains of liberalized markets and corporate-property relations.[13] Inequality and poverty in the USA and the UK, under the watch of centrist or left-leaning neoliberalism, as we will see, did not decline at all. Rather, poverty levels remained constant at higher scales than in the 1970s as inequality continued its upward trajectory.

Yet there is a common, unifying vision that renders neoliberalism meaningful across its diversity of sources and its various mutations—and this vision is certainly informed by and built on classical laissez-faire economics, though much else besides. This is despite neoliberalism's conceptual variations and its practical need to adapt itself to the political institutions and cultures that hold sway in specific national and regional contexts upon which it encroaches. What is this unifying vision? There are five main strands to it.

1. There is the idea that only private ownership of the means of production and the active empowerment of markets in goods and services and labour-power can deliver economic efficiency and material prosperity. This is because the market mechanism, as Hayek tells it, is the only rational means of allocating resources in a society, since this is governed by objective laws of competition.[14] The "laws" of the market are, from the neoliberal perspective, omniscient (albeit fragile—and thus in need of the protection of the state), because they allow the co-ordination of every economic act without the need for a director or co-ordinator (i.e. political authority). In Hayek's vision, the market was god-like, in that this functioned as a universal mind (hence a totalizing knowledge), in contrast to the finite minds of mere people (whether as individuals or as a collective), which owned mere opinions. So, for Hayek, whereas society (including politics and government) gives us relativism, the market gives us objectivism, which renders it as unknowable, sacrosanct, and therefore unquestionable.[15]

   The omniscience of the market for neoliberalism stands especially in sharp distinction to the supposedly irrational allocation of resources by the *illiberal* state (whether communist, fascist, socialist, nationalist, or social-democratic). This is because this is governed by the finite, fallible, and self-interested choices of political leaders, which may also be placed in the service of particular interest groups or at the mercy of majority rule and its (for neoliberals) inherently inflationary demands.[16] Neoliberalism thus does not support a "minimal state", as is commonly thought. There is, in fact, "scant evidence of neoliberal reforms ever leading to a 'smaller' or 'weaker' state in any meaningful sense, even if certain functions have been removed from the state via policies of privatization and out-sourcing".[17] Nor is there any evidence that any neoliberal ideologue or politician has ever sought one.[18] Such is unsurprising, because neoliberalism supports only a minimal *welfare* state (since an expansive one would hamper capitalism),[19] just as it supports a strong, expansionary interventionist state in the service of capitalism.

2. Neoliberalism is committed to the view that markets are the guarantor not only of economic rationality but also of rationality in other spheres of society—including and especially politics and government. This is inspired especially by Hayek's big idea that the laws of the market are omniscient in that they generate objective knowledge and universal benefits in contrast to other human endeavours that are governed by merely relativistic motives and values. As Stephen Metcalf points out, this treats the market as

   > less a human contrivance, to be manipulated like any other, than a force to be studied and placated. Economics ceases to be a technique—as Keynes

> believed it to be—for achieving desirable social ends, such as growth or stable money. The only social end is the maintenance of the market itself. In its omniscience, the market constitutes the only legitimate form of knowledge, next to which all other modes of reflection are partial, in both senses of the word: they comprehend only a fragment of a whole and they plead on behalf of a special interest. Individually, our values are personal ones, or mere opinions; collectively, the market converts them into prices, or objective facts.[20]

This is the essence of free-market fundamentalism in that the market is regarded not merely as a way of efficiently organizing economic life but also of validating all human affairs. Indeed, the market ought to *govern* all human affairs, from this perspective, since a deity must be worshipped and obeyed, not merely consulted with.[21] All things social should avoid bucking the market, certainly. But these should also be shaped by or made to resemble markets or treated as if they were some kind of market. The neoliberal project of economizing everything was thus integral to Hayek's Big Idea. This was a manifesto "for the transformation of society, and not simply for the expansion of the market".[22]

And so it has come to pass. The neoliberal utopia today is indeed one in which all political and cultural institutions are made to resemble markets, or are disciplined by market forces, or are turned into commercial enterprises.[23] Our world is indeed one in which virtually all human acts are regarded as in essence economic acts or acts of competition—as was theorized by abstract neoliberalism.[24] Exporting market rationality into the state has the virtue for neoliberals of imposing the competitive ethos and thus cost-efficiency on the functions of public administration. This explains the fondness of neoliberal governments to install quasi-markets in the state sector along with charismatic leaders, entrepreneurial visionaries, and a rafter of technocratic experts and methods brought in from the private enterprise sector. Such is to be accomplished where actual markets, privatization, and outsourcing, though desirable, are impractical, so as to impose competitive wage-discipline on employees and rationalize service delivery.[25]

3. According to neoliberalism, not only are markets the only rational way of organizing economic life (and of stemming inefficiency in institutions beyond the market), but they are also indispensable to personal liberty. This is because markets not only release individuals to pursue their rational self-interest as buyers and sellers (hence allowing economic freedom to flourish) but also foster in them self-reliance, by compelling them to take responsibility for their own welfare. In the absence of the incentives generated by private ownership and market rewards and protected from its deficits by generous welfare states that are intended to abolish social injustice (i.e. lack of consumer opportunities for some owing to unemployment or low-paid work), individuals would be deflected from the work ethic, from economic enterprise, and

from self-reliance. Moreover, private ownership and the market mechanism, according to neoliberalism, also safeguard individual liberty in another way. This is by acting as a bulwark against the encroachments of coercive state power on civil society, on familial autonomy, and on the rational pursuit of self-advantage.[26]

4. Neoliberalism is also animated by a broader ethical vision of the "good society" than is provided by classical economics. This is one in which market freedoms will generate not only universal economic benefits but also the wider benefits of democratic citizenship more generally. In Milton Friedman's words: "Economic freedom is an essential requisite for political freedom".[27] Hayekian neoliberalism (which especially influenced the neoliberal pioneer governments of Thatcher and Reagan in the UK and the USA) discovers the roots of social order not merely in *homo economicus* (i.e. markets) but also in families. Whereas the market sustains individual liberty, the traditional institution of the family is the source of moral virtue, according to Hayek.[28]

   In this neoliberal imaginary, there is, therefore, no legitimacy accorded to a role for state or government in acting to build and sustain a public democracy, by means of the allocation of social rights, in order to reduce market-generated inequalities. This is ruled out for two reasons. Firstly, this is because such action would simply be coercive—the imposition of state power on free markets and individual liberty. The rational distribution of rewards determined by free individual responses to objective market forces would be disrupted and perverted by politically motivated confiscations that would penalize the enterprising and successful. Egalitarianism, for neoliberalism, is incompatible with freedom.[29]

   Secondly, this is because neoliberals regard competition and competitiveness as absolutely central moral values (i.e. as the source of impulse, imagination, enterprise, creativity, and excellence)—and competition generates winners and losers.[30] Indeed, the virtue of competition sits alongside those of liberty (freedom) and individualism in the neoliberal moral universe, all of which are interrelated and secured by free markets.[31] For neoliberalism, therefore, inequality is acceptable, even indispensable, since this is the consequence of market competition between free agents. Conversely, diminishing the rewards of individual competitive success (e.g. by redistributive taxation) would be unjust, because this would impinge on the liberty of the successful, from the neoliberal perspective.[32] By doing so, this would also disincentivize enterprise, innovation, and effort, and therefore undermine wealth-creation, slowing economic growth and perpetuating poverty.[33]

5. Neoliberalism in all its forms is animated by a particular vision of the primary purpose that the politically interventionist state must dispense for capitalism. This is to ensure that its agents (the propertied) are free from coercion—where coercion is defined permissively as interference with the free pursuit of market rewards and unlimited accumulation of wealth. Liberty, for

neoliberalism, is defined narrowly and negatively as freedom from coercion so defined.[34] This means that the defence of liberty requires protecting the market and capitalist property from the pressures exerted on parliament by democratic citizenship—that is, pressures for redistributive justice, or unaffordable welfare reforms, especially those emanating from the propertyless majority.[35] The pressures exist because competition necessarily generates inequality, and the necessity of inequality places democracy in opposition to liberty, according to neoliberalism.[36] The danger of democracy is that it "may simply lead by its own logic to socialism".[37]

For Hayek and his disciples, capitalism and the market, not democracy, guarantee individual liberty, which is why the state must defend them.[38] Remarkably, then, neoliberalism sees no role for "free institutions, universal suffrage, freedom of conscience, congregation, religion and press" in defending society against illiberal forces. Rather, for Hayek, "the market provides all necessary protection against the one real political danger: totalitarianism. To prevent this, the state need only keep the market free".[39] This means that democracy has for neoliberals a lesser status than capitalism, so that this may be set aside or suspended where this poses a threat to individual liberty (i.e. to capitalist markets and property).[40] Democracy is not, Hayek opines, "an ultimate or absolute value", whereas liberty is.[41]

Not only that, capitalism and the market safeguard democracy, whereas democracy cannot safeguard capitalism and the market, from the neoliberal perspective.[42] A democracy without capitalism and markets is simply self-negating, according to neoliberalism, since this would mean communism, socialism, or fascism.[43] For neoliberalism, furthermore, extra- or non-parliamentary political or social movements, forms of grassroots activism or direct action, and collective methods of social protest, these are regarded suspiciously—as harbingers of mob rule.[44] All of these should be contained by state power.

This reveals that a profoundly antidemocratic tendency lies right at the heart of neoliberal theory since its origins.[45] Antidemocracy is not a potential of neoliberalism but is integral to its philosophical underpinnings. And this renders neoliberalism inherently sympathetic to authoritarian politics in order to defend "liberty". For neoliberals, the ultimate guarantor of markets and capitalist property, faced with the challenge of mass democracy, is exactly political violence meted out by the repressive arm of the state—of which there are plenty of historical cases.[46]

This also necessitates placing executive authority for overseeing capitalism beyond the reach of parliaments in the hands of apolitical professional managers in the unelected machinery of state and in non-state agencies affiliated to the state using "objective" technocratic processes (testing, ranking, target- or metric-setting, auditing, etc.).[47] Such has, as Davies observes, opened up a "new institutional sphere between market and state conventionally understood, that can be analysed in terms of networks of 'governance' or 'governmentality' that redistribute state functions into various new administrative units".[48]

Neoliberalism as *realpolitik*

So far, I have mostly (but not wholly) addressed neoliberalism as political philosophy or as political ideology, teasing out its consequences. But, of course, neoliberalism is also political governance. As such it may also be identified with a specific set of policies that were intended to deliver on the prescriptions of neoliberalism as political ideology. This is neoliberalism as *realpolitik* rather than in theory or as philosophy. Pioneered by right-wing governments in the UK and USA in the 1980s, "actually existing" neoliberalism was internationalized in the 1990s and 2000s. This was just as corporate free-trade capitalism became globally consolidated with the crisis and subsequent demise of communism or state socialism and the discrediting of Keynesian economics that supported social democracy in the West.[49]

In practice, neoliberalism as state policy sought to reinvigorate national economic competitiveness by placing itself unambiguously and enthusiastically in the service of mega capital and corporate enterprise. This has committed ruling parties to a form of class warfare from above whereby the political process is converted into a mechanism to squeeze welfare systems, emasculate the trade unions, promote labour market flexibility, liberalize finance and trade, empower MNCs, privatize public goods and services, and reduce taxation on business and wealth.[50] Ultimately, the secret of capitalist renewal, from the perspective of neoliberal powerholders, is to bring about an anti-egalitarian redistribution of allocative resources. This is away from labour or from income from wages and the "social wage" (i.e. welfare benefits) towards capital, or out of public hands and into private ones.

Neoliberalism in office is also committed to expanding or enlarging the role of the market in society (not simply empowering existing markets) in order to increase the scope or range of profit-making. This is by means of the commodification or consumerization of culture and leisure. Neoliberalism has also sought to "modernize" the state (i.e. financialize, commercialize, entrepreneurialize, and impose technocratic managerialism on it), not merely to limit states to the role of market defenders and facilitators.[51] This is intended to render the state itself more cost-efficient (and hence less burdensome on private capital) and more conducive (on-message) to the dispensing of neoliberal goals.

Neoliberalism's goal of building a social order that would insulate capitalist property and markets from democratic accountability has made it an imperial project in postwar international politics. As Quinn Slobodian has shown, this was the case from neoliberalism's 1920s and 1930s origins. From the start, neoliberalism was as much a global undertaking as it was a national one, because it was recognized that constitutionalizing the rule of property and markets internationally would buttress the same processes at home. And so neoliberalism committed itself from its origins to the project of enshrining the absolute primacy of rights of property and markets in the inter-state system and world economy, immunizing these rights from the challenge not merely of communism, but also post-colonial governments and movements in the Global South, socialism, unionized labour, and national citizenship. So-called globalization since the 1980s is the practical accomplishment of this project.

This is where the politics of the neoliberal pioneers (von Mises, Hayek, Röpke, Wilhelm, Buchanan, Haberler—the so-called Geneva School) merge with those of neoimperialism, since the goal of neoliberalism's originators was not simply the political constitution of liberalized markets worldwide but reconsolidation of the West's rule over those markets in a decolonizing world.[52] The Geneva neoliberals distinguished between two modes of domination: *imperium* (the rule of the state over a national territory—preferably that of a business-friendly state) and *dominium* (the worldwide rule of supranational regulatory political organizations on behalf of capitalism). An important role of the latter was to reign-in the former, so as to hold national governments to the straight-and-narrow of pro-market policies. This required supranational institutions of worldwide governance (the International Chamber of Commerce and the League of Nations in the interwar period; the UN, EEC, EU, OECD, in the postwar period) to be converted into legislators of neoliberal policies internationally. This has of course come to pass. Most recently, of course, this has generated new global steering organizations (i.e. GATT, the WTO) in pursuance of the same goals.[53]

These politics were bound to reproduce a world order in which the South remained subordinate to and exploited by the North, as was their intention. This was by virtue of the logic of comparative advantage and unequal exchange that flows from a one-fits-all rubric of "free" competition between the capitals of the West and those of the Rest, especially where the former reserves the right to set aside or restrict free trade rules imposed on the latter if these threaten to undermine their advantages. Thus, as Adam Tooze rightly says:

> For the Geneva neoliberals, Empire never went away; it was simply rebranded as the "global market." Neoliberalism was predicated on protecting private capital from democratic forces and the influence of individual nations by creating supranational organizations with little oversight to regulate and extract resources from the Global South, thus perpetuating the economic exploitation of Empire under the name of neoliberal free-trade.[54]

Slobodian's meticulous historical research shows that the neoliberal globalists of the Geneva School were exactly set on this project ("empire without colonies") aimed at reconstituting the dominance of the former colonial powers over the decolonized world in the postwar setup. Indeed, for some of them, this project was motivated by explicit endorsement of racial hierarchy in world systems.[55] But, even where neoliberals did not explicitly endorse racial hierarchy, its reconstitution was nonetheless necessitated by the West's postwar imperative of maintaining an international division of labour that preserved this in practice. Securing a world order that, despite decolonization, preserved the economic exploitation of the "under-developed" countries and their peoples (mainly those "of colour") by capitalist corporations from the "developed" (White-majority) countries was, after all, the neoimperial project of Western powerholders, including neoliberal globalists.[56]

Notably, the Geneva neoliberal pioneers, as Slobodian recounts, spearheaded Western opposition to calls by the decolonized nations in the 1960s for a fairer global trading system (based in part on economic protectionism for the former colonies alongside its dismantling in the West) that would protect them from the ravages of asymmetrical competition.[57] Simultaneously, as Arun Kundnani persuasively argues, the imposition of liberalized trade or open markets (i.e. unequal exchange) by the US-led Western powers on the Global South, especially since the 1980s, has been accompanied by their construction of increasingly punitive immigration controls at home to control global labour supply. Neoliberal immigration policies were needed to restrict access of formerly colonized peoples to the Western world so as to protect the hierarchical international division of labour that the imperialism of free market competition was establishing. The interface of neoliberalism and neoimperialism in sustaining and deepening worldwide inequalities, including those of racial-class, is the focus of this book.

Moreover, alongside these developments, as Jessica Whyte has shown,[58] neoliberals agitated successfully against the global postwar, post-colonial movement for the universalization of collective social-democratic rights, on the grounds that these were incompatible with the rights of property. As became enshrined in the UN charters, "rights to housing, food, education and medical care" were, as Whyte puts it, "supplanted by a narrow focus on civil and political rights".[59] Either that, or these were downsized to minimal entitlements,[60] so that these would present no challenge to global economic inequalities or capitalist profits. The solution to world poverty, class disadvantage, and economic underdevelopment in the Global South was thus framed not as the worldwide promulgation of social justice (i.e. economic, social, and welfare rights—or *redistributive* rights) but as promoting the economic growth treadmill and the expansion of the world market—the internationalization of "trickle down" theory. This was just as the World Bank tied the measure of what counted as living in poverty to a pitiless dollar-a-day threshold.

Now, the illiberalism of neoliberalism *in practice* appears at odds with the claims of neoliberalism *as theory* to be a liberating force. Neoliberalism, as political philosophy, promises that empowering and protecting (rather than liberating or freeing) the market and capitalist enterprise will not only maximize economic freedom but also protect individual liberty from the collectivizing ambitions of state power. Capitalism and the market, according to abstract neoliberalism, guarantee individual rights of citizenship, in part by counteracting illiberal tendencies of state authority, obstructing the state's capacity to deliver on illiberal designs.

However, neoliberalism in practice could never deliver on these ideals, because philosophical neoliberalism was self-contradictory to the core. Rather than rolling-back state power and authoritarian government, it was bound to consolidate them, as it has. Researchers have thus documented the ascendancy of "authoritarian" neoliberalism as a worldwide phenomenon, albeit to differing degrees, in different parts of the world, depending on the interface of global and local pressures and forces.[61] Authoritarian neoliberalism may be defined as a mode of governance of "contemporary capitalism . . . which tends to reinforce and rely upon practices that seek to marginalize, discipline and control dissenting social groups and oppositional politics rather than strive for their explicit consent or co-optation".[62]

William Davies usefully distinguishes between three successive phases of neoliberalism as political practice that have led to the dominance of the present hyper-authoritarian modes.[63] These are those of "combative neoliberalism" (1979–89), "normative neoliberalism" (1989–2008), and "punitive neoliberalism" (2008–). Combative neoliberalism gives us the assault on socialism, social democracy, welfare politics, and unionized labour, by the right-wing neoliberal pioneer governments. This also gives us the demise of those modes of politics in the West that neoliberalism waged its war upon.

Normative neoliberalism is where the new politics consolidates itself internationally. Having won the war (against socialism and social democracy), now neoliberalism seeks to secure its empire, by inscribing the ethos and "rules of the game" of free-market fundamentalism everywhere, not only in economy and government but also in society and culture. As Davies expounds:

> The neoliberal *telos* became a constructivist one, of rendering market-based metrics and instruments the measure of all human worth, not only inside the market but, crucially, outside it as well. . . . Concepts such as 'human capital' offered a new lens through which to analyse and calculate decision-making in non-market contexts. The virtue of markets was their competitive quality, which provided a normative procedure through which value and knowledge could be ascertained. According to this logic, all spheres of human activity should therefore be reconstructed around the standards of competition, so as to ensure that valuable products, services, artefacts, ideas and people were discoverable. The task of government was now to ensure that 'winners' were clearly distinguishable from 'losers', and that the contest was perceived as fair.[64]

Normative neoliberalism was the age of technocratic managerialism in state and government and in the expanding network of non-democratic institutions of governance beyond and around the state that sought to consolidate and deepen marketization. This is the period that sees concerted efforts to entrepreneurialize all non-market domains and to legitimize inequality as the necessary price of competition and of competitive success. Such provided space for "progressive" (Third

Way) variants of neoliberalism to assume centre-stage, since these were more "natural" conveyors of a normative neoliberalism than were those right-wing pioneers that were associated with class war to generate its conditions of possibility.

Finally, punitive neoliberalism characterizes our present times. This is the consequence of the failure of the neoliberal project to revitalize capitalism, as was its primary goal, which eventually ferments the Great Financial Crash of 2007/09 and the austerity decades that followed. Austerity radicalizes neoliberalism's war on public welfare and the remnants of the social state, facilitating a hardening and accelerating of its authoritarian bent. This leads to a re-centring of law and order politics as the only line of defence of neoliberal governance against the multitude of disenfranchised, distressed, and resentful at the hard edge of class inequality, whose ties with normative order may be weakened.

At the same time, all of neoliberalism's technocratic methods of rationalizing the functions of state and government, of distributing resources on the basis of competitive bidding, and of mobilizing people to give more for less in return, are deployed increasingly punitively. This is under the impress of economic "hard times" to help revive an anaemic capitalism by means of ever-greater savings and belt-tightening. The authoritarianism of the present phase of neoliberalism resembles that of its combative first phase. But, even so, there is a difference between the two, for as Davies rightly points out, the

> worldview of the neoliberal pioneers, which pitted free-market capitalism against all varieties of non-capitalist system, has mutated into something equally paranoid and simplistic, but now apparently self-destructive. In contrast to the offensive against socialism, the 'enemies' targeted now are largely disempowered and internal to the neoliberal system itself. In some instances, such as those crippled by poverty, debt and collapsing social-safety nets, they have already been largely destroyed as an autonomous political force. Yet somehow this increases the urge to punish them further.[65]

Neoliberalism in *realpolitik* has thus degraded individual citizenship rights worldwide, just as it has eroded social and welfare entitlements. Yet, assaults on labour rights, on employee rights, and on welfare rights of all kinds, which have been intended to "liberate" capitalism and the market from non-market "interferences", were made possible only by virtue of expanding the coercive functions of state power. So, as the "social state" receded, the coercive state expanded. This is because neoliberalism guarantees "liberty" by enforcing through the exercise of state power the rights of property and the marketplace, which are incompatible with rights broadly conceived. These are incompatible because the capitalism that neoliberalism empowers is hostile to social and welfare rights, just as it is indifferent to all other rights of citizenship except those of property ownership and commodity exchange. But, once social rights are rolled back, in favour of narrowly economistic individual rights, even the latter must fail, for all those outside the higher (propertied and professional-managerial) classes. This indeed has come to pass, as this chapter will show.

The profoundly anti-democratic tendencies of "actually existing neoliberalism", as these have been institutionalized in state and government in the USA and elsewhere, are rooted in the Hayekian vision that the "good society" is a market economy unencumbered by a rights-conferring polity whose moral basis resides in a privatized morality of family values and authority. The neoliberal imaginary also betrays an affinity with neoconservatism and right-wing populism, since all are allergic to the interventionist rights-based state and supportive of "family values" as the basis of moral order.[66] Neoliberal powerholders have sought to responsibilize parents for educative, healthcare, childcare, and other welfare functions that were once dispensed or aided by the state. This is an agenda endorsed by neoconservatism. Both share a commitment to reinvigorating traditional (i.e. familial) authority in opposition to public democracy.[67] Both mobilize religion and patriotism to build popular support.[68]

Now, the paradox of the neoliberal world is that international capitalism has, in recent times, appeared as unassailable, even though it has piled misery upon a vast swathe of the global population, and its success even in its own strictly economic terms of reference is limited—as I intend to show. Neoliberalism, though its intellectual or ideological origins can be traced to the 1920s, was forged as state *realpolitik* owing to the collapse of the long postwar economic boom (1948–73), and from the crisis of the Keynesian model of state-regulated social-welfare capitalism that was its political driver in the advanced economies. Not only has neoliberalism as political governance failed to usher in a new era of universal prosperity, however; it has also failed to match the levels of economic growth that characterized the preceding era of social democracy and Keynesian demand-side economics that ruled in the West from the late 1940s until the early 1970s.

Neoliberal policies, even though these are globalized, have gone furthest among the developed countries of the UK and USA, where these have been accompanied since the 1980s by increasing income and wealth inequality between rich and poor (i.e. a hardening of class polarization) and seemingly intractable problems of unemployment, economic marginalization and social exclusion.[69] However, they are rendered universal policies (and problems), albeit unevenly distributed across the face of the world, in the context of combined but unequal development, under the endless ratchet of international capitalist competition.[70] Neoliberalism's war on social rights, and its dismantling of the social-welfare conferring state, has indeed been a major driver of such widening inequalities worldwide. Consequently, this "nihilistic disintegration of the social compact", as Wendy Brown describes it, has generated, in places such as the USA, a multitude of the "economically abandoned and racially resentful", an atomized, displaced "populace seething with rancour, rage and resentment, not to mention material needs".[71] Neoliberalism's assaults on democracy and public welfare, and its abandonment of a protective regulatory role in labour markets, have spawned in this rancorous multitude a mirror-image of its own self-declared distrust of and alienation from remote "big" politics and government.

My own book *Modernity and the Pandemic* examines the impact of these decivilizing mechanisms of neoliberal capitalism (widening inequality, the retreat of the social state, hyper-competition in the labour market, the disintegration of the social bond) in nurturing egoistic and resentful individualisms suspicious of state authority that compromised public compliance with pandemic NPIs and vaccination.[72] This multitude of the disenfranchised are, on Brown's account, opened up to the influence of those who promulgate right-wing populisms suffused with ultranationalism and (in the USA) Christian fundamentalism.[73] This is as they seek refuge in traditional values suffused with an embattled xenophobia nurtured by the hyper-competition that free markets unleash. And so, as Brown puts it, neoliberalism "plants the seeds of a nationalism it formally abjures".[74]

The end of neoliberalism?

On some accounts, this global upsurge of the far right (exemplified by the success of Trump in the USA and the support for Brexit in the UK) even spells the ruination of neoliberalism, in the sense that this exposes its illiberal terminus in the Other of this nationalistic populism.[75] More speculatively, this has even led some political analysts to propose that our current age is witnessing the literal demise of neoliberalism.[76] This is on the grounds that these new incarnations of right-wing populism (e.g. "America First" Trumpism in the USA; Brexit nationalism in the UK) stand in opposition to the "globalization" of liberalized markets (including those in migrant and off-shored labour) and the de-nationalized cosmopolitan values that neoliberalism supposedly upholds.[77] As Kyle McGee expresses the argument:

> This new political enclosure raises from a different vantage the question of the end of neoliberalism that has been touted since Trump's election. If the reconstitution of the body politic raises this question, it is not because a macroeconomic regime of international exchange is on the verge of falling apart. It is because borderless global neoliberalism encounters a body politic not necessarily sympathetic to its goals.[78]

Indeed, on some accounts, the new body politic that confronts neoliberalism is manifestly unsympathetic to neoliberalism's goals. Thus, according to William Davies:

> Insurgent conservative movements, such as those which drove Brexit and the rise of Donald Trump in 2016, are antagonistic to many core tenets of the neoliberal state, and represent a danger to the ambition to anchor sovereign powers in "apolitical" centres of expertise such as the European Commission.[79]

From this perspective, whereas neoliberalism serves only deterritorialized interests (those of the cosmopolitan corporate elite), and whilst it recognizes only the territory of "global dispersion and placelessness", the new assertive right-wing nationalisms of the Trumpist and Brexit movements are committed to a contrary project. This is to re-embed political governance and capitalist economics in national territorial space, purportedly to serve the interests of the feet-of-clay ordinary folk.[80] For this reason, some left-wing analysts, notably the philosopher Slavoj Žižek, argued that a victory for Trump over arch-neoliberal machine politician Hillary Clinton in the 2016 presidential election would be the better outcome, on the grounds that this would rupture neoliberal hegemony, from which more progressive political currents might emerge.[81] The growing appeal of Bernie Sanders' populist socialism to many Americans (which compelled Trump's presidential successor, Joseph Biden, to commit to partially restoring those workers' rights that Trump had overturned) may indeed support this analysis.[82]

Trump, on this interpretation, won the White House in 2016 by explicitly denouncing globalization, cosmopolitanism, and the corporate (economic) and technocratic (political) elites, and by promising to defend American industry and jobs from unfair foreign competition.[83] Trumpism thus situated itself on the side of the browbeaten American working class faced with an unpatriotic, remote, global-facing neoliberal elite. In doing so, it contrasted the pro-migration interests of the latter (to undercut the wage levels of locals with the import of bargain-price overseas labour) with the anti-migration needs of the former (to defend wages, jobs, and access to slimmed-down social services). Similarly, Brexiters, on this account, secured their "yes" vote to leave the EU in 2016, and later the pro-Brexit Tory party were elected to office in 2019 to deliver severance from Brussels, on the promise that this would restore national sovereignty, deliver national renewal (putting the "great" back into Britain), and reaffirm a "Britain for the British" (i.e. closed borders to migrants from the EU).[84]

But these events (the challenge to state authorities of ascendant right-wing nationalisms) do not mark end times for neoliberalism, for a number of reasons, though they have germinated even more authoritarian versions. These reasons are as follows.

1. Neoliberalism has never simply been antithetical to nationalism and national chauvinism.[85] This is because, even in the "global" age, neoliberal polities have to administer territorial nation-states, which rely for their stability mostly on the domestic economy, on home-based and home-grown capitals, rather than income repatriated from the overseas operations of the MNCs. Neoliberal politicians and governments of high-income countries favour liberalized markets worldwide not because they see themselves (or rather those they serve) as a rootless, nationless elite, with global rather than local interests, but because they (rightly) see worldwide trade liberalization as empowering

the national capitalisms they serve. Moreover, the real interests of corporate bosses and MNCs are not transnational or borderless or "spaceless". These remain rooted in territorial space, as I will show in the next chapter.

Nor can neoliberal polities simply disregard national citizenries in the service of capitalist internationalization, even if they were so inclined, since they are compelled to secure for themselves some degree of legitimacy amongst those they purportedly represent. Neoliberals are compelled to alliance-build with at least some national citizenship groups or sections of the national society if they are to keep their grip on office. Ultranationalists and neo-conservatives are not excluded from the process if these are regarded as "on-message" with neoliberal fundamentals—such as the absolute primacy of markets and property, the sovereign consumer, "family values"—as they are. Quinn Slobodian and Dieter Plehwe, for example, discuss alarming cases of EU alliance-building in recent times, between neoliberal technocrats and radical "ethno-nationalist, identitarian, and Alt-Right" groups, to secure common goals.[86]

2. Neoliberalism has rarely legislated open borders for foreign workers and their families, in sharp contrast to its perpetual enthusiasm for free trade in money and commodities. So, when Joshua Cohen inquires if "it is reasonable to attempt to understand whether neoliberalism and its attachment to market fundamentalism is able to cloak itself and reconsolidate itself (or, at least, its key economic tenets, minus globalisation of labour) in the language or performance of right-populism by political elites",[87] the answer is, surely, yes. This is because there are precedents.

   The pioneer New Right neoliberalism's of Reagan in the USA and Thatcher in the UK could hardly be described as de-nationalized or cosmopolitanized regarding immigration and asylum policy. Both sought to restrict people inflows from poorer countries just as they extolled liberalized markets in capital and commodities.[88] So-called progressive (centre-left) neoliberalism in Britain under New Labour governments in the early 2000s did open the UK's borders to worker-migrants from Eastern Europe, true.[89] But such pro-immigration policies have hardly been typical globally under neoliberal governance. Certainly, these were in sharp contrast to borders that were closed to Eastern Europeans in the leading EU countries at the time.[90] Nor indeed were pro-immigration policies typical even of New Labour in office.[91] And, of course, the EU has been, since the 1990s, a "Fortress Europe", erecting insuperable barriers to legal entry for black- and brown-skinned peoples from the middle-income and lower-income countries.[92]

3. Unsurprisingly, then, nor has neoliberalism in power generally furthered the cause of cosmopolitanism over and against ethnic privilege or outright racism, as it claims. This is obscured by the neoliberal polity's noisy rhetorical

commitment to anti-racism. Neoliberalism represents racism as merely attitudinal, a matter of prejudicial, irrational, ignorant beliefs, because that fits with the individualist worldview it espouses. Not only that, but neoliberalism (in its more reactionary modes) also denigrates and dismisses the views of radicals who argue that there is more to racism than personal error or malice. Neoliberal anti-racism has spawned a vast, lucrative (of course) diversity-appreciation industry intended to educate racists out of their racism. But even though RAT and the like have undoubtedly helped some people (the willing and acquiescent) to recognize their own biases or prejudices, it has not put a dent in racism. Nor could it, because racism's causes are structural, not attitudinal, and neoliberal anti-racism functions to deflect attention away from the real causes, preventing their recognition.[93]

Racism and xenophobia are, for example, institutionalized in immigration and asylum rules and practices favoured by the neoliberal polity. This is because these are not targeted on all foreigners but on those from the so-called developing countries. Such anti-immigration policy in turn nurtures the popular racism and xenophobia that RAT and related enterprises seek to challenge, since its actuality (and the manner of its representation by politicians and the corporate media) conveys a negative sense of migrants as troublesome, threatening, parasitic, bogus, potentially violent and criminal. Deviance in the neoliberal imaginary is given a black or brown face.[94]

Racism and xenophobia are also institutionalized in neoliberal anti-welfare and criminal justice practices, which also feeds into popular racism. Neoliberalism's war on welfare "dependency culture" has tended to disproportionately stigmatize and penalize minorities—especially black people. For they, owing to the combined impacts of structural classism and racism, are most dependent on welfare support in the high-income countries. Simultaneously, neoliberalism's punitive law and order politics have focused on these same minorities, criminalizing them in unprecedented numbers, especially in the USA, where they have been especially targeted for mass incarceration. This is because the neoliberal polity's war on welfare exactly necessitated a parallel war on crime and disorder aimed at the growing numbers of the marginalized, disenfranchised, and potentially resentful, amongst whom black people were especially overrepresented.[95]

At the deeper level of world systems, there are of course those of statism and capitalism, divided up by nation, region, and class. These systems, which are defended by the present regimes of neoliberal and neoimperial rule, are grotesquely asymmetric. They are also inevitably racialized. This is because the hierarchic architecture of world systems reflects deep-seated ethnic divisions and inequalities as well as those of social class, since these arise from the interface of class stratification and uneven global economic development from unequal exchange.[96]

As we have seen, black- and brown-skinned people, especially those in subordinate class positions, are particularly marginalized, oppressed, and exploited in the white-majority high-income countries of the Global North. This is to the benefit not of working-class white people (the usual target of liberal RAT) but capitalism, its superordinate class of property owners and corporate employers, and therefore its neoliberal overseers.[97] As Arun Kundnani explains:

> This is partly because racism weakens class struggle by dividing white workers from most of the world's working people. More fundamentally, race provides a means by which capitalism can more intensively exploit certain categories of worker—the enslaved, the indentured, colonised peasantries, migrant workers—as well as justify discarding peoples deemed superfluous to the economy.[98]

The racialized class exploitation of minorities in Western countries has been made possible by a particular postwar pattern of immigration. This is one where people from low-income countries (often ex-colonies) were recruited by governments and employers into low-status jobs (especially vulnerable to insecurity, casualization, and downsizing) at the base of the class structure, at lower rates of pay than would be accepted by "natives", thereby forming a racialized fraction of the working class.[99]

As the overwhelming majority on planet Earth, these peoples are also overwhelmingly situated in the low-to-middle income countries, mostly in the Global South, where the vast bulk of them are vulnerable to the worst excesses of capitalist exploitation, including by corporate employers whooping it up on the opportunities provided by neoliberal-sponsored "globalization". These worldwide structures of advantage and disadvantage, of domination and subordination, have their genesis in the colonial era, of course. But owing to the inheritance of inequality, these have since become *emergent*; that is, recursively generated *structural* properties of capitalist world economy and international state system. Involuntary placement of people in these structures constrains or enables their life-chances, depending on which side of the divides they are situated in.[100]

4. The free-market fundamentalism imposed by the Washington Consensus on world economy and polity since the 1980s has always been one-sided. Structural adjustment programmes of radical marketization and the deregulation of cross-border trade and finance have always been aimed primarily at countries of the Global South rather than those of the Global North. This is so that the benefits of unequal exchange and comparative advantage can be harvested by (mostly) Western MNCs. The USA and the EU throughout the neoliberal era have resorted to protectionist policies (tariffs, quotas, subsidies, tax breaks, non-tariff restrictions, etc.) to insulate certain industrial sectors and agriculture from foreign competition, just as they

have been the beneficiaries of the battering down of trade barriers across the developing world. As I will show, globalization, as this is represented by neoliberals, as denoting a borderless world economy, has always been mythical in part.

5. The record in government of Trumpism in the USA and of Brexit Toryism in the UK has hardly confounded neoliberalism. This is perhaps clearest in the British case. My book *The Pandemic in Britain* shows that the Brexit nationalism of the Tory right was and is deeply ingrained with utopian ideas of neoliberal globalization.[101] Brexit, it was asserted, would release the UK from constraints on internationalized trade associated with EU membership, since membership constituted the bulk of British trade within the Union, limiting potential opportunities on the world stage—such as lucrative trade partnerships with the USA, India, China, and other Southeast Asian countries. EU release would, therefore, allow British capitals to prosper in global seas, as they did in the nineteenth-century laissez-faire era. As Adam Kotsko rightly observes: "The fact that this deal is an impossible fantasy only highlights the degree to which neoliberal standards are shaping Brexiteers' thinking".[102] Brexit would also supposedly release UK capitalism from the residual binds of EU labour market regulation and human rights law. Such would offer the possibility of a further diminution of civil liberties, of social liberalism, to the advantage of propertied elites.

   The performance of the Brexit Party in office betrayed its utter continuity with neoliberalism in another way. This was regarding its appalling pandemic response. The COVID-19 pandemic elicited a policy response from the UK government that may be described as "British exceptionalism".[103] This was detrimental to the cause of public health protection, leading to thousands of unnecessary deaths. The negative consequences of policy failure were exacerbated by the weaknesses of the UK public health system (NHS) generated by decades of under-resourcing under successive neoliberal governments.[104] Key features of British exceptionalism included (1) deferred lockdowns; (2) incautious fast-tracked reopenings; (3) ambivalent or tepid public-health messaging; (4) failure to restrict or close borders; (5) failure to mandate public mask-wearing for most of the pandemic; and (6) reliance on entrepreneurs or business leaders rather than public health professionals to lead on developing a functioning test-and-trace system, with predictably negative results. I will briefly address the first five.

   Each of them is attributable to the baneful influence of neoliberalism on the Brexit government. Initial and then later resistance to lockdowns was animated by the imperative to keep Britain "open for business", even though business was closing elsewhere.[105] Incautious de-escalation of lockdown restrictions was animated by the imperative to restore as quickly as possible Britain's "openness" for profit-making. Indeed, this was to ensure that British business was restored faster than anywhere else that matters, so that there was no comparative competitive disadvantage for home-grown or home-based capitals *vis-à-vis* those of competitor countries.[106] For exactly the same reasons, an aspect of the resolute defence of Britain's "openness for business" was also maintaining borders that were open to anyone and everyone who would bring commerce to UK shores and who would convey it from those shores to elsewhere.[107]

As for communicative ambivalence, this may be read as a strategy to either undermine physical distancing norms that could not be evaded or to disincentivize the public from sticking to the practices these norms enforce once the norms are removed. This of course was in order to break down public resistance to post-lockdown fast-tracked full capitalist restoration or normalization.[108] Finally, as for mask-scepticism, this was a curiosity in that, unlike other aspects of exceptionalism, this hardly served the cause of unshackling capitalism from the constraints of physical distancing. Unlike physical distancing, mask-wearing has little impact on economic life. Not only that, mask-wearing, if legally mandated by government, is a strategy for trying to evade physical distancing controls, or even to release them, by way of providing an alternative to them. However, mask-scepticism may be read as the expression of economic liberalism and consumer libertarianism thwarted by physical distancing. This was a case of displacement.[109]

Trumpism in office in the USA shows its continuity with neoliberalism in ways both similar and different to the UK Brexiters. There is here a stronger case for seeing the Trump presidency as some kind of break with neoliberalism. However, as Ray Kiely suggests, if so, this is "less a wholesale break from neoliberalism and more a shift to a renewed form of right wing neoliberal populism".[110] The right-wing populist aspect is arguably manifest in Trump's embrace of economic protectionist policies, his willingness to wage trade wars with China, and his ditching of NAFTA (which demonstrated his willingness to pull the USA out of supranational neoliberal trading organizations and treaties).

However, the examples of policy continuity with neoliberalism considerably outnumber the supposed breaks, whereas certain of the supposed breaks are arguable. Trumpism in office did not counter labour market deregulation or de-unionization. This did not seek to address zero-hour contractualization or casualization of labour whereby millions of workers are denied pensions, sick pay, holiday pay, a minimum living wage, etc.[111] Indeed, under Trump's presidency, there was a rafter of further attacks on employee rights and conditions of work.[112] Trump's government remained committed to privatization (including of infrastructure), budget cutting on the social and welfare aspects (though this was short-circuited by the pandemic), low rates of taxation on property, businesses, and the wealthy—all of which were at odds with his anti-corporate election campaign rhetoric. Trumpism did nothing to reverse technocratic managerialism in the US state and his presidency was marked by a further diminution of constitutional checks on executive decision-making that were evident under the Bush Junior and Obama presidencies.[113]

As for one of Trump's supposed breaks with neoliberalism, the termination of NAFTA, this was replaced by USMCA. But USMCA was a neoliberal free-trade deal (and organization) quite similar to the one it replaced in most respects, albeit with minor tweaks and adjustments to the eligibility criteria for avoiding tariffs that would benefit US automobile manufacturers especially. USMCA strengthened intellectual and digital property rights and raised the bar for immunity from prosecution for e-companies regarding content on their online platforms. Freer markets were legislated for in agricultural products with zero tariffs.[114]

Trump himself is neoliberalism personified in that he conformed to Hayek's romantic ideal of the ultra-rich entrepreneurial visionary who supposedly trail-blazes change in society from elevated heights simply by acting on his or her fancies or convictions.[115] As for Trump's presidential style, this was in a sense so neoliberal it was almost a caricature of neoliberalism. This was in the manner of treating the job of leading the US state as virtually the same as bossing a corporation, so that citizens and public officials alike were related to as if they were merely company employees. Trumpism in office was the brazen personification of corporate America, of "USA Plc." This was neoliberalism out in the open, in plain sight, devoid of self-reflection, without any attempt to disguise itself.[116] Trump's flagship Office of American Innovation, for example, explicitly stated its purpose as "fixing government with business ideas" and running the country "like a great American company".[117]

Even Trump's rants against globalization betrayed a hyper-neoliberal sentiment. This was because the target of his ire was not free trade but what he saw as *unfree* trade to the detriment of US big business and its employees. As Kotsko rightly says, Trump "is not offering us a way out of the endless competition of neoliberalism—he is offering to give us the pure form of neoliberal competition for the first time".[118] Trump was as committed to trade liberalization as his predecessors, including in the sense that this must be made to work especially to the advantage of American capitalism. This was continuity, not rupture, with US foreign economic policy. Notably, then, even though NAFTA was replaced by USMCA under Trump's watch, the rest of the supranational architecture of worldwide neoliberal governance (the WTO, IMF, World Bank, etc.) was untouched (excepting Trump's spat with the WHO), even by critique. Above all else, though, Trumpism represents the wildest and purest spirit of neoliberalism. This is because at the centre of Trump's worldview is the absolute primacy of endless, eternal competition and of the imperative of always being on the winning side in that competition.[119] This is the real meaning of Trump's "America First".

But, even if it were true that Trumpism represents a break with so-called globalization, this would raise the question of the relationship between "globalization" and neoliberalism. Is so-called globalization really integral or indispensable to neoliberalism? It is an article of faith that it is. But this orthodox view is based on a perception of neoliberalism as simply "the revival of classical liberalism".[120] This is a utopian interpretation of world capitalism as both nationless and self-sustaining. If this interpretation were correct, neoliberalism would indeed be simply the political and ideological expression of a globalized laissez-faire capitalism. But the interpretation is false.

As we have seen, neoliberalism recognizes that markets cannot regulate themselves and so cannot survive or prosper without political interventions. At the same time, neoliberalism has shown itself quite capable of mutation and adaptation. Therefore, greater or lesser versions of nationalistic neoliberalism seem possible, ranging from those which are moderately protectionist, up to those which oversee virtually autarkic national economies. Nationalistic neoliberalism would preserve all aspects of the hard programme of market and property fetishism alongside restrictions on cross-border exchanges. At the extremis, in a world where markets are curtailed by national borders, such neoliberalisms would likely struggle to secure domestic legitimacy for themselves, because the capitals they represent would not be able to exploit or extract resources internationally through the imperialism of free trade. And so, living standards would plummet; profits would slide. However, this raises the spectre of a revival of overtly imperial and colonial competition between states to reclaim a share of global resources inaccessible by trade. Neoliberalism, anti-democratic to the core, is capable of fashioning such a world.

Modes of inequality

I have asserted that the neoliberal age is one of massive inequalities in the distribution of economic rewards and that neoliberalism has reigned over a world in which these inequalities have increased dramatically. Indeed, neoliberalism as a form of politics and governance, I contend, cannot be absolved of responsibility for widening these inequalities. But it is commonly said that inequality is unimportant so long as the economic growth this supposedly supports reduces poverty. What does inequality matter, J.R. Rogers inquires, if everyone has enough to eat and a roof over their head?[121] The argument assumes either that inequality and poverty are unrelated or that inequality is even associated with poverty reduction (as Rogers does). However, our world of accelerating wealth and income disparities is also one in which the poor remain in greater numbers than ever before.

The empirical data I will mobilize in this chapter illuminating global poverty and inequality reveals primarily the reality of class polarization across the world. Under neoliberal-sponsored "globalization", the winners are mostly Western MNCs, capitalist elites, and the super-rich. This is as members of the higher professional-managerial class have held their position. The losers are the global working class and the poor, including the working poor (and, in the West, BAME workers and the minoritized poor). Moreover, this is especially workers and the poor in the postcolonial world and the feminized working class everywhere, as I will show.

Inequalities of class and of "race" (or rather of racialized class) are reproduced to a large degree by transmission through the family line.[122] Mike Savage estimates that in the high-income countries half of the wealth of the propertied elite is inherited rather than "earned" through "work" (i.e. by means of commodity production or commercial activity). Such is supported, as Melinda Cooper shows, by neoliberalism's retrogressive taxation policies. These subsidize the rich, functioning as a kind of covert privatized welfare support system for the propertied, just as public welfare for the poor and commonfolk has been scaled down, on the grounds that this deters work and encourages dependency.[123] As Cooper writes: "Tax deductions, exclusions, preferences, exemptions, deferrals, and credits are all deliberate departures from a baseline rate of income taxation", which function as "an instrument of wealth generation in the hands of the rich".[124] This has led to the resurgence of "dynastic wealth", or of capital-gains wealth, in traditional nuclear families, or rather in those of the elite. This monopolization of wealth as familial property is shielded by the neoliberal state and jealously guarded by anti-tax activism and demonization of social spending on the "undeserving".[125]

More radically, as Andrew Sayer argues, class inequalities are generated by the propertied elite's appropriation of an ever-growing share of the world's economic resources as *unearned* income. Properly speaking, the rich do not obtain half their wealth as unearned income (e.g. through inheritance or tax gifts or other subsidies) but *all of it*. This is as profits from the exploitation of wage-labour in capitalist productive enterprises, rent from the monopolization of land, interest from savings, speculation in financial markets and on commodity price movements, and so on.[126] The propertied and capitalist elites either *appropriate* wealth generated by those who work to produce use-values or *redistribute* it into their own hands through forms of enterprise that are unproductive because they do not generate use-values.

Feminized inequality

Now, inequalities (especially those generated by class relations in our market society) are the main focus of this book. This is because, as I have argued elsewhere, class divisions have by far the greatest efficacy in generating economic inequalities and income poverty, whereas relations of class exploitation also explain gender and "racial" hierarchies.[127] But, even so, there are also gender inequalities between males and females, which are especially impactful on working-class women and even more so on working-class women "of colour". A few words on gender stratification and gendered injustice are therefore in order. As I argue in my *Emergentist Marxism*, gender inequality is not explainable by a system of patriarchy, as many feminists argue. This does not exist and persist because it serves the interests of men in subordinating or exploiting women. Rather, this is quite simply a function of the economic-class exploitation of labour by capital, which has become an emergent structure of gendered inequality in its own right.[128] How does this work?

The sexual division of labour confronts individuals as an anterior material social environment, existing apart and prior to their own existence. It functions to apportion individuals to specific gender roles independently of their will (men as principally, not exclusively, "breadwinners" in the labour market, and women as primarily, not exclusively, "carers" in the family). This structure provides substantial, indeed indispensable, economic benefits for capitalism, in two main ways. Firstly, because it allows the reproduction costs of labour-power to be "privatized" (i.e. conducted by women without monetary recompense in the domestic sphere), hence protecting profits.[129] Thus, worldwide:

> Women do at least twice as much unpaid care work, such as childcare and housework, as men—sometimes 10 times as much, often on top of their paid work. The value of this work each year is estimated as at least $10.8 trillion—more than three times the size of the global tech industry.[130]

Secondly, because it provides employers with an ideological resource (sexism) to rationalize a horizontally and vertically segregated (by gender) labour market, the casualization of female labour, and the payment of especially low wages to women in sweated industries and feminized jobs, on the grounds that these are supplementary to the "family wage" earned by their male partners.[131] The lowest-paid jobs are indeed feminized (e.g. social care, childcare, catering, classroom assisting, retail, clerical, call centres, personal service, cleaning).[132] Little wonder, then, that across the capitalist world economy, "gender inequalities in labour markets are remarkably persistent and deeply embedded across diverse development paths".[133]

World capitalism has made women simultaneously winners and losers. On the one hand, capitalism's expansion across the globe has depended on a massive influx of women into the workforce who had traditionally been dependent on husbands, fathers, and male relatives. As such, this has given women a measure of independence from men—a progressive development. Especially in the HICs, women have been able to secure professional-managerial posts, in increasing numbers, though these are not usually the top jobs.[134] Yet this is a progressive development with a retrogressive aspect. This is because women of the Global South are also coerced into entering the labour market by the necessity of avoiding destitution in the context of the undermining of the peasant economy by corporate land grabs and by the impossibility of raising a family on a single ("breadwinner") wage.[135] On the other hand, combining paid work with domestic roles has made the lives of women increasingly difficult as they try to reconcile work and family life.[136]

This burden is inseparable from the workings of world capitalism. In all countries, from HICs to LICs, women are paid less than men for the same jobs.[137] The gender gap in income from wages or salary between the sexes is around 20–24 per cent on average worldwide.[138] Presently, this is 12.7 per cent in the EU (with wide variations between member countries),[139] 18 per cent in the USA,[140] and 13.1 per cent in the UK.[141] In all countries, from HICs to LICs, women remain underrepresented in the higher professions, in politics, and in business, and are corralled in occupations that are amongst the lowest paid. Only 25 per cent of MPs and 27.5 per cent of managers worldwide are women, for example.[142] The majority of women workers are in the service sector—many in jobs that used to be relatively well-paid, high-status men's jobs, but which have been deskilled and demoted in the job hierarchy (e.g. banking administration, secretarial and clerical work).[143] The vast majority of women workers in developing countries are in the informal sector (where jobs are precarious, without employment contracts, and without legal rights such as sick pay, holiday pay, or pensions).[144]

Whether they are in the formal or informal sector, however, women are especially concentrated in jobs that have bare subsistence wages (if that), primitive working conditions, and long hours. These include in sweatshops working shifts from 12 hours up to 36 hours in FEZs or EPZs where contractors serving the MNCs have set themselves up.[145] Many others are being paid a pittance to do jobs that have traditionally been done without pay by women in their own homes (e.g. domestic servants of the wealthy).[146] Women worldwide are disproportionately in part-time employment (owing mainly to having to juggle paid work and domestic labour) where the gender pay gap is at its widest. The impact of this on women who are lone mothers is obviously particularly severe.[147] On some estimates, as much as 70 per cent of the world's poorest are female,[148] though this figure is rightly disputed by the World Bank and by other analysts.[149]

Even so, the global feminization of poverty is undeniably real, and this is obviously related to the global feminization of employment.[150] The UN predicted that 383 million females would live in extreme poverty by the end of 2022 compared to 368 million males.[151] In fact, the reality today is rather worse:

> In 2024, the global extreme poverty rate, defined as living on less than $2.15 per person per day, was 9.8 per cent for females compared to 9.1 per cent for males. Overall, 24.3 million more females live in extreme poverty compared to males. By 2030, a projected 8.1 per cent of females (compared to 7.6 per cent of males) will linger in extreme poverty, missing the SDG target. Ending extreme poverty for women and girls will take an additional 137 years if this trend continues. The situation is even worse when considering the $3.65 and $6.85 international poverty lines, with 25.4 per cent and 47.5 per cent of females living in poor households in 2024 and little change expected by 2030.[152]

However, although this asymmetrical structure of gender relations sustains capitalism, this provides only illusory benefits for most men, that is, *working-class* men. This is because so-called advantages (e.g. higher wages earned by male workers *vis-à-vis* female workers or greater numbers of men in formal sector jobs compared to women) are often simply lesser inequalities than those endured by female workers rather than privileges as such. Working-class males derive no benefit from the fact that working-class women are paid less than they are, for example. Such reduces the household income of working-class families, which usually are made up of dual-earning couples, mostly male and female cohabitees. Not only that, but the monetary under-valuing and casualization of female labour-power also exerts a downward pressure on wages and incomes overall across the working class, to the detriment of men as well as women, widening economic inequalities and helping reproduce income poverty.[153] The proportion of jobs taken by male workers worldwide in the informal sector is astronomical (at 86 per cent) and only a few percentage points lower than for females (at 91 per cent).[154]

Other supposed benefits of "male privilege" (such as more leisure time and fewer domestic responsibilities than is typical for women) may also be questioned. In a certain sense, these may be considered an advantage (though arguably a marginal one) for men, but in a deeper sense not so. This is inasmuch as both males and females would benefit from the socialization of childrearing under an expansive, inclusive welfare state, which even social-democratic supported capitalism ruled out, let alone the present neoliberal version. In any case, these "privileges" are considerably outweighed by the disadvantages of class subordination that the gendered division of labour acts to preserve.

How is the gendered division of labour reproduced? Not primarily owing to sexist attitudes or beliefs. It is unlikely that the ideology of women's proper place which this gendered class structure sustains was ever accepted uncritically by all people—not even in the latter part of the nineteenth century where it corresponded better to the empirical reality of the worldwide division of labour than it does today. Nonetheless, this shapes still the perceptions of many, although not most, men or women. Yet male chauvinism remains causally efficacious, albeit weakly so, in shaping the life-chances of women, not least because it feeds into discriminatory practices in the occupational sphere (where most employers are male), and sometimes into oppressive or exploitative behaviour by individual males in the home. Situated as it is within the context of capitalist market society, the radical fringe of sexist ideology (which holds that women are the subordinates of men, servicing male needs) has contributed to the commodification of women as passive sex objects and to various other forms of sexual exploitation.[155]

But, even so, the commodification of sex is driven not by "men" but by capitalism. Moreover, sexist ideology is reproduced only by virtue of the gendered division of labour that serves capitalism. This emergent structure exerts directional pressure upon people of both sexes to accept it as a fact of life and to act in ways that ensure its persistence from one generation to the next. One important reason for this is that people remain immersed from birth in family units in which women do most of the housework and childrearing (even as they hold down paid jobs) and men perform a larger or more economically significant role in work outside the home (since women are more likely to have part-time jobs owing to childcare duties). This is part and parcel of the inherited or "emergent" social environment that by virtue of its causal powers of constraint and enablement exerts directional pressure on people to act in particular ways. Consequently, men and women are socialized to see this gendered division of labour as the "normal" state of affairs, even if some partially or totally break with its legitimatory ideology (sexism).

But, of equal importance, there is the simple fact that people encounter a labour market that *objectively* offers higher rewards for men than women for doing the same jobs (horizontal segregation) and which segregates lower-paid women's occupations from higher-paid men's occupations (vertical segregation—the "glass ceiling"). This makes it rational for men and women to stick to their "traditional" roles, whether they accept them as legitimate or not. Such is especially true of working-class men and women. This is because their market situation discourages swapping gender roles around, where doing so would incur poorer life-chances for themselves and their dependents. Thus, emergent social structures (in this case the gendered capitalist labour market) exert directional pressure on their agents to act in ways that reproduce them. Gender disadvantages at work and in the family are reproduced by virtue of the opportunity costs that are attached to social conduct challenging traditional gender roles.

Neoliberalism and injustice in the UK

I will now address the chronically reproduced emergent structures of economic inequality and of income-deprivation of world capitalism that disadvantage people on the wrong side of them and empower those on the right side of them. I will begin with the UK. Here, the inheritance of inequality and the reproduction of poverty has radicalized in the neoliberal era.

Wealth disparities narrowed in the postwar period prior to the neoliberal era, by contrast. "By 1979 the share of the top 1 per cent, which had been around three-quarters, was closer to one-fifth. The share of the top 0.1 per cent, which had been a third, was by 1979 around 7 per cent", whereas the share of the top 10 per cent remained stable.[156] Between 1936 and 1938, the richest one per cent of the population owned 56 per cent of the national wealth whereas the richest five per cent owned 88 per cent of it. The lower 90 per cent of the population, during this period, owned only 12 per cent of total wealth. By 1971, however, the share owned by the richest one per cent had fallen to 31 per cent, whereas the share owned by the richest five per cent had fallen to 65 per cent, just as the share going to the bottom 90 per cent increased to 35 per cent.[157] Since the mid-1970s these trends have been reversed. Between 1976 and 1999, the share of national wealth going to the top 10 per cent of households increased from 57 per cent to 71 per cent (excluding the value of dwellings). Simultaneously, the share going to the bottom 50 per cent declined from 12 per cent to just three per cent. This was according to data presented by *Social Trends*.[158]

Since the turn of the century, it has become more difficult to track the trend of wealth inequality in the UK, because there has not been continuity in the way the data is gathered, and it appears that the rich are increasingly adept at masking the full extent of their riches, as well as having greater opportunities to do so. Nonetheless, the evidence appears to support continuation of the trend of hardening wealth disparities since 2000. On this timescale, the richest 10 per cent of households increased their pickings, from 48 per cent to 52 per cent of national wealth,[159] whereas the share going to the bottom 50 per cent, according to the ONS, dropped back to nine per cent from 12 per cent.[160] This was in the period up to 2010. Since 2010, however, the process has levelled off owing to the damage inflicted on share price values and bonuses by the great crash and recession. Between 2010 and 2018, the top 10 per cent increased their share, but only fractionally, from 43.56 per cent to 44.59 per cent of the total, whereas the bottom 50 per cent saw their share decrease, also fractionally, from 9.61 per cent to 8.48 per cent.[161] These figures are inclusive of the value of dwellings. Nonetheless, the super-rich, the top 0.1 per cent, the corporate elite, escaped the crisis virtually unscathed, doubling their share of national wealth between 1984 and 2013.[162]

Turning now to trends in income inequality and poverty in the UK in the neoliberal era. Here the evidence of growing disparities and of worsening poverty over the long *durée* is clear. Prior to this, in the first few decades of the postwar period, the share of national income of the top 10 per cent of households fell from 33.2 per cent to 26.1 per cent, whereas the share of the next 60 per cent increased from 54.1 per cent to 63.5 per cent. However, over this period, the bottom 30 per cent were not the beneficiaries of the income redistribution that took place. Between 1954 and 1974, their share did not increase at all, though nor did it fall, fluctuating between 10.8 per cent and 12.1.[163] By contrast, in the period from 1979 to 1997, the top 20 per cent of earners saw their income grow by 2.5 per cent per annum compared to 1.1 per cent for those in the third quintile of earners and 0.8 per cent for those in the lowest quintile. This trend was interrupted under the New Labour years, though it was not reversed. Between 1997 and 2010, the top 20 per cent of earners increased their annual income by 1.7 per cent whereas the bottom 20 per cent increased theirs by the same amount.[164]

The number of people living below the official poverty line (as defined as disposing of an income of less than 60 per cent of average earnings) rose from four million to 14 million between 1979 and 1997, whereas the proportion of households below average earnings increased from 59 per cent to 63 per cent over the same period, just as average income increased.[165] As the New Economics Foundation reported in 2014,

> the UK saw a dramatic rise in levels of economic inequality during the 1980s; it has continued to rise since, although at a slower pace. Recent data shows that the richest one per cent of households in the UK now earn around 150 times more than the poorest one per cent of households. Wealth inequality has also risen considerably, with the top 1 per cent now having more wealth than the bottom 50 per cent put together".[166]

Between 1981 and 1992, the proportion of people living in households of less than 60 per cent of average income increased from 15 per cent to 25 per cent, just as average income increased.[167] Between 1981 and 1993, the poorest 10 per cent of the population experienced a 4.1 per cent decline of income, and the poorest 50 per cent a 2.9 per cent decline of income, whereas the richest 10 per cent increased their level of income by nearly five per cent.[168] According to *Social Trends*, these trends towards increasing income differentials between rich and poor continued, albeit at a lesser pace, between 1994 and 2001.[169] Research by Brewer *et al.* confirmed this, indicating increasing income inequality from 1997 to 2000 (under the first New Labour government).

By the late 2000s, still under New Labour's watch, income inequality had "reached levels last seen in the 1920s". This was "driven by a growing share of income going to the richest, in particular the top one per cent". During the period from 1975 to 2008, "income inequality among working-age people has risen faster in the UK than in any other OECD nation . . . such that the UK now ranks as one of the most unequal countries in the OECD".

> The UK has a net income inequality index of 0.341, and is only exceeded by Portugal (0.344), Israel (0.376), USA (0.378), Turkey (0.411), Mexico (0.466) and Chile (0.501). . . . The average annual income in the UK for the top 10 per cent of the population in 2008 was roughly £55,000; for the bottom 10 per cent, it was just £4,700—a ratio of 12:1. This is up from a ratio of 8:1 in 1985, and significantly higher than the average income gap in developed nations of 9:1.[170]

At the same time, according to DWP statistics, between 1979 and 2000, the number of people in poverty increased from 7.1 million (or 13 per cent of the population) to 13.3 million (or 23 per cent of the population).[171] However, between 2000 and 2005, the latter increase was offset, owing to the impact of New Labour's modest reforms of the benefits and taxation systems.[172] Hence, according to the Joseph Rowntree Foundation, the proportion of people in poverty declined marginally under New Labour, from 23 per cent to 20 per cent between 2000 and 2005. This was a temporary respite though. Since then, these modest gains have been dissolved by another upward spike in poverty rates between 2005 and 2007 that restored the level to 22 per cent of the population, and still climbing.[173] Overall, in the period between 1979 and 2008, under the impact of the three main planks of neoliberal reforms—financial liberalization, social security tightening, and labour market deregulation—"the number of people living in poverty . . . almost doubled, from 7.3 million people in 1979 to 13.5 million in 2008".[174]

In the aftermath of the Great Financial Crash of 2007/09, the process of growing inequality levelled off. But this was owing to a more rapid depreciation of income from wages than of income from welfare benefits owing to the recession. This was possible because the poorest of the poor derive a much greater proportion of their income than others from welfare.[175] The poorer became poorer but so did many average income earners. Since 2007 the proportion of the population in poverty has been static, with minor fluctuations either way. This was still 22 per cent in 2018/19 as it was in 2007/08.[176] Indeed, as analysis by the Social Metrics Commission has shown, "over the course of the last two decades, the overall rate of poverty in the UK . . . has sat stubbornly between 21% and 25% of the UK population".[177] But, in terms of raw numbers, there are more people living below the official poverty line today (14.3 million according to the Social Metrics Commission) than at any other time in the postwar period.[178]

Neoliberalism and injustice in the USA

What about trends in the structural emergence of inequality and poverty in the USA over the same period? Here some of the patterns are even more severe than in the UK. In the pre-neoliberal postwar period, between 1947 and 1977, rates of income inequality were stable, with minor fluctuations. The bottom 40 per cent of earners marginally increased their share of national income, whereas the top 10 per cent saw their share marginally decrease.[179] Between 1977 and 1997, by contrast, the top five per cent of American households increased their annual income after taxes by 43 per cent, the top one per cent by 115 per cent, while the bottom 60 per cent saw no improvement in real income at all, despite a sharp increase in the number of dual-earning families. Moreover, the bottom 20 per cent witnessed an absolute decline of around nine per cent over the same period.[180] In the mid-1970s, the share of national income going to the top fifth of American households was 45 per cent, whereas by 2018 this had increased to 52 per cent. The median income of the top-tier households increased by 64 per cent from 1970 to 2018, whereas the income of the lowest-tier households *fell* by one per cent over the same timeframe.[181] "Between 1979 and 2007 the share of income of the bottom 80 percent of the population fell by between 10 and 30 percent, while that of the top 1 percent increased by 130 percent".[182]

Thomas Piketty's exhaustive research concluded that over the course of three decades (1994–2014) the income growth of the poorest 50 per cent of the population was virtually zero compared to a 300 per cent rise for the wealthiest one per cent.[183] Between 1980 and 2016, just as the share of national income accruing to the top one per cent of householders increased from 10 per cent to 20 per cent, the share accruing to the bottom half declined from 20 per cent to 13 per cent.[184] On a longer timescale, from 1971 to 2016, the incomes of the top tenth of households grew 80 per cent more than those of middle-income households and 120 per cent more than the bottom half of households.[185] Between 1989 and 2016, the share of pre-tax national income going to the top 10 per cent of earners increased from 43 per cent to 50 per cent, whereas the share going to middle-earners declined from 42 per cent to 37 per cent and the share going to low earners (who made up half of all earners) fell from 15 per cent to 13 per cent.[186]

Wealth disparities in the USA are even wider than disparities of income and have shown the same tendency to increase in the neoliberal era. Again, the pattern before the consolidation of neoliberalism was for wealth disparities to reduce rather than increase. From the mid-1920s through to the end of the 1970s, the share of national wealth owned by the super-rich, the top 0.1 per cent of the population, fell from 25 per cent to eight per cent of the total. Since the early 1980s, however, this trend has been reversed, as the share of national wealth owned by this propertied elite has risen inexorably, reaching 22 per cent of the total by 2013.[187]

> In 1989, the United States had 66 billionaires and 31.5 million people living below the official poverty line. A decade later, the United States had 268 billionaires and 34.5 million people living below the official poverty line.[188]

In 1989 as well the richest five per cent of American households enjoyed a share of national wealth that was 114 times above the median, whereas by 2016 their share was 248 times higher.[189] At the tail end of the 1980s, the top tenth of families owned 67 per cent of total wealth whereas the bottom half owned just three per cent. By 2016, however, the top tenth of families had increased their share to 77 per cent, whereas the share owned by the bottom half of families had declined to only one per cent.[190]

Research conducted by Saez and Zucman showed that "almost all of this increase is due to the rise of the share of wealth owned by the 0.1% richest families, from 7% in 1978 to 22% in 2012, a level comparable to that of the early twentieth century". Moreover, according to Saez and Zucman, "over the 1986–2012 period",

> the average real growth rate of wealth per family has been 1.9%, but this average masks considerable heterogeneity: for the bottom 90%, wealth has not grown at all, while it has risen 5.3% per year for the top 0.1%, so that almost half of aggregate wealth accumulation has been due to the top 0.1% alone.[191]

America's richest householders "are also the only ones whose wealth increased in the years after the start of the Great Recession" of 2007/09.

> From 2007 to 2016, the median net worth of the top 20% increased 13%, to $1.2 million. For the top 5%, it increased by 4%, to $4.8 million. In contrast, the median net worth of families in lower tiers of wealth decreased by at least 20%. Families in the second-lowest fifth experienced a 39% loss (from $32,100 in 2007 to $19,500 in 2016).[192]

The outcome of all of this, as Barbara Ehrenreich noted in 2003, is widespread hardship alongside unprecedented riches in the wealthiest country on the planet:

> The Economic Policy Institute recently reviewed dozens of studies of what constitutes a 'living wage' and came up with an average figure of $30,000 a year for a family of one adult and two children, which amounts to a wage of $14 an hour. This is not the very minimum such a family could live on; the budget includes health insurance, a telephone, and childcare at a licensed center, for example, which are well beyond the reach of millions. But it does not include restaurant meals, video rentals, internet access, wine and liquor, cigarettes and lottery tickets, or even very much meat. The shocking thing is that the majority of American workers, about 60 percent, earn less than $14 an hour.[193]

The OPM in the USA unfortunately offers very little purchase on the reality or extent of the hardship faced by America's working poor. This is because it is based on an absolute baseline rather than on a culturally sensitive one, which drastically undersells poverty. US poverty is calculated by comparing a person's income to a fixed threshold. This threshold is the amount of income needed to cover the most basic of needs. The threshold was set in the 1960s and has not since been changed. This was pegged at three times the cost of a minimum food diet adjusted for family size and inflation (i.e. of food prices).[194] The rationale for this was that back then (in the early 1960s) one-third of family income was typically spent on food. But this is no longer the case. The proportion of income an average American family spends on food has since shrunk to just 15 per cent, because the prices of non-food consumptive items have increased much faster than of food items, so that the OPM has become arbitrary.[195]

Now, such a measure does not accommodate income from subsidies or benefits (e.g. housing or nutritional assistance, tax credits). Nor does it incorporate a host of everyday elementary living expenses (transport, medical bills, medical insurance, childcare support, taxes, etc.)—the cost of most of which have increased much faster than food prices. And, of course, there is no place for exceedingly basic cultural or leisure needs (e.g. the occasional vacation, day trip, or cinema outing). Nor is this threshold linked to national median income or to increases in general living standards as a culturally relative measure of poverty would be. Consequently, whereas the OPM in the 1960s set the poverty line at roughly 50 per cent of median income, today it is setting official poverty at under just 28 per cent of median income.[196] This effectively renders invisible tens of millions of Americans who, on a reasonable and culturally relevant definition of poverty, are very poor indeed, and who would have been recognized as poor in the 1960s. Ehrenreich's working poor are effectively airbrushed out of the picture.

Given that the OPM has since the 1960s become outmoded and invalidated, ever more so with each passing decade, massively under-representing real deprivation, and with the undersell also increasing with each passing decade, the persistence and magnitude of poverty in the USA that it reveals on its own terms is remarkable. The long postwar boom that coincided with the Keynesian-welfarist model of capitalism saw the official poverty rate as defined by the OPM halve from 22 per cent in 1960 to 11 per cent by 1973.[197] Since then, in the neoliberal era, progress has stalled over the long *durée*, as the poverty rate has fluctuated with the ups and downs of the economy, failing to maintain the steady downward trajectory of the earlier era. OPM rates climbed back up to above 15 per cent owing to the recessions of the early 1980s and 1990s, receding in the periods in between, though without falling back to the level of the early 1970s.

> The poverty rate wavered between 11 and 12 percent for the rest of the decade [after 1973] and then rose rapidly to 15.3 percent by 1983. It gradually fell to 12.8 percent by 1989, then climbed back over 15 percent by 1993. The 1996 poverty rate was 13.7 percent.[198]

The 1990s boom left one in eight Americans below the poverty line, whereas the percentage of Americans living in absolute poverty (i.e. on less than 40 per cent of median earnings) rose from 4.9 per cent in 1989 to 5.1 per cent in 1998.[199] Poverty then climbed continually from 1999 to 2010, again topping 15 per cent by the end of the period. The Great Recession increased the number of those living below the official poverty line by four million to 44 million, or 14.3 per cent of the population, the highest it had been for 15 years. This also brought about a 4.2 per cent drop in median household income.[200] Most recently, though, poverty has ebbed again, dipping from 14.8 per cent in 2014 to 10.5 per cent in 2019, this resulting from a mini-boom. Thus, after more than 45 years (and most of those under neoliberal governance) "official" (i.e. state-misrecognized) poverty marginally bettered the 1973 rate.[201] The reality, of course, is that poverty in America has increased *substantially* since the 1980s. Even on the official count, in 2018, the officially acknowledged American poor numbered more than 38 million, or one in seven Americans.[202] In 1973 they numbered 23 million.[203]

Neoliberalism and the workers

The structural emergence of widening economic inequalities in the neoliberal era also manifests as a general process of redistribution of income for or from wages to income for or from capital. Across the OECD, for example, just as neoliberal reforms started getting phased in, capital growth began to outstrip wage growth. This was from the 1980s onwards. "For the Group of Seven (G7) major industrial economies, the OECD estimates that the 'share of capital income' grew from 31.9 percent in 1975–9 to 33.9 percent in 1990".[204] This is indeed an international trend:

> The labor share of income in 35 advanced economies fell from around 54 percent in 1980 to 50.5 percent in 2014. . . . Developing economies have also experienced the same phenomenon, albeit to a lesser extent. Available studies suggest that the labor share of income fell from 39 percent in 1993 to 37.4 percent in 2014, a drop of about 4 percent.[205]

The OECD reported trends are supported by data gathered by other organizations. Most notably, according to UNCTAD's *Trade and Development Report 2022*, labour's share of total income *vis-à-vis* capital in developed countries shrank from 62.5 per cent in 1980 to 56.5 per cent in 2020. The report also conveyed a lesser reduction in labour's share of total income *vis-à-vis* capital's in the developed countries over the same period, from 54.7 per cent to 51.7 per cent.[206] Between 1980 and 2000 (the period in which neoliberalism became ascendant in politics and government in the West), the reduction in labour's share and increase of capital's gain was 4.4 per cent in the developed countries compared to 0.5 per cent in the developing countries. Between 2000 and 2020 (a period in which neoliberalism became globally ascendant), by contrast, the rate of redistribution of income from labour to capital in the developed world slowed (to 1.6 per cent), just as this accelerated in the developing world (to 2.5 per cent).

In the USA, on a longer timescale, workers have been especially hard hit, suffering a decline of the median wage of eight per cent between 1973 and 1998, despite recording productivity gains of 46.5 per cent for employers over the same period. This was even though the US economy enjoyed a 1990s growth boom that ought to have boosted wage growth.[207] According to Joseph Galbraith, four-fifths of American families witnessed an absolute fall in their income of five per cent during the recession-ravaged 1980s.[208] Robert Brenner estimated that between 1979 and 1990 hourly real wages in the US economy fell by an average of one per cent a year.[209] On Robert Heilbronner's calculation, the real weekly income of an American worker in 1990 was 19.1 per cent below the level reached in 1973.[210] As a result, "the average real income of families was only a few percentage points higher in 1993 than in 1973, and that largely because so many more spouses were working".[211]

The long American boom of the 1990s did nothing to reverse these trends, this benefitting only the top third of families. This was noted even by the IMF: “One strong development of the current expansion has been the steady decline in labour’s share of national income”.[212] Average wages for American non-supervisory employees working in all industries and services, other than government and agriculture, were less in 1997 (at the peak of the US boom) than they were in 1973.[213] By 2000, the poorest tenth of American workers were still earning just 91 per cent of the earnings they used to enjoy three decades earlier.[214]

Alongside these trends has also been a tendency for average working hours of waged or salaried workers to increase, so that incomes have declined relative to the expenditure of labour-time. The average working week in the USA increased by 20 per cent (or from 40.6 hours to 48.4 hours) between 1973 and 1985.[215] Employees were on average working the equivalent of more than a month extra (an additional 164 hours per year) in 1996 compared to 1976.[216]

> Between 1970 and 1990, the share of employed-for-pay U.S. men who worked more than 48 hours in the Census reference week rose from 15.4 to 23.3 percent. Between the 1980 Census and 2005 American Community Survey, the share usually working more than 48 hours per week rose from 16.6 to 24.3 percent. We find that increases in long work hours were greatest in detailed occupations (and industries) with (a) rising residual wage inequality and (b) slowly-growing real compensation at ‘standard’ (40) hours.[217]

This trend exists for female workers as well as male workers, and for lower-income as well as higher-income workers:

> The average worker worked 1,868 hours in 2007, an increase of 181 hours from the 1979 work year of 1,687 hours. This represents an increase of 10.7 percent—the equivalent of every worker working 4.5 additional weeks per year. . . . Annual work hours grew more among women (20.3 percent) than among men (4.4 percent) from 1979 to 2007, primarily because women increased their weeks per year in the paid workforce.[218]

Workers at the lower end of the pay scale have experienced the highest increases in annual working hours between 1979 and 2007 whereas those at the middle have experienced the next highest increase. The bottom fifth saw an increase of 22 per cent over this period, the next fifth saw an increase of 15.2 per cent, and the middle fifth saw an increase of 10.9 per cent. By contrast, the top 80–95 per cent of earners experienced an increase of annual working hours of 4.3 per cent whereas the top five per cent experienced an increase of 7.6 per cent over this period.[219] This trend has been accompanied by workplace speedup or intensification of work (along with increasing levels of stress and fatigue), with survey data reporting employees experiencing a significant increase in the tempo of work between 1977 and 2006.[220]

The trend towards diminishing income returns from work for ordinary workers has continued into the 2000s. Whereas "average real after-tax household income for the one percent of the population with the highest income grew by 275 percent between 1979 and 2007. . . the inflation-adjusted median income for working-age households declined by over $2000 between 2000 and 2007".[221] Hence labour's share of national income (i.e. the share that is composed of wages) *vis-à-vis* capital's (the share that goes to profits) has declined at a faster rate than has happened internationally:

> The decline in labor share of income in the United States since the turn of the millennium has been particularly marked. Official data from the Bureau of Labor Statistics (BLS) suggest that, while the labor share had already started to decrease in the 1960s, three-fourths of the entire post-1947 decline occurred between 2000 and 2016. The steepest part of the decline—from 63.3 percent in 2000 to 56.7 percent in 2016—followed a moderate downward drift in the 1980s and early 1990s, and a slight recovery in the late 1990s.[222]

The declining share of income accruing to labour and the increasing share accruing to capital in the USA is partly a story of boardroom excess. Hence: "In 1980 the top managers of the 300 biggest US corporations had incomes 29 times larger than the average manufacturing worker—by 1990 they were 93 times larger".[223] By 2018, though, the incomes of typical American CEOs were 278 times larger than those of ordinary wage-earners.[224] Widening capital-labour differentials are accumulative owing to increasingly asymmetrical competition between employees and employers in each cycle of social interaction generating structural emergence over recent decades. This of course is aided by neoliberalism's support of deregulated labour markets and its retrogressive taxation policies. The tendency for the competition between capital and labour to become ever-more asymmetric stems from the widening power gap between the two generated by the emergent inequalities.

The same downward pressures on workers' living standards have been experienced in the UK, albeit with less draconian results than in the USA. Average earnings from wages in the 1970s and 1980s grew 2.9 per cent annually, but these slowed to 1.5 per cent in the 1990s and just 1.2 per cent in the 2000s.[225] This occurred as workers recorded average productivity gains for their employers of 4.9 per cent between 1982 and 1990, and 2.3 per cent between 1997 and 2007, compared to 1.9 per cent between 1973 and 1979.[226] This is suggestive of greater intensification of work. And so it has been. In 1997, 23 per cent of employees reported working at very high speeds for most of the time, whereas by 2001 this had increased to 38 per cent, and by 2010 to 40 per cent.[227]

Workplace intensification continued to rise between 2012 and 2017. "Most notably, the proportion of workers in jobs where it was required to work at *very high speed* for most or all of the time rose by 4 percentage points to 31 per cent in 2017".[228] This trend is especially pronounced among public sector workers, since by 2012 53 per cent of them, compared to 30 per cent of them in 1992, reported higher work intensities.[229]

> Teachers and nurses are two professional groups that have experienced especially high levels of required work intensification. By 2017, a remarkable 92 percent of teachers strongly agreed that their job requires them to work very hard, up from 82 percent in 2012. Nine out of ten teachers, and nearly three quarters of nurses report that they often or always come home from work exhausted.[230]

Intensification of work has gone alongside the stalling of the postwar tendency for annual average working hours to decline, according to a report by the New Economics Foundation. The average full-time week fell from 46 hours in 1946 to 40 hours by 1979. This was owing to a "combination of increased pay and productivity, strong collective bargaining and increased labour market regulation from government". Since 1980, however, "this trend faltered following labour market deregulation, reduced collective bargaining and slower earnings growth for low-income workers", so that "the average full-time week fell by just 2.5 hours to an average of 37.5 hours by 2016".

Indeed, the average working week in the UK for full-time workers has been virtually static from the 1990s right up until the cusp of the novel coronavirus crisis: in 1992, it was 38.1 hours; in 2019, it was 37.4 hours.[231] Between 1983 and 1995, the average working week even increased by an hour,[232] and so has since reduced only marginally, by less than an hour. This was despite continued productivity growth that outstripped pay rises up until the financial crisis of 2007/09. If trends of the first three decades of the postwar period had continued, the UK would have been on target to reach a 30-hour week by 2040.[233] "If the pre-1980 trend had continued, workers would now be working half a day less than they do today, roughly in line with annual working hours in Germany".[234]

From 2008 to 2014, in the context of the global financial crisis and its aftermath, real median weekly wages in the UK dropped by 10 per cent whereas the real median hourly wage dropped by eight per cent.[235] By April 2011, "average real hourly wages were 4 percent lower than they were at the start of the recession", with 70 per cent of workers adversely affected, with 21 per cent of workers seeing their wages cut absolutely, and 12 per cent seeing their wages frozen.[236] According to the TUC's analysis of ILO data, UK workers saw income from wages decline by an average of one per cent a year from 2008 to 2015. This was as inflation rose faster than pay. This placed the country in 101st place internationally for wage growth and compared poorly with higher-income EU states such as France and Germany, which experienced increases in real pay over the period.[237] The pay drop was owing not simply to a combination of wage freezes and wage cuts imposed by employers but, in rarer cases, the re-employment of full-time workers on part-time contracts with lower salaries.[238]

The period of most precipitous decline was from 2010 to 2013, where real average wages fell by 2.2 per cent annually.[239] This was remarkable insofar as the assault on wages was sustained even though the UK economy managed to maintain high employment and low unemployment after the initial shock of the crash.[240] By 2018/19, even though the great recession had ended, average wages showed little sign of recovery from the squeeze of the earlier period, as employer gains were consolidated in the context of slow productivity growth. Thus, real earnings for workers were "still 3% below where they were in 2008 and . . . 13% (or £3,500 per year) below where we might reasonably have expected based on rates of growth in the years prior to the crisis (of around 1.4% per year)".[241]

Neoliberalism and injustice worldwide

But what of the international picture regarding the structural emergence of wealth and income disparities and poverty trends in the neoliberal epoch? Well, the past few decades have witnessed not only the radicalization of wealth and income inequalities within most national borders and across the globe but also the obdurate persistence of brutal subsistence poverty for billions on the wrong side of the North–South divide.[242] Opinions differ on the question of whether or to what extent subsistence poverty has reduced internationally under "globalization". Under the World Bank's definitions and measures, there is a case for saying that it has, and majorly so, from around 1.9 billion in 1990 to 741 million by 2017, or from 37 per cent of world population to under 10 per cent.[243]

However, the World Bank's timeframe for poverty trends leaves the 1980s out of the equation—which is where neoliberal "globalization" gets started. World poverty increased in the 1980s, even under the Bank's own metrics, despite the fact that there were substantial falls in China where a large proportion of the poor (20 per cent) are to be found.[244] The World Bank's definition and measure of poverty is also deeply problematic, based as it is on an arbitrary dollar value. Moreover, it instructs about trends only at the absolute basement of the poverty range rather than illuminating trends across the whole poverty spectrum, for which different measures are needed.

Now, poverty, if this is understood in *absolute* terms, as the World Bank understands it, as having an income below a fixed sum that is necessary for bare subsistence, ought to diminish wherever there is economic development or "modernization" of whatever shape or hue. Employers are, after all, compelled to pay their workers at least enough to live on and be capable of working or else they would have no one to employ. And so poverty reduction, under these terms, ought not to be portrayed (as it is by apologists of capitalism and neoliberalism) as a dizzying triumph of a benign economic system abounding in "freedom of opportunity". On the contrary, it would be miraculous if there was not poverty reduction in the context of world economic development and decolonization. Nor, reasonably, can poverty reduction be made a gift of "globalization", or of trade liberalization (i.e. neoliberalism), or even of capitalism *per se*, though it is presented as such by the World Bank, by neoliberal politicians, by the corporate media, and by free-trade economists. Rather, this is the result simply of the global spread of the industrial mode of economic development.

Before neoliberalism

This can be demonstrated by examining the economic world before neoliberalism was hegemonic. The period from 1948 to 1973, in which unrestricted markets did *not* hold sway, but in which they were more regulated and in which there was more state involvement in the economy, witnessed the postwar boom. This was an unprecedented period of industrial expansion that saw the world economy grow by 350 per cent.[245]

> Country after country experienced enormous economic growth. The American gross national product grew until it was three times as great in 1970 as it had been in 1940; German industrial output grew five-fold from the (depressed) level of 1949; French output four-fold. Even the miserable, long declining British economy was producing about twice as much at the end of the long boom as at the beginning. The new era of growth was not confined to the existing industrialised countries. Japan, still thought of as a third world type country in the 1940s, resumed its pre-war industrial growth; until, with a thirteen-fold increase in its industrial output, it was the second largest western economy after the US. Russia's economy grew likewise, until its industrial output was about seven times as high in the mid-1970s as in the mid-1940s. . . . By the end of the great boom . . . there were industrial centres across the globe, the rural population had shrunk to small minorities in the advanced economies.[246]

The period of the boom was one where trade liberalization and privatization was partially hemmed-in by various factors. There were constraints on the operations of *multinational* capitalism. These included the closing-off of a significant part of the world to Western business by Cold War partitions (with US and European corporations and foreign direct investment barred from the communist world and from those developing countries pursuing state socialism) and a wave of expropriations of foreign-owned (i.e. European and US) enterprises in the so-called Third World under decolonization. These included too fixed exchange rates on capital and other controls on financial transfers under Bretton Woods as well as tariffs and other forms of regional and national protectionism to safeguard vulnerable or vital domestic industries against foreign competition or takeover. "In Europe and the United States, whole sectors were closed to foreign companies".[247]

Under communism in Eastern Europe,[248] and under various forms of state socialism or state capitalism in various parts of the "Third World",[249] there was industrial development and therefore poverty reduction before the era of unfettered capitalism. This was despite the contradictions of authoritarian planning and the inefficiencies of command economics. This was also despite concerted efforts by the capitalist North (and the USA in particular) to choke it off by various means—economic, political, or military—in defence of their geopolitical and business interests.[250] Nor could US support for corrupt and profligate regimes in the developing world derail economic progress under boom conditions, despite the huge instabilities this also generated across the Global South. This support (overt and covert) was forthcoming to those "Third World" governments who were Cold War allies in the fight to contain socialism or Soviet influence, or could be counted on to suppress labour rights and maintain economic monocultures beneficial to the post-colonial metropoles, or were virtual vassal states of the USA in regions of crucial economic or strategic importance to American capitalism.[251]

In the Soviet bloc, extreme poverty was more-or-less abolished by the 1970s owing to a combination of state welfare, full employment policies, and subsidized prices for consumer goods.[252] This was despite the huge demands placed on the Soviet economy by the arms race with the USA and NATO and its consequential subordination of the consumer goods sector to the producer goods sector under sustained Cold War pressures to accumulate heavy industry.[253] In the developed Western world, it was the same story. Under social democratic governance (which forged the so-called postwar compromise between corporate capital and organized labour and mixed economies of capitalist market and state plan), there was prodigious industrial growth. This saw the end of bare subsistence poverty in most of the advanced economies, though relative poverty rates likely grew as the incomes of the better-off expanded faster than those of the least well off.[254]

Neoliberal ideologue, Samuel Brittan, of the *Financial Times*, by contrast, claims "unprecedented increases in world living standards" from 1950 to 1995 as global free-market capitalism's (and hence neoliberalism's) gift to the world. Huge increases in GDP per capita growth, life expectancy and literacy, he says, are bounties flowing from "world capital markets and free trade".[255] Greg Palast brilliantly conveys the fundamental historical flaw of this argument:

> Before 1980, virtually every nation in his [Brittan's] Third World survey was either socialist or welfare statist. They were developing on the "Import-Substitution Model" by which locally owned industry was built through government investment and high tariffs, anathema to the free

> marketeers. In those Dark Ages (1960–80) of increasing national government control and new welfare schemes, per capita income grew 73 percent in Latin America and 34 percent in Africa. By comparison, since 1980, the Reagan/Thatcher model has seen Latin American growth come to a virtual halt—growth of less than 6 percent over twenty years—and African incomes decline *by 23 percent*. Now let's count the corpses: from 1950 to 1980, socialist and welfare statist policies added more than a decade of life expectancy to virtually every nation on the planet. From 1980 to today [i.e. the early 2000s], life under structural assistance has gotten brutish and decidedly shorter. Since 1985, in fifteen African nations the total number of illiterate people has risen and life expectancy fallen—which Brittan attributes to "bad luck, not the international economic system.[256]

Yet the Golden Age before neoliberalization should not be idealized. The postwar boom was radically unbalanced, characterized by combined but uneven development. The world benefited, but the advanced economies benefited most from the expansion and these were the engine driving the world economy forward. As Nigel Harris expounds:

> Rising real incomes in the advanced capitalist countries provided expanding markets for the increasingly sophisticated and highly priced output. And it ensured the profit rates on new investment that continuously sucked in an increasing proportion of the world's new savings. Both labour and capital were dragged out of the backward countries to service the economies of the advanced. The trade between advanced capitalist countries provided the dynamo for an unprecedented expansion of world trade and output in the period after 1948, and for an ever-greater concentration of capital in the hands of the rich countries. What had been seen by imperialists as the division of labour between the manufacturing advanced and the raw material exporting backward countries was overtaken by a division between the relatively self-sufficient advanced enclave and a mass of poor dependents.[257]

The prevailing wisdom in the Global North during this period (and indeed since) was that free trade was something to be imposed on the underdeveloped world rather than on itself. This was because the logic of unequal competition or asymmetric trade would open up the decolonized countries for capitalist exploitation and allow the expropriation of local resources as corporate property. This would allow the preservation of a world economy in which the former colonies were bound by the law of comparative advantage to produce cheap unrefined primary goods in low-tech noncapital-intensive industries for export to the developed world and to act as net exporters of capital and commodities to the

Global North rather than as net importers to support domestic industrialization and consumption.[258]

However, these agendas were resisted by the newly decolonized countries committed to breaking this pattern of the *development of underdevelopment* that flowed from colonial history and from unequal exchange. This pattern was where mass poverty and economic backwardness in the Global South were recognized as being the legacy of its political and economic subordination to the developed capitalist states during the colonial age. Underdevelopment was *one-sided* development of the colonies by the imperial powers, and deliberately so. This was to dissolve economic self-sufficiency (hence create dependency on exports from the Western metropoles), destroy competition for these foreign imports from local industries (thereby creating monopolies in local markets for the products of the colonial powers), and convert local producers into mere suppliers of cheap raw materials and basic foodstuffs for consumption in the North.[259]

The postcolonial countries on securing independence were thus saddled with economic monocultures (e.g. in copper, tin, rubber, tea, coffee, sugar, tropical fruits) that yielded insufficient revenues to break the cycle of underdevelopment. Hence the solution, as most saw it, was to try to pursue independent (of the world market) paths of national economic development, on the grounds that trade liberalization would undermine development because this would mean subordination to unequal competition and unfair exchange. This strategy was pursued under the auspices of state subsidization or management or ownership of industry, because only the state could raise and co-ordinate the necessary resources. Central planning or direction of the national economy appeared to be the only strategy that stood a chance of allowing under-developed former colonies or satellites or dependencies to build diversified economies and protect new enterprises and domestic markets from the forces of unequal international exchange.[260]

For many underdeveloped countries, although this strategy met with success, it was limited and precarious success. This was for the simple reason that it just was not possible to mobilize sufficient local resources to build a range of industries that would achieve "all-round" economic development or national economic self-sufficiency or international standards of competitiveness. Small, poor countries, carrying the colonial heritage of chronic underdevelopment, could hardly mobilize the scale of investments that large capitalist MNCs could. This was particularly when set in price competition with each other for the custom of those MNCs that control the bulk of world trade and when subject to the ups and downs of the primary goods markets in minerals and foodstuffs.

The problem was exacerbated by the fact that the dependence of the advanced economies on the staple commodities produced by the poorer ex-colonies or satellites had been reduced before the start of the postcolonial age, just as the colonies won for themselves formal political independence, thus diminishing their bargaining position in the postwar economy. This occurred as the imperial states withdrew into economic autarky in the 30-year crisis period of war and slump from 1914 to 1945.

> Raw materials from agricultural countries had been indispensable for industrial production in the West before the First World War, and colonial control was an important way for industrial powers to ensure their own supplies and block access to their rivals. But now there were synthetic substitutes for most raw materials—artificial fertilisers, synthetic rubber, rayon, nylon, plastics. A parallel transformation of agriculture in Western Europe and North America reduced food imports from the rest of the world. By the late 1950s withdrawal from colonies in Africa and Asia was no longer the threat it would have been to the industrialists of the European countries. Companies which had made their fortunes from plantations and mines of the Global South began to diversify their investments into new lines of business.[261]

MNCs, which have come to "dominate global resource procurement, manufacturing and trade during the twentieth century",[262] were simply better placed to force down the prices of the primary exports of the poorer countries. This generated further obstacles to solving the dependency trap, since this relied on raising the capital to invest in new industries that would produce more sophisticated products yielding better returns in the world market.

Further obstacles to breaking the dependency trap stemmed from the fact that foreign MNCs enjoy "privileged access to Western capital, expertise gained through long-term activity, state-of-the-art technology for the efficient processing of commodities" and membership "of established worldwide distribution networks". In all of these areas, the enterprises and governments of underdeveloped countries are radically disadvantaged, "unless they can earn or borrow sufficient foreign exchange to . . . buy the technology and expertise from the West". Yet this technology and expertise is increasingly expensive relative to the prices that can be levied for the export of primary goods that would fund these acquisitions.

> Ever since their constitutional independence countries have been urged to diversify away from dependence on the cash crops and mineral exports which they inherited from colonialism. But that is a risky business involving a move away from proven foreign-exchange earnings attached to existing links with world markets and areas of expertise in which limited resources have been concentrated. Moreover, if developing countries seek the obvious remedy of moving along the production chain into processing and manufacturing where profits are higher, they tend to find progress difficult, due, firstly, to technological difficulties and, secondly, to import tariffs which protect Western manufacturers from outside competition. Thus, even if a Third World

> country succeeds in obtaining the capital, technology and expertise required to become a manufacturer rather than a raw material producer, the chances are its prospects will still not be good. . . . They might finance the training of their own personnel, which is a long-term project, but even then, they will have to keep up with technological advances and ultimately compete with Western multinational corporations for mass consumption markets. Access to large-scale markets is crucial for the economies of scale to apply, and Third World markets remain small in terms of purchasing power.[263]

Herein, in this dynamic, lies the origin of the indebtedness of many of the lesser developed countries to the big Western banks since the 1970s,[264] and which has for them further choked-off economic advance under the weight of crippling interest repayments.[265] For faced (under the cumulative logic of unequal exchange or comparative trade disadvantage) with steadily falling prices of their export staples *vis-à-vis* those of high-tech or industrially refined imports from the developed capitalist world, many were forced (or were enticed) to borrow heavily on unfavourable terms to preserve growth or to avoid radically suppressing domestic consumption.[266]

Yet this strategy was persevered with during the postwar boom and beyond because the alternative (openness to the world market—as demanded by neoliberal commonsense) appeared to render the prospects of industrial success even more precipitous. This perspective was supported by historical precedents; the only countries which successfully industrialized after the capitalist world economy was consolidated were those (e.g. the USA—from the latter nineteenth century, and Japan—from the 1950s) that deliberately embraced protectionist policies.[267] It was eventually abandoned not necessarily owing to the ideological appeal of neoliberal free-market nostrums to the governments of indebted countries, but because the collapse of the USSR and its Eastern bloc satellites left them hanging out to dry. Suddenly, they were cast adrift, without political protection or economic patronage, and confronted by a US-led alliance committed to scaling back social democracy and statism at home in favour of liberal democracy and marketization and bent on imposing free-trade fundamentalism internationally.

In any case, the limits of import-substitution-oriented industrialization under central planning were exposed, since this version of state capitalism, even though it had generated growth for a period, had not for those countries that embraced it broken the cycle of dependency. Indeed, for these countries, growth was slowing. This was because locally generated investments were spread too thinly in the pursuit of all-round development. Consequently, industries lagged further behind international standards of competitiveness carried by MNCs that could pull in investments from across the globe and focus these on specific product lines.[268]

> With slender resources any switching of emphasis from cash-crop production tended to create a rapid reduction in foreign exchange earnings to the

> detriment of all imports including the very production technology on which industrialization programmes depended. . . . Tariff barriers imposed to protect indigenous industry from imported finished goods also served to stimulate the setting up of local assembly plants by foreign companies intent on maintaining their export sales.[269]

Capitulation was inevitable, since acquiring further loans to service debt repayments or acquiring development aid or FDI were made conditional (by the World Bank, the IMF, the WTO, and the US Treasury) on free-market reforms. Thus, import-substitution was superseded by the World Bank's and IMF's so-called SAPs,[270] which later in remarkable Orwellian-speak were renamed as PRSs.[271]

These imposed on poor and indebted countries of the Global South an array of conditionalities that they needed to sign-up to in return for aid or FDI or bank loans or rescheduling of repayments on existing loans. These conditionalities, of course, came straight out of the neoliberal textbook: cutting social and welfare spending; scaling down the state—including by reducing the salaries and entitlements of public-sector employees; privatizing public enterprises; deregulating currency and finance markets; permitting foreign acquisitions of local industries; lifting restrictions and levies on cross-border capital transfers; dismantling protectionist import-tariffs; and abolishing price controls on life-sustaining goods such as primary foodstuffs, power, and water.[272] Neoliberalism alongside corporate mega-capitalism was internationalized.

Prior to that, the history of underdevelopment and under-investment left many of the former colonies stuck between a rock (the economic limits of autarky) and a hard place (submission to unequal competition). Nonetheless, there was growth and development and poverty reduction in the Global South in the post-war period before full-scale capitalist internationalization in what the World Bank referred to as the "centrally planned economies". GDP expansion in the developing world (excluding China, South Korea, South Africa, and Vietnam) was a respectable 7.1 per cent per annum from 1961 to 1970. This was above the world average of 5.4 per cent. This was also higher than the average for the developed countries (of five per cent) and for the Soviet bloc countries (of 6.7 per cent).[273] Such demonstrated that the shackles of underdevelopment were not insuperable roadblocks to economic progress—not in the context of a rapidly expanding world economy.[274]

Indeed, the few success stories of the Global South during the boom and after were achieved by those governments pursuing a particular version of the national state-managed development model, not by adopting neoliberal remedies. These were those which ditched import-substitution-oriented industrialization in favour of export-led industrialization.[275] This was the strategy of Japan (from the late 1960s), the East Asian "tigers" (the so-called NICs), and most recently China, for example. Here economic take-off was achieved not by trying to build a broad diversified industrial base that would cater for domestic consumption and ease dependence on foreign imports, or by submitting to finance and trade liberalization. Rather, it was achieved by massive state-planned and state-mobilized (and in the case of China often under state ownership) capital investments in specific targeted sectors of the economy geared towards export trade growth.[276] The fledgling industrial sectors favoured by these policies were able to progress and prosper and achieve international parity *because* they were protected from overseas competition at the hands of more technologically advanced capitals in the developed economies.

Japan led the way in pioneering this export-led model that the NICs were to follow, switching from an earlier import-substitution model that took it some way along the road to industrialization. Consequently, by the 1970s, Japan had the world's second-biggest economy, half the size of the USA's, just as "its governments systematically discouraged wholly owned FDI . . . and restricted it to a low level".[277] However, breaking the cycle of the development of underdevelopment that has been structured by the world capitalist system is a puzzle that few countries in the Global South have solved, whatever national economic policies they have adopted. Indeed, the fact that the NICs (and now the so-called BRICs) have taken major strides in that direction may further diminish the chances of others following suit. This is owing to the intensification of global competition that this has brought about along with market saturation and pressures of overproduction.

Nonetheless, despite the imbalances generated by uneven economic development, by Cold War politics, by the negative impacts of the capitalisms of the developed North on those of the developing South, including those of US-led imperialism, the postwar boom was long enough and strong enough to raise most national boats, even the poorest of these, and to raise the living standards of most within their borders. This period before neoliberalization thus witnessed the greatest reduction of extreme poverty across the planet, from approximately 63.5 per cent of the world's population in 1950 to 31 per cent by 1980.[278]

Neoliberalism and world poverty

I have noted that the pre-neoliberal era of world economy witnessed the greatest gains in worldwide poverty reduction of the postwar period. Since then, in the neoliberal age, extreme poverty, on the World Bank's definition, has been reduced further across the world, indeed majorly reduced. Nonetheless, this remains substantial, even on these limited terms of reference. The World Bank informs us that today there are around 689 million people living in conditions of *extreme* poverty, or approximately nine per cent of the world's population.[279] The organization's measure of absolute poverty (or international poverty line), from 2015 to 2022, was an income of $1.90 per day, up from $1.25 in 2008, $1.08 in 1993, and from $1.02 in 1985.[280] But this is an inadequate baseline, because hardly anyone anywhere could possibly have even their basic needs met on this level of income. Moreover, the upwards adjustments in the base dollar rate have not kept up with increases in the cost of living virtually anywhere in the world.

These are reasons to call into question the validity of the World Bank's grandiose claims that even severe subsistence poverty has been *drastically* cut in the era of "globalization". This measure is also static in as much as any meaningful definition of subsistence poverty anywhere in the world ought to relate this to median income levels in the countries in question and by making cross-national comparisons of GDP capacity. This is because poverty is also relational and contextual. Poverty ought to mean having access to a level of income that is insufficient to participate in the economic and cultural life of a society that is available to the "typical" or "average" person in that society. But this is not how the World Bank estimates poverty.

Another reason to dispute the World Bank's claim, according to critical economists, is major problems with their counting methods.[281] How did the World Bank settle on its own measure of absolute poverty? Well, first they found out the official national poverty lines of a sample of LICs and MICs. Second, they worked out the average poverty line from across the sample and converted the figure into its equivalent in US currency. Finally, they gathered data from general household surveys of the countries in the sample on the percentages of people who were below the local national poverty lines.[282] By this method, back in 1985, the World Bank determined that the correct measure of poverty was living on less than $1.02 per day, whereas in 1993 they raised this to $1.08 per day, then to $1.25 in 2008, to $1.90 in 2015, and most recently to $2.15 in 2022.

Fair enough, it could be said—the World Bank ought to adjust the poverty line upwards over time to account for things like price inflation. So they should. But the trouble is that they do not seem to adjust it often enough or generously enough. So, arguably, they are short-changing the world's poor. It just does not seem plausible, for example, that a rise of barely more than a dollar in the poverty baseline over a period of more than 35 years (from 1985 to 2022) could be sufficient to keep up with general price inflation anywhere in the world. This may mean that the World Bank's "evidence" for declining global poverty is literally senseless, for the simple reason that the real value of $2.15 of spending power today is quite possibly less than the real value of $1.02 of spending power 37 years ago.

But there are other problems with how the World Bank defines and measures poverty. Firstly, it relies on the adequacy of the local national definitions of poverty lines. The World Bank takes as given all the local national poverty lines that are used by all the countries in its surveys. For all sorts of reasons, these tend to be stringent, under-estimating the level of income needed to avoid destitution. So, there is right at the start of the counting and calculating process a pressure to deflate the international poverty line that ends up as its outcome.

Secondly, it relies also on the adequacy of the local general household surveys from which data is collected on the numbers of people below the various national poverty lines—and these are often inadequate. These often do not follow a standard template and are of variable quality. They often are methodologically flawed. For example, often the questions addressed to householders neglect certain poverty indicators, which skew the data. Householders are also sometimes reluctant to admit they are facing destitution, since in many entrepreneurial societies and cultures (e.g. in East Asia and in India) there is a strong stigma attached to poverty.

Of course, there is also the problem that many of the poorest are not actually householders at all. Vagrants and the homeless are not included in the household surveys. There is also the problem that those governments which administer the surveys have an interest in minimizing poverty because high poverty rates may reflect badly on them by revealing inadequacies of their own economic or social policies. With that in mind, a tendency has been noticed for the recall times of the surveys to be abbreviated, from 30 days to just seven days. This may be because shorter recalls tend to give a more favourable result. These result in people reporting higher levels of household expenditure than is the case for longer recall periods.[283]

Finally, the data sets from which the World Bank calculates poverty have big gaps in them. Two countries—China and India—are the most difficult of all to extract reliable data from. The Chinese government has not co-operated at all with the World Bank. This is by refusing to participate in international surveys that would allow comparison of living costs or household expenditures in China with other countries in the sample. The Indian government, on the other hand, has co-operated only partially, by selective involvement. The Chinese data is further weakened by the fact that urban populations have not been included in making calculations of the overall poverty rate.[284] Yet millions of the poor have flooded into the cities in search of work, and it is plausible to think that a lot of them remain very poor. There are good reasons for thinking that breakneck hyper-urbanization has generated masses of working poor.

For some critics, these inadequacies of methods of data collection and analysis (and other issues) are such that, at least from the 1990s through to the early 2000s, it was simply not possible to be certain whether real poverty was going up or down. All that could be said with confidence was that there was an awful lot of it and that this was devastating to the lives of the poor.[285] This is especially important, because China was responsible for around 90 per cent of the supposed decline in extreme poverty from the start of the 1980s up until the 2000s.[286] Indeed, on some estimates, in as much as there were poverty reductions in the 1980s and 1990s, these were almost entirely attributable to developments in China and India.[287] Even taking the World Bank's poverty data at face value, it is clear that poverty reduction is not a genuinely global trend but has been and remains localized and regionalized, reflecting the combined but uneven development of the world economy. Large parts of the world (in sub-Saharan Africa, the Middle East, and in Central Asia and Latin America) have not progressed in terms of human development.

These issues impact negatively not only on the accuracy of the official poverty trends but also on estimates of trends in global inequality. These counts have been shown to be based on methods of data collection and analysis that are most conducive to generating the desired (i.e. positive) results. These do not, for example, measure relative income differentials between top earners and bottom earners, both within and across national borders.[288] In any case, taking China out of the equation, there was for a long time scarcely any improvement for the life-chances of the world's poorest in the era of capitalist internationalization. This was from the 1980s up to the start of the new century,[289] although there has been progress since, which has been threatened in recent times by the COVID-19 crisis.[290] But China's poverty achievements (whatever they are) have little to do with neoliberal free-market policies or capitalist internationalization. These were achieved by state-capitalist methods: massive public investments in infrastructure and housing and industry, partial (at least) state ownerships of the biggest companies, epic investments and subsidies in economic target areas under the five-year plans, plus virtually self-enclosed consumer markets and selective doses of trade protectionism.[291]

The World Bank estimated that in 2008 there were 1.4 billion people living below its then poverty line of $1.25 daily.[292] That was roughly 20 per cent of the world population. They also estimated that 2.6 billion people were then living on an income of under $2 a day, more than one-third of the total.[293] In the early 1970s, by comparison, the ILO estimated that the total number of very poor people in the world was 700 million, whereas the World Bank put the number at 800 million.[294] Now, half of the global population (around 3.6 billion people) were thought by the World Bank to live on an income of less than $2.50 per day in 2008.[295] This was the equivalent of $2.50 purchasing power in the US market, not local marketplaces. The OPM in the USA was at the time, by comparison, an income of below $10 per day, whereas today the US FPL—which is the cut-off threshold for a range of welfare benefits—is $35 a day.[296] Now, roughly 97 per cent of the population of the developing world had an income of less than $10 per day in the mid-2000s.[297] Today around 80 per cent of the world's population does,[298] whereas almost half of the world's population have to get by on less than $5.50 a day.[299]

The figure of $5.50 per day is an interesting one. This is because the World Bank itself somewhat let the cat out of the bag, where it admitted that half of the world's population (i.e. that portion of it earning less than this amount) suffers as it puts it from "severe hardship".[300] So, even on a highly conservative estimate of subsistence poverty (i.e. an income of less than $2.50 per day at 2008 prices or of $5.50 a day at 2015 prices), which itself would scarcely be sufficient to secure the necessities of life for most people in most places, at least half of the world's population has been living under such a condition, and probably considerably more.

Even though the World Bank sees free-market capitalism's victory over poverty as imminent, if economic growth continues (a rather big "if), the lie is also revealed by the realities that the term "hardship" denotes. These are just a few of them. One in three people worldwide do not have safely managed access to clean drinking water (2.2 billion) and half (4.2 billion) do not have access to safely managed sanitation services.[301] One-third of children worldwide under five years of age are under-nourished and half lack essential vitamins and nutrients.[302] We have, therefore, what ought to be (from the World Bank's perspective) the incomprehensible phenomenon of widespread child "food poverty", despite the fact that (according to them) there is nowhere near as much *actual* child poverty.

Neoliberalism and global inequality

Addressing now the structural emergence of wealth and income trends in the world economy—what are we to make of these? Even though there is at least a case for seeing extreme poverty as having been reduced in the neoliberal era (though not for imagining that poverty levels are less than astronomical), this is certainly not true of inequality. Indeed, for the most part, the World Bank and pro-globalization economists concede the case but represent growing inequality as the necessary price to be paid for eliminating global poverty.[303] This is the infamous "trickle down" theory writ large. Today, more than 80 per cent of the world's population live in countries where earnings-differentials have been widening during the age of untrammelled capitalist internationalization.[304] Thus, inequalities *within* most countries have grown. The OECD reports: "In the 1980s, the richest 10% of the population in OECD countries earned seven times more than the poorest 10%. They now earn nearly ten times more".[305]

Inequalities *across* borders have also increased. At the close of the 1960s, "the gap between the richest and poorest fifths of the world's population stood at 30 to one, in 1990 at 60 to one, and in 1998 at 74 to one".[306] As Gabriel Zucman's recent review of a range of wealth surveys shows:

> Evidence points toward a rise in global wealth concentration: For China, Europe, and the United States combined, the top 1% wealth share has increased from 28% in 1980 to 33% today, while the bottom 75% share hovered around 10%. Recent studies, however, may underestimate the level and rise of inequality, as financial globalization makes it increasingly hard to measure wealth at the top.[307]

The wealthiest 10 per cent of the global population today monopolize 86 per cent of global wealth, and the top one per cent possess 46 per cent, whereas the lower 50 per cent have access to less than one per cent of the total.[308] The richest

20 per cent of the world's population today enjoy 75 per cent of total income, whereas the lower 40 per cent have to get by on just five per cent.[309]

A major international survey published in 2011 investigating trends in income distribution right across the OECD over several decades—*Divided We Stand: Why Inequality Keeps Rising*—found that, since the mid-1980s, in a vast majority of OECD countries, "the household incomes of the richest 10% grew faster than those of the poorest 10%".

> The Gini coefficient, a standard measure of income inequality that ranges from 0 (when everybody has identical incomes) to 1 (when all income goes to only one person), stood at an average of 0.29 in OECD countries in the mid-1980s. By the late 2000s, however, it had increased by almost 10% to 0.316. Significantly, it rose in 17 of the 22 OECD countries for which long-term data series are available, climbing by more than 4 percentage points in Finland, Germany, Israel, Luxembourg, New Zealand, Sweden, and the United States. Only Turkey, Greece, France, Hungary, and Belgium recorded no increase or small declines in their Gini coefficients. However, the ratio varies widely from one country to another. It is much lower than the OECD average in the Nordic and many continental European countries, but reaches 10 to 1 in Italy, Japan, Korea, and the United Kingdom; around 14 to 1 in Israel, Turkey, and the United States; and 27 to 1 in Mexico and Chile.[310]

The survey noted that first-world income inequality first began to widen in the UK and USA (the two neoliberal pioneers of the developed world) in the late 1970s and early 1980s, but thereafter the trend was internationalized.

> The latest trends in the 2000s showed a widening gap between rich and poor not only in some of the already high inequality countries like Israel and the United States, but also—for the first time—in traditionally low-inequality countries, such as Germany, Denmark, and Sweden (and other Nordic countries), where inequality grew more than anywhere else in the 2000s.[311]

A fundamental aspect of the inequality gap, as revealed by another recent OECD study, is the growing disparity between income from median wages and from typical corporate-executive salaries. Typical pay for CEOs across the OECD is now almost 300 times higher than median wages whereas 20 years earlier it was 20–30 times higher.[312] This OECD study also found that growth in global inequalities within and between the 34 member countries was interrupted by the financial crisis of 2007/09, but that these have since resumed their upward climb, so that the average earnings gap between the top 10 per cent and the bottom 10 per cent is now at a record postwar high of almost tenfold.

Emblematic of these developments, in the decade since the financial crisis, the number of billionaires in the world has doubled. From 2016 to 2018, the number of billionaires owning as much wealth as the poorest half of the global population dropped from 61 to just 26. Moreover, the world's richest increased their riches by 12 per cent just as the poorest half of the world's population saw their wealth fall by 11 per cent over this same period. By 2015 a new landmark in world-class inequality was reached. This was that the wealthiest one per cent of the world's population acquired for the first time more wealth than everyone else put together.[313]

World inequality and the interstate system

But what of the reproduction of emergent economic inequalities between nations in the neoliberal era? These need to be considered alongside those of social class. Is there here evidence of convergence or divergence? I will conclude this chapter by addressing this matter.

Owing to the asymmetries of "globalization" (by trade, by production, by investment—which will be explored in the next chapter), the neoliberal era has reinforced longstanding trends of postwar world economic development for the income gap between most developed countries (mostly in the Global North) and the LDCs (mostly in the Global South) to grow. "In 1980, the mean incomes in developing countries were 12.6 percent of those of the industrialized world; in 2000, these relative incomes had increased to 14 percent".[314] This may be claimed as a triumph for "globalization's" capacity to reduce the gap between LICs (or LDCs) and HICs, albeit an exceedingly modest one. But even this would be illusory.

Such raw figures mislead, because this apparent minor improvement in the fortunes of the developing countries has been, as was pointed out in the previous chapter, driven by a handful of NICs and BRICs, chief among which has been China—none of which has achieved these results by strict adherence to neoliberal free-market nostrums. GDP growth in the developing world from 1980 to 2000, if India and China are taken out of the picture, reduces from a yearly average of 2.4 per cent to just 0.7 per cent. Moreover, even though the developing world increased per capita income by 53 per cent over this same period, the corresponding gains in poverty reduction in the Global South were much more modest. From 1987 to 1999, for example, the World Bank estimated a reduction of absolute poverty globally of just 5–6 per cent.[315] This data is inconsistent with the ideology of growth-driven convergence.

Rather, the pattern has been mostly divergence—or convergence for a few alongside divergence for many others. Only a select number of countries have since World War Two managed to significantly close the income gap between the most developed ones and the rest. Even China, the big economic success story of the past few decades, had (by 2014) achieved a per capital income that was only one-seventh of the USA's. And this was despite spectacular rates of growth—averaging over 10 per cent, seven per cent per annum higher than the US economy managed to achieve—over the past 35 years.[316]

The majority of countries have remained stuck either in the so-called "middle-income trap" (with per capital incomes three-to-five times lower than in the USA) or in "poverty trap" (with per capita incomes 10–50 times lower than in the USA). The industrialized countries had a level of daily per capita income that was 6.2 times higher than non-industrialized countries in 1960, which was a reduction from 6.5 times higher in 1950. However, by 1980, the gap had increased back up to 6.5 times, and by 2000 this was 6.7 times higher.[317] Latin America and Africa have fared particularly badly since the 1980s. "After almost doubling per capita income from 1960 to 1980, Latin American economies barely maintained their 1980s levels, and that also over a 20-year period. Africa did worse, as its per capita incomes declined by 12 percent" over this stretch.[318]

There are other indicators of divergence. "In 1980, median income in the richest 10 per cent of countries was 77 times greater than in the poorest 10 per cent; by 1999, that gap had grown to 122 times".[319] The average earner in the USA (the archetypal HIC) had during the 1950s and 1960s an income 50 times bigger than that of average earners in the world's poorest country. By 2000, this was 70 times larger. But, if the average income of US earners is compared with that of earners in the tenth-poorest country, the divergence is even more radical. In 1960, the average American earned 23 times more than the average earner in the world's tenth-poorest country; by 2000, this was 45 times more. Comparing and contrasting the world's twenty richest and twenty poorest countries yields the same result. Whereas the richest ones were 23 times wealthier than the poorest ones in 1960, by 2000, they were 36 times wealthier.[320] Similarly, as was reported by the UN's *Human Development Report of 1999* and the World Bank's *World Development Report of 2000/2001*:

> The income gap between the fifth of the world's population living in the richest countries and the fifth in the poorest countries was 74 to 1 in 1997, up from 60 to 1 in 1990 and 30 to 1 in 1960. . . . The average incomes in the richest 20 countries is 37-times the average in the 20 poorest countries—a gap that has doubled over the past 40 years.[321]

These trends have continued unabated in the new century. Income differentials between the richer and poorer countries have continued to climb.[322] Today, the world's LDCs, 47 in number, contain within their borders 14 per cent of the world's population, but more than half of the world's poorest people. These are those people who live on \$2.15 a day or less. These LDCs account for just 1.3 per cent of world gross product (WGP). They have "been diverging over a long time from other (non-LDC) developing countries", let alone the developed ones.

> In 1990, the gross national income (GNI) per capita of other developing countries was three times higher than that of LDCs. Nowadays, it is almost six times higher. While in the early 1990s the labour productivity of these LDCs corresponded to 25% of that of other developing countries, at present it amounts to just 18%.[323]

Imperialism, underdevelopment, and dependency theory

The stark inequalities which exist between the developed HICs, on the one hand, and the MICs and LICs, on the other hand, would appear to lend credence to the key tenets of dependency theory. Yet the success of the NICs in navigating a route out of underdevelopment has radicalized a backlash against this body of work in sociology and political science. This backlash had its origins in the post-war boom, since this provided evidence that escape from economic backwardness was possible within a dynamic and growing world market.[324] However, in recent times, even though dependency theory has not been explicitly revived by means of new scholarship informed specifically by its concepts, there is much new work that is consistent with its arguments and perspectives and goals.

Dependency theory sought to explain the persistence of North–South divisions and racial-class inequalities in world economy in terms of the history of Western imperial domination and colonial exploitation. This told a story of how imperialism and colonialism generated the "development of underdevelopment" outside the West, just as this fuelled its opposite for the colonial powers, because the ascendancy of the West depended on colonial exploitation and extraction. Dependency theory also explained how the West could exploit the colonial legacy (i.e. the inheritance of emergent structural advantage alongside disadvantage) to preserve its dominance in world systems in the post-colonial era. This diagnosed a shift from imperialist domination and colonial extraction to neoimperialist and postcolonial extraction that has ever since maintained asymmetrical economic development alongside racialized class hierarchies across international state system and capitalist world economy. New work that seeks to grasp worldwide inequalities in relation to racial capitalism and postcolonial imperialism can certainly be counted as continuing this tradition.[325]

The industrial success of Japan, then of the East Asian "tigers", Latin American countries such as Mexico and Brazil, and most recently of China and India, has of course empirically confounded Andre Gunder Frank's argument for the "impossibility of development" in the "periphery" of the world system.[326] Frank considered the emergent structural advantages of the West *vis-à-vis* the Rest in world economy (established first as colonial legacy and then reproduced from generation to generation by the accumulative dynamic of unequal exchange) as insuperable barriers to economic progress in the Global South. But Frank's error has not invalidated dependency theory, as the critics have asserted. I will consider the arguments of one of these critics—Alex Callinicos—to establish the case.

Callinicos reads the success of the NICs as a straightforward refutation of dependency theory, which he dismisses as "Third Worldism". As he puts it: "One only has to utter the word 'China' to indicate what's wrong with the Third Worldist understanding of imperialism—though twenty years ago, 'South

Korea' would have done as well".[327] However, dependency as a concept would not necessarily support the economic determinism that belied Frank's own negative political judgements of the prospects of development in the Global South. Rather, this would support the rather less radical conclusion that the asymmetrical power structure of capitalist world economy places fundamental constraints on autonomous industrial growth outside the advanced economies, but without cancelling this out altogether. This, for example, was Arghiri Emmanuel's view. The author of *Unequal Exchange* was happy to

> give due acknowledgement to the recent wave of industrialization in the Third World and to the fact that annual growth rates of industrial production in some of these countries are higher than those prevailing in the advanced countries (which are) themselves higher than had ever been known before.[328]

These emergent structural constraints would not be uniform or undifferentiated in their impacts. Rather, these would be experienced as greater or lesser constraints in different parts of the world. Their degrees of impact (the stringency or otherwise of the constraints) would be mediated by specific regional, local, or national factors. These would include (1) the level of natural resources (human, mineral, and otherwise) at the disposal of state authorities to mobilize for growth; (2) the geopolitical positioning of a country in the world state system (whereby its strategic value may offer it opportunities to win patronage from the West—as for example Japan and the Asian "tigers" did); and (3) the success or otherwise of governments in formulating innovative national development strategies that may ameliorate or blunt or circumnavigate the structural constraints imposed by relations of economic domination and subordination.

Some countries that were formerly of the underdeveloped world, but which made of themselves the NICs or the "newly emerging markets" (NEMs), were simply better placed than others resource-wise to achieve industrial take-off, and these were also able to able to learn political lessons from the failed development projects of other countries. This, for example, was by innovating the all-resources-in-few-baskets approach of export-driven industrialization as potential solution to the unpalatable alternatives of submission to trade liberalization versus autarkic centrally planned all-round industrialization. That the concept of dependency through the development of underdevelopment retains relevance, despite the economic success stories of certain former "Third World" countries, is upheld by the relative paucity of those success stories. For every success story, there are many other stories (those of the manifold "failed states") that have not turned out well, and which appear to have few prospects of doing better. This is why the underdeveloped world is still with us—or why our world is, as Callinicos himself puts it, one of "malign neglect and partial industrialization".[329]

Nor does the fact that the world capitalist economy is one in which the bulk of foreign investment and trade circulates between the advanced countries and a handful of NICs or NEMs (as vast swathes of the Global South are mostly bypassed by capital and trade flows) count as a refutation, as Callinicos imagines it, of the concept of unequal exchange as a factor of underdevelopment and dependency. Callinicos claims that dependency theorists

> cannot explain the actual patterns of foreign direct investment, which are the opposite of what the theory of unequal exchange would predict. . . . Far from the prosperity of capitalists (and workers) depending on the poverty of the Third World, the main flows of capital and commodities passed the poor countries by. And the largest concentrations of wealth remained in the Western economies.[330]

For sure, this evidence counts against a certain concept of unequal exchange, whereby "Third World" poverty is seen as generated by the bumping up of commodity prices beyond the reach of the poor by the high wages commanded by workers in the developed world. But this hardly refutes the concept of unequal exchange that lies at the heart of dependency theory. This is in the sense that the concept espouses the capacity of Western MNCs to use their control of world trade and their higher technological level to impose conditions of exchange (buying cheap and selling dear) on poor countries that generate for them market advantages and which help lock the poor countries into a one-sided dependency.

Nor does this mean that branches or subsidiaries of these MNCs do not sometimes secure for themselves higher profits than at home by virtue of exploiting the superabundance of cheap labour in the poor countries—so, in effect, making higher returns from the super-exploitation of labour overseas that is realized by selling the commodities in home markets. There is plenty of evidence that corporate super-profits are to be made by outsourcing the production of cheap commodities in developing countries in the FEZs or EPZs and then selling them at many times their production costs in developed consumer markets where aggregate purchasing power is much higher.[331] As Teresa Hayter pointed out in the 1990s:

> Although there are disagreements about this, it appears that the profits made abroad were generally considerably higher than the profits made in the metropolis. Even if they had not been, they could still have ensured that the average rate of profit for all industries was higher than it would have been. . . . There is . . . evidence that the return flows on capital invested in underdeveloped countries are higher than the return flows resulting from investments in Europe and thus might be considered 'abnormal'. For example, in 1960 the capital flows from the United States to Europe exceeded the return flows by $500 million, whereas for the underdeveloped countries the

> reverse was the case: the latter exceeded the former by $1,100 million. And, according to *US News and World Report*, in the five years 1956–61 there was a ratio of outflow from the United States of 147 per cent for Latin America, 164 per cent for the under-developed countries as a whole, and 43 per cent for Western Europe. This tends to vitiate the argument that the return flows from underdeveloped countries are 'normal' and 'natural', rather than the result of any form of super-exploitation or super-profits.[332]

Callinicos argues that workers in advanced economies tend to have higher productivity than those in poorer developing countries owing to higher investments by employers in the latest labour-saving and labour-enhancing technology. So, on the Marxist understanding, he says, even though workers in North America and Western Europe have higher wages, they tend to be *more* exploited than workers in the developing world, because they generate higher rates of surplus value in production. Thus, according to Callinicos, super-exploitation of workers outside the advanced enclaves of the world economy is mythology.[333]

But this conclusion is disputable. Workers in the EPZs may typically be using fairly old means of production (though this is not always the case), so that intensive exploitation by means of labour-efficiency-enhancing technology is less developed than in the advanced economies. However, this may be compensated for by what may be termed as *hyper-extensive exploitation*. Hyper-extensive exploitation boosts productivity by compelling workers to labour at a pace far greater than those in the developed enclaves and with fewer and shorter interruptions and for far longer periods (sometimes on long shifts of 36 hours) at bare subsistence remuneration. Indonesian workers producing Nike sportswear receive in wages just four per cent of the retail price of the products they manufacture, for example.[334] Workers in EPZ enterprises are also subject to military-style discipline and instant dismissal if they fail to deliver on output targets. Social intercourse is forbidden. Employers reduce costs by skimping on workspace (herding workers together in small workshops), ventilation, hygiene, basic health, and safety provisions. Workforces are feminized and overwhelmingly young, because older employees simply cannot maintain the tempo of work that is demanded—so that staff turnover is high.[335]

So, even if it were true that such hyper-extensive exploitation of labour in the EPZs could not, at least for a while, ensure rates of surplus extraction that could match those in the countries of the Global North, the concept of super-exploitation would still apply as moral critique. This is because labour regimes based on extensive exploitation are far more brutalizing or dehumanizing than those based on intensive (technologically mediated) exploitation. It seems a trifle odd, from a normative perspective, to describe Western workers who enjoy some access to consumer and leisure opportunities, who work shorter hours, who are mostly not barred from joining trade unions, and who have some entitlements beyond the wage packet, as more exploited than those who lack all of these things.

As I have said, Callinicos is correct to note that capital and trade flows from developed countries are to other developed countries at the expense of the poorer countries.[336] I have also pointed out that this, he thinks, refutes dependency theory's concept of underdevelopment.

> Far from the prosperity of capitalists (and workers) in the advanced countries depending on the poverty of the Third World, the main flows of capital and commodities (by far the largest share of world trade takes place between developed economies) pass the poor countries by. And of course the main concentration of wealth remains in the Western economies.[337]

But this pattern of FDI and commodity trade is also exactly what we might expect from the development of underdevelopment. This is because underdevelopment occurs where a multitude of poor countries are locked into the production of basic unrefined goods (mostly foodstuffs and minerals) in labour-intensive rather than capital-intensive enterprises for export to the developed and developing worlds. And the larger capital flows will travel along the high-value commodity chains. By the late 2000s, 75 of 154 countries, mostly former colonies, were still locked in what Felipe *et al.* describe as the "low product trap". This was in contrast to 34 countries in the "high product" and 35 countries in the "middle product" brackets. Those in the high-product bracket produce technologically sophisticated exports, drawing on high investments in research and design, quality of infrastructure, intellectual property rights, availability of natural resources, etc. Those in the "low product trap" are those

> countries whose export baskets contain a significant share of unsophisticated products that are poorly connected to other products. . . . Many of the products exported by these countries are nature-made and subject to decreasing returns.[338]

This pattern is also consistent with another feature of economic imperialism noted by dependency theorists in the 1970s and 1980s, which remains as pertinent today. This is the tendency of poorer countries to export much more capital to rich countries than vice versa, hence restricting investment in local industries and hampering economic progress. The reason for this capital drain from the underdeveloped to the developed world is twofold. Firstly, given the fact of underdevelopment in the home economy of poor countries, local capitalist elites can obtain bigger or more secure returns by means of capital export than by investing locally. As Daniel Gros puts it: "All in all it seems that global capital markets seem to be 'efficient' in the sense that capital goes where the return is highest".[339]

Secondly, there is also the tendency of subsidiaries of Western MNCs in poor countries to raise investment capital locally to fund their enterprises or their outsourcing rather than by pulling in finances from the parent company or from parent country banks, before then repatriating most or all of the profits back home.[340] Between 2000 and 2017, data indicates that net capital outflows from developing countries to developed ones fluctuated between $150 billion and $977 billion, with an annual average of $588 billion, "leaving many developing countries on a debt treadmill, financially exhausted".[341] As Jason Hickel reports on the findings of the GFI survey conducted by the Centre for Applied Research at the Norwegian School of Economics:

> In 2012, the last year of recorded data, developing countries received a total of $1.3tn, including all aid, investment, and income from abroad. But that same year some $3.3tn flowed out of them. In other words, developing countries sent $2tn more to the rest of the world than they received. If we look at all years since 1980, these net outflows add up to an eye-popping total of $16.3tn—that's how much money has been drained out of the Global South over the past few decades. To get a sense for the scale of this, $16.3tn is roughly the GDP of the United States. What this means is that the usual development narrative has it backwards. Aid is effectively flowing in reverse. Rich countries aren't developing poor countries; poor countries are developing rich ones.[342]

One of the biggest contributors to this outflow is repatriated profits, along with interest repayments on debts and mostly illicit capital flight. Writing at the start of the 1990s, James Petra and Morris Morley calculated that capital transfer from Latin American countries to the developed world and especially the USA was (at $100 billion) almost the equivalent in value terms of a third of Latin America's total foreign debt.[343] The USA has been the biggest recipient of all the developed countries of net capital inflows from the underdeveloped world. As Terry McKinley puts it:

> The upshot is that global savings are flowing in the wrong direction—namely, from both high-income and middle-income countries to, overwhelmingly, the largest rich country in the world. The US absorbs about two-thirds of global excess savings. As a result, poor countries, the ones most in need of capital inflows, are crowded out of global resource transfers. The current scale of transfers to the US far exceeds the doubling of aid to poor countries that rich countries are now considering. Many developing countries are already foregoing their own development in order to "invest" in the US economic expansion.[344]

But Callinicos does not recognize the dependency of underdevelopment in this pattern. This is because, he says, capital transfer or capital export from the LICs to the HICs is driven by the class interests of local economic elites in the former, rather than by the economic imperialism of states and elites in the latter.

Speaking of capital flight from Latin America to the USA and Europe, for example, Callinicos argues that this

> involves not so much a conflict between nation states, rich versus poor countries, but a class struggle, in which the Latin American bourgeoisie, increasingly integrated into international financial circuits, aligns itself with the Western banks and multinational corporations in demanding solutions which further open up their economies to the world market.[345]

Callinicos is correct to point out the complicity of capitalist classes (or of certain capitalist elites) in capital outflows from the LICs to the HICs. However, this too is exactly what would be predicted by dependency theory, properly understood. Why is capital flight from the poorer countries to the richer countries an attractive option for "Third World" elites? This is precisely because this promises higher returns on their investments than are likely to be made locally. This surely presupposes underdevelopment stemming from relations of asymmetrical dependency between the (mostly Western metropole) HICs and those LICs (or LDCs) mostly situated in the Global South.

Dependency theorists, and those influenced by their concepts, were also amongst the first to show that, in the postwar period, developmental aid flowing from the developed countries (mostly in the Global North) to the developing countries (overwhelmingly in the Global South) has also been an instrument of capitalist imperialism. This is in the sense that this is deployed to reinforce dependency and consolidate commercial enterprise and trade liberalization in developing countries to the particular advantage of their own MNCs.[346]

None of this is to say that dependency theory is without problems. Of course, the notion of a fixed "core" and "periphery" of the world system, which was at the centre of Frank's (and Wallerstein's)[347] versions of the theory, is a blind alley. This is because there are routes out of dependence or underdevelopment, even if these are limited and hemmed in. Moreover, lumping all countries outside the developed world into the category of "periphery" was also unhelpful because this effaced local national variations and differences between countries. As for the idea of a "semi-periphery" in world systems, this simply confused matters since all countries outside the centre or core of the system were deemed to be trapped into underdevelopment. All were simply "dependent". Nor was the concept of "dependency" without difficulties. This is because, in a sense, all countries are mutually dependent in an interlinked market economy, so that a contrast between the developed centres and the less developed or underdeveloped regions of the Global South conceived in those terms lacked clarity.[348]

Nonetheless, the central proposition of dependency theory (i.e. that the chronically reproduced structural constraints of capitalist world economy and international state system dominated by the advanced capitals and nations was and is a force obstructing industrial development and economic modernization in the Global South, thereby reproducing a racialized international division of labour) is upheld. Moreover, the concept of dependency could certainly be refined, thereby undermining the common criticisms levelled at it. This would be so that dependency refers explicitly to specific kinds of asymmetric dependencies foisted by the rich countries on the poorer countries and the logic of comparative trade advantage and disadvantage or unequal exchange that the colonial legacy has established—in effect, applying the concept to those relations between the developed and developing world (political and economic) that have generated and perpetuated the advantages of the former and the disadvantages of the latter.

Anthony Brewer claims that dependency theorists somehow have failed to notice "how capitalism works". This is, he says, because they affirm that "the impersonal mechanisms of the market maintain the dependence of some countries on others, without the need to use state power overtly". Such a view, Brewer says, is misplaced. Why is it? This is because he says: "There is no central planning agency in a market system, no overall purpose. . . . In the absence of state intervention, countries are not relevant units, at this level of analysis".[349] Yet the case studies of dependency theorists clearly do not disregard the political dimension of domination. And Immanuel Wallerstein's world systems theory does root the economic subordination of the periphery in the operations of state system actors as well as market power actors.[350] To this point may be added another. If Brewer cannot see how the impersonal mechanisms of the market may function to reproduce the racial-class power asymmetries of the contemporary world economic order, even without the overt exercise of state power, he has not understood Marx's theory of capitalism. Capitalism, unlike precapitalist systems of class domination, as Marx made clear, does not rest essentially on "extra-economic" coercion.[351]

****

In summary, the neoliberal and corporate-dominated world today confronts us as one of vast and growing inequalities in wealth and income. This is between HICs and LICs (or LDCs), between workers and employers, between social classes nationally (within borders) and internationally (across borders), and between global ethnicities. These are inequalities transferred across successive cycles of asymmetrical competition by virtue of emergent structures that frame and organize these advantages and disadvantages. The hierarchized patterns of social interaction these structures govern have the tendency to widen the inheritance of inequality intergenerationally. This is by institutionally enabling those already empowered and advantaged by these structures to consolidate and entrench their position *vis-à-vis* those who are institutionally dis-enabled. Consequently, our world, in the "global" age, is economically more unequal than ever before.

These inequalities, as I will show, are not functionally necessary to any rational economic order, just as they are injurious to the wellbeing and life-chances of those at the wrong end of these divides. This is because these are not accompanied by any discernible performance benefits at the strictly economic level, not even for capitalism as a system—unless further enrichment of propertied elites *per se* can be counted as a general economic benefit. Rather, vast, and growing, income and wealth disparities have coincided with major performance deficits of world capitalism alongside the rise of retrogressive political forces fuelled by resentment and despair among the disenfranchised and dispossessed.[352] These deficits include increased vulnerability to recessionary crises, sluggish growth, and falling returns on capital investments. I will add that even if it could be demonstrated that inequality is causally efficacious in reducing poverty (by spurring economic growth and the attendant "trickle-down" effect), which has not been demonstrated, this would hardly establish a moral case for inequality. This is because such would not establish that poverty reduction *requires* increased inequality. Certainly, poverty reduction in the period of the long postwar boom did not.

Our unequal world demonstrates that corporate order and its neoliberal mode of governance are simply incompatible with the cause of worldwide social justice. As such, global political economy, as it is presently constituted, is an obstacle to a universal humanism of rights. Inequality, where this does not even serve the cause of capitalist profitability, let alone that of more "neutral" economic goals, cannot be anything other than unmitigated, incontestable injustice. This ought to be recognized even by neoliberals. Hayek's entrepreneurial heroes grow fatter on a rentier zombie capitalism rather than by promoting economic development. There is no longer any room even for debate on the ethical case for accepting inequality as trade-off for poverty reduction.

Notes and references

1 See for example: Ther, P. (2014). Europe since 1989. Princeton NJ: Princeton University Press, pp. 18, 19.
2 Davies, W. (2016a). 'The New Neoliberalism'. New Left Review, 101 (online).
3 Tooze, A. (2018). 'Neoliberalism's World Order'. Dissent (online). (Summer).
4 Tooze (2018).
5 Davies, A.; Jackson, B. and Sutcliffe-Braithwaite, F. (eds) (2021). The Neoliberal Age? Britain since the 1970s. London: UCL Press.
6 Rose, M.D. (2019). 'Book Review: Globalists, by Quinn Slobodian'. Source (online). (15 July).
7 Rose (2019).
8 This has been made clear enough by a large body of recent scholarship. Outstanding studies include: Biebricher, T. (2019). The Political Theory of Neoliberalism. Pal Alto CA: Stanford University Press; Blalock, C. (2020). 'Mutant Neoliberalism and the Politics of Culture'. Law and Political Economy Project (online). (28 April); Bonefield, W. (2012). 'Freedom and the Strong State: On German Ordoliberalism'. New Political Economy, 17 (5), pp. 633–56; Brown, W. (2019). In the Ruins of Neoliberalism: The Rise of Anti-Democratic Politics in the West. New York NY: Columbia University Press; Bruff, I. and Tansel, C.B. (eds) (2020). Authoritarian Neoliberalism: Philosophies, Practices, Contestations. Abingdon: Routledge; Cahill, D. (2014). The End of Laissez-Faire? On the Durability of Embedded Neoliberalism. Cheltenham: Edward Elgar; Callison, W. and Manfredi, Z. (eds) (2019). Mutant

Neoliberalism: Market Rule and Political Rupture. New York NY: Fordham University Press; Chernomas, R. and Hudson, I. (2017). The Profit Doctrine: Economists of the Neoliberal World. London: Pluto Press; Cohen, J. (2020). 'Neoliberalism and Antidemocratic Politics'. H-Socialisms (online). (May); Crouch, C. (2011). The Strange Non-Death of Neoliberalism. Malden MA: Polity Press; Davies, W. (2014). The Limits of Neoliberalism: Authority, Sovereignty and the Logic of Competition. London: SAGE; Davies, W. (2016b). 'The Neoliberal State: Power Against "Politics"'. Goldsmiths Research Centre (online). (September); Foucault, M. (2004). The Birth of Biopolitics: Lectures at the College de France, 1978–79. M Sennelart (ed) New York NY: Picador; Gerber, D.J. (1998). Law and Competition in Twentieth Century Europe: Protecting Prometheus. Oxford: Clarendon Press; Gane, N. (2014). 'Sociology and Neoliberalism: A Missing History'. Sociology, 48 (6), pp. 1092–1106; Hay, C. (2001). 'The "Crisis" of Keynesianism and the Rise of Neoliberalism in Britain'. J. Campbell and O. Pedersen (eds) The Rise of Neoliberalism and Institutional Analysis. Princeton NJ: Princeton University Press; Mirowski, P. and Plehwe, D. (eds) (2009). The Road from Mont Pèlerin: The Making of the Neoliberal Thought Collective. Cambridge MA: Harvard University Press; Monbiot, G. and Hutchinson, P. (2024). The Invisible Doctrine: The Secret History of Neoliberalism (& How It Came to Control Your Life). London: Allen Lane; Slobodian, Q. (2018). Globalists: The End of Empire and the Birth of Neoliberalism. Cambridge MA: Harvard University Press; Slobodian, Q. (2024). Crack-Up Capitalism: Market Radicals and the Dream of a World Without Democracy. London: Penguin; Streeck, W. (2014). Buying Time: The Delayed Crisis of Democratic Capitalism. London: Verso.

9 Slobodian (2018), pp. 2, 3.

10 Biebricher (2019).

11 Lenz, T. (2017). The Rising Authority of International Organizations. German Institute of Global and Area Studies (online).. (1 September).

12 Biebricher (2019).

13 Creaven, S. (2023). The Pandemic in Britain: COVID-19, British Exceptionalism and Neoliberalism. London and New York NY: Routledge (Ch.3: 'Neoliberalism and the Crisis of Welfare', esp. pp. 67–70); Wayne, M. (2021). 'Roadmaps after Corbyn: Parties, Classes, Political Cultures'. New Left Review, 132 (September/October), pp. 37–65; Geismer, L. (2022). Left Behind: The Democrats' Failed Attempt to Solve Inequality. New York NY: Public Affairs; Jessop, B. (2002). From Thatcherism to New Labour: Neoliberalism, Workfarism, and Labour Market Regulation. Lancaster University: Department of Sociology (online); Jordan, B. (2010). Why the Third Way Failed: Economics, Morality, and the Origins of the "Big Society". Bristol: Policy Press.

14 4 Metcalf, S. (2017). 'Neoliberalism: The Idea that Swallowed the World'. Guardian (online). (18 August).

15 Hayek, F.A. (1945). 'The Uses of Knowledge in Society'. American Economic Review, 35 (4), pp. 519–30; Hayek, F.A. (2002). Competition as a Discovery Process. Mises Institute (online).

16 Hayek, F.A. (1944). The Road to Serfdom. London: Routledge and Kegan Paul; Hayek, J.F. (1948). Individualism and Economic Order. London: Routledge and Kegan Paul; Hayek, J.F. (1960). The Constitution of Liberty. Chicago IL: University of Chicago Press. See also: Mises, L. (1990). Economic Calculation in the Socialist Commonwealth. Ludwig von Mises Institute (online); Schmitt, C. (1996). The Concept of the Political. Chicago IL: University of Chicago Press; Schumpeter, J.A. (1976). Capitalism, Socialism and Democracy. 5th edition. London: Allen and Unwin.

17 Davies (2016b).

18 Brown (2019), p. 5.

19 Seldon, A. (1981). Wither the Welfare State. London: Institute of Economic Affairs.
20 Metcalf (2017).
21 Metcalf (2017).
22 Davies (2016b). See also: Brown (2019); Slobodian (2018); Dardot, P. and Laval, C. (2014). The New Way of the World: On Neoliberal Society. London: Verso.
23 Brown, W. (2015). *Undoing the Demos: Neoliberalism's Stealth Revolution.* New York NY: Zone Books; Dardo and Laval (2014).
24 Becker, G.S. (1958). 'Competition and Democracy'. Journal of Law and Economics pp. 105–9; Becker, G.S. (1976). The Economic Approach to Human Behavior. Chicago IL: University of Chicago Press.
25 Bowman, A. et al. (2015). What a Waste: Outsourcing and How It Goes Wrong. Manchester: Manchester University Press; Brown (2015); Cerny, P.G. (1990). The Changing Architecture of Politics: Structure, Agency, and the Future of the State. London: SAGE; Fourcade, M. (2011). 'Cents and Sensibility: Economic Valuation and the Nature of "Nature" '. American Journal of Sociology, 116 (6), pp. 1721–77; Hood, C. (1995). 'The "New Public Management" in the 1980s: Variations on a Theme'. Accounting, Organizations and Society, 20 (2/3), pp. 93–109; Power, M. (1997). The Audit Society: Rituals of Verification. Oxford: Oxford University Press; Rhodes, R.A.W. (1996). 'The New Governance: Governing Without Government'. Political Studies, 44 (4), pp. 652–67.
26 Friedman, M. (1962). Capitalism and Freedom. Chicago IL: Chicago University Press; Hayek (1944, 1948, 1960); Seldon, A. (1967). Taxation and Welfare. London: Institute of Economic Affairs; Seldon (1981).
27 Friedman, M. and Friedman, R. (1980). Free to Choose. London: Penguin, p. 21.
28 Brown (2019), Ch. 3.
29 Friedman (1962); Hayek (1960).
30 Brown (2015); Davies (2014); Dardot, P. and Laval, C. (2014). The New Way of the World: On Neoliberal Society. London: Verso.
31 George, V. and Wilding, P. (1985). Ideology and Welfare. London: Routledge and Kegan Paul, pp. 19–26.
32 Friedman (1962), Hayek (1960).
33 Friedman (1962); Hayek (1944, 1960); Joseph, K. (1976). Stranded on the Middle Ground. London: Centre for Public Studies.
34 Hayek (1960).
35 Blyth, M. (2013). Austerity: The History of a Dangerous Idea. Oxford: Oxford University Press; Metcalf (2017); Slobodian (2018); Whyte, J. (2019). The Morals of the Market: Human Rights and the Rise of Neoliberalism. London: Verso.
36 George and Wilding (1985), pp. 30–2; Slobodian (2018).
37 Slobodian (2018), p. 252.
38 Davies (2016b).
39 Metcalf (2017).
40 Brown (2019).
41 Hayek (1960), p. 26.
42 Metcalf (2017).
43 Davies (2016b).
44 Brown (2019).
45 Brown (2019); Slobodian (2018); Mirowski and Plehwe (2009).
46 Davies (2016a); Gamble, A. (1988). The Free Economy and the Strong State: The Politics of Thatcherism. 2nd edition. Basingstoke: Palgrave Macmillan; Gray (2015). False Dawn: The Delusions of Global Capitalism. London: Granta Books; Harvey, D. (2005). A Brief History of Neoliberalism. Oxford: Oxford

University Press; Mirowski and Plehwe (2009); Slobodian (2018); Valdes, J.G. (1995). Pinochet's Economists: The Chicago School in Chile. Cambridge: Cambridge University Press; Whyte, J. (2023). 'Neoliberal Economists Like Milton Friedman Cheered on Augusto Pinochet's Dictatorship'. Jacobin (online). (09/11). Examples include (1) the Thatcher government's deployment of a paramilitarized police to defeat strikes by the miners, dockers, and printers in the UK in the 1980s; (2) Friedman's and Hayek's support for the Pinochet dictatorship that destroyed Allende's social-democratic government in Chile; (3) von Mises' and Hayek's backing of European fascism from the Vienna of the 1920s and 1930s to see-off the threat to property of a revolutionary labour movement. Many others could be cited.

47 Brown (2015); Rhodes, R. (1996). 'The New Governance: Governing Without Government'. Political Studies, XLIV, pp. 652–67; Rose, N. and Miller, P. (2013). Governing the Present: Administering Economic, Social and Personal Life. John Wiley & Sons; Blyth (2013); Streeck, W. (2014). Buying Time: The Delayed Crisis of Democratic Capitalism. London: Verso.

48 Davies (2016b).

49 Indeed, the restructuring of capitalism as a world system was itself a key element in intensifying the economic crisis of the communist states of the Eastern Bloc that destabilized them politically. The prodigious resources that became available to corporate capital owing to the new international division of labour left the Stalinist regimes, which were committed to industrial self-sufficiency, at a growing competitive disadvantage, so that growing proportions of GDP were swallowed up as waste expenditures in trying to keep abreast of the USA and its allies in the arms race. See: Callinicos, A. (1991). The Revenge of History: Marxism and the East European Revolutions. Cambridge: Polity Press, Ch. 2.

50 Harvey (2005); Harman, C. (2008). 'Theorising Neoliberalism'. International Socialism, 117 (Winter), pp. 87–121.

51 Duménil, G. and Lévy, D. (2004). Capital Resurgent: Roots of the Neoliberal Revolution. Cambridge MA: Harvard University Press; Glyn, A. (2006). Capitalism Unleashed: Finance, Globalization and Welfare. Oxford: Oxford University Press; Harman (2008); Harvey (2005); Klein, N. (2007). The Shock Doctrine: The Rise of Disaster Capitalism. London: Allen Lane; Miller, D. and Dinan, W. (2008). A Century of Spin: How Public Relations Became the Cutting Edge of Corporate Power. London: Pluto Press; Saad-Filho, A. and Johnston, D. (eds) (2004). Neoliberalism: A Critical Reader. London: Pluto Press.

52 Slobodian (2018).

53 Slobodian (2018).

54 Tooze (2018).

55 Slobodian (2018) shows that Mont Pelerin Society neoliberals were supportive of white minority rule in South Africa and Rhodesia right up to the 1980s. Hayek was unusual in that he claimed he disapproved of apartheid. But he refused to support sanctions on the grounds that these would violate free trade.

56 Kundnani, A. (2023). What Is Antiracism? And Why It Means Anticapitalism. London: Verso.

57 Slobodian (2018).

58 Whyte (2019).

59 Whyte (2019), p. 6.

60 As Whyte (2019, p. 96) quotes from the ILO charter, the "right to enjoy minimum [Whyte's emphasis] standards of economic, social and cultural well-being".

61 Bruff and Tansel (2020).

62 Bruff and Tansel (2020), p. 2.

63 Davies (2016a).

64 Davies (2016a).
65 Davies (2016a).
66 Brown (2019).
67 Brown (2019); Cooper, M. (2017). Family Values: Between Neoliberalism and the New Social Conservatism. New York NY: Zone Books.
68 Brown (2019).
69 Belfield, C. et al. (2014). Living Standards, Poverty and Inequality in the UK: 2014. London: Institute for Fiscal Studies; Bourquin, P., Cribb, J., Waters, T. and Xu, X. (2019). Living Standards, Poverty and Inequality in the UK: 2019. London: Institute for Fiscal Studies; Brenner, R. (2002). The Boom and the Bubble: The US in the World Economy. New York NY: Verso; Brenner, R. (2006). The Economics of Global Turbulence: The Advanced Capitalist Economies from Long Boom to Long Downturn, 1945–2005. London: Verso; Callinicos, A. (2000). Equality. Cambridge: Polity Press; Callinicos, A. (2003). An Anti-Capitalist Manifesto. Cambridge: Polity Press; Collins, C., Hartman, C. and Sklair, H. (1999). Divided Decade: Economic Disparity at the Century's End. New York NY: UFE; Gilbert, A. (2007). 'Inequality and Why It Matters'. Geography Compass, 1 (3), pp. 422–47; Hurst, C., Gibbon, H.F. and Nurse, A. (2016). Social Inequality: Forms, Causes and Consequences. London and New York NY; National Statistics (2007). Social Trends, 37. London: Office of National Statistics, Ch. 5; Saez, E. and Zucman, G. (2014). Wealth Inequality in the United States since 1913: Evidence from Capitalized Income Data. Working Paper 20625: NBER Working Paper Series. Cambridge MA: National Bureau of Economic Research; Westergaard, J. (1995). Who Gets What? The Hardening of Class Inequality at the End of the Twentieth Century. Cambridge: Polity Press.
70 Duménil and Lévy (2004); Harvey (2005); Hertz, N. (2002). The Silent Takeover: Global Capitalism and the Death of Democracy. London: Arrow; Sklair, L. (2001). 'The Transnational Capitalist Class and Global Politics: Deconstructing the Corporate: State Connection'. International Political Science Review, 23 (2), pp. 159–74.
71 Brown (2019), pp. 179, 85.
72 Creaven, S. (2024). Modernity and the Pandemic: Decivilization, Imperialism, and COVID-19. London and New York NY: Routledge. See especially Ch. 3.
73 Brown (2019), Ch. 2 and Ch. 3.
74 Brown (2019), p. 117. See also: Mattei, C. (2022). The Capital Order: How Economists Invented Austerity and Paved the Way to Fascism. Chicago IL: University of Chicago Press; Savage, M. (2021). The Return of Inequality. Cambridge MA: Harvard University Press.
75 Colantone, I. and Stanig, P. (2018). 'Global Competition and Brexit'. American Political Science Review, 112 (2), pp. 201–18; Koltai, J. et al. (2019). 'Deaths of Despair and Brexit Votes: Cross-Local Authority Statistical Analysis in England and Wales'. American Journal of Public Health, 110 (3), pp. 401–6; McQuarrie, M. (2017). 'The Revolt of the Rust Belt: Place and Politics in the Age of Anger'. British Journal of Sociology, 68 (S1), pp. 120–52. Brown (2019) refers to the far-right resurgence as neoliberalism's Frankenstein monster. It is not clear if she thinks we are seeing end times for neoliberalism, however, or simply living in the social wreckage it has wrought.
76 Cohen (2020); Gerstle, G. (2023). The Rise and Fall of Neoliberalism: America and the World in the Free Trade Era. Oxford: Oxford University Press; Koltai, J. et al. (2019). 'Deaths of Despair and Brexit Votes: Cross-Local Authority Statistical Analysis in England and Wales'. American Journal of Public Health; McQuarrie, M. (2017). 'The Revolt of the Rust Belt: Place and Politics in the Age of Anger'. The British Journal of Sociology, 68 (S1).

77 Gerstle (2023); Lind, M. (2020). The New Class War: Saving Democracy from the Metropolitan Elite. London: Atlantic Books.
78 McGee, K. (2017). Heathen Earth: Trumpism and Political Ecology. Santa Barbara CA: Punctum Books, p. 36.
79 Davies (2016b).
80 McGee (2017).
81 Kotsko (2019).
82 Loomis, E. (2024). 'Biden's Labor Report Card: Historian Gives 'Union Joe' a Higher Grade Than Any President since FDR'. Conversation (online). (16 May). Biden's pro-labour credentials were, however, considerably overstated. See: Riley, D. and Brenner, R. (2022). 'Seven Theses on American Politics'. New Left Review (online), 138 (November/December).
83 Gerstle (2023).
84 Kotsko, A. (2019). 'Trump as a Neoliberal Heretic'. Philosopher (online). (30 August).
85 "Cool Britannia", for example, was an image or slogan that Third Way New Labour governments in Britain sought to wrap around itself, denoting a new high-tech entrepreneurial culture that would sustain the UK as an economic powerhouse in the twenty-first century.
86 Slobodian, Q. and Plehwe, D. (2019). 'Neoliberals Against Europe'. Callison and Manfredi (eds). Mutant Neoliberalism, pp. 89–111.
87 Cohen (2020).
88 Banti, R. (2015). Thatcher's Government Immigration Policy as an Example of National Priorities Maintenance in View of European Union. European Historical Studies (online); Caldwell, A.A. (2016). 'Today's Immigration Debate Rooted in "Reagan Amnesty," Experts Say'. PBS News (online). (23 August); Ford, R. (2024). 'Changing Attitudes, Changing Coalitions: The Politics of Immigration before and after Brexit'. Political Quarterly, 95, pp. 224–33; Maddux, T.R. (2005). 'Ronald Reagan and the Task Force on Immigration'. Pacific Historical Review, 74 (2), pp. 195–236; Pierre, C. (2023). '"Keep Britain White": Britain's Inherently Racist Immigration Laws'. National Center of Competence in Research (online). (1 February); Shabi, R. (2019). 'How Immigration Became Britain's Most Toxic Political Issue'. Guardian (online). (15 November). Shull, C. (2015). A Recession-Proof Industry': Reagan's Immigration Crisis and the Birth of the Neoliberal Security State. Faculty of Law: University of Oxford (online).
89 Consterdine, E. (2016). 'The Huge Political Cost of Blair's Decision to Allow Eastern European Migrants Unfettered Access to Britain'. Conversation (online). (16 November); Watt, N. and Wintour, P. (2015). 'How Immigration Came to Haunt Labour: The Inside Story'. Guardian (online). (24 March).
90 Consterdine (2016): Watt and Wintour (2015).
91 Gibney, M.J. (2008). 'Asylum and the Expansion of Deportation in the United Kingdom'. Government and Opposition, 43 (2), pp. 146–67.
92 Widom, H. (2022). 'Fortress Europe: The EU's Colonial-Era External Borders: Spain & Morocco'. School of International Service: American University (online). (12 April).
93 Kundnani (2023).
94 Kundnani (2023). See also: Creaven (2007). Emergentist Marxism: Dialectical Philosophy and Social Theory. London and New York NY: Routledge, pp. 264–5.
95 Chambliss, W. (1994). 'Policing the Ghetto Underclass: The Politics of Law and Law-Enforcement'. Social Problems, 41 (2), pp. 77–94; Currie, E. (1998). Crime and Punishment in America. New York NY: Henry Holt; Davies (2016a, 2016b); Parenti, C. (1999). Lockdown America: Police and Prisons in a World of Crisis.

London: Pluto Press; Wacquant, L. (2009). Punishing the Poor: The Neoliberal Government of Social Insecurity. Durham CA: Duke University Press.

96 Creaven (2007), pp. 263–4; Kundnani (2023).

97 Miles, R. (1982). Racism and Migrant Labour. London: Routledge and Kegan Paul; Callinicos, A. (1992). Race and Class. London: Bookmarks, pp. 35–9.

98 Kundnani, A. (2023b). 'There Are Two Kinds of Antiracism. Only One Works, and It Has Nothing to Do with "Diversity Training" '. Guardian (online). (29 June). See also: Callinicos (1992, pp. 34, 39); Creaven (2007), pp. 255–7.

99 Miles (1982).

100 Creaven (2007), pp. 263–4.

101 Creaven (2023), pp. 229–36.

102 Kotsko (2019).

103 Creaven (2023), pp. 10–13.

104 Creaven (2023), pp. 67–81.

105 Creaven (2023), pp. 22–48.

106 Creaven (2023), pp. 96–124.

107 Creaven (2023), pp. 125–55.

108 Creaven (2023), pp. 156–61.

109 Creaven (2023), pp. 174–86.

110 Kiely, R. (2021). 'Conservatism, Neoliberalism and Resentment in Trumpland: The "Betrayal" and "Reconstruction" of the United States'. Geoforum (online), 124, pp. 334–42 (p. 334).

111 Kyle (2017), p. 27.

112 McNicholas, C., Poydock, M. and Rhinehart, M. (2019). 'Unprecedented: The Trump NLRB's Attack on Workers Rights'. Economic Policy Institute (online). (16 October).

113 Kyle (2017), pp. 37–8, 45.

114 Anon (2024). 'The Primary Differences Between NAFTA and USMCA'. TACNA (online).

115 Monbiot, G. (2016). 'Neoliberalism: The Deep Story That Lies Beneath Donald Trump's Triumph'. Guardian (online). (14 November).

116 Milanovic, B. (2020). 'Trump as the Ultimate Triumph of Neoliberalism'. Global Policy (online). (14 May).

117 As cited by Wendy Brown (2019, p. 29).

118 Kotsko (2019).

119 Kotsko (2019).

120 Anon (2021). 'Is Donald Trump a Neoliberal?' Reddit (online). (20 October).

121 Rogers, J.R. (2021). Is Inequality a Problem? Law and Liberty (online). (10 August).

122 Savage (2021).

123 Cooper, M. (2024). Counterrevolution: Extravagance and Austerity in Public Finance. Cambridge MA: Zone Books. See also: Cooper (2017).

124 Cooper (2024), pp. 87, 102.

125 Cooper (2024) argues that growing class and racial-class inequality in the USA has thus been driven not so much by the elite appropriating higher surpluses generated in production from the exploitation of wage-labour (which has not been possible owing to weak profits in the "real" economy) but from the accumulation in elite families of asset-based, capital-gains wealth sustained by tax breaks and concessions funded by deficit spending by the neoliberal state.

126 Sayer, A. (2016). Why We Can't Afford the Rich. Cambridge: Polity Press.

127 Creaven (2007), pp. 214–79; Creaven, S. (2000). Marxism and Realism: A Materialistic Application of Realism in the Social Sciences. London and New York NY: Routledge, pp. 240–7.

128 Creaven (2007), pp. 230–49.
129 German, L. (1994). Sex, Class and Socialism. 2nd edition. London: Bookmarks, pp. 50–1.
130 Anon (2024). Why the Majority of the World's Poor Are Women. Oxfam International (online).
131 German (1994), pp. 51–2; German (2007). Material Girls: Women, Men and Work. London: Bookmarks, pp. 10, 92–3, 95.
132 Goldberg, G.S. (2010). Poor Women in Rich Countries: The Feminization of Poverty over the Life Course. Oxford: Oxford University Press.
133 UNRISD (2010). Combating Poverty and Inequality: Structural Change, Social Policy and Politics. Geneva: UNRISD Publications. (Ch.4: 'Gender Inequalities at Home and in the Market').
134 German (2007), p. 10.
135 Creaven, S. (2024). Contagion Capitalism: Pandemics in the Corporate Age. London and New York NY: Routledge, pp. 222–3, 229–30, 233–5; Madrick, J. (1997). The End of Affluence: The Causes and Consequences of America's Dilemma. New York NY: Random House, pp. 16–7. Madrick shows how, in the USA, declining wages for male workers since the 1970s has been a powerful impulse for the feminization of the US labour market, as female spouses and partners seek out employment to make up a family wage. If this is true of the USA, it is certainly applicable in poorer countries.
136 Benería, L., Berik, G. and Floro, M. (2015). Gender, Development, and Globalization: Economics as if All People Mattered. 2nd edition. London and New York NY: Routledge.
137 Scheider, J. and Gould, E. (2019). '"Women's Work" and the Gender Pay Gap: How Discrimination, Societal Norms, and Other Forces Affect Women's Occupational Choices—and Their Pay'. Policy Studies Institute (online). (20 July).
138 ILO (2022). Pay Transparency Legislation: Implications for Employers' and Workers' Organizations. Geneva: ILO.
139 Boll, C. and Lagemann, A. (2021). Gender Pay Gap in EU Countries. Rome: European Commission; Eurostat (2022). Gender Pay Gap statistics. EU (online). Not adjusted for part-time and full-time employees.
140 Kochhar, R. (2023). The Enduring Grip of the Gender Pay Gap. Pew Research Center (online). This is the per hourly rate for all employees, whether full-time or part-time.
141 Devine, F. (2024). The Gender Pay Gap. Westminster: House of Commons Library. (8 November); White, N.J. (2023). 'Gender Pay Gap in the UK 2023'. ONS (online). This is the rate for all employees. The gap between full-time employees is seven percent.
142 UNSDG (2024). 'Progress on the Sustainable Development Goals: The Gender Snapshot 2024'. UN Women and UNDEA (online), p. 13.
143 A process noted by two pathbreaking studies: Braverman, H. (1974). Labour and Monopoly Capitalism: The Degradation of Work in the Twentieth Century. New York NY: Monthly Review Press; Crompton, R. and Jones, G. (1984). White Collar Proletariat: Deskilling and Gender in Clerical Work. Basingstoke: Macmillan.
144 Christensen, M.A. (2019). Feminization of Poverty: Causes and Implications. Gender Equality. Cham: Springer International: Oxfam International (online). (2024).
145 Klein, N. (2005). No Logo: Taking Aim at the Brand Bullies. London: Harper-Collins ("No Jobs"); Pilger, J. (2003). The New Rulers of the World. London: Verso, pp. 17–21.
146 German (2007), p. 11.
147 Brown. J.B. and Lichter, D.T. (2004). 'Poverty, Welfare, and the Livelihood Strategies of Nonmetropolitan Single Mothers'. Rural Sociology, 69 (2), pp. 282–301.

148 Moghadam, V.M. (2004). 'The Feminization of Poverty and Women's Human Rights. SHS Papers in Women's Studies/Gender Research'. No. 2. UNESCO (online). (July).
149 Sanchez-Paramo, C. and Munoz-Boudet, A.M. (2018). 'No, 70% of the World's Poor Aren't Women, but that Doesn't Mean Poverty Isn't Sexist'. World Bank (online). (8 March). Burchi and Malerba (2023) draw on recent IDIS studies to estimate that between 54 and 63 per cent of the world's poorest are female. See: Burchi, F. and Malerba, D. (2023). 'The Gendered Nature of Poverty: Data, Evidence and Policy Recommendations'. Policy Brief 24. IDIS (online).
150 Chant, S. (2014). 'Exploring the Feminisation of Poverty in Relation to Women's Work and Home-Based Enterprise in Slums of the Global South'. International Journal of Gender and Entrepreneurship, 6 (3), pp. 296–316; Oxfam International (online) (2024). Although real, the concept of feminization of poverty has been ideologized by the World Bank to support specific neoliberal growth-oriented, trickle-down solutions to world poverty. See: Chant, S. (2016). 'Addressing World Poverty Through Women and Girls: A Feminised Solution'. Sight and Life, 30 (2), pp. 58–62.
151 UNSDG (2022). 'Progress on the Sustainable Development Goals: The Gender Snapshot 2022'. UN Women and UNDESA (online), p. 6.
152 UNSDG (2024), p. 8.
153 German (2007), p. 75.
154 UNSDG (2024), p. 7.
155 McGregor, S. (1989). 'Rape, Pornography and Capitalism'. International Socialism, 2 (45), pp. 9–25.
156 Alvaredo, F., Atkinson, A.B. and Morelli, S. (2017). Top Wealth Shares in the UK Over More than a Century. INET Oxford Working Paper No. 2017–1. Institute for New Economic Thinking.
157 Westergaard, J. and Resler, H. (1976). Class in a Capitalist Society. Harmondsworth: Penguin, p. 112.
158 National Statistics (2002). Social Trends, 32. London: ONS, p. 102.
159 Alvaredo et al. (2017).
160 ONS (2018). 'Wealth in Great Britain: 2014 to 2016'. London: ONS (online); ONS (2016). 'Wealth in Great Britain: 2010 to 2012'. London: ONS (online).
161 ONS (2019). Total Wealth in Great Britain: April 2016 to March 2018. London: ONS (online).
162 Alvaredo et al. (2017).
163 Atkinson, A.B. (1983). The Economics of Inequality. Oxford: Oxford University Press, p. 63.
164 Cribb, J., Joyce, R. and Philip, D. (2012). Living Standards, Poverty and Inequality in the UK: 2012. London: Institute of Fiscal Studies, p. 30.
165 Callinicos (2000), p. 135.
166 Green, B. and Shaheen, F. (2014). 'Economic Inequality and House Prices in the UK'. New Economics Foundation (online), p. 7. See also: Equality Trust (2018). 'How Has Inequality Changed? Development of UK Income Inequality'. ET (online).
167 National Statistics (2006). 'Social Trends, 36'. London: ONS, p. 81.
168 Goodman, A., Johnson, P. and Webb, S. (1997). Inequality in the UK. Oxford: Oxford University Press, p. 22.
169 Social Trends, 36 (2006), pp. 76–7.
170 Oxfam (2013). 'The True Cost of Austerity and Inequality: UK Case Study'. Oxfam Case Study (online). (September); OECD (2011). 'Divided We Stand: Why Inequality Keeps Rising. Country Note: United Kingdom'; OECD (2013). 'Crisis Squeezes Income and Puts Pressure on Inequality and Poverty'. OECD (online).

171 DWP (2012). Households Below Average Income Statistics: First Release (14 June). London: DWP; Howard, M., Garnham, A., Fimister, G. and Veit-Wilson, J. (2001). Poverty: The Facts. 4th edition. London: Child Poverty Action Group, p. 21.

172 Brewer, M. et al. (2006). Poverty and Inequality in Britain. London: Institute for Financial Studies.

173 Aldridge, H. et al. (2012). Monitoring Poverty and Social Exclusion 2012. York: Joseph Rowntree Foundation, p. 23.

174 DWP (2013). 'Households Below Average Income: An Analysis of the Income Distribution 1994/95–2011/12 June 2013'. GOV.UK (online). See Table 3, p. 74. Cited in Oxfam (2013). The True Cost of Austerity and Inequality: UK Case Study. Oxfam Case Study (online). (September).

175 Belfield et al. (2014), p. 57.

176 Joseph Rowntree Foundation (2020). 'UK Poverty Statistics: Poverty Levels and Trends'. JRF (online).

177 Social Metrics Commission (2019). 'Measuring Poverty 2019: A Report by the Social Metrics Commission'. SMC (online). (July), p. 20.

178 Full Fact (2019). 'Poverty in the UK: A Guide to the Facts and Figures'. Full Fact (online). (27 September). Full Fact's statistics are based on the Social Metrics Commission's new measures of poverty.

179 Apel, H. (2015). 'Income Inequality in the U.S. from 1950 to 2010—the Neglect of the Political'. Real World Economics Review, 72, pp. 1–145. See p. 6.

180 Collins et al. (1999).

181 Schaeffer, K. (2020). 'Six Facts about Economic Inequality in the U.S.' Pew Research Center: Fact Tank. (online). (7 February).

182 Trudell, M. (2012). 'The Occupy Movement and Class Politics in the US'. International Socialism, 133. (Winter), pp. 39–53. See p. 44.

183 Piketty, T. (2014). Capital in the Twenty-First Century. Cambridge MA: Harvard University Press.

184 Alvaredo, F. et al. (2018). 'World Inequality Report 2018: Executive Summary'. World Inequality Lab (online).

185 Kuhn, M., Schularick, M. and Steins, U.I. (2019). 'Income and Wealth Inequality in America 1949–2016'. Federal Reserve Bank (online).

186 Kent, A., Rickets, L. and Boshara, R. (2019). 'What Wealth and Income Inequality in America Looks Like: Key Facts and Figures'. Federal Reserve Bank (online).

187 Saez, E. and Zucman, G. (2014). 'Exploding Wealth Inequality in the United States'. Washington Center for Equitable Growth (20 October).

188 Collins et al. (1999).

189 Schaeffer (2020).

190 Kent et al. (2019). Similarly, according to Saez and Zucman, the share of national wealth going to the top 10 per cent of households increased from 64 per cent in 1987 to 77 per cent in 2012. See: Saez, E. and Zucman, G. (2014). Wealth Inequality in the United States since 1913: Evidence from Capitalized Income Tax Data. Working Paper 20625. NBER Working Paper Series. Cambridge MA: National Bureau of Economic Research, p. 56.

191 Saez and Zucman (2014), p. 1.

192 Schaeffer, K. (2020). 'Six Facts about Economic Inequality in the U.S.' Pew Research Center: Fact Tank (online). (7 February).

193 Ehrenreich, B. (2003). Nickel and Dimed: Undercover in Low-Wage America. New York NY: Henry Holt, p. 213.

194 Institute for Research on Poverty (2020). 'How Is Poverty Measured?' University of Wisconsin-Madison: IRP (online).

195 Greenberg, M. (2009). 'It's Time for a Better Poverty Measure'. Center for American Progress (online). (25 August 25).
196 Greenberg (2009).
197 Morrill, R. (2010). '50 Years of US Poverty: 1960 to 2010'. New Geography (online). (19 February); Chaudry, A. et al. (2016). Poverty in the United States: 50-Year Trends and Safety Net Impacts. (March). US Department of Health and Human Services: Office of Human Services Policy (online).
198 Plotnick, R.D. et al. (1998). The Twentieth Century Record of Inequality and Poverty in the United States. Discussion Paper no. 1166–98. Institute for Research on Poverty, p. 21.
199 Collins et al. (1999).
200 Eckholm, E. (2010). 'Recession Raises Poverty Rate to a 15-Year High'. New York Times (online). (16 September).
201 Morrill (2010); Chaudry et al. (2016); Semega, J., Kollar, M., Shrider, E.A. and Creamer, J. (2020). 'Income and Poverty in the United States: 2019'. United States Census Bureau (online). (15 September).
202 Fessler, P. (2019). 'U.S. Census Bureau Reports Poverty Rate Down, But Millions Still Poor'. NPR News (online). (10 September).
203 Miller, R.H. (1973). Characteristics of the Low-Income Population: 1973. Current Population Reports. Series P. 60, No. 98. US Department of Commerce and Bureau of the Census. Washington DC: Government Printing Office.
204 Harman, C. (1993). 'Where Is Capitalism Going?' International Socialism, 2 (58), pp. 3–57. See p. 53 for OECD data.
205 Manyika, J. et al. (2020). 'A New Look at the Declining Labor Share of Income in the United States'. McKinsey Global Institute (online). (22 May).
206 UNCTAD (2022). 'Trade and Development Report 2022: Development Prospects in a Fractured World'. UNCTAD (online).
207 Collins et al. (1999).
208 Galbraith, J. (1993). The Culture of Contentment. Boston MA: Houghton Mifflin Harcourt.
209 Brenner (2006), pp. 191–2.
210 Heilbronner, R. (1993). Twenty-First Century Capitalism. New York NY: W.W. Norton and Co.
211 Madrick (1997), pp. 16–7.
212 IMF (1999). Why Has Inflation in the United States Remained So Low? Reassessing the Importance of Labor Costs and the Price of Imports. IMF: Working Paper 99/149. New York NY: IMF Publications, p. 5.
213 Luttwak, E.N. (1999). Turbo Capitalism: Winners and Losers in the Global Economy. London: Harper-Collins, pp. 95–6.
214 Collins et al. (1999).
215 Hunnicut, B.K. (1990). Work Without End: Abandoning Shorter Hours for the Right to Work. Philadelphia PA: Temple University Press.
216 Schor, J. (1991). The Overworked American: The Unexpected Decline of Leisure. New York NY: Basic Books, p. 26.
217 Kuhn, P. and Lozano, F. (2005). The Expanding Work Week: Understanding Trends in Long Work Hours Among US Men, 1979–2004. Working Paper 11895. Cambridge MA: National Bureau of Economic Research, pp. 1–2.
218 Mishel, L. (2013). Vast Majority of Wage Earners Are Working Harder, and Not for Much More: Trends in US Work Hours and Wages over 1979–2007. Issue Brief #348. Economic Policy Institute. (30 January), p. 2.
219 Mishel (2013), p. 3.

220 Kalleberg, A.L. (2011). Good Jobs, Bad Jobs. New York NY: Russell Sage Foundation; Maume, D.J. and Purcell, D.A. (2007). 'The "Over-Paced" American: Recent Trends in the Intensification of Work'. B.A. Rubin (ed) Workplace Temporalities: Research in the Sociology of Work. Vol. 17. Bingley: Emerald Group Publishing Limited. Work intensification and job strain (employees experiencing exhaustion and stress from their work) is commonplace in the developed world, affecting on one estimate 30–40 per cent of the workforce. See: Steiber, N. (2014). 'Trends in Work Stress and Exhaustion in Advanced Economies'. Social Indicators Research, 121, pp. 215–31. Work intensification also affects a wide range of different occupational groups and has shown a secular tendency to increase within nations and internationally over the past few decades. As Green et al. (2021, pp. 3–4) observe, a wide range of surveys have recorded work intensification, far in excess of those which have not. See: Green, F. et al. (2021). 'Working Still Harder'. ILR Review, 20 (10), pp. 1–30.
221 Congressional Budget Office (2011). 'Trends in the Distribution of Household Income Between 1979 and 2007'. CBO Online. (25 October).
222 Manyika et al. (2019).
223 Harman, C. (1999). A People's History of the World. London: Bookmarks, p. 607.
224 Mishel, L. and Wolfe, J. (2019). CEO Compensation Has Grown 940% since 1978: Typical Worker Compensation Has Risen Only 12% During That Time. Economic Policy Institute (online). (14 August).
225 Taylor, C., Jowett, A. and Hardie, M. (2014). An Examination of Real Falling Wages. London: ONS, p. 3. See also: BBC News (2014). 'Drop in Real Wages Longest for 50 Years, Says ONS'. (31 January).
226 Hardy, J. and Choonara, J. (2013). 'Neoliberalism and the British Working Class: A Reply to Neil Davidson'. International Socialism, 140 (Autumn), p. 7.
227 Felstead, A. et al. (2013). Work Intensification in Britain: First Findings from the Skills and Employment Survey 2012. Economic and Social Research Council and UK Commission for Employment and Skills: University of Oxford.
228 Green, F., Felstead, A., Gallie, D. and Henseke, G. (2018). Work Intensity in Britain: First Findings from the Skills and Employment Survey 2017. ESRC and UKCES: University of Oxford.
229 Felstead et al. (2013).
230 Green et al. (2018).
231 ONS (2021). 'Average Actual Weekly Hours of Work for Full-Time Workers (Seasonally Adjusted)'. GOV.UK (online).
232 Harman, C. (1995). The Economics of the Madhouse: Capitalism and the Market Today. London: Bookmarks, p. 49.
233 New Economics Foundation (2019). 'Average Weekly Hours Fell Faster Between 1946 and 1979 than Post-1980'. NEF (online).
234 Dmitracova, D. (2019). 'UK Working Hours Would be Shorter If Pre-1980 Trend Had Not Been Derailed, New Study Says'. Independent (online). (12 September).
235 Machin, S. (2015). Real Wage Trends. Understanding the Great Recession: From Micro to Macro Conference. (September 23–24 2015). London: Bank of England, pp. 8–9.
236 Blundell, R., Crawford, C. and Jin, W. (2012). What Can Wages and Employment Tell Us about the UK's Productivity Puzzle? IFS Working Paper W13/11. London: Institute for Fiscal Studies.
237 Osborne, H. (2015). 'UK Workers' Wages Fell 1% a Year Between 2008 and 2015, TUC Says'. Guardian (online). (27 February).
238 Belfield, C. et. al (2014). 'Living Standards, Pay and Inequality in the UK: 2014'. Institute for Fiscal Studies (online). (15 July); Taylor et al. (2014).

239 Taylor, C., Jowett, A. and Hardie, M. (2014). An Examination of Real Falling Wages. London: Office of National Statistics, p. 3. See also: BBC News (2014). 'Drop in Real Wages Longest for 50 Years, Says ONS'. (31 January).

240 Elliott, L. (2017). 'Missing Wage Rises Give Lie to Picture of Full Employment'. Guardian (online). (15 February).

241 Cribb, J. and Johnson, P. (2018). '10 Years On—Have We Recovered from the Financial Crisis?' Institute for Fiscal Studies (online). (12 September).

242 Anand, S. and Segal, P. (2008). 'What Do We Know about Global Income Inequality?' Journal of Economic Literature, 46 (1), pp. 57–94; Deaton, A. (2013). The Great Escape: Health, Wealth, and the Origins of Inequality. Princeton NJ: Princeton University Press; Dikhanov, Y. and Ward, M. (2003). Evolution of the Global Distribution of Income in 1970–99. Proceedings of the Global Poverty Workshop: Initiative for Policy Dialogue. New York NY: Columbia University; Dowrick, S. and Akmal, M. (2006). 'Contradictory Trends in Global Income Inequality: A Tale of Two Biases'. M. McGillivray (ed) Inequality, Poverty and Wellbeing. Basingstoke: Palgrave Macmillan, pp. 91–122; Galbraith, J.K. (2007), 'Global Macroeconomics and Global Inequality'. D. Held and A. Kaya (eds). Global Inequality: Patterns and Explanations. Cambridge: Polity Press; Ghosh, J. (2019). 'The Uses and Abuses of Inequality'. Journal of Human Development and Capabilities, 20 (2), pp. 181–96; Greig, A., Hulme, D. and Turner, M. (2006). Challenging Global Inequality: Development Theory and Practice in the Twenty-First Century. London: Red Globe Press; Korzeniewicz, R.P. and Moran, T.P. (2009). Unveiling Inequality: A World-Historical Perspective. New York NY: Russell Sage Foundation; Milanovic, B. (2007). Worlds Apart: Measuring International and Global Inequality. Princeton NJ: Princeton University Press; Milanovic, B. (2010). 'Global Inequality Recalculated and Updated: The Effect of New PPP Estimates on Global Inequality and 2005 Estimates'. Journal of Economic Inequality, 10, pp. 1–18; Nye, H. and Reddy, S. (2003). 'Weaknesses of Recent Global Poverty Estimates: Xavier Sala-i-Martin and Surjit Bhalla'. Social Analysis (online); Pogge, T. (2007). Freedom from Poverty as a Human Right: Who Owes What to the Very Poor? Oxford: Oxford University Press; Pickett, K. and Wilkinson, R.G. (2009). The Spirit Level: Why More Equal Societies Almost Always Do Better. London: Allen Lane; Pogge, T. (2009). 'How World Poverty Is Measured and Tracked'. ResearchGate (online). (January); Pogge, T. and Reddy, S. (2009). 'How Not to Count the Poor'. Initiative for Policy Dialogue Working Papers Series (online); Reddy, S. (2006). 'Counting the Poor: The Truth about World Poverty Statistics'. Socialist Register (online); Reddy, S. and Pogge, T. (2002). 'How Not to Count the Poor: A Reply to Ravallion'. Social Analysis (online); Reddy, S. and Minoiu, C. (2007). 'Has World Poverty Really Fallen? The Review of Income and Wealth, 53 (3), pp. 484–502; Sengupta, R. (2006). 'Poverty and Inequality in the New World: Moving Forward or Backward? A Critique of "Globalization, Poverty and Inequality since 1980" by David Dollar'. Network-Ideas.org (online); Sengupta, R. (2010). 'Human Rights and Severe Poverty'. Economic and Political Weekly, 45 (17), pp. 85–93; Vandemoortele, J. (2002). Are We Really Reducing Global Poverty? New York NY: United Nations Development Programme: Bureau for Development Policy; Wade, R.H. (2004). 'Is Globalization Reducing Poverty and Inequality?' International Journal of Health Studies, 34 (3), pp. 381–414; Wade, R.H. (2007). 'On the Causes of Increasing World Poverty and Inequality, or Why the Matthew Effect Prevails'. New Political Economy, 9 (2), pp. 163–88; Wade, R.H. (2017). 'Global Growth, Poverty and Inequality: The Globalization Argument and the "Political" Science of Economics'. J. Ravenhill (ed) Global Political Economy. Oxford: Oxford University Press, pp. 319–55; Weller, C.E. and Hirsch, A. (2004). 'The Long and Short of

It: Global Liberalization and the Incomes of the Poor'. Journal of Post-Keynesian Economics, 26 (3), pp. 471–504; Weller, C.E., Hirsch, A. and Scott, R.E. (2001). 'The Unremarkable Record of Liberalized Trade'. Briefing Paper 113. Economic Policy Institute (online). (1 October).

243 World Bank (2020), pp. 2–3 (17).

244 Chen, S. and Ravallion, M. (2004). 'How Have the World's Poorest Fared since the Early 1980s?' World Bank Research Observer, 19 (2) (Autumn), pp. 141–6.

245 Callinicos (1991), p. 67.

246 Harman, C. (1984). Explaining the Crisis: A Marxist Re-Appraisal. London: Bookmarks, pp. 75, 76.

247 Jones, G. (2005). 'Restoring a Global Economy, 1950–1980. Working Knowledge: Business Research for Business Leaders'. Harvard Business School (online).

248 Callinicos (1991), pp. 46–7; McAuley, A. (2008). Development Strategy, Welfare Regime and Poverty Reduction in the Former Soviet Union. United Nations Research Institute for Social Development. UNRISD Project on Poverty Reduction and Policy Regimes, Country Overview. Paper No. 3.

249 White, G., Murray, R. and White, C. (eds) (1983). Revolutionary Socialist Development in the Third World. Brighton: Harvester Press.

250 The classic case of hostile encirclement being of Castro's Cuba. See: Binns, P. and Gonzalez, M. (1983). Cuba, Castro and Socialism. London: Bookmarks; Yaffe, H. (2016). 'Cuba Is Poor—But Who Is to Blame, Castro or 50 Years of US Blockade'. Conversation (online). (2 December). See: Hayter, T. (1990). The Creation of World Poverty. 2nd edition. London: Pluto Press, pp. 14–7 for a discussion of other cases of hostile encirclement and attempted destabilization.

251 Hayter (1990), pp. 109–14, for examples.

252 McAuley (2008).

253 The drive of the Soviet planners to safeguard national security in a hostile capitalist world led to a huge asymmetry of investments in accumulation compared to consumption. As Harman (1990, p. 33) reports, in 1928, 60 per cent of the USSR's output was of consumer goods and 40 per cent of producer goods. By the mid-1980s 74.8 per cent of the USSR's national income was devoted to accumulation and only 25.2 per cent to consumption. Despite this, living standards and absolute levels of popular consumption rose steadily up until the 1980s. Harman, C. (1990). 'The Storm Breaks'. International Socialism, 2 (46), pp. 3–93.

254 UN (2017). World Economic and Social Survey 2017: Reflections on 70 Years of Development Policy Analysis. New York NY: UN: DESA. For the UK, for example, Rowntree's famous York surveys found that absolute poverty rates declined from 18 per cent in 1936 to just 1.5 per cent by 1950. See: Coates, K. and Silburn, R. (1970). Poverty: The Forgotten Englishmen. Harmondsworth: Penguin, p. 46. For the USA, for example, data from the Social Security Administration indicates that the proportion of people in subsistence poverty declined from 33 per cent in 1948 to 11.5 per cent in 1975. See: Plotnick, R.D. et al. (1998). The Twentieth Century Record of Inequality and Poverty in the United States. Discussion Paper no. 1166–98. Institute for Research on Poverty, p. 21.

255 Brittan cited in Pallast, G. (2003). The Best Democracy Money Can Buy. London: Constable and Robinson, p. 149.

256 Pallast (2003), pp. 149–50.

257 Harris, N. (1974). India-China: Underdevelopment and Revolution. Durham NC: Carolina Academic Press, p. 171.

258 Amin, S. (1976). Unequal Development. Brighton: Harvester Press; Amin, S. (1977). Imperialism and Unequal Development. New York NY: Monthly Review

Press; Amin, S. (1978). Accumulation on a World Scale: A Critique of the Theory of Under-Development. Basingstoke: Harvester Press; Baran, P. (1973). The Political Economy of Growth. Harmondsworth: Penguin; Emmanuel, A. (1969). Unequal Exchange: A Study of the Imperialism of Trade. London: New Left Books; Hayter (1990), pp. 49–53, 66–71.

259 Frank, A.G. (1978). Dependent Accumulation and Underdevelopment. Basingstoke: Macmillan; Frank, A.G. (1970). 'The Development of Underdevelopment'. R.I. Rhodes (ed) Imperialism and Underdevelopment. New York NY: Monthly Review Press; Frank, A.G. (1981). Crisis: In the Third World. London: Heinemann; Frank, A.G. (2008). 'The Development of Underdevelopment'. M. A. Seligson and J. T. Passe-Smith (eds) Development and Under-Development: The Political Economy of Global Inequality. London: Lynne Rienner Publishers; Frank, A.G. (1971). Capitalism and Underdevelopment in Latin America. Harmondsworth: Penguin; George, S. (1979). Feeding the Few: Corporate Control of Food. London: Institute of Policy Studies; George, S. (1976). How the Other Half Dies. Harmondsworth: Penguin; Galeano, E. (1973). The Open Veins of Latin America: Five Centuries of the Pillage of a Continent. New York NY: Monthly Review Press; Griffin, K. and Ghose, A.K. (1978). 'The Roots of Underdevelopment: Reflections on the Chinese Experience'. Modern China, 4 (3), pp. 23–38; Hayter (1990), pp. 46–53; Hoogvelt, A. (1982). The Third World in Global Development. London: Macmillan; Magdoff, H. (1978). Imperialism: From the Colonial Age to the Present. New York NY: Monthly Review Press; Magdoff, H. (1972). 'Imperialism without Colonies'. R. Owen and B. Sutcliffe (eds) Studies in the Theory of Imperialism. London: Longman; Rodney, W. (1972). How Europe Underdeveloped Africa. London: Bogle-L'Ouverture; Spybey, T. (1992). Social Change, Dependency and Development. Cambridge: Polity Press, pp. 158–80; Sutcliffe, B. (1972). 'Imperialism and Industrialisation in the Third World'. Owen and Sutcliffe (eds), pp. 171–2; Wallerstein, E. (1974). The Modern World System. New York NY: Academic Press; Wallerstein, E. (1979). The Capitalist World Economy. Cambridge: Cambridge University Press.

260 Harman (1999), pp. 560–2; Petras, J. (1977). 'State Capitalism and the Third World'. Development and Change, 8, pp. 1–17.

261 Harman, C. (2009). Zombie Capitalism: Global Crisis and the Relevance of Marx. London: Bookmarks, p. 183.

262 Spybey (1992), p. 169.

263 Spybey (1992), pp. 169–70.

264 George, S. (1988). A Fate Worse Than Debt. London: Penguin; e Gomm, R. (1986). 'Development, Under-development and Migration'. P. McNeill and C. Townley (eds) Fundamentals in Sociology. London: Hutchinson, pp. 407–8.

265 Susan George (1988, p. 12) estimated Third World debt as totalling around $1 trillion by the mid-1980s. Despite campaigns since to "drop the debt", and some debt relief measures at the close of the 1990s and in the mid-2000s, for the most part re-scheduling of repayments, the situation since remains fundamentally unchanged, indeed is worsening. As Hickel (2017) notes: "Developing countries have forked out over $4.2tn in interest payments alone since 1980—a direct cash transfer to big banks in New York and London, on a scale that dwarfs the aid that they received during the same period". By 2020, total debts for the developing or "emerging" countries had grown from $1 trillion in the mid-1980s to around $11 trillion, with $3.9 trillion due for repayment that year. See: Kharas, H. (2020). 'What to Do about the Coming Debt Crisis in Developing Countries'. Brookings Institute (online). (13 April). As reported by the Jubilee Debt Campaign Group, debt for developing countries more than doubled in the 2000s, leaving more than 50 countries at risk of

defaulting on repayments. External debt payments "as a share of government revenue [have]. . . more than doubled from 6.7% to 14.3% since 2010 and were at their highest level since 2001". Moreover, "even without taking full account of the impact of the coronavirus pandemic, there has been a sharp jump in the number of poor countries in debt distress since 2018". See: Elliott, L. (2020). 'Debt on Developing Countries Has Doubled in Less Than a Decade'. Guardian (online). (16 August).

266 These are the primary economic factors of underdevelopment theorized by dependency theorists. But for many the economic mechanisms that reproduced the inequalities and asymmetries of the world economy were buttressed by political mechanisms—the policy actions of the leading state actors in the advanced or developed world, led by the USA. In this sense, underdevelopment was also a story of neoimperialism, of political subordination of the underdeveloped world to the leading states, overwhelmingly those in the Global North (though Japan broke into the exclusive club), which was enshrined in the global governance of the G7, the UN, and the WTO. Neoimperialism is the subject of Ch. 3. However, a few observations on its economic aspects at this point are in order.

A fundamental instrument of economic neoimperialism in the postwar period has been the use and misuse of development aid. Development aid flowing from the developed enclaves (mostly in the Global North) to the developing countries (overwhelmingly in the Global South) has been deployed to reinforce dependency and consolidate commercial enterprise and trade liberalization in developing countries. As such, although aid could not be said to have been economically non-beneficial to poorer countries (aid is better than non-aid), the benefits have tended to be limited, insufficient to dent dependency relations, and have conferred greater advantages (economic, political, and ideological) on the givers than on the receivers.

The ideological benefit to the developed states of donating aid to the less developed or underdeveloped ones is that this legitimizes the economic status quo and the predominant position of the leading nation-states and their superordinate classes within it. It establishes the rhetorical commitment of the rich countries to assisting the poor countries in becoming rich countries—and it does this cheaply, since aid donations are equivalent to a tiny proportion of their GDP. Aid can also "be seen as a means of maintaining . . . a common interest between the elites of underdeveloped countries and the metropolitan countries, or as a kind of bribe to help to make it worth their while to continue to co-operate with the drain of capital from their countries" (Hayter, 1990, p. 83).

Such aid has also been used politically by Washington to reward "friendly" states for compliance to pro-capitalist free-market reforms (including openness to multinationals and their products) just as its withdrawal penalizes "unfriendly" ones for non-compliance. The politics of aid has also been used to deter countries from "going socialist", or embracing other forms of politics (whether nationalist or religious—for example, Arab nationalism or radical Islamism) considered anti-Western, or to coerce them to abandon these politics, or to secure them as geopolitical allies in Cold War and other imperial rivalries (such as against China and Russia in recent times). It has even been used to destabilize unfriendly or "off-message" governments by provoking popular discontent with them.

Aid, therefore, is a tool or weapon in global power politics, in the promulgation of free enterprise and the reproduction of the capitalist world system and attendant world political order. Such aid has also tended to be in the form of loans rather than grants (albeit at lower rates of interest than typical loans), so that the donator banks derive profits from it. Moreover, such aid is "tied", in the sense that a condition of receiving it is that it is used to purchase commodities (development-supporting goods or services or expertise) from the donating country (usually its MNCs) and is used to support only approved projects. This creates aid monopolies, hence inflated prices for the commodities that are purchased with the aid or provides the companies supplying the commodities with an opportunity to offload outmoded or unsafe products that cannot be sold in the markets of the developed world. This also channels the aid disproportionately into infrastructural projects (communications, transport, power, hydration) that would improve the accessibility and profitability of these countries for foreign MNCs. In the neoliberal age, aid has also been "tied" to or made conditional on governments agreeing to administer the IMF's structural adjustment programmes (SAPs) of radical marketization and privatization of all aspects of social life.

See: Arnold, G. (1985). Aid and the Third World: The North/South Divide. London: Robert Royce Ltd; Cammack, P. (2004). 'What the World Bank Means by Poverty Reduction, and Why It Matters'. New Political Economy, 9 (2), pp. 189–211; Escobar, A. (2012). Encountering Development: The Making and Unmaking of the Third World. Princeton NJ: Princeton University Press; Hayter (1990), pp. 82–96; Hayter, T. (1971). Aid as Imperialism. London: Pelican; Hayter, T. and Watson, H. (1985). Aid: Rhetoric and Reality. London: Pluto Press; Linear, M. (1985). Zapping the Third World War. London: Pluto Press; O'Brien, R. and Williams, M. (2013). Global Political Economy. Basingstoke: Palgrave Macmillan; Riddell, R.C. (2007). Does Foreign Aid Really Work. Oxford: Oxford University Press; Tarp, F. and Hjertholm, P. (2000). Foreign Aid and Development: Lessons learnt and Directions for the Future. London: Routledge; Taylor, M. (2004). 'Responding to Neoliberalism in Crisis: Discipline and Empowerment in the World Bank's New Development Agenda'. S. Soederberg and P. Zarembka (eds) Neoliberalism in Crisis, Accumulation, and Rosa Luxemburg's Legacy. London: Emerald; Waeyenberge, E.V. (2010). 'Tightening the Web: The World Bank and Enforced Policy Reform'. K. Birch and V. Mykhnenko (eds) The Rise and Fall of Neoliberalism: The Collapse of an Economic Order? London: Zed Books.

267 Indeed, Britain's own Industrial Revolution was fuelled by ruthlessly protectionist policies, protecting domestic markets from overseas competition, including the notorious Navigation Acts of 1799. Protection of home industries was combined with the deployment of military power to force free trade on economically weaker countries. See: Hayter, 1990, pp. 50–1, 69–70.

268 Harman (2009), pp. 207–11, 217–25; Harman (1999), pp. 589–97; Callinicos, A. (2009). Imperialism and Global Political Economy. Cambridge: Polity Press, pp. 183–4.

269 Spybey (1992), pp. 161–2.

270 Pallast (2003), p. 150.

271 Bello, W. (2003). Deglobalization: Ideas for a New World Economy. London: Zed Books, p. 43; Harman (1999), p. 594.

272 Pallast (2003, Ch. 4, pp. 141–204) describes the negative impacts of these SAPs or PRSs on the poor and ordinary folk of a few poor countries who bore the brunt of radical marketization. Pallast also reports "coming by" confidential official World Bank planning documents that set out that these policies would generate mass popular unrest (dubbed the "IMF riots") that the authorities would need to deal with "resolutely".

273 UN (2017). World Economic and Social Survey 2017: Reflecting on Seventy Years of Development Policy Analysis. New York NY: UNDESA, p. 28.

274 This encouraged some left-wing scholars to (prematurely) announce the "death of dependency" and falsity of underdevelopment. The tendency was most pronounced in the work of Marxist political theorist Bill Warren. For him the concept of dependency was redundant in the post-colonial age, since this related "almost entirely to political control of one country by another", which was no longer tenable.

For Warren, the success of the NICs demonstrated that the world was entering a post-imperialist condition. As he put it:

> Within a context of growing economic interdependence, the ties of dependence (or subordination) binding the Third World and the imperialist world have been and are being markedly loosened with the rise of indigenous capitalisms; the distribution of political-economic power within the capitalist world is thereby growing less uneven. Consequently, although one dimension of imperialism is the domination and exploitation of the non-communist world by a handful of major advanced capitalist countries (the United States, West Germany, Britain, France, Japan, etc.), we are nevertheless in an era of declining imperialism and advanced capitalism.

This informed Warren's view that in the post-colonial age international capitalism (and the predominant position within it of the advanced nations of the Global North) posed no barriers to development in the Global South. Hence: "Insofar as there are obstacles to this development, they originate not in current imperialist-Third World relationships, but almost entirely from the internal contradictions of the Third World itself". See: Warren, B. (1973). 'Imperialism and Capitalist Industrialization'. New Left Review, 1 (81) (online). (September/October). See also: Warren, B. (1980). Imperialism: Pioneer of Capitalism. London: New Left Books, pp. 9–10, 150, 176, 182. More on this later.

275 Harris, N. (1987). The End of the Third World: Newly Industrializing Countries and the Decline of an Ideology. London: Pelican.

276 Callinicos (2009), pp. 183–4; Harman (2009), pp. 218–9, 243–5; Harman (1984), pp. 94–7; Harris (1987), pp. 30–69; Jinjun, X. (1995). 'The Export-Led Growth Model and Its Application in China'. Hitotsubashi Journal of Economics, 36 (2), pp. 189–206; Koko, A. (2002). Export-Led Growth in East Asia: Lessons for Europe's Transition Economies. Working Paper No. 142. European Institute of Japanese Studies. Stockholm School of Economics; Lin, L.-W. and Milhaupt, C.J. (2011). We Are the (National) Champions: Understanding the Mechanisms of State Capitalism in China. The Peter A. Allard School of Law. Allard Research Commons; Szamosszegi, A. and Kyle, C. (2011). An Analysis of State-Owned Enterprises and State Capitalism in China. Washington DC: U.S.-China Economic and Security Review Commission.

277 Jones (2005).

278 Roser, M. and Ortiz-Ospina, E. (2017). 'Global Extreme Poverty'. Our World in Data (online).

279 World Bank (2020), p. 2.

280 Since September 2022 this has been elevated to $2.15 a day.

281 Nye and Reddy (2003); Pogge (2009); Pogge and Reddy (2009); Reddy and Pogge (2002); Reddy and Minoiu (2007); Sengupta (2006, 2010); Weller and Hersh (2004); Vandemoortele (2002); Wade (2004, 2007).

282 Wade (2004).

283 Wade (2004).

284 Wade (2004).

285 Pogge (2009); Reddy and Minoiu (2007); Wade (2004, 2007).

286 Wade (2004, 2007). See also Wade, R.H. (2006). 'Globalisation Isn't Working'. Prospect Magazine, 124 (July 22).

287 Wade (2004, 2007); Vandemoortele (2002).

288 Weller and Hersh (2004).

289 According to the World Bank, between 1980 and 1993 world extreme poverty excluding China fell by only 6.9 per cent, from 29 per cent of the world's poor to

27 per cent. Between 1993 and 2002 it had fallen 14.9 per cent, so that the proportion of the world's poor excluding China was reduced only to 23 per cent from 29 per cent. Since then, progress has quickened, so that world poverty outside China halved between 2002 and 2015. See: Roser and Ortiz-Ospina (2017). These are much less impressive results than the overall picture inclusive of China headlined by the World Bank.

290 World Bank (2020), p. 5. Their estimate was that the crisis has likely pushed 88 million below the poverty line in 2020 and would push a further 35 million below in 2021.

291 Cendrowski, S. (2015). 'China's Global 500 Companies Are Bigger Than Ever—and Mostly State-Owned'. Fortune (online). (22 July); Weightman, W. (2018). 'Why China Won't Abandon Its Controversial Trade Policies: Protectionist Policies Play a Key Role in China's National Strategy'. Diplomat (online). (24 May).

292 Chen, S. and Ravallion, M. (2008), 'The Developing World Is Poorer Than We Thought, But No Less Successful in the Fight Against Poverty'. Policy Research Development: Paper No. 4703. Washington DC: World Bank, pp. 31, 36.

293 Chen and Ravallion (2008). Indeed, as Chen and Ravallion noted, just as the number of people living under $1 a day declined from the 1980s through to the 2000s, at the same time "the number of people in the world living on less than $2 a day rose, so that there has been a marked bunching up of people living between $1 and $2 a day". Chen, S. and Ravallion, M. (2004). 'How Have the World's Poorest Fared since the Early 1980s?'. The World Bank Research Observer, 19 (2) (Autumn), pp. 141–69. Again, China was at the centre of this dynamic. Breakneck industrialization and urbanization took 300 million Chinese people out of severe poverty on the World Bank's numbers, but this was won by creating a new mass of the working poor hovering precariously above the $1 daily rate. The "great achievement" of neoliberal capitalist globalization is thus the replacement of a mass of absolutely impoverished rural farmers with a mass of slightly less impoverished proletarians.

294 Hayter (1990), p. 18.

295 Chen and Ravallion (2008).

296 Hayes, A. (2020). 'Federal Poverty Level (FPL)'. Investopedia (online). (13 October).

297 Ravallion, M., Chen, S. and Sangraula, P. (2008). 'Dollar a Day Revisited'. World Bank Economic Review, 23 (2), pp. 163–84.

298 Shah, A. (2013). 'Poverty Facts and Stats'. Global Issues (online). (7 January).

299 World Bank (2018). 'Nearly Half the World Lives on Less than $5.50 a Day'. World Bank (online). (17 October).

300 World Bank (2018).

301 United Nations Children's Fund and World Health Organization (2019). Progress on Drinking Water, Sanitation and Hygiene: 2000–2017: Special Focus on Inequalities. New York NY: UNICEF and WHO.

302 UNICEF (2019). 'The State of the World's Children: Children, Food and Nutrition'. UNICEF (online).

303 This is not the case for all, though. Some World Bank analysts and laissez-faire economists have heroically discovered evidence even for declining, albeit minor, reductions of global inequality in the neoliberal era, although these results are undermined by the methodological flaws already described. See, for example: Bhalla, S. (2002). 'Imagine There's No Country: Poverty, Inequality, and Growth in the Globalization Era'. ResearchGate (online); Dollar, D. and Kraay, A. (2004). 'Trade, Growth and Poverty'. Economic Journal, 114 (493), pp. 22–49; Sala-i-Martin, X. (2002). 'The Disturbing "Rise" of Global Income Inequality'. Working Paper 8904.

National Bureau of Economic Research. (April); Wolf, M. (2004). Why Globalization Works. New Haven CT: Yale University Press.

304 UNDP (2008). Human Development Report 2007. New York NY: UNDP, p. 25.

305 Keeley, B. (2015). Income Inequality: The Gap Between Rich and Poor. Paris: OECD Publications, p. 3.

306 Harman (1999), p. 607.

307 Zucman, G. (2019). 'Global Wealth Inequality'. Annual Review of Economics, 11, pp. 109–38. See p. 109.

308 Credit Suisse (2013). Global Wealth Report 2013. Geneva and New York NY: CS Research Institute, pp. 21–2.

309 UNDP (2008), p. 25.

310 OECD (2011), p. 22.

311 OECD (2011), p. 22.

312 OECD (2015). 'In It Together: Why Less Inequality Benefits All'. OECD (online).

313 Oxfam (2018). 'An Economy for the 99%. Oxfam Briefing Paper'. Oxfam org.com (online). For summary see: Elliott, L. (2019). 'World's 26 Richest People Own as Much as Poorest 50%, Says Oxfam'. Guardian (online). (21 January).

314 Peterson Institute for International Economics (2002). 'The Pattern of Economic Growth, 1950–2000'. IIE (online), p. 17.

315 PIIE (2002), p. 23.

316 Maria, A. and Wen, Y. (2015). 'Trapped: Few Developing Countries Can Climb the Economic Ladder or Stay There'. Federal Reserve Bank of St Louis (online). (7 October).

317 PIIE (2002), p. 18.

318 PIIE (2002), p. 21.

319 Weller and Hersh (2004), p. 471.

320 PIIE (2002), p. 24.

321 UNDP (1999). Human Development Report 1999: Human Development in this Age of Globalization. New York NY: UNDP, p. 3; Kanbur et al. (2001). World Development Report 2000/2001: Attacking Poverty. New York NY: World Bank, p. 3.

322 OECD (2011).

323 UNCTAD (2020). 'The Least Developed Countries Report 2020: Productive Capacities for the New Decade'. UNCTAD (online). (3 December).

324 Warren (1973, 1980).

325 See: Alami, I. (2019). Money Power and Financial Capital in Emerging Markets. London: Routledge; Ashiagbor, D. (2021). 'Race and Colonialism in the Construction of Labour Markets and Precarity'. Industrial Law Journal, 50 (4), pp. 506–31; Koram, K. (2022). Uncommon Wealth: Britain and the Aftermath of Empire. New York NY: Hachette; Tilley, L. and Shilliam, R. (2021). Raced Markets. London: Routledge. The authors show how racism is ingrained in international finance and labour markets and how colonial methods of extraction gave rise to offshoring, outsourcing and corporatization—key features of the "new" world economy. This kind of work is also continuous with that of radical "black Marxism" authors such as CLR James, Franz Fanon, Walter Rodney, Manning Marable, and Cedric Robinson.

326 Frank (1970, 1978, 1981).

327 Callinicos (2009), p. 5.

328 Emmanuel (1969). Quote is from: Emmanuel, E. (1974). 'Myths of Development Versus Myths of Underdevelopment'. New Left Review (online), 1 (85). (May/June).

329 Callinicos (2009), p. 178.

330 Callinicos (2009), pp. 179–80.
331 Klein (2005); Pilger (2003), pp. 17–20.
332 Hayter (1990), pp. 74–5.
333 Callinicos (2009), pp. 179–80.
334 Klein (2000); Pilger (2003).
335 Klein (2000); Pilger (2003).
336 Callinicos (2009), pp. 179–80.
337 Callinicos, A. (1991). 'Marxism and Imperialism Today'. International Socialism, 2 (50), p. 21.
338 Felipe, J., Kumar, U. and Abdon, A. (2010). How Rich Countries Became Rich and Why Poor Countries Remain Poor: It's the Economic Structure . . . Duh! Working Paper no. 644. Levy Economics Institute (online), pp. 2, 10–11, 29.
339 Gros, D. (2013). 'Why Does Capital Flow from Poor to Rich Countries?' World Economic Forum (online).
340 Barnet, R.J. and Muller, R.E. (1974). Global Reach: The Power of the Multinational Company. New York NY: Simon and Schuster; Frank (1978); Erel, I., Jang, Y. and Weisbac, N. (2019). 'The Corporate Finance of Multinational Firms'. Brookings Institute (online). (10 November); Hayter (1990), pp. 71–82; Jang, Y. (2017). 'International Corporate Diversification and Financial Flexibility'. Review of Financial Studies, 30 (12), 4133–78; Joffe, M. (2017). 'Why Does Capital Flow from Poor to Rich Countries?—The Real Puzzle'. Real World Economics Review, 81 (30 September), pp. 42–62; Lucas, R. (1990). 'Why Doesn't Capital Flow from Rich to Poor Countries?' American Economic Review, 80 (2), pp. 92–6; Moran, T. (1978). 'Multinational Corporations and Dependency: A Dialogue for Dependentistas and Non-Dependentistas'. International Organisation, 32 (1), pp. 79–100; Santos, T. (1970). 'The Structure of Dependence'. American Economic Review (May), pp. 231–9.
341 UNCTAD (2020). Topsy-Turvy World: Net Transfer of Resources from Poor to Rich Countries. Policy Brief No. 78 (May). UNCTAD (online).
342 Hickel, J. (2017). 'Aid in Reverse: How Poor Countries Develop Rich Countries'. Guardian (online). (14 January).
343 Petras, J. and Morley, M. (1990). US Hegemony under Siege: Class, Politics and Development in Latin America. London: Verso, p. 197.
344 McKinley, T. (2006). The Monopoly of Global Capital Flows: Who Needs Structural Adjustment Now? Working Paper No. 12. International Poverty Centre: UNDP, p. 2.
345 Callinicos (1991).
346 Arnold (1985); Cammack (2004); Escobar (2012); Hayter (1971, 1990); Hayter and Watson (1985); Linear (1985); O'Brien and Williams (2013); Riddell (2007); Tarp and Hjertholm (2000); Taylor (2004); Waeyenberge (2010).
347 Wallerstein (1974, 1979).
348 Brewer, A. (1990). Marxist Theories of Imperialism: A Critical Survey. London: Routledge, pp. 196–7.
349 Brewer (1990, p. 197).
350 Wallerstein (1974, 1979).
351 Marx, K. (1973). Grundrisse. Penguin: Harmondsworth, p. 507. This is because capitalism is a mode of production that separates the workers from all livelihood-sustaining property.
352 Brown (2019); Savage (2021).

2 Neoliberalism, globalization, and zombie capitalism

How are the asymmetries of the world economic order set out in the previous chapter to be explained? Why are they radicalizing in the neoliberal era? One answer—which is a good answer—is that this is an inevitable consequence of unfettered markets that neoliberal ideology asserts must deliver the opposite results and which the neoliberal politics of the Washington Consensus is forever seeking to expand and consolidate, both internationally but especially in the Global South. Regulated markets (in labour-power, finance capital, property ownership, and trade in commodities and services) grant workers everywhere a measure of protection from employers by placing controls on capitalist appropriation and exploitation. These also afford weaker or less developed countries, their economies, their industries, their workforces, their social-welfare and healthcare systems, some measure of protection from the trap of unequal exchange. Deregulated markets, by contrast, undermine these protections.

The neoliberal politics of unfettered capitalism therefore radicalize and complexify the postwar, postcolonial pattern of combined yet *uneven* economic development worldwide, just as these harden wealth and income disparities within and across national borders, as this chapter will explore. Yet, far from reinvigorating the capitalist world economy, neoliberal governance has presided over an economic system that is increasingly zombified by virtue of its corporate mode, its dominance by mega-capitals (the MNCs and occasional TNCs), as this chapter also will show.

Zombie capitalism is not only insatiable (and boosted in its appetites for "wealth creation" or "shareholder value"—including by means of the colonization of all things for commodification that can be made money out of—by neoliberalism's free-market mantras) but is also fragile, unstable, crisis-prone, with tendencies towards stagnation. The combination of a greed unchecked by rational controls, and its self-endangerment by virtue of parasitism's own economic unsustainability, this ensures that zombie capitalism cannot coexist with any politics other than those which will deliver more of the same—more inequality, asymmetry, commodification, appropriation, and so on.

DOI: 10.4324/9781003597346-3

The relevance of Marx

Here it is necessary to turn to Marx. Marx's critique of political economy (his theory of the "laws of motion" of the capitalist mode of production) allows us to understand why neoliberal-driven capitalist internationalization has delivered these unhappy (and for the naïve among neoliberal ideologists unexpected) results.

In the three volumes of *Capital*, Marx applies and develops his general theory of socio-historical materialism to making sense of what makes capitalism tick as a historically specific system of political economy. For Marx, the trajectory of modernity, as of premodernity, is determined primarily by processes of economic rationalization, and by the class struggle that arises from the structural contradictions of class-divided modes of production.[1] Capitalism is theorized as a historically specific mode of production, which is characterized by two main structural cleavages. Firstly, the internal division of the non-producing owners (bourgeoisie or capitalist elite) into competing units of capital in a system of generalized commodity production. Secondly, the separation of productive workers (proletariat—i.e. industrial workforce) from the means of production and the resultant alienation of their labour-power in exchange for the money-wages necessary to secure their access to means of subsistence.[2]

For Marx, these structural cleavages of the capitalist mode establish the relations between capitalist owners and non-owning workers as both oppressive and exploitative. Since members of the working class do not own or possess or otherwise exert power of control over the means of production they are compelled or at least pressured to sell their labour-capacity to the capitalist owners or controllers in return for the wages that would grant them access to subsistence goods. Consequently, the workers must surrender power of command of their labour-time and labour-power to the superordinate capitalist class; and, in doing so, they must also simultaneously submit to exploitation at the hands of their employers as appropriation of unpaid labour-time. On the CRT understanding of social systems, these structural cleavages of the capitalist mode are emergent, since these do not arise spontaneously from daily social practices or human agency. Rather, these are *reproduced* cross-generationally, by virtue of asymmetric competition between workers and capitalists, as this is supported by anterior structures that have arisen from previously materialized human agency.

Marx's analysis of capitalism theorizes the specific social form that class exploitation here takes. Under capitalism, exploitation of labour does not take the form of appropriated *product* (direct extortion of goods and services), as was the case in precapitalist and non-capitalist societies.[3] Rather, this takes the form of appropriated *value* (i.e. expropriation of unpaid labour-time embodied in commodities that are produced by the workers but owned by their employers). Value is specific to economies based on generalized commodity production,[4] referring to the *socially necessary* labour-time that is embodied in commodities—or as Marx puts it, "the labour time required to produce any use-value under the conditions of production normal for a given society and with the average degree of skill and intensity of labour prevalent in that society".[5] Market competition between owners ensures that goods and services and labour-power do not exchange in accordance with the *physical* or *concrete* labour-time that goes into their manufacture but in accordance with the socially *average* labour-time that prevails in a particular branch of production.

The competitive interactions in the marketplace between owners to maintain or increase their profits at each other's expense compel them to reduce production costs to the social average that prevails in their sector of business. Marx refers to this dynamic as the law of value.[6] This means that the workers are subject to increasingly rationalized techniques of surplus-appropriation (i.e. continual re-divisions of labour and introduction of new labour-enhancing technology to increase labour productivity). In other words, under capitalism, competition between business enterprises to safeguard market shares and profitable returns ensures that owners are driven to constantly increase the rate of exploitation of the workers to accumulate capital for reinvestment in increasingly efficient production.[7] Such explains the expansionist dynamism of capitalism (of which Marx was fully cognizant—his *Communist Manifesto*, co-authored by Frederick Engels, written in 1848, predicts the internationalization of the capitalist mode),[8] but also its barbarism. This is its capacity to pile up ever more colossal productive wealth (in the hands of a small elite) alongside its opposite (the meagre pittances of the have-nots) and its ruthless objectification of the world, as nature and human beings are reduced to the status of resources in pursuit of the self-expansion of value.

Marx's theory has typically been misrepresented as positing the inevitability of capitalist collapse owing to its inner contradictions.[9] It has also been mistakenly read as positing an inexorable linear process of growing inequality between capitalists and workers, and of working-class immiseration or pauperization (these resulting from inter-capitalist competition), which would reputedly drive the workers into socialist revolution.[10] Thus, Marx's theory is sometimes considered as invalidated especially by the postwar boom of 1948–73 and associated developments in the West (generalized affluence, consumer culture, welfarism, post-capitalist corporatism and managerialism, post-industrialism, and so on).[11] This is because this not only extended capitalism internationally but also drove up general living standards—especially in the developed world (where productivity gains from mass production radically lowered the price of consumptive means). Absolute poverty virtually disappeared in the developed countries, and class inequalities were somewhat reduced during the Golden Age.

However, Marx was fully aware that capitalism goes through periods of boom, in which low unemployment strengthens the bargaining position of workers, which may lead to wage increases. Marx thus rejected the idea (popular amongst socialists and anarchists as well as bourgeois commentators in his own day) that workers could never earn more than the bare minimum needed to keep them alive. Rather, Marx was explicit that working-class income from wages was regulated by the general level of development of the productive forces in any specific society and the popular cultural expectations this regulated.[12] As Marx put it, "the value of labour is in every country determined by the satisfaction of certain wants springing from the social conditions in which people are placed and reared up", that is, the "traditional standard of life".[13]

Yet Marx also argued that increased labour productivity under capitalism would not necessarily raise wages in absolute terms; rather, workers had to win these benefits of economic growth through their struggles with capital. Thus, for Marx, workers could improve their absolute consumption under capitalism by means of trade union action for improved wages.[14] But, at the same time, irrespective of the movement of absolute wages, Marx affirms that

> it does not follow from this [i.e. from the tendency under capitalism for investment in capital to increase faster than investment in labour-power] that the fund from which the workers draw their revenue is diminished *absolutely*; only that it is diminished *relatively*, in proportion to their total output.[15]

Under these circumstances, with rising labour productivity, the workers would be able to purchase a greater *volume* of commodities with their wages but a lesser *proportion* of the total mass and value of commodities produced by their labour. Now, this is precisely what has happened since Marx's day in the advanced economies, especially during the long postwar boom. Here the constant upgrading of labour-saving technology and redrawing of the division of labour, in tandem with the success of trade union organization and action in ensuring that the workers at least benefit somewhat from increased productivity, has meant that living standards through wages in the West increased substantially in absolute terms, even though the workers' share of what they produced fell.[16] For this reason, Marx's theory of class polarization is not at all discomfited by the rise of the affluent consumer society of the 1950s and 1960s.

Nor does the moderate decline in class inequality in the developed countries during the Golden Age count as a refutation of Marx. This is because Marx's theory specifies the necessary relationship between capital and wage-labour in a "pure" market economy. His purpose was to see how capitalism behaves if left to its own devices, in order to establish its underlying economic "law of motion". This was a model of capitalism considered in abstraction from politics or culture.

Therefore, Marx's theory does not consider (and thus does not rule out) the possibility that the capitalist state may assume the role of intervening in the marketplace in order to ease, manage, or reduce market imbalances, or ameliorate class conflicts over distribution of the social product between capital and labour, or provide certain social goods that both workers and capitalists would benefit from, so as to stabilize capitalist relations of production. Instead,

Marx's argument is that growing inequalities between capital and labour are bound to occur in an *unregulated* capitalist economy (governed only by its own internal dynamics). This is clearly not the same as saying that trade unions and governments cannot successfully temporarily resist or even reverse these divisive impacts of market forces. The period of the boom, I would contend, is empirical-historical demonstration of Marx's point.

Nonetheless, resistance to the inequality-generating mechanisms of capitalist competition, whether by workers or by reformist governments, encounters formidable emergent structural constraints. This is because if it were to be wholly successful, this would undermine capitalism (and hence would be resisted by the organized power of the capitalism-friendly or at least capitalism-acquiescent state). Since capital is appropriated labour-time realized in exchange-value and translated into profit, inequality by class is internal and necessary to the system. Moreover, working-class resistance may be blunted or undermined by the basic structural asymmetry of power between the contending (owing and non-owning) classes.

In a competitive market, capitalists are driven to increase the rate of exploitation of their workers to boost their profits. And over the trade cycle as a whole, workers and capitalists rarely (if at all) confront each other as equals, because the former (unlike the latter) obviously do not own or control the means of labour. Capitalists are macro-agents by virtue of their money-power and control of the means of wealth-creation. Workers are micro-agents by virtue of the fact that they possess only their labour-capacity that they are coerced to alienate in return for the means of life. Successful working-class resistance to capitalist exploitation—in the sense of moderating or tempering it—can therefore be achieved only by means of collective organization and struggles, or by electing reformist governments to office, since this reduces the power asymmetry integral to labour markets, even though this cannot guarantee success.

Now, the limited, modest redistribution of wealth and income that occurred especially during the postwar boom in the advanced countries was largely the result of government and trade union *intervention* in the economy. Western governments, under the auspices of Keynesianism, sought to counteract market forces in the interests of social cohesion. This was by redirecting some resources away from capital and towards the working class and the poor through the taxation and welfare systems. This was the policy of compensating the propertyless with a "social wage"—and this was considered economically affordable (for capitalism) by state managers owing to the massive expansion of GDP growth that allowed high capitalist profits to coexist with rising real wages.[17]

Under boom conditions of unprecedented longitude, the trade unions also took advantage of labour shortages under conditions of virtual full employment to wrest wage and other concessions (i.e. a range of workplace entitlements) from employers on behalf of workers—and capitalist resistance to these was muted by the fabulous productivity gains allowed by high-tech assembly-line

Fordism and the new export opportunities afforded by the expanding world market. In short, a degree of wealth and income redistribution occurred *in spite of* rather than *because of* capitalism, just as wage growth was made possible by economic exceptionalism under social-democratic governance. But, to reiterate the key point, Marx's theory does not state that governments or other collective actors cannot intervene against capitalism in order to redistribute wealth and income (in the interests of national cohesion or other public goals). Rather, Marx's theory would establish that *capitalism* itself has no inbuilt redistributive mechanism. So, left to its own devices, capitalism would not reduce income disparities between owners and workers, and would be likely to widen these, because of the mutual alienation of the units of capital in a system of competitive accumulation.

Nonetheless, Marx undoubtedly did believe that in the *long-run*, as ageing capitalism ran into the limits imposed by its own property relations, there would be a strong tendency for a growing polarization of income and wealth differentials between capitalists and wage-workers. This would be a tendency for growing class inequality, not any "iron law" of absolute working-class impoverishment. Any balancing act between the opposed interests of capital and labour (such as that established by the postwar compromise) would, from a Marxist standpoint, be made possible only by highly favourable economic circumstances (such as those afforded by the postwar boom). But these would be unstable and ephemeral owing to the contradictions of the capitalist mode. This understanding of postwar economic prospects would be wholly consistent with Marx's theory of capitalism as a system of class exploitation driven by blind competition.

This is highly significant. For, if Marx is right, his theory retains revolutionary significance today. This is because popular feelings of injustice are motivated as much by *relative* deprivation (i.e. inequalities that are perceived as indefensible) as by objective states of absolute deprivation. And Marx's theory of capitalist development is consistent with the reality of capitalist development in the postwar world. The period of the postwar boom (1948–73) saw what turned out to be a temporary interruption of the dynamic of hardening or widening class disparities between the propertied elites, on the one hand, and the working class and poor, on the other. This was at least in those HICs that embraced the mixed economy of state enterprise and private enterprise, the expansionist welfare state, state-regulated labour markets, and Keynesian demand-management policies. These policies also provided fertile conditions for strong, robust labour unions to be consolidated that were capable of somewhat effective defensive actions against employer encroachments.

But, in the decades since the 1980s, with the onset of the neoliberal revolution in state policymaking, in response to the mid-1970s crisis of "organized capitalism", the longstanding trend for wealth and income inequalities to grow has been renewed.[18] This is for reasons diagnosed by Marx's critique of capitalism. This would establish that markets liberated from the constraints of organized labour unions or reformist governments (i.e. deregulated, liberalized markets), under today's "disorganized capitalism",[19] would show a strong tendency to radicalize market-power asymmetries, hence generating pressures towards social disequilibria and social conflict. Indeed, since the radicalization of market-power asymmetries between capital and labour wrought by trade liberalization would (in the context of a capitalist world economy) apply as much across borders as within, Marx's theory would also predict widening income gaps between richer and poorer countries. Such would generate downsizing pressures on wages and labour rights and social-welfare systems everywhere, though with greater or lesser impacts on workers and the poor in different parts of the world.

By contrast, according to supporters of the Washington Consensus, and contrary to Marx, liberalized markets could in theory generate generalized prosperity and reduce imbalances between economic actors (countries, enterprises, workers, consumers, etc.). But this would be the case only if those economic actors encountered each other in the marketplace as equally endowed in terms of access to allocative resources. Yet neoliberalism supports a convergence theory of world economic development, based on the ideas of neoclassical economist Robert Solow, according to which "poor nations will have a *natural* tendency to steadily *approach* the income levels of industrialized countries".[20] The theory is based on a tautology. In a world based on trade liberalization, it is claimed, prices of the factors of production (land, capital, and labour-power), and hence wages and income levels, will equalize. But this will happen, Solow says, only if the poor countries grow much faster than the rich ones over the long *durée*—and it is this which is assumed by convergence theory to be integral to capitalism. This faster growth of undeveloped or lesser-developed countries, for convergence theory, is developmental law. This is because, it is assumed, in a world economy the advanced productivity-enhancing technologies researched and developed in the rich countries at considerable cost will be shared internationally, allowing the poorer countries with lower wage rates and smaller amounts of social spending to make bigger strides.[21]

This neoliberal utopia is not the world economy that actually exists. In the real world, liberalized markets can only exacerbate unequal exchange. This is owing to the anterior or emergent structural imbalances of world economy between the Western postcolonial metropoles and their multinational corporations/enterprises (MNCs or MNEs) that dominate world trade and production and the large bulk of semi-industrialized countries and their generally smaller, less capital-intensive industries of the Global South. "Free" inter-capitalist competition where some "players" wield much bigger sticks than others cannot correct market-power imbalances. Indeed, because this uneven "playing field" allows those with access to the lion's share of resources (capital, market share and reach, research and development, labour-enhancing technologies, etc.) to outcompete those without, the tendency is for unencumbered markets to reinforce the dominant position of the former. This explains why the emergent structure of the world economy today does not at all correspond to the abstract "convergence" models of free-market economists. This also undermines the globalization theory, which typically is supportive of neoliberalism's free-market dogmas.

Neoliberalism and globalization theory

"Globalization" has become all the rage in business studies and the social sciences since the 1990s, at least at the level of economic processes. According to this, since the 1980s, capitalism has essentially globalized. This means that world trade, investment, and production have become or are becoming *trans-nationalized* or *de-territorialized.* Hence, *trans-state capitalism* is, according to globalization theory, either an established fact or one that is at least on the horizon.[22] This "globalization", it is said, is driven primarily by technological change and innovation. This is especially by the "communications revolution" (hence virtually mediated stock exchanges and finance markets that instantaneously shift capital to the four corners of the earth) and "weightless" production (carried by computerization, automation, cybernetics, and the worldwide web). But it is also carried by the "new capitalism", consumerist and corporate, of global leisure and tourism, and of "footloose" (i.e. totally mobile) mega-corporations. As such, this globalization is said to have drawn each corner of the globe into a fully *integrated* global marketplace—or to be well along the road to doing so.[23]

This, on some accounts, has generated a world economy where production and exchange is driven by global consumerism and "sign-value" (i.e. the purchasing decisions of a burgeoning urban-based global citizenry for reasons of identity- and status-affirmation).[24] For virtually all globalization theorists, however, the ascendancy of the world market and global economic integration has completely or at least substantially subordinated the nation-state to a capitalism that is supposedly *trans*national. This is because "global" enterprises—or "stateless corporations" (as *Business Week* dubbed them)[25]—have emancipated themselves from reliance on any state or states in particular. This allows them to curtail or even undermine the capacity of governments to implement policies that would place any kind of limits on commodification, consumer-driven growth, and corporate profits.[26]

Most hyperglobalists regard so-called globalization as a good thing because the subordination or disciplining of nation-states by the market ensures that the citizen-as-consumer is empowered. Collective state actors, owing to transnationalization, cannot impinge on individual market actors. These supportive hyperglobalists are thus champions of free-market *capitalism*, hence of neoliberalism. "Globalization" is, for them, exactly trade liberalization, privatization, and financial reregulation writ large on a world scale—and these developments will (if supported by a politics that disposes of the interventionist social-democratic or socialist state) guarantee worldwide economic growth and prosperity, expand consumer opportunity, and substantially abolish world poverty.[27] As arch-neoliberal then UK prime minister Tony Blair put it when patronizing the Seattle anti-capitalism protestors in 2000:

> World trade is good for people's jobs and people's living standards. These protests are a complete outrage.[28]

Yet a minority of hyperglobalists regard this "globalization" as disastrous by virtue of exactly those same economic processes and policies lauded by neoliberals (i.e. trade liberalization, unrestrained cross-border capital flows, deregulated labour markets, subordination of state to market). These, they hold, trap the world's poor in poverty, empower the corporate elite and developed countries, and widen wealth and income disparities worldwide.[29]

But globalization theory is false, because so-called globalization is partly mythical.[30] As Emmanuel Todd rightly says: "The debate about 'globalization'... is in part disconnected from reality because we too often accept the orthodox representation of commercial and financial exchanges as being symmetrical and homogeneous".[31] This can be empirically substantiated by examining patterns or trends in the main cross-border exchanges (i.e. in trade, investment and production) since World War Two up until the contemporary period. This is the period beyond the financial crisis of 2007/09 and up until and beyond the COVID-19 pandemic. These flows over many decades are some distance from being "symmetrical" and "homogeneous". Nor are these "borderless" or trans-nationalized. These are not generating or sustaining an economically integrated world in any straightforward kind of way.

World trade

Starting with international trade. This doubled between 1960 and 1990, which could be suggestive of globalization. Yet, despite this, by 1990, 80 per cent of world output was still for domestic or national markets rather than for export.[32] By 2015, a further 25 years down the line, approximately 30 per cent of the value of world GDP (WGP) was traded internationally whereas 70 per cent is still bought and sold within national borders.[33] Now, the share of world trade of the developed countries (especially of North America, Japan, and the European Union) was 72 per cent of the total in 1990—so that the rest of the world had only 28 per cent.[34] By 2012, however, the developed world's share of world trade had diminished to around 56 per cent,[35] whereas by 2017 those countries of NATFA, the EU, and AFTA or the ASEAN accounted for 58 per cent of the total.[36] This was because, according to the WTO, the share of world trade going to developing countries increased from 26 per cent in 1995 to 39 per cent in

2014.[37] This, they suggest, demonstrates globalization at work—which is a force for the growing global *integration* of trade.

Further progress in equalizing world trade has stalled since 2012, however. By 2020, the developing world's proportion of it was 44 per cent, the same as for eight years earlier,[38] whereas by the end of 2022 it had declined to 42 per cent.[39] Of much greater importance, the apparent globalization of trade was almost entirely owing to just a select few countries joining the club over the past 20 or so years (China, India, Argentina, Brazil, and so on). In fact, the rise of India, but especially of China, has been responsible for nearly all world trade growth outside the developed world over this period. China increased its share of world export trade from just one per cent in 1980 to 13 per cent by 2011,[40] and to 14.4 per cent by 2022's end.[41] "In 2021, manufactured goods accounted for about 70 per cent of total merchandise exports from developing economies, with China accounting for almost half of the total exports of manufactures of the group".[42] India has increased its share of world export trade from 1.8 per cent in 2005 to 2.6 per cent in 2022.[43]

This means that 85 per cent of world trade today is circulated in very specific places—North America, the European Union, developed Oceania, Southeast Asia, China (or rather specific coastal regions of China), India, and one or two other BRICs—rather than being globally diffused. By contrast, the share of world export trade of that part of the Global South that cannot be counted as among its handful of economic success stories (i.e. the so-called *under*developed world) was just 16 per cent at the start of the 1990s. Yet, in the early 1960s, these "Third World" countries enjoyed a 24 per cent share.[44] Today, just 20 countries monopolize almost three-quarters of export trade in goods or merchandise. These are all either the developed countries or NICs and BRICs—namely, the USA, Canada, China, Hong Kong, Japan, Russia, Mexico, Brazil, India, Singapore, Taiwan and South Korea, the UK, plus seven of the EU nations (Germany, France, Belgium, Spain, Italy, the Netherlands, and Switzerland).[45] Not only that: "Only a few developing economies significantly increased their share in world exports of goods and services from 2011 to 2022"—just eight in total, whereas only nine (namely, China, India, Mexico, Brazil, Turkey, Saudi Arabia, Thailand, Vietnam, and Indonesia) convey a significant share of global exports of goods and services. From 2011 until 2022, the share of international trade of the world's LDCs has scarcely shifted above 0.9 per cent.[46]

This pattern of divergence rather than convergence is even more marked for export trade in IP services and in services generally—the so-called cutting edge of "post-industrial" capitalism. This is most asymmetric in IP, with 92 per cent of world trade in these services circulating within and dominated by the developed countries. As the WTO reports: "39% of exports are from EU, 34% from US, 11% from Japan and 8% from other developed countries".[47] Trade in services generally is also dominated by the developed world (with a 41.3 per cent share),[48] whereas the share of most of the rest circulates to the newly emergent NICs and BRICs (especially of China, India, and the East Asian "tigers" of the Pacific Rim). Thus:

> In 2019, developing economies' share of world services exports (US$6.1 trillion) was 30 per cent (US$1.83 trillion). The highest share of world services exports was recorded by developing Asia at more than 24 per cent. The top three services exporters are China (4.6 per cent), India (3.4 per cent) and Singapore (3.5 per cent). They account for more than 40 per cent of developing economies' services exports.[49]

The top 10 services exporting countries (six of which are in the Global North—plus Japan, China, India, and Singapore) even increased their share of world export trade from 51.8 per cent to 56.1 per cent from 2010 to 2022.[50]

Even though the "contribution of developing economies to trade in services grew by more than 10 percentage points between 2005 and 2017", this was "mainly concentrated in five economies. The share of least developed countries remains small".[51] Ever the masters of credulity and understatement when it comes to admitting the development failures of world capitalism, the WTO observes that the "participation of developing countries in services trade is *not yet* [my emphasis] inclusive".

> A close look reveals that trade is very concentrated, with the same five economies ranking both as leading services exporters and importers, although in a different order. In 2017, China was the leading services trader, followed by Hong Kong (China), the Republic of Korea, Singapore and India. These five Asian economies accounted for 56.7 per cent of developing economies' exports and 58.1 per cent of imports.[52]

Not *yet* indeed—or rather simply not so. The share of trade in services of 125 other developing countries was just 10.7 per cent for exports and 16.1 per cent for imports in 2018. But, not in the least bit deflated by the fact that this "not yet" has so far taken more than 70 years *not* to materialize since the end of the colonial period, or by the lack of any sign that this happy state of affairs is on the way, or by the fact that the development failures outnumber the successes by 25:1, the WTO instead heroically assumes that global inclusivity is merely deferred. This is just as it lauds the five's "impressive trade performance. . . . From R&D and IP-related services to ICT services, professional services and finance". Yet even the successful five, the WTO admits, "make up only 14.2% of exports and 17.3% of imports" in the global marketplace.[53]

The pattern of world trade, I contend, does not look terribly global. These statistics do not support the idea that global integration of trade *has* happened. This is contrary to the claims of the hyperglobalists or globalization boosters. Nor indeed do these statistics support the lesser notion that global integration of trade *is* happening or is *in the making*. Rather, the pattern revealed is triadic, evidencing more a regionalization rather than globalization of world export trade, as flows of goods and services are chased by "price signals" to those places where consumer markets are most profitable.

Regionalization of trade is most marked in the developed economies of North America and Europe. Trade within the EU accounts for 63 per cent of its exports, whereas trade within the NAFTA (now USMCA) zone accounts for half of its exports. Most of the rest of EU export trade flows, firstly, to NATFA (USMCA) countries, and, secondly, to the ASEAN countries. Most of the rest of NATFA (USMCA) countries export trade flows, firstly, to the EU, and, secondly, to the ASEAN countries. Trade within the ASEAN bloc, by contrast, accounts for 24 per cent of its exports, with the bulk of the rest flowing to either the NATFA (USMCA) region or the EU or China.[54] This patterning is contrary to the claims not only of hyperglobalists but arguably also of moderate globalists or self-styled transformationalists.

World production

But enough has now been said about international trade. I will now focus on world goods production. Is there *here* evidence of global integration, either as fact or as process? The following statistics may cast some light on this issue. Between 1990 and 2005, the level of manufacturing taking place in developing countries rose from 19 per cent to 30 per cent of the world's output.[55] So, on the face of it, this is a sign of a growing global diffusion of industrial production from the wealthier Global North to the poorer Global South. Now, this is not indicative of "globalization" in the sense of accomplished fact, since, after all, 71 per cent of manufacturing output was still in the advanced economies by the mid-2000s. Indeed, three-quarters of it was in 2004 concentrated in just 21 countries.[56] But at least this might be indicative of a globalizing dynamic at work—and one that is leading towards economic globalism.

However, even the lesser argument of moderate or cautious globalists does not really fit the facts. This is because only five countries—China and certain of the Southeast Asian "tigers"—accounted for 62 per cent of the increase in industrial goods production in the whole of the developing world between 1980 and 2005. Most of the rest was accounted for by the other BRICs in Central Asia and Latin America. Elsewhere, across the Global South, there was little evidence of industrial growth.[57] Again, as was the case for international trade, this indicates that the pattern of industrialization in the developing world does not, as this first appears, provide evidence in favour of economic globalization. Not only that, since "production" is not simply of goods, of course, but also of services, a decline of the HICs' control of the former is not necessarily indicative of erosion of their primacy in the world economy generally. Far from it. The Global North's dominance of international trade in services is in fact indicative of its control of output from services.

In any case, since the mid-2000s, manufacturing industry worldwide has become if anything more concentrated in fewer industrial centres than before, even though the most recent pattern does at least reveal erosion of the developed countries hitherto total dominance of world goods production. Just 10 countries accounted for around 72.2 per cent of WGP from manufacturing in 2017, for example.[58] Despite the "post-industrial" shift of the developed countries away from goods-production industries and towards service industries, six of the top 10 manufacturing countries in the world today remain the HICs, five of them in the Global North, whereas the others are either NICs or newly emergent BRICs.[59] This further centralization and concentration of industrialization (rather than its globalization), which also finally broke the primacy of the advanced or developed countries in manufacturing, was almost wholly driven by China's continued breakneck economic expansion and the USA's and Japan's relative decline as "factory" economies. In 2000, China accounted for 6.5 per cent of the world's industrial goods production, whereas the USA accounted for 26.3 per cent and Japan 18.3 per cent of it. By 2017, China was responsible for 27.5 per cent of global factory output, whereas the USA's share had fallen to 17 per cent and Japan's to 7.6 per cent.[60] Today, China's share is 28.4 per cent, whereas the USA's share is 16.6 per cent, and Japan's share is 7.2 per cent.[61]

Approximately 70 per cent of world trade and 25 per cent of world production is carried out by MNCs or MNEs), and their sales account for 50 per cent of WGP.[62] As Lesley Sklair points out, the majority of these MNCs are Western companies, hailing from the Global North. Consequently, their predominance in the world economy is also the predominance of the West or of the Global North.[63] Nonetheless, as Alan Rugman has shown, the West by no means monopolizes corporate power. By the start of the twenty-first century, although a large majority of the biggest MNCs were US or European, a significant number of South Asian companies had joined this elite capitalist club. "Of the fifty largest MNEs in manufacturing, twenty-five have their home region in North America, fifteen in Europe, and ten in the Asia-Pacific".[64]

Now, so too are the investments and sales of these mega-corporations heavily concentrated in their home regions. Thus, a triadic regionalization of corporate capitalist power is being consolidated in recent decades, not its globalization. This is where the bulk of production and sales of the MNCs is carried out in their home region within the Triad. By contrast: "Extremely few MNEs operate globally; nearly all are regionally based".[65] Even the "global" ones make the bulk of their sales within the Triad (spreading these across North America, the European Union, and Southeast Asia) rather than outside. According to statistics gathered at the close of the 1990s, 85 per cent of the output of these corporations (whether from goods or services) is produced in their home countries and home regions and just 15 per cent overseas by their foreign subsidiaries.[66]

World investment

These statistics too appear to challenge the views of both hyperglobalists and moderate globalists. Neither production nor sales have been globalized—and the present trends do not, as far as can reasonably be supposed, support the view of a definite move in that direction. Rather, these indicate less a global pattern and more a regional one. But what about cross-border money flows? Is world investment globalized or becoming global? Does this differ significantly to the patterns for trade and production? I will now peruse a range of empirical data that may cast light on this issue.

There has certainly been a massive increase in cross-border investment in the postwar period—and this has been especially pronounced since the 1990s.

> Foreign direct investment shot up: flows of it rising from $37 billion in 1982 to $1,200 billion in 2006; the cumulative stock of FDI rose from 4 percent of world gross domestic product in 1950 . . . to 36 percent in 2007.[67]

For the OECD the stock of incoming FDI as a proportion of world GDP (WGP) increased from 28.8 per cent in 2009 ($12.32 billion) to 44.3 per cent ($22.12 billion) in 2017. The OECD's stock of outgoing FDI increased from 36.6 per cent ($15.66) to 50.5 per cent ($25.22 billion) over the same period.[68] Nonetheless, the global imbalances in the distribution of FDI are striking.

In 2015, the developing world—which has 83 per cent of the global population—received around 45 per cent of inward Foreign Direct Investment (FDI), according to the UN. Thus, the developed countries, including those of North America, Japan and those of the EU—which have almost 17 per cent of the world population—obviously received the larger share of 55 per cent.[69] In 2016, they did even better, by increasing their share of inbound FDI to 59 per cent of the total,[70] whereas in 2017 and 2019 they did a little worse, by taking a 50 per cent and 52 per cent share, respectively.[71] The pandemic-stricken year of 2020 especially hit inward FDI for the HICs relative to the developing world (with this dipping to 31.3 per cent of the total).[72] But the pre-pandemic distributional pattern was more-or-less restored in 2021, as the developed countries recovered 50 per cent of it, only for them to fall back again in 2022, especially relative to "developing Asia", in what has been a turbulent (pandemic-impacted) period for global overseas investment.[73]

The pattern of recent years for FDI flows internationally is thus an unstable, volatile, one, as one would expect from the machinations of free-market capitalism. However, despite these fluctuations in the proportions of who gets what, or what goes where, the pattern nonetheless looks remarkably and resiliently asymmetric in favour of the developed world. This is because per head of population, investment in the developed world has remained throughout several times higher than in the developing world. Yet there has been a longer-run tendency since

2007 for the global distribution of FDI inflows to shift away from the Global North and towards the Global South—or at least certain parts of the Global South. From 1986 through to 2007, the proportion of FDI going to developed countries averaged 68.5 per cent per annum.[74] From 2008 to 2014, though, this has been reduced to an average of 48.5 per cent per annum,[75] and from 2015 to 2021 to an average of 42.5 per cent per annum (though if non-inclusive of the possibly anomalous year of 2020 this would be 51.5 per cent).[76]

These statistics do support, on the face of it, a globalizing dynamic at work, at least in terms of FDI,[77] though this tendency may have stalled since 2015—if we are to consider 2020 and 2022 as anomalous. However, the initial phase of capitalist internationalization under the spur of neoliberal policies in the 1980s and 1990s led to a massive increase in inequality of world investment to the advantage of the developed countries. At the start of the 1960s, developing countries (which, of course, includes those that are not developing) received half of world's incoming FDI.[78] By contrast, with the consolidation of the neoliberal "globalization" era, from 1986 to 1990, the proportion of world FDI going to the developed countries reached an all-time high of 82 per cent per year on average, and this was running at 69.2 per cent over the course of the 1990s.[79] So, in 1960, there was an "even split" between the developed countries and the rest in the distribution of world FDI (though investment per head of population was five times higher in the former), whereas in 2018 the share going to developing and transitional economies was 55 per cent.[80] From a longer historical view, then, the levelling gains of supposed globalization look much less impressive. Between 2015 and 2019, the developed world absorbed an average of 51.8 per cent of total world FDI.[81] This was marginally more than was the case six decades earlier.

But, indeed, if one considers *all* cross-border capital flows (not simply FDI), the asymmetry between the Global North and the Global South widens further still. In 2018, for example, the developed countries received 70 per cent of all capital inflows. Not only that, the imbalance within the developing world itself over who gets what is even more marked in terms of total capital investment funds than in terms of FDI inflows. The cluster of NICs and certain of the BRICs referred to by the UN as "developing Asia", for example, received 39.4 per cent of the FDI that went to all developing countries in 2018 (an especially good year for the developing world up to then *vis-à-vis* the developed world in terms of FDI shares), yet that same year received three-quarters of total capital investments bound for the developing world.[82]

These FDI statistics, which seemingly indicate a tendency since the mid-2000s for a more even global pattern of foreign investment, may in fact disguise a growing *inequality* of world FDI allocation. This is because almost two-thirds of FDI that goes to the developing world is received by just a few countries. These are, of course, the NICs and BRICs, which the World Bank in recent years has dubbed the newly emerging markets (NEMs).[83] These select few countries received, in 2015 for example, almost two-thirds of the total that went to the developing world. Now, one can finger-count these countries: China and Hong Kong (which alone had 18 per cent that year), Singapore, Taiwan, Korea, India, Brazil, and Mexico.[84] By 2018, of the top 20 countries receiving incoming FDI, 10 were developed, whereas the others were mostly NEMs. The USA was by far the biggest recipient, with around 21.5 per cent of the total, followed by China (12 per cent) and Hong Kong (10 per cent). Of the top 10 countries for receiving FDI in 2018, half were developed, whereas the other half were made up of NICs and BRICs. Together, these received approximately 79.3 per cent of the total.[85]

These statistics reveal also major intra-regional imbalances. In recent years, by far the biggest recipient of FDI in the developing world has been "developing Asia". In 2012, this received 27.5 per cent of it. But by 2018, the portion of it going to this part of the world had grown to 39.4 per cent.[86] And in 2022 these countries received almost half of it—a spectacular result for this part of the Global South.[87] But even here—the most dynamic part of the developing world—the asymmetries in resource allocation are radical. Almost three-quarters (73 per cent) of FDI received by "developing Asia" in 2018 went to just four countries or territories: China, Hong Kong, India, and Singapore.[88] Similarly, in 2022, just five countries or territories (China, Singapore, Hong Kong, India, and the United Arab Emirates) accounted for almost 80 per cent of it.[89] The same pattern is true of Latin America and the Caribbean. These regions received 11.3 per cent of world FDI in 2018. But 71 per cent of this went to just three countries: Brazil, Mexico, and Argentina.[90] In 2022, Latin America and the Caribbean were in receipt of 16 per cent of world FDI, but with Mexico, Brazil, and Argentina taking 78 per cent of it.[91]

There is also a problem with these FDI statistics. This is that they disguise the fact that quite a lot of so-called foreign direct investment is actually a form of economic imperialism. This is basically in two ways. Firstly, because the subsidiaries of (mostly Western) MNCs operating in poor countries actually raise a lot of capital for investment in the host countries themselves.[92] But this is then counted as foreign direct investment being brought into the poor host country by the MNC. As the UN's 2019 *World Investment Report* observes: "A significant part of investment between developing countries (South–South FDI) is ultimately owned by developed-country MNEs".[93] Thereafter, the profits made by the MNC are then exported or repatriated to the MNC's home country or home region, which partly explains why the poorer countries are net exporters of capital.[94]

Secondly, a lot of FDI is also used to buy-up or buy-out existing enterprises rather than generating new ones, and so amounts to the foreign appropriation of "resources for development" rather than the generation of additional investment in them. This may be called neoliberal imperialism. This amounts to a transfer of ownership—from local ownership to ownership by a foreign MNC. This is so-called "brownfield" or "merger-and-acquisition" (M&A) FDI, which may be preferred by foreign MNCs and other investors to "greenfield" FDI owing to the lower financial risks and higher profits. This has often involved the privatization of formerly publicly owned industries, often infrastructural (power, water, communications, and so on), but often other sectors such as media and banking.

> In developing countries, the share of cross-border mergers and acquisitions in FDI was about 10% in the mid-1980s and increased to more than a third at the beginning of the 2000s. The lion's share of the increase in cross-border M&A is explained by the privatization of state enterprises that took place during the 1990s in many developing countries. The share of cross-border M&A in FDI also increased markedly in industrial countries.[95]

Neoliberal-driven capitalist internationalization has thus also driven a worldwide merger-and-acquisitions boom, the majority of which in the developing world have been acquisitions. In the 1980s, virtually all FDI going to the developing world was greenfield. But, since the 1990s, FDI from M&A began to increase. Between 1991 and 1998, it rose from an average per country of just $40 million compared to $260 million for greenfield (approximately 14 per cent of total FDI) to $700 million compared to $1,300 million for greenfield (around 54 per cent of total FDI). By 2006, M&A FDI going to the developing world was approximately $1,110 million on average per country compared to $2,600 million for greenfield (around 43 per cent of the total).[96]

A body of research has found that brownfield FDI is much less advantageous for the recipient economies than greenfield FDI. Compared to greenfield investment, it tends to have lower benefits; indeed, it may have negligible benefits or even negative impacts on the host country's economic development.[97] This is for reasons that ought to be obvious:

> Foreign entrants may exploit the superior position in the global marketplace, on which their internationalization is based, to crowd out domestic entrepreneurs. Associated product market power will also result in higher entry barriers for domestic entrepreneurs. Moreover foreign entrants may also absorb a disproportionate share of domestic factor endowments (e.g., finance, managerial and skilled labor), raising the costs of entrepreneurial entry.[98]

In any case, ignoring the problem of how much FDI is genuine and adding value to the local economies into which it is exported, if we exclude the NICs and BRICs, so that our focus is on the so-called Third World, what we find is that the share of world investment received by this part of the world has been *falling* for decades. For example, it fell from 50 per cent in 1960 to 25 per cent by 1974, and then to just 17 per cent by 1988.[99] This has meant that, by the mid-1990s, more than 80 per cent of total foreign investment ended up in just 12 countries—in North America, Western Europe, and the Pacific Rim—and this pattern has changed significantly since then only because China (and one or two others) have gate-crashed the development party.

By contrast, by the close of the 1990s, the 48 poorest LICs or LDCs attracted just half a per cent of total world investment.[100] Since then, more than 25 years later, the basic situation remains incorrigible. From 2010 until 2018, FDI flows to the LDCs still make up less than two per cent of total world investment. The LDCs, which are home to 14 per cent of the world's people, had just 1.8 per cent of global inward FDI in 2018—and this has been static since 2010. The average incoming FDI to the LDCs from 2000 to 2018 was just 1.3 per cent.[101] Most recently, in the period from 2019 to 2022, this has averaged 1.96 per cent per year. This minuscule increase in the LDCs' share of world FDI in comparison with the preceding decade has occurred despite a fall (albeit minor) in the value of inbound FDI over these past few years.[102] Such reflects the weakness of the overall international investment climate pre- and post-pandemic. The LDCs suffered lesser downswings in inbound FDI from the pandemic than other parts of the developing world because their access to these finances has always been severely constrained.

The hardest-hit continent has, of course, been Africa, home to almost 17 per cent of the world's population. Whereas in 2016, the whole of the developing world (excluding the NICs) received just 15 per cent of total world investment, Africa was especially marginalized, since it got just 3.1 per cent.[103] Africa in 2018 received 3.5 per cent of global FDI inflows compared to 3.9 per cent in 2012, and has received on average 3.8 per cent of the total from 2012 to 2018.[104] Indeed, on the cusp of the pandemic, the continent's share of world FDI had scarcely shifted in 20 years, fluctuating between a low of 2.6 per cent in 2007 to a high of 4.6 per cent in 2009, and averaging just 3.4 per cent up to 2019.[105] Since then, from 2019 to 2022, Africa's receipt of incoming global FDI has increased marginally to 3.9 per cent on an average year. However, as is noted in UNCTAD's *World Investment Report 2023*, this was inflated by 2021's anomalously record share of 5.2 per cent caused by "a single intrafirm financial transaction in South Africa".[106] This doubled the continent's inflow of FDI in 2021. "Excluding that transaction, the increase in Africa [of inbound FDI] is moderate, more in line with other developing regions".[107] Africa also suffered a drastic cumulative 67.6 per cent fall in incoming FDI from 2014 to 2020.[108] Even excluding 2020 from the sums (the most impactful year of the pandemic), the decline over this period was 57.6 per cent.

But Latin America and the Caribbean's developmental woes since the 2000s have also continued. In the mid-2000s, these regions (home to almost 8.5 per cent of the world's population) had between them an 8.6 per cent share of global FDI, which was actually a lower level than 10 years earlier.[109] Fuelled by a primary commodities boom, however, they increased their share to 20.1 per cent by 2013, eliciting much talk by the WTO and World Bank of newly emerging markets and another economic miracle.[110] But, with the inevitable collapse of the boom (which those in primary commodities markets are especially vulnerable), their share of global FDI had plummeted to 8.1 per cent by 2017.[111] Not only that, they experienced a cumulative 27 per cent drop in inward FDI between 2014 and 2018.[112] Reversal of this trend in 2019 (which saw a 10 per cent increase of inbound FDI) was then extinguished by the pandemic (generating a 45.4 per cent slump in 2020).[113]

These statistics indicate that *global* investment does not exist. More seriously, they do not even demonstrate that a *trend towards* genuinely global investment exists. Rather, the data appear to indicate reinforcement of the pattern of regionalization or triadization of world economy, which is also suggested by other indicators. Owing to asymmetrical capital flows, nearly two-thirds of the globe is virtually bypassed by overseas (mostly Western) FDI and capital flows generally.[114] The problem for the globalization theorists, therefore—whether these be hyper or moderate globalists—is that much of the world and its population is simply superfluous to the profit-driven needs of the capitalist world economy. And so, they are just not included. These become impoverished backwaters populated by "unpeoples".[115]

Asymmetrical patterns of FDI confirm that globalization is myth. But other empirical data demonstrate that even the trend for world FDI to expand has stalled in recent times—so that so-called globalization has hit the buffers. This was apparent even before the Great Financial Crisis of 2007/09 and the austerity decade that ensued. This was due to the impact of low-profit rates and weak GDP growth in retarding cross-border capital flows. Global net inflows and outflows of FDI as a proportion of WGP were lower in 1985 than they were in 1970. Thereafter, though, the secular trend was upwards, despite ebbs and flows, reaching a peak of 10.81 per cent of world output in 2007—more than 13 times higher than in 1985.

This trajectory was far from a smooth ride, however. In response to the crises of the early 2000s, from 2000 to 2003, the value of world FDI fell by almost 57 per cent. Thus, it was not until 2006 that its value surpassed the pre-crises thresholds.[116] Moreover, since the 2007 peak, net FDI inflows and outflows as a proportion of world output have entered a long period of decline. The rate was lower in 2018 than it was in 1994, whereas the rate in 2019 scarcely surpassed that of 1998, and was almost three-and-half times lower than in 2007.

Average FDI (net inflows and outflows) as percentage of world GDP 1970–2019[117]

1970–1979	0.9877
1980–1989	1.2988
1990–1999	3.0717
2000–2010	6.4409
2011–2019	4.9939

Owing to the global pandemic, total global inflows and outflows of FDI combined dipped to just 2.5 per cent of world GDP in 2020. This was the lowest level since 1989. Since then—in 2021 and 2022—recovery of global cross-border financial transfers has been weak. In 2021, inbound and outbound FDI flows were equivalent to just 4.6 per cent of global GDP. In 2022, these were equivalent to only 3.7 per cent of global GDP.[118]

Fifteen or so years earlier, the Great Financial Crisis of 2007/09 triggered a drop of 53 per cent in the volume of global FDI (16 per cent in 2008 and 37 per cent in 2009).[119] The recovery from these crises years was also painfully slow and undermined with setbacks. Modest upswings in 2010 and 2011 and 2013 were undone by bigger downswings in 2012 and 2014.[120] Only by 2015 were FDI global flows restored to the (low) levels of the crisis years (2008 and 2009), and this required an unexpected (and as it turned out anomalous) 38 per cent increase from the year before. But these cross-border transfers were still much below the 2007 level. And no sooner were the investment losses recovered than they were reversed owing to the ongoing "fragility" (as the UN's *World Investment* Reports regularly put it) of the world economy.

For three consecutive years (2016 to 2018) levels of global FDI registered declines, indeed often sharp contractions. Worldwide, it fell by two per cent in 2016, by 23 per cent in 2017, and by 13 per cent in 2018.[121] In 2019 there was only a very modest recovery, of just three per cent, which was below the average of the previous decade, and some 25 per cent below the 2015 level.[122] Global FDI flows then plummeted in 2020, by 42 per cent, so that it was at its lowest level since the 1990s, and more than 30 per cent beneath the "investment trough that followed the . . . financial crisis".[123] The following year, however, witnessed a 64 per cent upswing of FDI flows "from the exceptionally low level of 2020", as transfers that were extinguished owing to pandemic restrictions were freed up for release. But the post-pandemic boost did not continue into 2022. Instead, global FDI flows dipped by 13 per cent owing to (as the authors of UNCTAD's 2023 *World Investment Report* put it) "the war in Ukraine, high food and energy prices, and debt pressures".[124] Consequently, global FDI in 2022 remained 28 per cent lower than it was in 2015.

During the period from 2016 to 2018, FDI flows to the developing world registered an overall drop of 14 per cent, whereas those to the LDCs fell by 16 per cent.[125] Pandemic-afflicted 2020 then saw further falls of 12 per cent for the developing countries (37 per cent in Latin America and the Caribbean and 18 per cent in Africa) and of a calamitous 77 per cent for the "transitional economies".[126] Yet the biggest casualties of the decline of world investment of recent years in the runup to the COVID-19 pandemic and during its calamitous first year have been the developed countries. Here FDI inflows dropped by 54 per cent between 2016 and 2019 and then by a further precipitous 69 per cent in 2020.[127] This is what has led in most recent years to a sharp (if perhaps temporary) swing in the balance of FDI shares in favour of the developing world and away from the developed world, albeit from a drastically shrinking pot of investment funds.[128]

Post-pandemic recovery of global FDI flows has since been fitful and unstable. A post-restrictions boost was inevitable, but this certainly has not exceeded expectations. The developed world rebounded from the crisis with a 134 per cent increase of inbound FDI in 2021, only to see a 37 per cent drop the following year. The developing world benefited from the unshackling of world capitalism from COVID-19 restrictions to a far more modest degree, however. There was an increase of FDI inflows of 30 per cent in 2021 (carried largely by developing Asia), which then slowed dramatically to just four per cent in 2022.[129] FDI inflows to the LDCs increased by just 13 per cent in 2021, only to be obliterated by a greater fall of 16 per cent in 2022.[130] World capitalism today is in poorer shape than at any time during the postwar era.

Of course, neoliberalism itself as a political project fully understands that trade and financial liberalization is not a force of economic convergence or integration, despite its rhetoric to the contrary. Its purpose is exactly to confirm and reproduce the international market-power asymmetries and to deepen or extend these as far as possible. This is because neoliberalism is the politics of mega-capitalism that dominates the world economy and also of the state managers of the Western Alliance whose function is to serve this mega-capitalism (especially their "own" MNCs in the world market). The state managers of the largely Western HICs (and hence political governance in the Global North) have formed a strategic alliance with corporate-capitalist power for mutual advantage. This is both internationally (against rival competitors in the Global South) and locally (against working classes and labour unions or other popular forces that would disrupt optimal competitiveness through profit-maximization).

Neoliberalization driven by the state managers obviously defends and extends the interests of their own national MNCs internationally and attracts inward investments from the MNCs of other developed countries. This protects the prosperity and advantaged position of these countries (and their locally based industries) in the international state system *vis-à-vis* the others, and hence stabilizes the rule and privileges of their state elites. This explains the radical disconnect between neoliberalism as *politics*, on the one hand, and neoliberalism as *ideology*, on the other. Neoliberalism as utopian ideology legitimizes this political project by representing it as something other than it is. This is as a politics that is about undermining world poverty, encouraging worldwide democratization (which is represented as a natural consequence of the export of trade liberalization),[131] and levelling income and wealth disparities everywhere—all of which are supposedly bounties flowing inevitably from the "dynamism of the market".

Capitalist globalization and the interstate system

As we have seen, a fundamental claim of globalization theory is that the new mega-capitalism has escaped dependence on the state system and therefore undermines the capacity of national governments to adopt policies that are in the least obstructive to or constraining of corporate profit-making. This, it is claimed, is largely the consequence of two developments. Firstly, the unprecedented mobility across national borders of money-capital (where billions or even trillions can pass through national turnstiles at the touch of the "send" button on a computer keyboard). Secondly, the structural power of the "nationless" MNCs (represented as TNCs) in the world economy because they control the bulk of the world's resources and have the capacity to pick and choose which countries they will invest in and set up operations in.

Since the MNCs or TNCs and finance capital are mobile or "footloose, say the globalists, they can set-up in or transfer funds to countries that better serve their interests in high profits and low costs and exit those countries that serve these interests less well. Nation-states are forced to compete to attract inward investment from the MNCs or TNCs and state managers must keep international speculators and financial markets onside. They cannot therefore afford to levy high taxes to fund expansive welfare programmes.[132] Nor can they do this by increasing government borrowing. Nor can they afford to lower interest rates to stimulate demand-led growth.[133] They cannot even afford to introduce a decent minimum wage.

If states attempt to "buck the market" in these ways, their credit-worthiness rating will suffer, so that interest charges on debts increase and loans are harder to acquire. Moreover, "global capitalists" will simply take their resources to where governments offer low interest rates and low taxes and can guarantee a high-skilled but "affordable" workforce. This means, it is argued by globalists of all hues, that national governments are no longer in charge economically of what happens to or within the countries they administer. The economic stability or prosperity of the territories they rule is determined not by themselves but by the market and by international capitalism. Governments in practice are forced to share sovereignty over national affairs with the mega-capitals. If they want economic stability and prosperity (which after all will also stabilize the state), they must work with international capitalism and market forces rather than against. This means that the role of government is to outcompete or outbid rival states in ensuring that the "supply-side" of things (labour skills, wage rates, taxation policy, employment law, infrastructure, etc.) is as attractive to corporate investment as possible.[134]

For these reasons, it is claimed, national governments are forced to define their role as serving above and beyond all else the interests of the MNCs or TNCs and global financiers.[135] If they are to attract (as they must) the trade custom, R&D, expertise, investment revenues and employment opportunities afforded by mega-capital, they are compelled to adopt exactly the kinds of economic policies that the big corporations would like to see. Hence: "Whatever the difference in partisan outcomes, all governments have been pressed in the same direction . . . [i.e. to] curtail state spending and interventions".[136] In practice, this means ensuring that the price of labour-power is "competitive" (hence legal restrictions on the labour unions) and lowering the cost of the "social wage" (hence abandoning policies of progressive taxation, welfarism, nationalization, and full employment). "The new international economic environment has undercut the partisan strategies of the left and right based respectively on broadly 'Keynesian' and 'monetarist' fiscal and monetary policies".[137] Or, as aspirant UK prime minister Tony Blair put it, shortly before winning his first electoral stint in 1997, since "the determining context of economic policy is the new global market . . . the room for manoeuvre of any government in Britain is already heavily circumscribed".[138]

Such policies demanded by the MNCs or TNCs and by the "footloose" financiers are then exactly the neoliberal ones: low rates of taxation on business and wealth; labour market deregulation—that is flexible working, temporary contracts, and so on; privatization of profitable state assets; dismantling of controls on the free movement of capital and goods; downsizing of the welfare state; legal restrictions on the rights of trade unions to cause economic "disruption" through excessive industrial action. Neoliberal ascendancy is thus, according to the globalists, the inevitable consequence of "global" capitalism's dominance of the state system; it reflects the disempowered state, which is converted into a mere means of serving the imperatives of the marketplace. This renders neoliberalism passive—the creature of mega-capital—according to its apologists and some of its left-wing critics. Neoliberalism expresses the crisis of competence of the nation-state that results from its drastically reduced autonomy in the sphere of economic policy-making. This in turn erodes its legitimacy and authority in the eyes of the citizenry who can perceive its weakness and lack of independence of action from market forces.[139] This may indeed (as it arguably has done) generate widespread popular disillusionment with politics and government. These are the pessimistic claims of the left globalists in particular.

Now, powerful as the thesis of the "declinist" or even "disempowered" state appears, faced with the ever-growing structural pressures of so-called globalization, it is far from being convincing. Indeed, it has been subject to damaging criticism, which in my view is decisive in dispelling it. However, before considering these critiques that seek to recover a rather more empowered state than neoliberalism allows, it is worth reiterating a more fundamental problem associated with the idea of the disempowered state. This is simply that, as I have demonstrated, globalization itself is myth. This raises the problem of what exactly the state (or interstate system) is supposed to be subordinated to and how. The point is important because, according to neoliberalism, the contemporary interstate system is under the thumb of a world capitalist economy that is borderless. Indeed, subordination of the interstate system is, from this perspective, the consequence of the transnationality of capitalism.

But, as we have seen, empirical data illuminating trends in the distribution of production, trade, and finance worldwide lend no support to the idea of a trans-nationalized capitalism. To this I would add: the idea that MNCs are "stateless corporations" (i.e. TNCs) is also largely mythical. Such hugely exaggerates the global reach and diffusion of these mega-capitals that would supposedly explain their capacity to browbeat even governments of developed countries into acquiescence with their commercial interests. Back in the real world, scarcely any MNCs can be counted as TNCs. Not only that, transnationalization as a tendency of corporate evolution in world capitalism has actually stalled for more than a decade. As UNCTAD's *World Investment Report 2020* concedes

> The average Transnationality Index (TNI) of the top 100—the relative shares of their foreign assets, sales and employees—has stagnated in the last decade around 65 per cent, in line with a global loss of momentum for FDI. . . . The stagnation is explained in part by the change in composition of the list, with new emerging-market entrants starting out at lower levels of internationalization. In addition, few MNEs in the top 100 have broken through the "glass ceiling" of transnationality.[140]

This can be read as the "economic" case against the thesis of the powerless state. But what of the "political" case? As the sceptics point out, the interstate system cannot be disempowered because it is integral to the capitalist world economy, for two main reasons. Firstly, this is because states retain their monopoly on the means of destruction (military power) and of judicial authority. This renders them indispensable to the maintenance of social order and hence of economic order. Secondly, this is because the national state remains in possession of sufficient authoritative and allocative resources to exercise a measure of control over economic processes and relations with its own borders, despite the contrary claims of the globalists. Indeed, in recent decades, it could even be said that the capacities of the state to intervene in the marketplace to secure economic or other goals has been enhanced rather than diminished. This is because since World War Two states have sought to re-empower themselves (or rather re-embed or re-consolidate their powers) by means of alliance-building, international cooperation, and the formation of multi-lateral partnerships and associations in various supranational political organizations that are all about global "governance" of the world economy.

Recent decades have seen a dramatic increase in the capacity of states to control the global environment by cooperating with each other. The postwar creation of a range of international governmental organizations (IGOs) or interstate supranational organizations and associated treaties and their signatories (such as GATT, the IMF, the World Bank, the UN, NAFTA or USMCA, AFTA, the EU, the ASEAN) does not necessarily evidence that the autonomy and competence of the nation-state is declining. Rather, this may more plausibly be indicative that nation-states (or rather some of them) are becoming more competent at asserting their interests on the international stage.[141]

This shows that different states have reached an understanding that they have common interests that are best served through multilateral agencies. This also shows that they have found ways to pursue their particular interests through collaboration rather than through unilateral action. So, for example, international coordination of currency exchange rates can enhance state autonomy rather than diminish it by imposing a measure of order or stability on cross-border exchanges. In particular, the growth of supranational political organizations is evidence that a particular group of states—the USA and its metropole allies—have constructed international regimes that help preserve a particular geometry of global power relations. So, for example, the UN, the IMF, the World Bank, and the WTO, these are not simply neutral international bodies concerned with the welfare of all nations. Rather, they are US- and Western-dominated institutions that allow the more powerful states to assert both common interests and particular interests against weaker, more dependent states.

So, to suggest that so-called globalization necessarily undermines state autonomy is to lose sight of the ways in which states empower themselves against the vagaries of global forces (including the world market) through collective action. International relations theorists of the Realist School have pointed out that the world capitalist economy depends on the maintenance of law and order worldwide.[142] In short, the economic order of global markets is contained or embedded within the political order of states. States have a monopoly on the means of violence and the legal right to exercise it. They are, as participants in a system of states, collectively invested (to varying degrees) in maintaining some kind of global order through power-balancing. Moreover, states provide police and legal protections for the wealth and property of those MNCs that are situated within their borders from rival states and rival firms and from alienated labour and the propertyless.[143] States as well secure the social and normative conditions and relations of commodity exchange more generally, including by the judicial administration and policing of contracts. Unless this is done, what is called economic globalization (in reality, worldwide competition between capitals and class conflict between capital and labour incentivized by emergent asymmetries in the distribution of allocative resources) could degenerate into violence, banditry, and war.

The military and political capacities of states also provide their citizens with relative security. Such is made necessary in a world made dangerous by national rivalries without which even a semblance of economic stability would not be possible.[144] Only states can provide citizens with security, internally and externally, whether by means of the dispensing of legal entitlements, or the provision of social-welfare rights, or the protections afforded by police and military forces. Capitalist markets and business firms obviously cannot provide these securities, since their function is simply the business of economic exchange between private actors in pursuit of individual gain, not the provision of public goods to service collective goals. The absence of military conflicts between the leading states since World War Two is explained by globalists as resulting from global economic integration that disassociates economic interests from national politics.[145] This is illusory because the disassociation of the two is much less than globalists think. The military functions of states may *seem* less significant in the postwar world compared to before, because these are exercised less often than previously.

But this is arguably a measure of the relative effectiveness of the international relations of state actors since World War Two in maintaining a balancing of powers that has secured world order in its political and economic aspects.[146] As Kenneth Waltz puts it: "Possession of power should not be identified with the use of force, and the usefulness of force should not be confused with its usability. . . . Power maintains an order; the use of force signals its breakdown".[147] Where state actors withdraw from international relations, so that state powers no longer are deployed to "balance" or "stabilize" inter-state competition, as occurred in the 1914–45 period, the system dissolves into anarchy and violence. This 1914–45 period that was characterized by depression and war among the Great Powers was in fact preceded by the first wave of so-called globalization. During this period (from the mid-nineteenth century up until the outbreak of the Great War) world trade grew by 900 per cent, whereas by the 1890s half of the total investments of the UK (still the world's biggest economy) were exported overseas.[148] Yet this period of growing international economic "interconnectedness" or "integration" through foreign trade and overseas investments did nothing to arrest the world's plunge into war driven by the intersection of inter-imperial and inter-capitalist rivalries.

The interstate system also continues to play a key role in regulating and stabilizing the world market, whereas particular states prop up the largest of their "own" corporations when they run into difficulties. Since the 1970s, as noted by David Gordon, in response to economic liberalization, and to head-off or ameliorate recessionary pressures in the world economy, "the role of the state has grown substantially". Moreover, "state policies have become increasingly decisive on the international front, not more futile. . . . And . . . everyone including transnational corporations has become increasingly dependent upon coordinated state intervention for restructuring and resolution of the underlying dynamics of crisis".[149]

In response to the East Asian crisis that broke out in 1997, and its spread to Latin America and Russia in 1998, massive bailouts organized by the IMF totalling more than $179 billion (and by Japan totalling $30 billion) eventually stabilized these economies.[150] At the same time, co-ordinated state intervention in the financial markets by Western governments led by the USA prevented (albeit narrowly) these meltdowns from dragging the developed world into crisis.[151] Trillion-dollar bailouts of the corporate banks in the Global North prevented a collapse of the financial sector and a far more severe global depression than perhaps would otherwise have been the case in 2007/09.[152] Trillion-dollar state and central-bank subsidization of a wide swathe of big corporations was rolled-out to head-off a potentially even bigger global economic slump than 10 years earlier provoked by the COVID-19 pandemic.[153] Here a number of observations are pertinent.

(1) Even the lone or stand-alone nation-state can still actively buck the world market and oppose the forces of international capitalism when it has to. The case of Malaysia provides a relatively recent example. Hardly a central player in the world economy, Malaysia was nonetheless able to weather the Asian economic crisis of 1997–98 (in sharp contrast to other "tigers") by resorting to counter-market measures. Basically, there was here an abrupt turn towards protectionism—imposing controls on the movement of capital into and out of the country—in express disregard of the free-market dogmas of the Washington Consensus.[154] Other recent examples of "market-bucking" state action include those of Argentina and Venezuela. In both cases, in response to economic crisis, the governments defaulted on their debts.[155] This, according to neoliberalism, is the cardinal sin, tantamount to economic suicide. Yet, in both cases, although the defaults helped trigger sharp contractions in GDP, the withdrawal of foreign investments and currency devaluations, economic calamity did not come to pass. Foreign investments did not dry up. Capital flight and currency collapse did not manifest. Both countries continued to be regarded as profitable sites by international financiers and MNCs.

(2) By the end of the 1980s, as Ruigrock and van Tulder have pointed out, at "least 20 companies in the 1993 *Fortune* 100 would not have survived as independent companies if they had not been saved by their respective governments in the last decade and a half".[156] Such rescues (whether by means of subsidy, non-market loans, or temporary nationalizations) characterized the economic crises of the 1970s and 1980s. Even though more bankruptcies were tolerated by governments in the 1990s and 2000s, there were still major bailouts,[157] and these have as we have seen mushroomed in response to the financial meltdown of 2007/09 and the subsequent novel coronavirus pandemic. In the teeth and claw of the pandemic, hundreds of billions have been thrown at the corporate sector, much of which has found its way into the pockets of shareholders and executives. The reason for this "bailout culture" of neoliberal governance of contemporary mega-capitalism is clear enough. Rescues of the corporate sector have been indispensable tools for blunting the impact of recessionary crises, preventing these spiralling into global depressions, just as has state-coordinated financial stimulus measures to boost lending by the banks to kickstart corporate investments and consumer spending.

(3) Whenever MNCs set themselves up in any specific country, they are dependent on the patronage of the host nation-state, just as they are dependent on the support of their "own" state in their home markets. Nation-states

provide corporations with access to the resources and safeguards they need: infrastructure (energy sources, water supplies, transport, communications); stable currencies and exchange rates; skilled labour-power; secure labour markets and acquiescent workers; access to supply chains; tax concessions; legal protections of their property; an effective police force to ensure industrial peace and armed forces to safeguard national security, etc.[158] Not every state can guarantee these conditions. Indeed, it is quite often only the more developed countries that can. This explains why the MNCs largely confine the bulk of their business activities to their home countries and home regions—hence the regionalization or triadization (not globalization) of corporate power already discussed.[159]

Moreover, MNCs also rely on their own home nation-states to help them gain access to foreign markets and to bat for their interests in negotiations with foreign states within which they have set up operations or in which they wish to set these up. As we have seen, so-called globalization is not a process that generates "stateless corporations" (or *trans*national or *trans*-state capitalism). Rather, this is a process whereby MNCs seek to dominate overseas markets by establishing partnerships with foreign states that bind these to supporting their goals.[160] This means, as Stopford and Strange observe, that very "few firms can operate in a genuinely borderless world". Rather, they must operate within an international state system in which governments, "both host and home . . . continue to play a crucial and, perhaps paradoxically . . . increasing role".[161] This role is in securing and extending their interests in competition and sometimes cooperation with the rival firms of rival states. This establishes the relations between states and capitals as one of "structural interdependence" rather than one of the utter dependence of the former on the latter.[162] Such gives governments, especially of the advanced or developed countries, considerable leverage to influence the decisions of the international corporate elite.

This leverage exists also because MNCs cannot simply "up stumps" whenever they encounter government policies of which they disapprove or other unexpected obstacles to profit-maximization. MNCs establish themselves in local national economies by placing themselves at the centre of complexes of enterprises that are cultivated as suppliers, distributors, retailers, etc.[163] "Neither individual firms nor states but *industrial complexes* constitute the centre of gravity of the international restructuring race".[164] Therefore, for an MNC to exit a particular country where its operations are heavily consolidated would involve major liabilities. These would include: writing-off considerable investments (premises, plant, machinery, etc.); abandoning networks of partners and clients; eschewing local sources of financing and of labour skills that are particularly weaned to its needs; and turning its back on a range of other benefits and concessions underwritten by the local state.[165] There are also the costs of establishing these complexes and negotiating these benefits from scratch somewhere else. This is not an undertaking that can be taken lightly or oft repeated. This, again, is exactly the reason why there are very few genuinely transnational corporations operating in the world economy today. This is why corporate enterprise tends to cluster within specific regional zones and national borders. MNCs simply cannot be as "footloose" as globalization theory asserts.

Globalization theory represents money as especially borderless and footloose, however. This is on the grounds that this has an immateriality or virtuality that industrial capital lacks. The notion of the deterritorialization of capital (i.e. of its independence from the state system) gains its strongest empirical case owing to the growing internationalization of finance.[166] Billions, it is said, may be shifted from one part of the world to another, at the flick of a switch, in the restless search of higher returns on investment, so that states and governments are at the mercy of financial speculators and must optimize local conditions for profit-making in order to attract the funds or deter their flight. Yet even in the case of finance capital the mobility in question is hugely exaggerated. This is because, as Susan de Brunhoff reminds us, "a global single market of capital does not exist". There is "no single world rate of interest" any more than there are "single world prices for produced goods".[167]

Nor is there a global currency. Rather, there are different national (or sometimes regional) currencies that do not convert into each other as equivalents—which largely reflects the varying strengths of the different *national* economies. This explains why finance capital does not circulate freely across the globe (instead concentrating especially in the HICs and a handful of developing countries) despite the opportunity allowed for total mobility by the "telecommunications revolution". What the technology allows the economics refuses. This demonstrates, as Dick Bryan points out, "the centrality of nationality within global accumulation"[168]:

> International finance . . . maintains national characteristics. It does not move systematically so as to equalise savings and investment. . . . A global financial system comprised of nationally designated currencies signals that globalisation cannot be devoid of a national dimension.[169]

(4) Nor is it the case that nation-states have been forced into serving international capitalism by promoting trade liberalization. Theorists of the "powerless state" stress how the irresistible power of global capitalism has forced states into adopting neoliberal policies. But so-called economic globalization was pioneered by some of the most powerful state actors, just as it has since been promulgated worldwide by US- and Western-dominated international organizations. In short, the internationalization of mega-capitalism was made possible by the intentional *agency* of government actors in building the three pillars of neoliberalism—deregulation, trade liberalization, and privatization. These "created the foundations for globalization", so that, as

Manuel Castells rightly says, "the global economy was politically constituted".[170] A fundamental problem with the globalist perspective, therefore, is that this tends to regard politics as the passive mirror of economics. Aside from the philosophical objections that can be made to economic determinism generally, this lets neoliberalism off the hook rather too easily. Rather than neoliberalism representing an accommodation or adjustment of state politics to a resurgent internationalizing capitalism, this was instead a major driver of capitalist internationalization. "Globalization was actively sponsored and promoted by powerful western governments, including and especially those of Reagan in the USA and Thatcher in Britain".[171]

Now, since deliberate state action was indispensable to unleashing the "runaway world" of free-market capitalism, it follows that deliberate resolute state action ought to be capable of bringing this world back under a measure of control that would restore limits to capital in the popular interest. For example, there seems no reason why the leading states of the Global North and Japan could not seek to secure international agreement to reign-in markets by imposing taxation on financial speculation (hence discouraging the destabilization of national currencies for financial gain), or de-penalizing protectionism for weaker economies, or re-instituting higher taxes on wealth to reduce inequalities. But the obstacle to this is simply that the dominant powers of the interstate system lack the *will* to contain capitalism—or, rather, they simply *do not wish* to confront capitalism. This is not because they are rendered powerless by "globalization", but because they positively identify with the agenda of corporate empowerment that "globalization" serves. It was, after all, this politics of preference—of commitment to untrammelled corporate exploitation of the world—that unleashed worldwide hyper-commodification in the first place.

(5) Finally, theorists of the "powerless state" exaggerate the *unique* nature of the pressures and constraints exerted by so-called economic globalization on national governments today. After all, capitalism has been afflicted by crises which have had an international impact since its birth. There have been plenty of major ones (1880s, 1930s, and 1970s) before the neoliberal age. This means that it is problematic to attribute the failure of the state to confront capitalism simply to the forces of "globalization". Capitalists have always resorted to economic sabotage—that is, withdrawing or withholding their money from a country—to get their way when faced with the challenge posed by left-leaning reformist governments. Capital flight and investment strikes are longstanding weapons of big business to try and deter or deflect such governments from even modest welfarist or redistributionist agendas.

Unfortunately, social-democratic governments have historically demonstrated very little willingness to confront or resist these tactics of economic destabilization, just as neoliberal governments have shown no inclination to do anything to provoke them in the first place. Rather, they have backed away from confrontation (and hence from social-democratic reforms), because fundamentally they are compromised by their reformism, which commits them primarily to capitalism and only secondarily to reforming capitalism.[172] In Britain, for example, this was the pattern (i.e. either capitulation or acquiescence to big capital) of every Labour government elected into office during periods of economic turbulence: the MacDonald governments of 1924 and 1929, Attlee's 1947 government, the Wilson governments of 1967 and 1974.[173]

This history demonstrates that the main barrier to state autonomy (though hardly an insuperable one) is simply *capitalism* rather than capitalist "globalization". But, again, if this is the case, there seems no good reason to suppose that corporate power has rendered states incapable of reintroducing the kinds of constraints on capitalism that existed in most of the developed countries right up to the start of the 1980s. Regulated labour markets, rent controls and social housing, restrictions on cross-border capital flows, progressive taxation of wealth and property and corporations, welfare inclusivity, public ownership of key utilities, de-commodification of public goods and services, etc.—none of this is beyond the power of the *collective* inter-government agency of the leading states.

Neoliberalism and zombie capitalism

I have described the new mega-capitalism that neoliberalism has helped export across the face of the planet as zombified. Corporate-MNC capitalism today is, I suggest, a *zombie capitalism*. A few words expounding on this proposition are in order before mobilizing evidence in its support.

The concept of "zombie banks" was applied by mainstream commentators to those financial institutions that ran-up spectacular debts through reckless lending during the bubble-boom of the 2000s, threatening to drag down the real economy by basically retrenching on lending, and requiring government bailouts to survive following on from the Great Financial Crash. The term "zombie *capitalism*", however, was coined by the radical political-economist Chris Harman in his book of the same name. This, for him, was not a description of the parasitism of particular lifeless corporations sucking in massive public funds in order to be resuscitated; rather, this was intended to describe the state of twenty-first-century capitalism as an international system. This was in the sense that this was a system that was "dead to achieving human goals and responding to human feelings"—a "Frankenstein's monster that has escaped from human control"; the "vampire that saps the lifeblood of the living . . . it feeds off".[174]

In a certain sense, of course, capitalism has always been zombified. This has been true of each and every stage of its development as an economic system—from classical laissez-faire capitalism from the 1780s to the 1880s, through to the monopoly-corporate mode of capitalism that became dominant in the first half of the twentieth century, and now on to the MNC-based mega-capitalism of the "global" era. This is in the sense that capitalism, as was diagnosed by Marx 150 years ago, is based on expropriation—of unpaid labour-time. Capital is not, as Marx pointed out, a thing (i.e. a store of money), or rather not *merely* a thing. Rather, capital is a social relation of economic exploitation. Capital, as he puts it, is "an independent social power, i.e. as the power of a part of society it maintains itself and increases by exchange for direct living labour".[175]

Such exploitation is, as we have seen, internal-and-necessary to capitalism, because the system is organized around two emergent structural cleavages: *vertically*, by the division between non-producing owners of the means of wealth-creation, on the one hand, and non-owning producers (waged or salaried employees of the owners), on the other hand; and, *horizontally*, by the division of the owning class into competitors for markets and profits in a system of generalized commodity production.[176] The vertical axis establishes capitalist class relations, rooted in ownership and non-ownership of property, since non-owners must sell their labour-power to employers in return for access to consumptive means. This constitutes the relationship between the classes as exploitative, because exploitation is the appropriation by employers from employees of unpaid labour-time in work, which is enabled by the fact that the non-owners have no means of livelihood except by alienating their labour-power in return for a wage. Capital is thus *parasitic* on living labour, the expenditure of the workers' labour-power as this is put to work. *Surplus value* (the difference between the price the employer pays in wages for the employee's labour-capacity and the value generated by the expenditure of the employee's labour-power in production) is, as Marx explains in *Capital*, the source and substance of capitalist profit.[177]

Capital, therefore, is also *dead* labour.[178] This is not simply because capital is the social relation that allows the vampire-like "sucking" of surplus labour-time (and hence surplus value) from living labour. Rather, this is also because capitalism is the accumulation by owners of the results of expended labour (i.e. the exchange-value embodied in commodities, the monies derived from their sale, and their re-investment in new means of production). The horizontal axis then compels capital to act *as capital*, because pressure of market competition between the non-producing owners incentivizes them to constantly seek out ways of maximizing the surplus-generating expropriation-through-exploitation process. As Marx puts it: "Capital exists and can only exist as many capitals", so that the "influence of individual capitals on one another has the effect precisely that they must conduct themselves as capital".[179] This constantly expands the object-world of dead labour (labour-diminishing technology to increase the rate of surplus value and a wealth of commodities beyond the affordability of the wages fund and impervious to the workers' needs) that confronts living labour as an oppressive power. This, as Marx argues, is the essence of alienated labour, which results

> from the fact that the worker is related to the product of his labour as to an alien object. For it is clear on this presupposition that the more the worker expends himself in work the more powerful becomes the world of objects which he creates in face of himself, the poorer he becomes in his inner life, and the less he belongs to himself.[180]

Nor, for Marx, could this "be otherwise in a mode of production in which the labourer exists to satisfy the needs of self-expansion of existing values, instead of, on the contrary, material wealth existing to satisfy the needs of development on the part of the labourer".[181] Capitalism is thus zombified in the sense that it is a vampire system. Marx is quite specific about this. "Capital . . . vampire-like, lives only by sucking living labour, and lives the more, the more labour it sucks . . . the vampire will not lose its hold . . . so long as there is a muscle, a nerve, a drop of blood to be exploited".[182]

Now, all systems of class domination are in a sense parasitic on the labour-capacity of the direct producers (since in all of them the income of the superordinate class is derived from the labour of the subordinate classes—whether this be the appropriation of rent as surplus product, or obligations to work on a landowner's estate, or tributary seizures of goods as tax).[183] But the parasitism or vampirism is most advanced and developed under capitalism. This is because capitalism, unlike non-capitalist and pre-capitalist modes of production, is governed by the law of value by which the owning class is coerced by pressure of inter-capitalist competition to increase or intensify the rate of exploitation of the non-owning employees. Thus,

> in so far as . . .[the capitalist] is capital personified, his motivating force is not the acquisition and enjoyment of use-values, but the acquisition and augmentation of exchange-values. . . . As such, he shares with the miser an absolute drive towards self-enrichment. But what appears in the miser as the mania of an individual is in the capitalist the effect of a social mechanism in which he is merely a cog. . . . Accumulate, accumulate! That is Moses and the prophets. . . . Therefore, save, save, i.e. reconvert the greatest possible portion of surplus-value or surplus product into capital. Accumulation for the sake of accumulation, production for the sake of production.[184]

This hyper-exploitation is achieved through the familiar capitalistic methods: investment in labour-saving technology, extension of the working week, extension of the working day, speed-up through workplace reorganization and increasing productivity targets, pegging pay increases below output gains, and so on.[185] These are intended, says Marx, to increase surplus value both relatively and absolutely.[186] By contrast, unlike under capitalism (where the law of competitive exchange dictates that there are no limits to the self-expansion of value), in pre-capitalist modes of class domination, the limits of exploitation were more stringent and relatively stable, since these were set by the finite consumption needs of the landowning elites. As Marx puts it, before capitalism, under feudalism, "the limits to the exploitation of the feudal serf were determined by the walls of the stomach of the feudal lord".[187]

However, there is more to contemporary capitalism, that is, to mega-capitalism, than vampirism. This additional aspect is what justifies designating the system as zombified. In horror folklore, vampires, like zombies in popular media culture today, share an insatiable appetite for consumption for its own sake, or consumption to satisfy a need that is experienced as compulsive and irresistible. Vampires, like zombies, must cannibalize the living to survive, just as capital must cannibalize living labour in order to self-reproduce and self-expand (and capital can survive only by self-expanding). Vampires, like zombies, grow stronger only through predation, as their victims are rendered weaker by it, just as capital grows bigger and fatter on predation as the workers are diminished by it.[188] In Marx's words, "the capitalist gets rich, not like the miser, in proportion to his personal labour and restricted consumption, but at the same rate as he squeezes out labour-power from others, and compels the worker to renounce all the enjoyments of life".[189]

Since World War Two, of course, capitalism's vampirism has become sustainable only by virtue of consumerism. Since the 1960s, indeed ever more so since then, accumulation for accumulation's sake is dependent on consumption for consumption's sake.[190] The success of the contemporary cultural incitement to consume (for reason of identity affirmation or status-differentiation or satisfaction of commodified hedonism) is what grows the global consumer marketplace. Capitalist vampirism has thus, since Marx's time, assumed a dual aspect. This is as capital's cannibalization of living labour in production, and as its conversion of people into consumers of capitalism-sustaining consumerism. Just as the bite of the vampire or zombie (where this is not fatal) converts the victim into a passive self-replicating extension of the biter's cannibalism (as victims are infected with the cannibal's need for compulsive consumption of blood or flesh), so too are workers turned into self-replicating agents of capital by means of enslavement by the culture-ideology of consumerism that binds them to the treadmill of production and the system of induced wants which sustain it.[191]

The consumer, in effect, is made an accomplice of capitalist consumerism, not simply because this allows capitalist consumption to continue (accumulation for its own sake), but because the consumer self-replicates capitalism's objectification of human beings as things to be used and exploited. Consumerism requires its agents to recognize "having" or "acquisition", not "being", as freedom.[192] It requires that people as consumers view other people as objects, whether as things to be consumed directly (e.g. as sexualized commodities and other types of property) or as the means to acquire consumptive means or to dispose of them. So, it would appear, the metaphor of the zombie or the vampire (or of the ghoul or werewolf) will equally suffice to illustrate the cannibalistic dynamics of capitalism today.

But there is a sense in which the term "zombie capitalism" better captures the reality of today's corporate mega-capitalism than is accomplished by invoking other ghoulish spectres. This is in the sense that it conveys a sense of a system that has exhausted itself in every aspect except elite empowerment and consumer exorbitance. Marx argued that no mode of production is ever superseded until its capacity to develop the productive forces and (along with this) promote human development or the further development of civilization is placed in jeopardy.[193] Where the inner strains or internal contradictions of a mode of production have developed up to such a point that its continuation threatens a future of almost permanent economic instability and crisis, posing a threat to the wellbeing of the bulk of humanity, and acts as a roadblock to social or cultural progress (so that tendencies towards barbarism are more pronounced), this mode can be legitimately regarded as a zombie economy. Indeed, where this mode poses a threat even to the viability of a life-sustaining planetary ecology,[194] the term becomes even more descriptively pertinent. This is the world we are in since the collapse of the postwar boom, as I will seek to demonstrate over the remainder of this chapter.

Zombie capitalism and the long downturn

Counterevidence to the zombification thesis would be faster growth and bigger profits in the neoliberal and "global" ages, irrespective of who are the beneficiaries. (As we have seen, trickle-down benefits of pro-capitalist reforms in recent decades are illusory). Has the neoliberal order at least succeeded in restoring levels of growth and of rates of profit in the world economy to those which prevailed before the mid-1970s crisis of Keynesian state-regulated capitalism? In short, is even *capitalism* as a system enhanced by neoliberalism? This, after all, was the main purpose of the neoliberal revolution that gave impetus to the expansionist border-hopping logic of mega-capitalism. This revolution's purpose was to resurge corporate enterprise by easing the shackles on profit-making generated by trade restrictions, by regulated labour markets, by "excess" public expenditures (including on welfare), by high levels of taxation on capital and wealth, and by unionized labour winning above-productivity wage rises.

But the answer is that these have not yielded the economic promised land—not unless one counts the radical boosting of the incomes of the super-wealthy as an economic benefit. For sure, this is experienced as highly beneficial by the corporate and propertied elites themselves. But this can hardly count as a universal benefit—or a "system" benefit. Productivity growth and GDP growth have been much less impressive in the new era of neoliberal-sponsored free trade and unbridled international competition than the earlier less liberalized and more state-regulated modes of political economy that preceded it. Comparing two periods, 1960–68 and 1979–88, for example, is instructive. In the USA, productivity growth per worker shrank from 2.6 per cent (1960–8) to 0.9 per cent (1979–88); in Japan from 8.8 per cent to 3.1 per cent; in Germany from 4.2 per cent to 1.9 per cent; in Italy from 6.3 per cent to 1.6 per cent; in France from 4.9 per cent to 2.4 per cent; and in the UK from 2.7 per cent to 2.6 per cent.[195] The same has been true of GDP growth, in both advanced economies and internationally. This too is a story of economic slowdown—and a slowdown that has also tended to radicalize with each passing decade in most parts of the world and across the OECD generally.

According to Robert Skidelsky's review of the international postwar economy, during the period he dubs as the "Golden Age" (1950–72), under the Bretton Woods system, the world annual average GDP growth was 4.8 per cent. This compared to 3.2 per cent during the subsequent neoliberal period (1980–2000), under the auspices of the Washington Consensus. Unemployment rates were also substantially lower in the earlier period compared to the later in the advanced economies.[196] GDP growth across the world, taken as an aggregate, that is, Gross World Product (GWP) fell from 4.7 per cent in the period from 1950 to 1979 (and from 5.1 per cent in the 1950s and 1960s) to 2.9 per cent from the 1980s up to 2019.[197] Since then, the pandemic and post-pandemic period (2020–22) has seen world GDP growth languish at just 1.4 per cent per year on average.[198] Worldwide GDP performance for 2022 was sluggish at 2.8 per cent, with OECD forecasts for 2023 and 2024 expecting no overall improvement (at 2.9 per cent and 2.7 per cent, respectively).[199] Thus, as the OECD reports, the global economy will remain "fragile" for the foreseeable future.[200] There will be low growth overall. And what little there is of it will be "highly dependent on fast-growing Asian economies".[201]

In comparison with our moribund age, as Skidelsky observes, the performance of world economy during the Golden Age was even more remarkable considering that there were only small pockets of industrial modernization across Southeast Asia during this period, spearheaded by Japan, South Korea, and Singapore. The later period, by contrast, has seen the inflation of average world GDP growth rates owing to massive industrialization in China and also in India. Per capita GDP growth in the developing world including China and India averaged 3.1 per cent in the 1980–2000 period compared to 2.1 per cent in the 1960–1980 period. By contrast, excluding China and India, per capita GDP growth averaged 2.5 per cent in the 1960–1980 period compared to just 0.7 per cent in the 1980–2000 period.[202]

Stephen Marglin and Juliet Schor estimate that, whereas the OECD countries enjoyed annual average growth of four per cent in the 1950s and five per cent in the 1960s, this had ebbed to three per cent by the 1970s and to just two per cent by the 1980s.[203] GDP growth across the OECD world, according to World Bank statistics, declined from 4.7 per cent in the 1960s and 1970s to 2.8 per cent in the 1980s and 1990s and to 2.1 per cent from 2000 to 2018.[204] Bounce back from the global pandemic for the OECD world has since then hardly been impressive. Average GDP growth for these 38 countries between 2019 and 2022 was just 1.5 per cent,[205] and this is projected to fall to 1.4 per cent in 2023 and 2024,[206] and to improve only to 1.8 per cent in 2025.[207] Virtually all the HICs (and all of the G7) have been hit by the general slowdown, as illustrated by the following table[208]:

GDP Growth (G7 + Sweden and Australia) 1950–2019

GDP growth	*1950–59*	*1961–69*	*1970–79*	*1980–89*	*1990–99*	*2000–09*	*2010–19*
USA	4.2	4.5	3.2	3.1	3.2	1.9	2.3
Canada	–	5.4	5.0	2.9	1.3	3.2	2.2
UK	3.2	3.4	2.7	2.6	2.2	1.7	1.8
Germany	8.0	4.6	2.9	2.0	2.2	0.8	2.1
France	4.7	5.7	4.1	2.4	3.1	1.5	1.4
Italy	–	5.8	4.0	2.5	1.5	0.5	0.3
Sweden	3.8	5.6	4.0	3.1	2.6	2.9	3.0
Japan	8.5	10.4	4.3	4.3	1.5	0.5	1.3
Australia	4.2	4.9	3.4	3.3	3.3	3.2	2.6

Even more so than for the OECD countries, the post-pandemic economic situation for the G7 has been precipitous. Average GDP growth for the G7 over the past five years (2019–23) has been just 0.72 per cent.[209]

GDP growth (G7)	*2019–23 (%)*
USA	1.92
Canada	1.30
UK	0.56
Germany	0.36
France	0.82
Italy	0.58
Japan	0.12

GDP average growth for Australia and for Sweden from 2019 to 2022 has been 2.97 per cent and 2.17 per cent, respectively, but with forecasts for 2023 and 2024 that would reduce these to 2.12 per cent and 1.58 per cent respectively over the five years, if these should pan out. If so, these would be their lowest GDP performance on record for a five-year span.[210] Across the Euro area, average annual GDP growth was 4.6 per cent in the period from 1961 to 1979 compared to 2.2 per cent from 1980 to 1999 and 1.7 per cent from 2000 to 2019.[211] For North America, average annual GDP growth was 4.1 per cent from 1961 to 1979 compared to three per cent from 1980 to 1999 and 2.4 per cent between 2000 and 2019.[212] For East Asia and the Pacific, average annual GDP growth was 6.7 per cent in the 1960s and 1970s compared to 4.4 per cent in the 1980s and 1990s and 4.5 per cent up until 2019 since then.[213] Across Latin America and the Caribbean, average annual GDP growth in the 1960s and 1970s was 5.7 per cent compared to 2.4 per cent in the 1980s and 1990s and 2.5 per cent from 2000 to 2019.[214]

The neoliberal era more than halved GDP growth in sub-Saharan Africa from 4.2 per cent in the period from 1961 to 1979 to just 1.8 per cent in the period from 1980 to 1999, though, unusually and counter-intuitively, the African subcontinent has fared better since the 2000s.[215] Nonetheless, the region experienced an unprecedented *fall* of GDP growth of 0.29 per cent between 1980 and 2000.[216] Only South Asia, driven by the huge accelerating state-sponsored industrializations of China and India, has bucked the international trend. Here average GDP growth from 1961 through to the close of the 1980s was 4.3 per cent compared to five per cent in the decades up until 2019.[217] In all these regions, the global pattern of economic slowdown has subsequently prevented a robust rebound from the pandemic. This is even the case in the South Asia region, which has been the most economically dynamic over several decades—the only powerhouse of world capitalism. In the Euro area, average GDP growth from 2020 to 2022 was barely more than one per cent,[218] whereas in North America it was 1.7 per cent.[219] In Latin America and the Caribbean, it has been only 1.4 per cent, whereas in sub-Saharan Africa it has been 1.9 per cent.[220]

This is a remarkably drawn-out period of slowdown verging on stagnancy. In East Asia and the Pacific, by contrast, average GDP growth was 2.94 per cent,[221] whereas in South Asia it was 3.4 per cent.[222] These are all rates of growth much below the 10-year and 20-year periods that preceded them in each of these regions. The global energy crisis that has been triggered by the Russo-Ukrainian war may explain the most recent post-pandemic sluggishness in part. But this can hardly account for the general depressionary pattern of which these recent indicators are a part. Forecasts for GDP growth for 2023 and 2024 expect more of the same in most places. In the Euro area, for example, a rate of only 0.9 per cent is predicted for 2023 and of 1.3 per cent for 2024.[223]

Alongside economic slowdown has been substantially lower returns on capital investment than were typical during the long boom. For the US economy, as Michael Roberts shows,

> there has been a secular decline in the . . . rate of profit from . . . 1965 to 2012; with the main decline between the peak of 1965 and the trough of 1982 (however you measure it). There was a rise in the rate between 1982 and 1997 (35 percent under the current cost measure and 12 percent under the historic cost measure). From 1997, the rate has been basically flat. The rate in the trough of the 2008 Great Recession was 11 percent (constant cost) and 6 percent (historic cost) *below* the 2001 trough.[224]

Since 1964, according to Roberts, the rate of profit in the US economy fell from 32 per cent to 19 per cent by 1982. It recovered partially after 1982, as neoliberal reforms were consolidated, rising to 25 per cent by 1997, before falling back to 20 per cent in 2009. This was followed by a weak recovery that increased the profit rate only partially to 23 per cent by 2012.[225] Between 1946 and 1965,

> the rate of profit was 11 percent above [the] average of the broadest measure and 15 percent above for the narrowest [i.e. of the whole period from 1946 to 2012]. In the neoliberal period from 1982 to 1997, the rate was still 9 percent below the average (broadest) or 18 percent below (narrowest) [of the 1946–2012 period]. The average for 1997 to 2011 was still below the overall average by 5 percent (broadest). It was 5 percent higher than the average for the narrowest measure from 1997 to 2011. But in this latest period, the rate in both cases was still below the 1946–65 golden age period by 10 percent and 15 percent, respectively. If historic costs are used, the results are no different. On the broadest measure . . . the average rate of profit from 1997 to 2011 was 23 percent lower [than the boom period average], whereas on the narrowest measure it was 16 percent lower.[226]

Similarly, on Robert Brenner's estimates, the rate of profit in the USA fluctuated from 15 to 32 per cent on investments between 1950 and 1970. Yet between 1980 and 2000 this rate was reduced by a third, so that this ranged from 10 to 20 per cent.[227] These are similar estimates to those drawn by Anwar Shaikh and Ertugrul Tomat in their exhaustive and forensic investigation of postwar economic performance in the USA from 1948 to 1980. This found that, during this period, the overall rate of profit "falls by almost a third" and the "corporate rate . . . by over 57 percent".[228]

The same pattern holds for the other developed economies. In Germany, the rate of profit fluctuated between 17 and 36 per cent from 1950 to 1970. Yet from 1980 to 2000 this was reduced to a third of the previous level, so that this ranged between 4 and 13 per cent. In Japan, from 1950 to 1970, the rate of profit fluctuated between 33 and 42 per cent. Yet between 1980 and 2000, this had more than halved, so that this ranged from 10 to 26 per cent. These are also Brenner's estimates.[229] As for the UK, Roberts calculates that here there was a fall in the rate of profit by 28 per cent between 1963 and 1975, followed by a period of recovery from 1975 to 1996, and then a further drop of 11 per cent between 1996 and 2008. Thus, the rate of profit in the UK has fallen "in a secular trend" since the mid-1960s.[230]

These empirical conclusions regarding dwindling profit rates since the boom are recorded by several other political economists and social scientists who have investigated the relationship between profit rates and capitalist crises. These researchers include, in addition to those already cited, as Chris Harman recounts, "Fred Moseley, Thomas Michl, . . . Gerard Duménil and Dominque Levy, Ufuk

Tutan and Al Campbell, . . . Edwin N. Wolff, and Piruz Alemi and Duncan K. Foley".[231] Their body of work reveals a

> certain pattern . . . for the whole business sector in the US . . . and . . . for manufacturing in the US, Germany, and Japan . . . [This] . . . is . . . that profit rates fell from the late 1960s until the early 1980s. There is also agreement that they partially recovered from about 1982 on, but with interruptions at the end of the 1980s and at the end of the 1990s, and never making more than half the decline since the long boom. According to Wolff, the rate of profit fell by 5.4 per cent from 1966 to 1979 and then "rebounded" by 3.6 percent from 1979 to 1997; Fred Moseley calculates that [the rate of profit] "recovered . . . only about 40 per cent of the earlier decline"; Dumenil and Levy that "the profit rate in 1997" was "still only half of its value of 1948, and between 60 and 75 percent of its average value for the decade 1956–65".[232]

From a wider international perspective, between 1965 and 1982, according to Roberts, the average rate of profit across the advanced or developed economies fell from 24 per cent to just 11 per cent.[233] As for the world economy taken as an aggregate, according to data mobilized by Joseph Choonora, the average rate of profit declined from 27 per cent in the mid-1960s to just 16.5 per cent by the early 1980s. This, as Choonora shows, has since gone through ups and downs but has not been restored to the level of returns of the boom. Between 1982 and 1995 the rate of return rose up to 20.5 per cent, before falling back to 18 per cent by 2002. Between 2005 and 2010, the rate dropped back from around 21 per cent to less than 17 per cent.[234]

IMF data cited by Harman correspondingly reveals a decline in the rate of capital accumulation worldwide from around 25.5 per cent in 1975 to 22 per cent in 1983. This was followed by a smaller recovery up to 24 per cent by 1990, but then a further dip to a then new low of 21 per cent in 2003. The downward trend in world savings over this period (i.e. since the collapse of the postwar boom) has been even more pronounced.[235] Similarly, World Bank statistics reveal alongside downswings and upswings a secular long-term decline in the level of gross capital formation (accumulation) as a proportion of global output. This fell from almost 27.9 per cent in 1974 to 24.6 per cent in 1982. A partial recovery brought this up to 26.6 per cent in 1989. Then followed a further long period of decline that reduced the level of accumulation to a new historical low of 23.3 per cent by 2002. A milder recovery then ensued which partially restored the rate of accumulation to 25.8 per cent by 2007. But the impact of the Great Financial Crisis pulled this back down to 23.4 per cent by 2009, whereas since then (up to 2019) the level of accumulation has recovered only half of the decline.[236]

Alongside the long slowdown and dwindling returns from capital investment, indeed as a consequence of these, has re-emerged the spectre of recessionary crises alongside escalating indebtedness (household, corporate and public). The global slump of 1974–76 was followed by others in 1980–82 and 1990–91, a catastrophic decade-long collapse of the economies of the former Eastern Bloc under neoliberal restructuring, and the virtual meltdown of the formerly dynamic South Asian "tiger" economies in 1997–98.[237] The crisis of Southeast Asian capitalism then spread to Latin America, with two of the biggest regional economies—Brazil and Argentina—plunged into their biggest recessions of the postwar period, dragging the rest of Central and South America down with them, and sucking 40 per cent of the world economy into crisis.[238] The EU experienced a decade-long period of economic stagnation in the 1990s (so-called "Eurosclerosis"),[239] whereas the US economy plunged into a prolonged recession again from 2001 to 2003 with the collapse of the dot.com bubble.[240] Meanwhile, total debt as a proportion of WGP increased from 70 per cent in 1989 to more than 140 per cent on the eve of the 2007/09 Financial Crash, just as public (state) debt "increased from 30 per cent [of WGP] in 1980 to more than 70 per cent by 2010".[241] By contrast, in 1974, on the cusp of the new period of crisis under neoliberalism, state debt worldwide was just 36 per cent of total output.[242]

Today, in the aftermath of the COVID-19 pandemic, UNCTAD's economists warn of a massive unfolding global debt crisis unless neoliberal governments of the Global North instruct their central banks to stop imposing financial austerity on world economy by pushing up interest rates (as they have been doing) in order to ease inflationary pressures. But, in fact the global debt crisis has long been gestating, as UNCTAD data itself shows. The cost of debt repayments as a proportion of state revenues for MICs, excluding China, increased from five per cent in 2010 to nine per cent in 2021. The cost of debt repayments for LDCs rose from four per cent to 11 per cent of state revenues over the same period. The top 20 indebted countries are facing debt-servicing costs that range from 22 per cent to 97 per cent of total government revenues.[243]

Just as these crises have unfolded, the World Bank's and IMF's imposition of its neoliberal SAPs (or PRPs) of radical marketization on the developing and undeveloped worlds, starting in earnest in the 1980s, were a dismal failure. These succeeded neither in reducing inflation nor in boosting growth—as was their stated purpose. Of 76 countries which implemented them throughout the 1980s and into the early 1990s only a handful recorded improved performance, whereas the majority performed worse than before.[244] The biggest SAP horror story (or market nightmare) was inflicted on Chile. Chile's SAP was the first and was to become the template for the others. This was under the Pinochet dictatorship lauded by the Thatcher (UK) and Reagan (US) governments for restoring "order" following a period of heightened class struggle that elevated Salvador Allende's socialist government into office and ended with Allende's murder by the army during Pinochet's coup. This was the first test-case of neoliberal remedies before neoliberalism became internationally hegemonic. This was indicative of developments to come right across the Global South, with similar results.

The case of Chile

Chile's SAP was organized around five key policies of neoliberalism. Firstly, re-establish the country as a profitable site for global enterprise by removing the existing barriers to capital movement. This necessitated abolition of taxes on wealth and capital and the withdrawal of restrictions on profits of foreign MNCs being repatriated back to home bases in the metropolitan centres. Secondly, abandon all state controls on prices (including subsidies on basic consumer goods), so that these can rise to "market levels". Thirdly, redirect national production towards the world market. This required export-driven production, in place of import-substitution production, which entailed the forcible conversion of subsistence agriculture into commercial agriculture. Fourthly, withdraw the state's activities in the economy. So, Pinochet's junta forced through large-scale privatizations and imposed substantial reductions in state spending on social services such as health, education, and welfare. Finally, neutralize the labour movement and the working class, in order to undermine opposition and resistance to these policies. Chilean neoliberalism was committed to barring strikes, outlawing trade unions, and scrapping laws safeguarding elementary health and safety at work.[245]

As Marcus Taylor points out: "The primary achievement of the repression was the decapitation of organised labour, the destruction of autonomous and politically active union movements, and the generalised suppression of political expressions of opposition". All of this was delivered by force of police jackboot and punitive labour code.

> In total, tens of thousands of activists were murdered, jailed or exiled. The repression was at its most intense in the immediate post-coup years, although it remained strong throughout the regime, with the period 1984–8 alone being marked by 163 murders, 446 cases of torture and 1,927 political arrests, all committed with legal impunity. Moreover, political violence was supplemented by an oppressive labour policy that involved the prohibition of strikes, the dissolution of unions (until 1979, when they were allowed to reconstitute in a controlled manner), suppression of wages and a reform of labour legislation that relaxed regulations and allowed a dramatic decrease in a firm's social security and tax benefits to workers.[246]

What were the effects of these policies? Firstly, the share of wages in total income fell from 63 per cent in 1972 to 41 per cent in 1976. Secondly, "in the agrarian sphere, 45% of peasants who had gained land in the Frei and Allende agrarian reforms, lost their property rights". Finally, unemployment was driven above 15 per cent over the same period.[247] As a result, by 1989, 42 per cent of Chile's population were reduced to poverty, with almost 15 per cent "living in conditions of indigence".[248] A decade later, by the close of the 1990s, the poverty rate had scarcely improved. This was only marginally lower at 40 per cent.[249]

The purpose of the SAP was to boost economic growth by making life as comfortable and secure as possible for capitalists (local and foreign) and as uncomfortable and precarious as possible for workers and the poor. Substantially reducing the share of national income going to wages and public welfare and increasing the share available for capital investments (under "shock therapy") was the central element of the strategy to secure that goal. Hence, Pinochet's neoliberalism was successful in delivering on its intent. The purpose was to force down wages to internationally competitive rates, shed surplus labour (whilst drastically curtailing the monies available for the reproduction of its owners and their families), and undermine disincentives to enter the labour market at bare subsistence levels of pay by cutting away the social security safety net.

But the positive outcomes that were supposed to flow from the "market therapy" were elusive. By 1981, eight years after the CIA-assisted military coup that brought Pinochet to office, GNP was still below the 1970 level,[250] whereas by 1991 Chile's debt had risen to almost half the value of GDP, according to the regime's own accounting. Indeed, the national debt was certainly higher, "as most of Chile's debt was concealed in foreign equity holdings".[251] The economy's GDP growth rate was 2.1 per cent per annum on average between 1974 and 1981, lagging most other Latin American countries.[252] Eventually, with the return of bourgeois civilian government after 1990 (though under the shadow of the pro-Pinochet military), Chile recovered enough from the effects of the initial neoliberal offensive to register an eight-year period of strong GDP growth averaging 6.98 per cent a year. In the Pinochet years (1973–90), by contrast, GDP growth was a modest 2.99 per cent per year on average, whereas it has averaged 3.96 per cent per annum over the neoliberal period as a whole (1973–2019). But, since 1998, the Chilean economy's GDP growth has slowed considerably, averaging 3.58 per cent per year up until and including 2019, and less than two per cent since 2014.[253]

The GDP gains in the boom 1990s were won based on the continued ruthless suppression of wage rates under civilian governments that preserved Pinochet's punitive labour code, so that the benefits of the economic boom were distributed highly unevenly. "In 1997, prior to the latest recession, the minimum wage had just regained its 1982 level and stood some 30% below its 1970 level".[254] Since then, from 1996 to 2010, the share of national income going to capital rather than to wages increased further, so that labour's share continued its long decline since Pinochet's coup.[255] Workers in the industrial sector generated productivity gains of 4.8 per cent per year on average between 1990 and 1998, whereas wage rates increased by only 3.6 per cent.[256]

Poverty declined from an astronomical 38.6 per cent in 1990 to 21.7 per cent by 1998. But this was merely returning the rate to the same level as in 1970.[257] Since then, however, poverty has continued to fall, so that the ILO estimated that this was 14.4 per cent in 2011. But this has not been achieved by the neoliberal aspects of government policy; rather, this was the consequence of other aspects that were intended to blunt neoliberalism's negative socio-economic impact on the workers and the poor. The reduction was largely brought about by a system of welfare transfers and subsidies introduced by the left-of-centre civilian neoliberal governments of the 1990s, not by expanding employment or rising incomes from wages. Today, "around 40 per cent of the population depends on cash transfers and subsidies provided by the state to achieve incomes above the poverty line". Without these, "21 per cent of the population are living in poverty" and as much again are placed only marginally above poverty.[258]

At the same time, rates of income inequality that skyrocketed under Pinochet remained amongst the highest in the world in the 1990s and second in Latin America only to Brazil. The share of national income of the lower 60 per cent of Chile's population was less than 25 per cent of the total in 1998—a decline of 1.6 per cent since 1987. The top tenth of Chilean earners in 1998 had an income 10 times larger than that of the bottom fifth of earners.[259] These inequalities of income have continued to grow since the 1990s, as they did during the 1990s.

> Despite the success in reducing poverty, concerns remain about the distribution of income, as inequality by several measures has not declined. The broad trends . . . reveal that it has actually risen over the period 1990–2011. Excluding the peak and subsequent decline in income inequality associated with the impact of the financial crisis in 2009, the overall trend is upward.[260]

Even though the most recent data (post-2014 up to the cusp of the pandemic) is suggestive of a decline of inequality, based on the Gini coefficient, this has been slight. Chile remains one of the most unequal countries in the world, in second place among the OECD nations, trailing only Mexico.[261] Thus, after almost half a century of neoliberalism in Chile, there remains little sign of the promised "trickle down" benefits of radical marketization.

Neoliberalism and capitalist crises

Yet trade liberalization, deregulation and untrammelled privatizations were exactly supposed to resolve the longstanding problems of capitalism (stagnation, immiseration, recession, falling profitability). These, according to the neoliberals, were going to usher in a new era of universal growth and prosperity, following the demise of the Keynesian model of capitalism—which was undone by its mid-1970s crisis of chronic stagflation and rising industrial conflict. Instead, as capitalism evolved into its mega-corporate mode, and as this mode driven by neoliberal politics conquered the world economy, the structural dissonance, and disequilibria (or, in Marxist terminology, the inner contradictions or strains) of the system have radicalized. Consequently, the world capitalist economy is more unstable and fragile today than at any time since the 1930s.

By contrast, during the Golden Age, economic downturns in the trade cycle were mild. These were not actual recessions, but so-called growth recessions,[262] in which the rate of growth slowed rather than stopping or contracting. This motivated 1960s economists and sociologists to claim that capitalism had overcome recessionary crises that had hitherto blighted its development and weakened its legitimacy.[263] John Samuelson, a Nobel Prize-winning economist, wrote in the 1960s that slumps were abolished, owing to the consolidation of mass consumerism, the expansion of the world market, and Keynesian methods of economic management. "The National Bureau of Economic Research", he claimed, "has worked itself out of one of its first jobs, namely business cycles".[264] Even after the long boom was a distant memory, even moderate temporary improvements in economic performance would still elicit the wildest optimism among Establishment economists. Thus, another Nobel Prize winner, Robert Lucas Junior, echoed Samuelson's sentiments in 2003, declaring that "the central problem of depression-prevention has been solved, for all practical purposes".[265] Four years later arrived the Great Financial Crash and subsequent long depression.

As previously noted, before COVID-19, the neoliberal epoch witnessed a succession of global economic crises (in the mid-1970s, the early 1980s, the early 1990s, the end of the 1990s, and then towards 2007's end. The Great Financial Crisis of 2007/09 was the biggest and deepest one since the depressive 1930s—until COVID-19. This triggered a worldwide recession (indeed possibly full-fledged depression) owing to the structural fragility of the world economy since 2007 and the more longstanding crisis of profitability and slow growth since the 1970s. As such, this was the sixth major international crisis in just 46 years. Since the start of the neoliberal "globalization" era up until the start of the new century, there have been no fewer than 139 financial crises of some shape or hue. The bulk of these of course did not trigger a meltdown of the real economy, but crash economics is a danger inherent in every major dip in the global stock exchanges and money markets. Now, in the whole 150-year history of capitalism right up to 1914, there were only twice as many financial crises as in this recent period. During the period from 1945 to 1971, by way of further comparison, there were only 38 financial crises.[266]

The great slump of 2007/09, subsequent long global depression,[267] and omnipresent "there is no alternative" (TINA)[268] politics of austerity that has blighted the lives of tens of millions in the developed world alone[269]—this was just the latest (drastic) episode in the decades-long pattern. The Great Crash added 61 million people to the dole queues worldwide,[270] including 22 million in the developed world, 7.5 million in the USA, and eight million in the "emerging economies".[271] Subsequently, as the ILO reported in 2014: "The bulk of the increase in global unemployment is in the East Asia and South Asia regions, which together represent more than 45 per cent of additional jobseekers, followed by Sub-Saharan Africa and Europe".[272] The World Bank estimated that 60 million people in the LDCs were dropped into destitution owing to the crisis by 2010's end, whereas the UN estimated that 100 million worldwide had been impoverished by the end of 2009.[273]

This evoked fears (in the context of the continued generalized economic stagnancy) that 2.8 billion people across the Global South hovering precariously above the World Bank's official poverty line could imminently be dragged back down beneath it, dissolving two decades of poverty reduction gains. In the event, this crisis of global immiseration was avoided, or rather a substantial worsening of it was. This was because a collapse of world recession into global slump was narrowly averted courtesy of "the largest global fiscal stimulus"[274] package ever undertaken, as was agreed by the G20—the price of which was to be the austerity decade that followed. Global slump was then delivered courtesy of the pandemic—the seventh major global economic crisis in just 57 years. The longer-term economic fallout from the COVID-19 crisis since 2020 (especially stemming from the failure of worldwide neoliberal governance to deal with it) has rendered the scenario of stagnancy collapsing into depression an even greater danger than it was in the aftermath of the Great Crash.

The purely economic damage of the 2007/09 crisis was substantial and prolonged. This chalked approximately $2 trillion off global GDP, or four per cent of world output, between March 2008 and March 2009.[275] It is also estimated that financial institutions saw losses of $2 trillion for the duration of the crash, while the combined losses from the financial crash and subsequent long global recession were more than $10 trillion in terms of world output. Ninety-one national economies representing two-thirds of world GDP experienced contractions in output in 2009. Europe witnessed a GDP fall of 10 per cent. The Middle East contracted by 11 percent. Latin America experienced a fall of eight per cent. North America endured a fall of almost three per cent. GDP in Asia as a whole (and in the Asian Tigers) did not contract but underwent a radical slowdown and virtual collapse of export earnings. Some 60 per cent of national economies had not fully recovered from the losses of output growth 10 years later. North America did not recover from its GDP losses until 2013. The EU did not recover from its own losses until 2018. From 2008 up until mid-2017, global government debt more than doubled, growing on average from 69 per cent to 164 per cent of GDP, averaging 105 per cent of GDP in the advanced economies, and topping $60 trillion overall. This contributed to a decade of weak and tardy growth almost up to the novel coronavirus outbreak.[276]

Yet by far the greatest harm inflicted on people and communities since 2008 has stemmed from neoliberal austerity policies to reduce huge budget deficits run up by multi-billion bailouts of the major banks than by the economic crisis provoked by the financial crash. Austerity policies, together with the long-drawn "jobless recovery",[277] have of course had a negative impact across class lines, damaging the well-being of tens of millions. But the impact of these on the poor and lower wage-earners has been savage, seriously damaging their life-chances in the longer term.[278] Nor did austerity succeed, in most countries, not for many years, even in lowering budget deficits, since the crisis itself massively increased public demand for those welfare services that were being cut to the bone. Nor, more importantly, did austerity trigger a new spurt of stable or healthy GDP growth. Rather, in most cases, public debt relative to GDP continued to build for years after the crash had subsided, owing to continuing poor economic performance.[279] Indeed, the post-crash deficit reduction programmes are more likely to have damaged growth, hence curtailing recovery, not least because their purely financial costs have been greater than whatever benefits austerity has yielded in terms of debt-reduction savings.

Martin Wolf's analysis of the relationship between GDP growth and austerity in the EU between 2008 and 2012 confirms this. This found "no evidence . . . that large fiscal contractions bring benefits to confidence and growth that offset the direct effects of the contractions. They bring exactly what one would expect: small contractions bring recessions; big contractions bring depressions". Similarly, Paul Krugman's analysis of the impact of austerity on economic performance in several EU member states showed that this was slowing recovery since "one euro of austerity yields only about 0.4 euros of reduced deficit, even in the short run". As Krugman concluded: "No wonder then that the whole austerity enterprise is spiralling into disaster".[280] But austerity was defended by Brussels—even as Germany and Austria registered better economic performance than across the EU by switching from financial austerity to financial stimulus.[281] And so austerity perpetuates, as it has done until today, at incalculable human and social cost (with supposed benefits that are projected into the future, and which for the better part of a decade showed no evidence of manifesting in the present), because neoliberal ideology dictates it must.

Explaining zombie capitalism

A remarkable feature of the longstanding crisis of capitalist world economy since the mid-1970s is that it took by surprise virtually every mainstream economist, whether of a neo-Keynesian or neo-classical orientation,[282] just as did the Great Crash of 1929 and the long 1930s depression that followed drop out of clear skies for establishment economists.[283] This was also true of the great financial crisis of 2007/09, despite the fact that this slump was the fifth major economic crisis to afflict the global system (or a substantial part of it) over the hitherto 30 years.[284] Yet this has not, for the most part, engendered a "return to Marx" in the Western academy, even though Marx is the most perceptive of the theorists of capitalist crisis.

An important exception to this pattern of neglect by academic economists, however, has been neo-Marxist historian and political economist Robert Brenner's capitalist crisis theory. Brenner's work deserves close attention because he has been one of the few theorists to diagnose the longstanding crisis of profitability which underpinned the financial meltdown of 200/709, and to predict its likely catastrophic effects. Brenner's argument is that this crisis was no mere crisis of "financialization", which has dragged down an otherwise healthy productive economy. Rather, this was rooted in an underlying structural crisis of over-competition and over-accumulation of world capitalism, and especially of the developed economies. This crisis, according to Brenner, ultimately has its roots in the failure of the successive international restructurings of capitalism of the 1970s, 1980s, and 1990s to restore average profit rates to the levels they enjoyed during the postwar boom.[285]

Brenner first developed his theory in an article he originally published in *New Left Review* in 1998. The article in question was an extended piece—which basically filled the whole content of that edition of the journal—entitled *The Economics of Global Turbulence*. Later, in 2006, Brenner updated and extended his analysis in a book of the same name. Now, Brenner is important for two reasons. Firstly, because he rejects the standard explanation of the current period of crisis, which discovers the whole reason for it in the behaviour of the banks and money markets. Secondly, because he also provides an explanation for it rooted in the deep structure of the postwar world capitalist economy. By doing that, Brenner was able to do something that hardly anyone else did. This was predicting the coming of the Great Financial Crisis of 2007/09 before it happened.

Brenner's theory extends the explanatory power of Marxist concepts in making sense of the boom and its demise. Marx diagnosed the cause of the long-run tendency of the rate to fall under capitalism as stemming from the pressures exerted by inter-capitalist competition on rival firms to lower output costs by increasing labour productivity. The primary means of achieving this is through progressively higher investments in labour-saving technologies. So, over time, the tendency is for the ratio of constant capital (i.e. the investment in means of production) to variable capital (i.e. the investment in labour-power) to increase, leading to what Marx refers to as a rising *organic composition of capital*.[286] But, since labour is the source of wealth, and since under capitalism labour-power is the source of capital, any increase in the value-composition of investments in dead labour *vis-à-vis* living labour will also have the unintended consequence of causing profit rates to fall. This is Marx's TRPF theory. As long as labour productivity is increased by means of a progressive tendency for capitals to elevate the ratio of investments in means of production rather than in labour-power, the tendency for the rate of profit to fall will manifest.

Pressure of competition incentivizes individual capitalists to innovate labour-saving means of production that, though advantageous to the capitalist enterprise that first innovates, has the unintended consequence of undermining the system as a whole. As Marx explains:

> No capitalist ever voluntarily introduces a new method of production, no matter how much more productive it may be, and how much it may increase the rate of surplus-value, so long as it reduces the rate of profit. Yet every such

> new method of production cheapens the commodities. Hence, the capitalist sells them originally above their prices of production, or, perhaps, above their value. He pockets the difference between the costs of production and the market prices of the same commodities produced at higher costs of production. He can do this . . . because his method of production stands above the social average. But competition makes it general and subject to the general law [of value]. There follows a fall in the rate of profit . . . which is wholly independent of the will of the capitalist.[287]

However, Brenner himself regards his account of the long downturn as an alternative to Marx's theory of organic crisis, which he rejects. But this is not so. Aside from mistakenly representing Marx's theory as "neo-Malthusian" (by virtue of its supposed positing of a "law" that capitalism is undermined by falling productivity),[288] Brenner accepts the common Marxist critique of Marx's account that no capitalist would invest in technological innovation to increase labour productivity if this would lower profits.[289] Marx's point, though, was exactly that the falling rate of profit was an unintended consequence of investment in labour-saving technology that was enforced by blind force of competition. In this process, the first capitalist firm to innovate would seize bigger profits at the expense of rivals by reducing its costs below theirs, whereas any firm that chose not to seek out innovation would be outcompeted and run out of business. Thus, actions that were beneficial to individual capitals were detrimental to capitalism as a system.[290]

Yet Brenner objects to Marx's theory because he says capitalist competition would tend to lower the value of capital-saving investments as much as labour-saving investments so that the organic composition of capital would not have a general tendency to rise.[291] But, as Chris Harman says, this argument being based on "simultaneous equations" modelling (a synchronic timeframe) is undermined by a temporal flaw. When new labour-saving technologies are brought in by an innovator capitalist this is before competition has generalized the use of the innovation and lowered its production costs. Those capitalists who innovate first would have higher costs on their investments than those who deploy the innovation latterly (which have to be deducted from profits), yet the latter would have already taken a hit on their profits due to the innovator taking their markets by under-cutting their prices.[292] Meanwhile, the competitive dynamic of generalized commodity production compels all capitals to be looking to fund initially expensive labour-saving technologies (compared with later investments in that same technology) with the goal of increasing productivity and thus reducing costs. This is because innovators (unlike followers) are the ones who have forked out the R&D costs that brought the new technology into use.

In short, diachronic, or temporal analysis, restores the TRPF, which appears undermined on the basis of simultaneity or synchronic analysis. So, contrary to

Brenner's own view, the logic of his own account of the collapse of the postwar boom—which proposes that this has been generated by the ratchet of intensifying inter-capitalist competition worldwide—would actually support Marx's theory of the TRPF as facilitated by a rising organic composition of capital. This is because "over-competition" (a concept that is at the heart of Brenner's theory) would indeed tend to increase the ratio of investment in capital relative to labour (hence generating Marx's organic crisis) as well as the other negative impacts proposed by Brenner's analysis.

Brenner begins his analysis by dividing the history of postwar capitalism into two phases. Firstly, there was what he terms the *long upturn*. This is basically the "Golden Age" corresponding to the postwar boom. This was, as we have seen, from the end of the 1940s to early 1970s. This was a period of record levels of growth—in output, productivity, wages, and investment. This was also a period of low if not negligible unemployment and only the mildest fluctuations in the business cycle.[293] Secondly, there was the period of global turbulence, or of the *long downturn*. And this, Brenner says, is the period we are still in, with no end in sight. The period of global turbulence starts in the 1970s as the long postwar boom peters out. This is a period characterized by declining levels of investment, productivity growth, and wage growth. This is also a period of depression-level unemployment as a permanent feature of the advanced economies, plus a series of major recessionary crises right across the world economy.[294]

The immediate cause of the long downturn, Brenner rightly points out, is the simple verifiable (and verified) fact that the rate of profit in the US economy, especially in manufacturing, not only fell sharply between 1965 and 1973 but also failed to recover thereafter. Such is supported by a wealth of empirical data mobilized by Brenner and other radical economists. This fall in profits was initially in the US economy but soon after in the advanced capitalist world as an aggregate. The reasons for the crisis of profitability, Brenner argues, are indissolubly integral to the dynamic of the capitalist economic system. Capitalism, Brenner reminds us, is a system of competitive accumulation. Capitalist firms compete to reduce costs in order to avoid being run out of business and to boost profits. This makes the system dynamic, so that the productive forces are developed at unprecedented pace. But it also renders the system vulnerable to recurrent economic crises and periods of stagnation. This is why these have been integral to the history of capitalism since its start—except, that is, for during the Golden Age, for reasons that Brenner explores.[295]

Why does inter-capitalist competition make the system prone to crises and stagnation? Brenner's answer, following Marx, is that this is because capitalism is by its nature individualized and unplanned. Each capitalist, in seeking to outcompete the others, cannot consider the system-wide effects of his or her actions. The overall effect of inter-capitalist competition for profits is beneficial only to those capitalists who come out on top in the competition. There are always winners and losers—and the losers tend to go bust or get taken over through mergers and acquisitions by the winners. However, not only does inter-capitalist competition generate as many losers as winners, but this is also detrimental to the system as a whole. The basic reason for this, as Brenner says, is that whenever firms introduce new technologies to boost their productivity, this renders obsolete the investments in technologies that have been made by their rivals, who therefore fail to recoup the profits they expected. Plant and equipment, which have been relatively newly introduced, often at great cost, fail to generate the expected revenues. As a result, all of these investments have to be written off, and new investments made in newer plant and equipment, also at great cost.[296]

So, because capitalism is based on unplanned individualized competition, this means any major technological innovation that reduces costs and increases output does not produce a general system-wide benefit. Rather, it benefits only those capitalists who pioneer the new technology, and it causes huge economic damage to everyone else. The irony of this situation, as Brenner observes, is that if the damage caused reaches a certain level of severity this ends up damaging even those companies that invested first in the new technologies that gave them initial economic advantage. This is because where firms go bust (as happens in the classical recession) this affects a whole lot of other firms that supply them or market their goods. And so, a general crisis arises whereby a recession may spill over into a full-fledged crash or slump. A general crisis means, of course, rising unemployment, whereas owing to rising unemployment, demand in the economy for all goods and services falls—including for the company that was first in introducing the cost-saving technology.[297]

Brenner applies this basic abstract model of capitalism to make sense of the behaviour of the postwar international economy—especially of the collapse of the long boom into the long downturn. The fundamental reason, he says, why the rate of profit fell, and has failed to recover, is ultimately the intensification of inter-capitalist competition on the global canvas since World War Two. The crisis stems, therefore, from the *internationalization* of inter-capitalist competition. This, he argues, has led to persistent problems of *overcapacity* and *overproduction* on a system-wide scale.[298] This has especially been the case in the manufacturing sector, beginning in the mid-1960s. (The long downturn, beginning in the 1970s, was, Brenner shows, sparked off not by problems in the finance sector, but by problems of industrial capitalism). Over-capacity means simply that the industrial sector can produce much more than it can sell, so that investments are not made or go to waste. Over-production means simply that the industrial sector is literally producing more output than can be absorbed by the market, so that goods go unsold. The problems of overcapacity and overproduction emerge, says Brenner, because inter-capitalist competition generates combined but uneven development across the world.[299]

After World War Two, the USA was by far the world's dominant economic power, responsible for almost half of world output. At the start of the 1960s, the USA was still contributing 40 per cent of global GDP, in a rapidly growing international marketplace.[300] The country's MNCs were the first ones, rapidly spreading their operations abroad, just as US goods flooded local markets everywhere. US economic dominance was undergirded by the Bretton Woods system whereby the US dollar became global currency into which all others were converted. However, since capitalism is never-ending competition, it was not long before American big business was challenged economically by other national capitalisms.[301] This is the crux of Brenner's theory. So it was, he argues, that the later-developing economies of Japan, Europe, and later Southeast and South Asia (or of their world-market facing corporations) began to challenge the USA's economic hegemony, starting in the 1960s and 1970s. This process of intensifying capitalist competition on the world stage between rival capitalist centres, argues Brenner, was the central cause of both the long boom and the long downturn.[302]

The Japanese, German, and other later-developing industrial economies were able to grow rapidly during the postwar boom. This was, as Brenner shows, by virtue of their ability to exploit the advantages of being followers of the USA—technologically, economically, politically, and militarily. They benefitted *technologically* from being followers of the USA because they could use plant and machinery that they did not have to develop themselves. American capitalism had borne the costs of developing the most advanced industrial technologies. But the other national capitalisms could simply import and use these new technologies at lower cost, hence building bigger profits.

The newly ascending national capitalisms benefitted *economically* from being followers of US capitalism because they could become participants in the world economy that US governments were building for the benefit of their MNCs. American capitalism had opened a world market to exploit, and other developing capitalist countries could try to get a share of that growing pie. The followers also benefitted economically because their lesser level of economic development ensured that their labour costs were lower than in the hegemon's domestic economy.[303] The newly developing (and war-recovering) capitalist countries could also benefit from large reserves of unemployed workers in the rural areas and attract chronically underpaid labourers from the underdeveloped agrarian economy into industrial work in the urban centres. These workers could be paid much less in wages than American workers who owing to the USA's international economic supremacy could win for themselves a standard of living that was much higher than anywhere else. This meant, Brenner's analysis shows, that the newly restored or newly rising capitalist economies of Europe and Southeast Asia were able to keep wage growth relatively low compared to productivity growth, whereas this was not the case in the USA.[304]

The newly emerging or newly renewing capitalist countries, Brenner argues, could also benefit from being followers of the USA *politically and militarily* to challenge US economic dominance. On the one hand, as theorists of the permanent arms economy also show,[305] the USA was bearing nearly all the military costs of maintaining the so-called "free world" against the threats supposedly posed by communism and socialism and social democracy across the face of the world—and especially in the developing world. To defend its worldwide economic and strategic interests, the US state established a huge military machine to be deployed all over the world in defence of the capitalist world market that its own MNCs dominated. However, the newly emerging or newly resurgent capitalist centres (especially Japan and Germany) were able to benefit economically from US military hegemony by enjoying a world market defended by US power without having to bear the costs of its upkeep themselves. This allowed these countries to avoid the heavy unproductive military expenditures undertaken by the US state, which meant that they could invest more in economic development and hence obtain a competitive edge in the civilian economy.[306]

On the other hand, as Brenner explains, to catch-up with the USA economically, these newly emerging or re-establishing economies were (in most cases) supported and protected by their own governments and banks in a way that did not happen in the USA. Especially in Germany and Japan, the state and the banks channelled huge resources into developing their own capitalist firms in key sectors oriented to export markets, so that they could challenge the American worldwide market supremacy. These governments also used tariffs to protect own industries from cheap imports until they were internationally competitive. In the USA, by contrast, there was more hostility to government involvement in the affairs of business, nurtured by the individualism of the general culture as well as by corporate suspicions over the diminution of private enterprise under an expanding social state. American MNCs also did not feel they needed protection or sponsorship by the US state, because their dominance of their local markets (by far the biggest in the world) and of world export trade was so great.[307]

As a result of these processes, during the first part of the postwar epoch, the German and Japanese economies were able to expand rapidly, placing themselves at the heart of larger regional economies, in Europe and Southeast Asia, and consolidating their own MNCs, which began to outcompete their US corporate rivals, eroding their profits. In Brenner's words:

> Between 1965 and 1973, manufacturers based especially in Japan, but also in Germany and in other parts of Western Europe, combined relatively advanced techniques and relatively low wages to reduce production costs sharply *vis-à-vis* those of US producers. On this basis, they dramatically seized increased shares of the world market and imposed on that market their relatively low prices.[308]

Their US competitors found themselves facing the double bind of lower prices for their output but with high costs because they were stuck with big investments in technology that was rendered obsolete by virtue of successful labour-enhancing investments elsewhere. Those that could no longer make the previous or expected rate of profit either had to scale back productive capacity or to accept significantly reduced rates of profit on their capital investments. Raising prices above costs to recoup profits was not possible because that would price their goods out of the market and further boost their international rivals.

Thus, as a consequence of this dynamic of intensifying worldwide inter-capitalist competition, US capitalism had to take the hit of reduced profit rates right across the board. However, owing to this crisis of specifically US capitalism, as Brenner tells it, there was also a system-wide crisis of overcapacity and overproduction—and this led to declining rate of profit right across the whole world economy. This happened as US firms could not sell their output faced with cheaper goods from elsewhere, and as market supply was boosted beyond demand by the greater productivity of German and Japanese firms. "Between 1965 and 1973, the US manufacturing sector sustained a fall in the rate of profit on its capital stock of over 40 percent".[309] At the same time, however, the average profit rates of the leading competitor economies of Japan and Europe taken as a whole held up, despite the US crisis, up to the start of the 1970s. Nonetheless, owing to the US crisis, the average profit rate across the manufacturing sectors of the G7 economies taken as a whole fell by about 25 per cent.[310]

Brenner's point is that the crisis of profitability of US capitalism led to a crisis of profitability of its major rivals which had begun to outcompete American business. The USA's rival economies could not (and did not), Brenner shows, protect themselves from the aggregate decline in profitability generated by the US crisis. The success of their manufacturers in outcompeting their US rivals could only increase system over-capacity in manufacturing, which would radicalize should US companies reduce the competitive deficit through restructurings. The US economy's lack of competitiveness led to its building up a huge balance of payments deficit. This in turn led to the collapse of the Bretton Woods system based on the dollar and gold and devaluation of the dollar in 1973 as the US government attempted to cheapen the price of US exports and increase the price of foreign imports entering the American market.

But, with the US dollar being devalued, German and Japanese companies found themselves saddled with significantly higher costs as those of their US rivals were lowered, and their exports were thereby made pricier in comparison with US imports.[311] The effect of the US currency devaluation was thus to drag down profitability right across the developed world, in effect by forcing German and Japanese firms to carry it as well—and by virtue of that to lower the rate of profit across the world economy as a whole.[312] This happened as the dollar devaluation basically restored parity of costs between US manufacturers and those from the leading competitor national capitals, if not tilting the scales in favour of the former. The fortunes of US corporate capitalism were revived (hence the American min-boom from 1995 to 2000), albeit weakly and partially, but only by exporting recession and stagnation to the USA's leading national competitors.[313]

This is Brenner's account of the origins of the crisis of profitability that began in the 1970s. But why has the crisis persisted? That it has done so is not a matter of serious question. This is established by a wealth of empirical indicators mobilized in this chapter. How does Brenner explain why the world economy is stuck in this long downturn? Now, an obvious solution to this crisis of profitability, Brenner observes, is that firms suffering from falling profitability in their lines of business would shift their investments into other, potentially higher profit lines, to alleviate overcapacity and overproduction in the over-saturated markets. But that did not happen, Brenner points out, because the big US, European and Japanese MNCs felt that their fortunes were better served by seeking improved efficiency in their own lines rather than by reallocating capital into other lines.

These companies had deployed in their own industries vast amounts of capital, prepaid or committed, so that they could use this for free. As a result, at least for a time, they could generate higher returns on investments in their own industries than they could by shifting money elsewhere. Therefore, it was far from irrational for them to err on the side of familiarity in terms of investments, despite reduced rates of profit on their total capital. Moreover, as Brenner tells, "these corporations maintained long-established relationships with suppliers and customers that could not easily, or without great cost, be duplicated in new branches of production". Perhaps most importantly, "over a long period of time, they had acquired hard-won specialized knowledge of production they could apply only to their own industries".[314]

One reason for the persistence of the long downturn, therefore, as Brenner explains, is simply that the big metropole based MNCs (of Europe, the USA, and Japan) found it more promising to stay in their own lines of business than to switch, and they did not abandon these lines unless they felt they had to. As a result, there was insufficient exit of investment capital from areas of the market with over-capacity and low profits to other areas where there was potentially higher demand and bigger profits.

A second reason for the continued relative stagnancy, however, was that, despite the reduced profitability in world manufacturing lines, the endless relentless process of inter-capitalist competition that had generated uneven development in the world economy continued apace. Indeed, the national-corporate capitalist rivalries that had generated the mid-1970s crisis of profitability intensified in the 1980s and 1990s. This happened as more countries underwent successful capitalist industrializations, turning themselves into low-cost producers of manufactured goods for the world market, typically organized as MNCs under state patronage. Initially, of course, it was the East Asian "tigers" (of Hong Kong, Singapore, South Korea, and Taiwan) which entered the fray. More recently, since Brenner penned his 1990s articles, it has been the BRICs, including and especially China,[315] that have made the biggest strides. So, not only was there, according to Brenner's analysis, insufficient exit of capital from over-saturated manufacturing lines, but there was also too much entry. Thus, intensifying international inter-capitalist competition simply radicalized the overcapacity that was holding down the rate of profit. This was, for Brenner, a second major reason why the crisis of profitability of the 1970s has continued to dog the system.

Finally, Keynesian policies, which became dominant in the advanced countries in the 1970s in response to crisis, and which survived in US government policy into the neoliberal era, also contributed to the worldwide perpetuation of overcapacity and overproduction. This was because these helped to prevent a decisive recovery of profitability and, in turn, of capital accumulation, in the 1980s and 1990s and beyond. Keynesianism may be defined as a form of macro government economic policy that seeks to maintain profitability by subsidizing the corporate sector and by raising consumer demand so that it matches the supply of goods in the marketplace. Keynesian policies would include those of full employment, deficit financing of the public sector, cheap credit to oil the wheels of industry, and using welfare spending to ensure there is enough money in people's pockets to absorb the output of the corporate sector. Now, much of this is anathema to neoliberals. But elements of Keynesianism—the corporate-supporting aspect (i.e. subsidization of big business and monetary or fiscal pump-priming to combat recessions)—are compatible with neoliberalism.

However, as Brenner points out, Keynesian policies prevented the bankruptcy of many inefficient ("high-cost, low-profit") corporations so that market oversaturation continued just as potentially more efficient ("lower cost, higher-profit") companies were prevented from replacing them. But, given their weak performance and sluggish profits, these corporations were not in a position whereby they could exploit government patronage so as to upscale levels of capital investment or boost growth and productivity. Instead, Keynesian policies intended to pump-prime the economy by accelerating aggregate demand to expand sales did not succeed in elevating goods supply enough to match demand. This meant that the huge budget deficits ran up by governments in the 1970s simply generated stagflation (i.e. small increases in output alongside big price hikes). Moreover, precisely by offsetting or blunting recessionary pressures that would otherwise generate conditions for a new boom, Keynesian policies helped undermine restoration of growth and profits across the world economy as an aggregate.[316]

Brenner tells us that it was only with the Clinton administration in the USA (1993–2001) that all of the world's leading states (and hence the world economy) ditched Keynesianism as general policy—though corporate-supporting Keynesian-style remedies would still be used to prevent recessions spiralling or deepening uncontrollably and bankrupting firms considered as indispensable to economic health. Instead, during the 1990s, governments in the USA and UK consolidated and completed the neoliberal revolution that they began in the 1980s, whereas most other states embraced fiscal and monetary austerity.[317]

Neoliberalism is, as we have seen (and as Brenner sees it), a political ideology and policy agenda that has sought to restore capitalist profitability by removing all fetters or constraints on corporate activity. So, neoliberalism has driven policies of budget balancing in the USA and UK, leading to sharp contractions of public and welfare spending. This has also driven policies of trade liberalization, of deregulated finance markets, of privatization of public utilities, and of deregulated labour markets right across the world. As such, neoliberalism has oiled the wheels of global capitalist expansion and colonization of world economy. But the ascendancy of neoliberalism worldwide, says Brenner, has not resolved the crisis of profitability that has bedevilled world capitalism since the 1970s. Rather, this has, as he put it, simply "brought the accumulated contradictions of the previous decades to the forefront".[318] Policies of fiscal austerity and labour market deregulation are intended to boost profits by squeezing the income of the public sector and of ordinary wage-earners. Such policies bolstered corporate employers to raise

> productivity growth . . . not so much by increasing investment in advanced plant and equipment as by radically cutting back on jobs and compelling the employees who remain to take up the slack. Holding down wages as they squeezed more output per person, they appropriated to themselves in the form of profits an historically unprecedented share of the increase that took place in non-financial GDP.[319]

These policies have therefore reduced the growth of domestic demand throughout the world economy. This has compelled the MNCs and national capitalisms everywhere to radically upscale their orientation to exports, to find new markets abroad to compensate them for the reduced (in relative terms) consumer demand at home. A further ratcheting-up of international competition was thus, for Brenner, the necessary consequence of the neoliberal revolution. The consolidation of an international capitalist economy dominated by MNCs that are looking to build overseas markets is the effect of the current phase of export-driven growth. But this, as Brenner shows, has paved the way for a further serious upsizing of international productive overcapacity. It is this which has made the "globalization" period of capitalist development since the 1980s one of long-standing relative stagnation and of heightened market instability.

Corporate mega-capitalism, Brenner reminds us, has piled up unprecedented resources through its plundering of the countries and peoples of the world. So much so that the biggest corporations have incomes larger than whole national economies. However, over-capacity owing to over-competition ensures that these astronomical surpluses cannot be ploughed back into the real economy.[320] So, instead, corporations have been incentivized to sink vast amounts of this surplus capital into the banks, just as this also fuels a boom in executive salaries and conspicuous consumer spending by the corporate elite.[321] At the same time, low rates of corporate profit encourage the big companies to borrow from the banks to fund their operations rather than sustain these from their own shareholder value.[322]

Also, simultaneously, institutions of global financial management and leadership (such as the World Bank and the IMF), along with the US Federal Reserve, have sought to contain the increasingly frequent fluctuations in the business cycle and outright recessions by pumping billons more into the banking sector. This is not only to shore up zombie banks but also to lower the cost of borrowing. Financial institutions (supported by neoliberal governments) have in turn strived to boost profits in an international context of limited opportunity for investment opportunities in the material economy but with huge excess liquidity by relaxing controls on lending (hence financial deregulation) and looking to exploit alternative (often virtual) avenues of money-making outside the productive economy.[323]

These radical reductions in the cost of borrowing brought about by the excess liquidity of the banks then triggered, as Brenner shows, the stock market bubble-booms of the 1990s and 2000s (especially the dotcom and telecommunications bubbles), and along with this an orgy of corporate fraud (insider-trading, false accounting, the disguise of bad debts, misappropriation of funds, etc.). This happened as easy credit which could not be profitably invested in the "real" economy was instead ploughed into real estate, hedge funds, junk bonds, subprime markets, the expansion of commerce, various forms of financial speculation by pension companies, insurance companies, and the like. The banks also used a lot of the excess liquidity to stimulate popular consumption, not only by granting cheap loans and easy credit to virtually everyone who applied for them but by actively encouraging or inciting people to take these out. This gave rise to huge stock market expansion, radical contractions in the level of savings, and the massive rise of private and civilian debt—company, consumer, and household.[324]

But, of course, Brenner points out, none of this did anything to resolve the underlying structural problem of system-wide overcapacity. Rather, it simply papered it over and hid it from view, under the effervescence originating in the immaterial enchanted economy of Marx's "fictitious capital". This meant, Brenner said, that it was only the booming markets in stocks and shares, mortgage lending and debt-funded consumer spending that were holding off a new international recession or something worse.[325] This was a precipitous situation because "bubblenomics" could not last.[326] The late 1990s American boom collapsed into the recession of 2000–01, undermined by a 42 per cent drop in the profit rate in corporate manufacturing from 1997 to 2002, which decimated most of the new dot.com and telecom companies.[327]

Then, in 2007/09, 10 years after the publication of *Economics of Global Turbulence*, Brenner's prediction panned out—the "something worse" than recession duly materialized as the unsustainable consumer and housing booms petered out amid radical stock market revaluations.[328] Banks, which had been major engines of bubblenomics capitalism, by providing easy and cheap credit to both corporations and consumers, and by ploughing masses of surplus money-capital into the expansion of banking and commerce itself, were caught up in a massive crisis of liquidity. This was because they found that their profits were undermined by the accumulation of bad debts by consumers and companies owing to reckless lending. The banks responded to this sudden and (for them) unexpected crisis of liquidity by stopping lending to each other, by stopping lending to companies, and by stopping lending to consumers. Consequently, the stock market boom collapsed into the biggest financial meltdown since the Wall Street Crash of 1929, plunging the world economy into the biggest recession since the 1930s, the effects of which were still being felt going into the COVID-19 crisis.[329]

Now, governments of the developed countries have since, of course, responded to the new period of crisis by pouring billions more into the financial system to save insolvent banks, increase liquidity, and kick-start lending. This, of course, created massive budget deficits—such as the one in the UK. These budget deficits then motivated the new politics of austerity (or rather their radicalization) as governments sought to recover the deficits through huge public spending cuts and by forcing on public sector employees wage freezes. But this response (of pumping tens of billions into the banks) is likely eventually to fund yet another speculative bubble-boom, followed by another crash, rather than end the crisis. This is because it does nothing at all to address the underlying problem acutely diagnosed by Brenner of system-wide overcapacity and overproduction spun from the ratchet of ever-intensifying international inter-capitalist competition.

Moreover, austerity politics also undercuts the consumer demand that is needed to turn corporate surpluses into sales and profits. Brenner himself was undecided on the question of whether or not the great financial crisis of 2007/09 and long depression that followed would be sufficient to create conditions for the restoration of capitalist profits to boom-time thresholds.[330] However, it is clear that it did not, since stagnation economics have remained, probably owing to the fact that massive government corporate bailouts prevented a level of capital destruction and depreciation that would be sufficient to end the crisis. So, the long downturn is likely to continue for the foreseeable future, so that the great financial crash of 2007/09 and long depression that followed it is likely to be repeated sooner rather than later. Indeed, looking beyond Brenner, another prolonged episode of recession economics could be upon us already, triggered by the ongoing economic fallout from the COVID-19 pandemic. This is fundamentally because, as Brenner and other perceptive critics of capitalism have argued, the system has reached its limits.[331]

Certainly, the damage that has been inflicted globally by the pandemic on capitalist profitability has been punitive, and this has generated significant knock-on harms on the real, material economy. By the spring of 2020, as the first wave of the pandemic began to recede, and the first lockdowns were being released, the world economy was already in a deeper recession than that sparked off by the 2007/09 financial meltdown. Significant hikes in unemployment were by then already officially logged in the USA, Australia, South Korea, Germany, and China, ranging from 4.4 per cent to 5.9 per cent. Statistics from the USA and

China showed on the same timescale a dramatic slump in revenues from retail trade, of 15.8 per cent in China up to March 2020, and of 6.2 per cent in the USA from February through to April of that first Covid year. Data also indicated sharp contractions in general household spending during the first lockdowns. According to the PM1, a reading of less than 50 on the scale indicates a contraction of sales activity. The reading for the EU in the spring of 2020 was just 26.4, for the USA 39.8, for China 43.0, and for Japan 33.8.[332]

The same picture existed for manufacturing in that period. Again, on the PMI, the EU then had a reading of 44.5, the USA a reading of 49.2, Japan a reading of 44.8, and China of 50.1. Factory output was also significantly hit, with a drop of 5.5 per cent in China from December through to February 2020, and of 1.1 per cent in the USA from February through to March 2020. The WTO predicted a decline in world merchandise trade of between 12.9 per cent and 31.9 per cent for 2020, whereas the IMF predicted a three per cent contraction of global GDP for 2020 and $9 trillion of losses for 2020 and 2021 combined. The IMF also predicted that the worst contractions of 2020 would occur in the Eurozone. Whereas the US economy was expected to shrink by 5.9 per cent that year, those of Italy and Spain (the then Covid worst-hit countries in the EU on the cusp of spring 2020) were expected to shrink by 9.1 per cent and eight per cent, respectively, with a 7.5 per cent contraction across the EU as a whole.[333]

As it transpired, the GDP contractions were not as precipitous as the doom-laden forecasters predicted. Nonetheless, world GDP declined by 3.2 per cent in 2020, by six per cent in the EU, by 4.4 per cent on average in the HICs, and by 3.4 per cent in the USA.[334] The UK economy, labouring as it was under Boris Johnson's chaotic but reputedly "charismatic" leadership, the ill-effects of Brexit-driven severance from the European single market, and mismanagement of the pandemic, did far worse than those other countries in the EU (Spain, Italy, France), which were hardest hit by the pandemic. Indeed, the UK fared worse than all the G7 countries. GDP fell by a precipitous 9.7 per cent in 2020. This was the biggest drop in output since "reliable" records began in 1948. It is reckoned to be the largest contraction of the British economy since 1921.[335]

Nor have the predicted "robust bounce-backs" in economic performance after the lockdowns were lifted and the NPIs were scaled down since materialized. Aggregate output for the HICs was forecasted in 2021 to recover its pre-pandemic trajectory only by the end of 2022 and to exceed this only by 0.9 per cent in 2024. Worse, "aggregate output for the emerging market and developing economy group (excluding China) . . . [was] . . . expected to remain 5.5 per cent below the pre-pandemic forecast in 2024, resulting in a larger setback to improvements in their living standards".[336] Global GDP was just 3.5 per cent higher by the end of 2021 than it was in 2019.[337] The USA's GDP was just 2.3 per cent larger on that same timescale.[338] The EU's GDP was 0.2 per cent smaller by the close of 2021 than it was in 2019,[339] whereas the GDP of the HICs taken as an aggregate was just 0.6 per cent higher.[340] As for the UK, recovery has been even slower. Here GDP was still 2.3 per cent smaller by the close of 2021 than it was in 2019.[341] Even prior to the Russo–Ukrainian war, world GDP growth (WGP) was predicted to slow down in 2022 (to 4.9 per cent), languishing below the 2021 level (of 5.9 per cent), and was predicted to slow further in 2023 and 2024 (to around 3.3 per cent).[342]

Yet even the economic fallout from COVID-19 is unlikely to shake world capitalism out of its doldrums. It may be that the only solution (i.e. temporary resolution) to the crisis would be a much more catastrophic event—such as another world war.[343] Such would destroy and devalue so much of the global capital stock that over-capacity would be ended. This is how the Great Depression of the 1930s was ended—by World War Two, not by Keynesian policies, technological advance, the cheapening of consumer goods by Fordist mass production, or the beginnings of "globalization", as capitalist mythology suggests.[344] But, even if there was another world war (which cannot be ruled out as globalization theorists assert), or some other catastrophe (such as a pandemic even more destructive than COVID-19 has been), assuming that humanity could survive these events, the world would be back in the same economic bind as today, facing the same emergent structural roadblocks as now, just 30 or so years in the future.

Marx's famous lines of the *Communist Manifesto* written back in 1848 seem remarkably prescient today. Indeed, this is even more so than when Marx penned them:

> Modern bourgeois society . . . [having] conjured up such gigantic means of production and of exchange, is like the sorcerer who is no longer able to control the powers of the nether world whom he has called up by his spells.[345]

More so than ever before, human progress depends on transcending zombie capitalism. The alternative modes of economic management of the system—Keynesianism and neoliberalism—have both failed to restore it. The global crisis of capitalism reaffirms the necessity of Marx and confirms the correctness of Rosa Luxemburg's famous judgement made from a German prison cell in the midst of the slaughter of World War One that the choice facing humanity reduces to either socialism or barbarism.[346] As Teresa Hayter commented at the start of the 1990s, in the teeth and claw of the new period of global crisis, and with neoliberalism newly ascendant: "Sometimes it seems as though we are well on the way to barbarism. But there is still a choice".[347] Barbarism (as an integral aspect of neoimperial order) is the subject of the remaining chapters of this book.

Notes and references

1 Marx, K. and Engels, F. (1970). The German Ideology. [1846]. London: Lawrence and Wishart. See also the famous preface in: Marx, K. (1976). A Contribution to the Critique of Political Economy. [1859]. London: Lawrence and Wishart. For defences of Marx's socio-historical materialism see: Callinicos, A. (1987). Making

History: Agency, Structure and Change in Social Theory. Cambridge: Polity Press; Cohen, G.A. (1978). Karl Marx's Theory of History: A Defence. Oxford: Oxford University Press; Creaven, S. (2000). Marxism and Realism: A Materialistic Application of Realism in the Social Science. London and New York NY: Routledge; Creaven, S. (2007). Emergentist Marxism: Dialectical Philosophy and Social Theory. London and New York NY: Routledge, esp. pp. 142–213.

2 Marx, K. (1976). Capital. Vol. 1. [1867]. Harmondsworth: Penguin; Marx, K. (1956). Capital. Vol. 2. [1885]. Moscow: Progress Publishers; Marx, K. (1971). Capital. Vol. 3. [1894]. Moscow: Progress Publishers.

3 Marx (1971), p. 791.

4 Marx, K. (1976), pp. 165–6.

5 Marx (1976), p. 129.

6 Marx (1976), p. 131.

7 Marx (1976), pp. 739, 742.

8 Marx, K. and Engels, F. (1967). The Communist Manifesto. [1848]. Harmondsworth: Penguin.

9 See for example: Crosland, A. (1956). The Future of Capitalism. London: Jonathan Cape; Dahrendorf, R. (1959). Class and Class Conflict in Industrial Society. Stanford CA: Stanford University Press; Strachey, J. (1956). Contemporary Capitalism. London: Gollancz.

10 This is encouraged by the apocalyptic passages in the Manifesto rather than anything that appears in Marx's theoretical output.

11 Baudrillard, J. (1970). The Consumer Society: Myths and Structures. London: SAGE; Bell, D. (1973). The Coming of Post-Industrial Society. New York NY: Basic Books; Strachey (1956); Crosland (1956); Dahrendorf (1959).

12 Marx, K. and Engels, F. (1973). Selected Works. Vol. 3. Moscow: Progress Publishers, pp. 13–30.

13 Marx and Engels (1973), pp. 71–2.

14 Collier, A. (2004). Marx. Oxford: Oneworld, p. 153.

15 Marx, K. (1968). Theories of Surplus Value. Vol. 2. [1905]. Moscow: Progress Publishers, p. 566.

16 Mandel, E. (1983). 'Economics'. D. McLellan (ed) Marx: The First 100 Years. London: Fontana, pp. 204–8.

17 This was seen by Dahrendorf (1959, pp. 64–5) as an aspect of the "institutionalization of class conflict" that reconciled the working class to what he saw as a post-capitalist industrial order.

18 Westergaard, J. (1995). Who Gets What? The Hardening of Class Inequality in the Late Twentieth Century. Cambridge: Polity Press.

19 Lash, S. and Urry, J. (1987). The End of Organized Capitalism. Cambridge: Polity Press; Lash, J. and Urry, S. (1993). Economies of Signs and Space. Cambridge: Polity Press.

20 Institute for International Economics (2002). The Pattern of Economic Growth, 1950–2000. Ch. 2, p. 22. IIE.org (online).

21 IIE (2002), pp. 21–3.

22 Globalists may be considered as "cautious globalists" (globalization is happening) or as "hyper-globalists" (globalization has happened)—though the "boosters" (as Callinicos calls them) predominate. See: Callinicos, A. (2001). Against the Third Way. Cambridge: Polity Press, p. 19. Globalists may also be distinguished between enthusiasts and critics.

23 Albrow, M. (1996). The Global Age. Cambridge: Polity Press; Bauman, Z. (1998). Globalization: The Human Consequences. Cambridge: Polity Press; Crouch, C.

(2004). Post-Democracy. Cambridge: Polity Press; Fitzgerald, N. (1997). 'Harnessing the Potential of Globalisation for the Consumer and Citizen'. International Affairs, 73 (4), pp. 731–43; Forrester, V. (1999). The Economic Horror. Cambridge: Polity Press; Friedman, T. (1999). The Lexus and the Olive Tree: Understanding Globalization. New York NY: Farrar, Straus and Giroux; Giddens, A. (2002). Runaway World: How Globalisation Is Shaping our Lives. London: Profile Books; Gray, J. (1998). False Dawn: The Delusions of Global Capitalism. London: Granta; Hay, C. and Marsh, D. (2000). 'Demystifying Globalisation'. C. Hay and D. Marsh (eds) Demystifying Globalisation, Basingstoke: Palgrave Macmillan; Held, D. and McGrew, A. (2002). Governing Globalisation. Cambridge: Polity Press; Held, D. and McGrew, A. (eds) (2003). The Global Transformations Reader: An Introduction to the Globalisation Debate. Cambridge: Polity Press; Held, D. and McGrew, A. (2007). Globalization Theory: Approaches and Controversies. Cambridge: Polity Press; Holloway, J. (1995). 'Global Capital and the Nation State'. W. Bonefeld and J. Holloway (eds) Global Capital, National State and the Politics of Money. London: St Martin's Press; Holton, R. (2005). Making Globalisation. Basingstoke: Palgrave Macmillan; McMichael, P. (2000). Development and Social Change: A Global Perspective. Thousand Oaks CA: Pine Forge Press; Klein, M. (2005). No Logo: Taking Aim at the Brand Bullies. London: Harper-Collins; Marshall, A. and Horsman, M. (1997). After the Nation State: Citizens, Tribalism and the New World Disorder. London: Harper-Collins; Ohmae, K. (1990). The Borderless World: Power and Strategy in the Interlinked World. New York NY: Harper Business; Ohmae, K. (1995). The End of the Nation-State. New York NY: Free Press; Reich, R. (1991). The Work of Nations: Preparing Ourselves for 21st Century Capitalism. London: Simon and Schuster; Rosenau, J.N. (1997). Along the Domestic-Foreign Frontier: Exploring Governance in a Turbulent World. Cambridge: Cambridge University Press; Sklair, L. (1995). The Sociology of the Global System. Hemel Hempstead: Harvester Wheatsheaf; Sklair, L. (2002). Globalization, Capitalism and Its Alternatives. Oxford: Oxford University Press; Waters, M. (1995). Globalization. London and New York NY: Routledge; Wolf, M. (2004). Why Globalization Works: The Case for the Global Market Economy. New Haven CT: Yale University Press.

24 Baudrillard (1973); Bauman (1998); Waters (1995). This is the so-called "global postmodern".

25 Harman, C. (2009). Zombie Capitalism: Global Crisis and the Relevance of Marx. London: Bookmarks, p. 257.

26 Left-wing globalists who accept this perspective include Klein (2005)—who refers explicitly to "footloose" MNCs shifting effortlessly from place to place in search of the most favourable markets and employing "rootless" workers along the way; and Holloway (1995)—who accepts the absolute and immediate "within seconds" mobility of money-capital thesis. But this is also axiomatic for Bauman (1998) and Marshall and Horsman (1997).

27 Friedman (1999); Ohmae (1990, 1995); Wolf (2004).

28 Blair quoted in Pallast (2003), p. 142.

29 Bauman (1998); Gray (1998); Marshall and Horsman (1997); Sklair (1995, 2002).

30 For excellent critiques of globalization theory, from various sceptical standpoints, see: Anderson, P. (2000). 'Renewals'. New Left Review, 2 (1), pp. 11–4; Bull, H. (1979). 'Natural Law and International Relations'. British Journal of International Studies, 5 (2), pp. 171–81; Callinicos (2001); Castells, M. (1996). The Rise of the Network Society. The Information Age: Economy, Society, and Culture. Oxford: Blackwell, pp. 135, 137, 140; Creaven, S. (2005). 'Recovering Marx for the Twenty-First Century'. Journal of Critical Realism, 4 (1), pp. 128–66; Gilpin, R. (2001). Global Political Economy: Understanding the International Economic

Order. Princeton NJ: Princeton University Press; Gilpin, R. (1981). War and Change in World Politics. Cambridge: Cambridge University Press; Gordon, D. (1988). 'The Global Economy'. New Left Review, 168 (March/April), pp. 43–65; Harman, C. (1996). 'Globalisation: A Critique of a New Orthodoxy'. International Socialism, 2 (73), pp. 3–34; Harman (2009), pp. 257–70; Kozul-Wright, R. and Rayment, P. (2004). 'Globalization Reloaded'. No. 167. United Nations Conference on Trade and Development; Mann, M. (1994). 'As the Twentieth Century Ages'. New Left Review, 168 (March/April), pp. 26–22; Mosley, L. (2006). 'Globalisation and the State: Still Room to Move?' New Political Economy, 10 (3), pp. 355–62; O'Rourke, K.H. (2001). 'Tariffs and Growth in the Late 19th Century'. Economic Journal, 110 (463), pp. 456–83; Osterhammel, J. and Petersson, N.P. (2005). Globalization: A Short History. Princeton NJ: Princeton University Press; Ruigrok, W. and van Tulder, R. (1995). The Logic of International Restructuring: The Management of Dependencies in Rival Industrial Complexes. London: Routledge; Stopford, J.M. and Strange, S. (1991). Rival States, Rival Firms: Competition for World Market Shares. Cambridge: Cambridge University Press; Waltz, K.N. (1999). 'Globalization and Governance'. Political Science and Politics, 32 (4), pp. 693–700; Waltz, K.N. (1979). The Theory of International Politics. New York NY: McGraw-Hill; Zolo, D. (2002). Invoking Humanity: War, Law and Global Order. New York NY: Bloomsbury; Weiss, L. (1998). The Myth of the Powerless State: Governing the Economy in the Global Era. Cambridge: Cambridge University Press; Williamson, J.G. and O'Rourke, K.H. (1999). Globalization and History: The Evolution of a Nineteenth-century Atlantic Economy. Cambridge MA: MIT Press; Wood, E.M. (1998). 'Modernity, Postmodernity, or Capitalism?'. R.W. McChesney, E.M. Wood and J.B. Foster (eds) Capitalism and the Information Age. New York NY: Monthly Review Press.

31 Todd, E. (2004). After the Empire: The Breakdown of the American Order. London: Constable, p. 15.
32 Hirst, P. and Thompson, P. (1999). Globalization in Question: The International Economy and the Possibilities of Governance. 2nd edition. Cambridge: Polity Press.
33 WTO (2015). International Trade Statistics 2015. WTO (online), p. 19.
34 Marfleet, P. (1998). 'Globalisation and the Third World'. International Socialism, 2 (81), pp. 91–130.
35 WTO (2015), p. 26.
36 WTO (2018). 'World Trade Statistical Review 2017'. WTO (online), p. 50.
37 WTO (2015), p. 24.
38 SDG Pulse (2020). 'International Trade in Developing Economies'. SDG Pulse (online); UNCTAD (2020). 'Handbook of Statistics 2020'. UNCTAD (online).
39 SDG Pulse and United Nations Conference on Trade and Development (2023). 'Economic Transformation Progress Towards the SDGs through Trade'. SDG Pulse and UNCTAD (online).
40 WTO (2013). 'World Trade Report 2013'. WTO (online), pp. 57–8.
41 Ma, Y. (2023). 'China's Share in Global Exports 2016–2022'. Statista (online). (4 December).
42 SDG Pulse and UNCTAD (2023).
43 Nim, D. and Goh, K. (2023). 'India is Beginning to Punch Its Weight in Global Exports'. Economic Times (online). (8 June).
44 Marfleet (1998).
45 International Trade Centre (2019). 'Trade Map: Trade Statistics for International Business Development—2018'. ITC (online); UN (2020). 'International Trade in Developing Economies'. UNCTAD (online).

46 SDG Pulse and UNCTAD (2023).
47 WTO (2020). 'World Trade Report 2019: The Future of Services Trade'. WTO (online), p. 30.
48 SDG Pulse and UNCTAD (2023).
49 SDG Pulse (2020).
50 SDG Pulse and UNCTAD (2023).
51 WTO (2020), p. 6.
52 WTO (2020), p. 32.
53 WTO (2020), p. 33.
54 WTO (2018), p. 12.
55 Dunn, C. (2009). 'Myths of Globalisation and the New Economy'. International Socialism (online), 121 (Winter).
56 Dunn (2009).
57 Dunn (2009).
58 Perry, M. (2019). 'World's Top 10 Countries by Share of World Factory Output, 1970–2017'. Flourish: Data Visualisation and Story Telling (online). (5 July).
59 Drolia, A. (2023). 'Distribution Pattern of the World Manufacturing Output'. PRASA (online). (7 July); Safeguard Global (2023). 'Top Ten Manufacturing Countries in 2023'. SG Resource Center (online). (15 September).
60 Perry (2019).
61 Drolia (2023); Safeguard Global (2023).
62 Stefanovic, Z. (2008). 'Globalization: Theoretical Perspectives, Impacts and Institutional Response of the Economy'. Economics and Organization, 5 (3), pp. 263–72. See pp. 267–8.
63 Sklair (2002).
64 Rugman, A. (2005). 'Globalization and Regional International Production'. J. Ravenhill (ed) Global Political Economy. Oxford: Oxford University Press, p. 269.
65 Rugman (2005), p. 270.
66 Wood, E.M. (1998). 'Modernity, Postmodernity, or Capitalism?' R.W. McChesney, E.M. Wood and J.B. Foster (eds) Capitalism and the Information Age. New York NY: Monthly Review Press.
67 Harman (2009), p. 255.
68 OECD (2019). 'OECD International Direct Investment Statistics, 2009–2018'. OECD (online), pp. 18–9.
69 UNCTAD (2016). The World Investment Report 2016: Investor Nationality—Policy Challenges. Geneva: UNCTAD, p. 4.
70 UNCTAD (2017). The World Investment Report 2017: Investment and the Digital Economy. Geneva: UNCTAD, p. x.
71 UNCTAD (2018). The World Investment Report 2018: Investing in Sustainable Energy for All. Geneva: UNCTAD, p. 61; UNCTAD (2020). The World Investment Report 2020: International Production Beyond the Pandemic. Geneva: UNCTAD, p. 61.
72 UNCTAD (2021). The World Investment Report 2021: Investing in Sustainable Recovery. Geneva: UNCTAD, p. 72.
73 UNCTAD (2022). The World Investment Report 2022: International Tax Reforms and Sustainable Development. Geneva: UNCTAD, p. 7.
74 UNCTAD (2002). The World Investment Report 2002: Transnational Corporations and Export Competitiveness. Geneva: UNCTAD, p. 7.
75 This calculation is distilled from the UNCTAD World Investment Reports from 2003 to 2014.
76 UNCTAD (2015–2022).

77 See also: UNCTAD (2015). The World Investment Report 2015: Reforming International Investment Governance. Geneva: UNCTAD; UNCTAD (2018). The World Investment Report 2018: Investment and New Industrial Policies. Geneva: UNCTAD; UNCTAD (2019). The World Investment Report 2019: Special Economic Zones. Geneva: UNCTAD. See also: UNCTAD (2016, 2017).
78 Hoogvelt, A. (2001). Globalization and the Post-Colonial World: The New Political Economy of Development. 2nd edition. London: Palgrave Macmillan, p. 77.
79 UNTACD (2002), p. 7.
80 UNTACD (2019), p. xiii.
81 UNTACD (2016, 2017, 2018, 2019, 2020).
82 UNTACD (2019), p. 12.
83 This is a constant of the period here under review—as is noted by all of the UNTACD world investment reports (UNTACD, 2015–22).
84 UNTACD (2016), pp. 4–5.
85 UNTACD (2019), p. 4.
86 UNTACD (2019), p. 49.
87 UNCTAD (2023a). Regional Trends—Developing Asia. UNTACD (online). The developing world took 70 per cent of global FDI in 2022. This result suggests that the developed countries "anomalously" reduced share of 2020 may not be anomalous, after all. Time will tell. Even so, per capita FDI inflows remain 3.5 times higher in the developed countries than in the developing ones.
88 UNTACD (2019), pp. 40–1.
89 UNTACD (2023a).
90 UNTACD (2019), p. 49.
91 UNCTAD (2023b). 'Regional Trends—Latin America and the Caribbean'. UNTACD (online); UNCTAD (2023c). The World Investment Report 2023: Investing in Sustainable Energy for All. Geneva: UNTADC, p. 13.
92 Hayter (1990), pp 77–9; Barnet and Muller (1974).
93 UNCTAD (2019), p. xi.
94 Hayter (1990), pp. 77–9; Barnet and Muller (1974).
95 Calderon, C. and Loayza, N. (2004). 'Greenfield Foreign Direct Investment and Mergers and Acquisitions: Feedback and Macroeconomic Effects'. World Bank (online), pp. 15–6.
96 Harms, P. and Meon, P.-G. (2011). 'An FDI Is an FDI Is an FDI? The Growth Effects of Greenfield Investment and Mergers and Acquisitions in Developing Countries'. Working Paper No. 11. EconStore (online), p. 27.
97 Danakol, S.H. et al. (2017). 'Foreign Direct Investment via M&A and Domestic Entrepreneurship: Blessing or Curse?' Small Business Economics, 48 (3), pp. 1–30; Neto, P., Brandao, A. and Cirqueira, A. (2008). 'The Impact of FDI, Cross Border Mergers and Acquisitions and Greenfield Investments on Economic Growth'. (October). Research Gate (online).
98 Danakol et al. (2017), p. 3.
99 Hoogvelt, A. (1997). Globalisation and the Post-Colonial World: The New Political Economy of Development. London: Palgrave Macmillan.
100 Pilger, J. (1999). Hidden Agendas. London: Vintage, p. 75.
101 UNTACD (2019), pp. 66, 67.
102 UNTACD (2023c, pp. xv, 6; 2022, p. 16; 2021, p. 80).
103 UNTACD (2016), p. 4.
104 UNTACD (2019), pp. 34, 35.
105 UNTACD (2014, p. 37; 2020, p. 28; 2019, p. 28; 2018, p. 34; 2017, p. 44; 2016, p. 38; 2015, p. 32).

106 UNTACD (2023c), p. 10.
107 UNTACD (2022), p. 12.
108 UNTACD (2021, p. 28; 2020, p. 38; 2019, p. 28; 2018, p. 34; 2017, p. 44; 2016, p. 38; 2015, p. 32).
109 UNTACD (2014, p. 61; 2020, p. 46; 2019, p. 48; 2018, p. 50; 2017, p. 57; 2016, p. 51; 2015, p. 58).
110 UNTACD (2014), p. 61.
111 UNTACD (2018), p. 50.
112 UNTACD (2019, p. 48; 2018, p. 50; 2017, p. 57; 2016, p. 51; 2015, p. 58).
113 UNTACD (2020, p. 56; 2020, p. 46).
114 Harman (1996).
115 These are, respectively, Noam Chomsky's and Mark Curtis's terms for the anonymous victims-at-a-distance beyond-our-borders of American and Western economic and political domination. See: Branfman, F. (2012). 'When Chomsky Wept'. Salon (online). (17 June); Chomsky, N. (2012). 'Recognizing the "Unpeople"'. Truthout (online). (7 January); Curtis, M. (2004). Unpeople: Britain's Secret Human Rights Abuses. London: Vintage.
116 UNTACD (2010). 'World Investment Report: Investing in a Low Carbon Economy'. UNCTAD (online), p. 3.
117 World Bank (2023a). 'Foreign Direct Investment, Net Outflows (% of GDP)'. World Bank (online); World Bank (2023b). 'Foreign Direct Investment, Net Inflows (% of GDP)'. World Bank (online).
118 World Bank (2023a, 2023b).
119 UNCTAD (2010), p. 3.
120 UNCTAD (2011, p. x; 2012, p. xi; 2013, p. ix; 2014, p. ix; 2015, p. x; 2016, p. x).
121 UNCTAD (2017, p. x; 2018, p. 2; 2019, p. x).
122 UNTACD (2020). 'World Investment Report 2020: International Production Beyond the Pandemic'. UNTACD (online), p. 11.
123 UNCTAD (2021). 'Global FDI Flows Down 42% in 2020'. Investments Trends Monitor (online), Issue 38. (January).
124 UNCTAD (2023), p. xiv.
125 UNCTAD (2017, p. x; 2018, p. 2; 2019, p. x).
126 UNCTAD (2021).
127 UNCTAD (2017, p. x; 2018, p. 2; 2019, p. x; 2021).
128 UNCTAD (2020, p. 8) predicted that the greater negative economic impacts of the COVID-19 crisis looking ahead would likely be the developing countries. "Developing economies as a group are expected to see a larger decrease in the range of 30 per cent to 45" of FDI in 2021. This did not come to pass.
129 UNCTAD (2023c), p. xv; UNCTAD (2021), p. x.
130 UNCTAD (2023c), p. xiv; UNCTAD (2022), p. x.
131 In the midst of the neoliberal age of capitalist "globalization", less than half of the countries of the world, according to Freedom House and the Economic Intelligence Unit, can be reasonably classified as being under democratic governance (in the limited liberal sense of democracy). This is by virtue of being subject to free and open elections of rulers or governing parties, relatively free of political corruption, with developed civil rights entitlements, formal legal equality, and so on. Many others that are classed as democratic are "flawed democracies" (i.e. with corruption in the political and legal apparatuses and processes, undeveloped rights cultures, factionalized electoral competition, under-representation of minorities in party, government and state). According to the Pew Research Center, only 20 per cent of countries have "fully consolidated democracies". See:

Desilver, D. (2019). 'Despite Global Concerns about Democracy, More Than Half of Countries Are Democratic'. Pew Research Center (online). (14 May); Freedom House (2019). 'Freedom in the World 2019: Freedom in Retreat'. Freedomhouse.org (online); Economist Intelligence Unit (2021). 'Democracy Index 2020: In Sickness and in Health?'. EIU.org (online).

This explains the high levels of popular dissatisfaction with democracy across the world. Or, rather, of popular dissatisfaction with liberal democracy—the only form of democracy that capitalist states, superordinate classes, and economic elites will easily tolerate in the corporate-global world. According to polls conducted by the Pew Research Center, across 27 countries classed under the Polity criteria as full democracies, only 45 per cent of people expressed satisfaction with the way that democracy was working in their own countries, whereas 51 per cent expressed dissatisfaction. Public discontent was mostly due to perceptions that "elections bring little change, that politicians are corrupt and out of touch, and that courts do not treat people fairly". This discontent was also shaped by perceptions that economic opportunities to improve living standards were unfairly blocked and monopolized by remote uncaring elites. In Europe, other discontents centred on concerns about immigration, dissatisfaction with the EU, and favourable views of populist parties (of left and right). See: Wike, R., Silver, L. and Castillo, A. (2019). 'Many Across the Globe Are Dissatisfied with How Democracy Is Working'. Pew Research Center (online). (29 April).

132 Giddens, A. (1994). Beyond Left and Right: The Future of Radical Politics. Cambridge: Cambridge University Press.
133 Held, D. (1991). 'Democracy and Globalization'. Alternatives, 16, pp. 201–8; Held, D. (1991). 'Democracy, the Nation-State and the Global System'. Economy and Society, 20 (2), pp. 138–72.
134 This is the "competition state" theory, as Luke Martell describes it. See: Martell, L. (2010). The Sociology of Globalization. Cambridge: Polity Press.
135 Gourevitch, P. (1986). Politics in Hard Times: Comparative Responses to International Economic Crises. Ithaca NY: Cornell University Press; Garrett, G. and Lange, P. (1991). 'Political Responses to Interdependence: What's "Left" for the Left'. International Organization, 45 (4), pp. 539–64.
136 Gourevitch (1986), p. 33.
137 Garrett and Lange (1991), p. 541.
138 Blair quoted in: Callinicos, A. (2001). Against the Third Way. Cambridge: Polity Press, p. 16.
139 Rosenau, J.N. (1990). Turbulence in World Politics. Brighton: Harvester Wheatsheaf.
140 UNCTAD (2020), p. 23.
141 Keohane and Gilpin (1987).
142 Gilpin (1979).
143 Harman, C. (1991). 'The State and Capitalism Today'. International Socialism, 2 (51), pp. 3–56; Stopford and Strange (1991).
144 Bull (1979).
145 Harris (1987), p. 202.
146 Waltz (1979).
147 Waltz (1979), p. 185.
148 Harman (1996), p. 6.
149 Gordon (1988), p. 63.
150 Frontline (2014). 'Timeline of the Panic'. PBS: Frontline (online).
151 Frontline (2014).

152 The final liability of the US government's rescue of its big banks in the aftermath of the 2007/09 financial crisis has retrospectively been estimated at between $498 billion and $4.6 trillion. See: Harbert, T. (2019). 'Here's How Much the 2008 Bailouts Really Cost'. (21 February); Taibbi, M. (2019). 'Turns Out That Trillion-Dollar Bailout Was, in Fact, Real'. Rolling Stone (online). (18 March). The cost of the UK government's bailout of its own corporate-finance sector was estimated at £850 billion by the end of 2009, though part of this was repaid over the next few years. See: Grice, A. (2009). '850bn: Official Cost of the Bank Bailout'. Independent (online). (4 December).
153 Barmes, D. (2020). 'Bank of England Provides £7.5 Billion in Big Business Bailouts—Hidden from Public View'. Positive Money (online). (April); Eisinger, J. (2020). 'How the Coronavirus Bailout Repeats 2008's Mistakes: Huge Corporate Payoffs with Little Accountability'. ProPublica (online). (7 April); Whoriskey, P., MacMillan, D. and O'Connell, J. (2020). '"Doomed to Fail": Why a $4 Trillion Bailout Couldn't Revive the American Economy'. Washington Post (online). (5 October).
154 Callinicos (2001), p. 109.
155 Argentina defaulted in 2001, in response to the Latin American slump that was triggered by the Southeast Asian financial crisis of 1997/98.
156 Ruigrock, W. and van Tulder, R. (1995). The Logic of International Restructuring: The Management of Dependencies in Rival Industrial Complexes. London: Routledge, p. 218.
157 Harman (1995), pp. 64, 65–6; Harman (2009), pp. 233–4.
158 Stopford and Strange (1995); Harman (1991), pp. 8, 12, 34–5.
159 Ruigrock and van Tulder (1995).
160 Harman (1991), pp. 33, 35.
161 Stopford and Strange (1991), p. 1.
162 Harman (1991), p. 13.
163 Harman (1991), pp. 12–3.
164 Ruigrock and van Tulder (1995), p. 164. My emphasis.
165 Harman (1996), pp. 14–5, 19; Harman (2009), pp. 258–9.
166 Hence, globalism acquires a superficial plausibility by virtue especially of the massive expansion of FDI since the 1980s This increased from four per cent of the value of world output in 1982 to 36 per cent by 2007 (Harman, 2009, p. 255).
167 de Brunhoff, S. (1999). 'Which Europe Do We Need Now? Which Can We Get?' R. Bellofiore (ed) Global Money, Capital Restructuring, and the Changing Patterns of Labour. Cheltenham: Edward Elgar, p. 50.
168 Bryan, D. (2001). 'Global Accumulation and Accounting for National Economic Identity'. Review of Radical Political Economy, 33 (1), pp. 55–77.
169 Bryan (2001), p. 61.
170 Castells (1996), p. 147.
171 Creaven (2005), p. 158. See also: Anderson, P. (2000). 'Renewals'. New Left Review, 2 (1), pp. 11–4; Callinicos (2001), p. 7; Castells, M. (1996), pp. 135, 137, 140.
172 Birchall, I. (1985). Bailing Out the System: Reformist Socialism in Western Europe 1944–1983. London: Bookmarks.
173 Cliff, T. and Gluckstein, D. (1996). The Labour Party: A Marxist History. 2nd edition. London: Bookmarks; Miliband, R. (1961). Parliamentary Socialism: A Study in the Politics of Labour. London: Merlin Press.
174 Harman (2009), p. 325.
175 Marx, K. (1934). 'Wage Labour and Capital'. [1849]. K. Marx and F. Engels (eds) Selected Works of Marx and Engels. London: Lawrence and Wishart, pp. 256–6.

176 Marx (1976, 1956, 1971).
177 Marx (1976), pp. 272–3, 279–80, 300–1.
178 Marx (1976), p. 342.
179 Marx, K. (1973). Grundrisse. [1939]. Harmondsworth: Penguin, p. 414.
180 Marx, K. (1963). Early Writings. T. Bottomore (ed) London: Penguin, p. 122.
181 Marx (1976), p. 582.
182 Marx (1976), p. 342.
183 Marx (1976), pp. 325, 344–5, 346.
184 Marx (1976), pp. 739, 742.
185 Harman (1995), pp. 48–52.
186 Marx (1976), pp. 1021, 1024.
187 Marx quoted by Harman, C. (1989). 'From Feudalism to Capitalism'. International Socialism, 2 (45), pp. 35–88. See p. 37.
188 Malone, T. (2018). 'The Zombies of Karl Marx: Horror in Capitalism's Wake'. Literary Hub (online). (31 October).
189 Marx (1976), p. 741.
190 Baudrillard (1970); Bauman, Z. (2007). Consuming Life. Cambridge: Polity Press.
191 Sklair, L. (2012). 'Culture-ideology of Consumerism'. G. Ritzer (ed) The Wiley Blackwell Encyclopedia of Globalization. Oxford: Wiley-Blackwell.
192 Bauman (2007).
193 Marx, K. (1973). 'A Contribution to the Critique of Political Economy'. K. Marx and Engels, F. (1973). Selected Works. Vol. 1. Moscow: Progress Publishers, pp. 503–4.
194 Foster, J.B. (2002). Ecology against Capitalism. New York NY: Monthly Review Press.
195 Harman (1995), p. 88.
196 Skidelsky, R. (2009). Keynes: The Return of the Master. London: Allen Lane, pp. 116, 118, 126.
197 DeLong, B. (1998). Estimating World GDP, One Million B.C.—Present. University College Berkeley CA: Department of Economics. (24 May); World Bank (2020). GDP Growth (Annual %)—World. World Bank.org (online).
198 World Bank (2023). 'GDP Growth (Annual %)—World'. World Bank (online).
199 OECD (2023a). 'Restoring Growth'. OECD Economic Outlook (online). (November).
200 OECD (2023b). 'A Long Unwinding Road'. OECD Economic Outlook (online). (June).
201 OECD (2023a).
202 Herring, C.R. (2002). East Asian Financial Cooperation. New York NY: Columbia University Press, p. 16.
203 Marglin, S.A. and Schor, J.B. (1990). The Golden Age of Capitalism: Reinterpreting the Postwar Experience. Oxford: Clarendon Press, p. 1.
204 World Bank (2020). 'GDP Growth (Annual %)—OECD Members'. World Bank (online).
205 World Bank (2023). 'GDP Growth (Annual %)—OECD Members'. World Bank (online).
206 OECD (2023b).
207 OECD (2023a).
208 Carlin, W. (1993). West German Growth and Institutions, 1945–90. London: University College London; Clark, D. (2020). 'Annual Growth of Gross Domestic Product (GDP) in the United Kingdom from 1949 to 2019'. Statista (online). (12 November); Country Economy (2020). 'France GDP—Gross Domestic Product: GDP France

1960'. Countryeconomy (online); Crafts, N.F.R. (1994). The Golden Age of Economic Growth in Western Europe, 1950–73. Warwick Economic Research Papers, No. 427. Department of Economics: University of Warwick; Eichengreen, B. and Ritschl, A. (2008). Understanding West German Economic Growth in the 1950s. SFB649 Discussion Paper 2008–68. University of California and London School of Economics (18 November); Fukao, M. (2003). 'Japanese Financial Deregulation and Market Discipline'. E. Demaestri and P. Masci (eds) Financial Crises in Japan and Latin America. Washington DC: Inter-American Development Bank; Gov.au (2001). 'Australia's Century since Federation at a Glance'. Treasury (online); O'Neill, A. (2021). 'Annual GDP Growth for the United States 1930–2020'. Statista (online). (5 January); Payne, C. (2011). 'Economic Revival of West Germany in the 1950s and 1960s'. E-International Relations (online) (7 August); Winslott-Hiselius, W. (2014). 'Annual GDP Growth in Sweden, 1950–2010'. ResearchGate (online). (July 2014); Trading Economics (2020). 'United Kingdom GDP Annual Growth Rate 1956–2020'. TE (online). Accessed: 09/01/21; Trading Economics (2020). 'France GDP Annual Growth Rate 1950–2020'. TE (online). Accessed: 09/01/21; World Bank (2020). 'GDP Growth (Annual %)—United Kingdom'. World Bank (online); World Bank (2020). 'GDP Growth (Annual %)—United States'. World Bank (online); World Bank (2020). 'GDP Growth (Annual %)—Australia'. World Bank (online); World Bank (2020). 'GDP Growth (Annual %)—Canada'. World Bank (online); World Bank (2020). 'GDP Growth (Annual %)—France'. World Bank (online); World Bank (2020). 'GDP Growth (Annual %)—Germany'. World Bank (online); World Bank (2020). 'GDP Growth (Annual %)—Italy'. World Bank (online); World Bank (2020). 'GDP Growth (Annual %)—Japan'. World Bank; World Bank (2020). 'GDP Growth (Annual %)—Sweden'. World Bank (online).

209 Statista (2024). 'Gross Domestic Product (GDP) Growth Rates of G7 Countries from 2000 to 2023'. Statista (online).

210 Statista (2024). 'Australia: Real Gross Domestic Product (GDP) Growth Rate from 2018 to 2028'. Statista (online).

211 World Bank (2020). 'GDP Growth (Annual %)—Euro Area'. World Bank (online).

212 World Bank (2020). 'GDP Growth (Annual %)—North America'. World Bank (online).

213 World Bank (2020). 'GDP Growth (Annual %)—East Asia and Pacific'. World Bank (online).

214 World Bank (2020). 'GDP Growth (Annual %)—Latin America and the Caribbean'. World Bank (online).

215 World Bank (2020). 'GDP Growth (Annual %)—Sub-Saharan Africa'. World Bank (online).

216 Herring (2002), p. 16.

217 World Bank (2020). 'GDP Growth (Annual %)—South Asia'. World Bank (online).

218 World Bank (2023). 'GDP Growth (Annual %)—Euro area'. World Bank (online). World Bank (online).

219 World Bank (2023). 'GDP Growth (Annual %)—North America'. World Bank (online).

220 World Bank (2023). 'GDP Growth (Annual %)—Sub-Saharan Africa'. World Bank (online).

221 Macrotrends (2023). 'East Asia & Pacific GDP Growth Rate 1961–2024'. Macrotrends (online).

222 World Bank (2023). 'GDP Growth (Annual %)—South Asia'. World Bank (online).

223 OECD (2023b).

224 Roberts, M. (2016). The Long Depression: How It Happened, Why It Happened, and What Happens Next. Chicago IL: Haymarket Books, p. 24.

225 Roberts (2016), p. 22.
226 Roberts (2016), pp. 24–5.
227 Brenner (2006), p. 7.
228 Shaikh, A.M. and Tonak, E.A. (1994). Measuring the Wealth of Nations. Cambridge: Cambridge University Press, p. 124.
229 Brenner (2006), p. 7.
230 Roberts (2016), p. 24.
231 Relevant contributions include: Alemi, P. and Foley, D.K. (1997). 'The Circuit of Capital, US Manufacturing and Non-Financial Corporate Business Sectors, 1947–993'. (online). (September). See p. 16; Duménil, G. and Lévy, D. (2005). 'The Real and Financial Components of Profitability (United States, 1952–2000)'. Review of Radical Political Economics, 36 (1), p. 82–110; Harman, C. (2007). 'The Rate of Profit and the World Today'. International Socialism, 115 (Summer), pp. 141–61; Harman, C. (2008). 'Economic Crisis: Capitalism Exposed'. Socialist Review (February); Kliman, A. (2008). 'A Crisis at the Centre of the System'. International Socialism, 120 (Autumn), pp. 61–76; Kliman, A. (2009). '"The Destruction of Capital" and the Current Economic Crisis'. Socialist Democracy (online); Michl, T. (1988). 'Why Is the Rate of Profit Still Falling?' Working Paper No. 7. Jerome Levy Economics Institute. (September). SSRN e-Library; Moseley, F. (1991). The Falling Rate of Profit in the Postwar United States Economy. Basingstoke: Macmillan. Moseley, F. (1997). 'The Rate of Profit and the Future of Capitalism'. Review of Radical Political Economics, 29 (4), pp. 23–41; Moseley, F. (2009). 'The US Economic Crisis: Causes and Consequences'. International Socialist Review, 64 (March/April); Moseley, F. (1999). 'The Decline of the Rate of Profit in the Post-War United States Economy: Due to Increased Competition or Increased Unproductive Labour?' Historical Materialism: Research in Critical Marxist Theory, 4 (1), pp. 131–48; Shaikh, A. (1999). 'Explaining the Global Economic Crisis'. Historical Materialism: Research in Critical Marxist Theory, 5 (1), pp. 103–44; Tutan, U. and Campbell, A. (2005). 'The Post 1960 Rate of Profit in Germany'. Working Paper 05/01. Izmir University (Turkey): Department of Economics. EconPapers (online); Wolff, E. (2003). 'What's Behind the Rise in Profitability in the US in the 1980s and 1990s'. Cambridge Journal of Economics, 27 (4), pp. 479–99.
232 Harman (2009), pp. 195–6.
233 Roberts (2016), p. 60.
234 Choonora, J. (2018). 'The Political Economy of a Long Depression'. International Socialism, 158 (Spring).
235 Harman (2009), p. 232.
236 World Bank (2021). 'Gross Capital Formation (% of GDP)'. World Bank (online).
237 Harman (1999), pp. 587, 593–6. See also: Fermont, C. (1998). 'Indonesia: The Inferno of Revolution'. International Socialism, 2 (80), pp. 17–47; Fischer, S. (1998). 'The IMF and the Asian Crisis'. IMF (online). (20 March); Frontline (2014). 'The Crash: Timeline of the Panic'. Public Broadcast Service: WBGH Educational Foundation (online). Gyoung-Hee, S. (1998). 'The Crisis and the Workers' Movement in South Korea'. International Socialism, 2 (78), pp. 39–54; IMF (2000). 'Recovery From the Asian Crisis and the Role of the IMF'. IMF (online). (June); Kaufman, G.G., Krueger, T.H., Hunter, W.C. (1999). The Asian Financial Crisis: Origins, Implications and Solutions. New York NY: Springer; Corporate Finance Institute (2021). What Is the Asian Financial Crisis? CFI (online); Rasiah, R., Cheong, K.-C. and Doner, R. (2014). 'Southeast Asia and the Asian and Global Economic Crisis'. Journal of Contemporary Asia, 44 (4), pp. 572–80. Malaysia successfully countered the crisis by barring capital exports and declining IMF loans and austerity. See Callinicos, A. (2001). Against the Third Way. Cambridge: Polity

Press, pp. 84–5, 101–2, 109; Blustein, P. (2001). The Chastening: Inside the Crisis that Rocked the Global Financial System and Humbled the IMF. New York NY: Public Affairs.

238 Creaven, S. (2003). 'Marx and Bhaskar on the Dialectics of Freedom'. Journal of Critical Realism, 2 (1), pp. 63–94. See pp. 79–80; Harman, C. (2002). 'Argentina: Rebellion at the Sharp End of the World Crisis'. International Socialism, 2 (94), pp. 3–47. See also: Harman (2009), p. 230.

239 Callinicos, A. (1994). 'Crisis and Class Struggle in Europe Today'. International Socialism, 2 (63), pp. 3–48; Callinicos, A. (1999). 'Reformism and Class Polarisation in Europe'. International Socialism, 2 (85), pp. 3–26.

240 Choonora, J. (2009). Unravelling Capitalism: A Guide to Marxist Political Economy. London: Bookmarks, p. 86.

241 Roberts (2016), p. 63.

242 Roberts (2016), pp. 68, 107.

243 UNCTAD (2022). 'Trade Development Report 2022: Development Prospects in a Fractured World'. UNCTAD (online).

244 Sobhan, R. (1992). 'Rethinking the Market Reform Paradigm'. Economic and Political Weekly, 27 (30) (25 July), pp. 66–72.

245 Taylor, M. (2002). 'Success for Whom? A Historical-Materialist Critique of Neoliberalism in Chile'. Historical Materialism: Research in Critical Marxist Theory, 10 (2), pp. 45–76. See pp. 51–4.

246 Taylor (2002), p. 52.

247 Taylor (2002), p. 52.

248 Taylor (2002), p. 56.

249 Pilger, J. (1999), p. 64.

250 Taylor (2002), p. 54.

251 Pilger (1999), p. 64.

252 Taylor (2002), p. 54.

253 World Bank (2021). 'GDP Growth (Annual %)—Chile, 1961–2019'. World Bank (online).

254 Taylor (2002), p. 67.

255 Gammage, S., Alburquerque, T. and Durán, G. (2014). Poverty, Inequality and Employment in Chile. Geneva: International Labour Office (ILO), p. 7.

256 Taylor (2002), p. 67.

257 Taylor (2002), p. 68.

258 Gammage et al. (2014), p. 8.

259 Taylor (2002), pp. 67–8.

260 Gammage et al. (2014), p. 10.

261 BBC News (2019). 'Chile Protests: Is Inequality Becoming Worse?' (21 October).

262 Harman (2009), p. 233.

263 Harman (1984), p. 10; Harman (1995), pp. 78–9, 93.

264 Samuelson quoted in Harman (1995), p. 37.

265 Cited in Roberts (2016), p. 65.

266 Bordo, M., Eichengreen, B., Klingsbiel, D. and Martinez-Peria, M. (2001). 'Is the Crisis Problem Growing More Severe? Economic Policy, 32 (April), pp. 51–82.

267 Roberts, M. (2013). 'From Global Slump to Long Depression'. International Socialism, 40. (Autumn); Roberts, M. (2016). The Long Depression: Marxism and the Global Crisis of Capitalism. Chicago IL: Haymarket Books.

268 Bhaskar, R. (1993). Dialectic: The Pulse of Freedom. London: Verso, pp. 248, 265.

269 Bivens, J., Fieldhouse, A. and Shierholz, H. (2013). From Free-Fall to Stagnation: Five Years After the Start of the Great Recession, Extraordinary Policy Measures

Are Still Needed, but Are Not Forthcoming. Briefing Paper #355. Economic Policy Institute. (14 February); Caritas Europa (2014). The European Crisis and Its Human Cost: A Call for Fair Alternatives and Solutions. Caritas Europa: Crisis Monitoring Report 2014; Cummins, M. and Ortiz, I. (2019). Austerity: The New Normal—A Renewed Washington Consensus 2010–24. IPD, ITUC, PSI, EURODAD and BWP: Social Sciences Research Network (online). (October); Dao, M.C. and Loungani, P. (2010). 'The Tragedy of Unemployment'. Finance and Development, 47 (4), pp. 22–5; Hurd, M.D. and Rohwedder, S. (2010). Effects of the Financial Crisis and Great Recession on American Households. Discussion Paper 09/2010-406. Netspar: Network for Studies on Pensions, Aging and Retirement (online); International Labour Organization (2015). The Decade of Adjustment. A Review of Austerity Trends 2010–2020 in 187 Countries. ESS Paper Series (SECSOC) 53. (30 November). Leventi, C., Levy, H., Matsaganis, M., Paulus, A. and Sutherland, H. (2010). Modelling the Distributional Effects of Austerity Measures: The Challenges of a Comparative Perspective. Social Europe: The European Commission; Oxfam (2013). A Cautionary Tale: The True Cost of Austerity and Inequality in Europe. Briefing Paper 174. (September); Oxfam (2013). 'The True Cost of Austerity and Inequality: UK Case Study'. Oxfam (online). (September); Verick, S. and Islam, I. (2010). The Great Recession of 2008–2009: Causes, Consequences and Policy Responses. IZA Discussion Series: Paper No. 4934. (May).

270 Alexander, D. (2010). 'The Impact of the Economic Crisis on the World's Poorest Countries'. Global Policy (online). (27 January).

271 Dao and Loungani (2010), p. 3; IMF and ILO (2010). The Challenges of Growth, Employment and Social Cohesion. Joint ILO-IMF conference in cooperation with the office of the Prime Minister of Norway. Discussion Document (13 September), p. 4.

272 ILO (2014). 'Global Employment Trends 2014: The Risk of a Jobless Recovery'. ILO (online).

273 IMF and ILO (2010); UN (2009). Voices of the Vulnerable: The Economic Crisis from the Ground Up. New York NY: GIVAS (UN).

274 Alexander (2010).

275 Merle, R. (2018). 'A Guide to the Financial Crisis—10 Years Later'. Washington Post (online). (10 September).

276 Arias, M.A. and Wen, Y. (2016). 'Recovery from the Great Recession has Varied Around the World'. Regional Economist. Federal Reserve Bank of St Louis (online); Chatham House (2018). 'The Lasting Effects of the Financial Crisis Have Yet to Be Felt'. Chatham House (online); Chen, W., Mrkaic, M. and Nabar, N. (2019). The Global Economic Recovery 10 Years After the 2008 Financial Crisis. IMF Working Paper 19/83; Lund, S., Mehta, A., Manyika, J. and Goldstein, D. (2018). 'A Decade After the Global Financial Crisis: What Has (and What Hasn't) Changed?' McKinsey Global Institute (online).

277 ILO (2014). 'Global Employment Trends 2014: The Risk of a Jobless Recovery'. ILO (online).

278 Stuckler, D. and Basu, S. (2013). The Body Economic: Why Austerity Kills. New York NY: Basic Books.

279 McKee, M., Karanikolos, M., Belcher, P. and Stuckler, D. (2012). 'Austerity: A Failed Experiment on the People of Europe'. Clinical Medicine, 12 (4), pp. 346–50; Lane, J.-E. (2013). 'Austerity Politics and the EU Debt Crisis'. Comparative Government and European Policy, 11 (3), pp. 369–86.

280 Wolf and Krugman cited in Yanushevsky, R. and Yanushevsky, C. (2018). Applied Macroeconomics for Public Policy. San Diego CA: Academic Press, p. 87.

281 Yanushevsky and Yanushevsky (2018), p. 88.
282 Harman (2009), pp. 191–5; Ormerod, P. (1994). The Death of Economics. London: Faber and Faber.
283 Harman (2009), p. 9; Harman (1984), pp. 10–11; Harman, C. (1996). 'The Crisis of Bourgeois Economics'. International Socialism, 2 (71), pp. 3–56.
284 Colander, D. et al. (2009). The Financial Crisis and the Systemic Failure of Academic Economics. Kiel Working Paper 1489. Kiel Institute for the World Economy. See also Roberts (2016), pp. 1–2.
285 Brenner, R. (1999). 'Competition and Class: A Reply to Foster and McNally'. Monthly Review (online), 51 (7); Brenner, R. (2001). 'The World Economy at the Turn of the Millennium Toward Boom or Crisis?' Review of International Political Economy, 8 (1), pp. 6–44; Brenner (2002); Brenner, R. (2003). 'Towards the Precipice'. London Review of Books (online) 23 (3). (6 February); Brenner, R. (2004). 'New Boom or New Bubble?' New Left Review (online), 25 (January/February); Brenner (2006); Brenner, R. (2007), 'That Hissing? It's the Sound of Bubblenomics Deflating'. Guardian (online). (26 September); Brenner, R. (2007). 'Structure versus Conjuncture'. New Left Review (online), 43 (January/February); Brenner, R. (2008), 'Devastating Crisis Unfolds'. Against the Current (online), 132 (January/February); Brenner, R. (2009). 'Robert Brenner: A Marxist Explanation for the Current Economic Crisis'. Robert Brenner interviewed by Seongjin Jeong. Reproduced on Links: International Journal of Socialist Renewal (online). (22 January).
286 Marx (1976), Ch. 25. See especially Grossman (1992), Ch. 2.
287 Marx (1971), pp. 264–5.
288 Brenner (2006), p. 15.
289 Brenner (2006), pp. 21–2.
290 The explanatory form of Brenner's own account of long downturn since the 1970s is in fact very similar to Marx's classic TRPF theory. This is because both discover capitalist crisis as the unanticipated consequence of competition that generates over-accumulation of capital. In Brenner's analysis, over-accumulation is over-capacity wrought by the undercutting of the profits of those capitalist firms which have invested initially in new plant and technology by those who invest in that already developed means of production later. In Marx's analysis, over-accumulation is manifest in the rising organic composition of capital that results from competition between capitalists as technological innovations that raise labour productivity are generalized.
291 Brenner (2006), pp. 27–8.
292 Harman (2009), pp. 73–5.
293 Brenner (1998), Ch. 2; Brenner (1999).
294 Brenner (1998), Ch. 1, Ch. 3; Brenner (1999).
295 Brenner (1998), Ch. 1; Brenner (1999).
296 Brenner (1998), Ch. 1; Brenner (1999).
297 Brenner (1998), Ch. 1; Brenner (1999).
298 Brenner (1998), Ch. 3; Brenner (1999).
299 Brenner (1998), Ch. 3; Brenner (1999).
300 Patton, M. (2016). 'US Role in Global Economy Declines Nearly 50%'. Forbes (online). (29 February).
301 Brenner (1998), Ch. 3; Brenner (1999).
302 Brenner (1998), Ch. 1; Brenner (1999).
303 Brenner (1998), Ch. 3; Brenner (1999).
304 Brenner (1998), Ch. 3; Brenner (1999).
305 Kidron (1967); Harman (1984); Harris (1983).

306 This, on Harman's (1984, 1995, 2009) account of the long downturn explained the rising organic composition of capital that caused the TRPF to renew itself.
307 Brenner (1998), Ch. 3; Brenner (1999).
308 Brenner (1999).
309 Brenner (2001), p. 8.
310 Brenner (1998), Ch. 3; Brenner (1999).
311 Brenner (1998), Ch. 3; Brenner (1999); Brenner (2001).
312 Brenner (1998), Ch. 3; Brenner (1999).
313 Brenner (1998), Ch. 3; Brenner (1999); Brenner (2001).
314 Brenner (1999).
315 Brenner (2009).
316 Brenner (1998), Ch. 3; Brenner (1999).
317 Brenner (1998), Ch. 3; Brenner (1999); Brenner (2009).
318 Brenner (1999).
319 Brenner (2008).
320 A paradox of zombie mega-capitalism is that, even though this mode delivers low rates of profit on capital investments, it delivers as well unprecedented masses or volumes of wealth (which cannot be easily re-absorbed into the productive economy owing to over-capacity and low returns on investments) and concentrates this conspicuously in fewer hands. This sows the appearance of a successful and prosperous economy that belies the reality of long-term sluggishness and stagnation.
321 Described by Brenner (2003) as the first economic expansion in history driven by "yuppie consumption".
322 Brenner (2003) notes that the much-lauded American boom of the late 1990s—which saw rapid growth—occurred, despite the rate of profit in manufacturing falling by 15 per cent from 1997 to 2000, just as the rate of profit in the corporate sector as a whole fell by 23 per cent over the same period.
323 Brenner (1998), Ch. 3; Brenner (1999).
324 Brenner (2003). See also: Brenner (2002, 2004, 2007, 2009).
325 Brenner (1998), Ch. 3; Brenner (1999).
326 Brenner (2007).
327 Brenner (2003).
328 A forecast or warning repeated by Brenner (2007) on the cusp of the crash.
329 Brenner (2008, 2009).
330 Brenner (2009).
331 Harman (2009). See also: Harvey, D. (1982). The Limits to Capital. London: Verso; Harvey, D. (2011). The Enigma of Capital and the Crises of Capitalism. London: Profile Books.
332 Amaro, S. (2020). 'IMF Says the World Will "Very Likely" Experience Worst Recession since the 1930s'. CBNC News (online). (14 April); Lee, Y.N. (2020). '7 Charts Show How the Coronavirus Pandemic Has Hit the Global Economy'. CNBC News (online). (24 April); CNBC News (online). 'WTO Director-General Roberto Azevedo on Plummeting Global Trade'. (8 April).
333 Amaro (2020).
334 Congressional Research Service (2021). 'Global Economic Effects of COVID-19'. CRS Report (R46270). (10 November).
335 Harari, D., Keep, M. and Brien, P. (2021). Coronavirus: Economic Impact. UK Parliament: House of Commons Library. (17 December).
336 IMF (2021). 'World Economic Outlook: Recovery During a Pandemic'. IMF (online). (October).
337 IMF (2022). 'Real GDP Growth: Annual Percent Change'. IMF (online). Accessed: 07/07/22; World Bank (2022). 'GDP Growth (annual %) 1961–2021'. IMF (online).

338 World Bank (2022). 'GDP Growth (Annual %)—United States 1961–2021'. IMF (online).
339 World Bank (2022). 'GDP Growth (Annual %)—European Union 1971–2021'. World Bank (online).
340 World Bank (2022). 'GDP Growth (Annual %)—High Income 1961–221'. World Bank (online).
341 World Bank (2022). 'GDP Growth (Annual %)—United Kingdom 1961–2021'. World Bank (online).
342 IMF (2021).
343 As Brenner (2009) put it: "The bottom line, I think, is that to actually resolve the problem of profitability that has so long plagued the system—slowing capital accumulation and calling forth ever greater levels of borrowing to sustain stability—the system requires the crisis that has so long been postponed". Could the worldwide COVID-19 crisis constitute such a catastrophic "restorative" event? It would be interesting to hear Brenner's own views on that. My answer is that this cannot be ruled out, but it is unlikely, unless the virus mutates into radically more dangerous and vaccine-resistant forms, so that the ill-effects of the pandemic (economic and otherwise) are restored and radicalized.
344 As Brenner (2009) notes.
345 Marx and Engels (1967), p. 68.
346 Luxemburg, R. (2003). 'The Junius Pamphlet: The Crisis of German Social Democracy'. [1915]. Luxemburg Internet Archive: Marxists (online).
347 Hayter (1990), p. 123.

3 Neoimperialism and international relations

In the previous chapter I addressed one good explanation of how the structural asymmetries or imbalances in the world economy are reproduced. This was that these are the necessary effects of the unfettered markets that neoliberal governance has imposed internationally. But this is only part of the explanation. A second answer to this "how" question—which dovetails with the first—is simply *imperialism*. This is to be understood as the dynamic interface of two kinds of competition, economic (inter-capitalist) and geopolitical (interstate), in their evolving forms and connections, in the pre-neoliberal and post-neoliberal epochs, which together constitute the world order. This chapter is intended to grasp the relationship between neoliberal capitalist economics and neoimperial geopolitics in reproducing the structures of advantage and disadvantage, domination and subordination, of global political economy today.

Capitalism and inequality

A world economy that is structured by (for the most part) unregulated inter-capitalist competition is inherently unbalanced, and hence potentially dangerous and unstable politically, as well as ideologically volatile. Such an economy must generate, owing to the operation of its own structurally based generative mechanisms, vast and growing asymmetries between social classes within countries and across the world—and along with these a hardening of class grievances and antagonisms domestically and across borders. Thus, a capitalist world economy based on free trade is structurally incapable of eliminating world poverty and of delivering economic or social justice for most of the world's population.

Such an economic system must, if left to its own structurally generated "laws of motion", reproduce as well widening development and income gaps between the metropole countries and those "Third World" countries locked into underdevelopment and dependency in the system's periphery. This means that conflicts over the distribution of allocative resources are not simply those between possessing and non-possessing classes or between privileged minorities and

DOI: 10.4324/9781003597346-4

underprivileged majorities. Rather, these conflicts are also between various other constituencies of "haves" and "have nots" or those between "greater haves" and "lesser haves" on the international canvas—that is, between rival states, rival imperialisms and sub-imperialisms, and between the US-hegemon-led developed world and the rest. These conflicts are integral or internal-and-necessary to mega-capitalism because this mode is constituted by an international state system dominated by Great Powers (the mostly Western metropoles) which are committed to preserving an economic status quo that serves their national advantages in the global pecking order.

This means that the contemporary world order is socially malintegrated because it is structurally malintegrated at the levels of polity and economy. The real-world phenomenal or empirical effects of this are manifold. These include the "clash of civilizations" (especially between the Christian West and the Islamist East)[1]; international "blow-back terrorism" (the weapon of economically marginalized and politically disenfranchised non-state actors from usually poor countries against oppressor governments or states and their supposed civilian "accomplices")[2]; civil wars and border wars in the economic wastelands of the periphery; and inter-communal or ethnic group antagonisms everywhere (usually motivated by asymmetries of allocative or authoritative resources between minorities and majorities).[3] However, the social malintegration that world capitalism and its life-support system of interstate political governance generates is also more-or-less and for the most part politically contained for reasons that will be discussed in this chapter.

Not only is mega-capitalism integrally or structurally dissonant, but it has become ever more so in the era of neoliberalism, owing in part to the multiple failures of the neoliberal project. As we have seen, the neoliberal age has witnessed, as might be predicted, given the emergent structure of its global architecture, a hardening of wealth and income inequalities between rich and poor in most places. This is despite record levels of people in waged employment worldwide and the decline of those in subsistence farming—the traditional bastion of rural poverty. The world economy today is rooted in mostly urban-based wage-labour. In 1800 just three per cent of the world's population lived in towns and cities. Today, however, 54 per cent of the world's population does so.[4]

By 1980, the share of the world's economically active population employed in the industrial and service sectors surpassed for the first time that employed in the primary sector (mining, agriculture, fishing and forestry).[5] Today, just one-third of the world's economically active population still derive their primary livelihood from the land, from subsistence farming, though the absolute number of peasants, petty farmers, and landless rural workers is higher than ever before.[6] This represents a massive expansion of the world's working class. By the start of the twenty-first century, Marx's proletariat—those economic actors who derive the main part of their income from the commodification of their own labour-power—was poised to become the majority social class of global humanity.[7]

Such radical socio-economic disequilibria may be offset by other system-wide benefits, however. These are exactly those that were promised by neoliberal champions of boundless capitalism. Two are especially worthy of note—upon which the legitimacy of neoliberal politics arguably hinges. One of these is simply the gradual elimination of the most extreme forms of poverty, as the world's poor are pulled away from subsistence agriculture into paid employment, reducing the old peasantry to a residual or rump class, in effect proletarianizing the global workforce. The other is the supposed "trickle down" impacts of faster growth and bigger profits, which it was promised would flow from unleashing the "dynamism of the market" (i.e. maximizing capital freedoms).

Worldwide proletarianization has indeed substantially reduced "extreme" poverty (on the World Bank's definition). But the global rise of the world's working class, driven by capitalist internationalization and by post-colonial modernizations in the Global South, precedes the neoliberal age. This, indeed, had its biggest push during the postwar boom. Moreover, under neoliberalism, the reduction in the proportion of the world's population who are among the "very poorest" (on the World Bank's definition) has been, as we have seen, accompanied by a dramatic increase in the number of "working poor". This is the global multitude whose number often hover precariously (by the odd dollar or so) above the World Bank's arbitrary and pitiless poverty threshold. Finally, as also discussed in the previous chapter, neoliberalism simply has not delivered on its promise to restore dynamism to the world economy in the long period since the collapse of the postwar boom. Even if trickle-down economics was not ideological, the opportunities for it are curtailed by conditions of weak GDP growth, stagnant FDI, and fragile profits, which characterize our present times.

Neoimperialism and the interstate system

The analysis so far brings us to a second good answer to the questions of *how* (do the economic imbalances between and within countries exist) and *why* (are these radicalizing since the 1980s). This is because some account is needed of how the spectacularly economically unbalanced world (which even though this is, to be sure, one that is reproducible by the market mechanism alone at the level of economy) has not been rendered politically untenable by virtue of massive social dissonance and popular resistance. That is, how revolt of the impoverished masses of the Global South against the rule of the mostly Northern metropoles and of their own rulers who acquiesce with a world radically hostile to their interests has been avoided. This is the question of how a world of massive and growing economic injustice can be politically stabilized. Why has structural malintegration not given rise to social malintegration? Or, rather, how has this not given rise to the kind or intensity of social malintegration that would undermine the current world order?

As I stated at the start of this chapter, a good answer to this question is *imperialism*. Imperialism, as this has taken shape in the postwar world, is made in the interface of economic (inter-capitalist) and geopolitical (interstate) competition. This is under conditions where the protagonists have radically unequal access to authoritative and allocative resources on the international canvas. In its political aspect, neoimperialism is where national states compete with each other in the interests of their home-grown or home-based (albeit internationally facing) corporations and in order to draw inside their borders a greater share of the global investments of the MNCs.

Imperialism, more broadly conceived, is simply those political practices of state, government, and supranational governance that are intended to secure the dominance of certain groups over others in world affairs. These groups are, of course, property-owners, the corporate-managerial elite, and the capitalist class generally, but especially included are particular elements of these constituencies. These are, namely, those that shelter under the sovereignty of specific national governing authorities (i.e. which administer the HICs, mainly of the Global North). Imperial practices may include colonialism and those acts (generally of warfare and or its threat) that secure territorial acquisitions, or reduce unconquered territories to vassalage, as was the case in the classical age of empire when the European powers competed among themselves to divide up the world's resources. Or these practices may include those of diplomatic coercion and manipulation, of economic sanction (or sweetening), and of political destabilization or stabilization, aimed at governments or states that are seen as thwarting or obstructing imperial goals or acquiescing to them. These also include the establishment of normative and legal institutional frameworks enshrining worldwide economic orders that preserve the monopolization of resources by the propertied and monied generally and the lion's share of these in the hands of those of whose enterprises are crucial to the national economies of the Western metropoles.

Imperialism, from the CRT perspective, is not simply a set of practices or policies conducted by state-power actors, however. Rather, this is also an inherited structure of asymmetrical powers of command in the international state system that allows relations of domination and subordination to be reproduced intergenerationally. On the one hand, imperium exists by virtue of the imperial agency of people, since imperialism as structure has no interest in its own preservation. Relations, positions or roles in relations, and resource distributions governed by relations (which is what social structures are)—these are not self-generating or self-replicating, because (unlike people) these are not purposive or intentional systems. But, on the other hand, structures of dominium (like class structures of exploitation) do have efficacy insofar as they frame and incentivize those practices of people that remake them. Imperial structures (like those of class) supply their superordinate agents with vested interests in their reproduction. These vested interests are derived from their positioning of advantage in these structures and the opportunity costs of failing to defend them against the disadvantaged.[8] Imperial structures also grant their superordinate agents the institutional capacities (i.e. those of state authorization) to deliver on these vested interests.

In the analysis that follows I will focus on the imperial practices that neoimperial structures facilitate and incentivize.

Now, it is important to recognize, in this context, that the well-documented pattern of US political interventions and interferences in the sovereign affairs of a vast swathe of countries of the Global South since World War Two was never motivated simply by Cold War geopolitical and ideological rivalries. Such are the paraphernalia of trade embargoes, economic blockades, strategies of political destabilization aimed at non-compliant governments, and overt and covert support for repression of oppositionists by compliant governments and aspirant governments. The latter includes arming and training insurgents, supporting military coups, hostile encirclements with military installations, supporting international terrorist networks that have abducted and murdered opponents or dissidents across the world, military and financial and intelligence assistance for "friendly" regimes, and of course direct military interventions.[9] As David Harvey summarizes:

> The US has frequently relied upon domination and coercion and has not shrank from the liquidation of opposition. . . . Even internally, it has a history of ruthlessness that belies its attachment to its constitution and the rule of law. . . . It has been even more significantly ruthless abroad in sponsoring coups in Iran, Iraq, Guatemala, Chile, Indonesia, and Vietnam (to name but a few), in which untold thousands died. It has supported state terrorism throughout the world wherever it has been convenient. CIA and special forces units operate in innumerable countries. Study of this record has led many to paint a portrait of the US as the greatest "rogue state" on earth. There is a major industry in doing so.[10]

During the Cold War, all of this was only partly motivated by fears over Soviet expansionism (though anti-Soviet paranoia played a part). In short, this was no mere artifice of what Alex Callinicos has dubbed "superpower imperialism", though this is how its excesses were typically rationalized or legitimized.[11] On the contrary, this was motivated as much by a politics committed to ruthlessly binding the countries of the Global South to the world market (dominated especially by American MNCs, finance, and trade) and to capitalist property and class relations.[12] As Harvey rightly says:

> Within the "free world" the US sought to construct an open international order for trade and economic development and rapid capital accumulation along capitalistic lines. . . . In this sphere the US was not only dominant but also hegemonic in the sense that its position as a super-imperialist state was based on leadership for propertied classes and dominant elites wherever they existed. Indeed, it actively encouraged the formation and empowerment of such elites and classes throughout the world: it became the main protagonist in projecting bourgeois power across the globe.[13]

But this US-fabricated international order was also one in which the other developed capitalist nations would benefit. This was owing to the logic of comparative advantage in a system of free competition where they were sheltered from political disruptions of the market mechanism by the global projection of American political and military power. "A tacit global compact was established among all the major capitalist powers, with the US in a clear leadership role, to avoid internecine wars and to share in the benefits of an integrated capitalism in the core regions".[14]

Breaking free of the Cold War, with the decline of Soviet communism towards the end of the 1980s, the role of US military power in securing the "developing" world for the imperialism of unequal exchange and the rule of the US-led and Western metropole-dominated free trade could assume centre stage. As President George Bush Senior's 1990 *National Security Strategy of the United States* review put it:

> In a new era, we foresee that our military power will remain an essential underpinning of the global balance, but less prominently and in different ways. We see that the more likely demands for the use of our military forces may not involve the Soviet Union and may be in the Third World, where new capabilities and approaches may be required. . . . Since World War II, the threat posed by the Soviet Union has dominated much of our planning for the Third World. But we have . . . long identified specific interests independent of a Soviet factor. In the future, we expect that non-Soviet threats to these interests will command ever greater attention. . . . Third World conflicts may no longer take place against the backdrop of superpower competition. Yet many will, for a variety of reasons, continue to threaten U.S. interests . . . and place serious demands on our forces.[15]

Consequently, the US state's war on the Global South in the Cold War era was aimed not simply at national movements and governments that were formally (or informally) aligned with the USSR or committed to building Stalinist-type command economies. Rather, "wherever there was a conflict between democracy, on the one hand, and order and stability built upon propertied interests, on the other, the US always opted for the latter". US coercion and aggression were thus just as much aimed at left-of-centre governments as those that were "communist" or socialist. That is, it was mobilized to destabilize or destroy all of those embracing a policy spectrum of land reform in favour of the rural poor, increasing taxes on wealth and property, limiting foreign ownership, placing controls on the export of capital, and so on.

> The US therefore moved from the position . . . [in the post-1945 decolonization era] . . . of patron of national liberation movements to oppressor of any populist or democratic movement that sought even a mildly non-capitalist (let

> alone socialist or communist path) to the improvement of economic wellbeing. Social democratic populist attempts at modifying capitalism were often struck down (as happened to Bosch in the Dominican Republic, Goulart in Brazil, and, eventually, Allende in Chile). . . . And savagely dictatorial regimes, such as those in Argentina in the 1970s, the Saudis, the Shah of Iran, and Suharto in Indonesia, were unconditionally supported by US military and economic power since they supported US interests.[16]

Sometimes US military and other coercive interventions were aimed simply at governments or movements that were set on merely liberal-democratic reforms (i.e. free elections). This was because a preference of US foreign policy—especially though not exclusively in the Cold War era—was for regional "strongman" states (i.e. right-wing dictatorships) that were absolutely committed to private property and capitalist enterprise *without limits*, and hence which were resolutely set against the trade unions and pro-worker or pro-peasant reforms.[17] The main reason for this was that these would ensure against the rule of the "wrong" kind of government (i.e. "weak" government that would bend to popular pressures) and would better protect US corporate property, investments and profits in "emerging" markets. As US State Department lead policy strategist George Kennan observed in 1949, "it is better to have a strong regime in power than a liberal government if it is indulgent and relaxed and penetrated by communists".[18]

In Latin America, regarded by Washington as its own captive marketplace, this allowed foreign policy to be projected and translated as equivalent to US internal security policy from the Kennedy presidency onward. This meant that any socialist or social-democratic or nationalist movement or government in the subcontinent was viewed as communist or "ultranationalist" by default, hence opposed to US interests and bent on undermining US national security. As Lars Schoultz has argued, this licensed the US state in perpetually seeking to undermine "a perceived threat to the existing structure of socio-economic privilege by eliminating the political participation of the numerical majority . . . the popular classes".[19] This same point could be made with equal force with regard to US foreign policy in the Middle East, which has also been read through the "internal securitization" lens, and with the same purpose in mind.

So, at work in the postwar interstate system were two distinct but intersecting forms of imperialism—the bipolar imperialism of inter-state competition between the US-led alliance and the USSR and its allies, and the US-led imperialism of the developed countries (or HICs) that was imposed on the Global South. Thus, although superpower imperialism has gone with the demise of the USSR and its allies, the other axis of imperialism (the Global North's domination of the Global South) remains entrenched. This is why the post-Cold War (and neoliberal) world is one that has seen the continuation of US-led imperial power politics, indeed their extension into previously uncharted territories that were reigned-in at least in part by Cold War partitions.

But, since imperialism is, as Callinicos says, "constituted by the intersection of two forms of competition, namely economic and geopolitical",[20] the demise of bipolar superpower rivalries has led to a transformation of the system of imperialist competition since the 1990s. And so neoimperialism in the neoliberal world is reconstituted as a triadic political system based on three great power centres: those of the USA (presently the lone superpower), the EU, and South-east Asia (Japan and China—the latter being a regional power that has global superpower ambitions and which is likely to increasingly challenge worldwide US political hegemony).[21] This emergent triadic pattern is correspondence of power of authorization (political domination) to power of allocation (economic exploitation)—the latter of which is also triadic. This re-ordered international state system is thus the power container of the new mega-capitalism and of its neoliberal mode of governance. Its structural architecture is asymmetric in the sense of polycentric, with the USA leading the "metropole alliance" (Japan and the North Atlantic states).

Washington's present global primacy is due to: (1) its economic strength (a GDP almost as big as Japan's and the EU's combined)[22]; (2) its strategic control over access to the bulk of the world's energy supplies in the Middle East (derived from its military protection of the petrol-monarchies) upon which all of the other advanced capitalisms are dependent[23]; (3) its global policing role (primarily for the protection of the interests of its own MNCs in the world market, but which entails safeguarding world markets from which its "partners" also benefit)[24]; (4) its much bigger contribution than partner states to overall world military spending and to funding NATO that is integral to this world policing role[25]; and (5) its political domination of the various multilateral institutions and supporting agreements or treaties of global governance (UN, G7, OECD, GATT, APEC, World Bank, IMF, WTO, etc.) that "coordinate economic growth between the advanced capitalist powers and . . . bring capitalist-style economic development to the rest of the . . . world".[26] These US-dominated supranational organizations ensure that, in the post-Cold War world, Washington Consensus policies—that is, "the neo-liberal ground rules of open financial markets and relatively free access"[27]—are internationally endorsed and are ideologized as multilateral and consensual.[28]

In this hierarchical trilateral emergent structure, the developed countries (those of the North Atlantic and Japan especially) can be viewed in a certain sense as sub-imperial states, or as belonging to a particular class of sub-imperial state, under the leadership of the USA. This is because they are participants (as junior partners) under US hegemony in the "imperialism of free trade"[29] that reproduces their mutual advantages and the disadvantages of others in the world economy. They are, in short, the beneficiaries of asymmetrical market competition. These are states that can maintain themselves as among the first rank of "competitors on the world stage" because they are, by virtue of the inheritance of inequality, "absorbers" and "producers" of surplus capitals.[30] But these states are also sub-imperialisms in a geopolitical sense. This is inasmuch as they are mobilized through the US-dominated supranational organizations of political governance to endorse and support, indeed participate in, specific US economic or military measures intended to discipline or undermine "outlier" states.[31]

However, these sub-imperialisms have their own national interests, so that tensions and conflicts are also integral to the interstate system, though these are containable so long as the US hegemon can preserve its economic and military power, and hence its political authority over the other metropoles. But this political dominance cannot be guaranteed in the long *durée* owing to the continuing relative decline of US economic power as this is confronted by a centrifugal world order of rival nation-states all striving to out-compete each other. The USA's weakening economy *vis-à-vis* competitor capitalisms has manifested over several decades as a growing dependence on capital and commodities from overseas. There is thus the spectre of spiralling trade and balance-of-payments deficits in the US economy since the 1980s.[32]

Washington now oversees a dangerously (from the perspective of national economic stability) unbalanced US rentier capitalism that is especially vulnerable to capital flight and currency (dollar) devaluation in the event of a recessionary crisis. As Harvey noted two decades ago:

> The sheer volume of support to the US is astonishing. . . . Foreigners now earn over a third of US government debt and 18 percent of corporate debt (more than double the ratios in around 1980), and the US now depends on over $2 billion a day of net foreign investment to cover its continuously rising current account deficit with the rest of the world. . . . Any other country in the world that exhibited such a macro-economic condition would by now have been subjected to ruthless austerity and structural adjustment procedures by the IMF. But the IMF is the United States.[33]

This parlous state of US capitalism appears almost intractable since the neoliberal "shock therapy" that might cure it of its massive indebtedness (brutal austerity-driven restructuring) is unthinkable for its political leaders. Such is for other, lesser states, whose economies and peoples must be disciplined by being opened up for corporate exploitation. At the time of writing, the USA's balance of trade deficit with the rest of the world on its current account stands at an astronomical $1.69 trillion, up by $320 billion from 2022.[34] This is continuing on an upwards trajectory:

> The deficit has averaged $535 billion since 2000, much higher than in previous decades, when it accounted for well below 2 percent of GDP. The United States ran either a surplus or a small deficit through the 1960s and 1970s, after which a large deficit opened in the 1980s and continued to expand through the 1990s and 2000s.[35]

Decades of deficit finances have made the USA the biggest debtor country in the world. US national debt was around $5 trillion in 2006. By 2016 it was $14 trillion, and by 2020 it was $17.3 trillion. Presently (December 2023), it stands at $33 trillion,[36] having passed $30 trillion for the first time in February 2022.[37] The federal public debt-to-GDP ratio increased from 73 per cent in 2015 to 96 per cent in 2021,[38] and this is projected to increase to 100 per cent by 2028.[39] It rose from 36 per cent in 1981 to 64 per cent in 1996 and to 86 per cent in 2010.[40] If one includes in these figures intergovernmental debt (as well as public debt), this stood at 130 per cent of the USA's GDP as of 2020.[41] More than a third of US national debt is owed to foreign donors. Roughly 59 per cent of it is owed to foreign states and 41 per cent to overseas corporations and other investors.[42] The leading US debt national sites are Japan, China, and the UK.

The US state, faced with the relentless ratchet of inter-capitalist competition, and its declining economic primacy, will find that its power to solidarize its hegemony in the key geostrategic theatres of world systems (the EU, Indo-China, the Asia-Pacific, the Middle East and southcentral Asia—where the bulk of the world's oil resources are to be found—is under increasing strain.[43] Indeed, there is evidence that those strains have been building for several decades. This could explain, for example, why the US state has in the post-Cold War era become increasingly reliant on a "force first" method of pursuing its foreign policy goals. Monica Duffy Toft and Sidita Kushi refer to this as the increasing primacy of "kinetic diplomacy" over "diplomatic persuasion" in the way Washington conducts international relations. Kinetic diplomacy does not simply mean a growing reliance on state violence as a matter of first resort. Even more so, this is the threat of using state violence, which the authors describe as "force display". Although "force display" has been more frequent than actual force deployment right across the history of US foreign policy, the latter has been more common in recent decades. Indeed, "force activation" has even become more frequent than "force display" in the most recent years.[44]

This process of "force-first accelerationism" begins in earnest in the postwar era, Duffy Todd and Kushi demonstrate, but has been quickening since 1990. As Duffy Todd observes: "The rate of interventions has accelerated over time, and since the end of the Cold War. . . . We are increasing our levels of hostility while other states are de-escalating".[45] The authors estimate that, of 393 US military interventions overseas since American independence in 1776, 200 of these have been since World War Two. Of the latter, 86 were in the 44-year period from 1945 up to 1989, whereas 114 have been in the 34-year period since then. There have been 72 US overseas military interventions since 2000. During this most recent period, Washington's allocation of resources to serve the cause of diplomacy (i.e. the Department of State budget) has fallen steadily relative to its allocation of resources to support the cause of militarization (i.e. the Department of Defence budget).[46] "Traditionally, you think of diplomacy first and use of force as last. But we've seen a weakening of the Department of State and the strengthening of commanders-in-chiefs".[47] Today, Duffy Todd and Kushi point out, the US state's spending on the latter is 17 times higher than on the former.[48]

Unilateral and multilateral instrumentalism

The spectre of US hegemony under stress due to the relative decline of American capitalism may also be part of the explanation for Washington's resort to *unilateral* military interventions under especially the George Bush Junior presidency (but to a lesser extent also under the preceding Clinton administration) to reign-in outlier states. These are to be contrasted with the US state's supposedly more typical postwar "consensus-building" methods of enticing, bribing, or coercing multilateral support for military interventions through the agency of the UN and under the cloak of international law.[49]

The most notable examples of US unilateralism in the neoliberal age beyond its own regional backyard have been in the Balkans in 1995 and 1999, in Afghanistan in 2002, and in Iraq in 2003. Two examples. The Clinton administration's war on Serbia in 1999 was "under the aegis of NATO, without reference to the United Nations Security Council".[50] Bush Junior's administration did not seek out UN approval for Washington's war on the Taliban in 2002 in response to 9/11, and nor did he accept offers of assistance from NATO.[51] A greater willingness of the US state to deploy military force unilaterally outside its own regional theatre of influence in the Americas and Caribbean could indeed be symptomatic of its declining capacity to project political power globally by virtual of economic ascendancy. This is as weakening American capitalist power erodes its political dominance of the Western Alliance, making it harder to build multilateral support for acts of military or economic coercion against outlier states in regional hotspots.

David Harvey interprets what he calls the "new imperialism" of the US state in similar terms.[52] This is as consisting of Washington's growing resort to military muscle (and to unilateral militarism) stemming from the decline of America's "real" economy in manufacturing and services and the corresponding unbalanced ascendancy of its financial sector.[53] Such, argued Harvey, signalled a shift from a pre-neoliberal and neoliberal "consensus imperialism" to a neo-conservative "exploitative imperialism".[54] Writing on the cusp of the second Gulf War of 2003, Harvey opined:

> If hegemony weakens, then the danger exists of a turn to far more coercive tactics of the sort we are now seeing in Iraq. . . . The Bush administration's shift towards unilateralism, towards coercion rather than consent, towards a much more overtly imperial vision, and towards reliance on an unchallengeable military power, indicates a high-risk approach to sustaining US domination, almost certainly through military command over global oil resources. Since this is occurring in the midst of several signs of loss of dominance in

> the realms of production and now (though as yet less clearly) finance, the temptation to go for exploitative domination is strong. . . . It is in this context that we see the Bush administration looking to flex military muscle as the only clear absolute power that it has left.[55]

As for the content of this "more overtly imperial vision" of the Bush Junior administration, Harvey summarized this well:

> The open talk of empire as a political option presumably seeks to hide the extraction of tribute from the rest of the world under a rhetoric of delivering peace and freedom for all. Control over oil supplies provides a convenient means to counter any power shifts—both economic and military—threatened within the global economy . . . since Europe and Japan, as well as East and South-East Asia (now crucially including China), are even more dependent on Gulf oil than is the United States. If the US successfully engineers the overthrow of both Chávez and Saddam, if it can stabilize or reform an armed-to-the-teeth Saudi regime that is currently based on the shifting sands of authoritarian rule (and in imminent danger of falling into the hands of radicalized Islam), if it can move on (as seems possible from Iraq to Iran and consolidate its position in Turkey and Uzbekistan as a strategic presence in relation to Caspian Basin oil reserves (which the Chinese are desperately trying to buy into), then the US, through firm control of the global oil spigot, might hope to keep effective control of the global economy for the next fifty years.[56]

However, the supposed discontinuity of US imperial policy during this period with what went before and what has come since—that is, the shift from instrumental multilateralism to instrumental unilateralism—is perhaps overstated. This is despite the fact that Washington's accelerating "kinetic diplomacy" of recent decades cannot be denied. After all, Washington has not typically since World War Two sought UN approval for its many military interventions (whether directly or by proxies) or other CIA-orchestrated covert operations to bring about regime change, especially though not exclusively those in Latin America and the Caribbean. Stand-out cases include Guatemala (1954), Cuba (1961), the Dominican Republic (1965), Nicaragua (1979), El Salvador (1980), Grenada (1983), Panama (1989), and Haiti (1991).[57] These (and other acts of military aggression in Southeast Asia—most notably the Vietnam War) were certainly cases of imperial instrumental unilateralism. Four of those listed earlier involved full-scale invasions of other countries by US troops, without UN mandate.

To these historical facts might be added a further observation of relevance. President Bush Senior's *National Security Strategy* review (1990) explicitly sanctioned the US state "to act either in concert with our allies or, if necessary, unilaterally, where our vital interests are threatened",[58] just as did its predecessors. US imperialism attempted strenuously (albeit unsuccessfully) to secure UN legitimization for the second Gulf War of 2003 against Saddam Hussein's Iraq, just as did (successfully) for the first one of 1991. So, if Washington had been able to win UN backing for the second invasion, just as it did for the first, this too would also have been an exercise of instrumental multilateralism. Even so, it is true that the US state under Bush Junior's neoconservative rule made a dramatic turn towards crude unilateral military imperialism that in certain ways set it apart from its predecessors. This was inasmuch as it noisily and explicitly endorsed an explicitly imperial project of re-ordering the Middle East (and beyond that the wider world) along liberal-democratic capitalist lines.

If necessary, this would be by military means as a first rather than last resort, with or without the support of Washington's sub-imperial allies or the sanctioning of the UN or international law. Such was assertion of the right to engage in military action as "pre-emptive self-defence" (which is contrary to human rights law) to destroy rogue regimes.[59] Such was also an explicit avowal of "crusade imperialism" as humanitarian intervention, of imperialism as moral purpose—not only to purge the region (and world) of terrorism and "extremism" but also to demilitarize it (relieving governments of WMD), and implant free trade, private ownership, and "democratic values" everywhere—starting with Iraq.[60] A whole chapter of the Bush Junior administration's *National Security Strategy of the United States of America* that set out this global imperial vision eulogized the virtues of "free-market democracy", thus conflating democracy and capitalism, and rendering the latter as indispensable to the former.[61]

Now, before the Bush Junior administration, Washington's unilateral imperialism was something it did when this was considered necessary, not something it declared itself as committed to, no matter what. In the runup to the second Gulf War, those allies or partners who would not support or endorse Bush's new war on Iraq were browbeaten at the UN and castigated as being "against rather than for us" (i.e. the USA), as anti-American, as weak or unprincipled, as uncommitted to the humanitarian and anti-terror causes. This was as other governments were offered inducements to pledge military assistances to the upcoming campaign and acquiesce to US-tabled resolutions before the UN that would legalize regime change in Baghdad and warned of "consequences" if they did not.[62]

This project was to start but not necessarily end with regime change in Baghdad. Rather, this would, it was suggested, proceed to undermine other "rogue states" of the "axis of evil" (whose days were declared as being numbered). Other illiberal regimes in the Middle East—especially those in Tehran and Damascus and Tripoli—would need to toe Washington's line, or else risk either "humanitarian war" to rescue their peoples from tyranny, or a war of self-defence to eliminate WMDs that threaten world security, or both. Indeed, the Bush gang even appeared to have longstanding US ally, the Saudi monarchy, in their regime-change sights, inasmuch as Riyadh was deemed (post 9/11) to be supportive of global terrorism and needful of liberal democratization to stamp that out.[63]

This was a unilateralism of disregard and dismissal not only of Washington's major geopolitical rivals (China and Russia) but also of key states of the Western Alliance, a substantial part of the US political establishment (of both major electoral parties—Republican and Democrat—who favoured still multilateral imperialism), the overwhelming bulk of world public opinion (expressed in mass anti-war demonstrations in the West and beyond), and indeed of majority public views in the USA.[64] As John Bolton, one of Bush Junior's under-secretaries on security matters, expressed the neoconservative perspective on Washington's rightful role in international relations:

> There is no such thing as the United Nations. There is an international community that can be led by the only real power left in the world, and that is the United States, when it suits our interests and when we can get others to go along.[65]

Or, as the president's National Security Adviser (NSA), Condoleezza Rice, put the matter, even more concisely:

> We [the Bush Junior administration] . . . proceed from the firm ground of the national interest, not from the interests of an illusory international community.[66]

Yet 20 years beyond the events that led up to second Gulf War of 2003 that indeed secured regime change in Iraq, it is apparent, with the advantage of hindsight, that this unilateral turn of US imperialism was more a moment or page in the history of US foreign relations. This was not the start of a new era of supposedly post-neoliberal nationalistic military adventurism in which Washington would simply steer its own path in disregard of coalition-building. Regime change was not extended to Iran, or to Syria, under Bush Junior's tenure. Nor was this pursued by the Obama and Trump administrations that followed. Washington also quickly restored normal diplomatic service with Riyadh. The rhetoric of "liberalizing" and "democratizing" the wider Middle East, including by force of US arms if local regimes eschewed self-reform, melted away. The pattern of US foreign policy tilted away from direct first-strike or pre-emptive military interventions in the Middle East (beyond the borders of Anglo-American occupied Iraq) in favour of those by means of proxies and covert military assistances to forces that would obstruct the designs or counter the influences of hostile states such as Iran.

Multilateral instrumentalism (coalition-building and consent-mongering in the UN) was thus pretty much reconsolidated as the US state's go-to approach of first resort, with unilateral instrumentalism once again reserved as a weapon of last resort if alliance-building should fail. The reasons for the resetting are not difficult to comprehend.

Neoconservative unilateral imperialism had an insecure base even in the right-wing of the Republican Party.[67] This was also given a huge but momentary boost by the events of 9/11, which the neocons were able to exploit, but which was unlikely to survive far beyond wars in Afghanistan and Iraq that were legitimized by the politics of securitization. Not only that, the initial success of the regime-change project in Iraq was then undone by the long insurgency waged against the Anglo-American occupation that was its legacy. Predictably, Iraq became, after Saddam Hussein was toppled, very messy, and it did so very quickly—which also made the occupation a costly endeavour economically and politically for Washington.[68] This thwarted Bush's Junior's utopian neoliberal reconstruction plans in Iraq and ensured that additional military projects of re-ordering the wider Middle East by force of arms were simply unfeasible, economically and geopolitically, even for the administration's neocon hawks.

Beyond these factors, US unilateralism simply risked undermining the Western Alliance. This is because it opened up space for a new strategic alignment between France, Germany, Russia, and China—as this was forged in opposition to the Iraq war and other potential US wars of regime change in the Middle East.[69] The risk was very real because Washington's unilateral tilt was aimed especially at a part of the world upon which all of the USA's economic rivals were dependent for oil supplies, and this could hardly be viewed by any of them as serving any agenda beyond the US state's and US capitalism's narrow self-interest to the exclusion of all others. A key objective of Washington's multilateral instrumentalism in imperial policy is to head-off any prospect of the formation of a Eurasian bloc of states ranged against it. The continuation of Washington's unilateral imperialism and militarism would thus have presented a major risk of this spurring an unprecedented challenge to its global hegemony that could undermine it altogether.

More mundanely, but perhaps no less pertinently, unilateral imperialism is a hugely costly enterprise financially for an economically weakened superpower, faced with radical trade disequilibria and indebtedness, such as is the USA. Indeed, it is doubtful if this would be economically sustainable for the US state, especially faced with the challenge of an economically (and militarily) ascendant China, plus a more assertive Russia. Multilateral instrumentalism as imperial strategy, by contrast, allows for the financial burden of wars and militarism to be distributed across several nation-states in exchange for a share of the spoils (of order, security—and capitalist exploitation). In geopolitical terms, this also allows the US state to avoid or at least reduce over-extending itself militarily, so that it can deploy its military resources more strategically.

Washington's rebranding of NATO as an organization that can and should project power outside and beyond its traditional spheres—including as far as the Asia-Pacific region—fits with the multilateral instrumentalist agenda that has been re-consolidated since Bush Junior's tenure. So too, obviously, does Washington's more longstanding policy of enlarging NATO membership and persuading the European member states to better resource the alliance militarily. Under Bush Junior's presidency, by contrast, NATO was sidelined. The organization was viewed by his administration's neocons as bureaucratic and inefficient and was not called upon to support their wars, despite NATO leaders offering to pitch in for the Afghan campaign.[70]

Moreover, there is also Washington's most recent diplomatic success stories under the Joseph Biden administration to throw into the mix. These are those of building a vast sanctions-implementing coalition against Russia in response to its invasion of Ukraine and extending and intensifying its network of allied states in the Asia-Pacific ranged against China. These actions too appear to confound the perspective that the USA's unilateral imperialism is displacing or subordinating its multilateral imperialism in world affairs. Multilateral instrumentalism is hardly on its last legs, though the resurgence of unilateral instrumentalism cannot be ruled out, despite the comparative decline of America's economic status in the capitalist world economy. This is presently conveying a more aggressive and confrontational foreign policy aimed at China and Russia in particular. As we have seen, despite its relative economic decline, the US economy remains the world's largest, and with a higher per capita income than any other. This is still sufficient economic capacity to support global power projection.

US imperialism and global power projection

The neoimperial order of states today is organized and primed for war. Such is the most striking and alarming aspect of interstate competition. The most dangerous aspect of militarization is the nuclear aspect This is just as much the case today as it was in the age of bipolar superpower imperialism during the Cold War.

Nuclear neoimperialism

The FAS and ACA estimate that there are 12,500 nuclear warheads worldwide. These are presently monopolized by nine nation-states—the USA, Russia, China, France, the UK, Pakistan, India, Israel, and North Korea. Russia is the world leader for possession (owning 5,889 warheads), closely followed by the USA (which has 5,244 of them). Together, Washington and Moscow have 89 per cent of the world's nuclear stockpile and 86 per cent of its operational warheads. To put that into perspective, China, by contrast, has 410. However, sitting alongside the US nuclear arsenal are those of two of its closest Western allies, the UK and France, which between them have 515 warheads.[71] The appalling global hazard posed by this situation hardly needs stating. This is the consequence of the intensity of antagonism between the USA and the West, on the one hand, and Russia, on the other hand (which I will explore later). This is also owing to the fact that both Washington and Moscow have threatened to use nuclear weapons in the past (including against non-nuclear adversaries), whereas one (the US state) is the only one to have used them so far—against civilian targets.

There is little prospect of any major reduction of nuclear stockpiles and the potential for further expansion and proliferation. As the FAS reports: "France and Israel have relatively stable inventories. But China, India, North Korea, Pakistan and the United Kingdom, as well as possibly Russia, are all thought to be increasing their stockpiles".[72] Non-reduction, and indeed potential expansion and proliferation, result from imperial and sub-imperial rivalries in the interstate system. A few examples will suffice.

Russia has nuclear weapons because the USSR acquired them. And the USSR sought to acquire and stockpile nuclear weapons because its bitter political and ideological rival, the USA, had previously acquired them, used them, and was committed to building up its arsenal with the Soviet "communist" threat in mind. Winston Churchill, Britain's wartime PM, even urged US president Truman to terminate the USSR with a pre-emptive strike using A-bombs before the Soviets had a chance to join the nuclear club. Apparently, there were sympathetic ears in Washington, though this was a step too far for Truman, with World War Two barely two years finished.[73]

Nonetheless, the Pentagon generated nine different plans for a pre-emptive war to destroy the pre-nuclear Soviet state in the period from 1945 to 1949, each of which entailed targeting major Russian cities with A-bombs.[74] For example:

> The 1949 Dropshot Plan envisaged that the US would attack Soviet Russia and drop at least 300 nuclear bombs and 20,000 tons of conventional bombs on 200 targets in 100 urban areas, including Moscow and Leningrad (St. Petersburg). In addition, the planners offered to kick off a major land campaign against the USSR to win a "complete victory" over the Soviet Union together with the European allies.[75]

At the risk of understatement, there can be no doubt that the Kremlin had pressing "national security" reasons to acquire a nuclear deterrence capacity right from the start of the Cold War. And it is the same story for China, of course. Beijing was incentivized to embark on the nuclear road because in the 1950s Washington threatened (twice) to launch a nuclear strike on China if it attempted to retake Taiwan from the nationalists who grabbed it in 1949 after their expulsion from the mainland.[76]

The state of Israel self-purportedly acquired its own nuclear capacity to deter military aggression from its hostile Arab neighbours aimed at its destruction. But more likely it did so in order to safeguard its own post-1967 colonial acquisitions in Palestine from any prospect of these being reversed by conventional military action by countries of the Arab League. The regime in Iran is incentivized to acquire a nuclear deterrent for the same reason as the one in North Korea has already done so—because Washington has cast it as a "rogue state". Based on the fate of the Ba'ath regime in Iraq, Tehran surely understands what can become of so-called rogue nations, especially if they are located in parts of the world that Washington considers as geo-strategically vital. They become vulnerable to US-orchestrated projects of regime change. Equally, Pyongyang understands perfectly well that its best line of defence against US-enacted regime change is its possession of nuclear arms.

Base nation

The key aspect of the US state's de-territorialized power network is the dispersal of military bases across the globe, especially in theatres of strategic importance to the reproduction of its global hegemony. With the Cold War world 30 years past, Washington still maintains on conservative estimates 750 overseas military bases in 80 countries and colonies (and on less conservative estimates 800 plus) at a cost of between $80 and $100 billion.[77] However, as David Vine notes:

> The sheer number of bases and the secrecy and lack of transparency of the base network make a complete list impossible. The Pentagon's previously annual list of its bases, the *Base Structure Report*, is notoriously incomplete and, at times, inaccurate. The Pentagon has also failed to release the Congressionally mandated annual report since the Fiscal Year 2018 version, making an accurate list even more difficult than in prior years. Most observers assume the U.S. military does not know the true number of bases occupied by U.S. forces. . . . Creating a list is also complicated by how one defines and counts as a "base." Definitions are ultimately political (and politically sensitive). Frequently the Pentagon and US government, as well as host nations, seek to portray a U.S. base presence as "not a US base" to avoid the perception that the United States is infringing on host nation sovereignty (which, in fact, is frequently the case).[78]

At the end of World War Two, in comparison, the number of overseas American bases was 400.[79] Britain, France, and Russia, by contrast, have 30 foreign military bases between them.[80] China—painted by the US hegemon and its allies as a state threatening world security by "aggressively" asserting its own national interests against other countries in Southeast Asia—has only eight military bases outside its own borders and only one in a different country. Seven are built on artificial islands of Beijing's own making in the South China Sea.[81] This leaves no room for doubt that the USA is the world's dominant imperial power, and the only one presently with global reach—and one which is aggressively power-projecting in all of the key theatres of world competition.

The chief distributions and concentrations are as follows. Of those in Europe—to contain the threat of the former Soviet bloc but latterly that of post-Soviet Russia—the US state maintains 119 bases in Germany, 25 in the UK, 44 in Italy, four in Spain, and seven in Norway, which together host almost 60,000 troops.[82] US military bases are also spread right across Latin America and the Caribbean. This is to police Washington's client and vassal states, buttressing allies and deterring enemies, and on occasions engaging in covert operations against popular left-wing insurgency or in support of right-wing insurgency. There are approximately 76 of them—including nine in Honduras, eight each in Guatemala and Belize, six in Panama, five each in Peru, El Salvador, Costa Rica, and El Salvador, and three in Nicaragua.[83] There are another 34 in the USA's "unincorporated territory" (i.e. colony) of Puerto Rico.[84]

There are, of course, plenty of US military installations in the energy-rich Middle East and Central Asia regions—especially in the Persian Gulf. This is to buttress the oil monarchies, securitize oil fields and supply lines upon which US capitalism and its allies (but also their rivals—including China) depend. This is also to reign-in "rogue" states (i.e. those which are perceived as posing a threat to US control of these resources). Islamist Iran is today the primary target of these policing operations.[85] Previously, these have been aimed at Ba'ath Iraq and Nasser's Egypt—on the grounds that these states were implacably opposed to Israel and were ostensibly committed to working towards pan-African/pan-Arab unity in the region.[86] The exact number of US bases in the region is more difficult to ascertain than elsewhere owing to the deep groundswell of public opposition in the Arab world to the US military presence. But Bahrain is thought to have 12, whereas Saudi Arabia, Kuwait, and Turkey are known to have at least 10 each—the largest numbers. There are also at least six in Oman, four in Syria, three in the UAE, and two in Qatar and Jordan.[87]

Finally, there are a vast number of US military bases in Southeast Asia and Indochina (the Asia-Pacific or Indo-Pacific region), primarily to ring-fence China but also to contain China's ally North Korea. Up until the early 2000s, they functioned as well to neutralize the "communist" state of Vietnam.[88] Washington's China-facing military installations in the Asia-Pacific are arranged across two island chains that totally enclose Chinese coastal waters from north (Korean peninsula) to south (Malaysia and Indonesia). There are more than 120 US bases and other military installations in Japan, 73 in South Korea, and 313 across the region as a whole.[89] Alarmingly, several have been upgraded or upscaled in the past few years,[90] just as new ones are set up.[91] This is as the US state ramps up its military presence off the Chinese seaboard, ratcheting up its effort to box-in its main international rival.

Neoimperialism, NATO, and Russia

Since the collapse of the Soviet bloc, the global reach of US militarism and imperialism has also been extended to the far-flung fringes of Eastern Europe and the Balkans, and towards southern and Central Asia adjoining the Caspian Sea.[92] Especially since the Yugoslav civil war, US and NATO military bases have been implanted in former Soviet territories and satellites that have been pulled into the US camp by the lure of American money, ring-fencing Russia on its western and southern frontiers. The expansion of NATO deep into eastern Europe started under the Clinton presidency following the unification of Germany. Initially, in 1999, this drew the Czech Republic, Hungary, and Poland into the organization—which to be clear is a military alliance *against* Russia in the post-Soviet age. After that, during the 2000s, Romania, Bulgaria, Lithuania, Estonia, Latvia, Slovakia, and Slovenia (all countries of central and eastern Europe) were also NATO incorporated, along with Albania and Croatia in Southeast Europe. More recently, Montenegro (in 2017) and Macedonia (in 2020) have joined the club.

US and EU powerholders and opinion-formers tend to represent NATO expansion into eastern and central Europe as a benign process governed by the legitimate security interests and autonomous decision-making of the NATO-joining countries. They should not be refused, it is argued, because Russia has no business seeking to maintain its own security buffer among countries that would refuse the role. However, back in the real world of global geopolitics, the USA and the leading EU states have major interests in actively incentivizing NATO membership among the non-aligned through inducements of various kinds and in establishing conditions of membership that are within their reach. Not only that, though denied today by American politicians,[93] the USA under the Bush Senior presidency did make oft-repeated commitments to Russia's leaders (in the midst of the Soviet crisis of 1989–91 and during the negotiating round for the reunification of Germany) that NATO would not be permitted to recruit new member states beyond newly united Germany.[94] This was in explicit recognition of Soviet Russia's legitimate security interests in rejecting any such expansion of the military alliance into eastern and central Europe.

> US Secretary of State James Baker reassured Soviet Premier Mikhail Gorbachev "not once, but three times" that NATO would expand "not one inch eastward," in a February 9, 1990 meeting. Baker told the final Soviet leader that Washington agreed that, "not only for the Soviet Union but for other European countries as well it is important to have guarantees that if the United States keeps its presence in Germany within the framework of NATO, not an inch of NATO's present military jurisdiction will spread in an eastern direction".[95]

Other Western leaders also offered the same assurances—including Germany's Helmut Kohl, Britain's John Major and Margaret Thatcher, and France's Francois Mitterrand. They were scattered across a range of official communications between senior diplomats and statespersons during the negotiation process for re-unifying Germany which are in the public realm. This is revealed in documents published by the National Security Archive at George Washington University in Washington DC, which show that

> multiple national leaders were considering and rejecting Central and Eastern European membership in NATO as of early 1990 and through 1991, that discussions of NATO in the context of German unification negotiations in 1990 were not at all narrowly limited to the status of East German territory, and that subsequent Soviet and Russian complaints about being misled about NATO expansion were founded in written contemporaneous memcons and telcons at the highest levels.[96]

So, if there ever was, for the USA and its Western allies, a sincere undertaking not to expand NATO eastwards and southwards towards Russia's borders, which there almost certainly was not, this was abandoned almost from the start. Today, in the context of Russia's invasion of Ukraine, and the West's military support for Ukraine to repel the invasion, propaganda war demands that it is strenuously denied that any such commitment ever did exist.

Neoimperialism and the Soviet crisis

Denial is necessary because NATO expansion, pushing ever closer against Russia's borders, has been one aspect of US imperialism's strategy of neutralization of Russia through containment and encirclement. Such is motivated simply by the fact that Russia is a state with the potential to become a regional hegemon that would reset the distribution of economic rewards right across the Euro-Asia zone to the disadvantage of Washington and its closest allies.[97] This is why the Western Alliance spurned the opportunity for rapprochement with Russia following the dissolution of the USSR at the end of the Cold War. There was consequently no Marshall Plan to build alliances and dependencies with the post-Soviet governments as the Russian economy unravelled under the impact of successive rounds of ruthless neoliberal-sanctioned capitalist "restructuring" and market exposure. The imploding Soviet republics, including Russia, were abandoned to their fate.

Capitalist restoration, under these conditions, in the absence of massive capital transfers from the Cold War victors (the USA, the EU, and US-dominated global financial institutions) to cushion its impact, was tantamount to economic vandalism. Consumer goods companies had with each passing decade lagged increasingly behind the Western and Japanese MNCs in terms of labour productivity and levels of capital investment. This was owing to the resource-ceilings placed on them by mostly self-enclosed national economies and by the Soviet-era prioritization of heavy industry and armaments for investment. These were wiped out *en masse* under neoliberal "shock therapy" agitated for by the US Treasury, the

IMF, and the World Bank. The vast heavy industry and raw materials extractive sectors were simply too big for the needs of local national markets and not competitive enough to find foreign markets, so that these also contracted massively. Those which remained were left as virtual monopolies, so seized the opportunity to elevate prices and disregard contractual obligations to other companies in the dismembered Soviet economy. This meant that viable enterprises were also undermined because they were cut off from suppliers and buyers.[98]

The crisis was also one that engulfed the USSR's satellites in eastern and central Europe. These fell into a fully fledged economic depression at the end of the 1980s and remained stagnant for much of the 1990s:

> In Poland, where initial austerity measures were arguably the most severe as the country plunged headlong into "shock therapy" reform, gross domestic product on a constant U.S. dollar basis contracted more than 7% in 1991 and barely budged in 1992 and 1993, according to data from the World Bank. It wasn't until 1994 that the size of Poland's economy returned to where it sat in 1990 . . . Bulgaria's economy contracted each year from 1989 through 1993, while Romania's GDP dropped nearly 13% in 1991 and nearly 9% in 1992. Similar economic hardship plagued Hungary and the former Czechoslovakia.[99]

But, in Russia and its former republics, the heartland of the old Soviet Union, the economic crisis was especially acute:

> GDP fell by 40–50 percent in the early 1990s, industrial production by more. Agricultural production fell by less but rural poverty was worse. . . . The level of capital investment fell by 75 percent. . . . By the mid-1990s the average level of real wages had fallen by around a half. . . . Perhaps around a third to a half of the population fell beneath the poverty line, though in some groups it was much more. . . . For the mass of the population savings were destroyed by inflation. According to 1996 data half were now held by the top 2 percent of the population, 72 percent by the top 5 percent, and 97 percent by the top 30 percent. . . . The death rate rose from 11 to 15 per 1,000 between 1990 and 1995. For those of working age it rose by 50 percent. Disease, suicide, injury, stress and the search for relief in alcohol carried off enormous numbers of men in particular. By 1995 life expectancy for males had fallen several years to 58.6.[100]

The Soviet collapse and the rise of ethno-nationalist politics in Eastern Europe

These desperate economic times emboldened radical ethnicized nationalism, as the various ex-republics of the USSR competed with each other to shield themselves from the impact of the crash, hoarding resources, disbanding cross-border exchanges, withdrawing into enclaves of self-protection, and contesting borders with their neighbours. Nationalist parties and movements flourished everywhere, and communist provincial rule was replaced by typically authoritarian right-wing regimes, liberal-democratic or otherwise. Fifteen new multi-ethnic states emerged from the dynamic. Within the borders of the new states, disputes emerged over the distribution of resources between majority and minority community groups, with patterns of conflict and discrimination emerging. Inter-communal violence broke out episodically in the former Soviet territories in Central Asia and the Caucasus. Ethnic disputes and antagonisms here were "triggered or exacerbated by the impact of democratization and marketization". This was as "elite struggles over political power and resource distribution" underpinned conflicts that were "often treated as purely 'ethnic'".[101]

Right-wing nationalism and chauvinism became the default politics in post-Soviet Russia just as this was the case right across the former Soviet republics. Indeed, this was the pattern right across the former Soviet satellite states of eastern and central Europe. Czechoslovakia, for example, split-up into the separate states of Slovakia and the Czech Republic along ethnic lines, albeit relatively peacefully, owing to an already existent clear geographical line separating the two. However, the potential of ethno-nationalist politics to collapse into inter-communal violence was fully played out in Yugoslavia. Here civil wars and ethnic partitioning were orchestrated by nationalist demagogues committed not only to the carving out of new ethnic states but to contesting and extending the borders of these against their rivals. This generated mass expulsions of people from the lands of their birth, splitting the formerly multi-ethnic republic into separate ethnically purified states—Serbia, Croatia, Herzegovina, Montenegro, Bosnia, and Kosovo. Tens of thousands were killed in the process and hundreds of thousands were internally displaced.[102]

Putin's Russia

The depth of the post-Soviet crisis bolstered popular support for "strong" nationalist leaders such as Vladimir Putin in Russia (former head of the KGB in the Soviet era) and Slobodan Milošević, in Serbia, who promised to restore national pride and economic prosperity by rescuing these from those who had stolen or squandered them. In Putin's case, this was noisy commitment to the aim of erasing the memory of Russia's humiliating defeat by the USA and its allies in the Cold War. Putin's nationalist politics have ever since these origins in national trauma and calamity retained considerable public appeal in Russia,[103] especially but not exclusively among older demographic groups, not least because these have coincided with improvement of the country's economic fortunes and geopolitical standing in the world.[104] This is shown by Russia's present BRIC status in world economy and its success in regaining political leverage in the Caspian Basin (at the expense of the US state), restoring old alliances in Central Asia with former Soviet republics, and securing new allies such as China and Iran.

Now, Putin's supporters are drawn especially from those who bore the terrible hardships of the USSR's economic collapse under the impact of neoliberal remedies (in the absence of Western aid for reconstruction) and who subsequently witnessed the Western Alliance's exploitation of Russia's paralysis through weakness by driving ahead with NATO expansion into the former Soviet satellites and republics. Older Russians especially have little fondness for the USA and its Western partners, and they are divested of good reasons to trust their intentions towards Russia. Putin has undoubtedly exploited this situation to his own advantage. His presidency has been bolstered by a politics of securitization that has cultivated the idea of American and Western ill-intent towards the Russian people, and along with this a sense of grievance over entitlements stolen by others.

These politics have enjoyed considerable public appeal, not least because they are rooted in populist notions of the "theft of enjoyment" (as Slavoj Žižek represents these in psychoanalytical terms)—as a force of emotion rather than of reason.[105] Yet cultivation of anti-Western popular sentiments by means of state propaganda is not the same thing as their manufacture out of thin air. Russian distrust of the West is not simply a matter of phobic or paranoid fantasy, as the Western liberal imagination would have it, but has its basis in reality. This reality is the experience of the Cold War and of superpower competition with hostile Western powers in the Soviet era. But this reality is also current. This is the refusal of the US state to treat Russia as anything other than a dangerous imperial rival in the post-Soviet age.

Russia's ascendancy under Putin

Putin's regime is hated and feared by US leaders not because it is a "rogue" state in world affairs but because it has been relatively effective in constituting Russia as a sub-imperial state competitor to the USA within what it sees as its own sphere of influence. Thus, US attempts at alliance-building with the new central-Asian states on Russia's southern borders, to thwart Russia's own geopolitical goals– to extend its regional influence, build new allies, or restore old ones—have been only partially effective, faced with Russian counter-diplomacy. Indeed, these have been partially reversed. Consequently, so too so far have been Washington's attempt to obtain secure control of the bountiful oil and (even more so) gas reserves of the Caspian Basin on Russia's southern rim, or rather to secure control of pipeline routes westwards and southbound to NATO-aligned countries and to international waters, at the expense of Russia and China.[106]

The stakes of this interstate imperialist competition for control of the pipeline distribution system of Caspian oil are high—though perhaps not as great as they were thought to be in the 1990s, owing to the fact that the Caspian's energy wealth is not quite the bonanza of riches that was anticipated. Back then, "proven oil reserves" were

> estimated at between 16 and 32 billion barrels, comparable to the US's energy reserves of 22 billion barrels and more than the North Sea's 17 billion barrels. Total reserves could be as high as 179 to 195 billion barrels according to the US Energy Information Administration.[107]

But more recently, these estimates of the Caspian's oil wealth have been somewhat scaled down, though these remain significant.[108]

> Proven reserves in the Caspian Basin are 15.31 billion barrels of oil, or 2.7% of world reserves. . . . Estimates of possible petroleum reserves vary from as few as 20 billion to as many as 200 billion barrels of oil.

On the other hand, estimates of the region's potential as a major source of natural gas supplies have been upscaled since the 1990s. Today, the Caspian is "estimated to contain some 230–360 trillion cubic feet of gas, or 7% of world reserves".[109]

Initially, during the 1990s, under the Bush Senior and Clinton administrations, Washington was able to make significant inroads into the trans-Caucuses and Caspian areas. This was by way of exploiting the opportunity provided by the political paralysis of a post-Soviet Russia faced with its decade-long debilitating economic crisis. A significant US military presence was established in the region (starting in Uzbekistan) alongside increased "military cooperation" with the post-Soviet republics.[110] The goal was to "inculcate more political stability in the countries involved (through training local political elites, training and equipping security forces), strengthen their external security (through military presence, joint exercises, training), and to encourage and assist in the settlement of regional conflicts".[111] Much of this was under the general umbrella of NATO's PFP Programme:

> The PFP programme was designed to "improve practical military cooperation and common capabilities" and "to enable joint operations with NATO peacekeeping and humanitarian missions" among other functions. . . . On a practical level this has meant ongoing US military training programmes in the region under the Cooperative Threat Reduction (CTR) programme and the Foreign Military Financing programme, and border security activities. In 1997, as part of a well-publicized joint military exercise in the region, the US Army's elite 82nd airborne division sent 500 paratroopers parachuting into the territory, including an Uzbek-born marine.[112]

Washington also

> helped establish CENTRASBAT, the Central Asian Battalion, with members from Kazakhstan, Kyrgyzstan, and Uzbekistan . . . Uzbekistan, Central Asia's dominant power and the one country most willing to challenge Moscow's security monopoly in the region, has been singled out by Washington for closest military cooperation. Since 1998, the United States has pursued a close bilateral relationship with the Tashkent government, assisting Uzbekistan in its efforts to build important military infrastructure.[113]

On the same timescale, five Central Asian former Soviet republics (Uzbekistan, Georgia, Ukraine, Azerbaijan, and Moldova) were pulled into a new GUUAM alliance "aimed at strengthening the member states' economic and political ties with the West".[114] The deed was accomplished at NATO's 50th birthday bash in Washington. Indeed, NATO was itself proactive in overseeing the setting up of a GUUAM "peacekeeping" force. Three of the GUUAM states—Georgia, Uzbekistan, and Azerbaijan—withdrew themselves from the Russian-led CIS shortly before joining.[115]

Washington's military penetration of Central Asia was further extended under Bush Junior's administration. This was as a network of US bases "whose existence would have been unthinkable in the pre-September 11 days" were established right across the region (including those in Tajikistan, Uzbekistan, and Kyrgyzstan) in pursuance of the "war on terror" against the scattered remnants of Al-Qaeda and the Taliban as well as other Islamist groups.[116] Alongside these political events, Western energy companies were busy procuring PSAs and extraction rights with local states and companies across the Caspian—primarily those of and in Azerbaijan and Kazakhstan.[117] As was reported by the *Financial Times*, the US state was seeking to promote US and Western commercial penetration of the Caspian in pursuance of geopolitical as well as capitalistic interests. That is, "to develop the area's rich oil and gas deposits to the exclusion of Russia".[118]

US leaders were absolutely clear about the purpose of this alliance building on Russia's southern flank. As Bill Richardson, Energy Secretary under Clinton, explained:

> This is about America's energy security. . . . It's also about preventing strategic inroads by those who don't share our values. We are trying to move these newly independent countries toward the west. We would like to see them reliant on western commercial and political interests. . . . We've made a substantial political investment in the Caspian and it's important that both the pipeline map and the politics come out right.[119]

Since Putin, however, Russia's economic recovery has allowed Moscow to increasingly reassert itself geopolitically in its Asian "backyard", especially in the trans-Caucasus and Caspian delta. Moscow's aspiration to do so certainly predated Putin's presidency. As John Rees points out, its origins can be traced to the so-called Primakov Doctrine, "named after Russia's foreign minister from 1996 to 1998, which called for a strengthening of opposition to the influence of 'outsiders' in Russia's 'near abroad'". But this kind of geopolitics was mere aspiration before Putin. Under Putin's leadership, a version of Primakov has become active policy. Indeed, one of Putin's first foreign policy moves was a "new defence doctrine calling for stronger defence arrangements with the former Soviet states and a major increase in defence spending".

> At the January 2000 Confederation of Independent States summit Putin proposed, and for the first time the other CIS leaders accepted, a greater Russian role in co-ordinating defence "against terrorism". Thus Putin's coalition preceded Bush's by more than a year and a half. Putin will be well aware that closer co-operation with the Soviet successor states over "terrorism" can lead to greater co-operation in resisting US and NATO expansionism.[120]

This has come to pass. Moscow, despite Washington's counter-diplomacy, has managed to rebuild alliances with many of its southern neighbours (including those pulled into the Western Alliance in the 1990s)—and to the detriment of US economic and geopolitical interests. The "pipeline map" that preoccupied Bill Richardson could not, after all, be forged to the exclusion of Russia (or China).[121] Such exclusion depended especially on the continuation of Russian foreign policy timidity and indifference to Central Asia that characterized the Yeltsin era.[122]

> In the end . . . the region did acquire multiple pipelines, and plans exist to send Caspian oil and gas to all directions of the compass. Whereas the Russian monopoly on the export of energy was broken in the late 1990s . . . major export routes continue to traverse Russian territory. For example, the Russian government secured a 24 percent stake in the Caspian Pipeline Consortium (CPC), which built a large-volume (560,000 barrels/day) pipeline from Kazakhstan's Tengiz fields to the Russian port of Novorossiysk on the Black Sea. This pipeline opened in 2001 and through to 2010 remained the largest single oil pipeline out of the region with potential to double its capacity to over 1.3 million barrels a day.[123]

The chief outcome of Washington's pipeline politics in the Caspian was the construction of the Baku-Tbilisi-Ceyhan (BTC) pipeline at astronomical cost, which bypassed Russia and Iran, but which ended up being under-utilized. More effectively, Moscow was able to upgrade the biggest conduit of Caspian oil (the

CPC), invest in a major new pipeline, and improve commercial relations with Caspian energy producers.[124] Consequently:

> At a time when no major deals have been announced with Western companies, Russian and Kazakh firms agreed to production-sharing agreements on potentially large oil fields such as Kurmangazy, Tscentralnoye, and Tyub-Karagan. With respect to Turkmenistan, Russia can claim two major "victories." In 2005, Russia concluded a twenty-five year agreement to purchase Turkmen gas, a deal that promises to increase Turkmen gas shipments through Russian pipelines over ten-fold. In May 2007, Russia, Kazakhstan, and Turkmenistan announced agreement on plans to upgrade the Prikaspirski gas pipeline, ensuring in effect that Russia will be able to virtually monopolize the export of Turkmen gas for the foreseeable future.[125]

Meanwhile, penetration by Western energy commerce of Caspian oil and gas industries and assets ran into buffers that continue to frustrate it. Only in Kazakhstan did the government permit substantial privatizations and sell-offs of oil and gas industrial enterprises to foreign energy corporations (rather than conceding minority, non-controlling share ownership) as is demanded by neoliberal orthodoxy. Turkmenistan and Uzbekistan have preserved Soviet-style era state ownership of the country's energy resources and deterred foreign investment. In Azerbaijan, despite a rafter of PSAs, there is state control "of the majority of . . . oil and natural gas fields", under the ownership of a single national company, which also has the monopoly on negotiating PSAs.[126]

Working with Beijing, and boosted by growing Chinese capital investments in Central Asia, Putin also helped consolidate the "Shanghai Alliance" (of China, Russia, Kazakhstan, Kyrgyzstan, and Tajikistan) that predated his presidency, thereby strengthening trade and military links between the countries.

> Due to limited Western business interest in their markets, Central Asian countries have strived to attract investment by joining the Beijing-controlled Belt and Road Initiative (BRI) the Moscow-led Eurasian Economic Union, or other Chinese and Russian structures. The relationship with these blocs invariably makes these countries more beholden to China and Russia for commerce and capital, which compromises their economic autonomy.[127]

Simultaneously, the economic precarity and security fears of the former Soviet republics of Central Asia faced with the terrorism challenge of radical Islam allowed many of these to be enticed back into Moscow's open arms.

> Most Central Asian regimes view radical Islam as the single largest threat to their survival, and have launched security operations against the militants and their supporters, arresting thousands of real (and sometimes just imagined)

> enemies. Central Asian countries are generally poor, and the readiness of the militaries they inherited from the Soviet Union ranges from poor to practically non-existent. The fight against terrorism required that they seek assistance from whatever country could provide the most financial and military support. The answer most often came in the form of assistance from Russia, which also fought some of the same radical Islamic forces in Chechnya. Under the auspices of the Commonwealth of Independent States, the security and economic association of former Soviet republics, Russia and the Central Asian states held numerous counterterrorist exercises. But Russian aid came at a price: Moscow's weapons and money bought influence, if not outright dominance, in the region and solidified Russia's control over the Caspian's mineral resources.[128]

Most recently, Moscow succeeded in securing agreement among the Caspian states to deny all foreign countries any kind of a military presence in or around the Caspian Sea, which has obviously curtailed NATO's further encroachment on Russia's southern flanks.[129] But perhaps Putin's biggest success story was in turning GUUAM into GUAM, by pulling Uzbekistan (one of the main oil and gas producers of the Caspian) back into Russia's rival CIS alliance.[130]

Putin's Russia, in short, has prevented US imperialism getting exactly what it wants in southern and Central Asia. And the success of this politics of obstruction (of Washington) and of restoration (of Moscow's geopolitical standing in middle Asia) has been an ongoing and developing tendency of his presidencies.

US imperialism and cold war renewed

Much is written or spoken in the Western media about Putin's anti-Western paranoia, that is, his delusional belief that the USA and its Western allies are rabidly anti-Russian and are devoted to undermining Russia. However, if Putin's distrust of the West is rooted in a politics of unfounded paranoia, this is not specific to Putin, or even specific to the present Russian government. Rather, "many Russian policymakers appear to believe that the prospects for a stable, long-term accommodation with NATO are limited".[131] This "mistrust predates the tensions borne out of the Ukraine crisis; it is rooted in a perception of the current US-led international order as denying Russia the place it deserves while threatening Russian interests".[132]

Thus, according to IR analysts in the service of the US state, "Russia is likely to remain a US rival until at least 2030 because of its desire to change the US-dominated international order, its insistence on maintaining influence over its neighborhood, and its military buildup".[133] From the US imperial perspective, of course, any challenge to US hegemony or primacy in world affairs from a competitor state (challenge not in the sense of *overthrowing* US hegemony but *moderating* it), whatever the motives for it, is beyond the pale. This is just taken for granted—Washington's absolute right to rule or define the international order. By definition, for Washington, any politics of challenge rather than acquiescence can only be those of a "rogue" state—unless, apparently, the state in question is a peer-competitor. "Russia is not a peer or near-peer competitor but rather a well-armed rogue state that seeks to subvert an international order it can never hope to dominate".[134]

These discourses betray a remarkable absence of critical self-reflection by or among those who comprise the "collective West". For US strategy towards Russia since the end of the Cold War has scarcely differed from that during the Cold War. This has manifestly been governed by the imperative of, in the terminology of the RAND corporation,[135] to "over-extend" and "unbalance" Russia.[136] This is on the premise that Russia "remains a powerful country that still manages to be a US peer competitor in a few key domains", even if not overall. Therefore, the task of over-extending and unbalancing Russia is necessary to ensure that the US state continues to outcompete its rival in order to maintain its primacy everywhere in all domains. This goal is taken as axiomatic, despite the end of the Cold War, and the demise of so-called Soviet communism.

> Recognizing that some level of competition with Russia is inevitable, RAND researchers conducted a qualitative assessment of "cost-imposing options" that could unbalance and overextend Russia. Such cost-imposing options could place new burdens on Russia, ideally heavier burdens than would be imposed on the United States for pursuing those options.

The RAND researchers themselves freely acknowledge the basic continuity of this strategy towards Russia with those which characterized US Cold War politics in the Soviet era:

> The work builds on the concept of long-term strategic competition developed during the Cold War, some of which originated at RAND. A seminal 1972 RAND report posited that the United States needed to shift its strategic thinking away from trying to stay ahead of the Soviet Union in all dimensions and toward trying to control the competition and channel it into areas of U.S. advantage. If this shift could be made successfully . . . the United States could prompt the Soviet Union to shift its limited resources into areas that posed less of a threat. The new report applies this concept to today's Russia.[137]

RAND accordingly has set out a range of "cost-imposing measures" by which Washington and its allies may pursue the over-extending and unbalancing of Russia by "non-lethal" means. This, to be clear, is as a general strategy of actively nobbling a competitor nation-state, rather than in response to particular events (i.e. hostile acts by Russia against America or its allies). This is indeed a strategy of permanent warfare by non-violent means in peacetime. A central purpose of these "cost-imposing measures" is to ferment anxiety and alarm in Moscow, so as to elicit the Kremlin's expenditure or shifting of resources for self-defence that will weaken Russia's economy or overstretch its military and shift competition on to terrain that will benefit the US state. The hypocrisy in all of this is apparent. For Russia is castigated by the Western Alliance exactly for its militarism that "cost-imposing measures" are intended to facilitate.

These "cost-imposing measures" are helpfully classified by the RAND authors in accordance with type: economic, geopolitical, ideological and informational, air and space, maritime, and land and multidomain. The economic options include "expanding US energy production", "imposing deeper trade and financial sanctions", "increasing Europe's ability to import gas from suppliers other than Russia", and "encouraging the emigration from Russia of skilled labor and well-educated youth". These measures would all "stress Russia's economy, potentially constraining its government budget, and by extension its defense spending".[138] The geopolitical options include "providing lethal aid to Ukraine" (which would "exploit Russia's greatest point of external vulnerability"), "increasing support to the Syrian rebels", "promoting liberalization in Belarus", "expanding ties in the South Caucasus", and "reducing Russian influence in Central Asia".[139] The ideological and informational options include seeking to diminish faith of Russians in the electoral system, engineering "the perception that the regime is not pursuing the public interest", and "undermining Russia's image abroad".[140]

The options for air and space cost-imposing measures include "reposturing bombers within easy striking range of key Russian strategic targets" (which would have "a high likelihood of success and would certainly get Moscow's attention and raise Russian anxieties"); "reposturing fighters so that they are closer to their targets than bombers as a way to achieve higher sortie rates to compensate for their smaller payloads" (which would "likely concern Moscow even more than reposturing bombers"); "deploying additional tactical nuclear weapons to locations in Europe and Asia" (in order to "heighten Russia's anxiety enough to significantly increase investments in its air defenses"); "repositioning U.S. and allied ballistic missile defense systems to better engage Russian ballistic missiles" (which "would also alarm Moscow"); and pursue "other ways to get Russia to extend itself in strategic competition".[141]

> In terms of benefits, such developments would exploit Moscow's demonstrated fear of US airpower capabilities and doctrines. Developing new low-observable, long-range bombers, or simply adding significantly more of types that are already available or programmed (B-2s and B-21s) would be worrisome for Moscow, as would developing autonomous or remotely piloted strike aircraft and producing them in high numbers. All options would likely incentivize Moscow to devote ever-greater resources to making its command and control systems harder, more mobile, and more redundant.[142]

The options for maritime cost-imposing measures include "increasing US and allied naval force posture and presence in Russia's operating areas" (to "force Russia to increase its naval investments, diverting investments from potentially more dangerous areas"); "increasing naval R&D efforts" (in order to "impose anti-submarine warfare costs on Russia" by allowing "US submarines to threaten a broader set of targets or enhance their ability to threaten Russian nuclear ballistic missile submarines"); and "shifting nuclear posture towards SSBNs" (thereby forcing Russia "to invest in capabilities that can operate in a blue-water environment in two oceans").[143]

Finally, the options for land and domain cost-imposing measures include "increasing US forces in Europe, increasing European NATO member ground capabilities, and deploying a large number of NATO forces on the Russian border"; "increasing the size and frequency of NATO exercises in Europe"; "developing but not deploying an intermediate range missile"; and incremental investments in new technologies to counter Russian air defenses and increase US long-range fires" (in order to "significantly improve defense and deterrence while compelling increased Russian investment in countermeasures".[144]

RAND's researchers could hardly be accused of false modesty. Manifestly, some of the suggestive cost-imposing measures are actual rather than potential US policy. But the real significance of RAND's work in informing US imperial statecraft is not so much in shaping current or future US geostrategic politics but in casting light on the imperial mindset that guides these politics. Which options ought to be pursued and which not to undermine Russia is assessed on a wholly instrumental-strategic cost-benefit calculus. This is on the basis of which of these will cause most harm to Russia whilst posing least risk of incurring responses that would harm the USA.

There is no space here for any distinction between "fair" and "unfair" competition. Nor is there any place for the idea that competition should be hemmed-in by normative or ethical considerations. There is no recognition that Russia is not simply a rival of the US state but also a population of 143 million people. Or, rather, there is no consideration that this should moderate the US state's pursuance of war (in practice, a new cold war) by non-lethal means against its rival. Rather, the privations faced by the Russian people are just the "collateral damage" of the US state's efforts to over-extend and undermine Russia's state or government or economy.

Ukraine and the Western ideology of the Russo-Ukrainian war

One fundamental aspect of US geostrategic competition with Russia (namely, NATO expansion) is not conveyed in the RAND reports, however.[145] This is even though this would certainly fit with the RAND proposals of "increasing US forces in Europe" and "increasing European NATO member ground capabilities".[146]

NATO encroachment on Russia's borders has undoubtedly sowed the seeds of the present Russo-Ukrainian war that was triggered by Putin's invasion of Ukraine in February 2022. This is for the simple and obvious reason that the Russian state (whichever leader or government happens to be administering it) cannot possibly accept this state of affairs. This is not only for reasons of internal security and national self-defence but also owing to the stringent limits this places on the country's wider political and economic aspirations. These aspirations include those of realizing its potential to become a European leader state alongside the UK, Germany, and France, making of itself a key powerbroker in the Euro-Asian zone, and becoming one of the world's biggest economic players; that is, joining the exclusive club of the HICs.

There is nothing anomalous in these politics of securitization and of national self-assertion—not in a global system based on interstate competition and imperial politicking, as ours unfortunately is. Russia is simply too big in geographical terms, too abundant in natural resources, and too well placed geo-strategically, to accept a subordinate status in world affairs, as this is dictated by the USA and its Western allies.

Nonetheless, Russia's attack on Ukraine is typically ideologized in the West (by its politicians and media) as being little more than an incompetent attempt to annex its neighbour as part and parcel of a strategy to restore territories to a new Russian empire that were lost to the former Soviet one. This, as Robert H. Wade says, is the standard narrative of a "wicked revanchist Putin" assaulting an "innocent and unified Ukraine, as a first step to conquest of other parts of eastern and central Europe and restoration of the erstwhile Soviet Union".[147] Thus, Putin's war on Ukraine, as Western politicians constantly reiterate, is completely "unfounded", or totally "unprovoked", as if it could possibly be any such thing.[148] Indefensible it is, of course. But that is not the same as being unfounded. The invasion was also certainly provoked, though nor does that make it excusable.

Yet the battle for Ukraine, it is commonly said, is also a battle to defend "freedom" and "democracy" from Russian imperialism and tyranny.[149] This is also part of the rationale for the West's waging of proxy war via NATO against Russia in support of Ukraine. One might question the basic legitimacy of a call to arms on that basis, however. For would a non-democratic country be any less deserving of international support faced with invasion from a more powerful neighbour than a supposedly "liberal" or "democratic" one?[150] As an exercise of propaganda to mobilize a public in support of proxy war, this is not a matter of importance though. The purpose is simply to ideologize the conflict as one between good and evil because that justifies almost "anything goes" in support of the virtuous and blameless. Public opinion will be more persuaded to go along with the designs of power if these are placed in the service of idealized peoples and communities rather than real ones.

But Ukraine's democracy, which is to be defended by NATO proxy war for as long as it takes to defeat the invasion, irrespective of the economic and people costs, is a deeply flawed democracy, just as much as is Russia's. Indeed, arguably, more so. This is not so much apparent at the level of electoral politics and parliamentary representation. Rather, this is more a matter of the underlying political culture, the institutions of state, and the politics of the street. The far right (i.e. out-and-out fascists or neo-Nazis) have had in Ukraine a marginal presence in parliamentary assemblies during the post-Soviet era. This is quite unlike the case in other post-Soviet republics where far-right parties have tended to be a significant electoral force. Only once, in 2012, has an ultra-right party been elected to parliament on the proportional voting platform. The share of the popular vote of the radical right in national elections has rarely exceeded three per cent, whereas none of its presidential candidates has ever secured more than five per cent of the vote.[151] In the most recent 2019 election, a coalition of ultra-right parties secured just 2.15 per cent of the popular vote.[152]

Nonetheless, the political system is deeply unbalanced on the terrain of the right in that it is suffused with xenophobic ethnic nationalism. And this colours the politics of all of the elected parties and politicians. Indeed, since the not-quite-so-radical right is so strong in the political system, this may explain why there is much less electoral support for the fascistic ultra-rightists than might otherwise be expected. Even so, openly fascist electoral presence is far from zero in Ukraine:

> Far-right groups have also gained political currency in the past decade, none more chilling than Svoboda (formerly the Social National Party of Ukraine), whose leader claimed the country was controlled by a "Muscovite-Jewish mafia" and whose deputy used an antisemitic slur to describe Ukrainian-born Jewish actor Mila Kunis. Svoboda has sent several members to Ukraine's Parliament, including one who called the Holocaust a "bright period" in human history, according to Foreign Policy.[153]

Liberalism, as this is understood in the West, is relatively weak in Ukraine. There is no social-democratic, let alone socialist, tradition of politics. Moreover, the state has actively sought to promulgate an ultranationalist culture. This has involved nominating patriots from the past as national heroes who were often Nazi sympathizers, Holocaust deniers, Holocaust participants, and leaders of anti-Soviet militias in World War Two that collaborated with the Nazis[154]—and renaming streets, statues, plaques, and public buildings accordingly.[155] Those memorialized include Jew-murderers such as Roman Shukhevyich, "leader of a feared Nazi auxiliary police unit", and Yaroslav Stetsko, who infamously declared himself in favour of "the extermination of the Jews in Ukraine".[156]

The state has also funded children's camps run by ultranationalists to promote "patriotic education"—which includes instilling hatred of separatists and Russians as non-peoples, and providing basic military training in how to kill them.[157] Ultranationalism also manifests as discrimination against Russian speakers (indeed against other non-Ukrainian speakers) in what is a multilingual country and oppression of Russian minorities.[158] There is a high degree of censorship of the press in Ukraine (including book and film banning where these do not fit the ultranationalist mould) and persecution of dissidents and of critical journalists. There was (prior to Putin's war) compulsory military service up to 60 years of age.[159] As for antisemitism, this, unsurprisingly, in the years since the "pro-democracy" Maidan uprising of 2014, has been on the ascendant:

> The past three years [since before 2019] saw an explosion of swastikas and SS runes on city streets, death threats, and vandalism of Holocaust memorials, Jewish centers, cemeteries, tombs, and places of worship, all of which led Israel to take the unusual step of publicly urging Kyiv to address the epidemic. Public officials make anti-Semitic threats with no repercussions. . . . For the first few years after Maidan, Jewish organizations largely refrained from criticizing Ukraine, perhaps in the hope Kyiv would address this on its own. But by 2018, the increasing frequency of anti-Semitic incidents led Jewish groups to break their silence. Last year [2018], the Israeli government's annual report on anti-Semitism heavily featured Ukraine, which had more incidents than all post-Soviet states combined. The World Jewish Congress, the US Holocaust Memorial Museum, and 57 members of the US Congress all vociferously condemned Kyiv's Nazi glorification and the concomitant anti-Semitism.[160]

There are openly fascist militias operating at the street level in Ukraine that successive governments since the Maidan uprising have pandered to owing to their high degree of organization and command of weapons.[161] These are instrumental in organizing marches and rallies that celebrate or glorify Ukrainian collaboration with the Nazis in World War Two.[162] These are able to consolidate because they are facilitated by the nationalistic framework of mainstream politics and culture. They are also emboldened by Putin's invasion. Neo-Nazis are thus an integral part of Kyiv's burgeoning volunteer battalions for the Russo-Ukrainian war.[163] These militias then help tilt the political culture and political institutions of the country further to the right.

As April Gordon correctly observes: "While the electoral power of far-right groups is limited, they are nevertheless influential within their respective societies, and shape social and political discourse according to their ideological framework".[164] This is especially true of Ukraine. The ultra-right militias here have political and cultural clout well beyond their resources at the ballot box, in part because elected politicians and ordinary citizens are afraid of them.

> The DC establishment's standard defense of Kyiv is to point out that Ukraine's far right has a smaller percentage of seats in the parliament than their counterparts in places like France. That's a spurious argument: What Ukraine's far

> right lacks in polls numbers, it makes up for with things Marine Le Pen could only dream of—paramilitary units and free rein on the streets.[165]

The paramilitaries also have a presence in the armed forces. The Ukrainian army is the only one in the world which has a self-avowedly neo-Nazi battalion operating in it—the Azov,[166] which also operates as a street militia that has taken upon itself the task of maintaining "order" in civil society.[167] "Azov is . . . an official member of the Ukraine National Guard".[168]

As for the non-elected machinery of state more generally, ultra-right presence here is much greater than among the MPs. Fascists and ultra-rightists occupy positions of authority throughout, especially in the police and security services. Now, Ukrainian liberals have charted human rights abuses in Ukraine conveyed especially by the fascist militias. They have also decried the failure of state and government to address them. For example, as Vyacheslav Likhachev rightly says, ultra-right groups in Ukraine are

> aggressively trying to impose their agenda on Ukrainian society, including by using force against those with opposite political and cultural views. They are a real physical threat to left-wing, feminist, liberal, and LGBT activists, human rights defenders, as well as ethnic and religious minorities . . . [E]xtremist groups have become increasingly active. The most disturbing element of their recent show of force is that so far it has gone fully unpunished by the authorities. Their activities challenge the legitimacy of the state, undermine its democratic institutions, and discredit the country's law enforcement agencies.[169]

Quite so. But what is often missed by the critics is that it is the overall political climate of right-facing ethno-nationalism in Ukraine and the penetration of the state (especially of law enforcement) by ultranationalists and fascist sympathizers that is licensing the "neo-Nazi pogroms against the Roma" and "attacks on feminists and LGBT groups",[170] which state authority has been either unable or unwilling to confront.[171] Such explains the failure of state power to confront the perpetrators.

All of this was the case on the eve of the present war. None of this gets a press airing or political articulation in countries such as the UK, however, because this might de-legitimize in the public mind the West's bankrolling of Ukrainian "freedom" and "democracy" by force of arms. According to Western propaganda, by definition, nothing that Putin or the Kremlin have to say about the need to "de-Nazify" and "de-militarize" Ukraine can have any merit or veracity. For sure, it is true that rooting out Nazis and the paramilitaries was not Putin's motive for the invasion, as the critics say. But, even so, Putin's fig-leaf is based on something substantive, which is why it is effective in Russia as propaganda.

Ordinary Russians can buy into it because there is a case to answer. For, as Lev Golinkin points out,

> stories of Ukraine's dark nationalism aren't coming out of Moscow; they're being filed by Western media, including US-funded Radio Free Europe (RFE); Jewish organizations such as the World Jewish Congress, and the Simon Wiesenthal Center; and watchdogs like Amnesty International, Human Rights Watch, and Freedom House, which issued a joint report warning that Kyiv is losing the monopoly on the use of force in the country as far-right gangs operate with impunity.[172]

The ideological representation of the Russo-Ukrainian conflict in the West (as motivated solely by Putin's wish to crush Ukraine's brave new democracy under the wheels of his military in pursuance of his goal to emulate the empire of the Czars or the Soviets) has been necessary to legitimize the Alliance's bankrolling of Western proxy war (via NATO) against Russia in support of the Kyiv regime, so as to thwart Putin. Alas, given the corporate media's overwhelming tendency to merely reproduce the party line of political powerholders on matters of foreign policy—so that dissenting or critical voices are more or less silenced by being denied an outlet—the general publics in the Western countries have been rendered passively acquiescent.

There are no other representations of the conflict ready to hand that might be compared with the dominant narrative of the war and the West's role in it by which this narrative might be found wanting. After all, if Putin succeeded in annexing Ukraine, as Western ideology tells it, surely this would embolden this "new Hitler's" territorial ambitions further westwards in Europe. Who would be next if Ukraine should fall? Robert Pszczel, writing in the *NATO Review*, typifies this alarmist (and unfounded) view:

> February 24, 2022, is likely to engrave itself on the history template of the contemporary world. Russia's unprovoked, unjustified and barbaric invasion of Ukraine is not only a manifestation of a huge security danger that has shattered peace in Europe. More structurally, it has broken the entire security architecture built patiently on the continent over many decades, including international commitments agreed in the last 30 years. As the top UK general recently observed, it is dangerous to assume that the war on Ukraine is a limited conflict. This could be "our 1937 moment", and everything possible must be done in order to stop territorial expansion by force, thereby averting a war similar to the one that ravaged Europe 80 years ago. Mobilising our resources must start today.[173]

Certainly, the USA and its NATO partners have "mobilized their resources". They have provided Kyiv with astronomical sums of advanced weapons aid—either to secure Ukrainian victory (which so far has proven elusive) or at least to prevent a Russian victory or make it too costly. The US state alone has provided the equivalent of 42 billion euros of arms assistance in the period from January 2022 until July 2023. Over the same period, Germany has provided 17 billion, the UK 6.6 billion, Norway 3.7 billion, Denmark 3.5 billion, Poland three billion, and the Netherlands 2.5 billion. These are the biggest donors in absolute terms. France, Sweden, and Canada have stumped up a further 4.4 billion euros between them.[174]

Without this military support, the war would, in all probability, have been over in two or three months, Russian forces withdrawn, and civilian normalcy restored, following meaningful diplomatic negotiations, albeit under terms favourable to Moscow. Instead, at the time of writing, the war has dragged out for one-and-half years, at enormous human and economic cost, with no end in sight.[175] Projections by military specialists of the war's longitude vary from six months (optimistic scenario) to indefinitely (worst-case scenario), with several years being seen as a reasonable case scenario.[176] Many (including NATO commanders) do not consider a military solution as possible for either side. As General Mark Milley, Chairperson of the Joint Chiefs of Staff, cautioned US leaders,

> there has to be a mutual recognition that military victory, in the true sense of the word, is maybe not achievable through military means. And therefore, you need to turn to other means. . . . So when there's an opportunity to negotiate, when peace can be achieved, seize it, seize the moment.[177]

The real motives and purposes of Russia's war in Ukraine

Setting propaganda aside, the purpose of Putin's invasion was far more modest and realistic in geostrategic terms than territorial empire-building. This was, rather, intended to either render the Ukrainian government more compliant with Russian strategic and economic interests or replace it with one that would be more compliant. There was almost certainly no intention to annex Ukraine. Putin, an arch pragmatist, would understand the prohibitively high costs of such an endeavour—economically, politically, and militarily.

Since the Maidan "Revolution of Dignity" of 2014, which removed from office a Moscow-friendly government in Kyiv, the successor nationalist governments of Poroshenko and Zelenskyy in Ukraine have energetically pursued a policy of cutting ties with its Eastern neighbour in favour of pursuing economic and military alliances with the USA and against Russia. The military aspect of this alliance-building was of particular concern to Moscow, for reasons that are obvious, but which I will further describe. This was to be the security trigger issue that led to war. These facts have been obscured by a fog of obfuscatory rhetoric on all sides of the conflict—whether this be the Kremlin's bogus claim that the invasion was motivated by the need to "de-Nazify" Ukrainian politics (though detoxification would be a good thing), or Western claims that Russia's security concerns are a mere excuse for the prosecution of war for purely offensive rather than defensive purposes.

The prelude to the Russo-Ukrainian war was, in fact, decades in which the US strategy of containment through ring-fencing of Russia was being accelerated, especially under the presidencies of George W. Bush and Barack Obama. This was with the incorporation into NATO of Bulgaria, Rumania, and the Baltic Republics.[178]

> In November 2002, Bush backed NATO's invitation to seven nations—including former Soviet republics Estonia, Latvia and Lithuania—to begin talks to join the Western alliance. In 2004, with Bush as a driving force, the seven Eastern European nations joined NATO.[179]

Shortly afterwards, Bush Junior's US government courted longstanding Russian allies Georgia and Ukraine by making them recipients of generous Western aid.[180] This was just as it tore up the Anti-Ballistic Missile Treaty as the prelude to set up new surveillance installations and anti-ballistic missile bases in several NATO-aligned countries in Eastern Europe. Bush next

> called on NATO to give Ukraine and Georgia a so-called Membership Action Plan, a formal process that would put each on a path toward eventually joining the alliance. France and Germany blocked him and warned that further NATO expansion would spur an aggressive Russian stance when Moscow regained power. In the end, the alliance simply issued a statement saying the two countries "will become members of NATO". That compromise risked the worst of both worlds—antagonizing Moscow without giving Kiev . . . a roadmap to join NATO.[181]

The US- and EU-supported "pro-democracy" Maidan coup of far-right nationalist groups in Ukraine then chased out the democratically elected president Viktor Yanukovych in 2014, just one year before the next elections were due.[182] Yanukovych's presidency was mired in corruption and nepotism scandals. His government was (like its predecessor and successors) also a repressive and authoritarian one. Yanukovych was also implementing a neoliberal SAP ("elimination of tariffs, a wage and pension freeze, spending cuts, and the end of gas subsidies to Ukrainian households") in return for an IMF loan that was generating much hardship and discontent. But the immediate catalyst for the protests that led to the coup was Yanukovych's decision to abandon a free trade deal with the EU (with strings attached) in favour of a much better offer from Moscow (without conditionalities) that was also supported negatively by the threat of Russian trade sanctions. These matters brought a wave of popular protests to the streets that far-right militias were able to exploit through acts of violence and intimidation so as to destabilize and unseat the president.[183]

Before that, Yanukovych was inevitably dismissed by the West as a Moscow "puppet" for courting closer economic ties with Russia rather than the EU. But, in fact, Yanukovych sought to court both Russia and the EU and USA, or to acquiesce to the pressures coming from East and West for partnership, rather than pick sides between them. His was a balancing act necessitated in part by a sharply polarized country—with more than a third (in the Russian-speaking eastern provinces) rooting for closer alignment with Russia and the rest (in the Ukrainian-speaking central and western provinces) rooting for closer integration with the EU and USA.[184] This was not acceptable to the US state and its closest allies, however. They demanded an ally in Kyiv that would side with the West to the exclusion of Moscow,[185] which is exactly what the Maidan coup delivered. Such allowed the disregard of due democratic process in Ukraine that ousted Yanukovych to be ideologized by Western governments as a "democratic revolution". This was a new watershed in the degeneration of Russo-Ukrainian relations.

In preceding years, NATO expansion had reduced Russia's European security buffer with the West to just two states, Belarus and Ukraine. Consequently, for Moscow, preservation of friendly relations with Kyiv was rendered geo-strategically vital, which is why the loss of Yanukovych was such a blow. Now, as I have noted, Ukraine is a country divided between an anti-Russian and pro-EU and pro-US west and a Russia-leaning east. Such rendered it inherently unstable and ripe for a tug-of-war between the two sides. The Maidan coup of 2014 motivated Russia's retaliatory strategic annexation of Crimea, and a further escalation of tensions between the two countries, including border skirmishes. Meanwhile, Ukraine's pursuit of NATO membership, which the US state did nothing to deter, and for which it declared its support (along with support for Georgia's membership since 2008), raised the spectre of outright war between the two countries.[186]

Putin's Eurasian geopolitics and the Western response

Now, drawing Ukraine into NATO would be entirely consistent with US imperialism's established strategy of hostile encirclement and neutralization of a potentially dangerous regional hegemon. Neither Putin in Moscow nor Zelenskyy in Kyiv could be unaware of the stakes. Nonetheless, Putin did not yield to pressure from ultranationalist hardliners in the Kremlin who wanted him to invade Ukraine right there and then in response to Maidan to restore a pro-Russian government. This was even though Ukraine was militarily weak at the time and would have been incapable of repelling a Russian offensive. The reason was that Putin favoured a strategy of securing looser Russian influence (or softer diplomatic power) over the former Soviet republics in eastern Europe by means of courting the French and German governments to drive a wedge between the EU and the USA.[187] In short, Putin preferred a diplomatic solution to the security issues posed to Russia by Ukraine rather than a military one.

Prior to this strategy of courting the EU's leading states to weaken the Western Alliance, Putin had instead sought a direct rapprochement with the US state. This was less than two years into his first presidency. This was because Putin had determined that cooperation rather than outright competition with the USA was the surest way of modernizing the Russian economy and re-establishing post-Soviet Russia as a great power that would play once again a leading role in world affairs.[188] It was the failure of this strategy that led him to seek out a solution within Europe *against* Washington.

The events of 9/11 provided the Kremlin with the opportunity to rebuild relations with Washington on the basis of a shared securitization agenda. Putin grasped the mettle:

> After a rocky start with the Bush administration—marked by spy scandals and a dispute over U.S. intentions to build a missile defense shield and withdraw from the 1972 Anti-Ballistic Missile Treaty—Putin had worked hard to build a personal affinity with Bush, remove the sense of confrontation, underscore that the Cold War was finally over, and find some mechanism for transcending differences. After September 11, it seemed that the war against terrorism could be just that mechanism. Russia and the United States had finally made common cause.[189]

Détente began with a telephone call—from Putin to Bush Junior—warning of an imminent terrorist attack on the USA. Apparently, this warning was disregarded. Later, after 9/11, Putin provided the Americans with counter-terrorism intelligence to assist their war on the Taliban derived from the USSR's long struggle against the Islamist militias in Afghanistan.[190] In a move that would have been unthinkable in the Cold War era, Putin even "agreed that US planes carrying humanitarian aid could fly through Russian air space" and that "the US military could use airbases in former Soviet republics in Central Asia" in pursuance of the "war on terror".[191] The latter move was remarkably unilateral. There were and are no circumstances by which the US state would extend the same permissions to the Russian military. By these means, Putin sought to build trust between the two countries and secure a partnership of equals in global affairs.[192]

Trouble was that the USA, under Bush Junior's presidency, was happy to accept the counter-terrorism support from Russia (which facilitated the rapid defeat of the Taliban in Afghanistan), and to offer some in return, but was never going to accept an equal partnership of unequals on anti-terrorism strategy or anything else between the two countries. Intelligence-sharing with regard to terrorist attacks continued. But Bush's "war on terror" was soon stepping on the

Kremlin's toes. This was as new US military bases were set up in the former Soviet republics of Kyrgyzstan and Uzbekistan,[193] and as Bush's neocon government pursued regime change in Iraq (without UN approval and in disregard of international law), as well as casting Iran and North Korea as "rogue" states supportive of terrorism, despite Putin's objections. As Fiona Hill reported at the time:

> Putin prides himself on Russia's intelligence capabilities. Russian leaders think they know their enemy, and it is certainly not in Iraq, Iran, and North Korea. While Russian intelligence officials concede that U.S. concerns about Saddam Hussein's acquisition of weapons of mass destruction have merit, they feel the threat can be contained and managed. From its perspective, Russia sees Iran as a stabilizing force in the Middle East, the Caucasus, and Central Asia, not as a state sponsor of terrorism. North Korea is an unstable neighbor, but not a military threat. In other words, Bush's axis of evil is not Putin's.[194]

In particular, the US invasion of Iraq in 2003 "was a turning point for Putin", since for him "the war made a mockery of American claims of promoting democracy abroad and upholding international law".[195] At a G8 press conference in 2006, hosting Putin and Bush, Putin openly mocked his opposite number: "We certainly would not want to have the same kind of democracy as they have in Iraq, I will tell you quite honestly".[196] Relations between the two countries also plummeted because Bush was on the same timescale setting aside those longstanding American undertakings not to push NATO deeper into the former Soviet world, in disregard of Moscow's security concerns. The Baltic states were the next to be incorporated.[197]

Putin made one more diplomatic push to get "onside" with the Americans and reverse the trends towards escalating tensions between the two sides. This was as Barak Obama was installed in the White House in January 2009.

> At first, the reset fared well. . . . Moscow agreed to greatly expand Washington's ability to ship military supplies to Afghanistan via Russia. In April 2010, the United States and Russia signed a new START treaty, further reducing the U.S. and Russian nuclear arsenals. Later that year, Russia supported sweeping new U.N. economic sanctions on Iran and blocked the sale of sophisticated, Russian-made S-300 anti-aircraft missile systems to Tehran.[198]

Moscow's backing of Obama's Iran policy—a continuation more-or-less of Bush's casting of Tehran as a rogue state—was remarkable. Remarkable, in that Putin was not inclined to see Iran as a rogue state that was particularly supportive of terrorism, and he would see Russia's geopolitical interests as better served by alliance-building with Iran than by supporting the regime's international isolation. But Moscow subordinated these misgivings about US foreign policy and pursuance of its own regional interests to the goal of courting American favour for US-Russian bilateralism and American non-interference in the former Soviet republics.

But, again, as was the case with Putin's earlier overtures towards Bush Junior's administration, much more was offered than returned. Obama reiterated his total commitment to the NATO alliance. He "affirmed that NATO's door remains open to European democracies that meet the standards for NATO membership".[199] The Baltic state of Montenegro was invited to start accession talks. This was as "NATO pointedly listed other countries in the pipeline for membership: Macedonia, Bosnia-Herzegovina, and most controversially, Georgia".[200] Obama announced plans to modernize NATO by developing "a territorial missile defense capability, which is necessary to defend against the growing threat from ballistic missiles".[201] These events made it clear that there was to be no American recognition of Russia as a great power with a right to its own sphere of influence in the former Soviet territories—which was the purpose of Putin's diplomatic efforts towards Washington. Rather, Russia remained, from the US perspective, potentially a "rogue" state, which needed to be reined in.

These facts about Putin's foreign policy have tended to escape the notice even of critics who can see through the "Putin = new Hitler" nonsense that spews forth from the corporate media and Western politicians. Robert H. Wade, for example, refers to a clash of "two mega forces"—namely, "the US's long-standing assertion of 'primacy' or 'hegemony *vis-à-vis* all other states" versus "the Russian state's ambition to constitute itself as the centre of the Eurasian polity, culture and economy". As Wade rightly says: "This long-term drive is missed by the focus on Putin—his ambition and his state of mind".[202] But, although Wade is right about Putin acting in accordance with goals that transcend his regime, it is overstating the matter to regard these as serving a *territorial* imperial project. Doubtless, Jane Burbank, emeritus Professor of History and Russian and Slavic studies at New York University, is right to affirm: "Since the 1990s, plans to reunite Ukraine and other post-Soviet states into a trans-continental superpower have been brewing in Russia". Yet, it is doubtful, as she claims, that "a revitalized theory of Eurasian empire informs Mr Putin's every move"[203]—or at least that it did prior to his invasion of Ukraine. The agenda of the Kremlin ultranationalists was not shared by Putin. Evidence to the contrary is slim.[204] Events since then may have encouraged a rethink on Putin's part, however.

Rather, as Anatol Lieven explains, the goal of Putin's regime, after its rebuttals by the US state, was "to create a new security order in Europe with Russia as a full partner and respected power"—respected, that is, as an integral part of European civilization rather than as a separate Eurasian civilization.[205] Putin was wanting to draw Russia closer to the EU rather than maintaining the country as an outsider rival power on the fringes of Europe that looked especially to Asia to build influence. The goal was indeed to constitute Russia as a great power that was central to Europe and indeed central and southern Asia, but primarily through the methods of soft power.

> This Russian strategy was . . . an attempt to split the west, and cement a Russian sphere of influence in the states of the former Soviet Union. However, having a European security order with Russia at the table would also have removed the risk of a Russian attack on NATO, the EU, and most likely, Ukraine; and allowed Moscow to exert a looser influence over its neighbours—closer perhaps to the present approach of the US to Central America—rather than gripping them tightly.

This was not a politics that was endorsed by other Russian nationalists to Putin's right inside and outside the Kremlin for whom courting closer ties with the EU's leading states was a waste of time and for whom territorial imperialism was the rightful way of restoring Russia's place in the world. These ultranationalists were not set on Putin's vision of making Russia, as he put it in 2012, "an inseparable, organic part of the Greater Europe, of the wider European civilisation", which would fit he thought with the aspirations of the Russian citizenry. Despite repeated setbacks, though, Putin remained more-or-less committed to this project. So, for him, attacking Ukraine would have undermined this strategy, strengthening the US alliance with France and Germany and the associated politics of Russian containment rather than weakening them. Putin thus acquiesced to diplomatic pressure from Berlin to reign-in pro-Russian separatists in the Donbas in return for Franco-German commitments not to arm the government in Kyiv and to support an autonomous Donbas under Ukrainian sovereignty under the terms of the Minsk 2 treaty.[206]

As Lieven tells, however, Putin's strategy ran into the buffers of Western intransigence. Berlin and Paris did not honour Minsk 2 and probably never had any intention of doing so. Ukraine refused to entertain an autonomous Donbas region without any diplomatic leverage being exerted to the contrary by any of the Western powers. Kyiv's war against the separatists thus continued unchecked at the cost of thousands of lives. Indeed, in the runup to Putin's invasion, this was escalated, in reckless disregard of civilian non-combatants caught up in the fighting.[207]

But, even before military escalation in the Donbas, there were other provocative anti-Russian acts by the Poroshenko government, such as repression of Russian language-use among the Russian minorities.

> On 23 February [2014], the day after Yanukovych fled, *the first act* of the Ukrainian parliament was to revoke the legal status of Russian as a national language; and more broadly, to prevent regions from allowing the use of any other language than Ukrainian. The government set about blocking access to Russian news, TV channels and radio. All through the next months, the government, the

> broadcast media and large sections of the population chanted the motto *"One Nation, One Language, One People"*. These were blatantly belligerent acts towards a large minority. It is easy to understand why the many millions of Russian speakers felt under envenomed siege; and why they felt emboldened by support from the powerful state on their doorstep. The fact that language legislation was then not put into law did not suddenly "make everything right again". The efforts to marginalise Russian speakers continued.[208]

Indeed, it was language war that alienated the Russian speakers of the Donbas from Kyiv to such a degree that the separatist movement was born:

> The largely Russian speaking and Russian Orthodox believing populations of the eastern provinces of Donetsk and Luhansk voted in favour of independence from Ukraine. The government in Kyiv (mostly Ukrainian speaking and Catholic) launched a war against these provinces to crush their resistance.

Kyiv's cultural war on Russian speakers and its military war on the separatists also gave encouragement to those anti-Russian acts perpetrated by non-aligned radical nationalists, including members of the neo-fascist militia groups. These included the desecration of World War Two cemeteries in which the Red Army's war dead were buried.[209]

Yet Moscow's diplomatic efforts continued. The plight of the Russians in the Donbas under attack from the Ukrainian army and ultra-right militias (but defended by Russian pro-separatist militias—also often ultranationalist) did not lead Putin to recognize the self-declared autonomy of Donetsk and Luhansk from Ukraine. This was likely so he could avoid committing Russian troops to the Donbas in support of the separatists, which would not fit with the attempt to win over Paris and Berlin. Putin stuck to this course for eight years. To no avail. His regime was accused of covert operations in the Donbas involving Russian troops disguised as local fighters.[210] Moscow's proposed European Security Treaty, which "would have frozen NATO enlargement, effectively ensured the neutrality of Ukraine and other states, and institutionalised consultation on equal terms between Russia and leading western countries", was spurned.[211]

So, in February 2021, Putin finally "entered the on-going civil war [in Ukraine] in order to protect the Donbas republics from the stepped up Ukrainian military attacks" (which were likely sanctioned by the USA and NATO), "and on a scale big enough for it to replace the national government".[212] At the same time, other developments may have resigned Putin to the view that a final reckoning with Kyiv may be unavoidable.

> These included the US-Ukrainian Strategic Partnership of November 2021, which held out the prospect of Ukraine becoming a heavily armed US ally in all but name, while continuing to threaten to retake the Donbas by force.[213]

US imperialism and the politics of entrapment

This was obviously a hazardous game of imperial politics being played out by the US government, because keeping Ukraine "neutral" would always be for Russia an absolute national security issue that could not be crossed, irrespective of who happens to lead the government in Moscow, as Washington would know. It is even possible, if not probable, that the US government's refusal to concede Moscow's demands for a "neutral" demilitarized Ukraine, or to rule out granting the country NATO membership, was intended to goad Putin into making war on his neighbour. This diplomatic intransigence was, therefore, likely intended as a trap.

After all, faced with the same situation that Russia was encountering (i.e. hostile encroachment from a foreign power in its own regional sphere of influence), US governments would behave in exactly the same way as Putin's regime in Russia was threatening to behave—and in the end did behave. This is sanctioned by the so-called "Monroe Doctrine", according to which the US state reserves the right to take military action in its own "backyard" (Latin America or in the Caribbean) in defence of its national security interests.[214] As such, Washington would understand, based on its own imperial precedents, that Russian military action in Ukraine in response to NATO expansion into the country would be a reasonable case scenario.

There is certainly at least one precedent for considering the trap scenario as feasible—Operation Cyclone. Operation Cyclone was the US state's campaign of destabilization of the pro-Soviet government of Afghanistan in the 1980s and early1990s. This included arming and training for insurgency the Islamic mujahidin (out of which eventually emerged the Taliban) and the so-called Afghan Arabs (Jihadists recruited from the Middle East, including Al-Qaeda).[215] The goal of Operation Cyclone became not merely to destabilize the Soviet-allied government in Kabul, which was its initial purpose, but to lure the Kremlin into an internecine and fruitless war against the insurgents in support of its ally that would strain its economy and degrade its military.

As Walter Slocombe, of the US Department of Defence, explained it, "there was value in keeping the Afghan insurgency going", since this would draw the Soviets into their own "Vietnamese quagmire", which "we had every interest in making sure they got stuck" in.[216] This, of course, is exactly what transpired. Zbigniew Brzezinski, the US government's Chief National Security Adviser during the Carter presidency, lauded the operation for its role in triggering the Soviet collapse:

> We didn't push the Russians to intervene, but we knowingly increased the probability that they would. . . . That secret operation was an excellent idea. It had the effect of drawing the Russians into the Afghan trap. . . . The day that the Soviets officially crossed the border, I wrote to President

Carter, essentially: "We now have the opportunity of giving to the USSR its Vietnam war". Indeed, for almost 10 years, Moscow had to carry on a war that was unsustainable for the regime, a conflict that brought about the demoralization and finally the breakup of the Soviet empire. What is more important in world history? The Taliban or the collapse of the Soviet empire? Some agitated Moslems or the liberation of Central Europe and the end of the cold war?"[217]

According to Robert H. Wade, US strategic geopolitical planners were banking on the Kremlin taking the bait and going into Ukraine. Indeed, US imperial policy towards Russia since 2013 was based on engineering exactly this scenario, he argues.[218] This was based on recognition of the vital geostrategic importance of Ukraine to Russia's self-defence and its goal of becoming a Euro-Asian powerhouse. As Wade points out, the strategic value of Western dominance of Ukraine was apparent to US statespersons for decades before the present conflict. As Zbigniew Brzezinski argued in his book *The Grand Chessboard* back in the 1990s: "Ukraine, a new and important space on the Eurasian chessboard, is a *geopolitical pivot* because its very existence as an independent country helps to transform Russia".[219] As Wade elaborates:

> He [Brzezinski] explained that without Ukraine being integrated into or closely allied to Russia, Russia was a "predominantly Asian imperial state". Whereas Ukraine integrated into Russia gave Russia the opening to be (or resume being) "a Eurasian empire". So the long-held US aim has been to push Ukraine away from Russia, as a major step towards constraining Russian strategy, and more distantly Chinese strategy too, thereby sustaining US primacy.[220]

From this perspective, the destabilization of Moscow's Yanukovych "puppet" was the necessary opening gambit to securing this objective, since this made possible the drawing of Ukraine into the Western camp, which was a red line for Russia that could not be crossed.

If conflict-provocation was the goal of US state planners, there were clear signs that this was yielding results in the runup to Putin's invasion. Since the spring of 2021, there was another upscaling of Ukrainian military action against pro-Russian separatists in the Donbas region and of "retaliatory" Russian troop mobilizations close to the border, accelerating in October of that year.[221] Given the failure of Moscow's strategy of alliance-building with France and Germany to neutralize US influence in Europe and reverse NATO expansion, Putin was thus less inclined or less able to resist the demands of "told you so" nationalists in his government to switch to the military option. Military action might, after all, achieve what diplomatic manoeuvres had failed to deliver. This was to force Ukraine to abandon allying itself with the US state or, failing that, allow a more Russian-friendly regime to be installed in Kyiv.

Even so, Putin seemingly sought to avoid sending in the troops right up to the point that he did so. This was as he persevered with his attempt to secure French agreement for a diplomatic solution that involved obtaining Ukrainian agreement to abandoning pursuit of NATO membership and engaging in direct talks with the separatists over autonomy within Ukraine.[222] Putin also did plenty of sabre-rattling in the runup to the invasion. The opportunity for this was provided by the fact that his military build-up was "patient", drawn out, several months (almost four) in the making before the invasion was started. This was obviously in the hope that the drama of it would exert pressure for a diplomatic breakthrough so that it could be called off. As was reported by *Al-Jazeera* a couple of weeks before Putin sent the troops across the border:

> Since the failure of negotiations to resolve the crisis, it remains unclear where events are headed. For Putin, the best outcome would be for the West to meet his security demands, having been persuaded by Russia's military mobilisation that Moscow is serious and capable of launching an invasion.

Last-minute diplomacy was unsuccessful though. As the *Al-Jazeera* reporter went on to say, "the Biden administration does not seem willing to make such concessions and already denied a Russian request for written reassurances on Ukraine's neutrality".[223] Thus, diplomacy failed because Washington did not want it to succeed. This is for various reasons, most of which I have expounded elsewhere, but which I will reiterate here. What are these reasons?

Firstly, because the advantage to Washington of a Russo-Ukrainian war would be that it would "allow a radical upscaling of sanctions against Russia, setting back its economy for decades".[224] Secondly, because the privations of the war would offer opportunity to destabilize the Putin government, opening up the possibility of a weaker, more US-compliant successor regime.[225] In short, it would generate potential for regime change in Moscow.[226] Finally, because "this would seriously degrade the Russian military, by legitimizing NATO member states in providing Ukraine with massive amounts of advanced weapons aid, which could draw Russia into a prolonged and costly conflict".[227] This is exactly the trap scenario. Such, of course, has all since come to pass, except that Putin's rule remains intact, and the Russian state retains its capacity to re-tool its military and provide its people with the necessaries of life, despite suffering under the most punitive sanctions regime ever imposed on a country.[228]

But, if provoking Russia to wage war in Ukraine was indeed the US government's intention, as is likely, it is worth noting the risks this would pose (and which now are being posed) to political security and economic stability worldwide. These were and are astronomical. As I wrote on the eve of the war:

> Military aid for Kyiv from the West and NATO in the context of all-out war between Russia and Ukraine would risk military escalation and cross-border conflict-widening from Moscow. US-led economic sanctions against Russia

> may even bolster nationalist support at home for Putin. Moreover, sanctions on Russia and Western military involvement in Ukraine (via NATO) would inevitably beget Russian retaliatory action—including the suspension of energy supplies to Europe and beyond.[229]

Cross-border conflict widening has not yet transpired, but this remains a real danger, especially if the war starts going badly wrong for Russia. Putin has also retained a large degree of public support at home, despite war privations and sanctions,[230] and there have been no moves to unseat him from within the state apparatus. Ordinary Russians, after all, are hardly strangers to Western attempts to inflict economic harm on their country in order to coerce them into challenging their leaders, whereas these attempts may reinforce anti-Western sentiment rather than encourage anti-government sentiment or protest—as is the intention behind them. This has certainly been the case for Putin.[231]

Sanctions have also been less effective in degrading the Russian economy than these were expected to be by the IMF and World Bank, though these obviously have inflicted major damage.[232] And, of course, sanctions on Russia and Western military involvement in Ukraine (via NATO) have triggered aggressive Russian countermeasures. Sanctions and counter-measures together have indeed majorly disrupted energy supplies worldwide, at huge economic cost, with the EU particularly hard hit (though not as much as the UK),[233] because 45 per cent of its supply of natural gas is from Russia.[234] Yet, despite sanctions, EU imports of Russian liquefied natural gas increased by 42 per cent in 2022, at massively inflated prices.[235] This has accelerated those recessionary pressures on world capitalism that are stemming immediately from the COVID-19 pandemic, but which also reflect decades of weak growth culminating in the Great Financial Crisis of 2007/09 and long period of economic stagnancy that has followed.

But these risks (including nuclear escalation) manifestly are regarded by US imperialism as worth taking, just as much as they are acceptable to the Kremlin. This is just as much as the enormous cost of the war in terms of destroyed and damaged lives has been regarded as acceptable to the Western powers to secure their geostrategic goals, just as they have been to Moscow to preserve the remnants of Russia's defensive shield and strike a blow against US primacy. It is worth noting that the devastation caused by this clash of intransigents extends far beyond the theatre of war. Of particular concern is the impact of war and sanctions combined on global food security. As noted by the *Economics Observatory*:

> Before the war, Ukraine and Russia were together the world's largest exporter of wheat—responsible for over a third (36%) of wheat exports. They also exported more than half of the world's sunflower oil. Early predictions, including those in Economic Observatory, that the conflict would exacerbate global food insecurity have, sadly, proved to be correct. It has hit developing and emerging economies the hardest, as they rely more on Ukraine and

> Russia for fuel and grain imports. The Food Security Information Network highlights the war as a key force—alongside the pandemic, other conflicts and extreme weather—behind a staggering rise in the number of people who are food-insecure. Nearly 258 million people in 58 countries/territories were in food crisis or moderate-to-severe acute food insecurity in 2022—up from 193 million in 53 countries/territories in 2021. This is the highest figure on record since the organisation began reporting these data in 2017.[236]

Diplomatic roadblocks

That the US government intentionally sought to draw Russia into a trap—that of making war on Ukraine in order to destabilize the government and undermine its capacity to pursue its own geostrategic goals—has been evidenced by subsequent events. The first of these took place just one month after the start of the conflict, in early March 2022. The second followed just a few weeks later, also in March 2022. What may be described as non-events, which unfolded in the autumn of 2022 and in the summer of 2023, also provide compelling evidence that the Western powers are not interested in a diplomatic solution to the war.

The initial March events were diplomatic efforts involving the former Israeli prime minister Naftali Bennett that reportedly yielded an agreement between Putin and Zelenskyy to end the war. The terms of settlement were that Putin would agree not to order Zelenskyy's assassination, would not require Ukraine's disarmament, and would immediately withdraw Russian forces from Ukraine, in exchange simply for Ukraine's agreement to renounce NATO membership. The deal was revoked, however, because, as Bennett put it, the key Western powers (the USA, France, Germany, and the UK) "blocked" it, in favour of a more "aggressive" policy towards Russia.[237]

Then a few weeks later:

> Russian and Ukrainian officials met in Istanbul, Turkey, and followed up with virtual consultations. According to former U.S. officials speaking to *Foreign Affairs*, the two sides agreed on the framework for a tentative deal. Russian officials, including Putin, have said publicly that a deal was close following the Istanbul talks. But the negotiations ultimately failed after more Western pressure. Boris Johnson visited Kyiv in April 2022, urging Zelenskyy not to negotiate with Russia.[238]

The deal in question was similar to the one that Bennett brokered earlier in March. As was reported by Fiona Hill, a former US Security Council official:

> According to multiple former senior US officials we spoke with, in April 2022, Russian and Ukrainian negotiators appeared to have tentatively agreed on the outlines of a negotiated interim settlement: Russia would withdraw to its

position on February 23, when it controlled part of the Donbas region and all of Crimea, and in exchange Ukraine would promise not to seek NATO membership and instead receive security guarantees from a number of countries. But as Russian Foreign Minister Sergey Lavrov stated in a July interview with his country's state media, this compromise is no longer an option.[239]

According to Hill and Angela Stent of the US National Intelligence Council (who are both bellicose exponents of the Western view of Putin as being set on forging a Russian territorial empire out of the Slavic countries—if not beyond), this peace deal was close to being signed.[240] This was also the view of Turkish Foreign Minister Mevlut Cavusoglu.[241] But this was before UK PM Johnson showed up virtually unannounced in Kyiv in April 2022 for talks with Zelenskyy. Johnson's intervention was presumably at the behest of the US government since he spoke on behalf (he said) of the "collective West". His "surprise" house call was also his first ever visit to Ukraine. As was reported in the local media: "Following the arrival of . . . Johnson in Kyiv, a possible meeting between . . . Zelenskyy and . . . Putin has become less likely".[242]

And so, it transpired. Within three days of Johnson's visit, the Turkish peace plan was dead in the water, for officially stated reasons that are as questionable as they are troublesome. As Tamás Orbán conveys: "Officially, Ukraine left the peace talks because of the discovery of the Bucha massacre after the Russian army withdrew from the Kyiv area". However, "the bodies of the murdered civilians in Bucha were discovered on April 1st, while the talks continued until after Johnson's surprise trip" on 9 April.[243] This shows that the timeframe of events simply does not support the official Western version of reasons taken in response to these events. Johnson's visit was officially intended to convey the UK's (and presumably the bigger West's) "unwavering support" for Ukraine, and to pledge their continued commitment to providing sufficient weapons and financial aid to prosecute the war indefinitely. The message was backed up with the news that the UK would supply an additional £130 million of "sophisticated weaponry" beyond existing commitments.[244] But, according to *Ukrainska Pravda*, Johnson also conveyed to Zelenskyy two "simple messages" on behalf of Kyiv's Western backers:

> The first is that Putin is a war criminal, he should be pressured, not negotiated with. And the second is that even if Ukraine is ready to sign some agreements on guarantees with Putin, they [the Western powers] are not. Johnson's position was that the collective West . . . now felt that Putin was not really as powerful as they had previously imagined, and that there was a chance to "press him."[245]

The successful Ukrainian Kharkiv and Kherson offensives in the autumn of 2022 presented a further opportunity to look for a peaceful settlement, but this time from a position of negotiating strength for Kyiv. As Medea Benjamin and

Nicolas Davies point out, such would have been consistent with US president Joe Biden's own press-stated reasons for arming Ukraine.[246] Weapons aid, Biden wrote, is intended to allow Ukrainian leaders to secure the best possible negotiated end to the war from a position of military advantage.[247] Yet, despite military advantage, there were no peace talks. These were not attempted by Western leaders, because presumably their own real but unstated goals (Russia's defeat, regime change, or utter degradation of the Russian economy and military) were not yet accomplished.

Kyiv's military advantage then evaporated. Ukraine's deferred spring offensive of 2023, which was supposed to begin to roll-back the Russian invasion stalled, incurring major losses in soldiers and equipment (including NATO-provided weapons). This was having scarcely made any progress, foundering on Russia's well-prepared and heavily fortified defensive lines.[248] Consequently, the war has settled into seemingly intractable stalemate for the foreseeable future. Yet still there is no evidence of any US or British or EU support for seeking out a negotiated settlement.

So, the pattern is clear enough. No diplomatic settlement is to be entertained by the Western Alliance, irrespective of the state of the war. This is even though the chances of a Ukrainian victory are increasingly doubtful, if not unlikely, following the defeat of the Ukrainian summer counteroffensive of 2023. (Indeed, an eventual Russian victory is now seen by some international relations scholars as probable,).[249] As Benjamin and Davies rightly say:

> If Ukraine is not allowed to negotiate with Russia from a position of strength or from a position of weakness, what stands in the way of its total destruction? And how can Ukraine and its allies defeat Russia, a country whose nuclear weapons policy explicitly states that it will use nuclear weapons before it will accept an existential defeat?. . . . Are they [the Western powers] . . . simply praying that Russia will implode or give up? Or are they determined to call Russia's bluff and push it into an inescapable choice between total defeat and nuclear war?. . . . In place of a strategy to resolve the conflict, the United States and its allies welded the natural impulse to resist Russian aggression to a plan to prolong the war indefinitely. The results of that decision are hundreds of thousands of Russian and Ukrainian casualties so far and the gradual destruction of Ukraine by millions of artillery shells fired by both sides.[250]

Again, this seemingly irrational, arbitrary, incoherent, misguided Western intention to prolong the war indefinitely, as Benjamin and Davies see it, is likely because the real goal of NATO's proxy war is not ending a conflict that is inflicting devastation on Ukraine, alongside all of its other negative impacts worldwide, especially on the global poor, but undermining Russia and Putin, or both. As such, the policy may be rightly considered as a stranger to any humanitarian concern, and certainly recklessly dangerous, for reasons I have discussed.

Indeed, for Washington, the risks even of nuclear escalation in pursuit of these goals are deemed as acceptable.

This complacency may be encouraged by the dismissive risk-assessments of certain "expert" analysts close to the US government. According to Katherine Lawler, of the Independent Institute for the Study of War, for example, the likelihood of the Kremlin launching a nuclear attack faced with calamity is "astronomically low"—so much so it "should not even be seriously considered at this stage".[251] It should *not be seriously considered* even though Russia's self-defence policy explicitly authorizes the usage of nuclear weapons under circumstances where defeat would threaten the integrity of the state and where the Kremlin have threatened their usage. For non-aligned others, by contrast, the risk is credible, and even small risks (where these have astronomical consequences) must be taken seriously. As Jon Wolfsthal of the nuclear disarmament campaign group Global Zero opines:

> It would be dangerous to assume that Putin would never use nuclear weapons. . . . Blind faith in deterrence does not guarantee stability, nor does it take heed of the lessons of history—recent and more distant—that deterrence is fragile and can fail. . . . As financial and military pressures on Putin grow, the concern is that he will not think clearly or may put more emphasis on survival and the destruction of Ukraine than he does on alliances or friends.[252]

Even so, prolongation of the war, from the US perspective, would not be stupid or clueless, as Benjamin and Davies suggest it is. This is rather quite consistent with the goals of American imperialism.

The peace talks of March and April 2022 also confirm that Putin's invasion was not motivated by an intention to annex Ukraine, so as to incorporate the country into a Greater Imperial Russia, as the first step towards further imperial conquests in eastern Europe. This, as we have seen, is the dominant Western narrative on the war. Rather, the peace talks confirm the view of critics (myself included among them) that the purpose of Russia's war was instead to bring Kyiv to heel over militarization and NATO membership, or failing that to replace the Ukrainian government with one that would agree to reverse militarization and eschew NATO membership.[253] RIR scholar John J. Mearsheimer explains succinctly the supporting case for this perspective:

> First, the talks were directly focused on satisfying Russia's demand that Ukraine not become part of NATO and instead become a neutral state. Everyone involved in the negotiations understood that Ukraine's relationship with NATO was Russia's core concern. Second, if Putin was bent on conquering all of Ukraine, he would not have agreed to these talks, as their very essence contradicted any possibility of Russia conquering all of Ukraine. One might argue that he participated in these negotiations and talked a lot about

neutrality to mask his larger ambitions. There is no evidence, however, to support this line of argument, not to mention that: 1) Russia's small invasion force was not capable of conquering and occupying all of Ukraine; and 2) it would have made no sense to delay a larger offensive, as it would afford Ukraine time to build up its defenses.[254]

Postwar prospects

A perversity of the US state's imperial politics towards Russia from any unprejudiced point of view is shown in that even if it secures its ultimate goal—the undermining of Moscow as an imperial rival that could disturb or disrupt American global hegemony—this will likely not bring about any fundamental rapprochement between the countries from the American side of the fence. Even a weakened, more compliant, more Western-subservient Russia (post-Putin), would still be treated as an "outlier" state—and potentially a "rogue" state. Russia would still not be drawn to the Western bosom or invited to sit at Washington's top table of nations. The reason for this is simple enough to grasp. An imperial hegemon, such as is the US state, needs powerful enemies to solidarize its right to exercise hegemony. A powerful foe, a dangerous enemy, is needed to bind America's fractious allies to its right to legislate the international order.

Without such an enemy, there is no purpose in the Western Alliance *as a military coalition* under the US leadership umbrella (and Washington requires military force projection to safeguard its neoliberal economic order), because there would be no credible military threat to unite *against*, and so nothing to unite *for*. The greater the danger posed by so-called rogue states to international order, the higher incentive there is for the HICs to huddle under the protection of the US military. In the absence of this politics of securitization, there would, in short, be no reason for any government of the HICs to defer or acquiesce to the US state, as a kind of default. There would be no reason to do so because the international state system is constituted in relation to world capitalism as an essentially competitive rather than cooperative order.

This is what the politics of global securitization (rogue state ideology) secures for the imperial hegemon—legitimization of Washington's global power projection and solidarizing of the Western Alliance that buttresses this global power projection. So, if an enemy does not exist for Washington, one (at least one) must be invented. Much, after all, depends on the designation of a bogey state—including the vast profits of the arms industries, for example. But an enemy must also be *credible*. It must be a *state* (non-state enemies such as terrorist groups will not suffice). And it must be a potentially powerful state. Russia, I contend, will remain a credible candidate for the role, irrespective of the outcome of the war in Ukraine. This is by virtue of its size, resources, and geospatial location at the centre of everything.

US hegemony and strategic allies

But what of the US hegemon's strategic allies? Two are especially worthy of note. These are the metropoles of Europe (especially Germany, France, and the UK) and Japan. A few words on these junior partners of US imperialism are warranted.

The US–Japanese alliance

Of these strategic alliances, the one with Japan for mutual advance appears the most secure. Japan has been bound to US hegemony by its strategic decision to ally itself to the world's biggest economic and military power in exchange for its protection. The advantage for Japan is that this has (until fairly recent times) majorly reduced expenditure on self-defence, which would slow down investments in the country's civilian economy. This assisted Japan's ascendancy towards becoming the world's second-largest economy by the start of the 1980s. On the other hand, the advantage to the USA has been twofold. Firstly, this pre-empts any strategic alignment of Japan and China. Indeed, this places Japan at the centre of a network of states encircling China that are cultivated as allies by the USA. Secondly, this provides Washington with much of the technological means to sustain its vast military machine, since this is dependent on the import of a range of high-tech Japanese products and parts.[255]

With the rise of China as a regional great power, overtaking Japan as the biggest capital investor in Southeast Asia, this alliance is more likely to be strengthened rather than diminished, as tensions with China grow. Such is supported by contemporary events. But this has also generated political pressures in Japan for re-militarization, the renouncing of the pacifism clause of the postwar constitution (which forbids the use of war and the threat of war to settle disputes with other states and also the maintenance of sufficient armed forces to wage war),[256] even the acquisition of nuclear weapons.[257] In response, although the pacificism clause has not been abolished, it was substantially undermined (by means of "reinterpretation") by Japanese PM Shinzo Abe in 2014. This revision was carried out without parliamentary mandate or public consultation. It was formalized in 2015 by means of the adjustment of other laws.[258] Naturally, Washington declared its support for the move, since this opened the door for Japanese armed forces to be deployed alongside its own and those of other allies in defence of "international security" (i.e. US global hegemony) rather than solely in defence of Japan's own borders.[259]

The pacificism clause of Japan's constitution appears to rule out the maintenance of armed forces even for purposes of national self-defence. However, this is disputable, and it has always been disregarded by Japanese leaders, so that significant military forces (by land, sea, and air) have been maintained by the state since the end of the US occupation. But Abe's "reinterpretation", based on the concept of "collective self-defence", which permits Japan to engage in military action beyond its own borders in support of allies under attack, manifestly contradicts the pacificism clause. Any military action overseas can be falsely represented as one of self-defence. And "allies under attack" may not themselves be acting in self-defence but may instead be prosecuting war overseas to serve other purposes. This "reinterpretation" of the pacificism clause has effectively mandated the Japanese state to use or threaten to use war in pursuit of whatever its foreign policy goals happen to be—the same as virtually every state. Abe even declared in 2019 that the "reinterpreted" clause did not prevent Japan from acquiring long-range cruise missiles.[260]

The US–Japanese strategic alignment also contributes to growing tensions with other Asia-Pacific states that remain suspicious of Tokyo's intentions owing to Japan's colonial record and its leaders refusal to officially acknowledge the country's culpability for its colonial exploits.[261] Remilitarization of the Japanese state and the effective junking of the pacificism clause will not ease these suspicions. These are also contributing to growing tensions with Beijing, as is Tokyo's courting closer military alignment with the US state.[262] Yet there were also, in the 1990s and 2000s, growing strains on the US–Japanese alliance from within Japan. These have been fuelled by Japan's economic doldrums as the US economy pulls ahead. The poor economic situation in Japan naturally encourages those of its people who are experiencing the fallout to ponder if the partnership is actually serving their best interests. Such too has helped reinvigorate Japanese nationalism, which owing to Japan's subordinate status in the US–Japanese alliance, contains a strand of anti-Americanism. This has led some politicians to agitate for the abolition altogether of the pacificism clause (to allow restoration of national pride through re-armament) alongside the removal of the US military presence from Japan.[263] This has also led to calls from the start of the 2000s for the return of the US Yokota military base from American to Japanese control.[264]

Yet the most recent escalation of US–Sino tensions and hostilities (and of Beijing's growing assertiveness in pursuing its territorial claims—including on Japanese-run islands in the East China Sea—has for now further strengthened the strategic partnership between Washington and Tokyo.[265] These have led Tokyo to upscale its own military capacities and to seek out military partnerships beyond the USA—including those with the leading European states, Canada, and Australia.[266] These are precedents that could also help rejuvenate assertive Japanese nationalisms, including those that could strain the alliance with the USA, if these seek to contest Japan's subordinate status in the partnership. Washington too may come to see Japan's growing militarization and pursuit of multilateral military alliances as more a danger than a benefit to its global hegemony. Moreover, as US–Chinese relations continue to deteriorate, Tokyo will come under much pressure to distance itself from Washington and reorient towards Beijing, owing to Japan's greater (and growing) economic dependence on China than on the USA of recent times.[267]

Even so, for now, tensions that were apparent in the USA–Japan alliance on the Japanese side in the 1990s and 2000s have subdued into latency. The history of US–Japanese relations since World War Two is nonetheless instructive in showing the potential for fissures to re-emerge that might undermine the partnership. It ought to be recalled that, in the 1980s and early 1990s, US powerholders were casting Japan as a threat to American global dominance in a manner that was not dissimilar to how they are presenting "China peril" today. The context of this was the collapse of the postwar boom into the new period of global recession and slowdown from the mid-1970s. Tokyo was accused then by Washington of undermining the US economy through unfair trade practices that were tantamount to economic imperialism: maintaining a devalued yen that rendered US exports uncompetitive, blocking US imports through protectionist policies, and flooding US markets with cheap imports that undermined core American industries (and generated for the US economy huge balance of payments deficits). US political and business leaders also accused Japan of trying to "buy America" (through property and business acquisitions) and of free-riding under the US security umbrella to protect the world of liberal-capitalism from the Soviets (by low spending on arms and defence).[268]

These criticisms rapidly morphed into an attack on the Japanese state as Other. This may be described as "MITI Mania" or "Japan Inc. bashing". Japan's Ministry of International Trade and Industry (MITI) was thus accused of being a diabolical force of state-planned economic modernization dedicated to ensuring that Japan replaced the USA as the world's leading economy.[269]

> In Washington, explanations emerged that Japan was more different to the West—in terms of deviating from the principles of free trade and market capitalism—than previously assumed. New labels such as "development state" and "comparative capitalism" were created to re-define Japan in relation to existing economic theory. . . . The Japanese economy came to be seen as "different, closed and threatening". References to Japanese "unfairness", "cheating" and "economic warfare" became widespread . . . Japan had replaced the Soviet Union as the "exotic Other". The so-called revisionists who became influential during the first Clinton administration argued that Japan was "fundamentally different" and that dealing with Japan required a more confrontational approach than the rulebook of liberal democratic capitalism would ordinarily allow.[270]

The same kinds of messages were espoused in a rafter of dramatized journalistic and "academic" publications. In the process, racialized anti-Japanese sentiments were openly espoused by political and business leaders, which led to an upsurge of popular hostility (including acts of violence) in the USA towards Japanese persons, products, and businesses.[271]

This was the discourse of "Japan peril".[272] Much of it was groundless. Japan by then was not running protected markets—except in agriculture and perhaps in automobile parts (the latter is not clear).[273] The problem for the US economy was not so much that the yen was undervalued but that the US dollar was overvalued and that the US Federal Reserve was maintaining high interest rates to control rampant inflation. Nonetheless, the US state exerted its considerable diplomatic power to force its trade demands on Japan, thereby securing Japanese agreement to reduce exports of cars and steel to the USA and acquiescence to the imposition of US tariffs on a range of goods (especially electronic products) that forced up their prices in the American marketplace.[274]

The real basis of all this US conflict-mongering was simply that right up to and throughout the 1980s Japanese capitalism was outcompeting American capitalism. Consequently, during the period of the postwar boom (1945–73), indeed beyond, the Japanese economy was rapidly catching up with the USA's in terms of GDP volume and surpassing it in some branches of industry in terms of per capita output. Of particular concern to the US state was that Japanese industry was the first "to seriously challenge the American lead in high technology, including semiconductors, numerically controlled machine tools and other sophisticated electronics".[275]

This posed a threat not only to America's global economic primacy but also its global military primacy, since "Japan will be producing original technologies which the US government deems important for preserving America's global hegemony but which it will not be able to control".[276] As the US government was warned by the authors of the Gibbons Report:

> [I]f Japan becomes the world leader in high technology products, she will be driving us. She will control when certain technologies and processes—including those important for defense—can leave Japan. She will become the low-cost producer in any area which she wants; she will be able to target industry after industry, thus placing irresistible political pressures on the Congress to extend a web of Voluntary Restraint Agreements and Orderly Marketing Agreements to more and more products. *But each such restraint will only further burden the US economy, making it more sluggish and inefficient, and we will slip further and further into a "British disease" economy.*[277]

These tensions between the countries from the American side of the fence did not outlast the early 1990s. These eased when Japan's threat to US economic primacy dropped away in the decades since the collapse of the Japanese stock market in 1990. From this point, the Japanese economy experienced deeper and longer periods of recessionary crisis than did its American competitor and lagged further and further behind on GDP growth.[278] Suddenly Japan's high-tech industries ceased to be a threat to American global hegemony. This was as US capitalism placed itself to the forefront of digital computerization and internet and cyber technologies, just as MITA's investments in supercomputing, artificial intelligence, and media technologies ended up as dead ends.[279]

The lesson to be drawn from the USA–Japan trade war is twofold. Firstly, if Japan's economic fortunes were to be restored, just as this coincided with a dip in US economic performance, so that competition between them shifted again in favour of Japan, we can expect the American racialized phobias of "Japan Peril" to make a comeback, opening up potential fissures in the alliance that doubtless Beijing would seek to exploit. Secondly, even though the US hegemon welcomes the competition of free trade (since this empowers those national capitals already advantaged—that is, mostly those of the Global North), success of others in that competition is far from welcome. Rather, to outcompete US capitalism is an attack on the foundations of international order and security, which must be repelled. For this reason, as Nicola Nymalm points out, the US–Japanese conflict of the 1980s and early 1990s had the "potential of undermining the conceptual basis of their relations". Indeed, although "bigger spillovers affecting the security relationship were prevented, 'hegemonic war' between the United States and Japan had been considered a possibility".[280]

The US–Western European alliance

The US state's hegemony over Europe looks less secure than over Japan, though hardly endangered at present. There seems little prospect of this unravelling in the shorter or medium term. Europe, unlike Japan, after all, is not confronted immediately by the "China Peril" on its doorstep that is drawing Tokyo closer into Washington's embrace. The EU (and its predecessor the EEC) was forged not only to reign-in the kind of destructive interstate rivalries that had led to two world wars[281] but also to act as a counterweight to Soviet *and* American power. This was by unifying the constituent states in a relatively protected (from the greater economic power wielded by the two superpowers) single market zone.[282] Greater European alliance-building also served the USA, however, because this would—by modernizing and stabilizing the continent economically—help fuel the expansion of the capitalist world market and better repel the threat of Soviet communism in Europe. A further benefit of European integration, from the US standpoint, was that this would allow the economic resurgence of Germany without the risk of this reinvigorating German nationalism, German political domination of Europe, or the re-establishing of Germany as a great power that could challenge the USA.[283]

At the same time, the fact that "the EU is politically fragmented and its overall territorial logic remains indeterminate" allows Washington "all manner of levers to divide and rule and thereby frustrate the emergence of "Fortress Europe". This, as Harvey says, is by means of a "double strategy" of:

> (a) insisting upon the rules of neo-liberalism as the basis of exchange relations and capital flows (hence the importance of the WTO) and (b) keeping certain political and military levers in place whereby it can influence internal politics of the EU. This entails engaging with individual European states on a bilateral basis rather than with Europe as a whole, and cultivating special alliances (e.g. with Britain, Spain, and Italy as well as with the tier of Eastern bloc countries, with Poland at the centre).

As for NATO, the main reason why the US hegemon preserves the organization is

> because it keeps European military planning and development under US command. The US supports, for example, the idea that Europe should develop its own military rapid-response force but only on the condition that it remain under NATO command.[284]

But a major source of Washington's hegemony over postwar Europe was exactly the military protection it offered against the USSR and its satellites—a threat from the East which has considerably waned with the end of the Cold War. Russia, despite current events, is not a peer competitor, or even a near-peer competitor rival of the US state, as was the former USSR. Nor indeed does it pose the same magnitude of "security" danger to Europe as did the Soviet-led Warsaw Pact. For this reason, the securitization agenda by which US imperialism has sought to preserve its hegemony over the European powers (and which legitimates NATO) is vulnerable to challenge.

However, the ideological and propagandist framing of the current Russo-Ukrainian war in the West has for now resurrected the notion of immediate potent Russian security threat to its EU neighbours and therefore short-circuited that kind of challenge. How successful a politics of securitization can be in the longer term for binding the leading European states to acceptance of US political (and military) leadership may depend on the outcome of the Russo-Ukrainian war.

Neoimperialism and the Global South

Beyond the great regional hubs (USA, China, Japan, and the EU), the rest of humanity is dispersed in mostly vassal and client nation-states developed or underdeveloped, to varying degrees, to service the needs of the metropoles. These are the multitude of semi-developed (or "developing" or "emerging" as the World Bank would have it) countries, mostly in the Global South, which are turned into open markets for North American, European, and Japanese commodities, suppliers of key energy resources, and net exporters of capital, especially to the USA but also the other developed countries.

Now, the maintenance of this asymmetric geopolitical international structure of subordination (of the Global South to the US-led global North) crucially depends on the worldwide "projection" of US military capabilities (hence the vast global network of US military bases I discussed earlier), as those who do the projecting admit:

> The underdeveloped world's growing dissatisfaction over the gap between rich and poor nations will create a fertile breeding ground for insurgencies. These . . . have the potential to jeopardize regional stability and our access to vital economic and military resources. The situation will become more crucial as our Nation and allies, as well as potential adversaries, become more and more dependent on these strategic resources. If we are to have stability in these regions, maintain access to these resources, protect our citizens abroad, defend our vital installations, and deter conflict, we must maintain within our active force structure a credible military power projection capability with the flexibility to respond to conflict across the spectrum of violence throughout the globe.[285]

As I discussed earlier, many (indeed most) developing countries are poor, minimally industrialized to varying degrees, over-reliant on the limited export earnings to be made from a limited range of primary and unsophisticated products, and locked into a subordinate and dependent market position *vis-à-vis* the developed countries. This is whereby they are heavily dependent on imports of manufactured goods to function as even minimally industrial economies.[286] Even the economically successful countries of the Global South—such as the East Asian tigers, Brazil, Argentina, Mexico, India, and China—are unbalanced and not fully industrialized. This is inasmuch as these are unevenly developed (with advanced industrial enclaves alongside stagnating regions) and wage rates that are a fraction of those in the developed world—which is a major source of their attractiveness for investors.[287] This is also because these have a huge proportions of workers in the informal sector, in casualized employment,[288] and with large rural populations in at best semi-modernized agricultural sectors.[289]

These NICs and BRICs are also heavily reliant on the foreign earnings to be made from the exports of a limited number of usually high-tech companies (mostly to the developed world), which have been favoured by state support to render them internationally competitive. These countries thus produce much more for foreign high-income consumer markets than for their domestic ones since the latter are deficient in the purchasing power (given the suppression of wages to render exports inexpensive) required to sustain growth.[290] Outside the favoured capital-intensive companies driving export-driven growth, the rest of the economy remains relatively neglected, with labour productivity much lower than in the USA, Europe, and Japan.[291] These countries too are net exporters of capital to the developed countries, especially the USA.[292]

Included in the NICs/BRICs of course is China, which has emerged as the biggest economy in Southeast Asia, with a GDP second only to the USA,[293] but which shares the economic imbalances and vulnerabilities of the others. China is too large and powerful economically to be considered as anything less than a fully fledged imperial power in the making with aspirations for regional dominance and with the potential and ambition to challenge the USA for world leadership. Indeed, that China is prepared to pursue its own national interests in geopolitics, without kowtowing to the USA, is revealed by its willingness to loan money to poorer countries in the Global South (disregarding the IMF and its neoliberal conditionalities on capital transfers),[294] its drive to add military strength to economic strength (expanding and modernizing its armed forces), and its intention to reclaim full sovereignty over Taiwan, irrespective of Western opposition.[295]

Add to that China's alliance-building with North Korea, Cuba, Iran, and Russia (all of which are "off-message" states from the perspective of the Washington Consensus, and outside the US coalition—and the potential for growing conflict with the US hegemon and its closest allies is clear.[296] This is especially the case, given that one of these allies is Russia. Russia is, as we have seen, a sub-imperial state with regional ambitions, locked in a deadly war against NATO for strategically vital Ukraine, and engaged in geopolitical competition with the USA for influence in the Middle East (successfully so in Libya, Syria, and Iran) and control of the Caspian region. Russia is also one of the select emerging BRIC economies in control of vast natural mineral resources.

The Russo-Chinese alliance taking shape thus poses a major threat to what Washington dubs as the "rule-based international order" (i.e. US and Western primacy in world systems).[297] Indeed, the alliance is intended to contest that primacy. As Meyer zum Felde summarizes:

> Russia and China are united in their strategic aim to turn the current international order, which they perceive as dominated by the West and led by the US, into a multipolar world with zones of interests linked to the greatest powers. They are clearly backing each other while ganging up against the West and are increasingly coordinating their work, including through military exercises (which are key for developing trust, increasing military interoperability, and for sending strategic messages). While they are like-minded and similar in many regards, they are also complementary in the designs of their military-strategic postures. China is focusing on the maritime dimension with a long-term and strategic perspective, its aspiration being to become the world's leading great power by 2049 (the 100th anniversary of the Founding

> of the People's Republic of China). Putin's Russia is a continental land power and one of only two nuclear superpowers. . . . Both lead patriotic and heroic people who are fully behind them, with high levels of confidence to fight and win a patriotic war, if necessary. Both have felt humiliated by the West during their history, and still feel humiliated at the present time.[298]

The fact that Washington and its Western allies have been much less successful in isolating Russia in world politics for its war in Ukraine than is commonly asserted is doubtless due in some degree at least to Beijing's enhanced capacities for deploying soft (economic and diplomatic) power in the developing world. From the start of the conflict, many countries, ranging from 42 to 86, especially those of the Global South, have either abstained or absented themselves from UNSC resolutions condemning or sanctioning Moscow for the war.[299] In doing so, they are undoubtedly taking their lead from China's leaders. Beijing has refused to condemn Putin's invasion (indeed has described it as a defensive incursion) and withheld support for any of the UN-mandated sanctions imposed on Moscow for the war. Beijing has also maintained normal trade relations with Russia (indeed has increased trade with Russia since the start of the war) and provided the country with considerable economic resources (including machine parts and dual-use technologies) that could contribute indirectly to the Kremlin's war effort.

> Bloomberg reports that China imported 72 percent more Russian oil and gas in June 2022 than a year earlier, amounting to $6.4 billion. China has imported $25.3 billion in Russian energy between March and June 2022. Since the start of the war in Ukraine, China has overtaken Germany as the largest purchaser of Russian oil, and in June 2022, Russia replaced Saudi Arabia as China's largest crude oil supplier. . . . The *Wall Street Journal* reports that China's exports of microchips, other electronic components, and raw materials to Russia have more than doubled in the first five months of 2022, compared to the same period in 2021. Many of these exports have military applications. The *Journal* states that China may be backfilling orders from Russia for defense-related components after Western nations cut off exports to Russia's defense industrial base.[300]

Chinese leaders have consistently legitimized this stance on the conflict by laying the blame for it squarely on the USA and its European allies for driving NATO encroachment on Russia's borders in disregard of Moscow's legitimate security concerns. This is just as they rebuke Moscow indirectly by affirming the sanctity of all national borders.[301] Beijing has also sought to situate itself as a mediator and peacemaker in the conflict, just as it eschews (so far) providing Moscow with weapons aid.[302]

The contrast of all of this with the West's NATO proxy war in Ukraine, its supporting ideology of "unprovoked" revanchist Russian aggression, and its obstruction of a diplomatic solution to the conflict, could not be sharper. Predictably, for this same reason, Beijing's diplomatic efforts were certain to earn Washington's dismissive ire, as they have. US leaders have denounced these as unserious, insincere, and meddlesome,[303] and as steeped in "misinformation" about the Western Alliance and NATO's role in provoking the Russian invasion.[304] This is just as they warn of Chinese intentions to provide Moscow with military support and the dire consequences that would befall them if they did.[305] This "even-handed" (at the level of appearances) diplomatic approach of Chinese powerholders was bound to resonate positively with public opinion outside the developed world, whereas its curt dismissal by Western powerholders was not.

The USA–China imperial rivalry

As we have seen, the US state has been in recent years ramping-up its China-facing military presence across the Asia-Pacific, including by accelerating the ring-fencing of China by island chains of military bases. The beginnings of escalation in the projection of US power in the region can be traced to the Obama presidency's "pivot to Asia" (away, relatively, from Europe—which saw troop numbers halved between 2006 and 2020).[306] This refocused American geopolitical goals on Southeast Asia faced with China's economic and diplomatic (though not at that point military) ascendancy since the 2000s.[307] As the US Congressional Research Service recalls, Washington's "posture in the Indo-Pacific" has since then

> shifted toward prevailing in competition against peer or near-peer rivals—particularly the People's Republic of China (PRC). Since 2011, the United States has negotiated access to 12 new defense sites in the Philippines and Australia, constructed new installations in Japan and Guam, and expanded facilities at dozens of existing installations across the region. Congress' role in these developments has included, for example, appropriating over $8.9 billion for new military construction projects at Indo-Pacific sites since fiscal year (FY) 2020 and establishing infrastructure improvements as an investment priority through the Pacific Deterrence Initiative (PDI).[308]

The purpose of US military encirclement of China is to deter Beijing from using its growing economic, diplomatic, and military muscle to entice or coerce neighbouring states into its orbit (and out of the US camp) or successfully assert its territorial claims for disputed lands and waters against the counterclaims of rival local states. China's principal claim is for restoration of its sovereignty over Taiwan. This is on the grounds that the island was made part of the post-dynastic Republic of China (formed in 1912) following the end of the Japanese occupation in 1945.[309]

But, in 1949, Taiwan was annexed by Chinese nationalists, who having been defeated on the mainland by Mao Zedong's Revolutionary People's Army in the civil war that established the People's Republic of China (PRC), made their escape to Taiwan, which they renamed as the Republic of China. Now, Beijing would undoubtedly have retaken the island in the 1950s if its occupiers had not been defended by US military power.[310] Washington later conceded Beijing's legitimate right to sovereignty over Taiwan in the 1970s as it sought to normalize US relations with the regime so that it could focus on the Soviets.[311] But, owing to China's economic ascendancy in the post-Cold War era, and its consolidation as a peer or near-peer competitor of the USA, Washington's interest in honouring Beijing's right to the territory has evaporated. Instead, US leaders now recast themselves as defenders of Taiwanese autonomy and democracy and legitimize military encirclement of China on the grounds of deterring Chinese "unilateral attempts to change the status quo by force or coercion".[312]

Beijing's other territorial claims are over strategically and economically important island groups and waterways in the East China and South China seas. Here the Chinese case appears no stronger (but also perhaps no weaker) than those of neighbouring countries (Vietnam, Malaysia, the Philippines, Brunei, Japan, and Taiwan).[313] Beijing is probably correct in its historical claim that these waterways and islands were for centuries part of the Chinese Empire.[314] But the imperial acquisitions of antiquity or the middle ages of a defunct autocracy cannot count as *de facto* entitlements of a modern nation-state. Nor should military force or political coercion prevail in resolving the competing territorial claims of the rival states—though this is almost certainly how things will be decided (whether by US or Chinese power). The view of this author is that these matters are better decided on the grounds of geographical proximity.

Success in claiming ownership rights over these islands and waterways would, however, improve China's security situation *vis-à-vis* Washington and its regional allies. This is obviously an attractive objective if not imperative for the regime, especially given the USA's hostile encirclement. These seas are also major shipping lanes and fisheries and are suspected of harbouring major mineral deposits—so there are considerable commercial benefits at stake. As for reclaiming Taiwan, this would dramatically enhance the power of Chinese capitalism *vis-à-vis* its Western and Japanese competitors, especially in high-value markets. Taiwan is a major hub for microchip production upon which worldwide computerization and electronics depend.[315] Reclaiming Taiwan would also breach the US state's inner island chain of military bases and strike a major blow against American political hegemony right across southern and eastern Asia.

For the US state, of course, any erosion of its hegemonic status anywhere by a peer or near-peer competitor is interpreted as an existential threat (as the example of the US–Japanese trade war of the 1980s shows). This is even if there is from the rival in question no military aggression or challenge to US borders or interference with the USA's internal affairs. China's challenge to the USA exists simply by virtue of its economic ascendancy and willingness to convert this into diplomatic assertiveness in its own neck of the woods. This is assertiveness aimed at retaking what are believed to be entitlements that were lost owing to economic and military weakness. But Washington's 2022 National Security Strategy chooses instead to identify China's aspirations as "the most comprehensive and serious challenge to US national security".[316] This followed on from NATO's declaration of intent in 2021 to extend its focus to address security threats in the Asia-Pacific.[317] Competition itself, economic and diplomatic, where this appears to be succeeding, therefore, is sinister and intolerable, according to US leaders. Consequently, in response, the US military's ring-fencing of China is now so advanced that it would be well placed to blockade the country from the seaboard-facing southeast in the event of war.

This US military escalation of recent years is purportedly in response to China's upscaling of its own military capacities, to deter Chinese aggression, though clearly this is incentivizing exactly that which it is supposed to be reacting against and deterring—as US powerholders can scarcely be unaware. Indeed, NATO's proxy war in Ukraine has further fuelled Chinese militarization, for two reasons. Firstly, this is owing to NATO's self-declared plans to extend its remit to include the Indo-Pacific. "The added focus on NATO from Beijing comes as both China and the United States see Russia's invasion as a foil for future tensions between the two countries in Asia". Secondly, this is because this provides NATO with the opportunity of drawing unto itself greater military resources from its European members (including from those countries—Finland and Sweden—which have joined in response to the conflict), thereby freeing up the US state to project yet more force in Southeast Asia.[318]

China's military build-up and associated military assertiveness against the USA and its US-aligned neighbours in the disputed waterways may thus be plausibly regarded as a response to Washington's military encirclement rather than its cause. As for the growing number of reported clashes in disputed waters between China and its neighbours (Vietnam, the Philippines, Japan, etc.), it is also plausible that these are initiated by any one of the parties privy to the dispute rather than only one—China—as US propaganda war tells.[319] After all, those other countries claiming sovereignty of the disputed waterways and islands of the South China and East China seas have an interest in presenting Beijing as the sole aggressor in the dispute, just as does Washington. This is in order to draw US power ever more closely into their corner.

These ideas are simply not entertained by Western opinion-formers and powerholders, however.[320] But, as Andy Mok of the Center for China and Globalization in Beijing sensibly points out, there are good grounds for viewing US efforts to upscale its military encirclement of China and to isolate Beijing diplomatically by a fresh round of military alliance-building or alliance-hardening across the region as proactive rather than reactive measures:

> We only need to look at a map of US military assets to see who's the aggressor. It's not that China has numerous military bases surrounding the United States. It's exactly the opposite. So I think any reasonable observer would question this assertion whether China is really engaging in any sort of military provocations here. . . . This latest phase really just shows an increase in desperation on the part of the US because taking military measures usually is a last resort. Because it's risky and it's expensive. It's also very dangerous. . . . A country that has to resort to these measures, I think, clearly feels it is running out of options and is increasingly desperate to protect its rapidly eroding position in the world.[321]

Yet Mok exaggerates greatly the US state's declining influence in the Asia-Pacific zone. And desperation is unlikely to be the motivator of US aggression. Rather, for Washington's geopolitical strategists:

> The US military posture in the Indo-Pacific region . . . is reasonably well aligned with American interests and strategy already . . . [T]he future of America as an Indo-Pacific power should be bright, and the ability of the United States and allies to push back when needed against a rising China should be promising.[322]

Instead, the motive for US aggression is simply multilateral instrumentalism. This is how the imperial hegemon behaves when placed under threat of being outcompeted by a powerful rival owing to its conviction that the international order that its primacy serves is sacrosanct. Even so, the military build-up on both sides poses real dangers to regional security and stability, including by incentivizing the USA's subordinate allies ("security partners") to ramp-up their own military forces in anticipation of war.[323] Military escalation on both sides has been accompanied by occasional (not yet frequent) instances of confrontation between US and Chinese naval vessels and warplanes in the disputed waterways. These too naturally are represented by Western political leaders and the Western corporate media as those of unprovoked Chinese escalation and reckless aggression.[324] Doubtless they are portrayed in reverse by China's leaders and according to Chinese press reports.

What is clear, however, is that there would not be any military flashpoints at all (or at least far fewer and of less consequence) if there were no US warships and warplanes in those seas close to China's coast that Beijing claims as rightfully its own. From any unprejudiced viewpoint, then, it is these actions of the US state that are aggressive, provocative, and escalatory, rather than China's responses. But, whatever triggers individual military stand-offs between the two powers (and only the credulous would imagine that only one side is always culpable), aggressive US military encirclement of the world's second-biggest economic, and military power right on its own doorstep by virtue of base-building renders war between the two more rather than less likely. Such a war would draw in all those countries in the region that have allowed themselves to become accomplices of this high-risk US project of militarized boundary-drawing.

Outlier states and failed states

The large group of countries of the Global South that is home to the majority of the world's population includes those countries vulnerable to US-enacted or US-orchestrated or US-led neoimperial sanctions—denial of foreign credit, trade embargos, political destabilizations (e.g. funding or arming oppositionists or involvement in military coups), and direct military interventions, albeit usually as a weapon of last resort—if they fail to tread the free-trade path or if they disrupt the established geopolitical order of things. The poorer or weaker of these countries are especially vulnerable to political instabilities. Hence: "The most protracted and deadly ethnopolitical conflicts are likely to occur in poor, weak, heterogenous states like those of Africa".[325]

This is owing to the precarity of their economic situation, the consequential incapacity of government to dispense basic social functions or accommodate the minimal aspirations of many, and the acute internal conflicts this generates over access to resources. Such conflicts may then often be expressed in ethnic or tribal antagonisms, and where these are most acute dissolve the authority or legitimacy of the state altogether, so that people must fend for themselves. In short, in such cases, class conflicts over allocative rights may be experienced as ethnic tensions and antagonisms between groups, which when state authority fails may even degenerate into banditry and civil war.[326] Somalia, the Democratic Republic of Congo, the Central African Republic, and Rwanda are recent cases.[327]

These precarities or vulnerabilities of the poorer countries are radicalized owing to intensification of interstate economic competition under the whip-hand of neoliberal politics and the pressures this places on local states to retrench public services and redraw and draw-in the distribution of social or community entitlements. And so,

> ethnic and sectarian violence is ironically linked to the apparent triumph of economic globalization and institutional transformation—the opening of new markets for goods, services, capital, and people; the construction of new democracies; and the implementation of "state-shrinking" ideologies that have swept the globe. . . . And transition to the market and the pressures of globalization—increased demands for industrial competitiveness and rising

> external debt that weakens the state's capability and willingness to allocate resources—are associated with high levels of conflict and even violence. . . . [C]ultural violence erupts most vociferously where secular economic decline, neoliberal economic reforms, and institutional transformation have broken old "social contracts"—that is, where they have broken the rules and norms by which access to political and economic resources was once granted. Globalization and liberalization are thus "triggers" for cultural conflict.[328]

Indeed, where membership of a particular ethnicity confers market advantages over non-members, ethnic antagonisms fuse with class antagonisms or, in the experience or perceptions of those encountering these injustices, replace them, so that these become the main political drivers of conflict—or so it is argued.[329] These pressures or strains (resource stress, economic precarity—and intensifying struggles between groups over the distribution of entitlements) may even be motives for vulnerable states to wage war for territorial or economic advantage on other of their weak, underdeveloped neighbours—hence acting as minor sub-imperialisms in their own right. These border wars can be a way of alleviating the inner tensions and conflicts or deflecting these on to an external foe.

Such sub-imperial wars were also a legacy of the colonial period where antagonisms between clans and tribes were engineered by imperial authorities for purposes of divide and rule and where the clans or tribes were cut off from each other by colonial border-drawing. This has certainly been the case for inter-state conflict in Africa, where border wars are sometimes fought to "liberate" and reunite wider ethnic or tribal groups. Again, Somalia is a classic example.[330] Other economically stronger but nonetheless dependent or underdeveloped states may aspire to exploit the freedom afforded by not being under the exclusive control of a specific imperial state (as was the case in the colonial era). This allows them the latitude to manoeuvre between the great powers (and between different MNCs from the rival great powers seeking investment opportunities within their borders),[331] in order to try and make of themselves regional sub-imperialisms—as for example, Iran has tried to accomplish in the Middle East and Central Asia in recent decades,[332] since the Islamic Revolution.

Surveillance states

Scattered among the vassal states, dependencies and protectorates under the new deterritorialized imperialism are what may be termed "watchdog" or "surveillance" states. I will end this chapter by considering the role of such states in the neoimperial order under US hegemony. A particular focus will be on Saddam Hussein's Iraq. The next (and final) chapter will present a case-study of a second surveillance state: Israel. The Iraqi and Israeli studies will attempt to establish the general perspective by means of a focus on these specific examples.

Surveillance states are nation-states situated in areas of the globe that are of particular or vital economic or strategic value to US corporate interests and which are sanctioned to act as bulwarks against local forces (countries or movements) that may threaten these interests in exchange for economic patronage and military aid. These are thereby elevated to regional sub-imperialisms by their strategic role in policing or neutralizing their neighbours. Suharto's brutal military dictatorship in Indonesia responsible for between 500,000 and a million deaths in internal pogroms and up to 300,000 deaths during its invasion and occupation of East Timor was one such case. Suharto secured power through a US- and British-assisted coup that unseated Sukarno's popular democratic government on the trumped-up pretext that the Marxists of the KPI were themselves planning one. Thereafter, Suharto enjoyed US (and British) patronage for "stabilizing" Indochina in the Cold War era and after, firstly as a bulwark against communism, then latterly as a key ally against China, for which the regime was rewarded not simply with lavish military aid but by a blind eye being turned to its purging of dissidents and its war crimes in East Timor.[333]

The Middle East and watchdogs

The Middle East, owing to its vast concentration of energy resources, has been the region where US governments have perhaps sought most energetically to maintain such watchdogs. Almost 80 per cent of the world's total oil reserves are in OPEC countries, with more than two-thirds of that in those countries which are situated in the Middle East.[334]

Historically, the US economy has relied, to greater or lesser degrees, on oil exports from the Middle East, though some degree of reliance has been the norm since the late 1960s. By the start of the 1970s, a third of US oil consumption needs were met by imports from the region.[335] By the close of the 1990s, 52 per cent of the USA's energy needs were being catered for by imported oil.[336] In the early 2000s, around 60 per cent of US oil consumption was from imports, with around 21 per cent of this coming from the Middle East.[337] The Bush Junior administration's *National Energy Plan* of 2001 predicted that US oil consumption would rise by 33 per cent by 2020, which would require oil imports to increase by 30 per cent. This, the report said, would create "increased dependency on foreign powers who do not always have America's interests at heart", so that the Middle East "would remain central to world oil security" and the "primary focus of US international energy policy".[338] By 2015, however, US imports from the region were reduced to 19 per cent, owing to the USA's upscaling of domestic shale-oil production, which greatly downsized the country's total foreign imports.[339]

Nonetheless, for most of the postwar period, including most recently, these have been major volumes and hence real dependencies, which provide US governments with pressing interests in securitizing these energy sources for reason simply of economic national self-interest. Yet, in recent times, US foreign energy dependency has been in decline (owing to the shale-oil boom), and this is projected to continue, so that the US economy will soon achieve energy self-sufficiency.[340] In fact, energy self-sufficiency has been a longstanding goal of US policy exactly in order to help preserve its international hegemony.[341] And, if the USA can produce major volumes of oil beyond its domestic needs (and the USA is a major oil exporter), this creates the potential to render economic and geopolitical rivals more dependent on the US for their energy requirements. Notwithstanding these observations, US imperialism's interests in securitizing the Middle Eastern oilfields and controlling the regional supply chains remain firmly intact, for two main reasons.

Firstly, this is to prevent disruption of the international energy marketplace and hence ensure the stability of affordable world prices. "The oil market is still global, which means the price Americans pay for fuel is still set by global oil prices and is vulnerable to supply disruptions, wherever they occur".[342] Secondly, this is also because competitor capitalisms (such as those of the EU bloc and Japan) and international rivals (most notably, China) are very much energy-dependent on the Middle East, whereas potential enemy states (such as Russia) which are much less so would become much more powerful rivals to the US if they could secure greater control of these resources at Washington's expense.[343]

US control of Middle Eastern oil (and indeed attempts to control it elsewhere—especially in the Caspian) is primarily for strategic rather than economic reasons. Oil, as Simon Bromley rightly says, is for the USA a "strategic commodity".[344] From the US perspective, controlling access to the world's biggest oil reserves is a powerful lever for ensuring that it continues to get what it wants in world politics. This is by virtue of the capacity this bestows for economically disciplining existing competitors and rivals and for obstructing the ability of new rivals or opponents to challenge the USA economically and hence politically. Indeed, this has the further advantage of permitting the US state to cripple economically any "outlier" state in the Middle East that may be tempted to disrupt the security of oil supply or the stability of oil prices or the established balance of interstate power relations in the region in pursuit of its own national interests.

Up until the 1970s, US control of the Middle East's oil was secured by virtue of the direct corporate ownership or possession of much of the oil extraction and refining business across the region by its energy MNCs. Thus, the petrol-monarchs of the Persian Gulf were tied to US imperialism by virtue of minority share ownership in as well as executive board membership of the "Seven Sisters" (mostly US-owned or US-majority controlled oil companies that possessed refining and processing and extraction facilities and which owned drilling rights right across the region). They were, in effect, "coupon-clipper kings". Other rewards included receipt of tax revenues from the oil operations of these companies (which instead of being repatriated to their home governments were diverted into the coffers of the local kingdom-state) and of course military aid to prop up these deeply unpopular autocracies.[345]

Since then, however, direct foreign control of oil by Western (mostly American) energy companies has been largely replaced by state ownership in the various regional oil-exporting nations, though the Western oil corporations do still largely control sales and refining.[346] By the end of the 1970s, unfettered access of international energy companies to oil supplies worldwide was reduced from 85 per cent in the 1960s to just seven per cent.[347] Nonetheless US domination of the Middle East's oil has since persisted by means of a system of control through *indirect* influence, pressure and patronage. The petrol-monarchies (Saudi Arabia, Bahrain, the UAE, Oman, Qatar and Kuwait) are in effect still US vassal states by virtue of receiving copious US military aid and the security bulwark that the distribution of US military forces across the region provides them with against their own peoples and against their local state rivals.[348] The USA spends "$81 billion annually to protect oil supplies, mostly in the Gulf".[349]

Such patronage and the pressure to cultivate it is necessary because the rulers of the oil-kingdoms command little support outside elite and middle-class circles in the countries they rule because they are oligarchs, heading family-run absolutist states. They are opponents of any semblance of popular democracy, repressing all opposition to their rights of sovereignty, usually under the guise of extinguishing the threat of radical Islam. These states are almost wholly dependent on guest workers devoid of those entitlements of citizenship (economic, political, legal) beyond the cash nexus. "In the UAE, Qatar, Bahrain and Kuwait, migrants substantially outnumber the overall national population, while Saudi Arabia has most foreign workers overall with 12 million, compared with its national population of 20 million".[350] The cheap labour-power of these migrant workers supports the fabulous wealth of the elite and the high living standards and negligible taxes of the local middle classes.

The oil-monarchies are also rentier states because of the tax income they accrue from granting permissions for overseas companies to do business within their borders and the export dividends they receive by means of their monopoly of natural resources—in this case, of course, crude oil.[351] These regimes are themselves bulwarks against those popular or democratic movements that pose a threat to US access to oil in return for US protection (especially against secular nationalist or socialist movements—since historically these are recognized by the USA as posing the greatest threat to the political and economic status quo). But they are also rivals, competing with and intriguing against each other for regional influence, including by supporting rival insurgency or counter-insurgency movements or organizations in neighbouring countries (most recently, for example, in Libya, Syria, Tunisia, and Yemen).[352]

Of these absolutist states, Saudi Arabia, which straddles the biggest oil reserves in the Middle East, has been especially feted and rewarded for the watchdog role, and has been a virtual US protectorate since 1947.[353] This is despite the regime's covert support in recent times for Salafist Jihadist groups (which Washington has itself classified as terrorist) that operate to destabilize or obstruct its regional rivals.[354]

The case of Iraq

For a period, commencing at the start of the 1980s, Saddam Hussein's Sunni-controlled Ba'ath regime in Iraq was also made a US watchdog in the region, just as Iran under the Shah was feted beforehand.[355] The Iraq case warrants particular interest in the history of watchdogs because this shows what becomes of them if they should "go rogue", that is, upset the neoimperial pecking order of states under US hegemony. The Iraq case also merits close inspection because it also reveals the precarity of US imperialism's project of regional "stabilization" under terms and conditions favourable to its political and economic interests and to those of its allies. Neoimperialism is far from secure; it is ever a process and never a settled product.

Previously, Iraq was regarded by the USA as a potentially hostile power. This was owing to the regime's espousal of secular nationalism and Arab socialism and its dispute with Pahlavi-ruled Iran (a key US ally) over control of the Shatt-al-Arab waterway. This compelled Saddam's government to maintain the strategic alignment with the USSR at the tail end of the Cold War, though relations with the USA were also courted, as the regime sought to position itself between the rival superpowers, declaring itself non-aligned in the Cold War, just as Nasser's Egypt did before it. Nationalization of the country's oil industry in 1972 did not help alleviate Washington's concerns about the regime, motivating US and Iranian covert backing of Kurdish insurgents in Iraq. But the Iraqi government's concession of control of Shatt-al-Arab to the Shah in 1975 ended outright US hostility to the regime, facilitating withdrawal of US support for the Kurdish militias. It was the Iranian Revolution of 1979, toppling the USA's Pahlavi puppet, which convinced Washington of the strategic value of "friendship" with Baghdad, however.[356]

The Ba'athists were elevated to watchdog status because they had shown themselves adept at "stabilizing" a country riven with ethnic, religious, and social divisions, despite being based on Sunni minority rule over a big Shia majority and a dissident Kurdish minority. This was owing to the regime's brutal internal repression and highly efficient security apparatus. But it was also due to unusually (if partially) successful policies of economic modernization and industrial diversification that were built on the revenues from state-owned oil. These permitted Iraqis better average living standards than in most countries in the Middle East. These also underpinned relatively well-resourced social, educative, and healthcare services which were more advanced than any in the Arab world.[357] By contrast, an alternative Shia-dominated regime may, from the US perspective, be much less adept at reigning-in the factionalized population and would be vulnerable to being pulled into closer alignment with Iran given the close ethnic and religious ties between the countries. Iran, after all, was a Shia-Muslim country ruled by a Shia-dominated government.

Consequently, in 1982, Iraq was removed from Washington's list of terrorist-supporting countries and, in 1984, Washington restored full diplomatic relations with Saddam's regime.[358] This was accompanied with copious US economic and military aid, despite Saddam's human rights abuses (including poison gas attacks on Iranian troops and the Northern Kurds),[359] for performing the role of containing its Islamist neighbour and preventing the export of radical Islam. The US state tacitly endorsed (and publicly incited) the regime's invasion of Iran and the eight-year war (1980–88) that this brought. This was primarily to detach the Shatt-al-Arab waterway from Iranian control.[360]

Thereafter, Washington subsidized the regime with money and agricultural credits, which made it the USA's third biggest trading partner in the Middle East behind Israel and Saudi Arabia.[361] Washington also supplied Baghdad with weapons (indirectly through third-party intermediaries—including the ingredients of biological weapons) and dual-use technologies that could be converted for military use. Moreover, the regime was provided with US naval protection in the Gulf and satellite military intelligence to assist the prosecution of the war against Iran.[362] This escalation of US assistance was as the conflict started to go badly for the Ba'athists, in order to rescue them from defeat and avert the wrong kind of regime change in Iraq—that is, imposition by force of Iranian arms of a Tehran-friendly Shia government.

Despite eventual stalemate in the Iran–Iraq war, without appreciable gains by either side, US support for Iraq had the (for the US state) unwanted by-product of bolstering the sub-imperial political regional ambitions of Saddam's government, just as the cost of the war drastically weakened the Iraqi economy. This was the context behind Iraq's ill-fated invasion and occupation of Kuwait in the summer of 1990. This was ostensibly to settle an oil dispute. Kuwait was undermining world fuel prices with overproduction from its oil fields and organizing resistance in OPEC to Iraqi attempts to reduce supply, hence thwarting the regime's efforts to pay off its war debts. Kuwait was also illegally drilling in disputed oil fields on the Kuwait–Iraq border. But perhaps the Iraqi invasion was also motivated by a sense of deeper historical injustice. The coastal state of Kuwait—which, like modern Iraq, was a territory of old Mesopotamia—was a construct of British colonialism in the 1920s in order to landlock the newly independent Iraq by means of partition. Kuwait was generally regarded by the Arab "voice on the street" across the Middle East as rightfully a province of Iraq.[363]

Ba'ath Iraq's imperial adventure in Kuwait cost it dear, since Washington had no interest in a greater Iraq, with a bigger share of the region's oil resource, whereas the Kuwaiti monarchy was also a key US ally. The termination of the Cold War thus afforded Washington an opportunity to demonstrate to the Global South the dire consequences of upsetting the US-sanctioned geopolitical and economic order of things. The US state abruptly switched Iraq's watchdog status for a rogue state one and fast-tracked a virtual unilateral (in terms of military investment) war on the country under UN cover that virtually destroyed the civilian infrastructure (water, sewerage, transport, healthcare, power, and communications).[364] This killed on US estimates between 50,000–100,000 Iraqi combatants (on Israeli estimates between 150,000–200,000),[365] plus unaccounted numbers of civilians.[366]

This war was supposedly to force the withdrawal of the Iraqi army from Kuwait but really was intended to destabilize the country in order to try to bring about a coup against the leadership from within the ruling party.[367] Colin Powell, US Chairperson of the Joint Chiefs of Staff, advised the Bush Senior administration that Saddam's invasion was prompted by a legitimate border grievance and that he would likely withdraw his army from Kuwait once a government less hostile to Baghdad was installed. This, said Powell, would please "everyone in the Arab world".[368] Faced with overwhelming force, Saddam had shown his willingness to broker a withdrawal. Indeed, on the eve of the "Allied" air offensive, he had agreed to an unconditional withdrawal.[369] And, before the start of the ground offensive, he was starting to pull his forces out of Kuwait.[370] By contrast, the US state was set on war and did not enter serious negotiations to obtain a peaceful outcome.[371]

The coup, however, did not materialize. Rather, incited by President Bush Senior's call for the "military and the Iraqi people to . . . force Saddam Hussein . . . to step aside",[372] which was broadcast right across Iraq's airwaves, the country rose up on cue in rebellion against the regime. But, since US imperialism wanted leader change, not regime change, American forces were ordered to stand down, leaving the insurgents to their fate. Not only that, but US troops also demobilized the rebels by blocking their access to the regime's weapons stores, whilst simultaneously allowing pro-regime troops and helicopter gunships free movement across American lines to attack the insurgents.[373]

The ensuing brief and one-sided civil war between loyalist Ba'ath troops and a range of insurrectionary groups renewed Saddam Hussein's grip on power and killed 100,000 to 180,000 civilians.[374] The USA (supported faithfully as always by the UK) then subjected the country to 12 years of virtual economic blockade, along with an unprecedented "peacetime" campaign of ongoing air strikes in illegally constituted (under international law) "no-fly zones" in the north and south of the country, presumably as the continuation of the coup-facilitation strategy.[375] This locked Iraq's economy into the virtually pre-industrial state brought about by the 1990 war (in a country with modern needs and dependencies)[376] but otherwise was to no avail, since the sanctions regime accomplished nothing except a humanitarian disaster. This policy failure showed the limits of US imperial power and its policy machinations.

In the immediate aftermath of the war, a UN report warned of an impending health and welfare catastrophe in the general population unless the Iraqi government was permitted to make sufficient oil sales to begin fast-tracking the repair work on the essential economy. This estimated that the cost of repairing Iraq's civilian infrastructure to the prewar level was $22 billion.[377] Despite this, the Security Council (at the insistence of the US and UK governments) placed a punitive cap on the country's oil exports and deducted a third of the revenues for war reparations and "administrative" costs (including for the funding of UN weapons inspections).[378] This left the regime with just $2.2 billion of oil revenues in the first year after the war's end for potential reconstruction, whereas a minimum of $6.8 billion was considered as essential to avert the crisis.[379] Unsurprisingly, these terms were too much for Saddam's regime to stomach, as indeed they were likely intended to be. Denying the regime control of airspace within its own borders and subjecting the country to continual bombing raids in the no-fly zones was hardly likely to facilitate its full co-operation with UN resolutions.

This then legitimized the indefinite perpetuation of the ongoing US campaign to spur leadership change from within the Ba'ath inner circle by destabilizing and undermining the Iraqi economy. Thus, it took another five years for the UN Security Council to impose on the Iraqi regime the Oil-for-Food (OfF) programme, which permitted the regime to sell oil for the purpose of obtaining life-sustaining imports. This marginally eased the conditions of life for ordinary Iraqi citizens. However, the programme still imposed a ceiling on oil sales (as well as a rafter of other restrictions) that seriously hampered its supposed humanitarian goals, just as the sanctions regime continued to cripple the country economically, generating massive deprivation for the bulk of the population.[380]

Simultaneously, the US government and its UK echo-chamber exerted their diplomatic weight (and the threat of veto powers) on the Security Council to block all proposals for remedial actions outside the framework of OfF.[381] This was while propagandizing in the face of official studies and reports to the contrary that the human costs of the sanctions were exaggerated or wholly the fault of the regime's corruption or wilful refusal to co-operate with aid providers.[382] On some estimates, the economic sanctions and the punitive conditions of OfF were the main cause of up to if not more than half a million excess deaths of children under five between 1991 and 1998 and double that number in total mortalities.[383] More conservative estimates of sanctions-related child mortality during this period put this at a minimum of 107,000 and a "more likely" 227,000.[384] This was owing to malnutrition and disease caused by the chronic state of disrepair of electricity, water and sewage infrastructure, degradation of healthcare, lack of basic medical supplies,[385] and exposure to warzone contaminants such as white phosphorus and depleted uranium (DU) shell fragments.[386]

"Regime change" was eventually accomplished by means of a second US war. This time, unlike the first, the US aggression was unable to cloak itself under either international law or UN backing (the UN Security Council refusing to sanction it),[387] so this was nakedly (politically as well as militarily) a unilateral US enterprise endorsed by the usual suspects—the UK, inevitably, tailing the

USA.[388] Military unilateralism was instead justified by Washington and London on the pretext that the Iraqi regime was supposedly assembling WMD and sponsoring Islamist terrorist networks (including al-Qaeda) that would threaten regional and world security.[389] This was despite the fact that Saddam's regime had readmitted the UN weapons inspectors (rebranded as UNMOVIC) and for the most part co-operated with their work.[390] Moreover, this was even though the factual claims of clandestine Iraqi WMD-related military procurements were exposed as groundless.

This was also despite the fact that both notions (arming Islamists and assembling WMD capacities) were manifestly absurd, buttressed by a mountain of media-disseminated state propaganda, the UK Blair government's "dodgy dossier", forged documents, US secretary of state Colin Powell's bogus scare-mongering presentation before the UN, and the like.[391] The secular Ba'ath regime was a lifelong implacable enemy of political Islam and despised by the radical Islamicists. Given the utter economic devastation of the country, the comprehensiveness of the sanctions regime, plus the systematic work of the UN weapons inspectorate (UNSCOM), in dismantling the vestiges of the regime's WMD capacities and checking facilities and sites for evidence that these were being repaired (none of which was found), the notion that the regime could pose any kind of security threat to neighbouring states or the international community in the immediate or near future was risible.[392]

But the Iraqi case reveals the major difficulty of the US imperial project in the Middle East. One aspect of this is simply that regional watchdogs among the Arab states cannot be counted on. Watchdogs escape their leashes. Driven by Arab nationalism or by an exaggerated sense of their own importance to the hegemon, they can develop ideas above their station in the Washington-sanctioned pecking order of states. In the case of the oil-monarchies, the risk is not from Arab nationalism (not among the ruling elite), since this is auctioned away in exchange for huge economic sweeteners. Rather, this is from the fact that these regimes are inherently at risk from the threat of popular unrest from below, which may be inspired by Arab nationalism, or worse (from the US perspective) by pan-Arab nationalism, Islamism, or socialism.

This instability risk is a function of the fact that the Arab populations of these countries are for the most part economically impoverished and politically disenfranchised, non-beneficiaries of "development", resentful of the spectacular ever-growing wealth of the elites, and of their political conservatism in failing to support the cause of dispossessed or oppressed peoples elsewhere in the Arab world—most notably, the Arabs of Palestine. Obviously, they are resentful also of the role of American and Western imperialism in propping up these regimes, of foreign corporate-capitalist ownership or control of resources that may be considered as rightfully theirs (e.g. the great oil refineries), and of unconditional US and Western support for Israel. The latter is popularly viewed as illegitimate, an unlawful state that was imposed on Arab lands and peoples by force of foreign power, and which has since acted to dispossess and oppress the indigenes within its own borders and beyond. The Middle East is, for these reasons, a perpetual powder keg in a theatre where the USA (plus its leading rivals) require "stability" more than anywhere else.

US governments throughout the postwar period have been fully aware of this popular "street view" of the Arab masses on its regional role (and those of the Washington's vassal states) across the Middle East, and they have also tacitly conceded the validity of that view. In 1958, US president Dwight D. Eisenhower observed that hostility towards the USA came not from Arab governments but from "the people" who supported the goals of Arab nationalism and socialism. As the USNSC explained in the same year:

> In the eyes of the majority of Arabs the United States appears to be opposed to the goals of Arab nationalism. They believe that the United States is seeking to protect its interests in Near East oil by supporting the status quo and opposing political or economic progress.

This perception exists, as the USNSC put it, because

> our economic and cultural interests in the area have led not unnaturally to close US relations with elements in the Arab world whose primary interest lies in the maintenance of relations with the West and the status quo in their countries.[393]

The Iraq case also reveals a second aspect of the difficulty faced by US imperialism in the Middle East. This is confirmation of the limits of this project of regional pacification, whether by means of economic bribery (aid), economic coercion (sanctions), or military force (from the funding of insurgents to the waging of total war). The limits exist by virtue of the depth of resentment and hostility towards the US state and its proxies on the Arab street but also are due to the internecine interstate rivalries of the Arab ruling elites as they struggle amongst themselves for regional advantage. These rivalries are inherently destabilizing since they are energized by states (mostly patrimonial, autocratic, or authoritarian) whose ambitions are not reigned-in by democratic or constitutional or popular controls.[394] And so US efforts to exert control are not only confronted by mass popular anti-imperial sentiment (with the ever-present potential to combust into violent protest) but also unsettled or disrupted by the ever-shifting patterns of Arab statecraft (intrigues, conflicts, feuds, conspiracies alliance-making and breaking, support for insurgencies or counter-insurgencies, and so on), the results of which are complex and unpredictable.

Saddam's own rule in Iraq survived the US-led attempts to overturn it through systematic and ongoing violence, economic and military. Indeed, it was likely strengthened by it, as embattled populations tend to unite behind their leaders in times of profound national crisis, no matter how reprehensible they are. The Ba'ath state's capacity to survive in the face of concerted US efforts to destabilize and undermine it (as Washington shifted from a strategy of leader-change to regime change in the runup to the 2003 war) ensured that it was a focus of Arab street pride right across the Middle East. This could be imagined by the masses (and was so imagined) as the courageous defiance of a lone beleaguered nation, abandoned by its neighbours, battered and bloodied yet uncowed, facing down the brute power of an alien superpower intent on imposing its will.[395]

The subsequent US-led invasion of the country in 2003 (along with the accompanying TV-images of civilian casualties shown by local broadcasters such as *Al-Jazeera* but studiously airbrushed out of the Western media coverage) could only further incite these sentiments.[396] Outrage over the war and sympathy for and solidarity with a long-suffering Iraqi people facing overwhelming deployment of alien military force would then be replaced by rage and frustration stemming from the humiliation of military defeat. Such sentiments fuelled the long Iraqi insurgency waged by an array of Ba'athist, secular nationalist, socialist, Shia and Sunni Islamist groups against the Anglo-American occupying forces and the governments these propped up.

The postwar Iraqi regimes were initially the interim government stuffed with US appointees and latterly the heavily vetted federal governments emerging from 2005 and 2010 elections mired in electoral fraud and repression of oppositionists.[397] The resistance movement commanded popular support amongst both Shia and Sunni communities, since 69 per cent of Shias and 84 per cent of Sunnis were opposed to the occupation.[398] Within weeks of the US "liberation" of Iraq, major towns witnessed mass demonstrations demanding the immediate removal of coalition forces, which of course went unheeded. The popular insurgency made the country ungovernable, short-circuiting postwar reconstruction, and derailing attempts by the interim government to act on US commands to sell-off the country's oil and other key national enterprises to American MNCs alongside the fast-tracking of other deeply unpopular neoliberal reforms.[399] The Iraqi resistance eventually forced the withdrawal of Anglo-American troops at the behest of the federal government as it became apparent that this was the only way to quell the insurgency.

Since the federal government, like the US-dominated provisional authority before it, resorted to sectarian (on ethno-religious lines) divide-and-rule policies in order to hang on to power, Iraq degenerated into inter-communal violence and civil war between Sunni and Shia militias between 2006 and 2008.[400] This drew new recruits to the cause of Islamic Jihadism (including al-Qaeda) and sowed the seeds for the rise of the ISIS organization—a radical Jihadist paramilitary group set on establishing, for starters, a caliphate unifying the territories of Iraq and Syria. As Callinicos rightly observes: "Overthrowing Saddam gave the jihadis their greatest fillip since the Soviet invasion of Afghanistan".[401] ISIS came perilously close to bringing down the Iraqi and Syrian governments, despite the fact that the military resources at its disposal were a fraction of those of the regimes it challenged. Indeed, ISIS would have succeeded in doing so were it not for US-orchestrated coalition military operations against the organization in both countries.[402] This showed the precarity of the post-occupation governments in Iraq, hopelessly compromised in the popular mind by their connections with the long Anglo-American occupation, and riddled with cronyism, corruption, and inefficiency.

This, again, demonstrated the limits of the US imperial project in the Middle East. Its wars in Iraq to stabilize and pacify the region signally failed to deliver on these goals. On the contrary, these interventions radicalized the regional instabilities, giving rise since 2003 to hundreds of thousands of new civilian deaths,[403] along with millions of refugees.[404] Not only that, these geopolitical power-games also ended up drawing Iraq into closer alignment with Islamist Iran, the US state's *bête noire* in the Gulf and central-south Asia.[405] This was Washington's least wanted outcome, and one which US policy towards Iraq since the Iranian Revolution was intended to avoid. Most seriously, this outcome is one that has diminished the US state's "securitization" of the vast energy resources of the Middle East, which is the fundamental principle guiding the whole of its regional strategy.

Notes and references

1 Huntingdon, S.P. (1996). The Clash of Civilizations and the Remaking of World Order. London: Simon and Schuster.
2 Johnson, C. (2004). Blowback: The Costs and Consequences of the American Empire. 2nd edition. London and New York NY: Henry Holt and Co; Johnson, C. (2002). 'American Militarism and Blowback: The Costs of Letting the Pentagon Dominate Foreign Policy'. New Political Science, 24 (1), pp. 21–38; Briant, E. (2015). Propaganda and Counter-Terrorism: Strategies for Global Change. Manchester: Manchester University Press.
3 Chua, A. (2003). World on Fire: How Exporting Free-Market Democracy Breeds Ethnic Hatred and Global Instability. London: Willian Heinemann.
4 UN (2014). World Urbanization Prospects. New York NY: UN.
5 Satterthwaite, D., McGranahan, G. and Tacoli, C. (2010). 'Urbanization and Its Implications for Food and Farming'. Philosophical Transactions of the Royal Society B, 365, pp. 2809–20.
6 Douwe Van der Ploeg, J. (2008). The New Peasantries: Struggles for Autonomy and Sustainability in an Era of Empire and Globalization. London: Earthscan, p. xiv.
7 Harman, C. (1996). 'Workers of the World'. International Socialism, 2 (96), pp. 3–46. See especially pp. 6–8.
8 Opportunity costs would not merely be those which impinge on the material self-interest of political powerholders or the interests of economic powerholders they serve but those which undermine the authority, legitimacy, or competence of the states they administer.
9 The literature on US-enacted "regime change" alone (political destabilizations, covert operations, complicity in human rights abuses, military interventions) is vast. This is leaving aside literature addressing the other coercive aspects of US foreign

policy, including the equally significant phenomenon of "regime preservation". The latter includes support for drug oligarchs, neo-fascists, and terrorists in no fewer than 35 countries in the postwar period. Nicolas Davies helpfully chronicles these cases by way of indictment alphabetically. (Davies, N.J.S. (2014). '35 Countries Where the U.S. has Supported Fascists, Drug Lords and Terrorists'. Salon (online). (8 March). Indeed, this aspect is so voluminous that a large encyclopaedia is dedicated to cataloguing it all.

10 Harvey, D. (2003). The New Imperialism. Oxford: Oxford University Press, p. 38. The major industry in question documenting Washington's coercive, bullying, anti-democratic, and frequently murderous foreign policy history is not simply academic but even includes popular bestsellers, such as Vernon Coleman's Rogue Nation.

11 Callinicos, A. (1994). 'Imperialism Today'. A. Callinicos et al. (eds) Marxism and the New Imperialism. London: Bookmarks, p. 27.

12 Chomsky, N. (1992). Deterring Democracy. London: Verso, pp. 19–33, 139–77, 215–51. See also Chomsky, N. (2003). Hegemony or Survival: America's Quest for Global Dominance. London: Penguin.

13 Harvey (2003), pp. 54–5.

14 Harvey (2003), pp. 57–8.

15 White House (1990). National Security Strategy of the United States. (1 March). Washington DC: National Security Strategy Archive, pp. 15, 26, 6.

16 Harvey (2003), p. 59.

17 See especially: Blakeley, R. (2009). State Terrorism and Neoliberalism: The North in the South. London: Routledge; Blum, W. (2014a). Killing Hope: US Military and CIA Interventions since World War II. 3rd edition. London: Zed Books; Blum, W. (2014b). Rogue State: A Guide to the World's Only Superpower. 4th edition. London: Zed Books. See also: Chomsky, N. (2000). Rogue States: The Rule of Force in World Affairs. London: Pluto Press.

18 Quoted in Chomsky (1992), p. 49.

19 Schoultz, L. (1981). Human Rights and United States Policy Toward Latin America. Princeton NJ: Princeton University Press, p. 7. Cited in Chomsky (1992), p. 51.

20 Callinicos, A. (2009). Imperialism and Global Political Economy. Cambridge: Polity Press, p. 15.

21 Callinicos (2009), p. 17; Harvey (2003), p. 68.

22 $19.39 trillion in 2017 compared to $17.28 trillion for the EU and $4.87 trillion for Japan. Worldometer (2020). 'Population Comparison: China, EU, USA, and Japan'. Worldometer (online).

23 Callinicos, A. (2003). The New Mandarins of American Power. Cambridge: Polity Press, pp. 93–8; Klare, M. (2003). 'The Policies: Resources'. J. Feffer (ed) Power Trip: US Unilateralism and Global Strategy after September 11. London: Seven Stories Press, p. 58.

24 Bromley, S. (2005). 'The United States and Control of World Oil'. Government and Opposition, 40, pp. 253–4.

25 Almost 70 per cent of "defence" (i.e. military) spending by NATO's 30 member states is by the USA. The USA makes by far the biggest contribution (22.4 per cent) to NATO'S military and civilian budget compared to 14.7 per cent by Germany and 10.5 per cent each by France and the UK.

26 Harvey (2003), p. 55.

27 Harvey (2003), p. 68.

28 Harvey, D. (2005). A Brief History of Neoliberalism. Oxford: Oxford University Press, pp. 54–5; Callinicos (2009), pp. 169–70, 176; Wade, R.H. (2003). 'The Invisible Hand of the American Empire'. Ethics and International Affairs, 17 (2), pp. 77–88.

29 Callinicos (2009), p. 193.
30 Harvey (2003), p. 185.
31 Chomsky (1992, 2000, 2003); Blum (2014a, 2014b).
32 Todd (2004).
33 Harvey (2003), pp. 72, 206.
34 Fiscal Data (2023). 'What Is the National Deficit?' US Treasury (online). (30 September).
35 McBride, J. and Chatzky, A. (2019). 'The US Trade Deficit: How Much Does It Matter?' Council on Foreign Relations (online). (8 March).
36 Fiscal Data (2023). 'What Is the National Debt?' US Treasury (online). (December). Accessed: 22/12/2023.
37 Rappaport, A. (2022). 'US National Debt Tops $30 Trillion as Borrowing Surged Amid Pandemic'. New York Times (online). (1 February).
38 Central Intelligence Agency (2022). 'The Economy. The World Factbook'. Accessed: 09/07/2023.
39 Congressional Budget Office (2018). 'The Budget and Economic Outlook: 2018 to 2028'. CBO (online). (9 April).
40 CIA (2022); Labonte, M. and Leubsdorf, B. (2023). 'Foreign Holdings of Federal Debt'. Congressional Research Service (online). (9 June); Federal Reserve Bank of St Louis (2023). 'Total Public Debt as Percent of Gross Domestic Product'. FRED: Economic Research (online). (23 July).
41 FRED (2023).
42 Labonte and Leubsdorf (2023).
43 Todd (2004, pp. 14, 15, 21–2.
44 Duffy Toft, M. and Kushi, S. (2023). Dying by the Sword: The Militarization of US Foreign Policy. New York NY: Oxford University Press.
45 Cited in Stephenson, S. (2023). 'US Foreign Policy Increasingly Relies on Military Interventions'. Global Affairs (online). (16 October).
46 Duffy Toft and Kushi (2023).
47 Duffy Toft cited in Stephenson (2023).
48 Duffy Toft and Kushi (2023).
49 See especially: Callinicos (2003); Feffer (2003).
50 Callinicos (2002), p. 9.
51 Callinicos (2002), p. 10.
52 Harvey (2003).
53 Harvey (2003), pp. 62–80.
54 Harvey (2003), pp. 62–71, 72–81, 183–212.
55 Harvey (2003), pp. 74–5, 77.
56 Harvey (2003), pp. 77–8.
57 Blum (2014a, 2014b).
58 White House (1990), p. 26.
59 Callinicos (2003), pp. 14–8.
60 Callinicos (2003), pp. 18–34.
61 Callinicos (2003), pp. 4–6, 23–34.
62 Callinicos (2003), pp. 16–8, 76–9; Callinicos (2002), pp. 28–9; Harvey (2003), pp. 7–8, 200–1.
63 Harvey (2003), pp. 197–8.
64 Callinicos (2002), pp. 27–9.
65 Cited in Callinicos (2003), p. 74.
66 Cited in Callinicos (2002), p. 4.
67 Callinicos (2002), p. 28.

68 More on this later.
69 Harvey (2003), pp. 84–5.
70 Callinicos (2002), p. 10.
71 Davenport, K. and Kimball, D.G. (2023). 'Nuclear Weapons: Who Has What at a Glance'. ACA (online). (June); Kristensen, H. et al. (2023). 'Status of World Nuclear Forces'. FAS (online). (31 March).
72 Kristensen et al. (2023).
73 Maier, T. (2014). 'Churchill Urged Us To "Wipe Out" Moscow with A-Bomb'. International Consortium of Investigative Journalists.
74 Kaku, M. and Axelrod, D. (1999). To Win a Nuclear War: The Pentagon's Secret War Plans. Boston MA: Southend Press.
75 Kaku and Axelrod (1999), p. 71.
76 As I discuss more later in the chapter.
77 Vine, D. (2015). Base Nation: How U.S. Military Bases Abroad Harm America and the World. New York NY: Metropolitan Books.
78 Vine, D. (2021). 'Lists of US Military Bases Abroad, 1776–2021'. American University Digital Research Archive (online).
79 Rees, J. (1996). 'The New Imperialism'. Callinicos et al. (eds), p. 69.
80 Vine (2015).
81 Goodman, A. (2023). 'The U.S. Has 750 Overseas Military Bases, and Continues to Build More to Encircle China. An Interview with David Vine.' Democracy Now (online). (14 February).
82 Allen, M.A., Flynn, M.F. and Machain, C.M. (2021). 'Global US Deployment Data, 1950–2020'. Conflict Management and Peace Science, 39 (3), pp. 351–70; Vine, D. (2021). Lists of US Military Bases Abroad, 1776–2021. American University Digital Research Archive (online).
83 Alonso, C. (2021). 'What Are the Latin American Countries with the Most US Military Bases?' Mexican Center for International Relations (online). (6 September).
84 Allen et al. (2021); Vine (2021).
85 Weedon, A. and Fankhauser, J. (2020). 'Iran Is Surrounded by US Military Bases and Facilities. Here's a Snapshot'. ABC News (online). (10 January).
86 Vine (2015). Harvey (2005), pp. 16–25; Klare, M. (2005). Blood and Oil: The Dangers and Consequences of America's Growing Petrol Dependency. London: Penguin, pp. 40–1, 26–55, 74–112; Klare (2003), pp. 50–60; Harvey, R. (2003). Global Disorder. London: Robertson, pp. 117–21; Callinicos (2003), pp. 80–98.
87 Allen et al. (2021); Vine (2021). See also: Wallin, M. (2018). 'US Military Bases and Facilities in the Middle East'. American Security Project (online).
88 The US state's military encirclement of Vietnam following its failure in the 1964–75 war to preserve its puppet regime in Hanoi and prevent unification of the country under communist rule was accompanied by a 19-year trade embargo, refusal of war reparations, and withholding of reconstruction aid. Such was intended to prevent Vietnam recovering economically from the American war and destabilize its government. Washington eventually permitted normalization of diplomatic relations between the countries in 1995, having lifted the blockade the year before. Such was likely intended to head-off closer ties between Hanoi and Beijing in the post-Cold War era. Bilateral trade relations were restored between the countries in 1997, but, perversely, this was in exchange for Hanoi's agreement to compensate the US government for $140 billion of debts run up by the former US-backed regime. To this day, the US government has paid Vietnam not a dollar in war reparations and very little ($80 million) for battle zone decontamination—and this was a war that cost the lives of somewhere between 1.5 million and two million Viet Cong soldiers

and Vietnamese civilians, substantially damaged the country's civilian infrastructure, and decimated 3.1 million hectares of its forests through saturation-bombing (including by means of cluster bombs and the use of chemical weapons such as Napalm and Agent Orange). The US military left 800,000 tons of unexploded ordinances in Vietnam, which have since the end of the war killed 40,000 people and maimed a further 65,000. See: Bennett, T. (2022). 'Healing the Wounds of War in Vietnam'. Science for the People (online), 25 (3); Castelli, B. (1995). 'The Lifting of the Trade Embargo Between the United States and Vietnam: The Loss of a Potential Bargaining Tool or a Means of Fostering Cooperation?' Pen State International Law Review, 13 (2), pp. 297–328; Clinton, W.J. (1995). 'Remarks Announcing the Normalization of Diplomatic Relations with Vietnam'. American Presidency Project (online). (11 July); Clodfelter, M. (1995). Vietnam in Military Statistics: A History of the Indochina Wars, 1772–1991. Jefferson NC: McFarland Books; Gettleman, E.M. et al. (1995). Vietnam and America: The Most Comprehensive Documented History of the Vietnam War. 2nd edition. New York NY: Grove Press, pp. 479, 487; Morris, B.S. (2016). 'Agent Orange and Unexploded Bombs: America's "Human Rights" Record in Vietnam'. Vox (online). (2 June); Neale, J. (2001). The American War: Vietnam 1960–1975. London: Bookmarks, pp. 62–3; Sanger, D.E. (1997). 'Hanoi Agrees to Pay Saigon's Debts to the US'. New York Times (online). (11 March). Ungerfeld, S. (2014). 'The Lingering Killer: Agent Orange'. Themis, 2 (1/8), pp. 129–41; Vu, M. (2022). 'War Explosive Remnants Kill 40,000 People in Vietnam since 1975'. Hanoi Times (online). (16 December).

In most recent years, Washington has even begun courting Hanoi as an unlikely ally, exploiting Vietnam's territorial disputes with China in the South China Sea to draw it into a closer strategic partnership, including by strengthening military ties. This is an extension of the US state's regional strategy of thwarting Chinese ascendancy in defence of its own primacy by alliance-building with neighbouring states (Taiwan, Malaysia, Brunei, the Philippines—and now Vietnam), which resist China's claims over mutually contested waters and islands. See: Bicker, L. (2023). 'US Denies Cold War with China in Historic Vietnam Visit'. BBC News (online). (10 September); Marciel, S. (2023). 'From Foe to Friend: Explaining the Development of US–Vietnam Relations'. Stanford (online). (31 March); Tatarski, M. (2023). 'China Concerns Drive Historic Upgrade in US-Vietnam Relations'. Guardian (online). (12 September); Fyler, B. (2022). 'Vietnam Relations Are a Quiet US Victory Already'. Foreign Policy (online). (9 May).

89 Allen et al. (2021); Vine (2021). See also: Goodman, A. (2023). 'The US Has 750 Overseas Military Bases, and Continues to Build More to Encircle China. An Interview with David Vine.' Democracy Now (online). (14 February); Anon (2023). 'US Bases Positioned for War Against China'. Solidarity (online). (19 January); Military Bases (2023). 'US Military Bases in South Korea'. (online). Accessed: 18/07/23.

90 Nicastro, N. (2023). U.S. Defense Infrastructure in the Indo-Pacific: Background and Issues for Congress. Congressional Research Service. R47589. (6 June).

91 Four new ones in the Philippines, plus others in the Pacific islands, for example. See: Lendon, B. (2023). 'US Gains Military Access to Philippine Bases Close to Taiwan and South China Sea'. CNN (online). (4 April); Agencies (2023). 'US Military Will Have "Unimpeded" Access to Papua New Guinea Bases Under New Security Deal'. Guardian (online). (15 June); Reid, J. (2023). Surrounded: How the U.S. Is Encircling China with Military Bases'. Foreign Policy (online). (20 August); Marshall, T. (2023). 'USA Moves to Contain China with More Military Bases in the Philippines'. Geographical (online). (23 February); Sevastopulo, D. and Hille, K. (2023). 'How the US Is Deepening Military Alliances in China's

Backyard'. Financial Times (online); Darmawan, A.R. (2023). 'Jakarta Is Alert But Not Alarmed Over the US-PNG Defence Agreement'. East Asia Forum (online). (5 August); Nakamura, R. and Imahashi, R. (2023). 'US Military to Use Papua New Guinea Naval Base for 15 Years'. NIKKEA Asia (online). (19 July).

92 Klare (2005), pp. 113–45.

93 US Secretary of State, Antony Blinken, brazenly claims that "NATO never promised not to admit new members". See: Lee, M. and Cook, L. (2022). 'U.S. and NATO Reject Russian Demand that Alliance Not Admit New Members'. PBS News Hour (online). (7 January).

94 Savranskaya, S. and Blanton, T. (2017). 'NATO Expansion: What Gorbachev Heard. Declassified Documents Show Security Assurances Against NATO Expansion to Soviet Leaders from Baker, Bush, Genscher, Kohl, Gates, Mitterrand, Thatcher, Hurd, Major, and Woerner'. National Security Archive: Washington University. (12 December).

95 Savranskaya and Blanton (2017).

96 Savranskaya and Blanton (2017).

97 Callinicos (2003), pp. 63–4; Callinicos (2009), pp. 191–3; Cohen, S.F. (2006). 'The New American Cold War'. Nation. (10 July); Rees, J. (1999). 'NATO and the New Imperialism'. Socialist Review (June); Brzezinski, Z. (1998). The Grand Chessboard: American Primacy and Its Geostrategic Imperatives. New York NY: Basic Books, p. 74.

98 Harman, 2009, pp. 207–11; Haynes, M. (2002). Russia: Class and Power 1917–2000. London: Bookmarks, pp. 204–6.

99 Senior, A.S. (2019). 'How 1989 Reshaped Europe'. US News (online). (8 November).

100 Haynes (2002), pp. 205, 214–5.

101 Lapidus, G.W. (2005). Ethnic Conflict in the Former Soviet Union. Centre for International Security and Cooperation: Stanford University. See also: Aklaev, A. (2010). Causes and Prevention of Ethnic Conflict: An Overview of Post-Soviet Russian-Language Literature. Moscow: Russian Academy of Sciences: Institute of Ethnology and Anthropology.

102 Bozic-Robertson, A. (2001). The Politicization of Ethnicity as a Prelude to Ethnopolitical Conflict: Croatia and Serbia in Former Yugoslavia. Kalamazoo MI: West Michigan University; Carment, D. and James, P. (1997). Wars in the Midst of Peace. Pittsburgh PA: University of Pittsburgh Press; Cagnon, V.P. (2009). 'Ethnic Nationalism and International Conflict: The Case of Serbia'. International Security, 19 (3), pp. 130–66; Jourek, O.N. (1997). Ethno-Political Conflicts in Post-Communist Societies: Prospects for Resolution and Prevention in the Context of International Law. Cambridge MA: Belfer Center for Science and International Affairs, Harvard Kennedy School.

103 According to the Levada Center, a Russian, independent, NGO, polling and sociological research institute, Putin's personal approval rating in Russia has never dipped below 59 per cent since he first won the presidency in 1999, and this peaked at 89 per cent in June 2015.

104 Stone, N. (2007). 'No Wonder They Like Putin'. Times (online). (4 December).

105 Žižek, S. (1993). Tarrying with the Negative. Durham NC: Duke University Press.

106 Rees (1999), pp. 174–8; Klare (2005), pp. 150–61; Klare (2003), pp. 53, 57–8; Harvey (2003), pp. 118–21.

107 Rees (1999), p. 175.

108 Mehdiyoun, K. (2017). 'Ownership of Oil and Gas Resources in the Caspian Sea'. American Journal of International Law, 94 (1), pp. 179–89.

109 Mehdiyoun (2017), p. 87.
110 Rees, J. (2001). 'Imperialism, Globalisation, the State and War'. International Socialism, 2 (93), pp. See p. 21.
111 Valasek, T. (2003). 'US Policy Toward the Caspian and Black Sea Region'. Quarterly Journal, pp. 15–22. See p. 18.
112 Jaffe, A. (2000). 'US Policy Towards the Caspian Region: Can the Wish-List Be Realized?'. Baker Institute (online), pp. 1018. See p. 2.
113 Valasek (2003), pp. 19–20.
114 Rees (1999), p. 175.
115 Rees (1999), pp. 174–5.
116 Valasek (2003), p. 20.
117 Energy Information Association (2013). 'Overview of Oil and Natural Gas in the Caspian Region'. USEIA (online). (26 August).
118 Rees (1999), p. 175; Alam, S. (2002). 'Pipeline Politics in the Caspian Sea Basin'. Strategic Analysis (online), 26 (1).
119 Richardson cited in Rees (1999), p. 176.
120 Rees (2001), pp. 19–20.
121 Kubicek, P. (2013). 'Energy Politics and Geopolitical Competition in the Caspian Basin'. Journal of Eurasian Studies, 4 (2), pp. 171–80.
122 Kubicek (2013), p. 173.
123 Kubicek (2013), p. 174.
124 Kubicek (2013), pp. 177–8.
125 Kubicek (2013), pp. 178.
126 USEIA (2013).
127 Weitz, R. (2020). 'Continuity and Change in US Policies Towards the Caspian Region'. Middle East Institute (online). (2 April).
128 Valasek (2003), p. 19.
129 TASS (2018). 'Five Caspian States Agree Armed Forces of Other Nations Won't Be Present at Caspian Sea'. Tass Russian News Agency (online). (2 June).
130 Blua, A. (2002). 'Uzbekistan: Tashkent Withdraws from GUUAM, Remaining Members Forge Ahead'. Radio Free Europe & Radio Liberty (online). (18 June).
131 Frederick, B. et al. (2017). Assessing Russian Reactions to U.S. and NATO Posture Enhancements. Santa Monica CA: RAND Corporation, RR-1879-AF, p. 74.
132 Radin, A. and Reach, C. (2017). Russian Views of the International Order. Santa Monica CA: RAND Corporation, RR-1826-OSD, p. 85.
133 Cohen, R.S. et al. (2020). The Future of Warfare in 2030: Project Overview and Conclusions. Santa Monica CA: RAND Corporation, RR-2849/1-AF, pp. 36–8.
134 Dobbins, J., Shatz, H.J. and Wyne, A. (2019). Russia Is a Rogue, Not a Peer; China Is a Peer, Not a Rogue. Santa Monica CA.: RAND Corporation, PE-310-A, p. 8.
135 RAND, which self-declares as a "non-partisan", independent organization, committed to objective, value-free, interdisciplinary research in the service of public interests, grew directly out of the US military-industrial complex. See: RAND (2023). 'A Brief History of RAND'. RAND Corporation (online).
136 Dobbins, J. et al. (2019). 'Overextending and Unbalancing Russia: Assessing the Impact of Cost-Imposing Options'. RAND Corporation (online). (24 April). Research Briefs Series.
137 Dobbins et al. (2019), p. 2.
138 Dobbins et al. (2019), p. 3.
139 Dobbins et al. (2019), p. 4.
140 Dobbins et al. (2019), p. 5.
141 Dobbins et al. (2019), pp. 6–7.
142 Dobbins et al. (2019), p. 7.

143 Dobbins et al. (2019), p. 8.
144 Dobbins et al. (2019), p. 9.
145 Pezard, S. (2022). 'US Strategic Competition with Russia: A RAND Research Primer'. RAND Corporation (online). (January).
146 Dobbins et al. (2019), p. 9.
147 Wade, R.H. (2022). 'Why the US and NATO Have Long Wanted Russia to Attack Ukraine'. Global Policy (online). (30 March).
148 See for example: EU (2022). 'EU Statement Regarding Russia's Unprovoked and Unjustified Military Aggression Against Ukraine'. EU: Diplomatic Service (online). (28 February); Foreign, Commonwealth and Development Office (2023). 'It Is Right to Remain Focused on Russia's Unprovoked, Full-scale and Illegal Invasion of Ukraine: UK Statement to the OSCE'. GOV.UK (online). (14 December); White House (2023). 'On One Year Anniversary of Russia's Invasion of Ukraine, Biden Administration Announces Actions to Support Ukraine and Hold Russia Accountable. Briefing Room: Statements and Releases'. (24 February).
149 Webber, A. (2022). 'Did Boris Johnson Deliberately Scupper a Peace Deal in Ukraine?'. Unity News Network (online). (4 September).
150 Tsuruoka, M. (2022). 'Why the War in Ukraine Is Not about Democracy versus Authoritarianism'. Royal United Services Institute (online). (27 June).
151 Mierzejewski-Voznyak, M. (2018). 'The Radical Right in Post-Soviet Ukraine'. J. Rydgren (ed) The Oxford Handbook of the Radical Right. Oxford. Oxford University Press, pp. 861–2.
152 Terzyan, A. (2020). 'Towards Democratic Consolidation? Ukraine after the Revolution of Dignity'. Open Political Science, 3, pp. 183–91. See p. 186.
153 Ripp, A. (2022). 'Ukraine's Nazi Problem Is Real, Even if Putin's "de-Nazification" claim Isn't'. Think: Opinion, Analysis, Essays (online). (5 March).
154 Golinkin, L. (2019). 'Neo-Nazis and the Far Right Are on the March in Ukraine'. Nation (online). (22 February).
155 Ahren, R. (2019). 'Top Nazi Hunter Blasts Visiting Ukraine Leader for Ignoring Holocaust Complicity'. Times of Israel (online). (24 January); Golinkin, L. (2021). 'Nazi Collaborator Monuments in Ukraine'. Forward (online). (27 January); Ripp (2022); World Jewish Congress (2016). 'WJC Concerned by Ukraine's Decision to Rename Kyiv Boulevard after Ultra-nationalist Complicit in Murdering Jews During Holocaust'. WJC (online). (8 July).
156 Ripp (2022).
157 Karmanau, Y. (2018). 'Training Kids to Kill at Ukrainian Nationalist Camp: Radical Nationalists Gain Growing Clout in Ukraine with Tacit Government Support'. Associated Press (online). (28 November); Kuzmenco, O. and Colborne, N. (2019). 'Ukrainian Far-right Extremists Receive State Funds to Teach "Patriotism"'. Bellingcat Anti-Equality Monitoring (online). (16 July).
158 Golinkin (2019).
159 Webber (2022).
160 Golinkin (2019). See also: Associated Press (2019). 'Yiddish Author Monument Vandalized with Swastikas in Ukraine'. AP (online). (25 November).
161 Spencer, K. (2021). 'Examining the Threat of the Azov Movement in Ukraine'. Geohistory (online). (17 October).
162 Spencer (2021); Lipshitz, C. (2021). 'Hundreds in Ukraine Attend Marches Celebrating Nazi SS Soldiers'. Times of Israel (online). (4 May).
163 Ripp (2022).
164 Gordon, A. (2020). 'A New Eurasian Far Right Rising: Reflections on Ukraine, Georgia and Armenia'. Special Report 2020. Freedom House (online).
165 Golinkin (2019).

166 Anon (2022). 'Who are Ukraine's Far-right Azov Regiment?' Al-Jazeera (online). (1 March); Baczynska, G. (2015). 'Ultra-nationalist Ukrainian Battalion Gears Up for More Fighting'. Reuters (online). (25 March); Bennetts, M. (2018). 'Ukraine's National Militia: "We're Not neo-Nazis, We Just Want to Make Our Country Better"'. Guardian (online). (13 March); Dorel, O. (2015). 'Volunteer Ukrainian Unit Includes Nazis'. USA Today (online). (3 October); Kramer, A.E. (2015). 'Islamic Battalions, Stocked with Chechens, Aid Ukraine in War with Rebels'. New York Times. (7 July); Parfitt, T. (2014). 'Ukraine Crisis: The Neo-Nazi Brigade Fighting Pro-Russian Separatists'. Telegraph (online). (11 August).

167 Nemptsova, A. (2018). 'The Frightening Far-Right Militia That's Marching in Ukraine's Streets, Promising to Bring "Order"'. Daily Beast (online). (5 February).

168 Ripp (2022). See also Spencer (2021).

169 Likhachev, V. (2018). 'Far-right Extremism as a Threat to Ukrainian Democracy'. Nation in Transit Brief. (May). Freedom House (online).

170 Golinkin (2019).

171 HRW (2018). 'Ukraine: Investigate, Punish Hate Crimes: Violent Attacks by Radical Groups Increasing'. HRW (online). (14 June); Likhachev (2018); Miller, C. (2018). 'With Axes and Hammers, Far-Right Vigilantes Destroy Another Romany Camp in Kyiv'. Radio Free Europe and Radio Liberty (online). (8 June); Radio Free Europe and Radio Liberty (2018). 'Amnesty Says Attack on Gay Event in Kyiv Shows Police Inaction'. (11 May).

172 Golinkin (2019).

173 Pszczel, R. (2022). 'The Consequences of Russia's Invasion of Ukraine for International Security—NATO and Beyond'. NATO Review (online). (7 July).

174 Armstrong, M. (2023). 'The Countries Pledging the Most Military Aid to Ukraine'. Statista (online). (22 September).

175 Anon (2023). 'The Costs of Russia's War Are About to Hit Home'. Economist (28 September); Disney, R., Becker, S.O., Farzanegan, M.R. and Gholipour, H.F. (2023). 'In Time of War'. Economics Observatory (online). (28 April); Hartwell, C.A. and Vaaler, P. (2023). 'Empire Building Has Always Come at an Economic Cost for Russia—from the Days of the Czars to Putin's Ukraine Invasion'. Conversation (online). (13 October); Kilfoyle, M. (2023). 'What's the Global Economic Impact of Russia's Invasion?' Economics Observatory. (24 October); Lasocki, J. (2023). 'The Cost of War to Ukraine'. Rusi (online). (23 February); Williamson, H. (2023). 'Ukraine: Human Cost of Brutal Russian Invasion'. Human Rights Watch (online). (23 February).

176 Gould, J. et al. (2023). 'When Will the War in Ukraine End? Experts Offer Their Predictions'. Defense News (online). (13 February). end?

177 Benjamin, M. and Davies, N.J.S. (2023). 'The West's Disastrous Decision to Reject Peace in Ukraine'. Fair Observer (online). (18 August).

178 Mearsheimer, J.J. (2015). 'The Causes and Consequences of the Ukraine Crisis'. Uncommon Core Lecture: University of Chicago (online). (4–7 June).

179 Rohde, D. and Mohammed, A. (2014). 'How the U.S. Made Its Putin Problem Worse'. Reuters (online). (18 April).

180 Cornwell, S. (2008). 'U.S. to Announce Over $1 Billion in Aid for Georgia'. Reuters (online). (3 September); Henney, M. (2019). 'US Aid to Ukraine: How It's Changed under Trump, Obama and Bush'. Fox Business (online). (12 October).

181 Rohde and Mohammed (2014).

182 Denial that Maidan was a US-backed and perhaps US-planned coup is the default of opinion-formers in the West because that would lend credence to Putin's claims that his invasion of Ukraine was indeed justifiable or at least provoked. This would be

on the grounds of self-defence against a hostile Western proxy state of ill-intent on its western border. However, just as I was about to submit this book to my publisher, an article published in the New York Times, based on testimony from CIA insiders connected to covert operations in Ukraine, basically confirmed (albeit unintentionally) that Maidan was indeed a US-backed coup. See: Entous, A. and Schwirtz, M. (2024). 'The Spy War: How the CIA Secretly Helps Ukraine Fight Putin'. New York Times (online). (25 February). For a critical discussion see: Mate, A. and Blumenthal, M. (2024). 'Ukraine Exposed as CIA-MI6 Bridgehead'. Grayzone (online). (25 February). This testimony of the CIA operatives is as follows.

Firstly, right after (i.e. within a few hours) the events of Maidan deposing the elected president and his government, Valentyn Nalyvaichenko, the new head of Ukraine's intelligence services, summoned the heads of CIA and MI6 stations to his intelligence HQ for a midnight meeting, whereupon a "three-way partnership" was agreed, right there, right then. The notion that this was a "right there right then" agreement is of course fundamentally implausible. Rather, this demonstrates, of course, prior involvement and collusion of the CIA and MI6 with opponents of the Russian-friendly government—in this case with an opponent with links to the Ukrainian ultranationalist militias. Secondly, the "partnership" in question with the new Kyiv government generated in short order the installation of a CIA-supported network of spy bases (including 12 in secret locations on Russia's border) engaged in covert operations against Moscow. This spy network was, according to the CIA insiders, their "own baby". Finally, operatives of this network provided the CIA with "intelligence" that would legitimize Washington's upscaling of its new cold war demonization of Russia as a "rogue state", leading to hostile acts against Moscow, including new sanctions, and eventually NATO proxy war in Ukraine to prop up Washington's proxy state. The "intelligence" in question (quite likely disinformation—for the obvious reason that it was gathered by operatives of a government that was anti-Russian with every incentive to "frame" Putin) was that the Kremlin was responsible for shooting down Malaysian civilian airliner Flight 17 and of attempting to interfere with the 2016 US presidential election—the so-called Russia-gate scandal that aroused international condemnation.

183 Marcetic, B. (2022). 'A US-Backed, Far Right–Led Revolution in Ukraine Helped Bring Us to the Brink of War'. Jacobin (online). (2 July).

184 Marcetic (2022).

185 Consequently, as well as declining to rebut NATO membership for Ukraine and Georgia, "the Obama administration backed a plan that would have moved Ukraine closer to the EU and away from a pro-Russian economic bloc created by Putin. Critics said it was a mistake to make Ukraine choose sides" (Rohde and Muhammed, 2014). Yet this was intention, not error.

186 Mearsheimer (2015).

187 Lieven, A. (2023). 'For Years, Putin Didn't Invade Ukraine. What Made Him Finally Snap in 2022?' Guardian (online). (23 February).

188 Stent, A. (2021). 'The Impact of September 11 on US-Russian Relations'. Brookings Institute (online). (8 September).

189 Hill, F. (2002). 'Putin and Bush in Common Cause? Russia's View of the Terrorist Threat after September 11'. Brookings Institute (online). (1 June).

190 Hill (2002); Stint (2021).

191 Rhode and Mohammed (2014).

192 Stent (2021).

193 Stent (2021).

194 Hill (2002).

195 Rhode and Mohammed (2014).
196 White House (2006). 'President Bush and Russian President Putin Participate in Press Availability'. White House News: G8 Summit. (15 July).
197 Stent (2021).
198 Rhode and Mohammed (2014).
199 White House (2010). 'Fact Sheet: President Obama's Participation in the Nato Summit Meetings in Lisbon'. Office of the Press Secretary. (20 November).
200 Righter, R. (2015). 'NATO's Obama Problem'. Politico (online). (10 December).
201 White House (2010).
202 Wade (2022).
203 Burbank, J. (2022). 'The Grand Theory Driving Putin to War'. New York Times (online). (22 March).
204 For example, Hill and Stent's (2022) claim that Putin invaded Ukraine "because he believes that it is Russia's divine right to rule Ukraine, to wipe out the country's national identity, and to integrate its people into a Greater Russia", is based on a 5,000-word essay he wrote as recently as 2021 (in which he asserts that Russians, Ukrainians, and Belarusians have a common identity and heritage), rather than on actual Russian foreign policy during the Putin era, and in disregard of other things he has written. See: Hill, F. and Stent, A. (2022). 'The World Putin Wants: How Distortions About the Past Feed Delusions About the Future'. Foreign Affairs (online). (25 August).
205 Lieven (2023).
206 Lieven (2023).
207 Wade (2022).
208 Wade (2022).
209 Mortimer, C. (2017). 'Russia Asks Ukraine and Poland to Stop People Vandalising Soviet War Monuments'. Independent (online). (24 October).
210 Righter (2015).
211 Lieven (2023).
212 Wade (2022).
213 Lieven (2023).
214 The Monroe Doctrine was formulated as an article of US foreign policy in 1823. Its original intention was to deter specifically European colonial-motivated interferences in the Americas. Under this guise, the doctrine legitimized the annexation of Hawaii in 1842, the attempted annexation of the Dominican Republic in 1870, and the military occupation of Cuba following the American-Spanish war (1895–1902), which turned the country thereafter into a virtual US colony. Emboldened by the "Roosevelt corollary", which sanctioned the exercise of force also against "flagrantly" and "chronically" misbehaving Latin American nations in order to protect US economic interests, the Monroe doctrine was extended far beyond its supposed original purpose—to defend the Americas from Old World colonialism. Instead, as the USA began to consolidate itself as a great power, the doctrine was invoked and applied to assert Washington's own regional hegemony and its own imperial projects. This was much in advance of the Cold War period. As US secretary of State, Richard Olney expressed the matter in 1895: "The United States is practically sovereign on this continent, and its fiat is law upon the subjects to which it confines its interposition" (Herring, 2011, p. 307). See: Gilderhus, M.T. (2006) 'The Monroe Doctrine: Meanings and Implications'. Presidential Studies Quarterly, 36 (1), pp. 5–16; Herring, G.C. (2011). From Colony to Superpower: US Foreign Relations Since 1776. New York NY: Oxford University Press.

Subsequently, in the Cold War era, the Monroe Doctrine has been asserted to justify a large number of military and other interventions in the Americas in the

1970s and 1980s to destabilize governments that are perceived as threats to free trade, capitalist enterprise, corporate ownership, or liberal democracy—those in Cuba, Chile, Nicaragua, and Panama being the main examples. Alternatively, it has been invoked to stabilize those US-compliant authoritarian right-wing regimes in the Americas (such as those in El Salvador, Guatemala, and Honduras) that were threatened by domestic opposition or popular insurgency under "communist influence". See especially: Chomsky (1992, 2003); Dominguez, J. (1999). 'US-Latin American Relations During the Cold War and Its Aftermath'. J. Dunkerley et al. (eds) The United States and Latin America: The New Agenda. David Rockefeller Center for Latin American Studies: Institute of Latin American Studies; Smith, G. (1995). The Last Years of the Monroe Doctrine 1945–1993. New York NY: Hill and Wang.

In the post-Cold War era, under the Trump administration, the Monroe Doctrine has been invoked to justify possible military action against Venezuela's populist left-wing government and as necessary to deter Chinese "trade imperialism" (i.e. China's efforts to cultivate Sino-Latin American commercial relations) in the Americas. See: Taylor, A. (2019). 'What Is the Monroe Doctrine? John Bolton's Justification for Trump's Push Against Maduro'. Washington Post. (4 March); Gramer, R. and Johnson, K. (2018). 'Tillerson Praises Monroe Doctrine, Warns Latin America of "Imperial" Chinese Ambitions'. Foreign Policy. (2 February).

215 Coll, D. (2004). Ghost Wars: The Secret History of the CIA, Afghanistan, and Bin Laden, from the Soviet Invasion to September 10, 2001. New York NY: Penguin; Riedel, B. (2014). What We Won: America's Secret War in Afghanistan, 1979–1989. Washington DC: Brookings Institution Press.

216 White Jnr, J.B. (2012). The Strategic Mind of Zbigniew Brzezinski: How a Native Pole used Afghanistan to Protect His Homeland. LSU Scholarly Repository. Louisiana State University, p. 29.

217 Gibbs, D.N. (1998). 'Brzezinski Interview: 1998 Interview with Zbigniew Brzezinski on Afghanistan in Le Nouvel Observateur'. University of Arizona (online).

218 Wade (2022).

219 Brzezinski (1998). Cited by Wade (2022).

220 Wade (2022).

221 Funajole, M.P. et al. (2021). Unpacking the Russian Troop Buildup along Ukraine's Border. CSIS: Center for Strategic and International Studies (online). (22 April); Siebold, S. and Emmott, R. (2021). 'NATO Warns Russia over Ukraine Military Build-up'. Reuters (15 November).

222 Jankowicz, J. (2022). 'Rare Video Shows France's Macron Trying to Talk Putin Down from Invading Ukraine. 4 days Later, He Attacked'. Business Insider (4 July). Putin urged Macron to support or open negotiations with the Russian-majority separatists in the Donbas as a way of easing tensions so that he had a reason to avoid war. Macron's response? "We don't give a damn about the separatists' proposals".

223 Anon (2022). 'On a Collision Course: Russia's Dangerous Game in Ukraine'. Al-Jazeera (online). (9 February).

224 Creaven, S. (2024). Modernity and the Pandemic: Decivilization, Imperialism, and COVID-19. London and New York NY: Routledge, p. 54.

225 Wade (2022).

226 Western leaders and politicians rarely state this explicitly as being a major goal of economic sanctions and proxy war, but they have certainly hinted at it. But former British PM Boris Johnson has been rather more direct. He declared on 1 March 2022 that sanctions "we are introducing, that large parts of the world are introducing, are to bring down the Putin regime" (Wade, 2022).

227 Creaven (2023), p. 54.

228 Wade (2022).
229 Creaven (2023), p. 54.
230 Levada Center (2023). 'Putin's Approval Rating'. Yuri Levada Analytical Center (online). Accessed: 12/12/2023.
231 Western sanctions in response to Russia's annexation of Crimea in 2014 boosted rather than diminished Putin's popular approval in Russia. This reached its second-highest rate (87 per cent) in August 2014. The annexation itself elevated Putin's approval rating to almost 86 per cent in May 2014—the highest for six years. Before that, following Russia's short military campaign in Georgia in August 2008, Putin's approval rating was raised to 88 per cent in September of that year (his highest ever), up from 80 per cent in July. See: Levada Center online (2023); Anon (2014). 'Putin's Approval Ratings Soar to Six-Year High'. Moscow Times (online). (29 May); Anon (2014). 'Vladimir Putin's Approval Rating Soars to 87 Per cent in Russia'. Straits Times (online). (7 August).
232 Economist. (28 September 2023); Disney et al. (2023); Hartwell and Vaaler (2023).
233 Jha, S. (2023). 'Which European Nations Are Handling the Energy Crisis Best?' Al-Jazeera (online). (20 December).
234 Zettelmeyer, J. et al. (2022). 'Beating the European Energy Crisis'. International Monetary Fund (online). (December); Natural Gas Intelligence (2023). 'How Much of Europe's Gas Comes from Russia?'. NGI (online).
235 Singh, A. (2022). 'Europe's Import of Russian LNG Jumps 42% Amid Russia-Ukraine War: Report'. WION (online). (30 November).
236 Kilfoyle (2023).
237 Sharma, U. (2023). 'Ex-Israel PM Naftali Bennett Blames West for Thwarting Possibility of Peace Between Russia, Ukraine'. Firstpost (online). (6 February); Semonsen, R. (2023). 'Former Israeli PM: West Blocked Russo-Ukraine Peace Deal'. New Conservative (online). (7 February).
238 Semonsen (2023).
239 Anon (2022). 'Western Allies Led by UK's Johnson Sabotaged Tentative Ukraine-Russia Peace Deal'. Gulf Insider (online). (1 September). See also: Colchester, M., Grove, T. and Marson, J. (2024). 'Document From 2022 Reveals Putin's Punishing Terms for Peace'. Wall Street Journal (online). (1 March).
240 Sinclair, I. (2022). 'Did the UK Torpedo Peace Talks on Ukraine?' Stop the War Coalition (online). (17 November).
241 Hill and Stent (2022).
242 Gulf Insider (2022).
243 Orbán, T. (2023). 'Official: Johnson Forced Kyiv to Refuse Russian Peace Deal'. European Conservative (online). (27 November).
244 Carl, N. (2022). 'Did Boris Scuttle Peace Talks Between Ukraine and Russia?' Daily Sceptic (online). (1 September).
245 Balachuk, I. and Romaniuk, R. (2022). 'Possibility of Talks Between Zelenskyy and Putin Came to a Halt after Johnson's Visit—UP Sources'. Ukrainska Pravda (online). (5 May). For useful secondary reports see: Carl (2022) and Johnson, J. (2022). 'Boris Johnson Pressured Zelenskyy to Ditch Peace Talks with Russia: Ukrainian Paper'. Common Dreams (online). (6 May).
246 Benjamin and Davies (2023).
247 Biden, J. (2022). 'What We Will and Will Not Do in Ukraine'. New York Times (online). (1 June).
248 Sciutto, J. (2023). 'Western Allies Receive Increasingly "Sobering" Updates on Ukraine's Counteroffensive: "This Is the Most Difficult Time of the War" '. CNN (online). (8 August).

249 Mearsheimer, J.J. (2023). 'The Myth that Putin Was Bent on Conquering Ukraine and Creating a Greater Russia'. John's Substack (online). (27 November).
250 Benjamin and Davies (2023).
251 Lawler cited in Shinkman, P.D. (2023). 'Putin's Hollow Nuclear Threat'. US News: A World Report (online). (24 February).
252 Cited in Shinkman (2023).
253 Ironically, the course of the war (i.e. Russia's failure to win it faced with NATO's weaponization of Kyiv) has reshaped Putin's military objectives, however, in favour of partial annexation.
254 Mearsheimer (2023).
255 Callinicos (2009), pp. 215–6, 218.
256 This is Article 9, which states: "The Japanese people forever renounce war as a sovereign right of the nation and the threat or use of force as means of settling international disputes. In order to accomplish the aim of the preceding paragraph, land, sea, and air forces, as well as other war potential, will never be maintained. The right of belligerency of the state will not be recognized".
257 Harvey (2003), p. 145.
258 Slavin, B. (2015). 'Japan Enacts Major Changes to Its Self-defense Laws'. Stars and Stripes (online). (18 September).
259 Richter, J.P. (2015). 'Japan's "Reinterpretation" of Article 9: A Pyrrhic Victory for American Foreign Policy?'. Iowa Law Review, 1 (1223), pp. 1223–62.
260 Kyodo News (2019). 'Japan to Develop Air-to-ship Long-range Missiles' (online). (18 March.
261 Harvey (2003), pp. 145–55.
262 Smith, S.A. (2021). 'The Growing Risk for Japan in the US-China Rivalry'. Global Asia (online), 16 (4). (December).
263 Samuels, R.J. (2001). 'Kishi and Corruption: An Anatomy of the 1955 System'. Japan Policy Research Institute (online). Working Paper No. 83. (December).
264 Harvey (2003), pp. 145–55.
265 Rasheed (2023).
266 Reynolds, I. and Westcott, B. (2023). 'Japan Looks Beyond U.S. Alliance for Help to Deter China Military'. Japanese Times (online). (16 January).
267 Smith (2021).
268 Bix, H.P. (1985). 'The "Japanese Challenge": US-Japan Relations at Mid-decade'. Bulletin of Concerned Asian Scholars, 17 (4), pp. 27–33; Cornish, A. (2019). 'Lessons for Today from the U.S.-Japan Trade War of the 1980s'. NPR (online). (20 May); Satake, M. (2000). 'Trade Conflicts Between Japan and the United States over Market Access: The Case of Automobiles and Automotive Parts'. Asia Pacific Economic Papers, 310, pp. 1–32; Dahl, E.S. (2013). 'US American 'Japan Bashing' in the 1980s and Today's 'China Threat': Is History Repeating Itself?'. East Asia Security Centre (online).
269 Thierer, A. (2021). '"Japan Inc." and Other Tales of Industrial Policy Apocalypse'. Discourse (online). (28 June).
270 Nymalm, N. (2019). 'Washington's Old "Japan Problem" and the Current "China Threat"'. East Asia Forum (online). (11 September).
271 Thierer (2021).
272 Bix (1985).
273 Satake (2000).
274 Samuelson, T. (2018). 'How the US Outgrew 1980s Trade Anxiety over Japan'. Marketplace (online). (29 November).
275 Bix (1985), p. 30.

276 Bix (1985), p. 31.
277 Cited in Bix (1985), pp. 30–1. Emphasis in the original.
278 Nielson, B. (2022). 'The Lost Decade: Lessons from Japan's Real Estate Crisis'. Investopedia (online). (14 January).
279 Thierer (2021).
280 Nymalm (2019).
281 Callinicos (2009), p. 171.
282 History Editors (2010). 'Europe's Common Market Founded in Major Step Toward Economic Unity'. History (online). (9 February).
283 Ross, E. (2019). 'How the US Influenced the Creation of the EU'. The World (online). (28 January); Callinicos (2009), pp. 172–3; Al-Jazeera (2017). '1950s: Birth of the European Project' (online); Milward, A. (2006). The Reconstruction of Western Europe 1945–51. Berkeley CA: University of California Press, p. 46.
284 Harvey (2003), pp. 82–3.
285 Editorial of US Marine Corps Gazette (May 1990) cited in Chomsky (1992), p. 31.
286 As correctly diagnosed by the theorists of dependency and underdevelopment.
287 Giles, C. (2006). 'Warning over Cost Benefits of Emerging Economies'. Financial Times. (3 October); Harman, C. (2009). Zombie Capitalism: Global Crisis and the Relevance of Marx. London: Bookmarks, pp. 213, 221–2, 242, 251–3; Harman, C. (1999). A People's History of the World. London: Bookmarks, p. 596.
288 Harman (2009), pp. 252, 337–41.
289 Textor, T. (2020). 'Distribution of the Workforce Across Economic Sectors in China 2019'. Statista (online). (July 29); Plecher, H. (2020). 'India: Distribution of the Workforce Across Economic Sectors from 2010 to 2020'. Statista (online). (20 October).
290 Callinicos (2009), pp. 183–4; Harman (2009), pp. 218–9, 243–5; Harman, C. (1984). Explaining the Crisis: A Marxist Reappraisal. London: Bookmarks, pp. 94–7; Harris, N. (1987). The End of the Third World: Newly Industrializing Countries and the Decline of an Ideology. London: Pelican, pp. 30–69.
291 According to OECD data, only one of the NICs (South Korea) was among the top 35 countries for hourly labour productivity (in 30th place), whereas all of the top 20 places (bar one—Japan, ranked 20th) were filled by the advanced countries of the Global North. See: Johnson, D. (2017). 'These Are the Most Productive Countries in the World'. Time Magazine (online). (4 January).
292 Callinicos (2009), pp. 199–201.
293 China's GDP is $12.24 trillion compared to the USA's $19.39 trillion and the EU's $17.28 trillion. These are statistics for 2017. See: Worldometer (2020). 'Population Comparison: China, EU, USA, and Japan'. Worldometer (online).
294 China's central bank loans (or "development aid") to a large swathe of countries across the developing world have become immense in recent years. These "amounted to US$ 675 billion at the end of 2016, more than twice the size of loans from the World Bank". See: Vieira, H. (2018). 'China Is Investing in Developing Countries—What Is It Really Up To?'. LSE (online). (1 October). Much of the capital is devoted to infrastructural projects—in energy, transport, and communications. The purpose is geopolitical as well as economic—to make of donor countries new allies and dependents.
295 Callinicos (2009), p. 219.
296 Aliyev, N. (2020). 'Military Cooperation Between Russia and China: The Military Alliance Without an Agreement? International Centre for Defence and Security'. (1 July); Atalaya (2020). 'The US Considers China's Enemies as Allies in the Region'. Atalaya (online). (27 October); Dwivedi, S.S. (2012). 'North Korea-China

Relations: An Asymmetric Alliance'. North Korean Review, 8 (2), pp. 76–93; Simes, D. (2020). 'China-Russia Alliance on Horizon as Nuclear Arms Treaties Crumble'. Nikkei Asia: Asia Insight (online). (21 April); Enoa, A.J. (2019). 'China: Cuba's Latest Benefactor'. Dialago Chino (online). (5 November); Fassihi, F. and Myers, S.L. (2020). 'Defying U.S., China and Iran Near Trade and Military Partnership'. New York Times (onlinc). (11 July); Friedman, U. (2020). 'America Is Alone in Its Cold War with China'. Atlantic (online). (17 February); Smith, J. (2020). 'China's Xi Says Intends to Deepen Relations with North Korea: KCNA'. Reuters (online). (9 October); Standish, R. (2020). 'China, Russia Deepen Their Ties Amid Pandemic, Conflicts with the West'. RadioFreeLiberty and RadioLiberty (online).

297 Garamone, J. (2023). 'DOD Report Details Chinese Efforts to Build Military Power'. US Department of Defense (online). (19 October). The US State's Rhetorical commitment to a "rules-based" international order of its own artifice has not of course prevented it from flouting those rules wherever they obstructed its own interests. See: Sands, P. (2005). Lawless World: America and the Making and Breaking of Global Rules. Allen Lane, Penguin.

298 Meyer zum Felde, R. (2022). 'What a Military Alliance Between Russia and China Would Mean for NATO'. S. Kirchberger, S. Sinjen and N. Wörmer (eds) Russia-China Relations: Emerging Alliance or Eternal Rivals? Cham: Springer, pp. 245–6.

299 Of the six UN Security Council resolutions either condemning or sanctioning Russia's invasion of Ukraine, many countries (ranging from 32 to 73) have consistently abstained or absented themselves (10 to 13). These are in countries that are home to most of the world's population. The ASEAN countries have collectively refused to condemn Russia's actions, whereas most countries of the African Union have not supported the UNSC resolutions. Only 46 countries (out of 195) have pledged their support for the sanctions imposed by the USA and its Western allies. See: Fillion, S. (2023). 'With Caution and Tact: How Asian Countries Voted on Ukraine at the UN'. Interpreter (online); Gotz, E., Kaas, J.G. and Knudsen, P. (2023). How African states voted on Russia's war in Ukraine at the United Nations—and what it means for the West. Danish Institute for International Studies (online). (15 November); Haddad, M. (2023). 'Where Does Your Country Stand on the Russia-Ukraine War?' Al-Jazeera (online). (16 February).

Cambridge researchers have observed what they see as a polarization of world public opinion between "illiberal" or "undemocratic" countries that are sympathetic to China (and to Russia) and "liberal" ones that are not. This is, they claim, a division in the interstate system between a "Maritime Alliance" and a "Eurasian Bloc", which has been exacerbated by the Russo-Ukrainian war. The so-called Eurasian Bloc—which includes Russia and China and extends across central Asia, the Arab Middle East, and into Africa and Southeast Asia—is represented as being populated by majorities of intolerant, traditional, authoritarian people. This contrasts with the liberal, tolerant, rights-affirming majority of people who predominate in "our" part of the world.

I will not dwell on the ludicrously partisan ideological framing of this global divide. This establishes the "liberal" or "illiberal" mindsets of peoples based on: (1) whether they feel positively towards either the USA and the other Western countries or towards China and Russia—a rather unfortunate strategy, given that the former have exported imperialism and war to the developing countries as much as they have preached to them the virtues of "liberal values"; and (2) whether or not they uncritically endorse "freedom" (rights individualism) or "authoritarianism" (recognition of social or community obligations that impose constraints on personal autonomy).

For the Cambridge researchers, a civilization based on rights-individualism and "democratic capitalism" (as they misdescribe corporate rule) is beyond rational critique.

Rather, the substantial point that this research demonstrates is that of those countries of the "Maritime Alliance" in which most people hold a negative view of China and Russia, these are home to only 16 per cent of the world's population (1.2 billion). By contrast, of those countries of the "Eurasian Bloc" where most people hold a positive view of China and Russia, these are home to 84 per cent of the world's population (6.3 billion). Anti-China and anti-Russia publics dominate in only 59 of the world's 195 countries. See: Foa, R. et al. (2022). 'A World Divided: Russia, China and the West'. Centre for the Future of Democracy, University of Cambridge (online). (20 October).

300 US-China Economic and Security Review Commission (2023). 'China's Position on Russia's Invasion of Ukraine'. USCESRC (online). (30 November).

301 Anon (2023). 'Why China's Stand on Russia and Ukraine Is Raising Concerns'. AP News Wire (online). (20 February); Stent, A. (2023). 'China, Russia, and the War in Ukraine'. Internationale Politik Quarterly (online). (28 August); US-China Economic and Security Review Commission (2023).

302 Askew, J. (2023). 'Where Does China Stand on the Ukraine War?'. Euronews (online). (2 March).

303 AP News Wire (2023); Kine, P. (2023). 'US Dismisses China's Ukraine Peace Proposal as an Attempt to Distract'. Politico (online). (24 February).

304 Drozdiak, M. and Rynolds, I. (2023). 'China Is Learning from Putin's War in Ukraine, NATO Chief Warns'. Bloomberg (online). (31 January).

305 AP News Wire (2023); CBS News (2023). 'NATO Chief Urges China Not to Back Russia's War in Ukraine'. (22 February).

306 Allen et al. (2021); Vine (2021).

307 Nicastro (2023).

308 Nicastro (2023), p. i.

309 BBC News (2022). 'China and Taiwan: A Really Simple Guide'. (online). (8 January).

310 During the military clashes of 1954 and 1958 between the two countries, US protection of the Taipei regime extended to deploying American warships in the Strait of Taiwan and providing the Taiwanese nationalists with copious weapons aid, including fighter jets. Washington also declared its willingness to use atomic weapons against Beijing in the event of a Chinese invasion of islands claimed by the nationalists that were right on top of China's seaboard. See: Halperin, M.H. (1966). The 1958 Taiwan Straits Crisis: A Documented History. RAND Corporation. Daniel Ellsberg Archive (online); Crean, J. (2023). The Fear of Chinese Power: An International History. London: Bloomsbury Academic.

311 BBC News (8 January 2022).

312 To quote a joint press statement by NATO chief Jens Stoltenberg and Japanese PM Fumio Kishida in January 2023 (Drozdiak and Rynolds, 2023).

313 BBC News (2023). 'What Is the South China Sea dispute?'. (online). (7 July); Ratcliffe, R. and Hawkins, R. (2023). 'Risk of Miscalculation Rises in South China Sea as Beijing Ramps Up Aggressive Tactics'. Guardian (online). (29 September).

314 Anon (2023). 'Why Does China Claim Almost the Entire South China Sea?' Al-Jazeera (online). (24 October).

315 BBC News (8 January 2022).

316 Nicastro (2023), p. 1.

317 Standish, R. (2022). 'China Takes Aim at NATO'. Radio Free Europe and Radio Liberty (online). (11 May).

318 Standish (2022).
319 Incidents of confrontation in the eastern waters of the South China Sea between China and Japan in 2012 and 2013—which were the first serious escalation of conflict in the longstanding dispute over rights to the Diaoyu Islands for a while—were reportedly initiated by the Japanese. See: Rose, C. (2014). 'Tensions in Sino-Japanese Relations in 2012 and 2013: Plus ça change?' Foreign and Commonwealth Office: GOV.UK (online). (15 January). A further initial trigger-event was Japan's purchase from their private owner in 2013 three of the disputed islands. See: Anon (2013). 'Dangerous Waters: China-Japan Relations on the Rocks'. International Crisis Group (online). (8 April). From a longer historical perspective, there is the Council on Foreign Relations' very useful timeline of China's maritime disputes with Japan, Taiwan, the Philippines, and Vietnam. This has shown that the trigger-events for escalating tensions have come in equal measure from all sides. This shows as well that, mischievously, the US government has sometimes supported escalations from parties to the disputes other than China. See CFR (2023). '1985–2023: China's Maritime Disputes'. (online). Accessed: 17/12/23.
320 US Department of State (2021). China's Military Aggression in the Indo-Pacific Region. USDS (online). Without a hint of irony, Beijing is accused of "establishing overseas military bases", as well as "stealing resources in the South China Sea", "challenging neighbours in the East China Sea", "intimidating Taiwan", and "provoking tensions along the India-PCR border". China is also accused by the West of using soft economic power to assert its territorial claims in the disputed island chains. This is even though Japan has been doing exactly the same without censure. See: Yoshimatsu, H. (2017). 'China, Japan and the South China Sea Dispute'. Journal of Asian Security and International Affairs, 4 (3), pp. 294–315. The standard position in the West on the military arms race between the USA and China is set out by RAND authors. "The expansion of Chinese military activities and capabilities in the Indo-Pacific region has led the United States to increase its own military activities in the region". See: Frederick, B. et al. (2023). 'Managing the Escalation Risks of U.S. Military Activities in the Indo-Pacific'. RAND (online).
321 Rasheed, Z. (2023). 'In Bid to Counter China, US Ramps Up Effort to Boost Military Ties in Asia'. Al-Jazeera (online). (28 December).
322 O'Hanlon, H. (2020). 'Evolving the US Base Structure in the Indo-Pacific'. Brookings Institute (online).
323 Huxley, T. (2023). 'The War in Ukraine Unfolds Alongside a Military Build-up in the Asia-Pacific'. IISS (online). (15 September).
324 Rasheed (2023).
325 Gurr, R. (1994). 'Peoples Against States: Ethnopolitical Conflict and the Changing World System'. International Studies Quarterly, 38 (3), pp. 347–77. See p. 347.
326 Henderson, E.A. and Singer, J.D. (2000). 'Civil War in the Post-Colonial World, 1946–92'. Journal of Peace Research, 37 (3), pp. 275–99.
327 Allen, C. (1999). 'Warfare, Endemic Violence and State Collapse in Africa'. Review of African Political Economy, 26 (81), pp. 367–84; Emmanuel, N.G. (2012). 'Self-Help and Africa's Collapsed States'. ASPJ Africa and Francophonie (2nd Quarter), pp. 76–96; Matthews, S. and Solomon, H. (2001). 'The Challenges of State Collapse in Africa: The Case of the Democratic Republic of the Congo'. Africa Insight, 31 (3), pp. 24–31; Quaranto, P.J. (2008). State Collapse and Security in Somalia. Institute For Security Studies. (May 20).
328 Crawford, B. (1990). 'The Causes of Cultural Conflict: An Institutional Approach'. B. Crawford and D. Lipschutz (eds) The Myth of "Ethnic Conflict": Politics, Economics, and "Cultural" Violence. Berkeley CA: University of California Press, pp. 4–5.

329 See Chua (2003).
330 Quaranto (2008).
331 Callinicos (2009), p. 185.
332 Naturally, this has incurred US-orchestrated economic sanctions of greater or lesser intensity against the regime along with concerted ideological warfare to cast the country as a "rogue state" and, later on, under Bush Junior's presidency, as part of the "axis of evil" (alongside North Korea, Ba'athist Iraq, Libya, Syria, and Cuba) that was supporting international terrorism and posing a threat to world security. See: Callinicos, A. (2003). The New Mandarins of American Power. Cambridge: Polity Press, pp. 14–5.

The failure of the US occupation of Iraq (2003–2011) to "stabilize" the country has allowed the Iranian regime to increase its influence over its once antagonistic neighbour, so that a closer political alignment of the two under the leadership of Tehran is likely, as well as to consolidate Kuwait as an ally. This was always a likely result of Washington's ill-conceived regime-change project in Iraq, given that the majority of the Iraqi population, like that of Iran, are Shia Muslim, and given that the official ideology of the Iranian state is Shia Islam. The insurgency in Syria has also provided opportunity for Iran to consolidate favour with the Assad regime by supporting it economically and militarily in the civil war. This intervention is motivated by Tehran's strategic interest in ensuring that Syria is not pulled into the US–Western alliance by falling under the control of a sectarian Sunni-dominated government. The Iranian regime has also made itself the dominant influence on political affairs in Yemen and Lebanon, out-competing the Saudis. See: Arango, T. (2017). 'Iran Dominates in Iraq After US "Handed the Country Over"'. New York Times (online). (15 July); Gardner, F. (2019). 'Iran's Network of Influence in Mid-East "Growing"'. BBC News (online). (7 November); Sadjadpour, K. (2013). 'Iran's Unwavering Support to Assad's Syria'. CTC Sentinel, 6 (8), pp. 11–3.

Aside from influence-building in the Middle East, Iran has also successfully sought new allies, including Russia, China, India, the former Soviet republics in the energy-rich Caspian delta and Trans-Caucasus, whereas diplomatic and commercial relations with the EU have been re-established, opening up tensions in the Western Alliance that are reflected as disputes in the UN over how to relate to Iran. Iran has also sought new allies in the USA's backdoor of Latin America and the Caribbean. See: Antapoulous, P. (2018). 'The Unlikely Friends: Iranian–Latin American Relations and Washington's Anxiety'. Strategic Analysis, 42 (2), pp. 154–67; Greenwood, P. (2018). 'Landmark Caspian Sea Deal Signed by Five Coastal Nations'. Guardian (online). (12 August); Johnson, F. (2020). 'Iran Is Working Hard to Revive Anti-US Operations in Latin America'. Foreign Policy (online). (1 June); Simpson Jr, J.R. (2010). 'Russian and Chinese Support for Tehran'. Middle East Quarterly (Spring), pp. 63–72.
333 Bevins, V. (2017). 'What the United States Did in Indonesia'. Atlantic (online). (20 October); Budiardjo, C. and Liem, S.J. (1984). The War Against East Timor. London: Zed Books; Defert, G. (1992). East Timor: The Forgotten Genocide. Paris: Editions de l'Harmattan; Kiernan, B. (2003). 'The Demography of Genocide in Southeast Asia: The Death Tolls in Cambodia, 1975–79, and East Timor, 1975–80'. Critical Asian Studies, 35 (4), pp. 585–97; O'Brien, A. (2005). 'The US-Indonesian Military Relationship'. Council on Foreign Relations (online). (4 October); Pilger, J. (2003). pp. 17–47; Scott, P.D. (1985). 'The United States and the Overthrow of Sukarno 1965–1967'. Pacific Affairs, 58 (2), pp. 239–64; Simpson, B. (2018). 'US Promoted Close Ties to Indonesian Military as Suharto's Rule Came to an End in Spring 1998'. National Security Archive (online). (24 July).
334 OPEC (2019). 'OPEC Share of World Crude Oil Reserves, 2018'. OPEC (online).

335 Council on Foreign Relations (2021). 'Oil Dependence and US Foreign Policy 1850–2017'. SFR: Timeline (online).
336 Callinicos (2003), p. 94.
337 Mills, R. (2019). 'The US Isn't Protecting Oil Supplies from the Middle East, It Wants to Control Prices as Foreign Policy'. EURACTIV (online). (23 May); US Energy Information Administration (2021). 'Petroleum and Other Liquids'. EIA (online).
338 NEP (2001) cited in Callinicos (2003), pp. 94–5.
339 CFR (2021).
340 Yergin, D. (2013). 'Congratulations America, You're (Almost) Energy Independent'. Politico Magazine (online). (November); US Energy Information Administration (2020). 'Oil and Petroleum Products Explained'. EIA (online). (27 April).
341 CFR (2021).
342 Center on Global Energy Policy (2020). 'The US Isn't Energy Independent. Middle East oil Still Matters'. CGEP (online). New York NY: Columbia University. (10 January).
343 Mills (2019); Telhami, S. (2002). 'The Persian Gulf: Understanding the American Oil Strategy'. Brookings Institute (online). (1 March).
344 Bromley, S. (1991). American Hegemony and World Oil: The Industry, the State System, and the World Economy. Cambridge: Polity Press, p. 86.
345 Sampson, A. (1976). The Seven Sisters: The Great Oil Companies and the World They Made. London: Coronet.
346 Callinicos (2003), p. 98.
347 CFR (2021).
348 Mills (2019).
349 Mills (2019.
350 Chulov, M. and Safi, M. (2020). '"We're Poor People": Middle East's Migrant Workers Look for Way Home Amid Pandemic'. Guardian (online). (9 June).
351 Baker Institute (2019). The Politics of Rentier States in the Gulf. Washington DC: Baker Institute: Project on Middle East Political Science (online); Beblawi, H. (1987). 'The Rentier State in the Arab World'. Arab Studies Quarterly, 9 (4), pp. 383–98; Crystal, J. (1990). Oil and Politics in the Gulf: Rulers and Merchants in Kuwait and Qatar. Cambridge: Cambridge University Press; Gause, F.G. (1994). Oil Monarchies: Domestic and Security Challenges in the Gulf States. New York: Council on Foreign Relations Press; ILO (2020). 'Arab States: Labour Migration'. ILO (online); Lewis, B. (2000). 'Monarchy in the Middle East'. J. Kostiner (ed) Middle East Monarchies: The Challenge of Modernity. Boulder CO: Lynne Rienner Publishers; Winckler, O. (2000). 'Gulf Monarchies as Rentier States: The Nationalization Policies of the Labor Force'. Kostiner (2017) (ed).
352 Achcar, G. (2018). 'The Saudi Predicament'. New Socialist (online). (20 April).
353 Chomsky, N. (1977). 'Oil Imperialism and the US-Israel Relationship'. Leviathan, 1 (3) (Spring), pp. 6–9; Chomsky, N. (1983). The Fateful Triangle: The United States, Israel and the Palestinians. London: Verso, p. 463. As Gilbert Achcar (2018) rightly puts it: "The 'leader of the free world' has supported the least democratic, most misogynist, most fundamentalist country on the planet, the only one to have the Quran and the Sunna (deeds and sayings of the Prophet) instead of a constitution".
354 Gold, D. (2004). Hatred's Kingdom: How Saudi Arabia Supports the New Global Terrorism. Washington DC: Regnery Publishers; Pipes, S. (2015). 'The Scandal of US-Saudi Relations'. S. Pipes (ed) Nothing Abides: Perspectives on the Middle East and Islam. New York NY: Routledge; Posner, G. (2005). Secrets of the Kingdom: The Inside Story of the Saudi-US Connection. New York NY: Random

House; Stern, S. (ed) (2011). Saudi Arabia and the Global Islamic Terrorist Network: America and the West's Fatal Embrace. New York NY: Palgrave Macmillan (esp. Chs 2, 4 and 5).

355 The Pahlavi monarchy seized power in Iran following a CIA-backed coup against the secular-nationalist government of Dr Mohammed Mossadegh. Mossadegh had earned the ire of the US state by nationalizing the country's oil resources. See: Ritter, S. and Pitt, W.R. (2002). War on Iraq. New York NY: Profile Books, p. 11.

356 Rivers and Pitt (2003), pp. 13–14.

357 Moore, J. (2003). 'Saddam Hussein's Rise to Power'. Online News Hour. PBS (online). As Pilger (2002, p. 95) points out: "Before sanctions, Iraqis consumed more than 3,000 calories each per day; 92 per cent of people had safe water and 93 per cent enjoyed free health care. Adult literacy was one of the highest in the world, at around 95 per cent. According to The Economist's Intelligence Unit, 'the Iraqi welfare state was, until recently, among the most comprehensive and generous in the Arab world'". See: Campaign Against Sanctions in Iraq (2000). Starving Iraq: One Humanitarian Disaster We Can Stop. Cambridge: CASI, pp. 5–6; Economist Intelligence Unit (1998). Iraq: County Report 1995–96. London: EIU, p. 6.

358 Rivers and Pitt (2003), pp. 14–5.

359 Rivers and Pitt (2003), pp. 15–6. Human Rights Watch—an organization accused by the US government of sympathizing with Saddam Hussein's regime for opposing the second Gulf War—estimates "conservatively" that his regime was responsible for or involved in the killings of 250,000 Iraqi nationals in various purges, counterinsurgencies, or other conflicts over the course of its 25 years. However, these figures are inclusive of those that occurred in the violent civil war triggered by the US-led war on Iraq in 1991 and the regime's crushing defeat in that war. See: Human Rights Watch (2004). 'War in Iraq: Not a Humanitarian Intervention'. HRW (online). (25 January).

360 Rivers and Pitt (2003), p. 14; Esposito, J. (1997). Political Islam: Revolution, Radicalism, or Reform. Boulder CO: Lynne Rienner, pp. 56–8.

361 Cockburn and Cohen (1991), p. 5.

362 Cockburn and Cohen (1991), pp. 2–9; Friedman, A. (1993). Spider's Web: The Secret History of How the White House Illegally Armed Iraq. New York NY: Bantam Dell; Hiro, D. (1991). The Longest War: The Iran-Iraq Military Conflict. New York NY: Routledge. (See "Outside Powers"); Nonneman, G. (1986). Iraq, the Gulf States and the War. London; Phythian, M. (1997). Arming Iraq: How the U.S. and Britain Secretly Built Saddam's War Machine. Boston MA: Northeastern University Press; Pilger (2002), pp. 66–7, 68–70; Stork, J. and Wenger, M. (1984). 'US Ready to Intervene in Gulf War'. MERIP Reports, 125/6 (July/September), pp. 44–8; Timmerman, K.R. (1991). The Death Lobby: How the West Armed Iraq. New York NY: Houghton Mifflin.

363 Humphreys, R.S. (1999). Between Memory and Desire: The Middle East in a Troubled Age. Berkeley CA: University of California Press, p. 105.

364 The targeting of Iraq's civilian and industrial infrastructure by the "Allied" bombing was hardly humanitarian war (Pilger, 1999, pp. 52–3). This was, rather, as Andre Gunder Frank (p. 267) describes it, Third World War in the specific sense of being conducted by the North (and an assortment of bribed or coerced allies) against a semi-developed country of the South, and in the more general sense that this signalled "recourse . . . to military force and annihilation against any recalcitrant country or peoples—as long as they are poor, weak and in the Third World South". Thus: "With the conclusion of the Cold War, the Third World (hot) War is not to be fought between East and West . . . but between the North and the South".

See: Frank, A.G. (1992). 'Third World War: A Political Economy of the Gulf War and the New World Order'. Third World Quarterly, 13 (2), pp. 267–82. It has been estimated that this wanton economic vandalism rendered 1.8 million Iraqis homeless as well as sowing the seeds "for famines and epidemics". See: Foreign Affairs Select Committee (1991). The Economic Impact of the Gulf Crisis on Third World Countries. (March). London: FASC.

365 Brittain, V. (1991). 'Introduction'. Brittain (ed), p. ix; Morrison, L. (1991). 'The NHS and Its Patients: Casualties of the Gulf War'. Brittain (ed), p. 117; Pilger, 1999, p. 51.

366 Ian Lee's study (cited in Pilger, 1999, p. 53) estimated the number of civilian deaths resulting directly from the war as being as high as 250,000. See: Lee, I. (1991). Continuing Health Cost of the Gulf War. Medical Educational Trust: London. "This confirmed American and French estimates of 'in excess of 200,000 civilian deaths'" (Pilger, 1999, p. 53).

367 Cockburn, A. and Cockburn, P. (1999). Out of the Ashes: The Resurrection of Saddam Hussein. New York NY: Harper-Collins.

368 Chomsky, N. (1996). Power and Prospects: Reflections on Human Nature and Social Order. Boston MA: South End Press, p. 35.

369 Carroll, E.J. and La Rocque, G.R. (1991). 'Victory in the Desert: Superior Technology or Brute Force?' Brittain (1991) (ed), p. 55.

370 Brittain (1991), p. x.

371 Cockburn and Cohen (1991), pp. 18–24, provide details of Iraqi and third-party efforts to negotiate a withdrawal with the US government. Pilger also provides a detailed account of Saddam's fruitless attempts to extricate himself from Iraq and avoid the war. See: Pilger, J. (1994). Distant Voices. London: Vintage, pp. 132–90. These overtures were ignored or dismissed.

372 Cockburn and Cockburn (1999), p. 13.

373 Rai, M. (2002). War Plan Iraq. London: Verso, pp. 76–81; Pilger (2003), pp. 82–3; Cockburn and Cockburn (1999), pp. 23–5.

374 Moore, S. (2006). 'Two Mass Graves in Iraq Unearthed'. Los Angeles Times (online). (5 June).

375 Pilger (2002), pp. 79, 80–2. See also: Graham-Brown, S. (2001). 'No-Fly Zones: Rhetoric and Real Intentions'. Middle East Information Project. Global Policy Forum (online). (20 February).

376 As a UN report in the immediate aftermath of the war put it: "most means of modern life support have been destroyed or rendered tenuous. Iraq has, for some time to come, been relegated to a pre-industrial age, but with all the disabilities of post-industrial dependency on an intensive use of energy and technology". See: Ahtisaari, M. (1991). 'Report to the Secretary-General on Humanitarian Needs in Kuwait and Iraq in the Immediate Post-Crisis Environment by a Mission to the Area Led by Martti Ahtisaari, Under-Secretary-General for Administration and Management'. Report S/22366. (20 March). New York NY: UN. Paragraph 9.

377 Khan, A.S. (1991). 'Report to the Secretary-General Dated 15 July 1991 on Humanitarian Needs in Iraq Prepared by a Mission Led by the Executive Delegate of the Secretary-General for Humanitarian Assistance in Iraq'. Report S/22799 (17 July). New York NY: UN. Paragraph 29.

378 This was under the provisions of Resolutions 706 and 712. See: Johnstone, I. (1994). Aftermath of the Gulf War: An Assessment of UN Action. Boulder CO: Lynne Rienner Publishers.

379 Khan (1991), paragraph 29.

380 Global Policy Forum (2002). 'Iraq Sanctions: Humanitarian Implications and Options for the Future'. GPF (online). (6 August). See Ch.5.

381 GPF (2002), Ch.3.
382 GPF (2002), Ch.3.
383 Pilger (2002), pp. 62–3. The estimate of 500,000 is based on a study by UNICEF in co-operation with the Iraqi government. See: United Nations International Children's Emergency Fund and Government of Iraq (1999). Child and Maternal Mortality Survey 1999: Preliminary Report. New York NY: UNICEF. See also: Ali, M.M. and Shah, I.H. (2000). 'Sanctions and Childhood Mortality in Iraq'. Lancet, 355 (9218). (27 May), pp. 1851–7; Garfield, R. (2000). 'The Public Health Impact of Sanctions'. Middle East Report, 215 (Summer), p. 17; Mueller, J. and Mueller, K. (2000). 'The Methodology of Mass Destruction: Assessing Threats in a New World Order'. Journal of Strategic Studies, 23 (1), pp. 163–87. UN (1999). 'Report of the Second Panel Established Pursuant to the Note by the President of the Security Council of 30 January 1999 (S/1999/100), Concerning the Current Humanitarian Situation in Iraq'. UNSC (online). (30 March); Zaida, S. and Smith-Fawzi, M.C. (1995). 'Health of Baghdad's Children'. Lancet, 346 (8988). (2 December), p. 1485; WHO (1996). 'The Health Conditions of the Population in Iraq since the Gulf Crisis. Section 4: Impact on Child Nutrition'. WHO (online). (March).
384 Garfield (2000). Garfield subsequently re-calculated child-under-five deaths between 1991 and 1999 at 350,000, however. See: Richman, S. (2004). 'Iraqi Sanctions—Were They Worth It?' Global Policy Forum (online). (January). See also: Garfield, R. (1999). Morbidity and Mortality among Iraqi Children from 1990 Through 1998: Assessing the Impact of the Gulf War and Economic Sanctions. New York NY: Columbia University.
385 More than 30 social-science studies and surveys conducted in the 1990s, often drawing on data sets that were not provided by the Iraqi government, verified the link between economic sanctions and major health, wellbeing and welfare deficits, including excess child mortality. See: Cortright, D. and Lopez, G.A. (1999). 'Are Sanctions Just? The Problematic Case of Iraq'. Journal of International Affairs, 52 (2), pp. 735–55. One of these found that child mortality rates in Iraq rose from 58.9 per 1,000 since the mid-1980s to 91.0 in the first half of the 1990s and to 121.7 in the second half. See: Awqati, N.A. et al. (2009). 'Causes and Differentials of Childhood Mortality in Iraq'. BMC Paediatrics, 9 (40), pp. 1–9.
386 A range of medical studies have associated exposure to DU with leukaemia and other cancers as well as a range of other genetical, neurological, and reproductive ill-effects. See: Miller, A.C. and McClain, D. (2007). 'A Review of Depleted Uranium Biological Effects: In Vitro and in Vivo Studies'. Reviews on Environmental Health, 22 (1), pp. 75–89. As Hindin et al. (p. 17) report: "In aggregate, the human epidemiological evidence is consistent with increased risk of birth defects in offspring of persons exposed to DU". See: Hindin R, Brugge, D. and Panikkar, B. (2005). 'Teratogenicity of Depleted Uranium Aerosols: A Review from an Epidemiological Perspective'. Environmental Health, 4 (1), pp. 1–19.

Iraqi medics reported sharp and major increases in childbirth abnormalities and cancers in southern Iraq in the decade following the 1991 war that they attributed to DU poisoning and other metal-based toxins integral to modern weapons. See: Caputi, C. (2012). 'The Victims of Fallujah's Health Crisis Are Stifled by Western Silence'. Guardian (online). (25 October); Jamail, D. (2013). 'Iraq: War's Legacy of Cancer'. Al-Jazeera (online). (15 May); Johnson, L. (2002). 'Iraqi Cancers, Birth Defects Blamed on US Depleted Uranium'. Seattle Post-Intelligencer. (12 November); McKay, R. (2001). 'Depleted Uranium: The Horrific Legacy of Basra'. The Sunday Herald. (14 January); Neuffer, E. (2003). 'Iraqis Trace Surge in Cancers to US Bombings'. Boston Globe. (26 January); Taylor-Martin, S. (2003). 'How Harmful Is Depleted Uranium?'. St. Petersburg Times. (25 May).

These reports were supported by series of medical and public health studies. See: Alaani, S. et al. (2011a). 'Uranium and Other Contaminants in Hair from the Parents of Children with Congenital Anomalies in Fallujah, Iraq'. Conflict and Health, 2, pp. 5–15; Alaani, S. et al. (2011b). 'Four Polygamous Families with Congenital Birth Defects from Fallujah, Iraq'. International Journal of Environmental Research in Public Health, 8 (1), pp. 89–96; Al-Ani, Z., Al-Hiali, S. and Al-Mehimdi, S. (2010). 'Neural Tube Defects among Neonates Delivered in Al-Ramadi Maternity and Children's Hospital, Western Iraq'. Singapore Medical Journal, 31 (2), pp. 163–9; Al-Hadithi, T. et al. (2012). 'Birth Defects in Iraq and the Plausibility of Environmental Exposure: A Review'. Conflict and Health, 6 (1), p. 3; Al-Sabbak, M. et al. (2012). 'Metal Contamination and the Epidemic of Congenital Birth Defects in Iraqi Cities'. Bulletin of Environmental Contamination and Toxology, 89 (5), pp. 937–44; Busby, C., Hamdan, M. and Arabia, E. (2010). 'Cancer, Infant Mortality and Birth Sex-Ratio in Fallujah, Iraq 2005–2009'. International Journal of Environmental Research in Public Health, 7 (7), pp. 2828–37; Rajab, K., Mohammad, A. and Mustafa, F. (2000). 'Incidence of Spontaneous Abortion in Bahrain before and after the Gulf War of 1991'. International Journal of Gynaecological Obstetrics, 68 (2), pp. 139–44.

387 BBC News (2016). 'Chilcot Report: Tony Blair's Iraq War Case Not Justified'. (6 July); Bowcott, O. (2004). 'Was the War Legal? Leading Lawyers Give Their Verdict'. Guardian (online). (2 March); Burkeman, O. and Borger, J. (2003). 'War Critics Astonished as US Hawk Admits Invasion Was Illegal'. Guardian (online). (20 November); Curtis, M. (2004). Unpeople: Britain's Secret Human Rights Abuses. London: Vintage, pp. 33–46; Falk, R. (2004). 'The Iraq War and the Future of International Law'. Proceedings of the Annual Meeting (American Society of International Law), 98, pp. 263–6; Hirsch, A. (2010). 'Iraq Invasion Violated International Law, Dutch Inquiry Finds'. Guardian (online). (12 January); Lobe, J. (2003). 'Law Groups Say US Invasion Illegal'. One World News Centre (online). (21 March); Kramer, R., Michalowski, R. and Rothe, D. (2005). '"The Supreme International Crime": How the U.S. War in Iraq Threatens the Rule of Law'. Social Justice, 32 (2), pp. 52–81; Norton-Taylor, R. (2003). 'Law Unto Themselves'. Guardian (online). (13 March); Polity (2003). 'No Legal Case for War'. (8 March).

388 The 1991 Gulf War boasted a coalition of 34 countries—even though most provided token forces. The 2003 Gulf War was supported by a "coalition of the willing" of just six countries (the US, UK, UAE, Australia, Spain, and Poland), with only the UK providing significant military assistance to the USA (42,000 troops, several warships, and 100 plus warplanes). The US force numbered approximately 336,800 infantries, 55,000 air forces, and 61,000 naval forces. Only forces from the UK, Poland, and Australia actually took part in military operations against Iraq alongside the USA. See: Carter, L.B. (2005). Iraq: Summary of US Forces. CRS Report for Congress. Congressional Research Service: The Library of Congress. (28 November); Lorenz, J. (2003). The Coalition of the Willing. Ethics of Development in a Global Environment. Stanford University. (5 June).

389 As Chomsky (2006) points out, the US government ended up justifying the war on the grounds that it was pre-emptive—a war that was necessary to avoid a later one. This was despite the fact that preventative war was contrary to international law. See for example: UK Prime Minister's Cabinet Office (2003). Iraq—Its Infrastructure of Concealment, Deception and Intimidation. London: GOV.UK; Drogin, B and Richter, P. (2002). 'White House Backs Report of Link between Iraq, Sept. 11 Suspect'. Los Angeles Times. (2 August); Feldmann, L. (2003). 'The Impact of Bush Linking 9/11 and Iraq'. Christian Science Monitor (online). (14 March); Milbank, D. (2004). 'Bush Defends Assertions of Iraq-Al Qaeda Relationship'.

Washington Post (online). (18 June); Mitchell, A. (2002). 'Iraq and al-Qaida Connection'. NBC News (31 October); US Department of State (2003). Iraq: Failing to Disarm. US Secretary of State Colin L. Powell: Remarks to the United Nations Security Council. (5 February).

390 Baradei, M. (2003). The Status of Nuclear Inspections in Iraq: 14 February 2003 Update. Report by IAEA Director-General Dr. El Baradei. International Atomic Energy Agency. (14 February); Blix, H. (2004). Disarming Iraq. New York NY: Pantheon; Borger, J. (2002). 'US Hawk "Tried to Sully Iraq Arms Inspector"'. Guardian (online). (16 April); El Baradei, M. (2003). Mission Possible: Nuclear Weapons Inspections in Iraq. Report by IAEA Director-General Dr. El Baradei. International Atomic Energy Agency. (7 March). Rai, M. (2015). 'Iraq War Questions Chilcot Won't Ask, Let Alone Answer: The Untold Story of the U.N. Weapons Inspectors' Crucial "Work Plan", and How It was Undermined and Finally Buried by Bush and Blair'. Vredessite (online). (22 September); Usborne, D. (2003). 'Hans Blix versus the US: "I Was Undermined"'. Global Policy Forum (online). (23 April).

391 Al-Marashi, I. (2006). 'The "Dodgy Dossier": The Academic Implications of the British Government's Plagiarism Incident'. Middle East Studies Association Bulletin, 40 (1), pp. 33–43; Associated Press (2005). 'CIA's Final Report: No WMDs found in Iraq'. AP (online). (26 April); BBC News (2003). 'Bush Administration on 9/11 link'. (18 September); Bloom, D. (2016). 'How Tony Blair and Jack Straw Shaped the "Dodgy Dossier" on the Iraq War'. Mirror (online. (6 July); Buncombe, A. (2016). 'Chilcot Report: Student Whose Thesis Became Tony Blair's "Dodgy Dossier" Accuses UK of Systematic Failure'. Guardian (online). (6 July); Commission on the Intelligence Capabilities of the United States Regarding Weapons of Mass Destruction (2005). Report to the President of the United States. (31 March). Washington DC; Hammond, J.R. (2005). 'The U.S. "Intelligence Failure" and Iraq's UAVs'. The Yirmeyahu Review (online). (14 November); Jehl, D. (2004). 'Pentagon Official Distorted Intelligence, Report Says'. International Herald Tribune (online). (22 October); MacAskill, E. (2016). 'MI6 Stood by Bogus Intelligence Until after Iraq Invasion'. The Guardian (online). (6 July); Marquis, C. (2004). 'The Struggle for Iraq Diplomacy: Powell Admits No Hard Proof in Linking Iraq to Al Qaeda'. New York Times (online). (9 January); Pincus, W. and Jeffrey-Smith, R. (2007). 'Official's Key Report on Iraq Is Faulted: "Dubious" Intelligence Fuelled Push for War'. Washington Post. (9 February); Schwarz, J. (2018). 'Lie after Lie: What Colin Powell Knew about Iraq 15 Years Ago and What He Told the UN'. Intercept (online). (6 February); Warrick, J. (2002). 'Evidence on Iraq Challenged: Experts Question if Tubes Were Meant for Weapons Program'. Washington Post (online). (19 September); Williams, C. (2011). 'Learning to Redress Pre-emptive Deceit: The "Iraq Dossier"'. Sage Open (online), 1 (3), pp. 1–10. 'Official's Key Report on Iraq Is Faulted'. Washington Post (online). (9 February); Wilson, J.C. (2003). 'What I Didn't Find in Africa'. New York Times (online). (6 July).

392 Curtis (2004), pp. 47–67; Zunes, S. (2005). 'Targeting Iraq'. Feffer (ed), pp. 130–2; Miller, D. (2003). Tell Me Lies: Propaganda and Media Distortion in the Attack on Iraq. London: Pluto Press; Rai, M. (2003). War Plan Iraq: Ten Reasons Against War on Iraq. London: Verso, pp. 45–56, 57–64, 115–17; Rampton, S. and Stauber, J. (2003). Weapons of Mass Deception: The Uses of Propaganda in Bush's War on Iraq. London: Robinson; Ritter and Pitt (2003), pp. 21–77; Woodward, R. (2004). Plan of Attack. New York NY: Simon Schuster.

Now, Saddam's regime was not wholly compliant with the UNSCOM weapons inspections. This was partly owing to legitimate national security concerns, owing to suspicions that these were being used illegitimately for purposes of general intelligence gathering, espionage and covert operations, including intelligence-gathering for air strikes. (In fact, the regime's suspicions were wholly justified. UNSCOM was infiltrated by the CIA and was being exploited by the USA in exactly those ways). See: Gellman, B. (1999). 'US Spied on Iraq via UN'. Washington Post. (2 March); Tran, M. and Black, I. (1999). 'UN Spies Scandal Grows: American Officials Admit Iraqi Data Aided Air Strikes'. Guardian (online). (8 January).

However, the regime was mostly compliant with the weapons inspections, despite Washington's misuse of them. This led to UNSCOM's and the IAEA's judgement that Iraq was verifiably 90–95 per cent disarmed of WMD. The inspectorates also considered that Iraq was likely wholly (i.e. 100 per cent) disarmed by 1998—though this could not be proven owing to the lack or imprecision of record-keeping and the regime's decision to destroy some materials rather than surrender these to the UN (Ritter and Pitt, 2003, pp. 23–4). Thus, UNSCOM concluded in 1998, "the disarmament phase of the Security Council's requirements is possibly near its end in the missile and chemical weapons areas". Likewise, at the end of that same year, the IAEA reported that Iraq's nuclear weapons programme was "efficiently and effectively" eliminated (Pilger, 2002, p. 59). As chief weapons inspector Scott Ritter summarised the situation:

> By 1998, the chemical weapons infrastructure had been completely dismantled or destroyed by UNSCOM or by Iraqi compliance with our mandate. The biological weapons programme was gone, all the major facilities eliminated. The nuclear weapons programme was completely eliminated. The long-range ballistic missile programme was completely eliminated. If I had to quantify Iraq's threat, I would say zero. (cited in Pilger, 2002, p. 59).

393 Chomsky, N. (2002). 'Terror and Just Response' in Rai (2002), pp. 34–5.

394 Achcar (2018).

395 Saddam Hussein certainly carried the mantle of street pride in the Middle East and beyond in the "Third World" for his noisy espousal of Arab nationalism, his consistently inflammatory anti-Zionist rhetoric, and his disdain for the oil-monarchies. His invasion of Kuwait (and supposed defiance of US power) brought hundreds of thousands of people (many bearing his portrait aloft) to the streets in order to demonstrate their support right across the region. See: Brittain (1991), 'Introduction', p. xiv.

396 Rampton and Stauber (2003), pp. 201–2.

397 Alexander, A. and Assaf, A. (2005). 'Iraq: The Rise of the Resistance'. International Socialism (online),105; Alexander, A. and Assaf, A. (2005). 'The Elections and the Resistance in Iraq'. International Socialism (online), 106; Chehab, Z. (2005). Iraq Ablaze: Inside the Insurgency. London: IB Tauris; Dodge, T. (2010). 'The Ideological Roots of Failure: The Application of Kinetic Neoliberalism to Iraq'. International Affairs (online), 86 (6); Dodge, T. (2012). Iraq: From War to a New Authoritarianism (International Institute for Strategic Studies); Rogers, P. (2005). Iraq and the War on Terror: Twelve Months of Insurgency. London: IB Tauris.

398 Alexander and Assaf (2005).

399 Alexander and Assad (2005); Chomsky, N. (2006). Failed States: The Abuse of Power and the Assault on Democracy. New York NY: Metropolitan Books; Klein, N. (2005). 'Baghdad Year Zero'. N. Klein, B. Mealer, S. Watkins, and W. Laquer (eds) No War: America's Real Business in Iraq. London: Gilbert Square Books.

400 Herring, E. and Rangwalla, G. (2006). Iraq in Fragments: The Occupation and its Legacy. London: C Hurst and Company, esp. Ch.3.

401 Callinicos, A. (2014). 'Nemesis in Iraq'. International Socialism (online), 143.

402 Callinicos (2014). There was also concerted Russian military support for Assad's Syria against both secular insurgents in the civil war and ISIS.

403 Iraq Body Count (2021). 'Documented Civilian Deaths from Violence'. Iraq Body Count (online). Accessed: 28/03.2021; Iraq Body Count (2021). 'Analysis: From the Numbers'. Iraq Body Count (online). Accessed: 28/03/2021. According to IBC, conducted by US and UK researchers, the number of documented (not estimated) civilian deaths in Iraq from violence between March 2003 (the start of the second US war) and June 2017 ranged from a minimum of 175,792 to a maximum of 196,572. The verifiable tally from the 2003 war to the end of 2019 was between 185,593 and 208,677, whereas the number killed since the US withdrawal in 2011 was calculated at 91,710 by the close of 2019.

404 UNHRC (2007). Statistics on Displaced Iraqis Around the World. UNHCR (online). The number of displaced people was estimated by UNHCR at more than four million by the spring of 2007, with almost two million homeless in Iraq, and two million plus homeless in neighbouring countries.

405 Achcar (2018). To contain ISIS, the US government under the Obama presidency was also obliged to secure the co-operation of Iran, sanctioning the regime's cross-border military interventions against the aspirant caliphate.

4 Neoimperialism and surveillance states—the case of Israel

The world that confronts us today is, as I have shown, stunningly asymmetric. Wealth and income gaps between HCIs and LCIs and between rich and poor within and across national borders have increased substantially since the 1980s. This represents a reversal of postwar trends from the 1950s to the 1970s that saw a modest degree of economic convergence between social classes and countries. Part of the explanation for this state of affairs is, as I have argued, the internationalization of neoliberalism as state policy. This is because trade liberalization (corporate land grabs in the Global South by Western MNCs, privatizations of state or public assets everywhere, deregulated labour markets, the scrapping of price controls on staples, and so on) is a recipe to further advantage the already-advantaged, both locally and globally.

The other part of the explanation, however, is *neoimperialism*. As I argued in the previous chapter, neoimperialism (the chief agents of which are the US-dominated Western Alliance) preserves a hierarchical structure of international relations within which corporate-monopoly capitalism and its neoliberal governance perpetuate and extend worldwide injustices in the distribution of powers of command and reward. This is of course an emergent structure, not a predetermined one, nor one that is generated in the immediacy of social interaction. The emergent structure of neoimperial dominion over world affairs, since this institutionalizes massive inequalities in the distribution of powers of command and reward, imparts directional guidance to ongoing social interaction that would reproduce rather than undermine it. This is for the simple reason that this anterior structure grants those agents who are beneficiaries of imperial dominion the material resources and institutional capacities to outcompete those non-beneficiaries whose interests would be served by dismantling or transforming the neoimperial order.

This does not render neoimperial dominion as necessary, since structural conditioning as directional guidance is not structural determinism, so that the balance of power between the contestants is never static (e.g. as is evidenced by the ascendancy of the Chinese state and Chinese capitalism). Emergent advantages of superordinate groups derived from their positions and roles in structures may

DOI: 10.4324/9781003597346-5

be eroded over time. Moreover, the multitude of radical non-beneficiaries on the wrong side of the class (and racial-class and feminized-class) divides would be a force capable of disrupting or undermining its order, if they were to make common cause against neoimperialism. Yet making common cause is exactly what would be needed, since only massive collective struggles will switch the dispersed multitude of the oppressed and exploited from micro-agents to macro-agents who can challenge institutionally entrenched powerholders. Such is not apparent at the present conjuncture, alas. In its absence, therefore, neoimperial dominion will be reproduced through each cycle of socio-economic and socio-political interaction owing to asymmetrical competition between those with power and those without that the emergent structure distributes and facilitates.

As I also sought to establish in the previous chapter, a fundamental aspect of the neoimperial order and hence of neoimperial politics is the perpetuation of what may be termed as *surveillance states*. Situated in areas that are of key geostrategic or economic importance to the Western Alliance, these states are bankrolled by the USA to act as counterweights to local forces that might upset the present asymmetrical distribution of political powers and economic resources in global systems. Of all of the key (to US power) geostrategic theatres of global political economy, the oil-rich Middle East remains the most fundamental. However, inherent difficulties confront US imperialism's project to stabilize and securitize the region. This is as this is faced with the interstate rivalries of the Arab states, the mass hostility of the Arab street to the oil-sheikdoms in the Gulf (and to the US power that props them up), and the consequential unreliability of regional watchdogs in the Arab world.

Now, such explains the peculiar role of the state of Israel in the politics of Palestine and the Middle East. Since its formation in 1948, Israel has been crucial to the success (more or less) of this American project of regional stabilization and securitization in the interests of the "international community" (Western power). For this reason, this chapter is addressed to the task of analysing the nature and role of this particular surveillance state (or watchdog) in the Middle East. This necessitates foregrounding the Israeli-Arab conflict in Palestine in the analysis that follows, because Israel's watchdog role in the Middle East on behalf of US and Western power explains the roots of this conflict. Not only that, but this also explains the incorrigibility of the conflict (i.e. its imperviousness to a "diplomatic" solution). This is in the sense that the key powerholders that could broker a diplomatic solution (the US state and its closest allies) are not incentivized to do so, so that it perpetuates, in its present form, as it has done for 75 years.

Current events are exposing the deadly and tragic consequences not so much of decades of diplomatic failure but of the absence of serious diplomatic intent over Palestine. This is lack of intent first-and-foremost by the state of Israel but also by its US ally and its Western backers. As I write these words, American imperialism's tolerance of the Israeli state's colonial project in Palestine (and the other Western powers' acquiescence to the US state's toleration of this project) is manifested yet again in war.

Israel's latest (and biggest yet) military assault on Palestine, focused this time on Gaza, was triggered by an unusually successful (i.e. destructive) cross-border attack on Israeli soldiers and civilians by the militant Islamic Palestinian Hamas group. Hamas's attack of 7 October 2023 struck their biggest ever blow against Israel in their decades-long conflict, killing 1,139 people (375 military and police personnel, 695 civilians—including 36 children, and 71 foreign nationals), and taking 248 hostages.[1] Israel's retaliatory war, now almost into its third month, with no end in sight (since Hamas has retained significant if not major military operational capability), has been pursued in callous disregard of the civilian population and infrastructure of a land already decimated by sanctions, withholding of aid, and a 16-year economic blockade that contravenes international humanitarian law. The people of Gaza have been treated by the Israeli military as expendable fodder (unpeople) in pursuit of its war aims—which ostensibly are those of disabling or destroying Hamas and the other Palestinian militias of Gaza.

Even prior to the war, the situation in Gaza was dire, from a humanitarian perspective. On the eve of hostilities, 63 per cent of Gazans were facing food insecurity, 81.5 per cent were mired in subsistence poverty, whereas 46.6 per cent of the Strip's adults and 62.3 per cent of its adults under 29 years of age were unemployed. As was reported by the UNRWA in August 2023:

> The economy and its capacity to create jobs have been devastated, resulting in the impoverishment and de-development of a highly skilled and well-educated society. Access to clean water and electricity remains at crisis level and impacts nearly every aspect of life. Clean water is unavailable for 95 per cent of the population. Electricity is available up to an average of 11 hours per day as of July 2023. However, ongoing power shortage has severely impacted the availability of essential services, particularly health, water, and sanitation services, and continues to undermine Gaza's fragile economy, particularly the manufacturing and agriculture sectors.[2]

Israel's invasion of Gaza thus piled catastrophe on calamity. The UN's OCHA reported that, by mid-December 2023, this had killed 18,787 Gazans. These were overwhelmingly civilians, almost two-thirds of whom were women and children. Thousands of others were missing, many of whom would be buried under rubble. The OCHA further estimated that 50,589 people had been injured on this same timeframe.[3] By the start of December, the war had turned 1.4 million Gazans (80 per cent of the Strip's population) into internally displaced persons.[4] This was on top of the 5.9 million Palestinians—mostly jam-packed in refugee camps in Syria, Lebanon, Jordan, the West Bank, and Gaza—who had already been forced from their homes by Israel's previous wars and annexations in Palestine over several decades.[5]

By mid-November 2023, less than six weeks into the Israeli offensive, "half of Gaza's civilian infrastructure" was already destroyed, according to the UN Human Rights Office of the High Commissioner. As of 10 December, according to OCHA,

> over half of Gaza's housing units had been damaged or destroyed, as provided by the Ministry of Public Works and Housing in Gaza as well as hospitals, schools, mosques, bakeries, water pipes, sewage, and electricity networks. On November 4 and 5 alone, according to OCHA, seven water facilities across the Gaza Strip were directly hit and sustained major damage, including water reservoirs in Gaza City, the Jabalia refugee camp, and Rafah.

By 14 December, only one of 24 hospitals in northern Gaza was operational.[6] Across the Strip as a whole, 27 out of 36 were out of action before 19 December. "Those still open are only partly functional and under growing pressure due to both strikes and growing numbers of sick and injured patients arriving".[7] As for food production:

> Since the beginning of the Israeli military's ground offensive on October 27, satellite imagery reviewed by Human Rights Watch indicates that orchards, greenhouses, and farmland in northern Gaza have been razed, apparently by Israeli forces, compounding concerns of dire food insecurity and loss of livelihood. Satellite imagery indicates that the razing of agricultural land continued in northern Gaza during the seven-day ceasefire, which began on November 24 and ended on December 1, when the Israeli military was in direct control of the area.[8]

This destruction has been mandated and conveyed by what human rights lawyers describe as discourses of "genocidal incitement". These are those which openly express the intent to "destroy the Palestinian people under occupation" and for a "second Nakba" (mass expulsion or ethnic cleansing of the Palestinians from Gaza and the rest of Palestine).[9]

Simultaneously, as the war has unfolded, the Israeli military (Israeli Defence Force—or IDF) supported by the Israeli government have sought to restrict the media's capacity to report on the violence being perpetrated in Gaza and its dire humanitarian consequences. This is by means of border closures that shut out the international press (except those "embedded" or placed under the control of the IDF—who are barred from having dealings with Gazans and who must submit their reports to the military for vetting).[10] This is also by means of acts of lethal violence against those local journalists and their families who do not submit to demands to cease reporting and leave the war zone.[11] Consequently, as Paris-based Reporters Without Borders conveys,

> journalism is in the process of being eradicated in the Gaza Strip as a result of Israel's refusal to heed calls to protect media personnel. . . . Reporters there

> have no safe refuge and no way of leaving. They are being killed one after another. Since 7 October, the Palestinian territory has been subjected to a veritable eradication of journalism.[12]

According to the New York-based CPJ: "More journalists have been killed in the first 10 weeks of the Israel-Gaza war than have ever been killed in a single country over an entire year". The tally up to 21 December was "at least" 68 since the start of the conflict, 61 of these Palestinians, and three Lebanese. (Four were Israelis—killed by Hamas militants in their cross-border raid of 7 October).[13] "CPJ is deeply alarmed by the pattern of journalists in Gaza reporting receiving threats, and subsequently, their family members being killed", as Sharif Mansour, CPJ and Middle East and North Africa Programme Co-ordinator, puts it. As he continues: "The killing of the family members of journalists in Gaza is making it almost impossible for the journalists to continue reporting, as the risk now extends beyond them also to include their beloved ones".[14]

> CPJ is particularly concerned about an apparent pattern of targeting of journalists and their families by the Israeli military. . . . In at least one case, a journalist was killed while clearly wearing press insignia in a location where no fighting was taking place. In at least two other cases, journalists reported receiving threats from Israeli officials and Israel Defense Forces officers before their family members were killed. . . . More than half the deaths—37—occurred during the first month of the war, making it the deadliest single month documented by CPJ since it began collecting data in 1992. . . . The Israel-Gaza war deaths have taken place against a backdrop of growing censorship of media in the region, including at least 20 arrests as well as physical and online harassment of journalists. Media facilities have also been damaged or destroyed.[15]

Israeli ministers and politicians are complicit in this violence by virtue of tacit incitement. Rather than condemning the threats and killings, they have tended to lend support to the unfounded inflammatory statements of pro-Israel advocacy groups (such as Honest Reporting) which allege involvement or complicity of Palestinian and Palestinian-friendly journalists in Hamas's 7 October attacks.[16] By these means, journalists are cast as terrorists or terrorism-sympathizers, or they are (as Israeli PM Benjamin Netanyahu's own office put it) guilty of "crimes against humanity".[17] They then become legitimate targets for the army or civilian vigilantes.

What has been the "official" US and Western response to the carnage? Much verbal energy has been expended on statements of regret over the terrible harms that the war is perpetrating on Gaza, over the loss of civilian lives, and over the damage caused to vital life- and livelihood-sustaining services. (By contrast, there has scarcely been a whisper over the plight of Palestinian media workers).[18] These regrets are expressed by Western leaders who have hitherto acquiesced to Israel's (and Egypt's) unlawful, under human rights legislation, collective punishment of a whole civilian people in Gaza by means of economic blockade to secure their political goal of undermining Hamas. At the same time, tepid UN calls for a ceasefire to ease the humanitarian crisis are vetoed by Washington with the support or at least acquiescence of the usual suspects (notably the British government),[19] just as the US government fast-tracks shipments of munitions to Tel Aviv to retool the Israeli military.[20]

Western opinion-formers and politicians also urge "restraint" on Israel's conduct of the war in Gaza, whilst at the same time refusing to condemn the absence of restraint. After all, it is said, Israel has the right of "self-defence".[21] There is no mention by Western leaders of the fact that the lack of restraint in question is actually criminal. According to international humanitarian law, war crimes are those which focus violence on civilians and civilian services and facilities in pursuance of the goals of war. These include most obviously those which "provoke starvation deliberately" or which intentionally generate hunger in a civilian population by "depriving it of its sources of food or of supplies".[22] As the ICC (Rome Statute) mandates, depriving civilians "of objects indispensable to their survival, including wilfully impeding relief supplies" constitutes acts of war criminality.[23]

Israel's war in Gaza undoubtedly fits these criteria. The pattern of actions and their effects make this clear. Not only that, but members of the Israeli government have also made no secret of the fact that their strategy involves exactly denying the civilian population of Gaza access to "objects indispensable to survival"—such as power, fuels, water, sanitation, medical supplies, communications, medical facilities, and food. Several ministers have stated this openly.[24] This denial includes by actively, systematically, destroying these objects or their sources. Yet Gaza is a territory that is formally under Israeli jurisdiction, albeit by virtue of colonial annexation. As such, the Israeli state has a legal responsibility to safeguard the lives of those who live there.

The USA's and the West's refusal to exert any diplomatic pressure on the Israeli government to terminate its murderous invasion of Gaza, or even to moderate or suspend its violence in Gaza—indeed the US state's bankrolling of this violence—is instructive. This is inasmuch as this illuminates the real underlying nature of the relationship between these parties. Such is instructive in that Washington's tolerance of an Israeli military campaign bordering on *genocidal* criminality persists, despite the enormous risks this poses to the stability and security of the international order that US power seeks to uphold. What are these risks?

For starters, the war places Arab regimes in the Middle East under greater pressure from the "Arab street" to demonstrate meaningful solidarity with the beleaguered Palestinians. Beholden as they are to US power and patronage, this they are unable to willingly muster (even though they could conceivably be forced into it by popular unrest to self-preserve). This renders the Arab ruling elites more vulnerable to challenge from below. Israel's invasion of Gaza thus triggered massive demonstrations in Jordan and Egypt—two Arab countries which have energetically pursued normalized relations with Israel. Protests also quickly engulfed Lebanon, Morocco, and Bahrain. These protests were not simply expressive of hatred for Israel and support for Palestine but of discontent with Arab rulers and elites that have stifled local democracy and renounced pan-Arabism in favour of self-enrichment. In Egypt, for example, protestors "chanted for 'bread, freedom, social justice'", resurrecting the slogan of the 2011 Arab Spring protests, "voiced in an iconic focal point, that would have sent chills down the government's spine".[25]

Secondly, there is the danger of conflict-widening, of a bigger war, which would further disrupt energy supplies that have been destabilized by the Russo-Ukrainian war, plunging the fragile post-pandemic (indeed fragile pre-pandemic) world economy into deeper crisis. Such may draw the Arab regimes, however reluctantly, into conflict with Israel. The risk of armed confrontation between Israel and Iran is especially acute.

Israel is certainly conflict-widening in Palestine. Its war in Gaza has been accompanied by a dramatic increase in its military operations in the West Bank that appear almost intended to provoke retaliatory violence from the Palestinian militias (including Hamas cells) that would legitimize elimination of the PA.[26] Ten cities have been targeted—"Hebron, Halhul, Nablus, Jenin, Tulkarem, el-Bireh, Jericho and notably the centre of Ramallah, which is the administrative headquarters of the Palestinian Authority". Since 7 October, 4,800 Palestinians of the West Bank and East Jerusalem have been arrested and at least 313 killed, including 76 children. Palestinian banks have also been hit and $2.5 million of financial resources expropriated.[27] As the attention of the global media is fixed on events in Gaza, Jewish settler vigilante violence against Palestinian civilians (including kidnappings, beatings, murders, and kidnappings) and appropriations of Palestinian land and property have also accelerated.[28] This is as the settlers are emboldened by the escalation of Israeli political and military repression and the refusal of colonial authority to offer the victims any protection from threats and violence.

Beyond Palestine, the Gaza crisis has provoked an escalation of cross-border exchanges between the Israeli army and Hezbollah in southern Lebanon, which could escalate into full-scale war.[29] A second Israeli invasion of Lebanon is hence a real possibility. This is just as the Iranian-backed Houthi rebels that control much of Yemen have recently responded to the conflict by launching rocket and missile and drone attacks on Israeli-owned or Israel-bound ships passing through the Red Sea to exert leverage for a ceasefire and the end of the Israeli-Egyptian blockade.[30] This too could beget Israeli air strikes on Yemen,[31] if not US-led military action against the Houthi (thereby heading-off Israeli retaliation that would ramp-up tensions between Israel and Iran), in order to secure international shipping lanes that convey 15 per cent of the world's ocean-bound freight trade.

Yet, despite these escalating risks of global conflict and disorder, US support (albeit indirectly) for Israel's war on Gaza shows no sign of weakening. This is even though securing a ceasefire in Gaza would immediately de-escalate these risks. This shows that, for the US state, the risks associated with giving unconditional support to Israel are acceptable, despite the fact that these are certainly high-consequence risks, because Washington regards the benefits of the US–Israeli alliance to the cause of American global hegemony as greater than the risks it poses to that hegemony. These for the US hegemon are the benefits of a strong and reliable (and beholden to US power) surveillance state in the energy-rich Middle East that regards itself as the Other of the Arab world—a willing regional watchdog. How secure that judgement is only history will tell. This chapter will explore how the US–Israeli "special relationship" has licensed if not incentivized Israel as a sub-imperial state wedded to settler-colonialism, rooted in racism and ethnic cleansing, and how this has perpetuated 75 years of wretched internationally tolerated injustice for the Palestinian people.

US bankrolling of Israel

Of the regional US surveillance states, Israel is by far the most important, long lasting, and dependable—a role for which it has been especially well rewarded. Indeed, Israel is unique in that it has for much of its life been viable as a nation-state, economically and politically, only by virtue of US aid. The Israeli state has been by far the biggest cumulative recipient of US foreign aid since its establishment.[32] As Phil Marshall observes: "Although it contains only 0.001 per cent of the world's population, Israel has received over a third of all US foreign aid. By 1999 the accumulated total was over $90 billion".[33] Israel swallowed up a third of Washington's total foreign economic assistance budget from 1948 to 2000,[34] and almost half of its expenditure on foreign military assistance and 35 per cent of its foreign economic aid between 1978 and 1982.[35]

Up to and including 2020, successive US administrations

> have provided Israel with significant assistance in light of robust domestic US support for Israel and its security; shared strategic goals in the Middle East; a mutual commitment to democratic values; and historical ties dating from US support for the creation of Israel in 1948. To date, the United States has provided Israel $146 billion (current, or non-inflation-adjusted, dollars) in bilateral assistance and missile defense funding. . . . According to USAID Data Services as of March 2020, in constant 2018 US dollars (inflation-adjusted), total U.S. aid to Israel obligated from 1946–2018 is $236 billion. . . . At present, almost all US bilateral aid to Israel is in the form of military assistance, although from 1971 to 2007, Israel also received significant economic assistance.[36]

However, even today, Israel's reliance on purely financial assistance from the USA is hardly insignificant. Quite the reverse:

> To date, Israel has been the beneficiary of approximately $125 billion in U.S. aid, an unimaginable sum, more than any other country since WW II, and which is slated to further increase to some $165 billion by the end of the new ten-year aid package, in 2029.[37]

Economic aid has often taken the form of loan guarantees (allowing Israel to borrow from commercial banks at low interest rates). This programme is authorized to run through to the close of 2023. A total of $17 billion of such guarantees were granted to Israel between 2002 and 2006. And, as of 2020, Israel had issued $4.1 billion of US-backed bonds and may be entitled to issue up to $3.8 billion more.[38] In addition, of course, the USA has also provided Israel with considerable emergency economic assistance.[39] Yet, in recent times, financial aid has been scaled down from its hitherto dizzying heights. This is as the Israeli economy, subsidized to the hilt, has become more developed.[40] Even so, "US aid constitutes some 3 percent of Israel's total state budget and about 1 percent of its GDP, a highly significant sum".[41] Aside from financial aid, Israel has also benefited hugely from its trade relations with Washington. The USA is "Israel's single biggest trading partner (only the EU taken as a whole is larger), with bilateral trade in 2016 running at approximately $35.5 billion".[42] Washington's bilateral free-trade agreement with Tel-Aviv, signed up for in 1986, was its first. "Israel's hi-tech sector exists and flourishes largely because of the United States".[43]

So, whereas from its origins right up to the 1990s, the state of Israel actually depended on the US state for its economic viability, the present situation is more that Israel depends on the USA for its continued economic prosperity. Without US financial support, the country's overall living standards and per capita income would be significantly, if not majorly, reduced. Yet economic aid from the USA to Israel has been much less than the military aid that has been provided. Unlike financial support, this shows no sign of slowing down after 70 years.

> U.S. aid constitutes some 20 percent of the total defense budget, 40 percent of the IDF [Israel Defence Force] budget, and almost the entire procurement budget. There is no alternative to U.S. aid, except at the price of a change in the national order of priorities. Even if we were to assume that Israel can do without U.S. financing, no other country would be both willing and capable of supplying . . . weapons in such quantities even if . . . [these were] . . . paid . . .[for in] . . . cash, especially advanced ones, like the F35. There is simply no alternative to American weapons, and . . . [Israel's] . . . dependence on the United States is almost complete; the bitter truth is that without the United States, the IDF would be an empty shell.

Israel remained, in 2021, "the largest recipient of US Foreign Military Financing. For FY2021, the President's request for Israel would encompass approximately 59% of total requested FMF funding worldwide".[44] The current round of contracts was signed-and-sealed from agreements reached in 2016 extending right up until 2028:

> In 2016, the U.S. and Israeli governments signed their third 10-year Memorandum of Understanding (MOU) on military aid, covering FY2019 to FY2028. Under the terms of the MOU, the United States pledged to provide—subject to congressional appropriation—$38 billion in military aid ($33 billion in Foreign Military Financing grants plus $5 billion in missile defense appropriations) to Israel. This MOU followed a previous $30 billion 10-year agreement, which ran through FY2018. Israel is the first international operator of the F-35 Joint Strike Fighter, the Department of Defense's fifth-generation stealth aircraft, considered to be the most technologically advanced fighter jet ever made. To date, Israel has purchased 50 F-35s in three separate contracts, funded with U.S. assistance.[45]

Under the Trump administration, for financial year 2021, $3.3 billion in foreign military financing and $500 million in missile defence aid for Israel was granted congressional approval. Under the Defense, Commerce, Justice, Science, Energy and Water Development, Financial Services and General Government, Labor, Health and Human Services, Education, Transportation, Housing, and Urban Development Appropriations Act of 2021, $500 million in joint US–Israeli missile defence cooperation was provided (including $73 million for Iron Dome, $177 million for David's Sling, $77 million for Arrow III, and $173 million for Arrow II missile systems).[46] Yet Israel's military dependence on the USA extends much beyond the vast sums of weapons aid that it receives. For example:

> The United States provides technologies for the development of unique weapons systems that Israel needs, such as the Iron Dome and the Arrow rocket and missile defense systems. It mans the radar deployed in Israel which is linked to the global American satellite system.

The USA also supports Israel "in a variety of areas related to counter-terrorism, the cyber threat, and the prevention of the proliferation of WMD". It also stockpiles its own weapons in Israel, which the Israeli military may draw on if necessary, if for example faced with a national emergency. Moreover, the US military "conducts joint military exercises with the IDF, which provide it with the opportunity to learn some of the most advanced military tactics". Intelligence sharing between the two countries "is so broad and deep that Israel's capabilities would be totally different without the United States".[47] The US state has especially exerted its economic muscle and diplomatic energies to the task of preventing nuclear proliferation in the Middle East, to ensure that Israel remains the only nuclear-armed regional power. Correspondingly, Washington "has also provided a diplomatic shield from international efforts to deprive Israel of its purported nuclear capabilities".[48]

Such dependence on US patronage binds the country's leaders to the defence of US interests in the Middle East. This indeed was exactly its purpose. Such indeed was energetically proposed by Israel's founders when lobbying for the new state in order to court American favour. Now, the alliance of the Israeli enclave-state with the USA *against* the Arab world is guaranteed by its geo-political positioning *within* the Arab world, on land expropriated from Arab indigenes, and by the extension of its borders at the expense of neighbouring Arab states. Forged from colonialism and ethnic cleansing, the Israeli state must remain steadfast in its US watchdog role, because without having received US military and economic patronage (and the diplomatic support that Washington can muster for the country and its policies through the UN), its viability as a nation would have been undermined.

Without US economic aid, Israel would not have transitioned from underdeveloped largely agricultural economy to relatively industrialized one.[49] Without US military aid, Israel would not be able to generate the level of investments to maintain its technologically advanced military capabilities without dragging down its civilian economy. Even today, despite decades of state-driven (and US-subsidized) upsizing of the population,[50] the Israeli state contains within its borders just 6.7 million Jews,[51] whereas the Arab League countries (22 states spanning North Africa and the Middle East) is home to approximately 423 million people,[52] overwhelmingly Arab, a large proportion of whom dispute Israel's legitimacy. Of the 28 UN states which do not recognize Israel, 15 of these are Arab League members, whereas 10 others are members of the Organization of Islamic Cooperation.[53]

Zionism

Establishing an independent nation-state of Israel was the goal of the Zionist movement, which was the artifice of a relatively small number of right-wing pro-imperialist Jewish nationalists (notably under the leadership of Theodor Herzl and Chaim Weizmann) towards the end of the nineteenth century.[54] Zionism took shape as the politics and ideology of a restless Israeli nationalism in search of a national homeland, especially but not exclusively one that was fixated on the goal of establishing this in the biblical Holy Land where the ancient Hebrew kingdoms once ruled. This necessarily rendered Zionism as conveyor of a politics of *settler colonialism*, because the Holy Land (Palestine) had since the demise of the Roman Empire been almost completely emptied of Jews by the great diasporas that carried them right across Europe, to be replaced by

Palestinian Arabs. By the ninth century, a majority of the population of Palestine were Arabic.[55] By the beginning of the rule of the Ottoman Turks, there were only 1,000 Jews left in Palestine.[56]

Antisemitism and anti-Zionism

At this point, it is necessary to briefly pause the historical narrative. This is in order to establish and defend a couple of elementary points which in a rational world would not be anything less than axiomatic. These are those which powerholders in Israel and their overseas backers deny and have managed to obscure in order to delegitimize any thoroughgoing critique of the Israeli state and its colonial roots and policies. Firstly, the concept of "Zionism" (or "Zionist") is not one that was invented as a term of abuse by Israel-detractors in order to demonize Jewish citizens of Israel. On the contrary, this was openly espoused by those Jewish nationalists who were agitating for a Jewish nation-state in Palestine. Secondly, *Jewishness and Zionism are not the same thing*. Jewishness denotes a particular ethnicity and perhaps associated cultural and religious traditions, whereas Zionism denotes a specific political ideology (national settler-colonialism) and associated political project (to establish a racialized Jewish nation-state in Palestine).

Consequently, to be *for* or *against* Zionism (or for or against a nation-state built on Zionism—as the state of Israel was—or for or against a politics of Zionism as the modern state of Israel practises) has nothing to do with a politics of "race" or "creed"; that is, of being *for* or *against* Jews as an ethnic or religious group. To be opposed to or critical of Zionism (as many Jews in common with millions of other people around the world are) is not necessarily to be anti-Jewish. Anti-Zionism is not by default antisemitism. This is not to deny that an anti-Semite may also be an anti-Zionist, and vice versa. However, this would be a contingent association between the two, not a necessary one.[57]

Zionism and the origins of Israel

Zionism sought from the start to secure Jewish settlement of and dominance of Palestine by aligning its own colonial goals with those of higher imperial powers, initially Britain. This was by convincing British leaders that supporting the Zionist cause would be of benefit to their own interests, not only allowing them to solve their own antisemitism problem (by exporting it) but by securing a friend sympathetic to the imperial ideal in a region of vital strategic value to the British Empire. As Herzl put it:

> England with her possessions in Asia should be most interested in Zionism, for the shortest route to India is by way of Palestine. England's great politicians were the first to recognise the need for colonial expansion. . . . And so I believe in England the idea of Zionism, which is a colonial idea, should be easily understood.[58]

Zionism and the Holocaust

But Zionism was at first very much a minority affair amongst Jews. It had little support amongst the Jews of Western Europe and North America. Nor did it find many recruits among the Jews of Russia and eastern Europe. This was despite popular and institutional antisemitism in the host countries, especially in the East, where autocratic authorities and landowners would incite pogroms against the Jews in order to deflect popular grievances away from themselves and onto scapegoats. Disaffected or displaced Jews in the East tended to migrate where possible to the USA or Western Europe, not Palestine.[59] However, the events of the Holocaust understandably rendered the idea of a national Jewish homeland much more attractive to many ordinary Jews. This also gave Zionist politics a major boost, emboldening its lobbying power in the West.

The Zionist message that peaceful coexistence with the gentiles was a pipe-dream (because of widespread violent anti-Jewish racism in the diaspora so that the security of Jewish lives and property could be guaranteed only within the borders of a strong autonomous ethnicized national home-state) was for many confirmed by the Nazi genocide.[60] Yet the Zionist agitators ruthlessly exploited the Holocaust by, at the war's end, sending organizers into refugee camps full of hungry, desperate, disoriented Holocaust survivors distributing immigration certificates for Palestine, pressurizing them into on-the-spot decisions, without alternative options being presented.[61]

Despite these sorts of tactics, most of the Holocaust survivors preferred to migrate to the USA rather than Palestine. But they were denied that option due to ongoing stringent immigration rules (predating the war and running throughout its course) that were intended in part to support Zionist efforts to persuade or coerce them into opting for the Holy Land.[62] Six million Jews were murdered by the Nazis and the demographic fallout from that has been long lasting. The world Jewish population was around 16.6 million in 1939, on the eve of World War Two, whereas the number of Jews worldwide today is estimated at 14.7 million.[63] Thus, 70 years after the Holocaust, the Jewish people have not recovered demographically from catastrophic losses suffered in a period of less than three years. Even so, the majority of Jews remained resistant to the lure of an Israeli nation-state, or at least were resistant to the lure of being a citizen of one or living in one.

Today, around 59 per cent of the world's Jews live outside the state of Israel, mostly in North America, especially the USA (with 44 per cent of the total), with most of the rest (9 per cent) in Western Europe, especially in France, the UK, and Germany.[64] This is even though, under the "Law of Return", Israeli citizenship can basically be claimed by anyone living anywhere in the world who can show Jewish ancestry (or who is married to a Jew), with no fees levied for processing paperwork, and without residential obligations.[65] Jewish citizenship is not, under Israeli law, a right to be claimed. This is, rather, as befits Biblical mythology, a timeless or eternal existent right that merely needs to be taken up.

Zionism and the politics of oil

Before the events of the Holocaust, Zionist lobbyists anticipated that Britain would acquire possession of Palestine from Turkey following the dismembering of the Ottoman Empire during and after World War One. Consequently, they agitated for British support in encouraging Jewish settlement of Palestine in order to, as Weizmann put it, "develop the country, bring back civilisation and form a very effective guard for the Suez Canal".[66] The Suez watchdog proposal was especially attractive to British powerholders for geopolitical and economic reasons. Suez was the most important trade route connecting Asia and Europe, so that its control was of strategic importance to Britain and other colonial powers vying for regional leverage.

The canal was also becoming indispensable to the new politics of oil dependency in the industrial world as this made the transition from steam-power to oil-power. Transportation of British-owned Iranian oil was already a fundamental part of Suez's business.[67] The Anglo-Persian Oil Company was established in Iran in 1909 under private ownership following the discovery of oil there in 1908. On the eve of World War One, the British state acquired a controlling stake (of 51 per cent) in the company, in pursuance of Churchill's policy of making Britain "owners, or at any rate, controllers [of oil] at the source".[68] On the same timescale, in anticipation of other discoveries in neighbouring Iraq, Britain, and France vied for control of the country, with Britain getting the upper hand. British control of oil was thereby extended to Iraq's reserves once these were discovered in 1927. British ownership of half the supply was secured with the Red Line Agreement of 1928, under the auspices of the Iraq Petroleum Company, with the rest ceded to France and the USA.[69]

Securitization of the canal was thus indispensable to Britain's desire to obtain control of oil and to dominate oil-politics internationally. This was prescient from the imperial perspective. By the 1950s, two-thirds of traffic moving across Suez would be oil, though by then British control of it was largely replaced by US control.[70] Unsurprisingly, then, the Zionist project was endorsed by the British government in its Balfour Declaration of 2 November 1917. This announced Britain's intention to establish "a national home for the Jewish people" and gave the green light to Jewish immigration to Palestine on condition that the settlers accept British sovereignty over the territory. The new Jewish homeland would be protected from the Arab indigenes by British power, whereas the settler Jews in return would act as agents of British authority in the region—an arrangement that future UK prime minister Winston Churchill lauded as "from every point of view . . . beneficial and . . . especially in harmony with the truest interests of the British Empire".[71] Ronald Storrs, Britain's first colonial governor of Jerusalem, extolled Zionist-led Jewish settlement in Palestine for its role in "forming for England 'a little loyal Jewish Ulster' in a sea of potentially hostile Arabism".[72]

Zionism and Jewish settlement in Palestine

The Arab population of Palestine numbered 700,000 in 1918, whereas the Jewish presence was just 56,000.[73] Yet the British committed to facilitating Jewish settlement without consulting with the Arabs and in disregard of their contrary desires. Balfour himself at the time confided: "In Palestine we do not propose to even go through the form of consulting the wishes of the present inhabitants".[74] Naturally, this was a recipe for inter-community conflict in Palestine between Palestinian-Arab indigenes and settler-Jews, which often took on a racialized aspect, particularly because racism was cultivated in the service of the rival nationalisms and, later on, in support of separate independence struggles against British rule.[75]

Popular antisemitism in the Arab communities was certainly boosted considerably by the fact that Arab fears over British-backed Zionist colonialism were realized in the interwar years. This was as monied Jewish settlers from Europe, typically religious nationalists, bought up the estates of absentee or indebted landlords, and then expelled tenant Arab farmers from the land, forming a closed enclave economy rooted in "Jewish land, Jewish labour, Jewish produce" from which the indigenes were excluded.[76]

> In Palestine, with the very low standard of living of the Arabs compared to Europeans, and with widespread hidden and open unemployment, the means of excluding the Arabs was by closing the Jewish labour market to them . . . [T]he Jewish National Fund, owner of a big proportion of the land owned by Jews, including a large chunk of Tel Aviv, had a statute that insisted only Jews could be employed on this land . . . The Zionist trade union federation, the Histadrut (General Federation of Hebrew Labour), imposed on all of its members two levies: one for the defence of Hebrew labour and one for the defence of the Hebrew product. The Histadrut organised pickets against orchard owners who employed Arab workers, forcing the owners to sack them.[77]

The closed Zionist economy was made up of mostly agrarian-village communities, under the authority of leaders who imposed ethnic exclusivity on their members (the closed Jewish-only economy), and who enforced this by police methods, punishing Jewish and Arab transgressors alike. These methods included patrolling the Jewish-only markets, destroying the produce of Arab traders, shunning or shaming Jews who bought goods from Arab sellers, and vandalizing business premises of owners suspected of hiring Arab workers. As David Ben-Gurion, Zionist settler, political leader, and future Israeli prime minister, put it:

> Nobody must think we have become reconciled to the existence of non-Jewish labour in the villages. We will not forego . . . one place of work in the country.

> I say to you with full responsibility that it is less shameful to establish a brothel than to evict the Jews from their work in the land of Palestine.[78]

In the Zionist-Jewish enclaves, alongside economic exclusion of the Arabs was also their exclusion from schools and from housing.[79] Jewish-administered schools were for Jews only. Jewish-owned accommodation was for Jews only. Such segregationist policies elevated the living standards of the Jewish settlers as it depressed those of the Arab indigenes. For, although the Jews of British-controlled Palestine owned just 2.5 per cent of land,[80] this was the better land. Britain's imperial overlords, by contrast, did not enforce segregation of Jews and Palestinians in employment. They hired Arab workers alongside Jewish workers, including in the same employment sectors and workplaces. Therefore, in "a few workplaces there were both Jews and Arabs". For example,

> of the 5,000 or so railway workers of the early 1940s some four-fifths were Arabs and a fifth Jews. The oil refinery in Acre employed both Arabs and Jews, again the majority Arabs. The lowest echelon of the civil service also employed workers from the two communities.[81]

Even so, British authority pandered to Zionism by means of pay discrimination in favour of Jews and to the detriment of Arabs (with the latter earning around a third of the former),[82] and by placing Jews in the higher-status jobs. This operated as a classic case of divide-and-rule colonial policy, deflecting hostility of Jewish and Arab workers onto each other and away from British rule. Nonetheless, outside British administration and the larger-scale industry, the vast bulk of the workforce were partitioned along ethnic lines. "Some nine-tenths of all workers were in segregated workplaces".[83]

Zionist colonization, in establishing with British support enclave economies for settler Jews, access to which for indigenous Arabs was denied, sought to bind the settlers to the ethno-religious nationalism of their leaders. This was by means of the modest trickle-down material benefits (from Jewish propertied elites to landless Jews) that this colonial protectionism afforded. Landless Jews (whether wage-workers or tenant farmers) could shelter under the umbrella of a Zionist paternalism that protected their livelihoods from Arab competition in the labour market and in the various primary goods markets. The politics of exclusion also nurtured in the settlers a sense of their supposed racial or cultural superiority to those who were excluded (hence exclusive schools, etc.), as well as anxieties and fears over the threat posed to their lives and livelihoods by the resentful and jealous Arabs owing to their exclusion, as indeed was the intention.

On the other side of the barricades, the

> Zionist colonisation frightened the mass of the Arabs. It put their opposition to Zionism at the top of their agenda, making them ready to unite with the feudal landlords and religious parties . . . to stop Zionist expansion.

This rendered the Palestinian Arabs "prey to the influence of feudal reaction", as this was conveyed by religious nationalists who regarded opposition to Zionism as synonymous with opposition to a Jewish presence in Palestine.[84] Arab nationalists deployed crude antisemitism (such as the idea of a worldwide Jewish-Bolshevik alliance to rule the world) not only to bind the Palestinian commonfolk to their cause of securing an exclusive homeland in Palestine for its Arab inhabitants but also to court favour with British colonial rule. This was by representing themselves as more loyal and reliable servants of that authority than the Zionists could ever be. As Yu Haikal, one of the Arab leaders, expressed it:

> The Arabs do not fight Britain, and do not wish to damage her interests, but fight against the Jewish settlement and Zionist policy. If it were not for these two, the Arabs would live in friendship and peace with the English.[85]

There was thus a remarkable symmetry in the politics and ideology of Zionism and of Arab nationalism in Palestine as these evolved under British rule. This was in the sense that both set themselves the task of acquiescing to British imperialism in order to win for themselves its permission to establish an independent ethnically purified nation on behalf of Jews or Arabs once the British mandate had run its course.

The establishment of the Israeli state

But it was the Zionists who were favoured by the British. The Jewish enclaves in Palestine were indeed created as a colonial bridgehead under Zionist authority. They were also simultaneously set up as a colonial watchdog that would assist British pacification of the Arab indigenes, and so were placed under British military protection. This established the groundwork for the postwar elevation of the Jewish colonial settlement to ethno-nationalist state. From these inauspicious beginnings, the state of Israel was then born as a *colonial settler state*. This was as its implantation in Palestine in 1948 by force of US power was of course contrary to the wishes of the huge majority Arab population who understandably felt entitled to a nation-state of their own. With British dominance of the Middle East being supplanted by US designs of postcolonial neoimperial control in the region, the strategic value of a new state in Palestine was not lost on US leaders. Such a state would be inextricably bound to US corporate and geopolitical interests by virtue of its total dependence on American support (money, arms, and political leverage exercised through the UN).[86]

According to the USNSC in 1958, containing the threat of radical Arab nationalism to US control of oil supplies and markets in the Middle East necessitated continuing "to support Israel as the only strong pro-West power left in the Near East".[87] Nor, obviously, was this perspective lost on Israeli leaders. As was reported by the Jewish *Ha'avetz* newspaper in 1951: "Strengthening Israel helps the Western powers maintain equilibrium" in the region".[88] The "security" (i.e. Western control) of oil was regarded as especially endangered in the post-independence era by pan-Arabism or Arab socialism or by weak Arab leaders who allowed themselves to be pressurized into making concessions to the Arab street. As *Ha'avetz* put it: "The feudal regimes in the Middle East have had to make such concessions to the nationalist movements that they become more and more reluctant to supply Britain and the United States with their natural resources".[89] Such would raise the spectre of drastic price hikes to support national industrial development, heavier taxes levied on the US and European oil corporations, even the ending of drilling rights under nationalizations.

The Western powers had from the start of the oil-era reaped the gains of bargain-basement prices and bumper profits from their ownership rights and drilling concessions in the oil-producing countries of the Middle East. These were won in exchange for patronizing or propping-up local Arab elites and gifting them a (small) share of the profits.[90] But these advantages were less secure in the postcolonial world where Arab rulers could no longer blame the Great Powers for not spreading the revenues they drew from the black gold more widely. Under these circumstances, "securitization" of oil was in danger, because the Arab rulers could not be relied on to secure it for the benefit of the West or on behalf of the "world economy". Instead, they may do so for their own national interests, or for the benefit of the Arab world, or even on behalf of the Arab masses.

So, this was where a state of Israel could be of crucial assistance to the USA in particular and the West more generally. This was basically as an enclave state in the Middle East that would act to defend their interests where these fell under threat from Arab nationalism or Arab radicalism. To cite *Ha'avetz* again:

> There is no fear that Israel will undertake any aggressive policy towards the Arab states when this would explicitly contradict the wishes of the US or Britain. But if for any reasons the Western powers should sometimes prefer to close their eyes, Israel could be relied on to punish one or several neighbouring states whose discourtesy to the West went beyond the bounds of the permissible.[91]

The assistance could indeed be military (hence acting to discipline an unfriendly state or break up an alliance of such states on behalf of or in support of the USA and its allies). But it could also be diplomatic (hence alliance-building with pro-Western governments in the region in order to marginalize or isolate anti-Western governments or movements or offering them military aid).

Israel and the two-state solution

And so it came to pass. Washington obtained UN approval for its "two state" plan based on Resolution 181 (II).[92] This was to place under Jewish sovereignty 56.4 per cent of the territory,[93] even though the Jews made up 32 per cent of the population and owned just 5.7 per cent of the land.[94] The new Jewish state (Israel) would include in its borders 400,000 Arab Palestinians whereas the new Arab Palestinian state (in the remaining 43.6 per cent of the territory) would include 10,000 Jews.[95] This partition was manifestly favourable to the Jews of Palestine and disadvantageous to its Arabs. For that reason, it was endorsed (with reservations) by the Jewish Agency, just as it was opposed by the Arab Higher Committee of Palestine, the Arab League, and the Arab states. The latter endorsed a singular Arab-majority state in Palestine that guaranteed rights for Jews as a protected minority.[96] This, from any unprejudiced view, would have been the fairer solution.

> The Jewish Agency accepted the resolution despite its dissatisfaction over such matters as Jewish emigration from Europe and the territorial limits set on the proposed Jewish State. The plan was not accepted by the Palestinian Arabs and Arab States on the ground that it violated the provisions of the United Nations Charter, which granted people the right to decide their own destiny. They said that the Assembly had endorsed the plan under circumstances unworthy of the United Nations and that the Arabs of Palestine would oppose any scheme that provided for the dissection, segregation or partition of their country, or which gave special and preferential rights and status to a minority.[97]

But US leaders knew, in all likelihood, that the two-state plan would be cast aside by the Zionist leaders of the Jewish community at the first opportunity owing to the limits it placed on their colonial ambitions. They could hardly be unaware. Annexation of the whole of Palestine was certainly the intention of Zionism.[98] Chaim Weizmann declared as much in 1937 in response to an earlier British proposal (the Peel Commission's) to partition Palestine: "We shall spread in the whole country in the course of time . . . this is only an arrangement for the next 25 to 30 years".[99] As David Ben-Gurion reassured those of his supporters who regarded the 1948 partition plan as thwarting their goal of emulating the ancient Hebrew kingdoms:

> No Zionist can forgo the smallest portion of the Land of Israel. . . . [A] . . . Jewish state in part [of Palestine] is not an end, but a beginning. . . . Our possession is important not only for itself . . . through this we increase our power, and every increase in power facilitates getting hold of the country in its entirety. Establishing a state . . . will serve as a very potent lever in our historical effort to redeem the whole country.[100]

The Jewish-Arab civil war 1947/48

The partition's wretched injustice from the Palestinian-Arab perspective, together with its failure to satisfy Zionist-Jewish ambitions for a greater Israel, triggered an escalating wave of tit-for-tat inter-communal violence (bombings, shootings, roadside ambushes, etc.), usually conveyed by militia groups, and typically targeting civilians, civilian homes, villages, civic infrastructure, and crowded public places.[101] This was the start of the so-called Israeli-Arab civil war of 1947/48. In the runup to partition, in those areas where both communities co-existed, this pattern of reprisal and counter-reprisal escalated into bigger skirmishes, pitched battles, plus a blockade (of Jerusalem).[102] Each atrocity committed by one side ramped up the racial framing of the conflict by ethno-nationalists on the other side. This inflamed inter-communal racial hatred, reinforcing the sense that this was conflict between Jews and Arabs, or between antisemites and anti-Arabs, which further escalated the violence. The British colonial authority's refusal to discharge its duty of care to Palestine in the runup to partition (i.e. maintaining law and order through the deployment of military forces to prevent or break-up skirmishes) obviously fuelled the escalation of conflict since this ensured that the feuding encountered no constraint.[103]

Ominously, the Zionist militias (Haganah, Irgun, and Lehi), which were much better organized and trained than the Palestinian ones, made their plans for a war of "self-defence" of the imminent Israeli state against the Arab communities that disapproved of it, including by the compulsory conscription of new recruits. A hundred thousand were recruited before partition, with 25,000 of these were already armed and combat trained by then.[104] These Zionist militias, on the cusp of Independence Day, were also much better-resourced than the Palestinian ones. In their support, the Jewish Agency (of Palestine) could draw upon a military budget of $28 million to purchase weapons from overseas. In contrast, the Arab Higher Committee (of Palestine) had at its disposal a total budget of just $2,250,000 from which to fund Palestinian forces, owing to the lack of financial backing by the Arab states.[105] This already huge asymmetry of military resources available to the two communities thereafter grew substantially, so that the Palestinian fighters were increasingly outgunned by their Zionist counterparts. A further $129 million was fund-raised for the Zionist cause in the USA between October 1947 and March 1949, with $78 million of this devoted to arms procurements.[106]

The colonization of Arab Palestine

Partition was the final moment of British colonial rule of Palestine. Even before it was instituted, as the British wound down their colonial administration and withdrew their troops, there was unleashed on Palestine a massive, murderous, pre-planned round of Zionist-led, militia-delivered ethnic cleansing of the Arab indigenes.[107] This was backed up by fearful propaganda of atrocities being committed against Arab civilians who refused to flee their homes in order to hasten the exodus.[108] The UN prefers to describe what happened post-partition as simply "escalation" of civil war between the two communities.[109] Thus: "Fierce hostilities immediately broke out between the Arab and Jewish communities".[110]

However, the former state-of-affairs was very much more the reality than was the latter. The "escalation" in question was one-sided and purposive.

The Zionist operation that would ethnically cleanse Palestine was codenamed Plan D (or Plan Dalet) by its planners. The final operational version of it was agreed on 10 March 1948. The assault on the town of Haifa by the Haganah militia on 21 April 1948 exemplifies its *modus operandi*:

> At sundown . . . the Zionists hurled 60 pounds of explosives about 300 yards into the crowded Arab quarter. Barrel bombs, which were casks filled with gasoline and dynamite, rolled down the narrow alleys and crashed, creating an inferno of flames and explosions. Loudspeakers of the Haganah, the mainstream Zionist militia, broadcast "horror recordings" that filled the air with shrieks and anguished moans of Arab women, interrupted by a booming sorrowful voice that called out in Arabic: "Flee for your lives! The Jews are using poison gas and nuclear weapons!"[111]

Such propaganda was effective precisely because atrocities *were* being committed. One of these (and one of many) was perpetrated less than two weeks before the Israeli assault on Haifa by Menachem Begin's notorious Irgun militia in the Deir Yassin village.[112] As was reported by an observer from the International Red Cross:

> Everywhere it was the same horrible sight . . . there had been 400 people in this village—about 50 had escaped. All the rest had been deliberately massacred in cold blood, for, as I observed for myself, this gang was admirably disciplined and acted only under orders.[113]

At this point, the conflict could no longer be categorized as one of inter-community violence at all. Rather, this was now a war waged by the military forces of the new Israeli state against an entire unwanted civilian population of non-Jews.[114] Indeed, the speed by which the success of the operation was delivered was likely explainable by the fact that the Arab villages it was intended to "cleanse" were much less militarized than the Jewish ones. These settlements were populated largely by frightened non-combatants, and these were typically weakly defended or undefended by the embattled Arab militias. This may perhaps explain why each time a village was attacked the neighbouring ones did not rally to its defence, so that each one was quickly overcome.[115] Such was the inevitable consequence of the huge asymmetry of military resources available to the two sides after partition together with the failure of the UN to intervene as peace-enforcers. This provided Zionist leaders with the opportunity to secure *at once* their longer-term goal of turning the whole of Palestine into their own state.

The Zionist offensive drove the panic-stricken Palestinian civilians not only out of the new Israeli state but also out of their own new state (as sanctioned by the two-state partition). They were expelled into neighbouring territories or countries—Samaria, central Galilee, Mount Hebron, Jordan, Lebanon, and Syria. Those who could not be "absorbed" into local populations (i.e. those without money or possessions) were thereafter concentrated in vast impoverished refugee camps.[116] By the end, Plan D had delivered the destruction of 531 Arab civilian settlements, the occupation of 774 others, the looting of all (whether razed or occupied), and in excess of 15,000 deaths from more than 70 known massacres.[117] The campaign was enacted in a series of 13 military operations. Nine of these were explicitly stated as meeting the goal of either clearing or destroying Arab villages. Eight of these operations were conducted in areas that lay within territory that the UN had designated as belonging to the Palestinian state.[118] Plan D also involved the use of bacteriological weapons inasmuch as wells were poisoned in those settlements that were razed in order to deter anyone from returning.[119]

The response of the Arab League to the Israeli colonization was tepid and recalcitrant and undermined by national self-interest and a wish not to displease the USA. From the start of the crisis, the Arab states had demonstrated a reluctance to get involved directly—by committing their own armed forces to the aid of the Palestinian Arabs.[120] As we have seen, there was also little financial backing from Arab leaders for the Palestinian militias. However, under pressure of events (especially news of the Deir Yassin massacre),[121] a token military force was despatched to Palestine, supposedly to restore the Palestinian state that never was. This engaged the Israelis in cross-border skirmishes before being withdrawn in short order.

> Arab League armed forces, representing five countries, mustered a grand total of 15,000. . . . Their heaviest armour consisted of 22 light tanks and 10 Spitfire aircraft. The Zionists had 30,000 fully mobilised regular troops, at least 32,000 second-line troops, plus 15,000 settlement police and a "home guard" of 32,000. In addition there were between 3,000 and 5,000 in the Irgun. . . . There were military clashes—but key Arab governments were already in negotiation with the Israelis. . . . In any case, the ruling feudal families had no stomach for a fight. King Abdullah of Trans-Jordan received Golda Meir as soon as the "war" began. His negotiations with her and later Moshe Dayan soon revealed his true intentions. He was more than content to aid the Zionist sabotage of the UN partition agreement by grabbing the West Bank of the Jordan for himself. Abdullah's army was the best trained in the Arab League. His equivocation at the outset undermined morale for the rest.[122]

By the start of 1949, when the UN finally brokered a "ceasefire", 80 per cent of Palestine was in Israeli possession, including all the best lands and wealthier settlements. So too was half of the citrus groves, nine-tenths of the olive groves and 10,000 shops.[123] Those Arabs who were left on the fringes and margins of the new Greater Israel were left fearful for their lives and without hope of redress. This was owing to the US state's refusal to discipline or sanction the Israeli state for its land grab, and with the UN acquiescent in America's complicity, in effect accepting the destruction of Arab Palestine. And so, they also began their own exodus. As Tony Cliff observes: "Figures of land ownership testify to their elimination: in 1917 the Jews owned 2.5 percent of the land in the country. In 1948 it rose to 5.7 percent, and . . . [to] . . . about 95 percent in the pre-1967 [post-1949] borders".[124]

Those Palestinian Arabs who resisted expulsion and stayed put on their lands in Israel (around one-fifth of the pre-1948 population) were eventually granted citizenship.[125] But up until the late 1960s the benefits of the concession were undermined due to the Arab population being placed under martial law restrictions.[126] This was a period in which the Palestinian Arabs faced a "rigorous regime of military rule that dominated what remained of the . . . population in territory ruled by Israel". This subjected them to a battery of curfews, travel restrictions, expulsions, and "administrative" (i.e. without trial) detentions. This also enabled the state to "expropriate most Arab-owned land, severely limit its access to investment capital and employment opportunity, and virtually eliminate all opportunities to use citizenship as a vehicle for gaining political influence".[127]

The Absentee Property Act of 1950 authorized the state to seize the land and premises of absentee Arab owners displaced or expelled by the war. The follow-up Land Acquisition Act of 1953 sanctioned transfer of ownership of this property to the state. Similarly, under emergency powers legislation, Arab-owned land was effectively confiscated because it was situated in areas that were designated by the state as militarized zones closed-off to private citizens. This land too was later expropriated by the state.[128] Those Arabs who remained inside Israel's borders but were internally displaced from their home places within the country were classified as "present absentees". They too were usually denied the right of return and suffered forfeiture of land and other property. Internally displaced Palestinians today make up 25 per cent of Israel's Arab population.[129]

The racialization of Israeli citizenship

The ethno-nationalist leaders of the new Israel also passed the Citizenship Act of 1952, repealing the Palestinian Citizenship Order of 1925 that previously established all residents of Palestine as citizens. The Act established four routes for the acquisition of Israeli nationality—by birth, by residence, by return, and by naturalization. The Act effectively rendered stateless and nationless by law those Palestinian Arabs who had fled the violence or been ethnically cleansed beyond the borders of the new state. This was because it did not automatically grant nationals of the territory of Palestine Israeli citizenship. Whereas Jews could acquire Israeli citizenship through residence and exercise of the Law of Return, Arabs could do so only if they fulfilled four eligibility criteria. These were

(1) as previously holding Palestinian nationality; (2) as registered residents of Israel since 1949; (3) as still being registered residents of Israel on the day that the 1952 Act came into law; and (4) as residing in Israel, or in a territory that became part of Israel in the period from when the Israeli state was established and up to when the 1952 Act came into effect. Those Palestinian Arabs who fled from the fighting and the ethnic cleansing (which was most of the population) could not meet these criteria and so were rendered non-nationals, divested of citizenship rights, as was the intention of the Act.

This "denationalization" of the Palestinian indigenes thus established ethno-religious "Jewishness" as the marker of Israeli nationality. This is regarded by many legal scholars as in breach of international human rights law.[130] Returning Arabs could not acquire citizenship, only lesser residency status. This ensured that Israel would perpetuate as a country with a permanent large Jewish majority (around 79 per cent), therefore the dominance of Jewish ethno-nationalists in the state and government, despite the granting of citizenship in 1967 to permanent Arab residents of Israel.[131] To this day, Israeli law does not recognize Israeli nationality as such, only citizenship. Citizens of Israel are registered on identity documents in terms of ethnic affiliation—as Jewish, Arab, Druze, and so on.[132] This in effect establishes the indistinguishability of Jewishness and Israeli nationhood, hence the exclusive Jewishness of the Israeli state, as well as the sectarian ethnic partitioning of the citizenry into separate communities and citizenship groups of greater and lesser status.

This has allowed a proportionally greater part of the state budget to be allocated to Jews rather than Arabs. (Jews, 79 per cent of the population, claim more than 93 per cent of state resources.)[133] This has also resulted in the exclusion of Israeli Arab citizens from the political process except as atomized voters. (No Arab political party has ever participated in coalition government in Israel.) This also has institutionalized not only Jewish control of the economy (or rather its control by a Jewish elite) but also ethnicity-based advantages for Jews over Arabs in the labour market. Thus, the average Arab-Israeli employee today earns only 58.6 per cent of the income of the average Jewish-Israeli employee, whereas the gap between the two widens among those with higher education. In 2018, an "Arab with 0–8 years of education earned 86.5 percent what his Jewish counterpart earned, while an Arab with 16 years of education earned 66.2 percent of what a Jew with a similar education level earned".[134]

There is little residential or social mixing between Jewish and Arab communities. The children attend school in separate education sectors—with the Jewish schools much better resourced than the Arab ones. Annual spending per pupil in state schools was estimated at just $192 for Arab students compared to $1,100 for Jewish students in the mid-2000s.[135] Moreover, intermarriage of Jews and Arabs is prohibited by Jewish religious law, as well as heavily disapproved and morally sanctioned by both communities, and is policed informally (on the Jewish side) by citizenship groups. A survey in 2015 found that 97 per cent of

Israeli Jews would be unhappy if their son or daughter married a Muslim (i.e. Palestinian Arab) whereas 82 per cent of Israeli Muslims would be unhappy if their son or daughter married an Israeli Jew.[136] But Arab hostility to intermarriage is primarily hostility to interpersonal ties with members of a group which is seen as oppressive, whereas Jewish hostility to intermarriage is mainly hostility to interpersonal ties with members of a group which is seen as culturally inferior.

Between 1948 and 1967, most Arab Palestinians adopted the Establishment self-identification of "Israeli Arab" imposed on them by the Zionist state, since self-identification as Palestinian or Arab Palestinian would have risked state repression, given that public displays of non-Jewish nationalism were illegal. This classification "intentionally misrecognized" the connection and affinity of Palestinian Arabs with Palestine "as a territorial unit, thus facilitating the erasure of the term . . . from the Hebrew vocabulary", and rendering the term " 'Israel' . . . as a defining feature of 'its' Arabs".[137] A double-identity was thus constructed by the state for Israel's Palestinian Arabs: firstly, as *Arab*, a cultural identity, rather than a political one, hence a denationalized one; secondly, as *Israeli*, a political rather than cultural identity, but one which was emptied of national identification and allegiance.[138]

With the relaxation of martial and emergency laws from 1967, however, Palestinian Arabs gradually regained the confidence to express their real nationalist sentiments on self-identity, though a significant minority continued to self-represent as Israeli Arab owing in part to the weight of expectation in "official" social discourse in Jewish-dominated society.[139]

> While they [Palestinian Arabs] were allowed to become citizens, they were distanced from the center of power because the Israeli state was a Jewish state and Israeli national identity incorporated Jewish symbols and referents. . . . In official and popular culture, they ceased being Palestinians and were recreated as Israeli Arabs or Arab citizens of Israel. Expressing Palestinian identity by displaying the flag, singing nationalist songs, or reciting nationalist poetry was illegal . . . until only very recently. Self-identification as Palestinians, Israeli Palestinians, or Palestinian citizens of Israel has increased since 1967 and is now their preferred descriptor. It was only under the influence of the Intifada, however, that many Israeli Palestinians felt secure enough to refer to themselves publicly in this way (as opposed to choosing the term Palestinian only in anonymous surveys on identity.[140]

Since then, in all surveys, "the majority of Arab citizens define themselves as Palestinian rather than 'Israeli Arab'". Thus, after decades of self-identifying as Arabs who "belong" to Israel, they now self-identify as "Arabs of Palestine". A survey conducted in 2006, for example, found that 66 per cent self-identified as Palestinian either wholly or in part compared to 37 per cent who self-identified at least in part as Israeli.[141] By 2017, most were classifying themselves as “Palestinian in Israel” (most popular choice) and “Palestinian Arab” (second-most common), with only 16 per cent self-identifying as “Israeli Arab”.[142] Given the colonial history of the Israeli state, its sectarian ethnic character, and the subordinate status of its minority Arab citizenry (who remain ghettoized in the poorer communities and allocated the lower status jobs), this is an unsurprising result. The Israeli US watchdog state was consolidated, by necessity, as a virtual apartheid state.

Jewish support for Zionism

This (the consolidation of Israel as both proxy state and racial state) has profoundly deformed popular political consciousness among large numbers of Israeli Jews. This is by rendering millions of the citizenry supportive of the Zionist colonial project:

> US and Israeli university surveys of Israeli opinion conform that half of the Israeli population welcome Zionist settlement on the West Bank. Perhaps most strikingly of all, only 1 percent favour a political settlement with the Palestinians by withdrawing to pre-1967 borders. This implies the existence of a colonial mentality among the mass of Israelis—not dissimilar to that of white Rhodesians “under siege” from black Zimbabweans in the 1970s, the French in Algeria “under siege” from Algerian Arabs in the 1960s, or the Afrikaners “under siege” from blacks in South Africa.[143]

This explains how it is that a majority of Israeli Jews accept or tolerate the militarization of the state (including compulsory military service for Jews—but not for Israeli Arabs) and a permanent arms economy. This explains how it is that the electoral political process in Israel continually elevates into office, without exception, parties and governments and leaders committed to Zionism, the colonial project of a Greater Israel, irrespective of their other differences. Zionism and militarism are necessary, in the popular mindset, to ensure the safety of the citizenry faced on all sides by rabidly “antisemitic” Arab populations set on sweeping them into the sea. The political ideology of “securitization” that is spun by the Zionist state and media constantly reproduces popular phobias and anxieties and hostilities over the threat posed by the Arab Other to the very existence of a Jewish homeland.

The extent to which the Zionist leaders themselves believe in this political discourse of their own making is a matter of debate. It perfectly suits their political goals, however, that a large bulk of Israel’s Jews continue to believe in it. As Maxime Rodinson explains, Zionism—despite its own claims to be interested in “peaceful coexistence” with the Palestinian Arabs and hence of supporting a diplomatic solution to the Palestinian crisis—is simply incapable of being genuinely interested in or supportive of any such thing. This is because "normalization" of relations with the Arab world (in the sense of granting the Palestinian Arabs some kind of independent homeland, relinquishing some land for the purpose, and accepting even limited "rights of return" for those expelled from Palestine) would be the end of Zionism itself:

> An Israel . . . admitting a certain number of Arab refugees to her breast, abandoning some of her conquests, conforming to the decisions of the UN . . . would have meant . . . extinction of the proud dream of reviving the kingdom of David and Solomon. . . . The "normal" progress of events was fatal for Zionist Israel . . . Once the external danger disappeared, Messianic fervour would decline. The pioneer spirit was in jeopardy. . . . Zionist Israel throve on a bellicose atmosphere and the threat of danger.[144]

Zionism and expansionary Israel

Since the start, the Israeli watchdog has thus remained resolutely committed to its foreign policy role as US proxy, policing and reigning-in its Arab neighbours in exchange for US acquiescence to expansionist Zionism. Subsequent wars with Arab states in 1956, 1967, and 1973 resulted in the further territorial expansion of Israel and the consolidation of its territorial gains. These were represented by Zionist politicians as "defensive" wars to deter Arab military aggression but were in fact aggressive and proactive campaigns to build a Greater Israel.

In 1956, Israel invaded Egypt in order to seize possession of the Straits of Tiran in the Sinai Peninsula. This was the prelude to the ill-fated Anglo-French military expedition to seize control of the Suez Canal following Egypt's president Nasser's decision to nationalize it.[145] (Nasser had closed the Straits to Israeli shipping in 1950, blocking access to the Red Sea, in retaliation for Israel's colonization of Palestine in 1948).[146] The British and French governments claimed that part of the purpose of their invasion was to terminate the Israel–Egypt war; hence war and imperialism was "peacekeeping". In fact, the Anglo-French and Israeli plans were known to each other in advance and were likely part of a co-ordinated operation. But the partners, not quite grasping the real nature of postwar superpower imperialism, proceeded without the US government's agreement. US leaders disapproved of this resurgence of European colonialism, and of Israel's unsanctioned alliance with it. Fearful also that the Soviets would exploit the crisis to build regional influence, Washington made it clear that all must cease hostilities and withdraw their forces or face sanctions. This they did. Israel withdrew from Sinai in March 1957.[147]

In 1967, with Nasser again denying Israel access to the Straits of Tiran, the Israeli state again unleashed war on Egypt, and on Egypt's allies (Syria and Jordan) with a full-scale surprise attack. (This time, presumably, the watchdog had secured US approval for the invasion). The Zionist leaders claimed initially that the attack was reactive (in response to being attacked) but later conceded that this was "pre-emptive".[148] The Egyptian and Syrian defenders were caught off-guard; Egypt had not resolved to go to war, whereas the Israelis were set on it and had planned for it. Air strikes destroyed the bulk of the Egyptian and Syrian air-forces on the ground just as Israeli ground forces invaded Sinai and Gaza. With complete mastery of the skies, the war's outcome in Israel's favour was scarcely in doubt.[149] It was all over in six days. The outcome saw Israel expand its size threefold at the expense of its Arab neighbours. The Sinai Peninsula and the Gaza strip were taken from Egypt. The Golan Heights were taken from Syria. The Gaza Strip and the West Bank where masses of already displaced Palestinians were ghettoized were taken from Jordan. The 1973 Yom Kippur War then confirmed the territorial gains as Israel repelled Egypt's and Syria's attempt to reverse the results of the 1967 war.[150]

UN resolutions requiring that Israel return to its pre-1967 borders were ignored without consequence (with sanctions vetoed by the USA and UK).[151] This was just as the flow of US military and economic aid continued, indeed was upscaled.[152] The reason for this was that Israel's success in the 1967 war convinced Washington that the Zionist state was indeed the ideal regional watchdog, since it had by virtue of its victory demobilized the cause of pan-Arab nationalism that threatened to upset the regional status quo. The last thing that the US state wanted was an Arab victory in the war, because this would have boosted Egypt's attempt to build an Arab alliance against the West, raised aspirations for economic progress right across the Middle East, and thereby placed the petrol-monarchies under popular pressure to redistribute the benefits of their oil wealth. As the US State Department expressed it:

> Israel has probably done more for the US in the Middle East . . . than any of our so-called allies and friends elsewhere around the world since the end of the Second World War. . . . Here the Israelis won the war single-handedly . . . and have secured our interests as well as theirs.[153]

Israel's victory in the 1973 war—which confirmed its colonial land grab—generated similar benefits for the US-led Western Alliance. Again, an Arab victory may have caused a resurgence of regional-wide pan-Arabism, with political and economic fallout for the West. The victory also undermined the first concerted effort by the OPEC cartel of oil-producing nations to flex its muscles against the USA—not only economically but also politically. Formed in the 1960s, OPEC had not sought to challenge the oil-producers' subsidization of low energy prices for the benefit of others, until 1973. But now the OPEC countries banded together to demand a dramatic increase of prices.[154]

In addition, they demanded that Washington insist that Israel return to its 1948 borders, in effect to reign-in its watchdog. This was in response to Henry

Kissinger's sanctioning of $2.2 billion of emergency military aid for Israel during the 1973 war rather than the $850 million that was requested.[155] Kissinger described the OPEC demand as "crazy". However, this was backed up by an oil embargo.[156] This posed a huge threat to US control of oil, potentially undermining alliances with the petrol-kingdoms. It also generated calls from American oil corporations for the US government to scale back on its support for Israel and pressurize its leaders to relinquish the 1967 gains. But Israel's victory in the 1973 war short-circuited all of that, except for the oil price hike. This is why the US state under the Nixon presidency, rather than making concessions on Israel in response to OPEC's demands, instead dramatically increased the supply of arms to its ally to ensure that it prevailed.[157]

As Kissinger later claimed:

> The United States saved Israel from collapse . . . by our arms supply. And even while this was going on, Sadat [president of Egypt] was sending me notes every day saying that he knew there would have to be talks after the war and that he wanted me to come to Egypt to get the process of peace started as soon as possible. Some have claimed that it was American strategy to produce a stalemate in the 1973 war. This is absolutely wrong. What we wanted was the most massive Arab defeat possible.

This was to "break up the Arab united front", neutralize Soviet influence (since the USSR was courting the Arab world by supporting restoration of the original pre-1949 Palestinian state), and "enable Israel to deal separately with each of its neighbors".[158] The embargo indeed failed.[159] The Arab alliance was undone. This was not inevitable but was partly because some key players did not support the boycott and because the others—faced with 1973 defeat—allowed themselves to be "persuaded" by Washington that it was committed to negotiating with the Israelis a settlement on behalf of the Palestinians.[160]

The Palestinians were left without allies. Egypt abandoned pan-Arabism, and made its peace with Israel, paving the way for the US-brokered Camp David accords.[161] The Arab countries thereafter paid only lip service to the cause of a Palestinian state. Those harbouring the diaspora populations or with designs on adjoining territories where these displaced people lived came to view them as their own security risks, as a beacon for the discontents of their own subject peoples against their own rule, or as an obstacle to their own geopolitical goals.[162] This was partly because the 1967 and 1973 defeats licensed them to prioritize national self-interest over wider regional goals. Israel began its programmes of new settlement building in the unlawfully occupied territories, in defiance of UN resolutions, and again without consequence.[163] The number of illegal (under international law) Jewish settlers in the West Bank increased from 35,000 in 1984 to 64,000 in 1988 and to 130,000 by 1995.[164]

Political and economic impacts of the occupation

New militarily protected Jewish enclaves and hence new displacements of the already marginalized and dispossessed Palestinian Arabs thus became normalized in the occupied territories. This was as daily life was made an endless round of "beatings, shootings, killings, house demolitions, uprooting of trees, deportations, extended imprisonments, and detentions without trial",[165] all of which were aspects of the ongoing Israeli state campaign to undermine Palestinian nationalism. Plenty of the Jewish civilian settlers, typically religious nationalists, made themselves junior partners in the state oppression, forming militias, turning their settlements into armed camps, and meting out "discipline" to "disrespectful" villagers.[166] Economically as well, the Palestinian Arabs of the occupied lands languished, as they were caught between the rock and hard place of expanding population and lesser access to agricultural land or premises for business or paid employment. Lack of jobs compelled many (including the highly educated—up to degree level) to become daily guest workers in Israel, taking on the poorest paid and lowest status jobs that Israeli Jews did not want.[167]

As per capita GDP income in Israel grew tenfold between 1985 and 2012, it fell back for Arabs in the Israeli-occupied territories. By 2012, this was $32,000 in Israel compared to just $2,900 in the West Bank and Gaza Strip.[168] This was an 11-fold income gap, whereas in 1980 this was a nine-fold one. By the close of 2022, the per capita income gap between Israel and Palestine was the highest on record. This was $55,731 in Israel compared to $3,656 in the colonized territories—a 15-fold income gap.[169] Palestine is amongst the world's poorest places, in 139th place out of 194 countries internationally.

Palestine and the pandemic

Naturally, the drawing together of economic injustice and political repression has resulted in epidemiological injustice in the context of the COVID-19 pandemic. Such has been conveyed by the vaccine colonialism of the Israeli state. Israel's vaccine rollout may be considered the absolute world leader—until one considers that this was to the exclusion of the Palestinians in the occupied territories, in contravention with international human rights law and the terms of the Fourth Geneva Convention. As was reported by the UN in January 2021: "Israel has not ensured that Palestinians under occupation in the West Bank and Gaza will have any near-future access to the available vaccines".[170] This was as Israel began vaccinating its own citizens in these territories, with 20 per cent inoculated by the start of March 2021.[171]

The PA would thereafter have to rely mostly on donations not from Israel but from the COVAX programme, with additionals from China and the UAE, having received up until February 2021 a few thousand doses of Sputnik courtesy of Russia. Eventually, in June, having by then vaccinated 85 per cent of its own population, the Israeli government offered the PA 1.4 million surplus doses of Pfizer. But this was in exchange for receiving the same number of doses back from the PA when they received supplies from COVAX. Such was simply Israeli opportunism. Vaccination of Palestinians was still languishing at around 30 per cent, so that the PA was placed under pressure to accept a "new for old" deal with Tel Aviv. This collapsed because the Israeli government's Pfizer vaccines were so old they were on the cusp of their expiry date and could not have been distributed prior to that.[172]

Inequities of epidemiological outcomes between Israel and Palestine were thus unsurprising. The COVID-19 mortality rate per caseload volume in Palestine has been almost three times higher than in Israel. As of 15 March 2023, there were 621,008 recorded cases of infection in Palestine, whereas 5,404 Palestinians had by then been killed by the virus. This was a mortality rate of approximately 0.7 per cent per rate of infection. In comparison, by that same date, there were 4,806,715 recorded cases of infection in Israel, whereas 12,342 Israelis had by then been killed by the virus. This was a mortality rate of approximately 0.26 per cent per rate of infection.[173]

Diplomatic games—the myth of a "peace process"

Away from zones of displacement, oppression, and injustice, ineffectual and patently unjust "peace plans" brokered by the USA or UN (the Oslo Accords, Camp David, the Taba Summit, etc.) inevitably foundered precisely because they offered settlements that fell far short of the requirements of Resolution 242 and its successors. Not only were the peace negotiations radically and inevitably asymmetric in favour of Israel (given its unconditional US backing), but it is unlikely that there was any intention on the part of Israeli leaders to implement any one-sided agreements with the browbeaten Palestinian negotiators that may have resulted from them.

The purpose of the various phony "peace talks" was really to convey an *impression* of US-backed Israel's willingness to at least try to negotiate a settlement that would settle the Palestinian Question whereas in fact there was little willingness to give ground on anything fundamental for reasons I have stated. The "peace talks" may have also been motivated by US concern over renewed regional instability in the wider Middle East provoked by the Palestinian uprisings *(Intifadas)* of 1987 and 2000 and their brutal military repression by the Israeli state, since these provoked mass demonstrations and strikes in many Arab countries.[174] The convening of new US-brokered negotiations to settle the Israeli-Arab conflict therefore may have been intended to dampen down on growing unrest on the Arab street across the region. The timing of the initiatives certainly supports this interpretation.

Thus, the Oslo Accords of 1993 and 1995, based on Washington-brokered talks that started at the tail end of the first Intifada, brought the "two-state" settlement not one iota closer to fruition, offering mere scraps of land to the Palestinians. Nor did these offer redress to the three million homeless Palestinian refugees, that is, the survivors of the 1948 expulsion and their descendants.

> During the Madrid Peace Conference in 1991 and talks in Washington DC the following year, the Palestinian political delegation focused its efforts on negotiating an end to the illegal Israeli settlements in the occupied West Bank and Gaza Strip. Yet, in Oslo, Israel set aside all those issues—including settlements, the status of Jerusalem and refugees—for future negotiations. . . . The Oslo Declaration of Principles was not a peace treaty; rather, its aim was to establish interim governance arrangements and a framework to facilitate further negotiations for a final agreement, which would be concluded by the end of 1999.[175]

Instead, the deal brokered between Israel and the Palestinian Liberation Organization (PLO) extended Israeli formal recognition to the PLO as the legitimate representatives of the Palestinian people and elicited Israeli agreement to *limited* Palestinian political autonomy in the occupied territories of Gaza and the West Bank under Israeli sovereignty. "The Accords transferred control of major Palestinian cities and towns in the occupied West Bank and Gaza Strip to a newly-created Palestinian Authority (PA), an interim structure meant to oversee administration and internal security in these urban areas".[176] This was in exchange for the PLO's formal recognition of the state of Israel, as well as its commitment to "securitize" the refugee camps in order to demonstrate the commitment of the new PA to "law and order".[177] As the 1995 Accord states:

> In order to guarantee public order and internal security for the Palestinians of the West Bank and the Gaza Strip, the Council shall establish a strong police force . . . Israel shall continue to carry the responsibility for defense against external threats, including the responsibility for protecting the Egyptian and Jordanian borders, and for defense against external threats from the sea and from the air, as well as the responsibility for overall security of Israelis and Settlements, for the purpose of safeguarding their internal security and public order, and will have all the powers to take the steps necessary to meet this responsibility.[178]

The Accords also agreed to divide up the occupied West Bank into three non-contiguous regions (A, B, and C). In areas A and B, comprising 39 per cent of the West Bank, the PA would control most administrative functions, with one notable exception: Israel would continue to exercise full control over external security, giving it the right to intervene as it pleased for reasons of security, including if internal security failed. As for area C, making up 61 per cent of the West Bank, the Accords agreement was that control over this would also be handed over by Israel to the PA (again with the exception of external security). But this part of the agreement was never implemented.[179]

In effect, the Oslo Accords co-opted PLO leaders into functioning as a new layer of local political control of Palestinian refugees on behalf of the Israeli occupation, whilst leaving the illegal Israeli settlements untouched and all of the other fundamental issues undecided. Far from being a step towards a later settlement in accordance with UN resolutions, this was a means of derailing one, as was let slip by Benjamin Netanyahu in 2001 when making off-the-cuff remarks to an interviewer that he thought were unrecorded:

> They asked me before the election if I'd honour [the Oslo accords]. . . . I said I would, but. . . . I'm going to interpret the accords in such a way that would allow me to put an end to this galloping forward to the '67 borders. How did we do it? Nobody said what defined military zones were. Defined military zones are security zones; as far as I'm concerned, the entire Jordan Valley is a defined military zone. Go argue! . . . Why is that important? Because from that moment on I stopped the Oslo Accords.[180]

This wretched deal reflected the total dominance of the interests of US-backed Israel in the process. "Israel's red lines were the ones that counted, and if the Palestinians wanted a deal, they would have to accept them, too".[181] Israeli settlement building in the occupied territories post-Oslo, far from slowing, was accelerated. "By May 2003 there were over 200,000 Jewish settlers in the West Bank and some 180,000 in East Jerusalem—figures . . . double the total of the early 1990s when the Oslo accords were launched".[182]

No further progress was made in the Camp David talks of 2000 (the so-called "Clinton Accords"), with Israel refusing to concede on the fundamental minimum for any agreement to be brokered. This was simply concession on the principle of an independent Palestinian state situated between Israel and Jordan occupying the West Bank and Gaza Strip and of rights of return for Palestinian Arabs expelled from their land by the initial Zionist colonization of Palestine. Basically, the PLO was prepared to settle for a rump Palestinian state carved out of a parcel of land (just 22 per cent of former Palestine) under supervision by Jordan and Israel. This was, of course, a far cry from the original short-lived Palestinian state of 1948 that incorporated 45 per cent of the land within Israel's pre-1967 borders.

But the Israelis would concede initially only 73 per cent of the West Bank for the new Palestinian state. This was alongside an undertaking that "all going well" this would be permitted to grow (on Israeli estimates) to a maximum of 91 per cent (86 per cent on Palestinian estimates) of the West Bank in return for other land concessions from the Palestinians in the so-called "Green Line".

This would have left Israel's largest settlements concentrated on the better land intact—and legalized. This would also have entailed the Palestinians ceding nine per cent of the West Bank (which included one of the holiest Islamic shrines, the Al-Aqsa mosque) in return for one per cent of unspecified land. The Israelis also insisted on preserving or maintaining Jewish enclaves under Israeli sovereignty within the rump Palestinian state (including in Islamic East Jerusalem). At the same time, there would be Israeli sovereign control of new elevated transport routes (by road and rail) between the West Bank and Gaza and of Palestinian air-space. The new Palestinian state was also to be de-militarized, that is, maintain only token armed forces.[183]

This was, in short, a deal designed and intended to be rejected, though the PLO negotiators were prepared to swallow much of it. The subsequent Taba Summit of 2001, in the midst of the second Palestinian Intifada, could make no progress beyond the Camp David proposals, generating no signed agreements.[184] The Arab Peace Initiative of 2002 brokered by the Saudis and agreed by the Arab League (and re-endorsed by the League in 2007) then offered full normalization of relations with Israel by the Arab states in return for Israel's return to its pre-1967 borders, settlement of the Palestinian refugee crisis under the terms of UN Resolution 194, and its ceding of East Jerusalem as the capital of an independent Palestinian state. This was rejected out-of-hand by Israeli prime minister Ariel Sharon.[185] Thereafter, the Arab Peace Initiative was endorsed (but not acted on) by Sharon's successors Ehud Olmert and Shimon Perez,[186] before being initially "welcomed" by returning prime minister Benjamin Netanyahu in 2015, only to be dismissed by him in 2018.[187]

These disingenuous diplomatic games which are designed to reproduce the status quo (whilst appearing to struggle against it) perpetuate indefinitely. This is alongside the ongoing Israeli colony-building in the annexed territories and the accompanying cycle of conflict and strife: Palestinian protests and demonstrations, their violent dispersal by the Israeli security forces, leading to flare-ups of violence between the Palestinian militias and the Israeli colonists and defence forces, with the usual radically asymmetrical outcome in terms of damaged and lost lives. The cycle of protest and violence has not disturbed the ongoing illegal expropriation of Palestinian land and property in the occupied territories. Indeed, the process has accelerated, as the colonial settlers are emboldened by each of the clamp-downs on protest that demoralize and demobilize it for a while. Thus, at the time of writing the first draft of this chapter (mid-year 2021), there are "between 600,000–750,000 Israeli settlers living in at least 250 settlements (130 official, 120 unofficial) in the occupied West Bank and East Jerusalem".[188] This is an increase of between 63 per cent and 97 per cent since the early 2000s.

Recent twists in the "diplomatic" story are also worthy of mention. This is because these have also fanned the flames of Palestinian injustice-motivated discontent that have facilitated violent flare-ups over the past few years. These include US president Donald Trump's declaration in 2017 that the USA would hitherto recognize Jerusalem as the capital of Israel (followed by the relocation of the US embassy from Tel Aviv to Jerusalem in 2018),[189] plus his announcements in 2019 that the USA ought to recognize the Golan Heights as belonging to Israel[190] and that at least some Israeli settlements in the West Bank may not, after all, be illegal.[191] Trump's move was accompanied by his government's defunding of the UN Relief and Works Agency that provides aid for Palestinian refugees.[192] The tail-end of the Trump administration also saw the brokering of the Abraham Accords by which the United Arab Emirates and Bahrain agreed to normalize relations with Israel, hence further increasing the isolation of the Palestinians and their cause among Arab powerholders, as was perhaps part of their unstated intention.[193]

The recognition of Jerusalem as Israel's capital was, bizarrely, claimed by Trump to be a "long overdue step to advance the peace process", despite silence on the Palestinian goal of making their own capital in East Jerusalem. This was, he declared, on the grounds that previous US refusal to acknowledge Israel's "ancestral" right to the city was responsible for the failure to settle the Israeli-Arab conflict. As Trump put it: "It would be folly to assume that repeating the exact same formula would now produce a different or better result".[194] The formal rationalization of Trump's decision to recognize Jerusalem as Israel's capital was rooted in Biblical authority. This is Israel's transcendental right to the City of God that has its origins in a stateless world—a right which has miraculously survived the Jewish exodus from Palestine since before the Middle Ages.[195] At the same time, an "ultimate deal" that would finally end the Israeli-Palestinian conflict was Trump's promise to the world.[196] This, unsurprisingly, failed to materialize over the course of his presidency.

These shifts tilted the centre of political gravity in Washington even more radically (and certainly more openly and crudely) in favour of Israel's Zionist state, provoking much consternation worldwide, especially in Europe and the Middle East where politicians prefer to believe that there is such a thing as a "peace process". The content of Trump's declaration on the status of Israeli settlements in the West Bank and East Jerusalem was, of course, contrary to international law. But at least this (along with the Jerusalem declaration—which together have killed-off even the semblance of a peace process) renders transparent the US state's utter commitment to and complicity in the colonial project of its most important and valued watchdog.

Palestinian resistance

Owing then to the multiple failures of "diplomacy" over several decades has begun, out of desperation, for lack of alternative options, the current era of independent Palestinian do-it-yourself resistance to Israeli colonization and repression in its various forms. Most notable among these forms of resistance has been the great *Intifadas* (popular uprisings) of 1987–1993 and 2000–2005 in the occupied territories. As Benny Morris explains, the primary cause of the uprisings was an "all-pervading" sense of Arab "humiliation" owing to the long period of occupation since 1967. From the start, this was "a brutal and mortifying experience for the occupied", since the occupation was based "on brute force, repression and fear, collaboration and treachery, beatings and torture chambers, and daily intimidation, humiliation, and manipulation".[197]

Noam Chomsky conveys a forensic sense of daily life under the occupation from the perspective of the civilian occupiers in the Jewish settlements:

> The religious settlers in the West Bank, operating freely with army support, take pride in creating a pogrom-like atmosphere among the Arabs, who must be trained not to "raise their heads", this being the only way to treat Arabs, who "adore power" and will live with Jews only when "we show him that we are strong". . . . The settlers are quite open about the measures they take towards Arabs and the justification for them, which they find in the religious law and the writings of the sages. In the journal of the religious West Bank settlers we find, for example, an article [that] cites passages from the Talmud explaining that . . . law concerning "conquered" peoples is explicit . . . quoting Maimonides on how they must "serve" their Jewish conquerors and be "degraded and low", and "and must not raise their heads in Israel but must be conquered beneath their hand . . . with complete submission".[198]

This explains, as Chomsky recounts, a "standard bit of black humour in the Occupied Territories". This is that "Arabs should stop flying and begin walking on the ground, so they won't be shot so often when settlers fire into the air". Thus:

> The general character of the occupation is indicated by an incident in an Arab village in March 1982. Four settlers claimed that a stone was thrown at their car in the village. They fired "into the air", shooting one boy in the arm. Another boy was kidnapped, beaten, locked in the trunk of the car, taken to a Jewish settlement, and locked in a room where he was beaten "on and off" during most of the day, then taken to the military government compound in Ramallah, where the boy was held while the settlers went on their way. . . . Children and teenagers are often the main victims, since they are generally the ones involved in protests and demonstrations.[199]

The Intifadas

The first Intifada was largely led by community councils organized loosely affiliated to organizations (Fatah, Popular Front, Democratic Front, etc.) under the PLO umbrella, though Islamist groups such as Hamas and Islamic Jihad were also involved.[200] The various groups coordinated under the Unified National

Leadership of the Uprising (UNLU). The Intifada's aim was to render the occupied territories ungovernable so as to force Israel back to the negotiating table.

Initially, for a year or more, the first Intifada was remarkably free of lethal violence, indeed much violence at all—on the Palestinian side, that is. Rather, the resistance was largely peaceful, consisting of mass demonstrations, strikes, boycotts (of Israeli goods and stores and publicly owned transport), civil disobedience (including refusal to pay taxes), roadblocking, graffitiing, and so on. Tens of thousands of ordinary Palestinians took part, large numbers of them women and children. Acts of violence were confined mostly to stone-throwing (though there were also some isolated petrol-bombings) by disaffected youths, usually in response to attempts by the army and security forces to disperse crowds and break-up demonstrations. The illegal Israeli civilian settlements were not targeted. For a year, Hamas and Islamic Jihad acquiesced with the PLO and UNLU strategy of engaging in civil rather than violent protest.[201] By contrast, the Israeli colonial state authorities' response from the start was simply to radically upscale the level of violent repression that already was the norm with the aim of simply demoralizing the protestors into submission.

Some 80,000 troops were deployed to subdue the rebellion. Demonstrations and strikes were attacked and dispersed by the military and the police using live ammunition, plastic bullets, tear gas, water cannon, batons, and cudgels. Hundreds of roadblocks were setup to help administer curfews and exclusion zones. There were mass detentions, and there were hundreds of deportations. Parents of stone-throwing youngsters were arrested and handed exemplary fines. Collective punishments—such as shutting down schools and universities and shutting-off water and power and fuel supplies—were rolled out. Palestinian houses and shelters were bulldozed, and Palestinian stores and farms and allotments were vandalized. Olive and citrus groves were burned and trees uprooted. Palestinian goods were prevented from going to local markets and were blocked for export. Tax-refusers faced heavy fines, confiscations of property, and termination of licenses to trade. Israeli-Jew civilians from the illegal settlements participated in the repression, engaging in acts of "retaliatory" vigilante violence against their Arab neighbours. In the Intifada's first year, 142 Palestinians were killed, but there were zero Israeli deaths.[202]

Thereafter, the non-violent discipline of the popular resistance inevitably waned, and lethal acts of retaliatory violence became more common, since the peaceful methods of protest did nothing to moderate the state violence, strengthening the appeal of paramilitary-style methods for reasons of anger and bitterness. At the same time, the Intifada fractured, so that its cohesion was undermined, and it degenerated into intra-communal violence perpetrated by militants against Palestinians suspected of being informants and collaborators. Over the whole course of the Intifada, between 57,000 and 120,000 Palestinian Arabs were arrested; 120,000 at least suffered injuries from state violence—including between 23,600 and 29,900 children (who required medical treatment for injuries caused by beatings), whereas between 1,162 and 1,284 of them were killed by the army and police, including 241 to 332 children. By contrast, Israeli fatalities over the six years have been estimated at between 179 and 200 (100 of whom were civilians), with the number of injured thought to be 3,100.[203]

The first Intifada taught the dispossessed Palestinians that irrespective of the tactics that their resistance to the occupation may take (whether these be violent or non-violent), the response from the Zionist state is always the former—violence and terror as the first resort. Unsurprisingly, therefore, the second Intifada that broke out in 2,000 largely eschewed moderate methods. Rather, the resort to factionalism and paramilitarism was apparent from the start, though as before there was mass civilian popular participation in the uprising, especially at the beginning. The second Intifada was triggered by Zionist politician Ariel Sharon's and his supporters incursion "into the Al-Aqsa mosque—the most revered Islamic site in Jerusalem". This passed off without violence but was doubtless intended to be provocative, as it was.

> When mass protests began they were met once more with extreme violence from Israeli troops. . . . As in the uprising of 1987, most Palestinian combatants were armed with no more than stones. This did not prevent Israeli troops shooting to kill. By April 2002 the Palestinian Red Crescent Society estimated the death toll at 1,482, with over 19,000 injured.[204]

The initial protests of the Palestinians were mass civilian demonstrations in East Jerusalem. The Israeli army and security services responded as ever by violently dispersing these "riotous assembles" using tear gas and rubber-coated bullets as well as live rounds.[205] The demonstrations then spread to Gaza and the West Bank where these were again violently dispersed, including by means of the deployment of helicopter gunships against stone-throwing youths.[206] Within a few days, Israeli Arabs had joined the protest, with a general strike and demonstrations in northern Israel, including in the capital Tel Aviv. These too were met with the default excessive force of state powers, triggering street battles in which some protestors responded with stone-throwing, firebombing and small arms fire.[207] Mobs of Jewish civilians numbering in the thousands expressed their solidarity with the Zionist state with verbal racial taunting and threatening and by attacks on Arab property and civilians in the capital and other Israeli cities.[208]

By the end of the first day of protest, seven demonstrators had been killed and 300 injured. After five days, 47 Palestinians were killed and 1,885 were wounded. After the first month, 147 Palestinians were killed and 5,984 were injured. Unsurprisingly, Jewish casualties were, by comparison, modest. Two were killed in the first two days, whereas 12 were killed and 65 injured in the first month.[209] Amnesty International reported that virtually all of the Palestinian injured or killed by the Israeli military and security forces in this early stage of the Intifada were demonstrators or bystanders rather than combatants or militiamen, whereas 80 per cent of those killed were in gatherings that posed no threat to the lives of military or police personnel.[210]

After that, the Israeli state escalated the violence, not only clamping down on the civil protests but deploying tanks, artillery, and warplanes against the militia groups in the occupied territories. The militias responded with military-grade handheld weapons, sniper attacks, rockets, and roadside bombings.[211] This was the pattern until the end of the Intifada. Operation Defensive Shield in 2002 involved simultaneous Israeli military assaults on Palestinian refugee camps in the West Bank, including on PLO leader Yasser Arafat's Ramallah compound and the city of Jenin.[212] Operations Rainbow (which included opening fire on a civilian demonstration) and Days of Penitence followed in 2004, targeting camps in Gaza. These and other raids reduced the refuge settlements to ruins, rendering tens of thousands homeless, razing agricultural land, destroying greenhouses, water pumps, irrigation and sewage systems, and other civilian facilities.[213]

Human Rights Watch has estimated that the Israeli military destroyed 2,500 Palestinian homes in Gaza over the course of the Intifada. The attack on Rafah alone displaced 16,000 people and bulldozed 1,500 homes:

> The pattern of destruction strongly suggests that Israeli forces demolished homes wholesale, regardless of whether they posed a specific threat, in violation of international law. In most of the cases Human Rights Watch found the destruction was carried out in the absence of military necessity. . . . The pattern of destruction . . . is consistent with the goal of having a wide and empty border area to facilitate long-term control over the Gaza Strip. Such a goal would . . . greatly exceed the IDF's security needs. It is based on the assumption that every Palestinian is a potential suicide bomber and every home a potential base for attack. Such a mindset is incompatible with two of the most fundamental principles of international humanitarian law: the duty to distinguish combatants from civilians and the responsibility of an Occupying Power to protect the civilian population under its control.[214]

From this point, Israeli casualties became more common. This was as the resistance became far more militarized than in the first Intifada. And this was directed against both military and civilian targets, including across the Israeli border. Resistance also took the most radical but also saddest *sacrificial* form, that is, suicide attacks, in which again both Jewish civilians and security forces within and without Israel were targeted. The same style of resistance was to be seen against the agents of the Anglo-American occupation of Iraq a few years later, including by women and children. These were the tactics of those whose sense of hopelessness was so profound that they could see no future in their own lives except by making a political statement of the manner these were ended.

This was also the tactic of the militants of Hamas and Islamic Jihad. As reported by Amnesty International, by the close of the Intifada's first year:

> The overwhelming majority of cases of unlawful killings and injuries in Israel and the Occupied Territories have been committed by the IDF using excessive force. In particular, the IDF have used US-supplied helicopters in punitive rocket attacks where there was no imminent danger to life. Israel has also used helicopter gunships to carry out extrajudicial executions and to fire at targets that resulted in the killing of civilians, including children . . . Hamas and Islamic Jihad have frequently placed bombs in public places, usually within Israel, in order to kill and maim large numbers of Israeli civilians in a random manner. Both organizations have fostered a cult of martyrdom.[215]

Unlike the first Intifada, the second one thus impacted directly on Israeli society, causing substantial disruption of public life and the civilian economy, owing to the spectre of terrorist attacks real, threatened or imagined. This naturally fuelled public anxiety and outrage among many of Israel's Jews with regard to the threat posed by the incomprehensible "fanaticism" of those murderous Jew-hating Arabs fanned by media horror stories of the murder, kidnapping or beating of captured police or soldiers and of innocent Jewish civilians, including children. There were several such atrocities that made headline news in Israel, provoking the aforesaid public outrage and clamour for retributory sanctions against the terrorists.[216] One must not, after all, "reward" terrorists by negotiating or compromising with them.

Of course, in ethno-nationalistic Israel, critical self-reflection was, as usual, mostly conspicuous by its absence. This did not extend so far as acknowledging that, as history tells, such Arab terrorism is *retaliatory*, tit for tat, an eye for an eye, as Israel's biblically inspired Zionists ought to grasp. Nor, of course, did this acknowledge that Israel's innocent victims (including child victims) were but a fraction of those piled high on the Arab side of the barricades, who had been crushed beneath the wheels of Israel's illegal occupations for decades.[217] By the Intifada's end, in 2005, it has been estimated that 4,789 Palestinian Arabs had lost their lives (including 982 children) along with 1,000 Israeli Jews (including 119 children).[218] Since 2000 (the second Intifada's start), 2,120 Palestinian children have been killed by Israeli soldiers or settlers, whereas 134 Israeli Jewish children have been killed as a result of civilian attacks by Palestinian or Islamic militants.[219]

Terrorism and the militias

Even outside and beyond the Intifadas, modes of Palestinian resistance have generally become increasingly militarized, with guerrilla-style violence assuming centre-stage and becoming a kind of "low-intensity" constant. This is especially since the end of the first Intifada, which saw civilian demonstrations violently dispersed. The more recent period has witnessed the resort to terrorist tactics enacted by the various paramilitary organizations (bombings, sniper shootings, suicide attacks, kidnappings, hijackings, hostage-taking, assassinations, mortar and rocket attacks) aimed at civilian and military targets in the occupied territories and across the border in Israel. These have been conducted under the auspices of the radical splinters of the PLO and Fatah, as well as by Islamic Jihad and Hamas.[220]

This pattern of sporadic low-intensity guerrilla-style resistance has become normalized interspersed with sudden escalations of violence in response to triggers. This is as the prospects of a diplomatic solution have all but disappeared faced with the unfeasibility of a "conventional" civilian or military liberation struggle as this founders on the radical power asymmetry of the two sides and the willingness of the Israeli state to use military violence as a first resort to quell "disturbances" of all hues and types. On the scale of human rights, Jewish and Arab lives are of equal currency. All lives matter. But, under the Israeli state's *realpolitik*, only Jewish lives appear to matter. This incentivizes Hamas's cross-border incursions into Israel to take some of those Jewish lives, blameless or otherwise, in order to sow fear and alarm into Israel's Jews, so that they might pressurize their leaders to cut a deal.

What of the most recent flashpoints before the present war? A large-scale 2014 cross-border skirmish between Hamas and the Israeli military killed 73 Jews and 2,251 Palestinians (1,462 of them civilians and 551 of them children)[221] before a ceasefire was brokered by Egypt.[222] As always, the escalation from low-intensity repression and violence to high-intensity repression and violence had trigger events—in this case the kidnapping and murder of a Palestinian teenager by colonial settlers in revenge for the abduction and murder (perhaps by Hamas militants) of a couple of their own. The murder provoked incidents of stone-throwing by Palestinian youths and the inevitable security clampdown.[223] In the spring of 2018, Israeli soldiers opened fire with live rounds on mostly peacefully demonstrating Palestinians in response to a few stone-throwing youths at the Gaza-Israel border, killing 183 protestors and injuring in excess of 6,000.[224] This fuelled another major if brief (24 hours) skirmish between Hamas and the IDF in August of that year.[225] Rocket-launching into Israel was, as always, met with warplanes, bombs, shells, and missiles going the other way.

The next and last major flare-up of cross-border violence between Israel and Hamas before Israel's current full-scale invasion of Gaza took place in May of 2021. Hamas launched another round of missile attacks into Israel that were met with artillery bombardments of military targets and civilian infrastructure.[226] This was the culmination of a build-up of tensions in East Jerusalem in response to evictions of Palestinians from their homes to make way for Jewish settlers. As usual, Palestinian peaceful protests (legal challenges, sit-ins, demonstrations) were of no avail in shifting the course of events as the most recent property-grabs were legalized.[227] The usual heavy-handed security response to the protests (involving the use of water cannon, rubber bullets, and stun grenades) led to the usual outbreak of skirmishes that left hundreds of Palestinians injured.[228] This of course led to the escalation of protest and of its repression by colonial authority, including as always the deployment of lethal violence.[229]

Fatah and Hamas

Palestinian resistance over this period has also factionalized and splintered, with Hamas and Fatah vying for control of the movement and for popular support among the displaced peoples, with outbreaks of violence between the two organizations. The basis of the antagonism was the PLO leaders' continued commitment to the "peace process" under the terms of the Oslo Accords (despite their failure to deliver a settlement) and Hamas's rejection of them as tokenistic and demobilizing of the liberation movement in favour of renewed armed struggle against Israel. This conflict eventually led to Hamas's ousting of the PLO's Fatah-controlled PA in Gaza, so that today Hamas "runs" Gaza whereas the PLO-backed, Fatah-dominated PA "runs" the West Bank, though episodic (if tokenistic) efforts are made by both parties to restore the alliance.[230]

The basis of this split was Hamas's decisive (and for Israel and the West) unexpected victory over Fatah in the Palestinian Legislative Election of 2006.[231] This, according to international observers, was a free and fair election,[232] despite the fact that the Israeli security forces reportedly prevented Hamas from campaigning in or their supporters voting in East Jerusalem,[233] and arrested and detained many of its candidates and campaign workers.[234] The victory entitled Hamas to form and lead the next government of occupied Palestine. However, Hamas was reluctant to do this alone, instead attempting to coax Fatah into a Hamas-led national government.[235] This was in a fruitless attempt to head-off crippling Israeli and "international community" (i.e. US-led Western) sanctions intended to collectively punish the Palestinian electorate for making the "wrong" choice at the polls, destabilize the new authority, and undermine its popular support.[236] These sanctions included withholding of customs receipts and tax revenues and withdrawal of foreign aid.[237] Even more precipitously, Israel and Egypt restored their economic blockade of Gaza (implemented in 2005 as a supposedly anti-terrorism policy), curtailing the movement of workers and goods in and out of the Strip, causing unemployment and destitution to skyrocket.[238] The blockade has continued to this day, with relentlessly devastating effects on people's livelihoods in Gaza.[239]

But Fatah declined the offer of unity government, so that Hamas was forced to go it alone. Instead, Fatah embarked on a campaign of obstruction, including public sector strikes and violence, to undermine the new administration.[240] This was doubtless motivated by the idea that undermining Hamas in office would restore their own electoral fortunes and win enough favour from Israel, the USA, and the "international community" to end or reduce the blockade and other sanctions. Tit-for-tat violence between the two sides escalated until tentative agreement was reached in February 2007 to form a national unity government to arrest the deteriorating economic and security situation.[241] But this collapsed within four months, owing to Fatah's plot (in collaboration with Washington—which was to provide arms and training) to stage a coup to depose the Hamas-led government and replace it with an emergency one.[242] Fighting broke out between cadres of both sides in Gaza in June 2007, with Hamas prevailing and seizing control of all government offices and purging these of Fatah members and supporters.[243] Such has led to the partition of the occupied territories between Hamas-run Gaza and the Fatah-run West Bank and the overall dilution of the liberation movement that remains pertinent to this day.

But the deeper historical cause of this rupture between Fatah and Hamas that has further weakened the Palestinian cause was the PLO leaders' disastrous decision under the Oslo Accords to assume the role of policing the occupied territories on behalf of the occupying power in order to demonstrate its "fitness" to govern (hence clamping down on protest and cooperating with the Israeli security forces to stamp out armed resistance). This de-legitimized the PLO and Fatah for many Palestinians and boosted support for Hamas and the armed struggle, especially among the young radicals. This also enabled Israel and the USA to exploit the situation by recognizing only the PA under the PLO in the West Bank as lawful (in order to widen the split between the two), and to legitimize the stepping up of cross-border military operations in Gaza against Hamas, as well as the joint Israeli-Egyptian economic blockade of the Strip, with lesser risk of this inciting unrest in the West Bank.[244]

Delegitimization strategies

At the same time, the resort of Palestinian radicals of various militias to acts of violence against Jewish citizens has helped the Israeli state and its US backer to delegitimize the Palestinian resistance, hence weakening international support for the Palestinian cause. This is by representing this as the artifice of fanatical Jihadists, not so far removed from the likes of Al-Qaeda and ISIS, driven by murderous anti-Jewry, and set on establishing another Islamic autocracy.[245] This has allowed the watchdog state to legitimize at home and in the West its cross-border military operations that are intended to disable or destroy these organizations (and others such as the militant Shia Muslim Hezbollah group, which chased the Israeli army out of Lebanon in 2000,[246] ending the occupation there). This is by representing these campaigns as integral to the global war on terrorism in defence of liberal democracy.[247] Israel's cloaking of its colonial project as anti-terrorism is part of its ongoing campaign to undermine popular support for the Palestinian cause in the battleground of world opinion.[248]

This campaign has been accompanied by another that is worthy of note. This is one that is waged in the world of definitions and classifications. This is a police move in ideology to establish the supposed identity of anti-Zionism with antisemitism before the court of world opinion. This conflation of the two concepts has even been slipped into the IHRA's definition of antisemitism, which has been endorsed by a large number of governments, political parties, NGOs, and other institutions across the world. This declares that "denying the Jewish people their right to self-determination . . . by claiming that the existence of a State of Israel is a racist endeavor" would be antisemitic. Indeed, of 11 examples of antisemitic behaviour listed as part of the definition, this is one of seven which refer, whether directly or obliquely, to criticisms that might be made of the Israeli state.[249]

This is simply untenable. In the abstract world, denying any people their right of self-determination is oppressive and discriminatory. So, of course, the Jews have the right to self-determine. This is the case in the realm of ideals. But this has no bearing on the rightness or wrongness of how that right was exercised by Israel's founders in practice. Could it not have been realized in a multi-ethnic Palestinian state (rather than in an Israeli state), which was inclusive of Jews and Arabs? Why, in other words, did it require *Zionism*? Or why, to put it differently, did it require a specifically *colonial-settler* state in Palestine? Moreover, if it did require such a state, what entitled this right to prevail over the right to self-determination of the majority Arab population of Palestine who were expunged or expelled to make room for it? As has rightly been pointed out by Palestinian critics, the IHRA definition

> does not bother to recognise that under international law, the current state of Israel has been an occupying power for over half a century, as recognised by the governments of countries where the IHRA definition is being upheld. It does not bother to consider whether this right includes the right to create a Jewish majority by way of ethnic cleansing and whether it should be balanced against the rights of the Palestinian people. Furthermore, the IHRA definition potentially discards as antisemitic all non-Zionist visions of the future of the Israeli state, such as the advocacy of a binational state or a secular democratic one that represents all its citizens equally.[250]

Now, if this right to self-determine did not require Zionism to bring it about, the Jews of Israel would not have been divested of it if they had been denied *that* kind of state. Nor is it clear that the right of the Jews to self-determine established the moral case for *any* kind of *exclusive* political state for Jews. Why is there an automatic right to exercise sovereignty over a territory that was voluntarily abandoned in the premodern period for pastures anew by those who would claim it centuries later? By what right is that sovereignty exercised on behalf of a specific ethno-religious group in a land that was hitherto multi-ethnic? A principal example of the IHAR's definition of antisemitism is therefore, in my view, groundless. But, even if this were not so, there is another case to answer.

For, whether or not the state of Israel was conceived as a racial endeavour and continues to be one, this is a matter that can only be settled by history, not by assertive prejudgements—and there is certainly a historical case to answer. To deny that case on the grounds that Israel is a homeland for Jews whereas Jews have been and continue to be the victims of antisemitism appears as less than rational. Are victims of racism exempted from perpetrating racism? On this logic (that of setting aside history in order to avoid confronting power), would for example claiming that apartheid South Africa was a racial state also, by default, be racist? If not, is the difference between the two cases (colonial Israel versus apartheid South Africa) simply a matter of degree of oppression of a subordinate people—that is, such that under apartheid in South Africa black people were denied the vote whereas in Zionist Israel the Palestinian-Arabs are not? As I have shown, even Israel's Palestinian citizens are discriminated against by the state in all walks of life. In the none-too-distant past they have also been denied the vote.

This example of antisemitism thus arbitrarily claims exemption for Israel from the colonial record. This is indeed exceptionalism, since no one disputes that colonialism and the racism of empire is historically real, and exemptions are not claimed on behalf of other former colonial powers—such as the European ones. Since Israeli settler colonialism is real, and is undoubtedly animated by racial politics, this example of antisemitism would actually delegitimize virtually all academic work that has been critical of Israel. As Muhannad Ayyash rightly points out:

> The list of academic articles and books that would become anti-Semitic if we accepted this example is . . . astounding. It would include the writings of Hannah Arendt, Edward Said, Gilles Deleuze, Judith Butler, Joseph Massad, Achille Mbembe, Robert Wolfe, Angela Davis, Hamid Dabashi, Audra Simpson and many others. In fact, an entire academic journal, Settler Colonial Studies, would have to be removed from all of our libraries.[251]

Indeed, if one were to generalize the example, by reframing this as pertaining to racism rather than antisemitism, hence as a statement about any state that has practised colonialism, this would delegitimize as well indigenous studies and critical race theory.

This example of antisemitism even contradicts another of the IAHR's examples. This is the one that sees antisemitism lying in "applying double standards by requiring of it [Israel] behavior not expected or demanded of any other democratic nation". So, Israel's settler-colonial racism is perhaps real, after all, but Israel should not be put in the dock over this *realpolitik* because other nations have been sinners as well. Racism *in general*, on this logic, renders criticism of Israel's *specific* racism as antisemitic! As Ayyash puts it:

> By stating in the first example that no one shall point out the racist endeavour that underpins the Israeli state, it actually applies a different standard to the Israeli state. The first example dissolves the very equality of standards that this second example is alleging to promote.[252]

This is nonsense, of course. There would be double standards only if the critic of Israel's colonialism excused colonialism in countries other than Israel. I, for one, would require of any democratic nation that it does not practise colonial occupation, or unleash military assaults on civilian targets, or place a whole territory under blockade, when those who are under occupation resist, or discriminate internally on grounds of race or ethnicity or religion. I would also require any democratic nation to obey international law.

Nonetheless, despite these issues, Hugh Tomlinson is perhaps right in his legal judgement that

> understood in its own terms the IHRA Definition does not mean that activities such as describing Israel as a state enacting a policy of apartheid, as practising settler colonialism or calling for policies of boycott divestment or sanctions against Israel can properly be characterized as antisemitic.[253]

However, this is true in the world of logic but not in the world of politics. The main problem with the IHRA definition is that, owing to its lack of clarity or precision in its examples, together with its over-preoccupation with defence of the state of Israel, it licenses authorities to censure or suppress legitimate criticism of Israel, and operates to delegitimize support for the Palestinian people (whose own rights to self-determination are denied by Israel). This is as part of a strategy of risk-avoidance that is corrosive of free speech. This has also emboldened Israeli politicians, campaigners, and organizations allied to the Israeli state to agitate, successfully, for the adaptation of the definition worldwide, by governments, political parties, and public bodies of all kinds, despite its limitations.

Not so much in the drafting of the IHRA definition, therefore, but rather in the manner of its political appropriation; this is testament to the role of power (i.e. of the strategic alignment of the interests of the US and Israeli states that emboldens the pro-Israel lobby internationally) in ensuring the IHRA definition's global pre-eminence. This is shown by the fact that in the process, other, better, clearer, non-politized, non-partisan definitions of antisemitism were sidelined, including those proposed by internationally renowned Jewish scholars, such as the Nexus Document (ND) and the Jerusalem Declaration on Antisemitism (JDA). This was almost certainly because these did not represent anti-Zionism as anti-Jewish, and therefore could not be used to legitimize Israel and de-legitimize its critics.[254]

The IHRA definition may be interpreted as the ill-judged work of well-meaning liberals whose work has been shamelessly exploited by powerholders in the service of the US–Israeli alliance. But this would not quite fit the facts. The Bucharest Plenary that supposedly agreed on what became the IHRA definition (including its 11 examples of antisemitism) did not in fact agree on the illustrations, only on the definition. Yet spokespersons of the IHRA thereafter proceeded as if the examples were agreed at the Plenary, in disregard of the fact. The definition, then, is not actually the IHRA's in a certain sense but one that has been falsified by Israel-sympathizers inside and outside the IHRA. The IHRA definition was thus politicized from the start, and was subsequently weaponized by pro-Israeli powerholders and opinion-formers worldwide.[255]

Futures and prospects

A fundamental aspect of the neoimperial order is the perpetuation of what may be termed as *surveillance states*. Situated in areas that are of key geostrategic or economic importance to the Western Alliance, these states are bankrolled by the US state to act as counterweights to local forces that might upset the present emergent asymmetrical distribution of political powers and economic resources in global systems. Of these surveillance states, Israel has been, and will remain for the foreseeable future, the most important. As Phil Marshall rightly says, this particular watchdog is unique among modern nation-states, in that it is the only one that "has been established by means of the expropriation of an entire people".[256] Such explains the intractability and incorrigibility of the so-called Israeli-Palestinian conflict and its systematic misrepresentation by powerholders and opinion-formers in the West. The interests of the dispossessed Palestinian Arab population for redress and for justice (the restoration of stolen lands and livelihoods—and for an autonomous state) simply cannot be accommodated within the present neoimperial order of international relations under US hegemony.

Israel's cheerleaders certainly perfectly understand the dependence of Israel's Zionist project on US power and patronage. As one of these, Freilich, rightly says:

> Among the world powers, only the United States seeks to promote a settlement with the Palestinians on terms that are acceptable to most of Israel's population. No other state so consistently supports Israel's demands for security and recognition as the nation-state of the Jewish people, and its opposition to the so called "right of return". No other power so consistently defends Israel in almost every international organization and leads the battle against its delegitimization and diplomatic isolation. We saw how the great heroes in Jerusalem trembled when the United States merely abstained recently from a non-binding Security Council resolution on the settlements.[257]

Indeed. This is why the dispossession of the Palestinian indigenes (and their perpetual daily humiliation at the hands of colonial power) continues decade after decade alongside mild rebukes for Israeli settlement policy and the ritual of non-sanctions from the UN as these are vetoed by the USA and Britain. This is why the Intifadas and the other flare-ups and their violent suppressions repeat their cycles. This is why the present war will not be the last.

This is also why the conflict is represented by liberal-left opinion in the West in a "balanced" or "even-handed" way; that is, as one prosecuted by crazed fanatics on both sides. Or, more commonly, it is represented by Western liberals as prosecuted by fanatics on one side—that is, by the terrorists of Hamas and its predecessors, with their bombings and kidnappings and murders, motivated by visceral religious or racial hatred—which then incite the retaliation of intemperate, albeit justifiably enraged, state authority. (Naturally, of course, state violence against often civilian targets can never be acts of terrorism—not if the state in question is a key ally. The term is to be reserved for non-state actors that the West disapproves of.) Moreover, this is why the conflict is simultaneously ideologized by more right-wing opinion as a straightforward struggle between good and evil (in which the unfortunate Palestinian civilians are caught up in the crossfire), so that the Israeli state response to the wicked terrorists may be considered as at worst "heavy-handed" and "counterproductive". Thus, "caution" is urged, as the tanks and bulldozers and blockades do their work, although its disregard would be understandable and forgivable under the circumstances.

Are there solutions? The most obvious one—the resurgence of a project of Arab pan-nationalism (or pan-Arabism) by governments in the Middle East and beyond—has proven elusive. This project has melted away since the demise of Nasserism in Egypt. A unified Arab bloc straddling the larger part of the world's energy supplies would be able to exert huge pressure on the USA to reign-in its watchdog so that at last Israeli leaders are incentivized to entertain a two-state solution that would be acceptable to Palestinian leaders and enter into negotiations in good faith. A meaningful diplomatic process that aims to deliver a real two-state deal would either reduce the influence of radical Islamism in Palestine (which formally commits to a single multi-ethnic Palestinian state in place of Israel) or moderate it by bringing its supporters onside with the two-state solution.

This would be beneficial to the Jews of Palestine, indeed Jews everywhere, not simply the Palestinian Arabs, because it would dampen down on antisemitic passions in the Arab world and more generally, weaken the securitization agenda of Israeli leaders that has fuelled their racial politics and given this popular appeal, and render Israeli Jews much less vulnerable to violent attacks from disaffected supporters of Palestinian or other militias. A strong sense of pan-Arab unity certainly exists at the level of the Arab street. But this has foundered on the rock of interstate rivalries and intrigues among Arab political leaders and on US patronage of the key players (especially of the Gulf states and Egypt) in order to establish their ruling elites as allies.

In the absence of pan-Arab unity at the level of statecraft the solution to the conflict must seemingly come from within Israel itself—or from popular pressure exerted on American leaders from within the USA to reconfigure their relationship with Israel. Neither peaceful civil protest nor violent resistance (whether against military targets or civilians) from within Palestine will make a difference for the foreseeable future. Palestinian resistance to the occupation has often degenerated into organized or militarized acts of violence (terrorism) against civilian targets, indeed sometimes random and disorganized acts of violence, because of the failure of other strategies. These other strategies have failed because they are faced with the intransigence of a militarized semi-apartheid state which is backed by a superpower with the acquiescence of its allies. They have failed also because the leaders of the Arab nations have set aside the project of pan-Arab unity and abandoned the Palestinians to their fate. This form of resistance is morally indefensible, of course. It can never be right to make war on civilians, to murder or kidnap non-combatants, in response to state violence. Not only that, but it will also not win a battle for favour in the court of international public opinion.

However, this type of political struggle is at least comprehensible, given the historical context. Moreover, it is, in a sense, rational as well, given the failure of purely military struggle and peaceful protest alike. For the leaders of Hamas, targeting Israeli civilians may eventually undermine popular support for Zionism in Israel, so that the country's leaders come under pressure to concede more than a rump state. Certainly, this would appear to stand a better chance of success than feeding its combatants to Israel's military machine. The West's demonization of Hamas as a terrorist organization pays scant attention to the fact that its own historic failure to confront Zionism in Israel and its consequential acquiescence to Israel's illegal occupation of Palestine has undermined the so-called peace process that would end this state of affairs by non-violent means. Those people drawn to Hamas have no reason by way of precedent to believe that methods other than acts of terrorism have any chance of delivering them from the colonial rule of Israel.

This perspective does not belong only to the militants of Hamas. Rather, this is widely shared by civilians in the occupied territories. This is the stark truth that the West will not admit because it offends liberal sensibilities and illusions. The failure of diplomacy—as well as the fact that non-violent and violent resistance to the occupation has elicited the same response from the Israeli state (i.e. violent repression)—explains why armed struggle that is waged within Israel's borders actually commands a much higher degree of popular support among the displaced peoples of Gaza and the West Bank than a return to the negotiating table or non-violent struggle.[258]

In most recent times, public support for armed resistance to the occupation among the commonfolk has risen to an all-time high, with 79 per cent of Palestinians saying that they are in favour of it (by June 2023),[259] up from 50 per cent just the year before. In 2007, by contrast, two-thirds of Gazans did not support military struggle against the Israeli occupation, and only 20 per cent were in favour of terrorist methods (kidnappings, targeting of civilians, etc.) of prosecuting the armed struggle.[260]

> Findings regarding the peace process indicate a significant decline in support for the two-state solution and a considerable rise in support for an armed intifada. They also show a significant rise in the perception that the two-state solution is no longer feasible due to settlement expansion in the West Bank.[261]

The hardening of public attitudes in Palestine is unsurprising, given the diplomatic games of the "international community" in the service of the US–Israeli alliance that are intended to reproduce the status quo.

Yet support for armed resistance against Israel is not the same thing as popular support for Hamas, or not to the same degree. In Gaza and the West Bank, and across Palestine generally, public approval of Hamas has waxed and waned over the past 15 years, just as it has for Fatah. This is partly due to the feuding between the parties, which has obstructed the cause of Palestinian unity. This is also perhaps owing to suspicions of corruption and cronyism in the administrative machinery of government (though these suspicions are mostly aimed at the Fatah-controlled PA).[262] Naturally, this is mostly attributable to the fact that neither Hamas nor Fatah has managed to improve the dire political and economic situation faced by ordinary Palestinians who crave peace and prosperity rather than endless conflict, poverty, and oppression.[263]

Even so, despite the terrible hardships inflicted on Gaza by the Israeli-Egyptian blockade since Hamas's takeover 16 years before, remarkably, 57 per cent of Gazans express a "somewhat positive" view of Hamas today.[264] Public support for Hamas also tends to peak during periods of military confrontation with Israel, just as it simultaneously dips for the PA's Fatah leaders who reject joining the armed resistance. This shows that the popular legitimacy of Hamas is tied to its commitment to armed struggle against the occupation.[265] Not only that, but there is also bigger and less equivocal public support in Gaza and the West Bank for other radical political organizations other than Hamas (notably, Palestinian Islamic Jihad and Lion's Den) that favour the military struggle over the (so far) illusory diplomatic remedies. "About three quarters of Gazans express support for both groups, including 40% who see the Lion's Den in a 'very positive' light, an attitude shared by a similar percentage of West Bank residents".[266]

> A clear majority of respondents told PCPSR [Palestinian Center for Policy and Survey Research] that they support the formation of armed groups that don't take orders from the PA and that are not part of the PA security forces, but numbers were higher in Gaza, where 84% of respondents backed the concept, than in the West Bank, where 65% supported the idea.[267]

Such is indicative of the de-legitimization of the Fatah-led PA by virtue of its co-option in the service of the policing functions of the occupying colonial power.

Hamas is dismissed and denigrated as terrorist by the USA and Israel in order to legitimize the utmost repression of the organization by the methods of state terrorism. Terrorism is thus sanctioned in the name of combatting terrorism. This is the meaning of the Western Alliance's mantra "we cannot negotiate with terrorists". But, as I have noted, Hamas retains much public support in Gaza, even if for many Gazans this support is accompanied by a critical view of the organization. Or, at least, Hamas retains what may be termed as the acquiescence of much of the Gazan public, despite the negative perceptions of many who accept the organization and its right to govern.

Prior to Fatah's US-backed coup attempt, Hamas ruled Gaza and the West Bank by virtue of popular-democratic mandate, which has not since been overturned by electoral means. So, dismissal and demonization of the organization is tantamount to dismissal and demonization of its supporters; that is, of *Palestinians*, since many of these after all support Hamas. This allows the Zionists to conflate in their propaganda Hamas activists, Hamas supporters, and other Palestinian civilians, all of whom become diabolical or potentially diabolical, so that all can be treated as unpeople. This then licenses the Israeli state's severe and indiscriminate deployment of force in the occupied territories on combatants and non-combatants alike (including collective punishments such as the economic blockade, cutting off humanitarian aid or water or electrical supplies, and destruction of homes and civilian facilities) when faced with Palestinian resistance to its colonial order.[268]

None of this is new, of course. Israel's first prime minister, David Ben-Gurion, proposed exactly terrorism to win Zionism's war to expropriate the Arabs of Palestine in 1948. As he put it: "If we know the family, strike mercilessly, women and children included. . . . At the place of action there is no need to distinguish between guilty and innocent".[269] Terrorism, then, was at the root of the Israeli colonial state. These were the foundations on which it was built. And so it has continued. Arab terrorism in Palestine—such as that of Hamas and the other Palestinian militias—is made by Israel. Indeed, Israeli terrorism-backed colonialism in the occupied territories is not only the source of Palestinian terrorism, but it is by far the single biggest source of antisemitism in Palestine, in the Arab world, and internationally. So, if US and Western leaders were serious about combatting antisemitism worldwide, as they claim to be, they would be looking to reign-in Zionism rather than assiduously supporting and cultivating it.

But, of course, Western powerholders are not serious about confronting global antisemitism. Rather, they are committed to playing the "race card" in order to suppress a politics of opposition to the injustices meted out by Israeli state racism. Yet, for Israel's leaders, state terrorism has always been legitimized on the grounds that it is reactive or retaliatory. Such, for them, is necessary to deter terrorism. Consequently, before Hamas, the PLO was also dismissed as a terror organization, for the same reasons, and with the same results. And if Hamas were to fall, any successor political organization of the Palestinians committed to resisting the occupation would meet with the same fate. This is necessary because Zionism will never concede a Palestinian state, so that each and every political organization of the Palestinians that seeks to win one must be cast beyond the negotiating table.

Now, if there is to be an end to the conflict, such would seem to depend on a sea-change in public attitudes in Israel towards the Palestinian cause, even if this is most likely to be motivated by a kind of war-weariness from the perpetual cycle of conflict, so that the Israeli state is placed under systematic pressure to step back from the imperial-colonial path it has embraced from the point of its origin. There is even evidence that such sentiments are gaining some leverage in Israel. According to a poll conducted in 2011, for example, 58 per cent of Israeli Jews were in favour of Bill Clinton's (2001) version of two-state solution to the conflict compared to 47 per cent in 2003, whereas 70 per cent of them wanted to see the end of violence, up from 58 per cent a few years before. The same poll revealed much less support for the Clinton proposals among Palestinians, however, for obvious reasons.[270] Any two-state solution must grant the Palestinians more than the crumbs of a rump state.

Nonetheless, this perhaps is utopia, for the foreseeable future. This is owing to the emergent structural constraints of world politics under which Israel's leaders shelter, the economic and other privileges bestowed on Jews in Israel by the colonial history of the Israeli state, and the tenacious grip of the state-orchestrated racialized politics of fear in Israel. A major shift of Jewish public attitudes in Israel away from Zionism must confront the barriers imposed on popular consciousness (institutional and ideological) by Zionism itself. Israel's parliamentary democracy is degraded by virtue of being suffused by ethnic settler nationalism, which pervades and degrades the electoral process. This also pervades the Israeli press. Parliamentary politics in Israel has from the start been dominated by Zionist parties—those espousing either revisionist Zionism, or Labour Zionism, or religious Zionism.[271] This is why the democratic process continually recycles governments led by hawkish, belligerent nationalists committed to the colonial project. And this is why no Arabian-Palestinian party, or party supporting Israel's return to its pre-1967 borders, has ever made it into coalition government in Israel.[272] Such partly accounts for the Economic Intelligence Unit's recent classification (in 2022) of Israel as a "flawed democracy".[273]

Israel is not Zionist because such is a spontaneous outgrowth of Jewish public opinion. Rather, Israeli politics and media relentlessly cultivate attitudes favourable to Zionism in the popular mind. This is by marginalizing dissenting views, fear-mongering on the terrain of the securitization agenda, and demonization of the Arab street as implacably antisemitic. Such also extends to the state the capacity to crack-down on dissent among those Israeli Jews who oppose Israel's colonial occupations, or its violent suppression of Palestinian resistance, or its disregard of Palestinian civilian lives in its attempts to crush that resistance, without this generating widespread public outrage. The pattern is evident since the start of the current crisis. This is shown by the *de facto* curtailment in Israel of pro-Palestinian protests under threat of a zero-tolerance policing response.[274] This is also exposed by the political persecution of Palestinian-Israelis and Jewish Palestinian-sympathizers by other methods on the basis of their social media messaging or their expressing "likes" for the messages of others. These include summonses to disciplinary hearings, suspensions from university or college courses, dismissals from employment, late-night arrests involving unnecessary force on suspicion of "aiding the enemy" or "supporting terrorism", and so on.[275]

The postings in question do not condone or exonerate Hamas's cross-border attacks on Israeli civilians. Rather, they express disapproval of Israel's response to those attacks. To no avail. As Nareman Shehadeh-Zoabi, general director of the Israel-based independent human rights organization Adalah (Justice), reports:

> Any expression of solidarity with the Palestinian civilian victims, opposing the war on Gaza, or calling it a war crime is being perceived as support for terror or a terrorist organization. . . . These arrests and measures indicate that all institutions are now implementing the policy of [Israel's National Security Minister . . .] Ben Gvir, who sees Arab citizens as enemies. I can't make any distinction between Ben Gvir and the police, the attorney general, and the universities.[276]

Zionism's politics of fear-mongering and hate-mongering on the terrain of securitization is thus a powerful force short-circuiting popular support in Israel for the Palestinian cause—and perhaps this is an insuperable barrier to Jewish-Palestinian solidarity in Israel. If so, this begs the question: in the absence of popular pressure from within Israel to settle the Palestinian question, are there other possibilities?

As I have said, one of these could be popular pressure from within the USA to defund the Israeli military, as this is confronted with the horrors of state violence against Palestinian civilians that has characterized its responses to the Intifadas and the militias. Such may conceivably gain some traction looking ahead. This is because, as Israel's economic autonomy from the USA grows, this may cause its actions in the occupied territories to manifest a growing tendency to become more ruthless and brutal than they have been before. The Israeli state's prosecution of the present war in Gaza hardly confounds this possibility. Indeed, this raises the spectre of ethnic cleansing on a massive scale, if the Zionists were to decide to expel the Palestinians from the occupied territories altogether. Is Zionism capable of such a move? Yes, of course. The current war in Gaza may be about just that.[277] But if such a policy was enacted (or is being enacted), it might dramatically shift American public attitudes against Israel.

Yet any upsurge of popular pressure within the USA to reign-in the Israeli state will run into the buffers of US imperial policy (as this is embraced by both Republican and Democratic statespersons), a pro-Zionist corporate media, and the organized power of the pro-Israeli lobby in US politics that permeates all institutions.[278] As such, the "solution" may, alas, have to wait either for a dramatic resetting of global political economy—such as would be generated by the decline of US hegemony faced with the growing challenge of China perhaps—or even the drying-up of the Middle East's oilfields that would disincentivize the US state's interests in the preservation of a Zionist state in Palestine rather than a genuinely multicultural one for Jews and Arabs. Even so, the power of the pro-Israeli lobby in US politics will remain a force to be reckoned with, even in a resource-depleted world.

Notes and references

1 France 24 (2023). 'Israel Social Security Data Reveals True Picture of Oct 7 Deaths'. (15 December). Lurid media stories sowed by the Israeli authorities of Hamas militants murdering babies have since been shown to be unsupported, however.
2 UNRWA (2023). 'Where We Work'. UNRWA (online). (August).
3 UNOCHA (2023). 'Hostilities in the Gaza Strip and Israel'. Flash Update #69. OCHA (online). (14 December).
4 UN (2023). 'Israel-Palestine crisis: First evacuations from Gaza; outrage grows over refugee camp strikes. UN News (online)'. (2 November)
5 UNRWA (2022). 'Palestinian Refugees'. UNRWA (online).
6 HRW (2023). 'Israel: Starvation Used as Weapon of War in Gaza'. HRW (online). (18 December).
7 Farge, E. (2023). 'UN Agencies Voice Anger at Gaza Hospital Attacks, Deprivation'. Reuters (online). (19 December).
8 HRW (2023).
9 UN (2023). 'Gaza: UN Experts Call on International Community to Prevent Genocide Against the Palestinian People'. UNHROHC (online). Press release. (16 November).
10 Sherwood, H. (2023). '"Hugely Frustrating": International Media Seek to Overcome Gaza Ban'. Guardian (online). (12 December); Middle East Monitor (2023). 'Foreign Press Association Petitions Israel Supreme Court to Allow Journalists into Gaza'. MEM (online). (21 December).
11 McGreal, C. (2023). 'Israeli Military Accused of Targeting Journalists and Their Families in Gaza'. Guardian (online). (21 December); Reuters (2023). 'Gaza War "Most Dangerous Ever" for Journalists, Says Rights Group'. (19 December).
12 Cited in McGreal (2023).
13 CPJ (2023a). 'Israel-Gaza War Takes Record Toll on Journalists'. CPJ (online). (21 December).
14 CPJ (2023b). 'Father of Al-Jazeera's Anas Al-Sharif Killed in Gaza After Journalist Receives Threats'. CPJ (online). (11 December).
15 CPJ (2023a).
16 Farrell, P. and Smith, J. (2023). 'Israel Demands Answers from CNN, Associated Press, Reuters and The New York Times over Claims Freelance Photographers

"Embedded" with Hamas to Cover October 7th Attack'. Daily Mail (online). (9 November).

17 Cited in McGreal (2023).

18 Attiah, K. (2023). 'Where Is the Outrage Over Israel's Killing of Journalists in Gaza?'. Washington Post (online). (18 December).

19 UN (2023). 'Israel-Gaza Crisis: US Vetoes Security Council Resolution'. UN News (online). (18 October); Wintour, P. (2023). 'US Defies Appeals to Back UN Resolution for Urgent Gaza Ceasefire'. Guardian (online). (8 December); Gordon, H. (2023). 'U.S. Is Called Out Over Voting Against Gaza Ceasefire During the U.N. General Assembly'. Time (online). (13 December); Smith, D. (2023). 'Joe Biden's Reluctance to Call for Ceasefire May Leave Him at Odds with His Party'. Guardian (online). (22 December).

20 Beaumont, H. (2023). 'Protesters Block US Military Ship Allegedly Carrying Weapons for Israel'. Al-Jazeera (online). (7 November); Hammer, M. (2023). 'What to Know about U.S. Military Support for Israel's Gaza Offensive'. Time (online). (3 November).

21 Lederer, E.M. (2023). 'US Vetoes UN Resolution Backed by Many Nations Demanding Immediate Humanitarian Ceasefire in Gaza'. Associated Press (online). (9 December).

22 Article 54(1) of the First Additional Protocol to the Geneva Conventions (Protocol I) and article 14 of the Second Additional Protocol (Protocol II).

23 International Humanitarian Law Databases (1987). Protocol Additional to the Geneva Conventions of 12 August 1949, and relating to the Protection of Victims of International Armed Conflicts (Protocol I), 8 June 1977. Article 54: Protection of objects indispensable to the survival of the civilian population. ICRC: IHL Treaties (online). Accessed: 8/12/23.

24 HRW (2023).

25 Malik, N. (2023). 'As Gaza Is Bombed and Starved, the Arab World Is Watching—and it's Angry'. Guardian (online). (22 October).

26 McKernan, B. and Taha, S. (2023). '"The West Bank Will Ignite": Israel's Operations Spark Anger in the Territory'. Guardian (online). (24 October).

27 Anon (2023). '"Unparalleled": Israeli Army Raids Ramallah, More Occupied West Bank Cities'. Al-Jazeera (online). (28 December).

28 Mustafa, T. (2023). 'With All Eyes on Gaza, Israel Tightens Its Grip on the West Bank'. International Crisis Group (online). (24 November).

29 Sly, L. (2023). 'Creeping Escalation along Israel-Lebanon Border Brings Risk of Bigger War'. Washington Post (online). (19 November).

30 US Central Command (2023). 'Houthi Attacks on Commercial Shipping in International Water Continue'. Press release. (3 December); Turak, N. (2023). 'Houthi Attacks Rocking Red Sea Trade Routes Likely Won't End Anytime Soon. Here's What Could Happen Next'. CNBC (online). (21 December).

31 Michaelis, T. and Chen, H. (2023). 'Israel Ready to Act against Houthi Rebels if International Community Fails to, National Security Adviser Says'. CNN (online). (10 December).

32 Sharp, J.M. (2020). US Foreign Aid to Israel. Congressional Research Service. Report RL33222. (16 November).

33 Cited in Rose, J. (2003). Israel: The Hijack State. 3rd edition. London: Larkham Publishing, p. 6.

34 Rose (2003), p. 6.

35 Rose (2003), p. 20.

36 Sharp (2020), pp. ii, 2.

37 Freilich, C. (2017). Israel's Dependence on the United States Is Existential. Belfer Center for Science and International Affairs, Harvard Kennedy School. (7 February).
38 Sharp (2020), pp. 2–3.
39 Frelich, C. (2018). 'Has Israel Grown Too Dependent on the United States?'. Mosaic (online). (5 February).
40 Fisher, M. (2021). 'As Israel's Dependence on U.S. Shrinks, So Does U.S. Leverage'. New York Times. (24 May). However, Fisher rather overstates the degree of economic autonomy that Israel has obtained from the USA.
41 Freilich (2017).
42 Freilich (2018).
43 Freilich (2017).
44 Sharp (2020), p. 8.
45 Sharp (2020), p. ii.
46 Sharp (2020), p. ii.
47 Freilich (2017).
48 Freilich (2017).
49 Israel now ranks internationally 28th for GDP per capita income. "From 1985 to today, the Israeli economy grew by a factor of ten, as it expanded from agriculture to computer circuitry, biotechnology, pharmaceuticals, and aviation and communications products". Fisher, M. (2012). 'Here's a List of Countries with a Higher GDP Per Capita Than Israel'. Atlantic (online). (31 July).
50 As Sharp (2020, p. 31) explains: "Since 1973, Israel has received grants from the State Department's Migration and Refugee Assistance account to assist in the resettlement of migrants to Israel. Funds are paid to the United Israel Appeal, a private philanthropic organization in the United States, which in turn transfers the funds to the Jewish Agency for Israel. Between 1973 and 1991, the United States gave about $460 million for resettling Jewish refugees in Israel. Annual amounts have varied from a low of $5 million to a high of $80 million, based at least partly on the number of Jews leaving the former Soviet Union and other areas for Israel". A total of $58.4 million of US funds were issued to Israel under the scheme between 2012 and 2018. With the collapse of the Soviet bloc, many Russian Jews wished to emigrate to the USA. Acting on behalf of Israel, the US state refused their visa applications en masse, so that the influx of Russian Jews was redirected to Israel, where many would be resettled in the occupied territories.
51 Australian Jewish News (2020). 'Global Jewish Population Hits 14.7 Million'. Australian Jewish News (online). (21 April).
52 World Population Review (2021). 'Arab Countries 2021'. WPR (online).
53 Shah, S. (2020). '30 Countries, Including Pakistan, Still Do Not Recognise Israel'. News: International (online). (22 August). This has since reduced to 28, on my count.
54 Weinstock, N. (1979). Zionism: False Messiah. East Troy MA: Inklink; Bonds, J. et al. (1977). Our Roots Are Still Alive. San Francisco CA: People's Press, pp. 20–1, 24, 25–6.
55 Gil, M. (1997). A History of Palestine, 634–1099. Cambridge: Cambridge University Press, pp. 291–4.
56 Jewish Virtual Library (2021). 'Pre-State Israel: Under Ottoman Rule (1517–1917)'. JVL (online).
57 The point needs to be stressed because conflation of Jewishness and Zionism has become a political strategy of supporters and allies of the latter to deem any critique

of the state of Israel as racist without having to demonstrate this is the case. I will return to this issue later.

58 Quoted in Rose (2003), p. 36.
59 Weinstock (1979), p. 12.
60 Brenner, L. (1983). Zionism in the Age of the Dictators: A Reappraisal. Beckenham: On Our Own Authority.
61 Rose (2003), p. 40.
62 Rose (2003), pp. 40–1.
63 Australian Jewish News (2020). 'Global Jewish Population Hits 14.7 Million'. Australian Jewish News (online). (21 April).
64 Pew Research Centre (2016). 'Jewish Population by Country. Global Religious Futures Project'. Pew-Templeton (online); Sherwood, A. (2020). 'Europe's Jewish Population has Dropped 60% in Last 50 Years'. Guardian (online). (25 October). These statistics calculate Jewishness by religious affiliation. If based on ancestry (having a Jewish parent), the number would be much higher.
65 If the birth rate of Jews in the diaspora countries had not declined as they have since World War Two, as the birth rate of Jews in Israel has risen, Jewish non-nationals would outnumber Jewish nationals in far greater numbers.
66 Weizmann quoted in Bonds (1977), p. 29.
67 Kuiken, J. (2014). 'Caught in Transition: Britain's Oil Policy in the Face of Impending Crisis, 1967–1973'. Historical Social Research, 39 (4), pp. 272–90.
68 Sampson (1976), p. 72.
69 Black, E. (2004). Banking on Baghdad: Inside Iraq's 7,000-Year History of War, Profit, and Conflict. New York NY: John Wiley. See Ch.7; Kwarteng, K. (2012). Britain's Legacy in the Middle East: Iraq's Oil. Globalist. (24 February). 'Once Upon a Red Line—the Iraq Petroleum Company Story'. GEOEXPRO (online). (6 May); Paul, J.A. (2002). 'Great Power Conflict over Iraqi Oil: The World War 1 Era'. Global Policy Forum (online).
70 Sampson (1976), p. 77.
71 Quoted in Rose (2003), p. 38.
72 Cited in Cliff. T. (2000). A World to Win: Life of a Revolutionary. London: Bookmarks. Ch.1: 'Palestine'. See p. 15.
73 Mansfield, P. (1992). The Arabs. Harmondsworth: Penguin, pp. 172, 173, 174–5.
74 Quoted in Bonds (1977), p. 29.
75 Cliff (2000), pp. 8–21.
76 Rose (2003), p. 39.
77 Cliff (2000), p. 8.
78 Cited by Cliff (2000), pp. 8–9.
79 Cliff (2000), pp. 6–7.
80 Cliff (2000), p. 19.
81 Cliff (2000), pp. 12, 11.
82 Cliff (2000), p. 10.
83 Cliff (2000), p. 12.
84 Cliff (2000), p. 19.
85 Cited by Cliff (2000), p. 20.
86 Rose (2003), p. 44.
87 Chomsky (1983), p. 19.
88 Cited in Rose (2003), p. 21
89 Cited in Rose (2003), p. 21.
90 Sampson (1976), p. 245.

91 See Rose (2003), pp. 21–2.
92 UN (2016). 'Resolution 181 (II). Future Government of Palestine. A/RES/181(II). 29 November 1947'. UN (online). (18 October).
93 BBC News (2017). 'UN Partition of Palestine'. BBC (online).
94 Cliff (2000), p. 19.
95 Rose (2003), pp. 44–5.
96 Morris, B. (2008). 1948: A History of the First Arab-Israeli War. New Haven CT: Yale University Press, pp. 66–7, 68, 72.
97 UN (2008). The Question of Palestine and the United Nations. New York NY: UN, p. 9.
98 De Waart, P. (1994). Dynamics of Self-Determination in Palestine. Leiden: Brill, p. 138; Finkelstein, N. (2005). Beyond Chutzpah: On the Misuse of Antisemitism and the Abuse of History. Berkeley CA: University of California Press, p. 280; Flapan, S. (1988). The Birth of Israel: Myths and Realities. New York NY: Pantheon, pp. 8–9; Kamrava, M. (2011). The Modern Middle East: A Political History since the First World War. Berkeley CA: University of California Press, p. 83; Morris (2008), p. 75; McMahon, S.F. (2010). The Discourse of Palestinian-Israeli Relations. London: Routledge, p. 40; Masalha, N. (1992). Expulsion of the Palestinians: The Concept of 'Transfer' in Zionist Political Thought, 1882–1948. Institute for Palestine Studies (online), pp. 62, 107; Morris, B. (2011). Righteous Victims: A History of the Zionist-Arab Conflict, 1881–1998. New York NY: Knopf Doubleday, p. 138; Segev, T. (2000). One Palestine, Complete: Jews and the Arabs Under the British Mandate. New York NY: Henry Holt and Company; Rogan, E. (2012). The Arabs in History, 3rd edition. London: Penguin, p. 321; Shourideh C.M. (2014). Stateless Citizenship: The Palestinian-Arab Citizens of Israel. Leiden: Brill, p. 126; Slater, J. (1994). 'The Significance of Israeli Historical Revisionism'. R.A. Stone and W.P. Zenner (eds) Critical Essays on Israeli Social Issues and Scholarship. Vol. 3. New York NY: State University of New York (SUNY) Press, p. 182.
99 Masalha (1992), p. 62.
100 Morris (2011), p. 138.
101 Karsh, E. (2002). The Arab–Israeli Conflict—The Palestine War 1948. Oxford: Osprey Publishing, p. 30; Morris, B. (2004). The Birth of the Palestinian Refugee Problem Revisited. Cambridge: Cambridge University Press, pp. 65, 101; Morris (2008), p. 76; Pappe, I. (2006). 'The 1948 Ethnic Cleansing of Palestine'. Journal of Palestine Studies, 36 (1), pp. 6–20.
102 Gelber, Y. (2006). Palestine 1948. Brighton: Sussex Academic Press, pp. 24–6; Karsh (2002), pp. 35–8; Morris (2003), p. 163.
103 Karsch (2002), p. 30; Morris (2008), p. 76.
104 Hazkani, S. (2021). Dear Palestine: A Social History of the 1948 War. Redwood CA: Stanford University Press. See Ch.1.
105 Gelber (2008), p. 38; Laurens, H. (2007). La Question de Palestine. Vol. 3. Paris: Fayard, p. 33.
106 Morris, B. (2003). Histoire revisitée du conflict arabo-sioniste. Brussels: Editions Complexe, p. 240.
107 Initially, this was conceded even by pro-Zionist historians such as Danny Morris, who wanted an honest account of Israel's origins, backed by considerable evidence. But Morris later engaged in self-revisionism (whilst denying he was), in effect by claiming that ethnic cleansing would be an appropriate characterization of what happened in 1948 and 1949 in Palestine only if this was the pre-conceived policy of Israeli leaders, which he contended could not (despite Plan D) be proven. See: Hammond, J.R. (2016). 'Benny Morris's Untenable Denial of the Ethnic Cleansing of Palestine'. Foreign Policy Journal (online). (14 November). See also: Blatman,

D. (2016). 'Yes, Benny Morris, Israel Did Perpetrate Ethnic Cleansing in 1948'. Haaretz (online). (14 October).

108 Bonds (1977), pp. 65, 74; Hurst, D. (1977). The Gun and the Olive Branch. London, pp. 128–9, 138; Khalidi, W. (1996). 'Islam, the West, and Jerusalem'. Center for Muslim-Christian Understanding (online); Morris, B. (1986). 'The Causes and Character of the Arab Exodus from Palestine: The Israeli Defence Forces Intelligence Branch Analysis of June 1948'. Middle Eastern Studies, 21 (1), pp. 5–19; Morris, B. (2001). 'Revisiting the Palestinian Exodus of 1948'. E.L. Rogan and A. Shlaim (eds) The War for Palestine: Rewriting the History of 1948. Cambridge: Cambridge University Press, pp. 37–59; Morris (2003), pp. 242–3; Morris (2008), p. 116; Pappe (2006), pp. 6–20; Pappe, I. (2011). The Ethnic Cleansing of Palestine. Oxford: Oneworld; Rose (2003), pp. 45–6.

109 Or which is sometimes misdescribed as a Palestinian exodus at the behest of the Arab states to avoid getting caught up in the crossfire of an imminent Israeli-Arab war over Palestine.

110 United Nations (2016), p. 9.

111 Rose (2003), p. 48.

112 Begin became Israel's sixth PM (1977–83) following two stints as defence minister.

113 Jacques de Reynier cited in Hurst (1977), p. 128.

114 None of the ultranationalist Israeli militias (including Irgun) that prosecuted the conquest of Palestine were disbanded. They were all absorbed into the Israeli Defence Force (IDF).

115 Morris (2008), p. 400.

116 Bonds (1977), pp. 65, 74; Hurst (1977), pp. 128–9, 138; Morris (1986), pp. 5–19; Morris (2001), pp. 37–59; Pappe, pp. 6–20; Rose (2003), pp. 45–6.

117 PCBS (2007). 'Nakba (Catastrophe)'. PCBS Press Release (online). See also: Morris (2003), pp. 242–3, 342–60.

118 Khalidi, W. (1988). 'Plan Dalet: Master Plan for the Conquest of Palestine'. Journal of Palestine Studies, 18 (1), pp. 4–19.

119 Morris, B. and Kedar, B.Z. (2022). '"Cast Thy Bread": Israeli Biological Warfare during the 1948 War'. Middle Eastern Studies, 59 (5), pp. 752–6.

120 Pappe, I. (2000). La guerre de 1948 en Palestine. Paris: La fabrique éditions, p. 146.

121 Morris (2003), p. 239.

122 Rose (2003), pp. 48, 49.

123 Rose (2003), pp. 49–50.

124 Cliff (2000), p. 19.

125 Segev, T. (2007). 1967: Israel, the War, and the Year that Transformed the Middle East. New York NY: Henry Holt and Company; Feron, V. (2002). Palestine. Paris: Du Felin, pp. 37–40.

126 Lustick, I.S. (2017). 'Zionist Theories of Peace in the Pre-State Era: Legacies of Dissimulation and Israel's Arab Minority'. N.N. Rouhana and S.S. Huneidi (eds) Israel and its Palestinian Citizens: Ethnic Privileges in the Jewish State. Cambridge: Cambridge University Press, pp. 39–72.

127 Lustick (2017), p. 68.

128 Feron (2002), p. 94.

129 Pappe, I. (1992). The Making of the Arab-Israeli Conflict 1947–1951. London: IB Tauris, p. 72.

130 Mazen, M. (2015). 'The Implications of the Acquisition of a New Nationality for the Right of Return of Palestinian Refugees'. Asian Journal of International Law, 5 (2), pp. 356–86.

131 Davis, U. (1995). 'Jinsiyya Versus Muwatana: The Question of Citizenship and the State in the Middle East: The Cases of Israel, Jordan and Palestine'. Arab Studies Quarterly, 17 (1/2), pp. 26–7.

132 Schechla, J. (2004). '"Jewish Nationality", "National Institutions" and Institutionalized Dispossession'. Al-Majdal, 24 (24 December), pp. 32–42.
133 Munayyer, Y. (2012). 'Not all Israeli Citizens Are Equal'. New York Times. (23 May).
134 Bassok, M. (2018). 'Wage Gap Between Israeli Jews and Arab Counterparts Widens'. Haaretz (online). (24 April).
135 New Israel Fund (2005). 'Arab Sector: NIF Grantees Fight Discrimination in Arab Education'. NIF (online). (13 September).
136 Pew Research Center (2017). 'Intergroup Marriage and Friendship in Israel'. Pew Research Center: Religion and Cultural Life (online). (18 May).
137 Rabinowitz, D. and Khawla, A.B. (2005). Coffins on Our Shoulders: The Experience of the Palestinian Citizens of Israel. Berkley CA: University of California Press, pp. 54–5.
138 Kook, R.B. (2002). The Logic of Democratic Exclusion: African Americans in the United States and Palestinian Citizens in Israel. New York NY: Lexington Books, pp. 67–8.
139 Lowrance, S. (2006). 'Identity, Grievance and Political Action: Recent Evidence from the Palestinian Community in Israel'. International Political Science Review, (27 (2), pp. 167–90.
140 Torstrick, R. (2000). The Limits of Coexistence: Identity Politics in Israel. University of Michigan Press: Ann Arbor MI, p. 13.
141 Lowrance (2006).
142 Berger, M. (2019). 'Palestinians in Israel'. FP News (online). (18 January).
143 Rose (2003), p. 64.
144 Rodinson, M. (1982). Israel and the Arabs. London: Routledge and Kegan Paul.
145 Smith, S.C. (2016). Reassessing Suez 1956: New Perspectives on the Crisis and its Aftermath. London: Routledge.
146 Pierre, J.-M. (2014). 1956 Suez Crisis and the United Nations. London: Pickles Partners Publishing.
147 Smith (2016); Peden, G.C. (2012). 'Suez and Britain's Decline as a World Power'. Historical Journal, 55 (4), pp. 1073–96; Kyle, K. (2003). Suez: Britain's End of Empire in the Middle East. London: IB Tauris; Neff, D. (1981). Warriors at Suez: America Takes America into the Middle East. New York NY: Simon and Schuster.
148 As reported by the BBC Panorama (6 February, 2009).
149 Bowen, J. (2003). Six Days: How the 1967 War Shaped the Middle East. New York NY: Simon and Schuster.
150 Bowen (2003).
151 Resolution 242 and Resolution 338 (which re-iterated Resolution 242) as well as a range of others requiring nation-states not to recognize any changes in the pre-1967 borders. As of 2013, Israel had been condemned in 45 UN resolutions for actions or inactions concerning the Palestinian conflict and had been the subject of 131 in total. Between 1948 and 2017, 80 UNSC resolutions have criticized Israel for violations of UNSC resolutions, for breaches of the UN Charter, for abrogating Geneva Conventions (on human rights), and for other violations of international law. This is far in excess of any other country, including the USA's so-called rogue states. See: Welcome to Palestine (2017). 'United Nations Security Council Resolutions against Israel'. Welcome to Palestine.org (online). (29 August).
152 Rose (2003), p. 23.
153 Cited in Bonds et al. (1981), p. 116.
154 Hammes, D. and Wills, D. (2005). 'Black Gold: The End of Bretton Woods and the Oil-Price Shocks of the 1970s'. Independent Review, 9 (4), pp. 501–11.

155 Lacey, R. (1981). The Kingdom. San Diego: Harcourt Brace Jovanovich, pp. 410–11.
156 Graf, R. (2012). 'Making Use of the "Oil Weapon": Western Industrialized Countries and Arab Petropolitics in 1973–1974'. Diplomatic History, 36 (1), pp. 185–208; Lacey (1981), pp. 411–2.
157 Hughes, G. (2008). 'Britain, the Transatlantic Alliance, and the Arab-Israeli War of 1973'. Journal of Cold War Studies, 10 (2), pp. 3–40; Rose (2003), p. 18.
158 Kissinger, H. (1975). 'Kissinger Memorandum: "To Isolate the Palestinians"'. Middle East Report, 96 (May/June 1981). Middle East Research and Information Project (online).
159 Licklider, R. (1988). 'The Power of Oil: The Arab Oil Weapon and the Netherlands, the United Kingdom, Canada, Japan, and the United States'. International Studies Quarterly, 32 (2), pp. 205–26.
160 Office of the Historian (1976). Oil Embargo, 1973–1974. Foreign Service Institute: US Department of State.
161 Naidu, A.G. (1992). 'Camp David Accords: A Study in American Foreign Policy'. Indian Journal of Political Science, 53 (3), pp. 397–414.
162 Rose (2003), pp. 53–9. And so King Hussein of Jordan made war on Fatah in 1970 because he was fearful that his own country's largely Palestinian population would make common cause with the guerrillas to depose him. Before that, Nasser of Egypt, who symbolized pan-Arabism, betrayed it, by signing up to Kissinger's Rogers Plan, according to which Egypt would recognize Israel's 1967 borders in exchange for being handed back some scraps of land lost in the Arab-Israeli wars. Later on, President Assad of Syria sent his army into Lebanon to destroy an alliance of the Palestinian militias and Islamic left groups to overturn the ruling coalition of the Christian right.
163 Most recently, resolution 2334, passed in 2016, deplores the continuation of Israel's colonization of Palestinian territories and demands that Israel immediately ceases further settlement building. See: United Nations (2016). Israel's Settlements Have No Legal Validity, Constitute Flagrant Violation of International Law, Security Council Reaffirms. UN Security Council. 7583rd meeting. SC/12657. (23 December).
164 Morris, B. (2001). Righteous Victims: A History of the Zionist-Arab Conflict. London: Vintage, p. 567.
165 Ackerman, P. and DuVall, J. (2000). A Force More Powerful: A Century of Nonviolent Conflict. New York NY: Palgrave Macmillan, p. 407.
166 Chomsky (1983), pp. 123–32.
167 Ackerman and DuVall (2000), pp. 400–1.
168 Fisher (2012).
169 Country Economy (2023). 'Country Comparison: Israel versus Palestine'. CE (online). Accessed: 12/01/2023.
170 Cited in Martin, S. and Arawi, T. (2021). 'Ensure Palestinians Have Access to COVID-19 Vaccines'. Lancet, 397 (10276), pp. 791–2.
171 Human Rights Watch (2021). 'Israel's Discriminatory Vaccine Push Underscores Need for Action. Press Statement'. HRW (online). (19 March).
172 Anon (2021). 'Palestinian Authority Calls Off Vaccine Exchange with Israel'. Al-Jazeera (online). (18 June).
173 Worldometer (2023). 'Israel COVID—Coronavirus Statistics'. (online). Accessed: 27/04/2023; Worldometer (2023). 'State of Palestine COVID—Coronavirus Statistics'. (online). Accessed: 27/04/2023.
174 The active support for the Palestinians from the Arab street across the Middle East is in stark contrast with the tepid and equivocal support from the Arab rulers.

This has been revealed quite recently during the crisis engendered by President Trump's decision to recognize Jerusalem as Israel's capital and relocate the US embassy there. See: Abumaria, D. (2017). 'Palestinians Thankful for "Arab Street" Response to U.S. Jerusalem Move'. The Medialine: Trusted Mideast News (online). (14 December).

175 Daman, R. (2015). 'The Price of Oslo'. Al-Jazeera (online).

176 Daman (2015).

177 ProCon (2008). '1995 Oslo Interim Agreement'. Britannica (online). (24 April); Daman (2015).

178 ProCon (2008).

179 Daman (2015).

180 Levy, G. (2010). 'Tricky Bibi'. Haaretz (online). (15 July).

181 Waage., H.H. (2008). 'Postscript to Oslo: The Mystery of Norway's Missing Files'. Journal of Palestine Studies, 38 (1), pp. 54–65. See p. 63.

182 Marshall cited in Rose (2003), p. 3.

183 Pressman, J. (2003). 'Visions in Collision: What Happened at Camp David and Taba? International Security, 28 (2), pp. 5–43. See especially pp. 15–9; Wright, R. (2002). 'Was Arafat the Problem?' Slate. (18 April); Malley, R. and Hussein, A. (2001). 'Camp David: The Tragedy of Errors'. New York Review of Books (9 August); Sher, G. (2006). The Israeli-Palestinian Peace Negotiations, 1999–2001. London and New York NY: Routledge.

184 Pressman (2009), pp. 9–11.

185 BBC News (2002). 'Arabs Offer Israelis Peace Plan'. (28 March).

186 McCarthy, R. (2007). 'Olmert Gives Cautious Welcome to Arab Peace Plan'. Guardian (online). (30 March).

187 Ahren, R. (2015). 'Netanyahu Backs "General Idea" Behind Arab Peace Initiative'. Times of Israel. (28 May); Ravid, B. (2018). 'Netanyahu: Israel Will Never Accept Arab Peace Initiative as Basis for Talks with Palestinians'. Haaretz (online). (10 April).

188 Haddad, M. (2020). 'Palestine and Israel: Mapping an Annexation'. Al-Jazeera (online). (26 June).

189 Borger, J. (2017). 'Donald Trump to Recognise Jerusalem as Israel's Capital and Move US Embassy'. Guardian (online). (6 December); Landler, M. (2017). 'Trump Recognizes Jerusalem as Israel's Capital and Orders US Embassy to Move'. New York Times (online). (6 December); Plett Usher, B. (2018). 'Jerusalem Embassy: Why Trump's Move Was Not about Peace'. BBC News (online). (15 May).

190 Holmes, O. (2019). 'Trump Provokes Global Anger by Recognising Israel's Claim to Golan Heights'. Guardian (online). (22 March).

191 Borger, J. (2019). 'US Says Israeli Settlements No Longer Considered Illegal in Dramatic Shift'. Guardian (online). (18 November); Jakes, L. and Halbfinger, D.M. (2019). 'In Shift, US Says Israeli Settlements in West Bank Do Not Violate International Law'. New York Times (online). (18 November).

192 DeYoung, K. and Eglash, R. (2018). 'Trump Administration to End U.S. Funding to U.N. Program for Palestinian Refugees'. Washington Post (online). (30 August).

193 Cook, S.A. (2020). 'What's Behind the New Israel-UAE Peace Deal?' Council on Foreign Relations (online). (17 August); Norlen, T. and Sinai, T. (2020). The Abraham Accords—Paradigm Shift or Realpolitik? George C. Marshall: European Center for Security Studies (60). (October).

194 Landler (2017).

195 Plett Usher (2018). As evangelist Robert Jeffress, close to Trump's vice-president Mike Pence, put it: "God decided Jerusalem was the capital of Israel more than 3,000 years ago during the time of King David".

196 Landler (2017).
197 Morris (2001), pp. 341, 568.
198 Chomsky (1983), pp. 23–6.
199 Chomsky (1983), pp. 28–9.
200 Lockman, Z. and Beinin, J. (1989). Intifada: The Palestinian Uprising against Jewish Occupation. Cambridge MA: South End Press, p. 39.
201 Pearlman, W. (2011). Violence, Nonviolence, and the Palestinian National Movement. Cambridge: Cambridge University Press, pp. 107, 112; Seddon, D. (2004). 'Intifada'. D. Seddon (ed) Political and Economic Dictionary of the Middle East. London: Taylor and Francis, p. 284; Shlaim, A. (2000). The Iron Wall: Israel and the Arab World. London: Penguin, pp. 450–1; Vitullo Khoury, A. (1989). 'Uprising in Gaza'. Lockman and Beinin (eds), pp. 43–55.
202 Beitler, R.M. (2004). The Path to Mass Rebellion: An Analysis of Two Intifadas. New York NY: Lexington Books, pp. 114–6; Cronin, A.K. (2012). 'Endless Wars and No Surrender'. H. Afflerbach and H. Strachan (eds) How Fighting Ends: A History of Surrender. Oxford: Oxford University Press, pp. 417–33; Filiu, J.-P. (2014). Gaza: A History. Oxford: Oxford University Press, pp. 204–6; Nasrallah, R. (2013). 'The First and Second Palestinian Intifadas'. J. Peters and D. Newman (eds) The Routledge Handbook on the Israeli-Palestinian Conflict. London: Routledge, pp. 60–1; Pearlman (2011), pp. 14–6; Seddon (2004), p. 284; Shlaim (2000), pp. 450–1; Tessler, M. (1994). A History of the Israeli-Palestinian Conflict. Indiana University Press, pp. 677–8; Vitullo Khoury, pp. 46–7.
203 Cronin (2012), p. 426; Lopez-Ibor, J.J., Christodoulou, G., Maj, M. and Sartorius, N. (2005). Disasters and Mental Health. New York NY: John Wiley and Sons, p. 231; Nasrallah (2013), p. 56; Mearsheimer, J.J. and Walt, S. (2006). 'The Israel Lobby'. London Review of Books, 28 (6), pp. 3–12.
204 Phil Marshall cited in Rose (2003), p. 8.
205 Byman, D. (2011). A High Price: The Triumphs and Failures of Israeli Counterterrorism. Oxford: Oxford University Press, p. 14; Schindler, C. (2013). A History of Modern Israel. Cambridge: Cambridge University Press, p. 283; Sontag, D. (2000). 'Battle at Jerusalem Holy Site Leaves 4 Dead and 200 Hurt'. Chicago Tribune. (30 September); Klein, M. (2003). The Jerusalem Problem: The Struggle for Permanent Status. Gainesville FL: University Press of Florida, pp. 97–8.
206 Klein (2003), p. 97; Sher, G. (2006). The Israeli-Palestinian Negotiations 1999–2001: Within Reach. London and New York NY: Routledge, pp. 161–2.
207 Catignani, S. (2008). Israeli Counter-Insurgency and the Intifadas: Dilemmas of a Conventional Army. London and New York NY: Routledge, pp. 104–6.
208 Anon (2001). 'The Or Inquiry: Summary of Events'. Haaretz (online). (12 September).
209 Byman (2011), p. 14; Catignani (2008), pp. 100–6; Schindler (2013), p. 283; Sontag (2000); Klein (2003), pp. 97–8; Sher (2006), pp. 161–2.
210 Amnesty International (2001). 'Israel and the Occupied Territories: Broken Lives—A Year of Intifada'. AI (online). (13 November).
211 Philps, A. (2000). 'A Day of Rage, Revenge and Bloodshed'. Daily Telegraph (13 October); USA Today (2000). 'Israeli Copters Retaliate for Soldiers' Deaths'. (11 August).
212 Anon (2002). 'Arafat Siege Could End Soon'. CBS News (online). (29 April); United Nations (2002). 'Report of General-Secretary on Recent Events in Jenin, Other Palestinian Cities'. UN (online). (1 August).
213 PCHR (2004). 'Uprooting Palestinian Trees and Levelling Agricultural Land: The Tenth Report on Israeli Land Sweeping and Demolition of Palestinian Buildings and Facilities in the Gaza Strip'. PCHR (online).

214 HRW (2006). 'Razing Rafah: Mass Home Demolitions in the Gaza Strip'. HRW (online).
215 Amnesty International (2001).
216 BBC News (2004). 'Gunmen Kill Jewish Settler Family'. (3 May); Feldman, S. (2000). The October Violence: An Interim Assessment; Hershman, T. (2001). 'Israel's First Internet Murder'. Wired. (19 January); Israeli Ministry of Education (2001). 'Target: Israeli Children'. Wayback Machine Archive. (27 March); Staff and Agencies (2001). 'Two Israeli Boys Found Bludgeoned to Death'. Guardian (online). (9 May); Kalman, M. (2001). 'Two Israeli Teenagers Stoned to Death'. USA Today (online). (29 June); O'Sullivan, A. (2001). 'Hamas Terrorist Killed: Followers Threaten Revenge in Tel Aviv'. Jerusalem Post (25 November); Fisher, I. (2006). 'In Hamas's Overt Hatred, Many Israelis See Hope'. New York Times. (29 January); Stanage, N. (2002). 'Death of Innocents'. Sunday Business Post (3 February); Israeli Ministry of Foreign Affairs (2001). 'Suicide Bombing at the Ben-Yehuda Pedestrian Mall in Jerusalem'. (1 December).
217 The targeting of Palestinian children by the Israeli military (and by Israeli settlers) in the occupied territories has been a feature of the occupation since its 1967 start. See: UN (2015). Since 1967, Israel has systematically targeted Palestinians including children. UN: HRC 28th session—NGO Submission, Annex (Palestine Independent Commission for Human Rights). Since 2005 (the year that the second intifada ended) and up to the end of 2020, 1,393 have been killed. See: DfCI (2020). 'Child Fatalities: Distribution of Palestinian Child Fatalities by Month'. Palestine: DfCI (online). (22 September). Recent reports include the following: Amnesty International (2019). 'Israel and Occupied Territories 2019'. AI (online); Foreign Staff (2019). 'Israeli Snipers Targeted Children, Health Workers and Journalists in Gaza, UN Says'. Daily Telegraph (online). (28 February); Middle East Monitor (2018). 'Israel Killed 37 Palestinian Children This Year'. Middle East Monitor (online). (13 August); Parker, B. (2014). 'What's Not a Target for Israel?'. Al-Jazeera (online). (30 July); Pinna, M. (2019). 'Hebron's Palestinian Children Are Targeted, Says Israeli Army Veteran'. Euronews (online). (30 May).
218 B'Tselem (2010). 'Fatalities Data Base'. IICHROT (online). Israeli Information Center for Human Rights in the Occupied Territories (online). Accessed: 04/04/2020; Jewish Virtual Library (2009). 'Comprehensive Listing of Terrorism Victims in Israel'. JVL: Terrorism against Israel (online).
219 DCI (2020); If Americans Knew (2020). 'The Impact of the Conflict on Children'. IAK.org (online).
220 Atkins, S.E. (2004). Encyclopaedia of Modern Worldwide Extremists and Extremist Groups. London: Greenwood Press, p. 123; Beitler, R.M. (1995). 'The Intifada: Palestinian Adaptation to Israeli Counterinsurgency Tactics'. Terrorism and Political Violence, 7 (2), pp. 49–73; Chehab, Z. (2007). Inside Hamas: The Untold Story of Militants, Martyrs and Spies. New York NY: IB Tauris; Cordesman, A.H. (2006). Arab-Israeli Military Forces in an Era of Asymmetric Wars. London: Greenwood Press, p. 326; Davis, J. (2004). Martyrs: Innocence, Vengeance, and Despair in the Middle East. Basingstoke: Palgrave Macmillan; Hassan, R. (2014). Life as a Weapon: The Global Rise of Suicide Bombings. London and New York NY: Routledge; Hatina, M. (2001). Islam and Salvation in Palestine: The Islamic Jihad Movement. New York NY: Syracuse University Press, pp. 21–32.
221 UN (2015). 'Key Figures on the 2014 Hostilities'. OCHA (online). (23 June).
222 Sherwood, H. and Balousha, H. (2014). 'Gaza Ceasefire: Israel and Palestinians Agree to Halt Weeks of Fighting'. Guardian (online). (27 August).

223 Browning, N. (2014). 'Suspected Israeli Revenge Killing of Palestinian Triggers Clashes'. Reuters (online). (2 July).
224 UNHRC (2019). 'Report of the UN Commission of Inquiry on the 2018 Protests in the Occupied Palestinian Territory'. HRC (online). (28 February).
225 Eglash, R. (2018). 'After 24-hour Flare-up, Uneasy Calm Returns to Gaza and Southern Israel'. Washington Post (online). (30 May).
226 Al-Mughrabi, N., Farrell, S. and Heller, J. (2021). 'Dozens Dead as Israel and Hamas Escalate Aerial Bombardments'. Reuters (online). (11 May); Al-Mughrabi, N., Saul, J. and Ayyub, R. (2021). 'Israel and Hamas Both Claim Victory as Ceasefire Holds'. Reuters (online). (21 May); Al-Mughrabi, N. and Saul, J. (2021). 'Palestinians, Israelis Count Cost of 11-Day Fight'. Reuters (online). (20 May).
227 El Kurd, D. (2021). 'Young People Are Leading the Palestinian Protests in Jerusalem. And They Aren't Going Away'. Washington Post (online). (12 May); Alsaafin, L. (2021). 'What Is Happening in Occupied East Jerusalem's Sheikh Jarrah?'. Al-Jazeer (online). (1 May).
228 Farrell, S. and Ayyub, R. (2021). 'Israeli Police, Palestinians Clash at Jerusalem's Al-Aqsa, Scores Injured'. Reuters (online). (7 May).
229 Al-Mughrabi, N. and Heller, J. (2021). 'Jerusalem Violence Leads to Rockets, Air Strikes'. Reuters (online). (10 May).
230 Tahhan, Z. (2017). 'Hamas and Fatah: How Are the Two Groups Different?' Al-Jazeera (online). (12 October); Schanzer, J. (2008). Hamas vs. Fatah: The Struggle for Palestine. New York NY: St Martin's Press.
231 Weisman, S.R. (2006). 'Rice Admits that US Underestimated Hamas Strength'. New York Times. (30 January).
232 Pina, A.D. (2006). 'Palestinian Elections'. CRS Report for Congress (online). (9 February).
233 BBC News (2006). 'Israel to "Allow Jerusalem Vote"'. (10 January); Urquhart, C. (2006). 'Palestinians Allowed to Vote in East Jerusalem, but Israel Bars Hamas from Election'. Guardian (online). (16 January).
234 PSHA (2009). 'The Arrest and Detention of Palestinian Legislative Council Members'. PSHA (online). (15 March).
235 UN (2006). Chronological Review of Events Relating to the Question of Palestine. Monthly Media Monitoring Review. (January 1–31).
236 Erlanger, S. (2006). 'US and Israelis Are Said to Talk of Hamas Ouster'. (14 February). New York Times.
237 BBC News (2006). 'Israel to Impose Hamas Sanctions'. (19 February); CNN (2006). 'Israel Stops Payments to Palestinians'. (10 February); Erlanger, S. (2006). 'Hamas Leader Faults Israeli Sanction Plan'. New York Times. (18 February); Oxfam International (2006). Poverty in Palestine: The Human Cost of the Financial Boycott. Oxfam Briefing Note. (13 April); Sharp, J.M. and Blanchard, C.M. (2006). US Foreign Aid to the Palestinians. CRS Report for Congress. RS22370. (27 June); United Nations (2006). Chronological Review (January); Weisman, R.S. and Smith, C.S. (2006). 'US and EU Halt Aid to Palestinian Government'. New York Times. (8 April).
238 Sherwood, H. (2010). 'Israel Accused Over "Cruel" Gaza Blockade'. Guardian (online). (30 November); Hartberg, M. (2012). Beyond Ceasefire: Ending the Blockade of Gaza. Oxfam Briefing Note. (6 December); Human; United Nations (2006). The Gaza Strip: Situation Report. (31 January). UN: The Question of Palestine (online); BBC News (2006). 'Gaza Farmers Dumping Their Crops'. (17

March); United Nations (2006). 'The Gaza Strip: Situation Report'. (6 June). UN: The Question of Palestine (online).

239 Hartberg, M. (2012). 'Beyond Ceasefire: Ending the Blockade of Gaza'. Oxfam Briefing Note. (6 December); Human Rights Watch (2022). 'Gaza: Israel's "Open Air Prison" at 15'. HRW (online). (14 June); Holmes, O. and Balousha, H. (2019). 'Gaza's Generation Blockade: Young Lives in the "World's Largest Prison"'. Guardian (online). (12 March); Middle East Policy Council (2020). 'Egypt Criticized for Gaza Blockade'. MEPC (online).

240 Shikaki, K. (2007). With Hamas in Power: Impact of Palestinian Domestic Developments on Options for the Peace Process. Working Paper 1. Brandeis University. Crown Center for Middle Eastern Studies (online). (February).

241 Morro, P. (2007). International Reaction to the Palestinian Unity Government. CRS Report for Congress. RS22659. (9 May).

242 Goldenberg, S. (2007). 'US Plotted to Overthrow Hamas after Election Victory'. Guardian (online). (4 March); Rose, D. (2008). 'The Gaza Bombshell'. Vanity Fair. (3 March); Morrow, A. and Moussa al-Omrani, K. (2008). 'This "Bombshell" Took A Year Falling'. Inter Press Service: News Agency (online). (2 April); Segev, T. (2008). 'Bay of Pigs in Gaza'. Haaretz. (13 May); Toameh, K.A. (2008). 'Vanity Fair: Bush Approved Plot to Oust Hamas'. Jerusalem Post. (4 March).

243 Black, I. and Tran, M. (2007). Hamas Takes Control of Gaza. Guardian (online). (17 June); Scott, W. (2007). 'Abbas Dissolves Government as Hamas Takes Control of Gaza'. Washington Post (online). (15 June).

244 Charrett, C. (2020). The EU, Hamas and the 2006 Palestinian Elections: A Performance in Politics. London and New York NY: Routledge, p. 10; Holmes and Balousha, (2019); Middle East Policy Council (2020).

245 Thus, unsurprisingly, Hamas, like Hezbollah, is officially classified by Israel and the USA as a terrorist organization. This is owing to its refusal to renounce the military struggle for Palestinian liberation and its targeting of Jewish civilians as an aspect of that struggle. (Naturally, Israel's refusal to renounce violence in its efforts to maintain the occupation and its targeting of Arab civilians as an aspect of this violence has not placed its government on the USA's list of international terrorist organizations). At the time of writing, Australia, Japan, and New Zealand have stopped short of classifying Hamas as a terrorist organization, instead designating its military wing as such. Plenty of other countries have rejected the terrorist label for Hamas altogether, however—many of which are not among Washington's "outlier" or "rogue" states (e.g. Brazil, Switzerland, Norway, Sweden, Turkey, and Egypt). The UN also rejected a US resolution calling for condemnation of the organization as terrorist. The EU resisted listing Hamas as a terrorist organization but capitulated under US diplomatic pressure.

246 Callinicos (2003), p. 91.

247 The other aspect of Israel's and the US state's strategy of delegitimization of the Palestinian resistance is to represent it as motivated by antisemitic ideology. This can be counted on as a potent weapon in the propaganda war, given the events of the Holocaust and the persistence of genuine antisemitism across the world. Of course, elements of the politics and ideology of Hamas, Fatah, and Hezbollah can be legitimately construed as antisemitic, as can aspects of popular attitudes among the multitude of the Arab street. The targeting of Jewish civilians as part of the armed protests may be reasonably construed likewise. There are, of course, Jewish and American academics who insist that Hamas (and especially) Hezbollah are simply militantly and virulently anti-Jewish organizations. See for example: Gleis, J.L. and Berti, B. (2012). Hezbollah and Hamas: A Comparative Study. Baltimore MD: John Hopkins University Press; Wistrich, R.S. (2010). A Lethal Obsession: Antisemitism from Antiquity to the Global Jihad. New York NY: Random House.

These studies are devoid of nuance or context, however. For, if there was not an antisemitic aspect to the beliefs and actions of those motivated to resist, this would be miraculous. It would be miraculous, given the relentless cruelty and brutality of the Palestinian occupation and Israel's murderous assault on Lebanon. Not everyone is so politically adroit that they can distinguish between anti-Zionism and antisemitism. And it is easier to draw these analytical distinctions if you are outside the warzones rather than inside them at the receiving end of often racially aggravated state terrorism. Under these circumstances, it could even be argued that Hamas, Hezbollah, and Fatah could be a lot more antisemitic than in fact they are.

Leaders of these organizations insist that their political goals—whether these be the termination of Zionist Israel and its replacement with a single multi-ethnic Islamic-led state in Palestine (Hezbollah's present position; Hamas's former position), or simply the return of Israel to its before-1967 or even original 1948 borders, the establishment of an independent Palestinian state between Israel and Jordan, and deliverance on the right of return to Israel for dispossessed Palestinians (Fatah's position; also latterly Hamas's)—are anti-Zionist rather than anti-Jew. These organizations (not even Hezbollah) formally espouse a politics bent on ethnically cleansing the Jews from the Holy Land. Termination of Israel, for Hezbollah, is replacement of the Zionist state with an Islamic one, not expulsion of the Jews from Palestine. Jews who chose to stay in Palestine after the dismantling of the state of Israel would, its spokespeople have said, enjoy the status of a "protected minority" under Muslim majority rule. This may not be a sincere undertaking, but equally it might be.

Even the manifestly antisemitic pronouncements of certain of the leaders or spokespersons of these organizations (e.g. claims of a worldwide Jewish conspiracy or Holocaust denial) cannot be taken at face value. Rather than evidencing anti-Jewish phobias, these may reflect more a politics of frustration at the way that the Holocaust has been relentlessly exploited (as it has been) by Zionists and their US patrons to legitimize Israeli imperialism under the umbrella of "securitization". There is also the problem here of "reading-off" from such pronouncements of a handful of specific individuals a consistent racialized belief-system and attributing it to whole memberships and their constituencies of support. This is a form of racism based on preconceived notions of the meaning of Arab politics and mentalities. This is especially the case since Hamas and Hezbollah are necessarily clandestine organizations. Those who dismiss Hamas and Hezbollah as "rabidly antisemitic" are in no position to actually discover what their members or supporters think. Nor are these armchair critics interested in doing so.

Treatment of Jewish civilians as legitimate targets of violence, though horrible and indefensible from a human rights perspective, is arguably not motivated primarily or especially by religiously inflamed antisemitism either. This is more plausibly viewed as being motivated by an instrumental "calculus of harm". This is because, so great is the asymmetry in military capabilities between Hamas and Hezbollah, on the one hand, and the Zionist state of Israel, on the other hand, that a purely military war of the former against the latter would yield zero chance of success. Instead, this would likely rapidly degrade the resistance organizations. By contrast, a military campaign that includes targeting of civilians (alongside low-intensity guerrilla attacks on enemy combatants or installations) can be construed as better adapted tactically for success. This is because civilians are less risky targets and easier ones to hit than military personnel, whereas civilian casualties (if these are ongoing) might sap public confidence in Zionist politics and build up popular pressure on the Israeli state to make concessions.

248 Britannica (2021). 'Hamas: Conflict with Israel'. Britannica (online). The Israelis not only locked Gaza into a permanent blockade in 2007, after Hamas won the municipal elections ousting Fatah (hence resorting to the standard collective punishment of a whole people) but unleashed a fresh round of aerial bombardments of the Strip in

2008, and again in 2012. These were followed by full-scale invasions of the West Bank and Gaza in 2014. The ground offensives were intended to undermine Hamas but succeeded only in perpetrating yet more damage on the civilian infrastructures and yet more high numbers of civilian deaths. Hamas undoubtedly lost many fighters, but its paramilitary capacities survived the attacks. Finally, in 2018, border protests in Gaza over the blockade involving tens of thousands of people spurred a renewed Israeli air assault on positions in Gaza supposedly linked to Hamas's cross-border rocket attacks.

The "war on terror" was also the pretext of Israel's invasion of Lebanon in 1982—which, on conservative estimates, was responsible for 19,000 deaths and 30,000 injured. The terrorist act in question was an unsuccessful assassination attempt on the Israeli ambassador to London. This campaign was an especially brutal and indiscriminate one, even by Zionist precedents. Beirut was carpet-bombed into rubble. So too were many Palestinian refugee camps. Those that escaped aerial destruction were subjected to artillery bombardment and tank assaults, the resistance of a few fighters obliterated. The camps were then bulldozed, their fleeing populations (or rather the men and boys) rounded up and deported into vast internment camps, with the women and female children left to fend for themselves. Reporter Tom Segev described "refugees wandering amidst swarms of flies, dressed in rags, their faces expressing terror and their eyes bewilderment . . . the women wailing and the children sobbing". Other journalists reported "savage and indiscriminate beatings" of prisoners and bystanders and of arrestees being forced under the gun to chant "Long live Begin" (the Israeli prime minister's name).

The invasion secured its goal. This was the withdrawal of the PLO from Lebanon under the protection of a US peacekeeping force. But this did not end the bloodletting. The climax of the Israeli campaign was civilian massacres in the Sabra and Shatilla refugee camps, after the PLO had departed. The camps were sealed-off by the Israeli army. Then truckloads of Christian fascist Phalange and Haddad militiamen were allowed entry whereupon they systematically murdered all of the inhabitants right under the gaze of Israeli command posts a few hundred yards away. See Rose (2003), pp. 26–31.

249 IHRA (2016). 'Working Definition of Antisemitism'. Bucharest Plenary: Romanian Chairmanship. Press Release. (26 May).

250 Abdallah, S. et al. (2020). 'Palestinian Rights and the IHRA Definition of Antisemitism'. Letters. Guardian. (29 November).

251 Ayyash, M. (2020). 'The IHRA Definition Will Not Help Fight Anti-Semitism'. (23 November). Al-Jazeera (online).

252 Ayyash (2020).

253 Tomlinson, H. (2017). 'In the Matter of the Adoption and Potential Application of the International Holocaust Remembrance Alliance Working Definition of Anti-Semitism: Opinion'. Free Speech on Israel (online). (8 March).

254 Penslar, D. (2022). 'Who's Afraid of Defining Antisemitism?' Antisemitism Studies, 6 (1), pp. 133–45.

255 Stern-Weiner, J. (2021). 'The Politics of a Definition: How the IHRA Working Definition of Antisemitism Is Being Misrepresented'. Free Speech on Israel (online). (21 April).

256 Marshall in Rose (2003), p. 7.

257 Freilich (2017).

258 Policy and Survey Research (2022). Public Opinion Poll No. 84. (22–25 June). Palestinian Center for Policy and Survey Research (online). Fifty per cent of respondents supported armed resistance compared to 22 per cent who supported a return to diplomacy and 21 per cent who favoured non-violent protest. The poll also revealed a major upscaling in popular support for Hamas owing in part to its cross-border guerrilla attacks in Israel.

259 Policy and Survey Research (2023). 'Public Opinion Poll No. 88'. PCSR (online). (7–11 June).

260 Policy and Survey Research (2023). 'Palestinian Public Opinion Poll No. 24'. PCPSR (online). (14–20 June).
261 Policy and Survey Research (2018). 'Public Opinion Poll No. 70'. (27 December). PCPSR (online).
262 PSR (2018).
263 Policy and Survey Research (2019). 'Public Opinion Poll No. 71'. PCPSR (online). (13–16 March).
264 Cleveland, C. and Pollock, D. (2023). Polls Show that Majority of Gazans Were against Breaking Ceasefire: Hamas and Hezbollah Unpopular among Key Arab Publics'. Fikra Forum (online).
265 Krauss, J. (2021). 'Poll Finds Dramatic Rise in Palestinian Support for Hamas'. AP News (online). (15 June).
266 Cleveland and Pollock (2023).
267 Staff, T. (2022). 'Poll: 72% of Palestinians Support Forming More Armed Groups in West Bank'. Times of Israel. (15 December).
268 The rationales given by Israeli PM Benjamin Netanyahu's ministers for the reckless violence of the Israeli state against Gazan civilians confirm this. By their own words they damn themselves.

> I am vehemently opposed to lifting the blockade and letting goods into Gaza for humanitarian reasons. Our commitment is to the families of the murdered and to the kidnapped hostages—not Hamas murderers and the people who helped them (Energy Minister Israel Katz, 16 October).

Note that, by definition, the whole of the Gazan population are assimilated either to "Hamas murderers" or "the people who helped them".

> We are imposing a complete siege. No electricity, no food, no water, no fuel—everything is closed. We are fighting human animals and we must act accordingly (Defence Minister Yoav Gallant, 9 October).

Here commentary is almost superfluous. The targeting of the whole Gazan people is acceptable because they are all "human animals".

> For years, we have given Gaza electricity, water, and fuel. Instead of a thank you, they sent thousands of human animals to butcher, murder, rape, and kidnap babies, women, and elderly people. This is why we have decided to cut off the supply of water, electricity, and fuel (Energy Minister Israel Katz, 11 October)

Katz seemingly has forgotten that Gaza has been under blockade for 16 years that has seriously limited supplies of water and power. Aside from that, who are the "they" he refers to? Gazans! They are all guilty.

Statements by Israeli government officials in October and November 2023 in justification of what is in effect a war crimes policy (since that is what the deliberate targeting of civilians in war is) are notable for two assumptions. Firstly, that the shutting-off of all water and power supplies to the people of Gaza—and the withholding of humanitarian aid from them—is a perfectly acceptable response to the actions of an organization these people do not control and in which they play no part. Hence, arbitrary, collective punishment, is legitimate. Indeed, this is legitimate, irrespective of whether or not this furthers the goals of the military action—a wholly retributive logic. Secondly, where "limited" humanitarian aid for Gazans is permittable, this is only where this fits with or furthers military goals. Thus, there is actually no space at all here for any humanitarian endeavour whatsoever in the context of war. For examples, see Human Rights Watch (2023).
269 Ben-Gurion quoted in Chomsky (1983), p. 182.

270 Lidman, M. (2011). 'Support Growing for Two-state Solution'. Jerusalem Post. (28 December).
271 Bregman, A. (2002). A History of Israel. Basingstoke: Palgrave Macmillan, pp. 168–71.
272 The present PM, Benjamin Netanyahu, has been the country's leader for 15 years in the period from 1996 to 2021, occupying senior posts in government for many years prior to that. He was formerly an officer in a special reconnaissance unit of the IDF. His years as Israel's PM are notable chiefly for decades-long support for the resettlement of Jews in the occupied territories and his self-declared success in destroying the Oslo Accords.

Yitzhak Shamir was twice PM and spent eight years in the highest office. He was a leader of the Zionist paramilitary group Lehi, which plotted and organized political assassinations before and after independence, and which later joined the IDF. Shamir later became a Mossad operative before pursuing a political career that was notable in his stint as PM for his implacable resistance to entering peace talks to settle the Palestinian crisis. Shamir opposed and thereby undermined the Madrid Peace Talks. He later oversaw the violent suppression of the largely peaceful first Intifada.

Yitzhak Rabin also had two stints as PM in the period from 1974 to 1995. Rabin led paramilitary forces in the so-called Israel-Arab war of 1948/49 that destroyed the Palestinian state and turned most of the Palestinians into refugees. Later, he was commander of the IDF, which was to be trusted with policing the occupation. As commander-in-chief of Israel's armed forces, he led Israel to victory in the 1967 war that generated the occupied territories.

A measure of the fundamental unity of Israeli politics on the spectrum of right-wing ethno-nationalism is that Rabin (who was assassinated by a crazed gunman for entering into "peace talks" with the PLO) is today eulogized as a moderate, a peace-maker, supporter of the Oslo Accords, in contrast to others—such as Sharon, Netanyahu, and Shamir. This is despite his long Zionist track record and despite the fundamental unity of politics on the terrain of settler-colonialism that he shares with all of Israel's leaders. The repetition of leadership style and recycling of the same political "types" as leaders is testament to Israel's deformed democracy.
273 Economic Intelligence Unit (2022). 'Frontline Democracy and the Battle for Ukraine'. Democracy Index 2022 (online), p. 60.
274 Anon (2023). 'Israel Police Boss Threatens to Send Anti-war Protesters to Gaza "On Buses" '. Al-Jazeera (online). (19 October).
275 Bisharat, G., Ziv, O. and Zoubi, B. (2023). ' "This Is Political Persecution": Israel Cracks Down on Internal Critics of its Gaza War'. +972 Magazine (online). (17 October).
276 Quoted in Bisharat, Ziv, and Zoubi (2023).
277 "Whoever returns here, if they return here after, will find scorched earth. No houses, no agriculture, no nothing. They have no future". These are the words of Yogev Bar-Sheshet, deputy leader of Israel's Civil Administration, in an interview he gave inside Gaza. Cited in HRW (2023).
278 The strength of that lobby (and the willingness of powerholders to prostrate themselves before it) has been thrown into sharp relief during the present crisis by events on university campuses right across America. Here pro-Palestinian protestors against the war have faced unprecedented censure and sanction and denigration by agents of authority of various hues. The backlash has been of McCarthyite proportions. This is so much so that the basic civil liberties of protestors (not only free speech but also career prospects and the right not to be threatened with physical violence) have been undermined. See: Kane, A. (2023). 'A "McCarthyite Backlash" Against Pro-Palestine Speech'. Jewish Currents (online). (20 October).

Index

Note: numbers in **bold** indicate a table.

For Product Safety Concerns and Information please contact our EU
representative GPSR@taylorandfrancis.com
Taylor & Francis Verlag GmbH, Kaufingerstraße 24, 80331 München, Germany

www.ingramcontent.com/pod-product-compliance
Ingram Content Group UK Ltd.
Pitfield, Milton Keynes, MK11 3LW, UK
UKHW022347190926
475702UK00015B/2151

* 9 7 8 1 0 3 2 9 8 1 6 4 2 *